VATICAN II

EXPÉRIENCES CANADIENNES /
CANADIAN EXPERIENCES

Sous la direction de / Edited by

Michael Attridge, Catherine E. Clifford & Gilles Routhier

VATICAN II

EXPÉRIENCES CANADIENNES / CANADIAN EXPERIENCES

PRESSES DE L'UNIVERSITÉ D'OTTAWA / UNIVERSITY OF OTTAWA PRESS

Les Presses de l'Université d'Ottawa reconnaissent avec gratitude l'appui accordé à leur programme d'édition par le Département du Patrimoine canadien en vertu de son Programme d'aide au développement de l'industrie de l'édition, le Conseil des Arts du Canada, la Fédération canadienne des sciences humaines en vertu de son Programme d'aide à l'édition savante, le Conseil de recherches en sciences humaines du Canada et l'Université d'Ottawa.

The University of Ottawa Press acknowledges with gratitude the support extended to its publishing list by Heritage Canada through its Book Publishing Industry Development Program, by the Canada Council for the Arts, by the Canadian Federation for the Humanities and Social Sciences through its Aid to Scholarly Publications Program, by the Social Sciences and Humanities Research Council, and by the University of Ottawa.

www.press.uottawa.ca

Catalogage avant publication de Bibliothèque et Archives Canada

Vatican II : expériences canadiennes / sous la direction de Michael Attridge, Catherine E. Clifford & Gilles Routhier = Vatican II : Canadian experiences / edited by Michael Attridge, Catherine E. Clifford & Gilles Routhier.

(Religions and beliefs series, 1480-4700)
Comprend des références bibliographiques et un index.
Textes en français et en anglais.
ISBN 978-2-7603-0763-6

1. Concile du Vatican (2e : 1962-1965). 2. Église catholique--Canada--Histoire--20e siècle. 3. Canada--Histoire religieuse--20e siècle. I. Attridge, Michael, 1967- II. Clifford, Catherine E., 1958- III. Routhier, Gilles, 1953- IV. Collection: Religions and beliefs series

BX830.1962V373 2011 262'.52 C2011-901025-9F

Library and Archives Canada Cataloguing in Publication

Vatican II : expériences canadiennes / sous la direction de Michael Attridge, Catherine E. Clifford & Gilles Routhier = Vatican II : Canadian experiences / edited by Michael Attridge, Catherine E. Clifford & Gilles Routhier.

(Religions and beliefs series, 1480-4700)
Includes bibliographical references and index.
Texts in French and English.
ISBN 978-2-7603-0763-6

1. Vatican Council (2nd : 1962-1965). 2. Catholic Church--Canada--History--20th century. 3. Canada--Church history--20th century. I. Attridge, Michael, 1967- II. Clifford, Catherine E., 1958- III. Routhier, Gilles, 1953- IV. Series: Religions and beliefs series

BX830.1962V373 2011 262'.52 C2011-901025-9E

uOttawa

TABLE DES MATIÈRES / CONTENTS

Remerciements / Acknowledgements

Cet ouvrage a été publié grâce à une subvention de la Fédération canadienne des sciences humaines de concert avec le Programme d'aide à l'édition savante, dont les fonds proviennent du Conseil de recherches en sciences humaines du Canada.

Nous sommes également reconnaissants pour le soutien financier de l'Université St. Michael's College, du Fonds Gérard-Dion de l'Université Laval, Québec, et de l'Université Saint-Paul, par l'entremise de son programme de bourses pour la publication.

Nous souhaitons exprimer notre sincère reconnaissance à nos collègues des Facultés de théologie de l'Université St. Michael's College, à Toronto, de l'Université Saint-Paul, à Ottawa, et à ceux de la Faculté de théologie et de sciences religieuses de l'Université Laval, à Québec, pour leur soutien et leur collaboration à ce projet.

*

This book has been published with the help of a grant from the Canadian Federation for the Humanities and Social Sciences, through the Aid to Scholarly Publications Program, using funds provided by the Social Sciences and Humanities Research Council of Canada.

We are also grateful for the financial support of the University of St. Michael's College, the Fonds Gérard-Dion, Université Laval, Québec, and the Publication Grants Program of Saint Paul University.

We wish to express our sincere gratitude to colleagues at the Faculties of Theology at the University of St. Michael's College, Toronto; Saint Paul University, Ottawa; and the Faculté de théologie et de sciences religieuses, Université Laval, Québec, for their support and collaboration in this project.

Michael Attridge, Catherine E. Clifford & Gilles Routhier

INTRODUCTION

Le concile Vatican II est reconnu comme l'événement religieux qui a eu le plus grand retentissement au XXe siècle. Vu à l'échelle du Canada, son importance n'est pas moindre. En effet, non seulement c'était la première fois qu'un nombre significatif d'évêques canadiens participait à un concile œcuménique, mais ce concile s'est tenu au moment où la société canadienne entrait dans une période de grande mutation, où l'Église catholique du Canada était appelée à une transformation sans précédent et à trouver une nouvelle manière de se situer dans cette culture et cette société en évolution. Cette Église, dont la pierre de fondation avait été posée au début du XVIIe siècle et qui avait connu une véritable expansion depuis la seconde moitié du XIXe siècle, avait vécu pendant plus de trois siècles des legs du concile de Trente et des développements du catholicisme survenus dans le sillage de ce concile, qui avait marqué l'Église catholique d'une empreinte profonde et durable.

L'importance du concile Vatican II au Canada est donc indéniable et, plus de quarante ans après son ouverture, nous n'avons pas encore fini d'en prendre la mesure. Les études menées jusqu'ici ont permis de montrer tout l'intérêt de poursuivre les recherches si l'on veut comprendre l'évolution de l'Église catholique au Canada et prendre la mesure de la réception de Vatican II au Canada, phénomène complexe et aux multiples facettes. Cinquante ans après l'annonce du concile, il nous semblait important de relancer les études sur Vatican II et le Canada : l'histoire de la participation canadienne à ce concile, sa réception au pays et aussi l'interprétation que l'on en a donnée.

Vatican II apparaît comme le moment de la seconde fondation de la conférence épiscopale. En effet, malgré sa mise sur pied en 1943, les évêques n'avaient pas réellement eu l'occasion de se fréquenter, de travailler de concert, de partager leur vision de l'avenir du catholicisme au Canada. Vatican II leur fournit cette occasion. Pendant quatre ans, ils se côtoieront au quotidien, travaillant ensemble sur une base régulière. Il semblait donc approprié d'envisager la recherche sur Vatican II et le Canada en suscitant la collaboration d'universitaires des diverses régions du Canada et de plusieurs universités canadiennes.

Ce cinquantième anniversaire de l'annonce du concile, le 25 janvier 1959, allait fournir l'occasion à des professeurs de théologie au Canada de revenir sur cet événement, sa réception et son herméneutique au Canada. Cela nous semblait une opportunité à saisir pour engager un travail en commun sur un objet autour duquel les préoccupations de plusieurs collègues, quels que soient leur discipline ou leur intérêt de recherche, peuvent se retrouver. De là la proposition de lancer une recherche commune, patronnée par trois facultés de théologie canadiennes (University of St. Michael's College, Université Saint-Paul et Université Laval), autour du concile Vatican II au Canada.

Cette recherche s'est traduite par la tenue de trois rencontres scientifiques au cours de 2009. Le présent volume présente la plupart des communications données dans le cadre de ces rencontres.

Vatican II n'ayant pas été seulement une affaire d'évêques, la première partie de l'ouvrage approche le concile à partir de regards pluriels : celui des médias, acteurs influents au concile, même si les débats en assemblée et les travaux en commission leur demeuraient fermés ; celui des chrétiens non catholiques, désignés comme observateurs au concile mais en réalité y jouant un rôle très actif ; et celui des théologiens, que certains ont désignés comme les « ingénieurs » du concile.

La deuxième partie s'intéresse à l'activité de Canadiens, évêques ou théologiens, au moment du concile ou par la suite, et à l'expérience que ceux-ci ont faite au concile qui s'est avéré un tournant, non seulement pour l'Église catholique comme corps, mais aussi pour des personnes singulières, une expérience emballante, mais aussi traumatique, au moins pour ceux qui n'avaient pas imaginé que le concile pouvait emprunter la direction qu'il a prise.

La dernière partie examine la réception de Vatican II au Canada dans divers domaines d'activités : la liturgie et la catéchèse, la vie religieuse et la condition laïcale, l'œcuménisme et le respect de la liberté religieuse. On trouve là d'abord trois domaines qui avaient connu de réelles évolutions avant que Jean XXIII n'annonce son intention de convoquer un concile en 1959 : la liturgie (la réforme de la vigile pascale et le projet de réforme du bréviaire par Pie XII, les messes célébrées en soirée, l'introduction des messes dialoguées, etc.), la catéchèse (le projet de rédaction de nouveaux instruments catéchétiques au Canada, en remplacement du Catéchisme) et l'apostolat des laïcs (les mouvements d'Action catholique). De plus, les réformes conciliaires dans ces trois domaines sont celles qui ont affecté le plus immédiatement et le plus concrètement les fidèles, au lendemain du concile. Les deux derniers domaines, l'œcuménisme et la liberté religieuse, constituent des questions relativement nouvelles que les fidèles devaient encore apprivoiser, même si elles commençaient déjà à se poser au Canada, à la veille de Vatican II.

Ces divers essais, nous l'espérons, permettront de relancer la recherche sur le concile Vatican II au Canada et nous donnera d'apprécier davantage son passage dans notre histoire religieuse et sociale.

Michael Attridge, Catherine E. Clifford & Gilles Routhier

Introduction

The Second Vatican Council (1962–65) is recognized as the most significant religious event of the twentieth century, having a global influence. Its importance is no less significant when viewed from a Canadian perspective. In fact, this was the first time that a substantial number of Canadian bishops took part in an ecumenical council. Moreover, the Second Vatican Council was held at a moment when Canadian society was beginning to undergo a period of profound change, at a time when the Catholic Church in Canada was called to an unprecedented transformation due to its changing place within this evolving culture and society. The Canadian church, whose foundation was laid at the beginning of the seventeenth century and which had undergone a rapid expansion from the second half of the nineteenth until the middle of the twentieth, had lived for more than three centuries with the legacy of the Council of Trent and the developments spurred on by that council, which deeply marked the Catholic Church.

The importance of Vatican II in Canada is undeniable. More than forty years after its opening, we have yet to fully measure its impact. The studies written thus far have shown how important it is to examine the influence of this event in order to understand fully the evolution of the Catholic Church in Canada and to shed light upon the extent of the council's reception into the life and practice of the church, a complex and multi-faceted reality. On the fiftieth anniversary of the announcement of the council, the editors of this work considered it essential to encourage renewed attention to the study of Vatican II in Canada, including the history of Canadian participation in the council, Canadian interpretations of the council, and its reception in this country.

In retrospective literature about the council, Vatican II emerges as a moment for the second founding of the episcopal conference of the

Canadian Catholic bishops. Indeed, although the Canadian Conference of Catholic Bishops was first established in 1943, the bishops had not really had an opportunity to meet each other often, to work in common, or to share their vision of the future of Catholicism in Canada. Twenty years after the conference's inception, Vatican II thus provided an opportunity for a more intensive exchange between the bishops. Over a period of four years, bishops from across the country encountered one another daily and worked together regularly. It thus seemed appropriate for us to envision our own project of research into Vatican II in Canada as a collaborative effort that would bring together scholars from across the diverse regions of this country, and from several Canadian universities.

The fiftieth anniversary of the announcement of the council, on January 25, 1959, provided an occasion for scholars in theology from across Canada to revisit this event, its reception, and interpretation in Canada. We wanted to take advantage of this opportunity to invite the contributions of colleagues from across many disciplines and interests to gather together to reflect on a subject of common concern. An invitation went out from three Canadian faculties of theology (University of St. Michael's College, Saint Paul University, Université Laval) to undertake a common research project on Vatican II in Canada. The results of our research were shared within the context of three scholarly colloquia throughout the course of 2009, one in each of these respective universities. Most of the papers presented in these meetings are now offered in this volume.

Because Vatican II was not merely an affair of the bishops, the papers found in the first part of this work approach the event from a variety of perspectives, including those of the media, influential actors at the council, even though the debates *in aula* and the workings of the commissions remained closed to them; non-Catholic Christians, designated as official observers at the council and who in reality played a very active role; and theologians, who some have called the "engineers" of the council.

The second part of this book looks at the activities of Canadians—bishops and theologians—during and following the council, and at the experiences of those for whom the council became a turning point, not only for the Catholic Church as a body but also for individual persons. It was a thrilling experience for some, but for others a traumatic one (at least for those who could not have imagined that the council would take the direction it did).

The third and final part of this book examines the reception of Vatican II in Canada in different domains of the church's activity: liturgy, catechesis, religious life, the condition of the laity, ecumenism, and respect for religious liberty. Even before the announcement of the council by John XXIII in 1959, there had been significant developments in three of these areas: in the liturgy (the reform of the Easter Vigil and the plan to reform the breviary by Pius XII; the celebration of evening Masses; the introduction of dialogue Masses, etc.); in catechetics (plans to write new catechetical resources for use in Canada, to replace the catechism); and the apostolate of the laity (the movements of Catholic Action). Conciliar reforms in these three areas had perhaps a more immediate impact than others on the concrete life of the faithful in the wake of Vatican II. The two remaining areas, those of ecumenism and religious liberty, were relatively new issues with which Canadian Catholics would have to become better acquainted, even though they had become more pressing on the eve of Vatican II.

It is our hope that these diverse essays will stimulate a renewed interest in research and writing on the Second Vatican Council in Canada and will lead us to a greater appreciation of its significance in our religious and social history.

Michael Attridge, Catherine E. Clifford & Gilles Routhier

PART I

REGARDS PLURIELS SUR LE CONCILE / VARIOUS VIEWS OF THE COUNCIL

SECTION I

Vatican II Viewed by the Press / Vatican II vu par la presse

Reporting the Revolution: The *Western Catholic Reporter* and Post-Vatican II Reform[1]

Indre Cuplinskas,
St. Joseph's College, University of Alberta

Half a year after the closing of the Second Vatican Council, on April 19, 1966, the board of advisors of the weekly newspaper the *Western Catholic Reporter* met in the chancery office boardroom of the Archdiocese of Edmonton. The secretary recorded the following discussion:

> Father Mueller … stated that he had talked to two priests who were very vehement. These priests considered the paper too ambiguous. One priest stated that in their opinion the paper was not faithful to Catholic teaching. Both stated that if they were in control of [it,] something would be done about the format of the paper. Both specifically stated contraception as the main objection …. Sister Lillian stated that she felt people are confused. They

1 I am very grateful to Éloi DeGrâce, archivist at the Archives of the Roman Catholic Archdiocese of Edmonton for his assistance, to Douglas Roche for graciously agreeing to talk about his work with the *Western Catholic Reporter*, and to my colleague Richard Rymarz for commenting on the manuscript.

do not want to read about arguments; they want answers to the arguments and controversies. She stated that it will take time for people to understand, that when they read articles in the paper they assume that because it is a Catholic publication the printed article is the Church's position on the matter being discussed. They are very confused .... Sister Lillian stated that she would like to see a little more education on what the purpose of the paper is. Mr. Lemieux asked the Board if it was their opinion that the paper was not faithful to Catholic teaching. No one on the Board took this attitude.[2]

This discussion in an Alberta boardroom reveals the confusion that was common among Catholics in the years immediately following the council. Amid the turmoil people were taking sides regarding how the council should be understood and implemented. The discussion among the directors of a provincial Catholic paper also points to the important role media played in interpreting the council.[3]

This essay analyzes the *Western Catholic Reporter* (*WCR*) as a weekly newspaper created at the tail end of the council for the purpose of implementing the council's decisions through both the paper's structures and its publications: its *modus operandi* and its content, which espoused a liberal interpretation of the council in which the image of the people of God was central. This study focuses on the *WCR*'s mandate and method of operations in its early years (1965–68)—a period that reflects both the optimistic hopes and the tensions among Catholics in Canada after the closing of the council—and contributes to the larger ongoing debate about the proper interpretation of Vatican II in the Canadian context.

[2] Minutes of Meeting of the Board of Advisors to *Western Catholic Reporter* Held in Chancery Office Board Room, 19 April 1966, file: 1.6.22.3: Minutes 1965-1966, Archives of the Roman Catholic Archdiocese of Edmonton (ARCAE).

[3] The topic of the media and Vatican II has been examined from a number of different angles, categorized by Gilles Routhier thus: "examinations of the coverage of the Council itself and the work of journalists in this regard; explorations of the point of view of journalists regarding the practice of the Church in the area of communications; analyses of the mechanisms put into place during the time of the council, which assured the communication of religious news; studies of the position that the council itself took regarding mass media and social communication." Gilles Routhier, "Assurer la couverture dâu Concile Vatican II au Canada: Les initiatives de l'épiscopat canadien," *Études d'histoire religieuse* 68 (2002): 58–59.

The excitement, confusion, and uncertainty palpable among Catholics after the council were accompanied by a debate on how Vatican II should be understood and implemented. Opinions were hardly unanimous. For example, shortly after the council, polarization between liberal and conservative editors in the Catholic press in North America intensified.[4] This long-simmering debate has heated up again recently, with lines drawn between those who espouse a hermeneutic of rupture, insisting on charting their course on the broader "spirit of Vatican II,"[5] and those who espouse a hermeneutic of continuity, privileging the conciliar texts as the locus for the meaning of the council. John O'Malley, a proponent of a more expansive, event-centred understanding of the council, argues in his recent one-volume history of the council that, besides the obvious theological debates among the council fathers, there were undercurrents—the "issues under the issues"—one of which he identifies as "the style or model according to which … authority should be exercised."[6] O'Malley has in mind the relationship of centre and periphery in the Church, and, more specifically, the relationship between the papacy and the rest of the Church. The issue of the exercise of authority, however, surfaces at all levels of ecclesial life. The council as an event raised anew the question of the exercise of authority in the Church: for many Catholics, both lay and clergy, Vatican II signalled a change in these relations and called for greater dialogue, lay involvement, consensus and democracy in Church-based organizations, the *Western Catholic Reporter* being one among them.

Critics of O'Malley's interpretation of Vatican II, such as Matthew Lamb and Matthew Levering, contend that the council and its texts have been reduced to "products of power struggles between the lib-

---

4 Mary Lonan Reilly, *A History of the Catholic Press Association, 1911-1968* (Metuchen, NJ: Scarecrow Press, 1971),.254.

5 Richard John Neuhaus, "What Really Happened at Vatican II," *First Things* 186 (2008), http://www.firstthings.com/article/2008/09/001-what-really-happened-at-vatican-ii-30, accessed 3 October 2010; Matthew L. Lamb and Matthew Levering, *Vatican II: Renewal within Tradition* (Oxford and New York: Oxford University Press, 2008); John W. O'Malley, *What Happened at Vatican II* (Cambridge, MA: Belknap Press of Harvard University Press, 2008); John W. O'Malley and David G. Schultenover, *Vatican II: Did Anything Happen?* (New York: Continuum, 2007).

6 O'Malley, *What Happened at Vatican II*, 8.

erals and conservatives, with one side winning this passage and the other winning that."[7] In fact, it is journalists, first among them Xavier Rynne reporting on the council to the *New Yorker*, who are blamed for advancing this kind of interpretation of the council while it was still in session. Lamb and Levering argue that the real story of Vatican II is a theological one in which the Church's teachings underwent one more cycle of organic renewal and reform that placed emphasis on continuity rather than change.

Yet, in the first years after the council most Catholics focused on change, which they either favoured and fostered or criticized and eschewed. They had read about the debates and disagreements during the council and were thus exposed to pluralism in the Church in a way that most would not have experienced in their individual parishes or dioceses. These questions and new visions were only amplified by world events in the 1960s, when so many traditional values were being called into question, when the call for freedom was on the lips of youth, of women, of African Americans, and of European colonies in Africa and Asia.

During and immediately after the council, individual Catholics, organizations, and the Catholic press voiced their opinions as to what Vatican II meant and what Catholic life should look like in its wake. In 1965 both the Archbishop of Edmonton and the editorial team of the new *Western Catholic Reporter* unabashedly viewed the council as an event ushering in change, change that had to be supported, explained, and implemented. Unlike most of the Canadian Catholic press, the *WCR*, published in the Archdiocese of Edmonton, was a product of the council. It was founded as a medium to implement the teachings of the council, doing so not only through the information and views that were expressed in its pages but also in the paper's organizational structure and editorial policy. The resulting changes had much to do with transformations regarding, in O'Malley's words, the "style or model according to which authority was exercised."[8] The new *WCR* actively involved lay people and called for a freedom in reporting that Alberta's Catholics had not seen before.

7 Lamb and Levering, *Renewal within Tradition*, 7.

8 O'Malley, *What Happened at Vatican II*, 8.

Between 1919 and 1965 Catholics in Alberta read the Edmonton-based *Western Catholic*, which, until the 1960s had been edited by priests. By 1964 the paper needed a new editor and a new direction. In 1965 Archbishop Anthony Jordan of Edmonton invited Monsignor J. A. MacLellan, seventy-four years old, back to the helm of the newspaper that he had edited from 1927 to 1935.[9] While MacLellan was overseeing the *Western Catholic*, Jordan was developing a new plan.

Archbishop Jordan took on full responsibilities as the see's archbishop in 1964, at the age of sixty-three, presiding over the archdiocese in the turbulent years after the Second Vatican Council. The new archbishop participated in all four sessions in Rome[10] and took very seriously the renewal called for by the council fathers, embarking on a number of educational initiatives pertaining to the liturgy and the formation of the laity. He built on the work of his predecessor, establishing the archdiocesan liturgy commission. A few years after the council, the adult education commission was formed. For lay people who sought a degree in theology, Archbishop Jordan founded Newman Theological College.[11] These institutions allowed laity to engage in a systematic study of their faith. Only a tiny minority of Alberta's Catholics, however, would take advantage of these various educational opportunities. To reach all Catholics, other avenues had to be found for explaining the revolution that was taking place at the Second Vatican Council. Archbishop Jordan turned to the ailing archdiocesan newspaper, wondering how it could serve this purpose.

In his North America–wide search for a new editor, Jordan responded to a suggestion to contact Douglas Roche, a Canadian journalist in his mid-thirties working for the top-ranking New Jersey–based Catholic monthly magazine *The Sign*.[12] Archbishop Jordan contacted Roche

9 MacLellan was born in 1891. Edward Purcell, *Priests of Memory* (n.p., n.d.), 71. He had been the editor of the *Western Catholic* in its early days. Now, three decades later, he was asked to step in as an interim editor.

10 Bernard M. Daly, *Beyond Secrecy: The Untold Story of Canada and the Second Vatican Council* (Ottawa: Novalis, 2003), 218.

11 Newman College was founded in 1968. Frank Dolphin, *From Snow Shoes to E-mail: History of the Catholic Archdiocese of Edmonton* (Edmonton, 2002), 20–21.

12 J. G. Hanley to Reverend J. E. Crough, Catholic Information Centre, Edmonton, 8 September 1964; Paul Harris to Father J. E. Crough, 13 October 1964, file: 1.6.21:

in November 1964 during the third council session, and Roche agreed to come to Edmonton to take a look at the now forty-year-old *Western Catholic*. After examining the weekly, Roche proposed that Jordan launch a completely new paper that would better reflect the changes being wrought by the council. In agreeing to become the new paper's editor, Roche also saw his chance to run his own paper.

Roche brought with him extensive journalistic experience from a number of different newspapers: *The Toronto Telegram* (a secular daily), Cleveland's *Catholic Universe Bulletin* (a diocesan paper), and the Catholic monthly *The Sign*. Working in the United States, Roche explained that he came to understand more about reporting on the world events from a Catholic perspective, and he continued to be drawn to Catholic papers that were, in his words, "outward focused."[13]

Besides developing a Catholic perspective as a journalist, Roche also learned valuable lessons about the financial viability of Catholic papers during his time with the short-lived *Ensign,* a lay-operated Catholic weekly published in Montréal. Roche was asked to write a report on the *Ensign* after its failure to remain solvent in 1956. By his own account, Roche learned that for a Catholic newspaper to be viable its leadership had to have a good relationship with the local diocesan hierarchy, a "broad program of financing," and expert advice from an active board of directors.[14] All of these issues came to the fore when Roche became editor of the *WCR*, with the issue of financing proving to be the thorniest.

The first issue of the *WCR* came out in September 1965. Inspired by the council, the paper's editorial team placed the balance between freedom and authority in the Church at the centre of its editorial

---

"Archdiocesan Services: Western Catholic Press and the *Western Catholic*," ARCAE.

13 This was an attribute of the Catholic press that Roche had already highlighted in his honour's thesis as a student at St. Patrick's College, Ottawa. In this work on the apostolate of the Catholic Press, Roche analyzed a number of Canadian Catholic publications, evaluating the Montréal-based *Ensign* most positively because it did not simply dwell on internal Church issues. Douglas Roche, *Creative Dissent: A Politician's Struggle for Peace* (Toronto: Novalis, 2008), 42, 52, 57.

14 Ibid., 50. *Ensign* was a lay-operated Catholic weekly published in Montréal, 1948–56. For more on the history of the *Ensign*, see Peter McGuigan, "Robert Keyserlingk, Cardinal McGuigan and the Demise of the *Ensign*," *Catholic Insight* (February 2004).

policy. Moreover, the *WCR* sought to be more representative of the composition of the Church—in the catchphrase of the day: the people of God—than its predecessor had been. These goals were evident in the policies of the paper's staff, in the workings of the board of advisors, and in its relationship to the hierarchy.

As the paper's masthead declared, the *WCR* was published "For the People of God of Alberta." The people of God, arguably one of the dominant ecclesial images emanating from the council, was, of course, one of phrases used to describe the Church in the Dogmatic Constitution on the Church, *Lumen Gentium* (*LG*), and the title of the document's second chapter.[15] The council fathers debated its use and place in the constitution extensively.[16] Supporters argued for its expansiveness, inclusiveness, and rootedness in history: it linked the Church to the people of God of the Old Covenant; it was a concept that allowed for some connections between all peoples—theists, monotheists, Christians; and it was a way of speaking about all Christians in their fundamental equality as baptized persons before embarking on considerations of the hierarchy and the laity.[17] In the wake of the council, it was the concept of the people of God that captured the imagination of many Catholics, the editorial team of the *WCR* among them. They, too, were drawn to its potential for inclusiveness: by using the term on the masthead, the editors indicated their hope that the newspaper would appeal to Christians of various denominations.[18] The equality that the concept underscored resonated with a Church that was more open to what all of its members had to say. For Douglas Roche, one of the defining characteristics of the people of God was the liberty of the "sons of God" upon which *LG* insisted.[19] This liberty, in turn, challenged

15 For more on the debates surrounding the image see Alois Grillmeier, "The People of God," in *Commentary on the Documents of Vatican II*, vol. I, ed. Herbert Vorgrimler (Freiburg: Herder and Herder, 1967), 153–85.

16 See, for example, Giuseppe Alberigo, ed., *History of Vatican II*, vol. III (Maryknoll–Leuven: Orbis–Peeters, 2000).

17 Avery Dulles, "Nature, Mission and Structure of the Church," in *Vatican II: Renewal Within the Tradition*, ed. Matthew Levering and Matthew Lamb (Oxford: Oxford University Press, 2008), 25–36.

18 D. J. Roche, "Who We Are; What We Believe," *Western Catholic Reporter*, 9 September 1965.

19 *Lumen Gentium*, 9.

individual Christians to be responsible for their life of faith. Inspired by the idea of the people of God, the *WCR* advocated for a voluntary, enlightened, socially conscious, and activist Church membership and more egalitarian and transparent Church structures.

The first thing that Roche recommended was that Archbishop Jordan establish an independent newspaper that would, nevertheless, be owned by the archdiocese. Thus the paper embarked on a delicate balancing act that required it to maintain a credible amount of freedom to report on newsworthy items and at the same time pay due respect to Catholic moral and doctrinal truths. Roche was well aware that he would have to manœuvre between these two demands.[20]

To be a newspaper worthy of respect, the *Western Catholic Reporter* had to have freedom to report on newsworthy stories. As articulated in Roche's contract and in the very first issues, the paper was no longer an official organ of the hierarchy or "a press agent for the Church."[21] Independence and newsworthiness guided the *WCR* in matters of content. Roche pointed out to the Catholic Women's League (CWL) that the word "Reporter" in the newspaper's title was very consciously chosen because the paper was to report on the world around it, particularly on newsworthy items, not simply to list activities of Catholic organizations. It strove to be respected both by "Catholics and the general community for ... [its] ... objectivity ... [and] ... commitment to the art of journalism."[22] With this concern for the freedom of the press and emphasis on printing newsworthy items, the *WCR* joined the chorus of voices beginning to emanate from the Catholic Press Agency (CPA), which raised similar concerns with the National Catholic Press Department

[20] "If the paper is born at a propitious time in Christianity, it also comes at an hour of tension. For Vatican II, in probing the depths of the Church, has opened the way for steamrollers of criticism of every area of Church life. The volume of criticism voiced in the name of freedom has made many in authority in the Church nervous lest order and unity be sacrificed in pruning the accretions of age which have undeniably given a medieval character to the Church." D. J. Roche, "Who We Are; What We Believe," *Western Catholic Reporter*, 9 September 1965.

[21] D. J. Roche, "WCR and the CWL: Same Game; New Rules," *Western Catholic Reporter*, 3 February 1966; Agreement Between the Archdiocese of Edmonton and the Editor of the *Western Catholic Reporter*, "A Program for the *Western Catholic Reporter*," 13 February 1965, file: 1.6.22, ARCAE.

[22] Ibid.

and News Service (NC) run by the US Bishops' National Catholic Welfare Conference. Since the mid-1940s the CPA had been criticizing the NC for not always providing newsworthy items. During the council, the CPA became increasingly concerned that the NC was "controlling and withholding" news about the Church, in 1966 articulating its own task in Vatican II vocabulary: "This body of journalists [is] responsible for providing truth to the people of God …."[23] Roche was clearly not alone in his insistence on transparency and access to information.

The newspaper's freedom was rooted not just in the exigencies of the newspaper business but also, according to Roche, in the very "holy liberty of Christians."[24] Repeating this phrase like a mantra whenever he had the chance, Roche argued that this Christian freedom had to be at the very core of the Catholic press's identity. Moreover, he insisted that it was Vatican II that had rediscovered Christian freedom. Here was the council presented as the agent for change by reclaiming ancient teaching. The emphasis on Christian freedom challenged laity to become more responsible Church members.[25] The press had to both uphold this freedom and model it. Only a free press in the Church[26] could help to form a healthy Catholic public opinion that the Church so desperately needed in the postconciliar age.[27] In an August 1966 editorial entitled "New Use of Public Opinion," Roche perceptively wrote about the connection between public opinion and the new ecclesiology that he saw emerging from Vatican II. Sensing that some readers might find this vision of the Catholic press and laity novel, and therefore suspect, Roche peppered his argument with ecclesiastical authorities, lest he be seen as claiming something unprecedented.[28] Vatican II's emphasis on freedom and dialogue was altering relationships and responsibilities

---

23 Mary Lonan Reilly, *Catholic Press Association*, 244–48. Quoted in ibid., 248.

24 D. J. Roche, "*WCR* and the CWL: Same Game; New Rules," *Western Catholic Reporter*, 3 February 1966.

25 D. J. Roche, Memorandum to Canadian Catholic Press Editors, 11 February 1966, file: 1.6.22.3: Minutes 1965–1966, ARCAE.

26 D. J. Roche, "Who We Are; What We Believe," *Western Catholic Reporter*, 9 September 1965.

27 Appendix A, 1965, file: 1.6.22, ARCAE.

28 D. J. Roche, "New Use of Public Opinion," *Western Catholic Reporter*, 11 August 1966.

in the Church. Both hierarchy and laity were called to change the way they communicated and related to one another. In his article on public opinion, Roche further elaborated that, prior to Vatican II, directives were given from the top down, but now the bishops, "by giving new dignity to laity and emphasizing the role of authority as one of service ... had opened up a way for a flood of information and opinions and reactions to reach them."[29] Roche assumed that Catholics had to embrace their faith and their membership in the Church in a mature and conscious way because it was only mature and conscious Christians who would be able to take leadership positions in the postconciliar Church. This freedom rooted in maturity was at the core of the *WCR*'s vision of its mission.[30]

Despite this repeated emphasis on freedom, Roche was aware that the heady postconciliar liberty was not the only thing that defined the Catholic press. This new freedom embraced by the *WCR* was circumscribed by Church authorities and Catholic truth claims. In the *WCR*'s founding documents it was clearly stated that the editor determined the content of the paper, though he would be "responsible to Archbishop Jordan for the faithful reflection of official Catholic teaching."[31] To ensure that the newspaper was doctrinally orthodox a theological advisor was appointed. In the first years this position was held by Father Phillip Mueller, a twenty-seven-year-old priest with a degree from the Gregorianum who worked as a professor at St. Joseph's Seminary in Edmonton.[32]

Such were the optimistic ideals spelled out in the editorial policy: the production of a paper that respected Catholic teaching in the realm of faith and morals, but one that had the freedom to report on the world around it from the perspective of the renewal issuing from the Second

[29] Ibid.

[30] Roche even argued that other institutions such as the Canadian Catholic Conference News Service would benefit by making this freedom the cornerstone of their institution. See D. J. Roche, Memorandum to Canadian Catholic Press Editors, 11 February 1966, file: 1.6.22.3: Minutes 1965–1966, ARCAE.

[31] D. J. Roche, "Who We Are; What We Believe," *Western Catholic Reporter*, 9 September 1965.

[32] "Board of Advisors for *Western Catholic Reporter*," *Western Catholic Reporter*, 9 September 1965.

Vatican Council. This event was unquestionably perceived as one that was calling forth change in the Church.

The ideas emerging from Vatican II did not just guide the editorial policy of the paper but were also manifest in the views of those responsible for producing the paper. Like so many others enthused by Vatican II, the *Western Catholic Reporter*, published *for* the people of God produced *by* the people of God, insisted on greater responsibility on the part of the laity.[33] The editorial team was made up of lay Catholics trained as professional journalists. Working together on the first issues of the *WCR* with Editor Douglas Roche were Associate Editor Frank J. Dolphin, who brought with him his experience as a CBC journalist,[34] and Calgary Editor Fred T. Kanuka. Roche's former colleague from the Montréal-based *Ensign*, Stuart Lindop, was hired as the business manager. The *WCR* was not going to be an amateur operation.

One of the innovations of the *WCR* was to gather together a Board of Advisors that was selected as a cross-section of the people of God of Alberta for whom the paper was being published. According to the agreement between editor and archbishop, this "cross-section of the People of God of Alberta [was] empowered to set the overall tone of the paper. The editor [had] the editorial power, but could be relieved of his position with a two-thirds vote of non-confidence."[35] In the program for the *WCR* set out in 1965, the board was to include: "a professional journalist from the management level of a secular newspaper; an advertising executive, a lawyer, an accountant, a housewife, a nun, a theologian, [and] a priest."[36] The first board had thirteen members: ten from Edmonton and three from Calgary and other parts of Alberta. There were ten men and three women. Of the thirteen, five were clergy and

---

[33] The image of the people of God as articulated in *LG* emphasized that all the baptized together formed the people of God. On a popular level, however, this image was used to rally the laity. For a concise articulation of this position, see David R. Maines, Michael J. McCallion, *Transforming Catholicism: Liturgical Change in the Vatican II Church* (Lanham, MD: Lexington Books, 2007), 10–12.

[34] Roche, *Creative Dissent*, 83.

[35] Minutes of Meeting Held in the Office of *Western Catholic Reporter*, 17 December 1965, file: 1.6.22.3: Minutes 1965-1966, ARCAE.

[36] Agreement Between the Archdiocese of Edmonton and the Editor of the *Western Catholic Reporter*, "A Program for the *Western Catholic Reporter*," 13 February 1965, file: 1.6.22, ARCAE.

one was a nun. Over half were under fifty years of age. These members reflected the voice and power that each group they represented had in the Catholic Church of Alberta in the mid-1960s. The board was mature but youthful.[37] Most of its members were ready through the *WCR* to promote the renewal they saw emanating from the council.

In many ways the paper rode on the early euphoria and optimism of the council. In the words of Roche in his memoirs, "The paper was catching on, at least in important circles."[38] Who made up these important circles? Peers in the journalistic world and supporters of a progressive reading of Vatican II who rallied a mature and active laity to support changes in the liturgy and ecumenism. Other press agencies responded positively about the new weekly being published in Alberta. The *WCR* received laudatory reviews from *The Edmonton Journal* and the *Toronto Star*. South of the border, *Time* magazine devoted a half-page article to the new Western paper[39] and across the Atlantic in London *The Tablet* sang its praises.[40] For two years in a row, in 1967 and 1968, the Catholic Press Association, which evaluated press from all over North America, honoured the *WCR*, barely in its second year, with the first prize for "General Excellence" for papers with circulation up to 18,000.[41] In addition, in 1967, the paper garnered third place for Best Editorial Page. The judges were particularly impressed by "the content ... the solid way it relates a Church viewpoint to a broad national and international outlook and a lively concern for local public questions."[42]

---

37 "Board of Advisors for *Western Catholic Reporter*," *Western Catholic Reporter*, 9 September 1965.

38 Roche, *Creative Dissent*, 86.

39 *Time*, 8 April 1966.

40 Draft Letter, *Western Catholic Reporter* Board of Advisors to Bishops, August (?) [date unretrievable], 1966, file: 1.6.22, *Western Catholic Reporter*: Correspondence 1965, ARCAE.

41 "Catholic Press Association Awards," 58th Annual National Convention, 14–17 May 1968, The Neil House, Columbus, Ohio, file: *Western Catholic Reporter*, 1968, ARCAE.

42 "Catholic Press Association Awards," 57th Annual National Convention, 16–19 May 1967, King Edward Sheraton, Toronto, Ontario, General Editor: Rt. Rev. Msgr. Salvatore J. Adamo, file: 1.6.22, *Western Catholic Reporter*: Correspondence 1967, ARCAE.

Despite the accolades and interest, the paper faced substantial challenges in two areas in particular: finances and editorial policies. The same policies that elicited praise in some quarters were troubling to others. The people of God were not unanimous in their understanding of what the Church should look like and how it should operate.

The initial hope was to have a paper that would survive on subscriptions and advertising. Not a parochial paper, the *WCR* could solicit a substantial number of advertisements, the majority from local businesses in Edmonton and Calgary. The weekly managed to secure 18,000 subscriptions, but that was 7,000 short of the number that would make it financially viable.[43] Discussions among the board of advisors regarding the financial difficulties reveal a number of interesting tensions that the paper was experiencing. The ambition of running a paper that could survive on subscriptions was rooted in the new optimism regarding the laity and the active participation to which it was called by the council. The hope was that the laity would embrace the new ecclesiology and theology that the newspaper was intent on communicating. This happened among some sectors of the Catholic population, but not all.

The disappointing revelation that not all of the laity were embracing and engaging with the new ecclesiology and theology highlighted the weekly's need for active clerical support. From its inception, of course, the paper had the support of Archbishop Jordan, who willingly kept the *WCR* afloat in the first years as the paper struggled to expand its readership. There is a sense from the board of advisors' meetings, however, that a sizeable portion of the clergy had to be approached circumspectly in order to ensure their backing. Still, critics and supporters of the new paper were found among clergy and laity alike.

Some lay-clerical tension was evident in the discussions about the subscription drives in the first two years. Initially, priests were asked to

---

43 The overwhelming majority of subscriptions were from Alberta. For example, in 1967 from a total of 15, 850 subscriptions 11, 928 were from Alberta. Although the province had 372,000 Catholics, the *WCR* never managed to get much beyond 18,000 subscriptions, which, it should be noted, was more than double the subscribers that the *Western Catholic* had had. File: 1.6.22.3, Minutes 1967, ARCAE; *The Western Catholic Directory: Official Catholic Directory for the Province of Alberta* (Edmonton, AB: Western Catholic, 1965); Minutes of Meeting of the Board of Advisors to Western Catholic Reporter, 19 January 1966, file: 1.6.22.3: Minutes 1965-1966, ARCAE.

inform their congregations of the new *WCR* and to promote the paper by encouraging people to subscribe. The response was moderate; however, in one parish, the *WCR* ran a pilot project with a layman speaking to the congregation—this resulted in twice as many people subscribing. Consequently, the board of advisors discussed the possibility of asking laypeople to promote the paper in parishes. A number of the board members were cautious. What were their concerns? First of all, the board members wanted to ensure that clergy would not presume that their efforts had not been appreciated. Secondly, there were concerns about the time and the place at which laypeople should speak. Should they speak after the Mass? Could they speak from the lectern? Thirdly, some members worried about finding competent laypeople to talk about the subscription drive. These discussions give a glimpse of how the laity was trying to negotiate its way between its new found prerogatives and clerical authority and sensitivities.[44] Lay involvement in the subscription drive did not, however, solve the paper's financial challenges.

By 1966 it was becoming clear that the *WCR* would not be able to survive on subscriptions alone; therefore, a committee was struck to investigate the pros and cons of a parish coverage plan, in which parishes would pay for subscriptions for their members. This would guarantee funding for the paper, though it would undermine the ideal of an active laity consciously choosing to support the paper.[45] Moreover, this approach would require the explicit support of the parish pastor. During one of the meetings of the board of advisors, latent laity-clergy tensions seeped into the conversation. The members of the special committee had been canvassing parish priests to get a sense of the support that they could anticipate for a parish plan and reported that, in general, parishes had responded positively. In the discussion that ensued, however, it became clear that the board was very aware that the paper now needed the active support of pastors, and yet some board

[44] Eleven subscriptions resulted when the paper was advertised by clergy and twenty-five when the layman encouraged congregants to subscribe. Minutes of Meeting of the Board of Advisors to *Western Catholic Reporter*, 19 January 1966, file: 1.6.22.3: Minutes 1965-1966, ARCAE.

[45] Report of Committee Investigating the Pros and Cons of a 100% Plan as Applicable to the *WCR* submitted Archbishop. A. Jordan, 26 January 1967, file: *Western Catholic Reporter*: Correspondence 1967, ARCAE.

members felt that parish priests were becoming more reluctant to push the paper actively. Board member and former *Western Catholic* editor Monsignor MacLellan, a staunch defender of the clergy, remarked that he seemed to recall "at a previous meeting plans were made that would exclude the clergy, the laity would take over and run the show."[46] He also recalled Roche's earlier assurances that the paper would sell itself. MacLellan seemed to savour the fact that the lay leadership's hopes for the newspaper's success were foundering and that, chastened, the leadership was forced to turn to the clergy for help.[47]

This discussion among the board of advisors foreshadowed the mixed response that Archbishop Jordan received when he went to his priests to ask them to promote the parish coverage plan. In mid-March Jordan invited parish representatives to attend a meeting in which parishes would indicate whether or not they were willing to put their parish on the coverage plan. He had been told by board members that he needed two-thirds of the parishes to sign on to the plan to make it work. Therefore, Jordan must have been disappointed when less than half the parishes agreed to join the parish coverage plan—forty of the eighty-four representatives who had attended the meeting.[48] The board and Jordan had been adamant that the plan had to be accepted voluntarily: there was to be no compulsion. Despite the less than satisfactory results, Jordan took heart in the fact that this meeting was the first one in which a democratic process was used to come to an archdiocesan-wide decision.[49] Here was an example of the *WCR*, albeit indirectly, changing the very culture of the archdiocese, and bringing in the voice of the people of God, even when that voice did not support the newspaper. For the archbishop, the new ecclesiology of the people of God required

46 Meeting of the Board of Advisors of the *Western Catholic Reporter*, 1 February 1967, file: 1.6.22.3: Minutes, 1967, ARCAE.

47 In the detailed and colourful minutes of the board meetings, MacLellan came across as particularly defensive of clergy and sensitive to criticism of members of the Church hierarchy, whereas Roche felt that the *WCR* needed to report on substantiated criticisms of clergy as part of a move towards greater transparency and professionalism in Catholic press. Thus, when the laity were forced to turn to the clergy for help, as in this case, a reader of the minutes can detect that MacLellan relished the moment.

48 Archbishop Jordan to the Parish Priests and Parish Councils of the Archdiocese of Edmonton, 14 March 1967, file: 1.6.22.3: Minutes 1967, ARCAE.

49 Ibid.

that clergy and laity in the archdiocese have a more direct voice in some of the decision-making.

By 1968 another committee was in place to help guide the *WCR* in its work. Because concerns continued to be raised about the paper, especially that it was unnecessarily controversial and contentious, Archbishop Jordan "in consultation with the Edmonton Priests' Senate" appointed the Pastoral Review Committee.[50] Its task was to give "a periodic evaluation of the content of the paper from a pastoral viewpoint."[51] This was not, however, to be done in a vacuum. The committee was to read the five Catholic papers selected by the Catholic editors of North America as the all-round best papers being published, judging the *WCR* in light of its peers, not simply according to the preferences of committee members.[52] Thus, for example, when Roche asked the Committee for guidance on whether and how to report on the numerous clergy who were leaving the priesthood, committee members both gave their own opinions and referred to the aforementioned Catholic publications to see how the latter had handled the issue.[53]

All of these developments indicate that the editorial team's initial enthusiasm about producing a progressive paper that would be sustained by a like-minded laity and supportive clergy had to be tempered. Disagreements among Alberta's Catholics about what the council meant and the kind and degree of change that should be ushered in were present from the closing of the council onwards. The people of God to whom the paper was directed were not as unified as the editors might have hoped, and a good number were resistant to the plans the *WCR* had for their re-education.[54] This is particularly evident in the *WCR*'s

---

50 Memorandum of Agreement between Archbishop Anthony Jordan, OMI, Archbishop of Edmonton, and Douglas J. Roche, Editor of the *Western Catholic Reporter*, 1 June 1968, file: 1.6.22: *Western Catholic Reporter* 1968, ARCAE.

51 Ibid.

52 In the mid-1960s these were the *St. Louis Review*, the *National Catholic Reporter*, Cleveland's *Catholic Universe Bulletin*, the *Catholic Star Herald*, and the *Clarion Herald*. Archbishop Anthony Jordan, OMI, Archbishop of Edmonton, and Douglas J. Roche, Editor of the *Western Catholic Reporter*, Memorandum of Agreement, 1 June 1968, file: *Western Catholic Reporter*, 1968, ARCAE.

53 Report of the Pastoral Review Committee, 24 June 1968, file: 1.6.22, Western Catholic Reporter, 1968, ARCAE.

54 The initial program for the *WCR*, written up in 1965, did see the newspaper as a tool

attempts to woo unsupportive clergy in order that they would then coax laity to buy into the newspaper. The campaign was not always successful: critics remained.

Those who were loath to support the paper, including bishops, priests, and laypeople, were displeased with the general editorial thrust and the resulting content of the *WCR*. In the last year of his episcopacy, Bishop Francis P. Carroll of Calgary[55] responded to Roche's request that he encourage readership, insisting, "I do not think some articles are helping the renewal desired by the Vatican Council, and I do not care to assume responsibility for them."[56] The bishop's ambivalence, amplified by the hostility exhibited by segments of the clergy and laity, was disheartening. In board meetings anecdotes trickled in of priests who were concerned that the content of the weekly was too intellectual or contentious, or both. Some voiced concerns that youth should not be exposed to controversial stories about priests calling for their own unions, nor should young people be reading the numerous articles on birth control. The paper did not edify and clarify; rather it confused and scandalized, said its critics.[57]

Not even all board members agreed about the paper's content, and their disagreements spilled out into the paper itself. Evidently Monsignor MacLellan did not feel that his criticism of some of the content was being heeded. Accordingly, in August 1966, he penned a letter to the editor entitled "Profoundly Disturbed," voicing his concerns about "all the negative statements about clergy in the last issue." This MacLellan perceived as "highly harmful to the Church," and he thought that the paper would do better to focus, for instance, on the life of exemplary priests. He also recalled the advice he had received from a bishop while he was editor: "it is not so much what you put

for re-education. Agreement Between the Archdiocese of Edmonton and the Editor of the *Western Catholic Reporter*, "A Program for the *Western Catholic Reporter*," 13 February 1965, file: 1.6.22, ARCAE.

55 Bishop Carroll resigned in 1966 after thirty years in office. His successor, Bishop Francis Klein, was more supportive of the *WCR*.

56 Francis P. Carroll, Bishop of Calgary to Douglas Roche, 20 July 1966, file: *Western Catholic Reporter*, Correspondence 1967, ARCAE.

57 Minutes of Meeting of the Board of Advisors to *Western Catholic Reporter*, 19 April 1966, file 1.6.22.3: Minutes 1965–1966, ARCAE.

into the paper as what you keep out."[58] The matter did not end there. Another board member—the young theological advisor Father Phillip Mueller—sent in a response that was duly printed in the "Letters to the Editor" section. Echoing Roche's vision for the paper, Mueller defended the *WCR* and the need for honesty in order for the growth of a healthy public opinion in the Church. This exchange suggests that for a man such as MacLellan—an older clergyman who had shown enthusiasm for the council as editor of the *Western Catholic*—what was most troubling was the criticism directed at the Church.[59] He preferred renewal through positive examples rather than negative criticism. Roche and Mueller valued a wider spectrum of truth, be it positive or negative, and strove to help form Catholics who could cope with imperfect people, practices, and organizations without losing their faith in the Church. The fact that board members engaged in debate in the pages of the paper underscores how charged the atmosphere must have become. But the fact that the editor chose to allow this disagreement to be aired so publicly is also remarkable evidence of Roche's belief in openness and transparency.

Despite the criticism directed at the *WCR*, the editorial team, and many of the board members, did not see themselves as putting out a radical paper. Time and again, the weekly was described as moderate but progressive.[60] Roche, in his memoirs, insists that he was not looking for a fight.[61] But Roche was on a mission; he strove toward the proper implementation of Vatican II. Minutes from meetings indicate that Roche felt that he had to control his tone, because "he did not want to give the impression of attacking people—especially those who are not

---

58 Msgr. J. A. MacLellan, "Profoundly Disturbed," *Western Catholic Reporter*, 18 August 1966.

59 In an earlier letter to the editor, MacLellan had come to the defense of the CWL after Roche had challenged the organization to take part in more meaningful activity and take stands on the burning social issues of the day. Msgr. J. A. MacLellan, "A Defence of the CWL," *Western Catholic Reporter*, 17 February 1966.

60 "Policy Statement by Archbishop Jordan," *Western Catholic Reporter*, 6 September 1965; Minutes of Meeting of the Board of Advisors to *Western Catholic Reporter* Held in Office of Western Catholic Reporter, 19 January 1966, file: 1.6.22.3: Minutes 1965–1966, ARCAE.

61 Roche, *Creative Dissent*, 84.

doing enough to implement Vatican II here in Alberta."[62] Interestingly, in his memoirs, Roche insists that at the end of the day it was not the paper but the outcome of Vatican II that clergy antagonistic toward the *WCR* opposed. Roche was convinced that the *WCR* was an accurate interpreter of the intent of the council.[63] The *WCR* also faced the difficulty that so many newsworthy stories of the day dealt with controversial issues that many Catholics had not been used to seeing aired: priestly celibacy, contraception, relations with other Christian denominations. If it was going to report on the issues of the day, the *WCR* could not avoid controversy.

There is also evidence in the paper of self-censorship and struggles on how to approach some topics. In his memoirs, Roche recalls the struggle to frame a policy for reporting on priests who were leaving their ministry.[64] The archives contain Roche's correspondence on this matter with the pastoral review committee, in which the editor argued for more openness, particularly because many priests were leaving not because they "were at fault" but "as a form of protest against the institution."[65] The committee chair countered that, though it might be appropriate to discuss the phenomenon in general, it was more prudent and pastoral not to report on specific individuals, especially if they had been local priests known to the readers.[66] Here, again, two visions of the post–Vatican II Church were pitted against each other: while one called for a strengthening of the Church through openness to criticism, the other sought to build up the Church through positive examples and by shielding the faithful from troublesome developments.

---

62 Minutes of Meeting of the Board of Advisors to *Western Catholic Reporter*, 19 January 1966, file: 1.6.22.3: Minutes 1965–1966, ARCAE.

63 Roche, *Creative Dissent*, 84. Roche distinguishes between bishops and priests, indicating that bishops were more open to changes in the postconciliar Church because they had attended the council and, therefore, understood the task that lay before them. Priests, on the other hand, were less knowledgeable and, hence, more resistant.

64 Roche, *Creative Dissent*, 84–85.

65 Douglas Roche to Rev. L. Frizzell, Rev. F. E. Otterson, 9 May 1968, file: *Western Catholic Reporter*, 1968, ARCAE.

66 Rev. L. Frizzell to Douglas Roche, 15 May 1968, file: *Western Catholic Reporter*, 1968, ARCAE.

A second example of self-censorship, an unsigned handwritten note in the archives, from mid-1967, indicated that the *WCR* was loath to be too critical of Paul VI's encyclical of the same year on priestly celibacy, *Sacerdotalis Caelibatus*. The author of the note argued that, "In present situation, *WCR* cannot take a stand this critical of celibacy and authority. Better not to publish an editorial at this time." Suggestions, however, were made on how to respond more obliquely: the paper could publish responses from other newspapers and could include letters to the editor.[67]

These fragments give an indication of some of the negotiation in which the editorial team was involved as it judged what to print in the pages of the *WCR*. Despite its call for openness and freedom, the paper knew it had to tread carefully when it came to more controversial subjects, particularly when they pertained to clergy and authority.

Thus it is evident that the *WCR*'s structures and its *modus operandi* were very consciously products of the optimism that initially flowed out from the council. Those involved with the paper, whether part of the editorial team or members of the board of advisors, were convinced that they needed to model the new ecclesiology and liberty in the way that the paper operated.

The *WCR* put Alberta on the Canadian Catholic map. This usually conservative province was producing an edgy Catholic paper that was constructed on principles perceived to be emanating from the Second Vatican Council. How Vatican II was implemented depended very much on personalities: in Alberta it took an archbishop like Anthony Jordan, who was prepared to put his money and some of his authority on the line, paired up with an ambitious young Catholic layman like Douglas Roche to take up the challenge of producing a paper with high journalistic standards in a province that frankly barely had the Catholic population to support such a venture.

What does the creation of the *WCR* and its conscious attempt to embody the Second Vatican Council contribute to an understanding of the council itself? It shows that even on the ground among Alberta's Catholics the meaning of the council was contested. In its *modus*

67 Handwritten note, s.a., 4 July 1967, file: 1.6.22.3: Minutes 1967, ARCAE.

operandi, the *WCR* unquestionably sided with what O'Malley identified as "the style or model ... according to which authority should be exercised."[68] Despite its calls for change, the *WCR* was an exercise in both continuity and change in the early postconciliar era.

The paper emphasized greater lay involvement in the Catholic press, which had been growing steadily since World War II in the US and elsewhere.[69] The creation of the *WCR* was a return to a press with greater lay involvement that had been prevalent in the nineteenth and early-twentieth centuries.[70] What was new was that these calls for greater lay responsibility could be grounded in an ecclesiastically sanctioned shift in ecclesiology rooted in the image of the people of God.

In the end, the most contentious issue the *WCR* dealt with was the nature and extent of criticism that could be directed against Church hierarchy and Church organizations. The words "independence, liberty, and public opinion" loomed large for the *WCR*. The weekly did not call, however, for these ideals as embattled Catholics in an antagonistic secular environment, as might have been the case for the *Western Catholic* in 1919. Rather, the *WCR* wanted to contribute to building up independence, liberty, and public opinion *within* the Church. The *WCR* was joining the growing chorus for a robust public opinion in the Church. Challenges and questions were directed less *extra ecclesia* and more *intra ecclesia* by a newspaper that ironically did not want to be limited simply to intra-ecclesial matters.

68 O'Malley, *What Happened at Vatican II*, 8.

69 John G. Deedy, Jr., "The Catholic Press: The Why and the Wherefore," in Martin E. Marty, *The Religious Press in America* (New York: Rinehart and Winston, 1963): 65–123. Catholic Canada could boast of important English-language lay journalists, such as Henry Somerville and Murray Ballantyne, between the two world wars. Both Somerville and Ballantyne questioned the position of a number of Canadian bishops on the issue of the Canadian Commonwealth Federation, see Robert H. Dennis, "Beginning to Restructure the Institutional Church: Canadian Social Catholics and the CCF, 1931–1944," *Historical Studies* 74 (2008): 51–71.

70 Deedy, "The Catholic Press: The Why and the Wherefore," 77.

Le concile Vatican II dans la région de la Beauce : une fenêtre sur Rome à travers l'*Éclaireur-Progrès*

Marc Pelchat,
Université Laval

Nous disposons déjà, sur la couverture de presse de Vatican II, d'un bon nombre d'études qui nous éclairent sur la diffusion des idées et la réception des enseignements ou des décisions du concile[1]. Cependant, les études réalisées sur la couverture

[1] Jan Grootaers, « Le catholicisme du Québec et son insertion dans le milieu conciliaire », dans Gilles Routhier, dir., *L'Église canadienne et Vatican II*, Montréal, Fides, 1997, p. 447-453 ; Yves Therrien, « La couverture de Vatican II dans les quotidiens francophones du Canada (1959-1962) », dans *L'Église canadienne et Vatican II*, *op. cit.*, p. 145-164 ; Marc Pelchat, « Les revues canadiennes-françaises de dévotion et le concile Vatican II (1959-1962) », *ibid.*, p. 165-188 ; Gaëtan Baillargeon, « Les intellectuels québécois et Vatican II : de l'annonce du concile à son ouverture (1959-1962) », *ibid.*, p. 189-208 ; Yves Therrien, « La couverture de presse de Vatican II dans les quotidiens francophones du Canada », mémoire de maîtrise présenté à la Faculté de théologie et de sciences religieuses de l'Université Laval (1997), s'intéresse à la phase préparatoire ; Jean-Pierre Proulx, « Le quotidien *Le Devoir* et l'aggiornamento conciliaire : (1960-1970) », dans *Études d'histoire religieuse*, n° 63, 1997, p. 45-57 ; Réjean Plamondon, « Le service d'information de la CCC à Vatican II » et Pierre Hurtubise, « Vatican II : propos d'un témoin engagé », dans *L'Église canadienne et Vatican II*, *op. cit.*, p. 209-222 et 223-234 ; Jean-Claude Dupuis, « La revue *Relations* et le concile Vatican II », dans *Les Cahiers d'histoire du Québec au XX*e *siècle*, n° 6 (1996), p. 33-50 ; Roland Leclerc, « La couverture médiatique du concile par Radio-Canada : première réception au Canada français », dans *Vatican II au Canada : enracinement et réception*, Montréal, Fides, 2001, p. 261-272 ; Jérôme Coutard, « La presse québécoise et Vatican II de 1959 à 1962 : la construction

de l'événement conciliaire par des publications hebdomadaires en région sont beaucoup plus rares. Dans ce dernier cas, le regard porté sur l'événement, dans la durée, révèle une attention plus particulière à certains thèmes, dans les limites d'une population précise, possédant ses caractéristiques propres. L'importance du journalisme hebdomadaire en regard de la diffusion des idées auprès d'une population régionale ne saurait être négligée[2].

Pour illustrer la couverture de presse régionale du concile Vatican II, nous avons porté notre attention sur le journal l'*Éclaireur-Progrès*, publié à Saint-Georges de Beauce entre le 9 octobre 1958, avec l'annonce de la mort du pape Pie XII, et le 28 septembre 1966, une année après la fin de la dernière session du concile.

Pour situer l'importance de l'*Éclaireur-Progrès*, il faut voir que ce journal hebdomadaire occupe une place déterminante dans la région Beauce-Etchemin. Cette région s'est dotée d'une presse locale un peu plus tardivement que d'autres régions du Québec, mais son développement sera rapide. Un premier journal éphémère, intitulé *La Beauce*, fut publié à Sainte-Marie en 1891, rapidement suivi d'un autre, un peu plus durable, intitulé *La Vallée de la Chaudière*. La parution d'un journal appelé simplement *L'Éclaireur* débute à Beauceville en 1908. Celui-ci deviendra l'*Éclaireur-Progrès* en 1960, lors de sa fusion avec *Le Progrès de Saint-Georges*, fondé en 1944[3]. Le nouveau journal né de

---

d'une culture conciliaire », dans *Vatican II au Canada : enracinement et réception*, *op. cit.*, p. 245-260 ; Gilles ROUTHIER, « L'annonce et la préparation de Vatican II : réception et horizon d'attente au Québec », dans *Études d'histoire religieuse*, n° 63 (1997), p. 25-44 ; Gilles ROUTHIER, « Assurer la couverture du concile Vatican II au Canada : les initiatives de l'épiscopat canadien », dans *Études d'histoire religieuse*, n° 68 (2002), p. 57-72. La présente note a été réalisée grâce à la collaboration du professeur Gilles Routhier.

2 On doit à Yves MICHAUD ce qui semble être la première étude de la presse hebdomadaire régionale, à l'occasion d'un mémoire de maîtrise (1960) réalisé au Centre international d'enseignement supérieur du journalisme de Strasbourg et intitulé « La presse hebdomadaire au Canada français ». Il faut également signaler l'étude réalisée par Denis CHABOT, « L'exploration de la presse hebdomadaire québécoise : de l'apostolat à l'entreprise de presse », mémoire de maîtrise présenté à la Faculté des lettres de l'Université Laval (1989), qui tente une périodisation des phases de transformation de la presse hebdomadaire régionale, passant « d'une vision imprégnée d'une mission apostolique à une vision moderne de la presse conditionnée par les notions de tirage et de couverture du marché ».

3 Sur les activités reliées à l'information dans la région de la Beauce, voir Serge COURVILLE, Pierre C. POULIN, Barry RODRIGUE *et alii*, *Histoire de Beauce-Etchemin-*

cette fusion ne monopolise pas toutes les activités reliées à l'information dans la région Beauce-Etchemin, les villes régionales se dotant presque toutes d'une presse écrite. Cependant, le journal l'*Éclaireur-Progrès* va s'imposer comme l'un des plus importants hebdomadaires de la région en atteignant une bonne partie de la population de Beauce-Etchemin et, en particulier, toute la région économique de Saint-Georges de Beauce. On rapporte que le tirage hebdomadaire était de 9000 copies en 1968[4], ce qui laisse supposer que le nombre de lecteurs atteignait chaque semaine quelques dizaines de milliers dans les foyers où le journal pénétrait.

Il sera donc question ici de la couverture de la nouvelle religieuse dans l'*Éclaireur-Progrès*, témoignant de l'importance de la présence du catholicisme dans la vie quotidienne des Beaucerons. Cependant, nous nous arrêterons plus particulièrement à l'impact de l'événement conciliaire tel que reflété dans le journal hebdomadaire sur une période de huit années, de l'automne 1958 à l'automne 1966. Nous mesurerons l'importance de cette information et caractériserons son évolution, en mettant en évidence les sujets d'intérêt et les thèmes ayant le plus retenu l'attention.

La présence de l'actualité religieuse dans l'*Éclaireur-Progrès*

Notre intérêt, dans cette étude, se porte principalement et presque exclusivement sur l'écho conciliaire dans un média régional d'information. Cependant, il importe de situer la diffusion des idées provenant du concile Vatican II par rapport à l'importance de l'information religieuse dans ce média beauceron. En effet, on repère facilement dans les pages de l'*Éclaireur-Progrès* la forte présence de l'actualité religieuse et de ses

---

Amiante, Québec, Les Éditions de l'Institut québécois de recherche sur la culture et les Presses de l'Université Laval (collection « Les régions du Québec », 16), 2003, p. 390. On peut aussi consulter France Bélanger, Sylvia Berberi, Jean-René Breton, Daniel Carrier, Renald Lessard *et alii*, *La Beauce et les Beaucerons. Portraits d'une région 1737-1987*, Saint-Joseph-de-Beauce, La Société du patrimoine des Beaucerons, 1990, p. 277.

4 Source : Roger Bolduc, *Saint-Georges d'hier et d'aujourd'hui*, Saint-Georges de Beauce, 1969, p. 124. Roger Bolduc a été successivement professeur, libraire et journaliste. Résident de Saint-Georges de Beauce, il fut rédacteur en chef du *Progrès de Saint-Georges* de 1952 à 1954 et de l'*Éclaireur-Progrès* à compter de 1954.

thèmes. À titre indicatif, nous avons repéré 90 références explicites à des faits religieux dans 12 numéros de l'hebdomadaire sur une période de 3 mois, du début d'octobre à la fin de décembre 1958[5]. Cette actualité religieuse est d'abord et avant tout locale. Les statistiques paroissiales annuelles y prennent une place importante, avec l'indication du nombre d'« âmes », le nombre de communiants et de non-communiants, le nombre de baptêmes et de mariages. De même, les installations et les départs de curés ainsi que les résultats des élections de marguilliers se retrouvent régulièrement dans les pages du journal. Les événements liturgiques suscitent nouvelles brèves et photos : fêtes de Noël et messes de minuit, pèlerinages paroissiaux. Les comptes-rendus d'événements civils (inaugurations, mises au jeu d'événements sportifs), souvent publiés avec photos, mettent en évidence des membres du clergé.

On y trouve aussi fréquemment des messages ou des comptes-rendus à propos de réunions ou de congrès de confréries religieuses[6] et des mouvements d'Action catholique. On y donne également des nouvelles des missionnaires de la région ou on souligne leur passage dans la région beauceronne. On y annonce les prises d'habit religieux, les ordinations presbytérales, les cours de préparation au mariage. On y fait état des œuvres ou des institutions catholiques, telles que l'École des parents, l'hôpital, les commissions scolaires. On y traite assez souvent de l'école catholique et de l'éducation et on fait état à l'occasion de campagnes de moralité contre la mauvaise littérature. Les nouvelles de l'extérieur sont relatives aux événements touchant le Saint-Siège, comme la mort du pape Pie XII, en octobre 1959, qualifiée de « perte irréparable[7] » et suscitant des messages de sympathie publiés par des commerçants, ou les hommages rendus au pape Jean XXIII à l'occasion de son élection[8]. On parlera aussi du consistoire convoqué par le

---

5 Dans son analyse de la presse hebdomadaire québécoise réalisée en 1960 et citée précédemment, Yves Michaud soulignait la place importante prise par les informations religieuses « dans la presse semainière de langue française, 10,7 % de toute la matière à lire par comparaison à 0,7 % pour les nouvelles internationales, 1 % pour les nouvelles de la politique nationale, 3,8 % pour la politique provinciale ».

6 Enfants de Marie, Ligues du Sacré-Cœur, Ligue ouvrière catholique, Ordre des Filles d'Isabelle, Ordre des Chevaliers de Colomb, en particulier.

7 16 octobre 1958, p. 11.

8 30 octobre 1958, p. 1.

nouveau pape pour le 15 décembre 1958 afin de nommer de nouveaux cardinaux au Sacré Collège et d'en augmenter le nombre à la faveur d'une réforme[9].

Plus significatif encore, on retrouve périodiquement dans l'*Éclaireur-Progrès* des chroniques régulières telles que « Choisis bien ta vocation », la chronique colombienne ou la chronique « Dans le monde », reprenant divers communiqués de presse sur les événements civils ou ecclésiaux. On repère aussi une chronique de nouvelles brèves intitulée « À l'ombre de la métropole », qui rapporte divers événements régionaux, nationaux ou internationaux, assez souvent à caractère ecclésial. Particularité qu'il convient de souligner, le journal publie régulièrement des sommaires de la revue jésuite *Relations* et des résumés d'articles. On trouve aussi des articles de fond tirés d'ouvrages ou d'autres publications, sur des thèmes inspirés de fêtes religieuses, comme Noël et l'épiphanie, ou sur des sujets comme le communisme et la liberté religieuse ou la papauté. On ne s'étonnera donc pas que l'hebdomadaire beauceron fasse largement écho au concile qui sera bientôt convoqué par le pape Jean XXIII. C'est la manière dont il le fera qui va maintenant retenir notre attention.

Le concile Vatican II dans l'*Éclaireur-Progrès*

Les informations sur le concile viendront d'abord de l'extérieur, principalement de Rome, et seront tout simplement reprises dans le journal. L'annonce de la convocation du concile est publiée dans le numéro du 29 janvier 1959, à peine quelques jours après l'événement, dans le bloc de nouvelles portant le titre « Dans le monde », qui semble reprendre un communiqué de source non identifiée insistant sur l'unité chrétienne comme objectif à longue portée du concile voulu par le pape. Il faudra cependant attendre plus de six mois avant qu'une autre nouvelle, publiée le 27 août 1959, cherche à préciser l'objectif du concile, dont on dit maintenant qu'il poursuivra « l'union des catholiques ». Le numéro suivant, toujours dans la section intitulée « Dans le monde », corrigera le tir en précisant que « les frères séparés pourront se faire entendre[10] ». Cette même édition soulignera l'intérêt des anglicans du

---

[9] 13 novembre et 20 novembre 1958 ; 8 janvier 1959.

[10] 3 septembre 1959.

Québec pour le concile ainsi que leurs bonnes relations avec les catholiques. Il faudra ensuite attendre janvier 1960 pour que l'on commence à parler vraiment de la préparation du concile.

Une couverture médiatique en évolution : 1959-1966

Les deux tableaux suivants présentent schématiquement la couverture du concile par l'hebdomadaire beauceron. Le tableau I indique le nombre d'articles parus dans l'*Éclaireur-Progrès* en relation avec la chronologie des différentes phases du concile. Le tableau II répartit le nombre d'articles publiés en relation avec les thèmes abordés.

Tableau I : Nombre d'articles selon la phase conciliaire

Chronologie du concile	Nombre d'articles parus dans l'*Éclaireur-Progrès*
Phase antépréparatoire (17 mai 1959 - 5 juin 1960)	4
Phase préparatoire (6 juin 1960 - 10 octobre 1962)	6
Première session (11 octobre - 8 décembre 1962)	8
Première intersession (9 décembre 1962 - 28 septembre 1963)	17
Deuxième session (29 septembre - 4 décembre 1963)	1
Deuxième intersession (5 décembre 1963 - 13 septembre 1964)	6
Troisième session (14 septembre - 21 novembre 1964)	8

Troisième intersession 22 novembre 1964 - 14 septembre 1965	6
Quatrième session (15 septembre - 8 décembre 1965)	6
Phase postconciliaire 9 décembre 1965 -	13
Total	75

Tableau II : Répartition des articles par thème	
Liturgie	13
Œcuménisme	8
Jean XXIII	7
Paul VI	7
Éducation	7
Encycliques	4
Autres (brochure, timbre du concile)	4
Bilan 1re session	3
But du concile	3
Commission préparatoire	2
Morale	2
Cardinal Léger	2
Catéchisme	2
Documents conciliaires	2
Église vs monde	2
Séminaires et séminaristes	1
Collégialité des évêques	1

Théologie	1
Paroisse	1
Réception du concile	1
Cardinal Roy	1
Religieux et consacrés	1

Les années 1959-1960

En 1959 et 1960, les informations sur le concile proviennent presque totalement de l'extérieur, et des textes brefs sont réalisés à partir de courts communiqués émanant de Rome : l'ouverture du premier synode du diocèse de Rome (28 janvier 1960), la rencontre du pape et de l'archevêque de Canterbury, le docteur Ramsey (6 décembre 1960), l'audience solennelle donnée par Jean XXIII pour marquer l'ouverture de la phase préparatoire du concile (13 décembre 1960). À partir d'un communiqué officiel de la même source, on repère une nouvelle d'intérêt local : la nomination de Mgr Lionel Audet, évêque auxiliaire à Québec et originaire de la Beauce, comme membre de la Commission pontificale de théologie.

L'année 1961

À partir de 1961, l'information devient un peu plus volumineuse et la provenance locale est plus affirmée, en rendant compte d'initiatives québécoises et canadiennes en écho à ce qui se passe à Rome. On trouve ainsi, le 31 août 1961, un article portant sur la parution de l'édition canadienne-française, aux Éditions du jour, de l'encyclique *Mater et magistra* du 15 mai 1961, en soulignant la présence d'une introduction de Claude Ryan. On signalera de même, le 28 septembre 1961, la parution d'une autre édition de la même encyclique en format de poche aux Éditions Fides. On pressent que cette lettre pontificale annonce le ton ou le style du concile à venir tel que le souhaite Jean XXIII, en présentant la sollicitude universelle de l'Église et son souci de justice sociale pour tous les peuples.

L'année 1962

L'année 1962 sera encore plus fertile en textes portant directement sur l'événement conciliaire. L'*Éclaireur-Progrès* du 4 octobre 1962 fera écho à la publication par la revue *Relations* d'un dossier sur le concile qui s'ouvrira quelques jours plus tard (11 octobre 1962). L'édition du 11 octobre 1962, jour de l'ouverture de la première session, annonce la parution d'une publication sur le concile par Marcel Adam[11], *Qu'est-ce que le concile ?*, aux Éditions du Jour. Deux semaines plus tard (25 octobre 1962), la publication à grand tirage (125 000 ex.) d'une nouvelle brochure signée par le père André Bilodeau, o.m.i., *Le Concile, questions et réponses*, est annoncée aux lecteurs, en mettant en évidence qu'il s'agit du « plus grand événement du XXe siècle ». Le même texte sera repris dans l'édition du 1er novembre 1962. Plusieurs articles plus longs sont repiqués à partir d'autres publications et développent un aspect ou l'autre du concile, par exemple « la présence d'observateurs non catholiques au concile », dans un texte signé par Claude Ryan, qui met aussi en évidence que le rassemblement conciliaire a donné le signal d'un « rendez-vous mondial des théologiens[12] ».

On commence aussi à parler concrètement de réformes. Toujours dans l'édition du 1er novembre 1962, un article signé par l'abbé Guy Racicot s'interroge sur les réformes possibles et impossibles et avance prudemment que le renouveau portera davantage sur « l'Église totale » que sur des points particuliers, tout en soulevant quelques thèmes. L'édition du 13 décembre 1962, quelques jours après la fin de la première session, mettra en évidence le renouveau liturgique, en soulignant la nécessité d'une « vraie communauté, participante et agissante » au point de départ de toute adaptation liturgique. Un bilan des premières semaines du concile, dans l'édition du 6 décembre 1962 (texte non signé, repris d'une autre source), présente brièvement la méthode de travail adoptée, développe les travaux entrepris sur la liturgie et l'amorce de l'étude du deuxième schéma sur les sources de la Révélation. On y évoque aussi la réception de l'événement conciliaire dans le monde et

---

11 Marcel Adam fut envoyé par le quotidien *La Presse* pour couvrir le concile dès la première session.

12 Claude Ryan était l'envoyé de la Presse canadienne et de la Conférence des évêques au Concile.

le climat d'ouverture suscité par la présence des non-catholiques, qui ont répondu à l'invitation du pape, ainsi que la réception favorable au message de paix adressé au monde par les pères du concile.

L'année 1963

En 1963, divers articles reviennent sur des thèmes majeurs comme le progrès œcuménique et la « vraie nature du dialogue » pour l'unité (3 janvier 1963). On y retrouve notamment le rapport d'une intervention de Mgr Joseph De Smedt, membre du comité pour l'unité des chrétiens. Dans son édition du 4 avril 1963, l'*Éclaireur-Progrès* présente le résumé d'un thème développé par le père Émile Legault dans le magazine *Maclean's*, celui de l'ouverture au monde. Pour la première fois, on fait état des tensions parmi les pères conciliaires entre les tenants du *statu quo* et ceux qui « favorisent l'adaptation au temps présent ». Dans le même article, l'Afrique noire est présentée comme une force nouvelle dans l'Église. Le même texte sera repris le 18 avril et sous le même titre : « Les grands moments du concile ».

Pour une bonne partie des mois suivants, au printemps et à l'été 1963, les différents numéros de l'*Éclaireur-Progrès* parleront beaucoup du pape, en raison de la maladie et du décès de Jean XXIII. Ce sera l'occasion de publier sa biographie et de rappeler les circonstances de la convocation inattendue du concile. Il faut signaler ici la publication de l'un des tout premiers textes signés par un rédacteur local, sur l'événement conciliaire. En effet, le texte du 6 juin 1963, signé « R.B. », est dû à Roger Bolduc, rédacteur en chef de l'*Éclaireur-Progrès* pendant de nombreuses années. Dans son article intitulé « Le pape est mort », le citoyen de Saint-Georges rend hommage à sa « lutte au conservatisme stagnant », en montrant que Jean XXIII « a ouvert des voies nouvelles que le concile finira de paver en poursuivant l'œuvre d'un innovateur puissant qui aura réussi le double exploit de rapprocher les hommes entre eux et de les rapprocher tous de Dieu ». Au milieu d'autres regards sur l'héritage de Jean XXIII, on salue « l'arrivée d'un nouveau pape fait pour des temps nouveaux » (13 septembre 1963) et on fera mention (26 décembre 1963) du voyage du pape Paul VI en Terre sainte, événement sans précédent depuis 2000 ans.

Par ailleurs, le thème de l'œcuménisme et des relations entre les Églises chrétiennes sera abordé plusieurs fois encore, soit à l'occasion de l'évocation de la figure de Jean XXIII, soit à l'occasion de l'ouverture de la deuxième session, en septembre 1963. « Le peuple chrétien apprend à connaître et à aimer nos frères séparés » (21 novembre 1963), rapporte l'hebdomadaire en mentionnant le début de l'étude du schéma sur l'œcuménisme, dont il souligne l'importance en reprenant les propos de Réjean Plamondon, tirés du Bulletin d'information publié par la Conférence des évêques du Canada[13]. D'autres thèmes devenus dominants avec le déroulement du concile seront abordés de nouveau, comme celui de la liturgie, en annonçant la disparition prochaine de la langue latine au profit de la langue vernaculaire et un renouveau liturgique axé sur la participation des fidèles (12 décembre 1963). Un nouveau sujet, celui de la collégialité et des conférences épiscopales, sera présenté le 21 novembre 1963 comme « la question la plus importante qu'ait étudiée le concile », en reprenant un texte émanant du Service de presse de la Conférence catholique canadienne, dans lequel on fait état de la séance dramatique du 8 novembre, sur le fond de la confrontation entre les cardinaux Joseph Frings et Alfredo Ottaviani sur le « Saint-Office[14] ».

L'année 1964

La couverture de presse de l'*Éclaireur-Progrès* pour l'année 1964 va se désintéresser des grands débats conciliaires pour se concentrer davantage sur deux thèmes majeurs : les changements apportés à la liturgie et les transformations de l'enseignement religieux. Au chapitre de la liturgie, on rapporte l'extension du dimanche au samedi, le chantier de la préparation de nouvelles mélodies en langue française pour la liturgie eucharistique — dont les premières expérimentations sont

---

[13] Réjean Plamondon a été au service de la Conférence des évêques catholiques du Canada de septembre 1959 à mai 1966 comme directeur du Service d'information (secteur francophone). Ce service agissait comme une agence spécialisée de nouvelles religieuses. Le Service d'information des évêques a ainsi publié de nombreuses nouvelles touchant les travaux conciliaires et a notamment alimenté la presse régionale.

[14] Le cardinal Frings prononça un discours rédigé en grande partie par Joseph Ratzinger, le futur Benoît XVI, qui était son consultant (ou *peritus*) en théologie pour le concile. Ce texte traitait du Saint-Office défini comme trop conservateur tel qu'il était dirigé par le cardinal Ottaviani.

annoncées pour l'automne 1964 —, les premières messes célébrées face au peuple dont on prévoit la généralisation rapide, les modifications apportées au jeûne eucharistique et aux horaires des célébrations pour tenir compte de « la communion plus nombreuse » (31 décembre 1964). C'est pourtant le « nouveau catéchisme » et les modifications apportées à l'enseignement religieux qui vont surtout défrayer la chronique régionale en Beauce au cours de l'année 1964.

On dit du « nouveau catéchisme » qu'il « s'inscrit dans le grand renouveau religieux dont témoigne l'Église tout entière » (22 octobre 1964). L'Association des Parents-Maîtres fait publier une série d'articles sur le sujet, et l'*Éclaireur-Progrès* en poursuit la publication sur quatre numéros à partir du 22 octobre 1964. On y intercale un message du cardinal Paul-Émile Léger aux membres de la Croisade eucharistique, soulignant l'harmonie entre la réforme de la liturgie et des sacrements et « les orientations actuelles » de la catéchèse en « conformité d'esprit avec la Constitution conciliaire sur la liturgie ». Le 5 novembre 1964 est annoncée à Saint-Georges une soirée d'étude sur « la formation religieuse » sous le titre « Parents-maîtres et religion », en évoquant la nécessité d'un « renouvellement religieux en réponse à un manque de satisfaction devant l'enseignement religieux traditionnel ». Comme on peut le constater, la couverture de l'événement conciliaire se déplace vers les impacts locaux des réformes qui commencent à pointer et des inquiétudes ou des désaccords qui se manifestent petit à petit.

L'année 1965

À compter de 1965, à côté de la publication de nouvelles sur l'assemblée conciliaire ou rapportant certains gestes significatifs posés par le pape Paul VI, la réforme liturgique va désormais prendre beaucoup de place dans les pages de l'hebdomadaire. Le 11 février 1965, le compte-rendu d'une première réunion du comité régional de liturgie, rassemblant 400 personnes, donne la mesure des attentes dans ce domaine. On y annonce le début des modifications apportées aux célébrations liturgiques pour le 7 mars 1965 et le numéro suivant de l'hebdomadaire, publié le 18 février 1965, en précise le détail et les mesures transitoires tant que certains textes (canons, mélodies) n'auront pas été approuvés[15]. Les premiers débats autour des changements liturgiques et la dénonciation de « certaines expériences liturgiques non autorisées » commencent à trouver un écho, comme le texte du père Ovila Melançon à propos de la question de la communion à genoux ou debout (19 novembre 1965). On évoque le changement d'appellation de la confession (pour « sacrement du pardon ») et son importance en particulier pour les jeunes, les premières concélébrations paroissiales, la suppression de l'abstinence du vendredi (19 décembre 1965), ainsi que le nouveau rite du mariage (à l'intérieur de la messe, après la lecture de l'Évangile et l'homélie). On fait aussi un certain cas des modifications apportées à l'habit religieux (10 novembre 1965). Le journal s'intéresse de près aux changements de plus en plus visibles qui affectent la vie de l'Église et un monde ecclésiastique qui avait peu changé jusque-là, en maintenant sa force tranquille. On constate que cet échantillon de la presse hebdomadaire régionale qu'est l'*Éclaireur-Progrès* s'intéresse maintenant de plus en plus et surtout aux aspects pratiques de la nouvelle religieuse relative au concile, à travers les changements qui touchent directement les lecteurs.

À l'échelle plus large, l'année 1965 voit l'hebdomadaire annoncer le lancement par les Éditions Fides de la collection « L'Église aux quatre vents », dont les brochures diffuseront les principaux textes du concile à prix économique (25 mai 1965). Ce dernier reproduit, le 6 octobre 1965, des extraits substantiels du discours de Paul VI à l'ONU sur la paix, prononcé la veille à New York. On fait état de la direction moderne que Paul VI imprime au gouvernement de l'Église, en réformant la curie et en manifestant son désir de créer de nouveaux « ministères » ou dicastères pour l'œcuménisme, la liturgie, le mariage et la famille (24 novembre 1965). On va jusqu'à évoquer le rajeunissement du décor des appartements pontificaux comme symbole de la « direction du pape le plus moderne et le plus calmement efficace » du siècle présent. Dans la même édition de l'hebdomadaire, on trouve aussi l'écho des débats autour du *Schéma XIII* sur les rapports de l'Église avec le monde, la diffusion d'un « esprit de paix » par l'appel au désarmement et le refus « d'ajouter des condamnations supplémentaires du communisme ».

15 Il s'agit de la mise en application de la lettre apostolique en forme de Motu proprio *Sacram Liturgiam*, promulguée par Paul VI une année auparavant, le 25 janvier 1964.

L'année 1966

L'assemblée conciliaire terminée, les informations locales sur les lendemains du grand événement vont occuper l'avant-scène, même si on note encore la reprise d'articles publiés ailleurs, comme un texte du journaliste français Georges Hourdin, sur « Les problèmes qui confrontent l'Église à l'heure actuelle » (19 janvier 1966), publié quelques semaines après la clôture solennelle du concile le 8 décembre 1965. Hourdin y insiste sur la nécessité pour l'Église de se présenter aux « masses matérialisées, déchristianisées » dans « la nudité de la foi », pour qu'elles trouvent auprès du corps ecclésial « l'accueil intelligent et charitable dont elles ont besoin ».

Un thème local qu'il importe de relever est l'attention accordée au Décret sur l'œcuménisme mis en relation avec la visite de l'évêque anglican de Québec au Petit Séminaire de Saint-Georges à l'occasion de la semaine pour l'unité des chrétiens, avec la participation de Mgr Ernest Lemieux, président de la Commission diocésaine d'œcuménisme (2 février 1966). Un autre thème peu ou pas abordé jusque-là, en tant que tel, dans le journal beauceron, est celui du rôle des laïcs dans l'Église. C'est le cardinal Maurice Roy, à l'occasion d'une visite dans la Beauce sur « l'application du concile », qui place ce point au centre de sa réflexion, avec celui du dialogue entre les membres de l'Église et les institutions du diocèse, si l'on en croit le rédacteur de ce texte pour l'*Éclaireur-Progrès*, l'abbé Jean-Marie Vachon[16]. Maintenant que le concile est terminé, énonce l'archevêque de Québec, « les évêques désirent des contacts plus fréquents qu'autrefois avec les prêtres, les religieux et les laïcs, les paroisses et les régions, les organismes et les institutions du diocèse ; ils veulent aussi voir comment les contributions et les décrets du concile pourront s'appliquer à l'Église du Québec ». Il estime en particulier que « le concile a mis en évidence le rôle des laïcs dans l'Église ».

On trouvera dans les numéros publiés en 1966 quelques traces de controverses sur les transformations les plus visibles qui manifestent

[16] Jean-Marie Vachon, prêtre diocésain, a été pendant plusieurs années l'un des principaux artisans, avec l'abbé Luc Grenier, de l'application du renouveau conciliaire dans le monde de la pastorale paroissiale, de l'enseignement religieux et de la pastorale scolaire pour la région de la Beauce.

les changements inspirés par le concile. On note ainsi une controverse sur le port du « costume de ville » par les religieuses, les religieux ou les prêtres (23 février 1966) et une opinion très critique sur « la dégradation des valeurs chrétiennes à l'école », avec l'abandon du catéchisme qui « conduira bientôt à l'abandon des pratiques religieuses et au reniement de sa foi » (27 avril 1966). Derrière le refus de ce que certains appellent « l'école neutre », on décèle la conscience que de grands bouleversements sont déjà à l'œuvre.

Enfin, le journal ne manque pas d'annoncer la publication par la maison Fides d'une édition populaire des seize documents conciliaires (25 mai 1966). L'hebdomadaire mentionne régulièrement toute nouvelle publication accessible susceptible de permettre à la population de s'approprier les changements conciliaires, mais il est difficile d'évaluer l'impact de cette promotion.

En conclusion

La couverture de l'événement conciliaire par l'*Éclaireur-Progrès* illustre le cas particulier d'une population semi-rurale, pour laquelle l'Église catholique demeure une référence commune et un acteur social important, mais qui entre dans une période de transformations[17]. Le concile va marquer l'accélération de changements qui suscitent beaucoup d'espérance, mais aussi de l'incertitude et des contestations que l'on voit apparaître surtout à partir de 1965-1966.

Si la réforme liturgique lancée en 1964 semble bien accueillie et correspondre même à certaines attentes de changement, le renouveau catéchétique semble soulever autant d'inquiétudes que d'espérance[18]. En témoigne une lettre de protestation contre des modifications aux manuels scolaires qui bannissent les références religieuses dans les livres de français (10 novembre 1965). Les signataires y voient se profiler l'apparition de l'« école neutre », si peu conforme à leur vision de

---

17 Gilles Routhier, « L'Église après la Deuxième Guerre mondiale : renouveau et nostalgie », dans Serge Courville, Pierre C. Poulin et Barry Rodrigue, dir., *Histoire de Beauce-Etchemin-Amiante*, Les éditions de l'Institut québécois de recherche sur la culture et Les Presses de l'Université Laval (collection « Les régions du Québec », 16), Québec, 2003, p. 790-816.

18 *Ibid.*, p. 798.

la société. Cette lettre exprimant une position très critique sera suivie d'autres interventions semblables publiées régulièrement.

On doit aussi noter que si le concile correspond pour la majorité à la réforme liturgique et au renouveau de l'enseignement catéchétique, la question œcuménique suscite aussi de l'intérêt, si l'on se fie à l'importance que lui accordent les pages de l'*Éclaireur-Progrès* pendant cette période. La recherche de l'unité des chrétiens semble capter l'attention parce qu'elle est le symbole fort d'un changement d'attitude de l'Église, d'une ouverture au dialogue et à l'accueil de la diversité. Cet intérêt pour la question œcuménique dans un hebdomadaire régional au milieu des années soixante peut surprendre : il traduit un changement de perspective dans la manière de saisir l'Église catholique par rapport à l'époque précédente. On comprend peut-être confusément que l'Église catholique passe par une certaine dépossession pour un recentrement sur le salut en Jésus-Christ, vers lequel sont tournées toutes les Églises. On pressent que ce mouvement de conversion traduit une nouvelle attitude de l'institution ecclésiale et de ses pasteurs à l'égard du monde qui l'entoure.

Par contre, il peut être étonnant de constater que les responsables pastoraux locaux ne se sont pas manifestés dans la presse régionale avant la fin du concile. Les premières interventions d'acteurs ecclésiastiques diocésains pouvant être reliés au concile ne sont repérables qu'à partir de l'année 1966, dans les mois qui suivent la clôture de l'événement conciliaire. Ce qui a d'abord été un événement ecclésial inhabituel, un fait aux dimensions internationales, dont on a suivi à distance les possibles effets sur notre vision du catholicisme, n'a commencé que lentement à être perçu comme une expérience de transformation qui nous touche concrètement au plan local. C'est ce que manifeste aussi l'intérêt croissant pour les aspects pratiques des changements apportés par le concile ou perçus comme tels, touchant la liturgie, l'éducation catholique, la vie religieuse et presbytérale ainsi que les signes extérieurs de leur identité.

Il faudrait poursuivre le dépouillement de l'hebdomadaire après 1966 pour apprécier de manière encore plus complète comment un organe de presse comme celui-là a pu être le témoin de la diffusion du concile. Le regard que nous avons porté sur la période qui va de l'automne 1958 à l'automne 1966 montre déjà que l'hebdomadaire de Saint-Georges de Beauce a accompagné de manière continue une population qui, avec le concile, entre dans une période de bouleversements sur les plans social et religieux, en manifestant une grande disponibilité au changement, sans dissimuler des inquiétudes réelles qui vont en grandissant. La suite montrera que les bouleversements seront profonds.

Deux événements reliés au concile dans les médias québécois : « Foi et Constitution » à Montréal (1963) et Paul VI à L'ONU (1965)

Pierre C. Pagé,
Université du Québec à Montréal

C'est toujours par l'image médiatique que les faits religieux d'une société rejoignent le grand public, qu'il s'agisse de la population chrétienne active en Église ou de la population québécoise toutes sensibilités religieuses confondues. Au début des années soixante, la composition socio-démographique du Québec évolue rapidement, et la culture religieuse se modifie au rythme de la culture publique commune. Il est pertinent de jeter un regard critique sur deux événements qui ont constitué à cette époque des moments exceptionnels par rapport à l'activité régulière de la vie de l'Église au Québec. Ces deux faits médiatiques représentent des ruptures dans l'image collective coutumière du fait religieux que les médias avaient été appelés à diffuser.

Au moment où les travaux du concile Vatican II se déroulaient surtout à Rome, dans le cadre de commissions spécialisées, et où les médias avaient transmis l'image austère de la première session, ce fut toute une surprise pour le grand public d'apprendre la tenue en 1963 à Montréal, à l'Université McGill où étaient situées les facultés protestantes de théologie, de la *Conférence Foi et Constitution*, un congrès international majeur de théologie chrétienne, issu d'un organisme non catholique de Genève, le Conseil œcuménique des Églises. Les médias se retrouvaient très loin de la tradition des congrès eucharistiques populaires ou des classiques rencontres d'animation de la dévotion mariale ou de la dévotion au Sacré-Cœur. Ce n'était plus une activité d'encadrement des catholiques pratiquants, mais un rassemblement exceptionnel des autres chrétiens où, d'une doctrine à enseigner, la théologie devenait un lieu de débat entre des croyants en recherche.

Par ailleurs, dans une perspective culturelle, il n'est pas indifférent de rappeler que cette *Conférence Foi et Constitution* était d'abord tenue en anglais, dans un contexte spécialement caractéristique de la culture anglophone de Montréal et dans un lieu qui rassemblait les principales facultés anglicanes et protestantes de théologie. C'est pourquoi il s'impose à la recherche d'observer l'ensemble des médias, anglophones aussi bien que francophones.

Deux années plus tard, en 1965, on assiste à une nouvelle rupture dans l'image médiatique coutumière du fait religieux lorsque le pape Paul VI, inscrivant dans l'image pontificale la pratique des voyages internationaux, vient accomplir en terre nord-américaine une visite à l'ONU, une instance essentiellement politique. Aucune confusion n'est alors possible avec les voyages à caractère pastoral qui deviendront plus tard une tradition.

La présente analyse des deux événements repose sur une lecture de quatre quotidiens, *La Presse*, *Le Devoir*, *The Gazette*, *The Montreal Star*. Nous avons également consulté les multiples documents écrits qui ont été les témoins autorisés de la couverture télévisée dans les deux langues.

Notre propos est de construire une réflexion sur l'image médiatique des deux événements religieux et sur la représentation de l'institution ecclésiale concernée, en tenant compte du contexte socioculturel des années soixante au Québec. La portée théologique directe des commentaires journalistiques et des reportages, sans être ignorée, n'est pas l'objet premier de notre analyse.

I. La *Conférence Foi et Constitution*, à l'Université McGill, du 12 au 26 juillet 1963

La tenue de cette conférence internationale à Montréal sortait de tous les cadres connus de rassemblements à caractère religieux, pour toutes les confessions chrétiennes établies au Canada. Que le Conseil œcuménique des Églises (COE) tienne à Montréal la réunion statutaire de son instance théologique la plus importante, la *Commission Foi et Constitution*, c'était un précédent aussi bien pour le Conseil que pour le milieu québécois et canadien. C'était donc une innovation pour les professionnels du journalisme et, évidemment, pour le grand public, puisque ces instances n'étaient connues que des seuls spécialistes en questions religieuses internationales. L'événement a rassemblé plus de 450 participants, représentant 138 confessions chrétiennes membres (anglicans, protestants, orthodoxes) et des observateurs invités de l'Église catholique.

La question pertinente pour l'histoire des médias est de comprendre comment ceux-ci ont pu sensibiliser l'opinion publique aux travaux austères et aux enjeux de *Foi et Constitution*. On éclaire d'autant mieux ces débats si l'on garde en mémoire la simultanéité de cette conférence avec le déroulement, à Rome, du concile Vatican II, dont la deuxième session devait reprendre l'automne suivant et que les médias couvraient attentivement.

L'annonce discrète de la Conférence

Les premières traces journalistiques que l'on retrouve de l'événement se situent très tôt. Le 6 février, faisant écho à des communiqués de presse issus du COE, le journal *La Presse* annonce la tenue à l'été d'un « Colloque sur l'unité chrétienne ». Quelques semaines plus tard, le 2 mars, *The Gazette* annonçait dans un article de six colonnes : « Christian Unity / Two-Week Program / World Theologians To Attend Montreal Session ».

Mais dans les milieux catholiques, c'est un processus beaucoup plus subtil et efficace qui a pu sensibiliser les paroisses et les institutions. La revue *La Semaine religieuse de Montréal* a publié, au cours de l'hiver et du printemps, plusieurs articles sur l'œcuménisme (21 mai), aussi bien sur la mise en place d'une Commission diocésaine d'œcuménisme que sur la venue de la *Conférence Foi et Constitution* ou sur la participation catholique à une soirée œcuménique dans ce cadre, ou encore sur la création d'un Centre d'œcuménisme (11/6) jouissant d'une autonomie spéciale. Enfin, la *SRM* publie un communiqué du cardinal Léger (9/7) annonçant la tenue de la *Conférence Foi et Constitution* et invitant les chrétiens à soutenir l'événement par une prière écrite pour l'occasion. Deux autres articles viennent compléter le parcours : l'un, préparé par l'Office catholique national des techniques de diffusion, annonce une émission spéciale de télévision pour le 26 juillet, l'autre, pour faire la synthèse théologique du congrès (30/7). On doit ajouter un article complémentaire (13/8) où, dans un communiqué de la chancellerie, le cardinal propose une prière pour le Congrès mondial anglican qui doit se tenir à Toronto du 13 au 23 août. Il est donc évident que la conférence œcuménique internationale est soutenue activement par l'Église catholique diocésaine et que l'événement est intégré dans une vision spirituelle globale de recherche de l'unité des chrétiens.

Une solide continuité d'articles dans les journaux sur le déroulement de la Conférence

Il n'était pas évident que la tenue d'un long congrès de théologie puisse susciter une abondante couverture de presse. Il était également certain que la nature même des débats — un ensemble de questions théologiques — représentait un défi considérable pour les journalistes et les commentateurs. En effet, si c'était un domaine éloigné des événements généralement traités par les médias, c'était aussi un ensemble de discours sur des aspects du fait religieux et de son organisation ecclésiale qui s'éloignait radicalement des activités religieuses publiques, habituellement centrées sur des célébrations cultuelles. Il en découle que la couverture journalistique étoffée et de bonne qualité a forcément été le résultat d'un travail professionnel bien accompli et soutenu par une motivation au-dessus de la moyenne : le fait œcuménique a intéressé les journalistes qui ont pu, en conséquence, le transmettre au grand public. Les quatre journaux que nous avons analysés ont traité, chacun selon son style propre, l'ensemble des activités de la *Conférence*, depuis l'arrivée multicolore des participants jusqu'à la grande célébration publique qui s'est tenue exceptionnellement à l'Université de Montréal.

La Presse pouvait compter sur un chroniqueur spécialisé en questions religieuses, Marcel Adam, qui était le correspondant du journal à Rome pour le concile. Dès la veille de la *Conférence,* il commençait la publication d'une série de 16 articles couvrant tous les aspects et tous les événements. Son premier texte (11/7) donnait la structure du programme et présentait avec enthousiasme le rassemblement exceptionnel des Églises chrétiennes, dont il estimait le nombre à près de 200. Il est intéressant de noter que, dès cet article et pour toute la série, Adam crée un modèle visuel récurrent en coiffant ses textes du logo et du nom du Conseil œcuménique des Églises. La problématique œcuménique est formulée dès l'article suivant : « Cinq cents frères qui se réclament du même Père et de sa Parole sont divisés en 138 familles. » Et le texte pose les questions essentielles : l'unité progresse-t-elle ? De quelle unité parle-t-on ? Quelles sont les questions en litige ? Quelques jours plus tard (22/7), Marcel Adam considère que cette assemblée fait bouger des choses : « Après avoir scandalisé le monde, les chrétiens donnent un bel exemple de fraternité. » Il perçoit l'énergie immense déployée par les participants : « Certains délégués travaillent jusqu'à la limite de leurs forces nerveuses » (24/7). Il identifie certains obstacles : « La bureaucratie est un mal nécessaire dans l'administration moderne des Églises » (25/7). Mais Marcel Adam conclut (27/7) sa série d'articles en faisant sienne une conclusion du communiqué final : « L'unité approche à une allure plus rapide que notre aptitude à l'exprimer. »

En complément des chroniques de Marcel Adam, *La Presse* publiait, le 20 juillet, un article de fond (émanant de la CCC) intitulé « Depuis 50 ans, l'unité des chrétiens a progressé miraculeusement », consacré aux questions théologiques telles qu'elles furent exposées en conférence plénière par l'évêque anglican de Bristol, Mgr Oliver Tomkins. Celui-ci y formulait avec force que l'objectif du COE n'était pas seulement de développer une coopération des Églises, mais « de travailler à l'unité complète du peuple de Dieu ».

Le journal *The Gazette* pouvait compter sur un chroniqueur compétent, Fred Bruemmer, un journaliste expérimenté et capable de saisir les nuances de plusieurs questions théologiques. Il publia une série de

14 articles sur la *Conférence Foi et Constitution*, entre le 13 et le 27 juillet. Il insistait d'abord, dans deux articles, sur la recherche de l'unité qui animait les Églises et sur leur volonté d'universalité. En suivant les débats du congrès, Bruemmer fit rapport sur les divergences et nota : « Christian Tensions Not New » (17/7). Il souligna le besoin ressenti par les Églises protestantes et orthodoxes d'une plus grande participation de l'Église catholique (19/7). Bruemmer porta attention à l'évolution du Conseil œcuménique des Églises et précisa : « Problems Result from Growth » (20/7). La contribution du journaliste se fit plus pressante lorsqu'il commenta la présentation faite au congrès par le cardinal Léger et par le commentaire soulignant l'innovation : « Leger Breaks a Tradition » (22/7), indiquant le virage constitué par la première participation officielle d'un dignitaire de l'Église catholique à une réunion du COE. Tout le travail des délégués était jugé de grande valeur selon Bruemmer, il voyait l'appréciation qu'en donnaient les observateurs de l'Église catholique et il soulignait la capacité des délégués de marquer sereinement les différences, tout en recherchant une unité fondamentale (23, 25 et 26 juillet). La fin du parcours journalistique de Bruemmer indiquait que la démarche du congrès avait été un travail de lutte vers une clarification : « Struggle With Doctrinal Complexities » (27/7).

Le journal *Le Devoir* avait déjà une longue expérience des dossiers touchant le fait religieux et il avait régulièrement fait rapport sur les débats de la première session du concile. La *Conférence Foi et Constitution* est apparue tout naturellement comme un événement qui suivait la logique du rapprochement voulu par le concile, mais aussi comme une étape dans un cheminement où les Églises non catholiques avaient tracé la voie d'un dialogue entre chrétiens. Pour couvrir les deux semaines de ce congrès, *Le Devoir* ne disposait pas des mêmes moyens financiers que les autres quotidiens, et ses journalistes réguliers devaient assurer les affaires courantes. Un texte général adapté d'un communiqué de presse fut publié le jour de l'ouverture de la Conférence, le 12 juillet, et il en donnait le programme d'ensemble. Mais pour la suite, *Le Devoir*, utilisant un modèle qui lui était familier pour les affaires internationales, conclut une entente avec le quotidien français *Le Monde* en vertu de laquelle les articles de son journaliste spécialisé Henri Fesquet, correspondant à Montréal, étaient publiés par *Le Devoir* avant même d'être publiés à Paris. La contribution très documentée de Fesquet donna lieu à huit publications, tous les deux jours. Le premier article donnait une vue d'ensemble du mouvement œcuménique et présentait les spécialistes européens qui animaient les séances. Il fit état de la conférence inaugurale du pasteur Roger Mehl, professeur à Strasbourg, qui saluait les progrès de l'Église catholique en œcuménisme sous Jean XXIII. Mais il rappela aussi que Mehl formulait clairement les obstacles majeurs au dialogue venus des positions catholiques, notamment sur le mariage entre catholiques et protestants ou encore sur les insuffisances de la théologie du Saint-Esprit dans les Églises de la Réforme.

Le 22 juillet notamment, Henri Fesquet fit une place spéciale à l'action du cardinal Léger, mettant en dialogue les propos de Visser't Hooft, de George Johnston et de Léger. L'article de Fesquet publie de larges extraits des trois conférenciers. L'événement exceptionnel de leur rencontre à la même tribune publique, lors de la réunion de la fraternité chrétienne, réunissant 1400 personnes à l'Université de Montréal, est présenté par Fesquet comme un moment très solennel qui inspira cette phrase de Léger : « Cette veillée de famille est un signe des temps. » Fesquet a par ailleurs souligné les propos du pasteur Lukas Vischer, qui indiquait « la surprenante convergence » entre les thèmes traités à Vatican II et au Conseil œcuménique des Églises. Fesquet a noté la présence au congrès de Mgr Willebrands, bras droit du cardinal Bea au secrétariat pour l'unité à Rome. Enfin, Fesquet prenait soin de mentionner le dîner amical offert par le cardinal Léger aux dirigeants du Conseil œcuménique des Églises, aux observateurs catholiques, aux représentants locaux des diverses Églises chrétiennes et aux autres personnalités importantes. *Le Devoir* offrait ainsi à ses lecteurs une couverture approfondie, en synergie avec l'information européenne fournie par *Le Monde*.

Auparavant, le 17 juillet, Henri Fesquet avait publié une interview approfondie du cardinal Léger sur la situation de l'Église et de la foi au Canada, où Léger affirme « la difficulté de porter un jugement objectif sur le catholicisme canadien ». Et il précise : « Comme tant d'autres communautés chrétiennes, nous devons passer au stade d'une foi personnelle, lucide, consciente de ses responsabilités vis-à-vis des non-catholiques. » Il ajoute : « La foi est un dialogue avec Dieu qui peut se poursuivre dans le désert de Tamanrasset et même, ajoute le cardinal Léger avec un bon sourire, dans le décor du Vatican. » Évoquant les changements requis par l'évolution du Québec, il précise :

> La foi n'est pas une camisole de force. Elle n'est pas dans la pesanteur des institutions… Je suis convaincu que ce n'est pas la place des prêtres mais celle des laïcs, qui sont aussi l'Église, de faire partie des commissions scolaires ou d'assumer des tâches administratives. Mes initiatives en ce sens n'ont pas toujours été comprises…

Le journal *The Montreal Star* a publié 14 articles signés par Francis Allen et Michael Ballantyne, dont plusieurs mettaient en relief les interventions du cardinal Léger :

> History was made in the gleaming auditorium of the University of Montreal last night as Paul Emile Leger… This is the first time that a Prince of the Roman Catholic church has addressed such a gathering which included Protestant and Orthodox clergy and laymen (22/7).

Par ailleurs, la contribution du *Star* est significative en ce qui concerne les documents photographiques qui illustrent les événements. Plusieurs photos montraient l'évidence d'un lien amical de Léger avec l'archevêque anglican de Montréal et le directeur Johnston du United Theological College de McGill, ou de rencontres conviviales avec Athenagoras d'Elaia, le métropolite grec orthodoxe pour le Canada, et avec le pasteur Visser't Hooft, secrétaire général du COE. Dès le début de sa série, le *Star* accorde une place très importante à la Conférence (15/7) et en fait une manchette. À plusieurs reprises, le journal met en évidence le rôle des Églises orthodoxes russe, roumaine, grecque, syrienne et autres. En finale, le *Star* publiait à la une une photo de l'équipe de présidence de la Conférence et une synthèse mettant en relief la volonté commune de continuer à construire la paix entre les 138 Églises de 50 pays qui étaient représentées par plus de 500 délégués.

Des positions éditoriales en appui aux Églises

L'événement théologique de la *Conférence Foi et Constitution* a été répercuté comme un événement médiatique par les grands journaux quotidiens de Montréal. On constate aussi que non seulement les aspects sociaux ont intéressé les journaux, mais également le sens profond de cette actualité religieuse. C'est ce que trois éditoriaux ont voulu mettre en évidence. L'éditeur de *The Gazette*, Peter MacRae, indiquait dès le 12 juillet l'objectif de la rencontre : « Ecumenity To Key Protestant Meeting » et il commentait : « Deliberations which may alter the face of non-Roman Catholic Church and provide a springboard for more solid unity with the Vatican will get underway this weekend. » Gérard Pelletier, dans *La Presse* (20/7), disait son optimisme :

> De cette conférence œcuménique qui se tient dans nos murs, comme du concile Vatican II qui se rassemblera en septembre, ce n'est pas une impression de crépuscule qui se dégage, aux yeux bien ouverts, c'est la lumière d'une aube nouvelle.

Un deuxième éditorial de *The Gazette* (24/7) titrait « The Spirit That Stirs The Churches » : « Faced with the vast sea of human want and anxiety in the world today, the forces of Christianity have more compelling needs than to protect themselves from one another. It is in this larger spirit that the hope and the influence will lie. » Dans *Le Devoir* (29/7), Claude Ryan rattachait tout le processus de dialogue intensif qui venait de se tenir à un mouvement vers la pleine unité, dans son éditorial « La Catholicité redevenue familière » :

> Certes, l'accord est loin d'être complet entre protestants eux-mêmes, et davantage entre protestants et orthodoxes. Mais comment ne pas considérer ce travail de déblaiement et de mise en commun comme une étape nécessaire sur la route qui conduit à la catholicité pleinement réalisée ?

Et Ryan ajoute une observation sur les liens avec le catholicisme :

> Les représentants du Saint-Siège furent traités comme des frères. Ils furent invités officieusement à donner leur point de vue sur plusieurs thèmes étudiés. Ils constatèrent avec joie un effort des délégués en vue d'éviter les formules choquantes pour l'Église de Rome.

Ces trois témoins du milieu journalistique professionnel permettent de penser que l'événement socioculturel d'un congrès international fut aussi un élément majeur de réflexion sur la perception globale du christianisme.

Une large couverture de presse justifiée

Il n'était pas courant de voir un événement à contenu religieux multiconfessionnel tenu à Montréal occuper une telle place dans les médias. L'espace journalistique, le personnel affecté aux reportages, la place accordée aux chroniques dans la présentation des quotidiens, tous ces aspects médiatiques survenaient au début des années soixante, alors que surgissaient dans le milieu québécois des questions touchant la place de la religion dans les institutions[1].

C'est pourquoi un journaliste a senti le besoin de faire un retour sur la couverture des événements. Dans *La Presse* (27/7), Marcel Adam s'en explique longuement :

> Plusieurs lecteurs se sont probablement étonnés que les journaux, la radio et la télévision accordent une telle importance à des travaux de cette espèce. D'abord, les moyens d'information ne peuvent ignorer un événement aussi considérable qu'un congrès de 138 Églises chrétiennes qui tentent de se réconcilier, après des siècles de séparation. Nous assistons à un événement qui met en cause des millions d'individus et d'une certaine façon le cours de l'histoire [...] Les journaux d'inspiration chrétienne se doivent de collaborer à leur manière à une si grande œuvre. Car n'oublions pas que ces rencontres au sommet mettent en contact des spécialistes, des œcuménistes d'avant-garde. Et lorsqu'ils arrivent à s'entendre ou à faire l'unité, il n'est pas dit que le simple chrétien du troisième rang de Saint-Quelque-Part a évolué au même rythme, quand il n'en est pas resté aux préjugés anti-catholiques ou anti-protestants.

---

1 Toute la question de la place institutionnelle de l'Église avait été l'objet de plusieurs jours de débats publics, retransmis à la radio, en septembre 1961, lors d'un colloque de l'Institut canadien des affaires publiques (ICAP) sur le thème « L'Église et le Québec ». On y a notamment examiné la place de l'Église en éducation et on a évalué certaines initiatives de Léger qui avait créé des collèges à direction laïque. Les principaux conférenciers furent Vincent Harvey, o.p., Fernand Dumont, Louis O'Neill, Marc Lalonde, Laurier Lapierre, Bertrand Rioux, Vianney Décarie, Gilles-M. Bélanger, o.p., et Marcel Rioux. Voir : Coll., *L'Église et le Québec*, Montréal, Éditions du Jour, 1961. Durant la même période, les catholiques engagés dans la revue *Cité libre* publiaient des analyses réalistes sur la conjoncture sociale : « Feu l'unanimité » (oct. 1960), « Mgr Charbonneau et l'opinion publique dans l'Église » (janv. 1960), « Le Protestantisme canadien, le mouvement œcuménique » (août 1961) et plus tard, un numéro spécial, « Religion » (fév. 1967).

C'est la fonction sociale du journal dans le dossier religieux qui est ici l'objet d'une réflexion ponctuelle, au moment même où les médias d'inspiration chrétienne, spécialement en Europe, étaient engagés dans un processus approfondi de débat sur l'information religieuse, lors de leurs congrès annuels[2].

Le rôle de la télévision publique

Les réseaux anglais et français de Radio-Canada ont diffusé des émissions spéciales pour faire connaître les travaux de la *Conférence*. Ces émissions étaient annoncées dans les revues spécialisées *La Semaine à Radio-Canada* (13-19/7) et *CBC Times* (20-26/7). À la SRC, en plus de signaler des portions d'émissions religieuses régulières, on a mis l'accent sur une émission télévisée de 90 minutes consacrée à la Soirée de fraternité chrétienne tenue à l'Université de Montréal, diffusée le dimanche 29 septembre. Elle était présentée dans la revue de Radio-Canada par un article qui faisait suite à une longue présentation (4 col.) du congrès. À CBC, on a diffusé une émission spéciale de radio le 21 juillet sur la même soirée publique.

Dans le *Rapport annuel 1963-1964* (p. 30) de Radio-Canada[3], on donne un éclairage éditorial d'ensemble à la place accordée aux événements. En rappelant que « la quatrième conférence *Foi et Constitution* [...] a fourni la matière de trois émissions télévisuelles », on explique un contexte :

> Selon sa politique, Radio-Canada s'est efforcée de répartir équitablement le temps accordé aux diverses croyances. Le décès de Jean XXIII a donné lieu à plusieurs émissions spéciales, dont l'une a présenté les vues de représentants des fois catholique, protestante, orthodoxe et juive sur celui qu'on a appelé « le père de l'œcuménisme ».

---

2 On peut signaler que les travaux effectués en 1962 et 1963 par l'Union internationale de la presse catholique, lors de ses congrès internationaux, ont abordé régulièrement cette question, en soulignant une ligne de pensée essentielle : le journalisme catholique doit d'abord être du vrai journalisme. On peut consulter la revue *Journalistes Catholiques* pour les années concernées.

3 Pour les réseaux privés de radio et de télévision, les documents manquent pour en faire une analyse même minimale.

Durant ces années où les réalisateurs et les journalistes avaient comme arrière-plan d'information religieuse l'événement international qu'était le concile Vatican II, la radio et la télévision de Radio-Canada ont ainsi apporté à la *Conférence Foi et Constitution* une couverture qui semble avoir été appropriée. Le rôle de Radio-Canada comme service public n'a pas été l'objet de critiques concernant ces événements. Tout indique que la Conférence, comme fait religieux d'intérêt public, a été bien intégrée à la programmation d'information et que la distance critique souhaitable dans un média professionnel a été correctement respectée.

II. La visite officielle de Paul VI à l'ONU le 5 octobre 1965

Le rôle central de la télévision

La visite de Paul VI fut un événement médiatique d'une nature entièrement différente de ce que furent les reportages sur la *Conférence Foi et Constitution* ou sur les travaux du concile. Pour le voyage à l'ONU, rien ne pouvait être improvisé, le parcours était minuté, l'horaire des rencontres et des déplacements se devait d'être planifié conjointement par les responsables de l'Église et par les directeurs des réseaux de télévision. Tout devait être minutieusement prévu, la scénarisation des images ou le nombre de caméras mobiles, car la télévision, une fois en ondes, ne pouvait souffrir de retard ou d'improvisation. L'événement religieux ou politique se moulait dans le cadre d'un reportage-spectacle télévisuel. Malgré toutes ces contraintes, différentes de celles qu'impose un déplacement au milieu de foules religieuses, la visite de Paul VI à l'ONU fut une réussite complète, aux États-Unis, dans le monde entier par l'utilisation d'un satellite, et immédiatement au Canada et au Québec, où les réseaux étaient directement reliés aux réseaux américains de production.

Le voyage de Paul VI à l'ONU, effectué à l'intérieur d'une courte période de vingt-quatre heures, était un événement d'intérêt public international qui se situait à la jonction du fait religieux et du fait politique, comme un signe évident voulant montrer « l'Église dans le monde de ce temps ». La visite avait aussi une dimension conciliaire, puisque Paul VI avait momentanément quitté le concile en pleine session et revenait lui faire rapport le lendemain matin. La brièveté et la densité de cette visite officielle ont tout naturellement conduit les médias à mobiliser les ressources de la télévision. L'événement devenait un immense reportage télévisé, les médias écrits venant en appui et en prolongement réflexif sur les faits vécus collectivement. Cette dimension médiatique est devenue partie intégrante de la portée universelle du geste posé par le Pape.

L'événement médiatique du 4 octobre 1965 fut d'abord annoncé dans les deux revues officielles de Radio-Canada/CBC. Dans *La Semaine à Radio-Canada* (2-8 oct.), on trouve une présentation de trois pages, avec des photos de l'ONU et de Paul VI. Dans un texte sur « Le pape Paul VI aux Nations Unies », on situe l'événement dans son contexte international et surtout comme un fait susceptible d'intéresser tous les publics : « Quelle que soit l'allégeance religieuse de tous ces gens, ils attendent impatiemment l'illustre visiteur. » C'est pourquoi la programmation de Radio-Canada n'est pas décrite comme destinée aux seuls croyants, mais présentée « à leur intention comme à l'intention de tous les auditeurs et de tous les téléspectateurs de ses réseaux français » pour l'ensemble du Canada. Dans cette perspective, Radio-Canada se sent légitimée d'annoncer que la Société « consacrera tout son horaire du lundi 4 octobre à la visite de Paul VI aux Nations Unies ». Dans *CBC Times*, on annonce plus brièvement que les reportages vont présenter « Pope Paul VI with President Lyndon Johnson and his appeal for peace before the United Nations General Assembly ».

Si les télévisions canadienne et québécoise ont pu consacrer l'essentiel de leur programmation d'une journée entière, le 4 octobre, sans compter les rappels et les reprises, ce fut rendu possible par un mécanisme très complexe d'ententes avec les grands réseaux américains qui, seuls, pouvaient fournir l'équipement et le personnel technique pour une telle durée de diffusion. Le matériel des images multiples et simultanées captées par les réseaux de terrain devenait ainsi disponible pour les réseaux de diffusion, qui pouvaient faire certains choix mais surtout intégrer les commentaires originaux dont ils avaient confié la responsabilité à des journalistes et à des experts de leur choix. Ainsi en était-il de Radio-Canada comme de CBC. Les réseaux nationaux des autres pays, captant par satellite les images venues de New York, pouvaient les enrichir des points de vue propres à la culture de leur milieu. Pour ce qui est des émissions enregistrées par la SRC à Montréal, leurs archives, si elles ont été partiellement conservées, ne sont pas accessibles et notre analyse ne peut s'y reporter. Nous pouvons cependant recourir à des sources indirectes, celles des documents écrits de Radio-Canada et celles des journaux quotidiens des jours qui ont suivi.

Un regard rétroactif sur les reportages télévisés

Il n'est pas indifférent de lire le *Rapport annuel 1965-1966* de Radio-Canada/CBC. Ce genre de document, d'abord destiné au Parlement canadien, dont la partie essentielle est formée d'un rapport financier et d'une description du développement technique permettant de rejoindre tout le pays, est toujours d'une grande concision sur d'autres éléments comme la programmation offerte aux catégories de public. Dans un tableau des « Émissions représentatives », la très courte liste des cinq émissions d'information de la catégorie « Nouvelles » inscrit, aussi bien pour la radio que pour la télévision, la mention de la « visite de Paul VI aux Nations Unies » (p. 52).

Dans une autre catégorie que l'on désigne comme « les émissions d'intérêt particulier », un court texte résume une mission publique à l'égard du fait religieux :

> L'éventail des émissions religieuses s'est étendu des services religieux aux études sur le rôle de la religion dans la collectivité et dans le monde en évolution. Rappelons, entre autres émissions remarquables, *Ferment* avec Paul Tillich et l'évêque de Woolwich, de même que *Bilan de Vatican II*, dont la reprise a retenu un million d'auditeurs (p. 39).

Il est important de noter que, dans ce *Rapport* comme dans les articles des magazines sur la programmation, les émissions consacrées à la visite de Paul VI sont rattachées à la fonction d'information et affaires publiques. Cependant, dans la grande émission de synthèse des émissions religieuses, on a inséré des segments de la visite de Paul VI, ce qui a permis de les faire revoir par un nombre très élevé d'auditeurs.

L'évaluation des reportages télévisés par les journaux quotidiens

Deux journaux anglophones ont publié le 5 octobre des chroniques dans leur section « TV-Radio » évaluant la couverture télévisée de l'événement. Le journal *The Gazette* publie un article de Mark Blandford intitulé « Superb Coverage Of Visit » (p. 14). L'auteur souligne la coopération exceptionnelle entre les réseaux américains permettant une couverture parfaite et instantanée : « Peace among the networks, imagine ». L'événement semble assez exceptionnel pour que l'auteur insiste :

> The networks must be congratulated for their absolutely unique cooperation. It was a superb example of the achievement of collective thinking that the Pope was advocating… The most remarkable achievement, the greatest gift that the little glass eye had for us was the profile of a man who, for millions of people, emerged as the great man that he obviously is. There was more people watching or listening to the event than any other in history.

Dans *The Montreal Star*, la journaliste Patricia Pearce souligne la contribution spéciale de la télévision dans la perception d'un événement comme cette visite de Paul VI : « Medium Reveals Its True Talent » (p. 64) :

> Most of the camera coverage was polled, the differences coming in studio anchor comment. All had accomplished commentators, accompanied throughout the day by fluent representatives of the Roman Catholic Church — Bishop Sheen, R. Robert O'Donnell, Rev. Edward Heston. The Pope himself emerged on television a figure of unruffled dignity, with that fine capacity of too few — the ability to take TV in his stride as just a part of the world, never his master.

La journaliste souligne le rayonnement exceptionnel des reportages télévisés et les records d'audiences qui ont été atteints : « […] To allow 100 million people and sometimes 200 million via Early Bird to share what is being experienced only by some thousands of others at any given time, then it's a fine and wonderful thing indeed. »

Les journaux quotidiens, témoins attentifs des événements

Les quatre quotidiens que nous avons retenus pour cette réflexion sur l'événement ont apporté des contributions d'autant plus pertinentes qu'ils se savaient dans une situation claire de complémentarité avec la télévision. Ils ont ainsi résumé en quelques manchettes la perception générale du grand public, mais ils ont aussi consolidé la mémoire des faits par des photos nombreuses et évocatrices des déclarations et des rencontres. Ils ont également publié en totalité ou en extraits substantiels le texte de l'allocution à l'Assemblée générale.

Tous les journaux ont fait la manchette de la une, aussi bien le 4 que le 5 octobre, avec la thématique principale de la visite : « L'ONU est le chemin de la paix. » *Le Devoir* : « Nous allons à l'ONU encourager ceux qui tendent vers la paix » ; *La Presse* : « Avertissement solennel du pape : faire la paix ou périr » ; *The Gazette* : « No More War, War Never Again, Pope's Peace Plea To the World » ; *The Montreal Star* : « UN Last Hope For Peace – Pope ». Chaque fois, la première page des journaux était largement illustrée de photos montrant Paul VI, la foule durant ses parcours, ses interlocuteurs politiques, son intervention à l'ONU, ses conversations avec le président Lyndon Johnson, avec Jacqueline Kennedy, la foule au stade de New York, sa visite à la cathédrale St. Patrick et des documents évoquant l'atmosphère. Deux journaux ont publié un cahier de plusieurs pages de photos.

Parmi ce vaste reportage de photos, il est utile de signaler quelques images particulièrement significatives. Une photo publiée par *The Montreal Star* résume une situation unique dans l'histoire de la papauté contemporaine. Elle représente Paul VI à la tribune de l'ONU, lisant son discours devant un lutrin, alors que l'on voit, derrière lui et un degré plus haut que lui, les trois personnes en autorité à l'Assemblée générale : le président Amintore Fanfani, le secrétaire général, U Thant, et le sous-secrétaire, C.V. Narasimhan. Le Pape est ici intégré de façon normale aux structures de la société politique et il n'occupe pas la place éminente qui est toujours la sienne dans les rassemblements religieux.

Des éditoriaux en appui à la démarche de Paul VI

Lorsque le Pape accomplit en 1965 sa visite hautement symbolique aux représentants des gouvernements réunis à l'ONU, il s'apprête à faire compléter par le concile Vatican II la dernière étape de ses travaux. En même temps, il vient apporter aux autorités politiques internationales un message qui se situe dans le prolongement très net de son prédécesseur, Jean XXIII, dont le testament spirituel était largement exprimé dans son encyclique *Pacem in terris*, publiée peu de temps avant sa mort, en 1963, et six mois après son intervention médiatique dans la crise des missiles de Cuba. La personnalité de Paul VI comme leader international n'est pas bien connue encore, et c'est ce qui fait écrire au journal *La Presse* dans son reportage sur la visite à l'ONU que ce fut « un discours qui a *révélé* le Souverain Pontife » (5 oct., p. 1).

Les éditoriaux ont été unanimes et ils ont mis en lumière ce rôle de Paul VI et de l'Église dans la société internationale et dans le développement d'une culture de paix. *The Gazette* affirme : « Pope Paul is raising the Papacy to new dimensions in the modern world. At a time when the peace of the world is menaced, Pope Paul sees not only the danger, but the opportunity » (4 oct.). Le lendemain, *The Gazette* poursuit sa réflexion :

> It was in the spirit of the man of goodwill that Pope Paul VI appeared yesterday before the United Nations… He came as a man with nothing to ask, and everything to give. And he gave the United Nations, at a time when it is sorely tried and deeply perplexed, and often intemperately ridiculed and condemned, the weight of support from the most venerable office on earth (5 oct.).

Dans le *Montreal Star,* l'appui du Pape à l'institution internationale de l'ONU est clairement mis en relief : « Pope Paul also threw the vast moral weight of the Catholic Church behind the United Nations. The UN, he warned, "must never fail". We must seek to make it more perfect and equal to the needs which world history will present » (5 oct.).

Les commentaires publiés en éditorial par Claude Ryan dans *Le Devoir* sont davantage tournés vers une réflexion sur la conception de l'Église qui peut répondre aux attentes dans le monde de l'époque. Dans une perspective nettement inspirée par les débats conciliaires,

Ryan affirme : « La papauté doit plus que jamais s'élever au-dessus de sa fonction immédiate de gardienne des simples brebis installées dans le bercail, pour embrasser les soucis et les espoirs de tous les hommes de bonne volonté » (5 oct.). Le lendemain, dans un « Bloc-Notes » sur « Le retour de Paul VI à Rome », Ryan pousse plus loin sa pensée et donne une pleine dimension sociale à la mission de l'Église, toujours dans le contexte du concile :

> C'est donc dans la lutte contre l'injustice que doivent s'engager à fond les membres de l'Église… L'Église n'est vraiment et totalement elle-même que lorsqu'elle sort de son univers intérieur pour embrasser les préoccupations de tous les hommes, pour se mettre au service de toute l'humanité (6 oct.).

Comme on peut le voir, ces quelques exemples de commentaires éditoriaux publiés par les journaux indiquent que le message, verbal et non verbal, de Paul VI transmis par un geste immense de visite aux Nations Unies a été perçu correctement et reçu de façon positive. On ne trouve pas de traces d'une perception qui aurait vu cet événement comme une intrusion dans les affaires politiques ou comme un geste médiatique de prosélytisme. C'est le fondement même de l'institution onusienne qui était conforté par cette présence exceptionnelle.

III. Pour une mise en perspective historique

Les deux événements internationaux que nous avons retenus pour cette analyse médiatique mettaient en contact l'Église de l'époque conciliaire avec des institutions qui étaient indépendantes d'elle. Ils appartiennent à une époque qui est révolue, autant pour la structure de l'offre médiatique décuplée faite au grand public par la radio et la télévision que pour l'image de l'Église catholique et des autres Églises chrétiennes dans la société. Caractéristiques des années soixante, les deux faits religieux sont représentatifs d'une vision nouvelle qui situait l'Église catholique « dans le monde de ce temps », le monde des autres religions et le monde de la politique internationale. Pour certains chrétiens à l'esprit plus traditionnel, c'était sans doute un moment de plus dans le sentiment de rupture qui a affecté plusieurs autorités ecclésiastiques soucieuses de conserver une sorte de « pureté » doctrinale ou sociale, une sacralisation par la mise à part, hors du monde, de l'institution ecclésiale. Au contraire, d'autres pouvaient voir dans ces gestes de 1963 et 1965 un lien intime, spirituel, mais aussi affirmé publiquement d'une Église solidaire des sociétés, et qui a été répercuté mondialement par les médias.

Ce fut un lien harmonieux entre une Église libre et les médias au service d'une opinion publique qui s'est développé à l'occasion d'événements exceptionnels. Mais la relation avec les médias durant la période suivante fut plus imprévisible et elle fut marquée par de nombreux soubresauts, notamment à compter des réactions internationales des chrétiens lors de la publication de l'encyclique *Humanae Vitae* de 1968[4]. Le ciel sans nuages des relations entre l'Église et les médias s'était assombri de plusieurs signes de tempêtes. Cependant, un autre événement hors catégorie, en 1984, la visite de Jean-Paul II au Canada, fut couvert entièrement par la télévision, d'un océan à l'autre. Mais la vie de l'institution ecclésiale n'est pas faite des seuls événements rassembleurs exceptionnels. Les décisions institutionnelles comme les comportements des chrétiens, au fil des décennies, ont pu donner matière — comme c'est une chose normale dans tous les domaines d'intérêt public — à un regard critique des médias. Ils avaient tout naturellement à jouer leur rôle, essentiel dans la société (comme dans l'Église, selon ce qu'affirmait déjà Pie XII en 1950), d'animation de l'opinion publique comme fondement d'une participation de ses membres.

Pour la visite de Paul VI à l'ONU en 1965 et pour la *Conférence Foi et Constitution* en 1963, les médias québécois que nous avons analysés — quatre journaux quotidiens et la télévision — ont compris ces événements comme des *faits d'intérêt public* et les ont traités comme tels, avec les règles professionnelles habituelles gouvernant l'information et les affaires publiques. On n'a pas visé à s'adresser de façon spécialisée à des auditoires religieux ou à des groupes spécifiquement croyants. Les reportages sur ces faits à contenu religieux étaient traités dans l'intérêt de tous les lecteurs ou de tous les auditeurs pris globalement avec leur

---

[4] J'ai analysé cette question dans un article que j'ai publié récemment : « L'image médiatique de l'Église et l'opinion publique au Québec : deux décennies paradoxales de mutations (1968-1984) », dans *Études d'histoire religieuse*, vol. 75, Trois-Rivières, Société canadienne d'histoire de l'Église catholique, 2009.

diversité de perceptions qui nécessitait les explications journalistiques normales. Le fait religieux sortait alors de la « page religieuse » du journal ou du magazine religieux de la télévision pour entrer de plein droit dans les manchettes et dans les faits de société qui animaient l'actualité. On expliquait les événements à un grand public, quelle que soit sa religion. Ce positionnement éditorial pour transmettre et expliquer l'information a été justifié correctement par les médias eux-mêmes à la fin de ces séries de reportages.

Globalement, la couverture a été très professionnelle et elle s'appuyait sur une documentation abondante et sur une variété d'entrevues pour assurer une pluralité de points de vue. Pour *Foi et Constitution*, les enjeux œcuméniques ont été bien expliqués, des témoins spécialisés ont été entendus, des rappels historiques et culturels ont été formulés, et le ton a toujours semblé approprié pour faire saisir le sens de l'événement. À cet égard, on peut considérer que, pour l'ensemble des reportages, les couvertures de langue anglaise et française ont été équivalentes, avec les différences de style et d'accent qui découlent de la tonalité générale de chaque média et de sa clientèle.

Les longues heures de reportages télévisés et radiophoniques lors de la visite de Paul VI à l'ONU ont constitué un moment exceptionnel dans l'histoire de la télévision nord-américaine par l'ampleur des équipes de production résultant d'une mise en commun amicale entre les grands réseaux américains. En même temps, l'utilisation d'un nouveau satellite de communication a permis, en première mondiale, de créer un auditoire universel de très grande envergure. La visibilité en direct de l'événement fut immense dans de nombreux pays.

Ce fut le cas au Canada et au Québec par les soins de Radio-Canada/CBC. Les trois blocs de reportages — celui du matin montrant l'arrivée du pape, celui de l'après-midi présentant la séance de l'Assemblée générale des Nations Unies et celui du soir apportant la grande célébration populaire au stade de New York — ont totalisé, selon la programmation anglaise ou française, plus de huit heures de diffusion. Il faut encore ajouter les émissions de commentaires diffusées la veille et le lendemain. En l'absence d'une vérification dans les archives de Radio-Canada ou des agences de sondages, il est difficile d'évaluer le nombre d'auditeurs de la télévision et de la radio. On peut cependant se faire une idée approximative en considérant qu'une émission spéciale de 90 minutes diffusée par Radio-Canada pour tracer le *Bilan du concile Vatican II*, et qui comprenait des extraits de la visite à l'ONU, a été regardée — et, qui plus est, en reprise — par un million de personnes, selon le *Rapport annuel 1965-1966* de Radio-Canada.

Le rôle des journaux ne doit pas être sous-estimé pour autant. La possibilité de voir à tout moment des textes et surtout des photographies d'événements intéressant le public est toujours d'une portée immense. Il suffit pour s'en convaincre de voir, dans le métro ou l'autobus, la première page de certains journaux au lendemain d'événements sportifs ou politiques pour constater la permanence de l'image imprimée dans la culture populaire. Dans cette perspective socioculturelle, on se doit de retenir pour la mémoire historique certaines photos tirées des reportages des deux faits que nous avons analysés. Au début des années soixante, il n'était certes pas anodin de voir les journaux de juillet 1963 montrer le cardinal Léger — dont l'image des années cinquante comportait quelquefois un certain caractère « princier » — dans une situation nouvelle, issue du concile, où la fraternité avec les autres croyants l'emporte sur l'image d'autorité, où la convivialité souriante est l'indication d'une volonté de rapprochement avec les responsables des autres Églises chrétiennes. À l'occasion de la *Conférence Foi et Constitution*, les journaux ont multiplié les photos de personnalités venues d'autres pays et appartenant à d'autres confessions chrétiennes, et portant souvent des signes vestimentaires de leur responsabilité ou de leur milieu religieux. Cette présence médiatique quotidienne a beaucoup fait pour que l'opinion publique accueille favorablement la pluralité des appartenances religieuses, surtout en ce qui concerne les protestants et les orthodoxes, dont les Églises étaient vues avec méfiance par les catholiques des décennies précédentes. L'image nouvelle inscrite dans les journaux rendait familier le pluralisme chrétien[5].

---

[5] Immédiatement après le concile, la radio a poursuivi pendant deux décennies le travail d'information et d'éducation à la culture religieuse, notamment lorsque Radio-Canada a diffusé pendant cinq ans une tribune téléphonique intitulée « Le Père Legault vous écoute » puis « Les grandes religions », deux émissions réalisées par Jean-Charles Déziel. Voir Pierre PAGÉ, *Histoire de la radio au Québec, information, éducation, culture*, Montréal, Fides, 2007, p. 264 ss.

La visite de Paul VI à l'ONU en 1965 entrait dans une séquence d'événements politiques internationaux qui avaient occupé l'espace médiatique avec intensité depuis le début des années soixante. Rappelons pour mémoire quelques faits largement médiatisés dans le monde et spécifiquement au Québec : l'élection de John F. Kennedy en 1960 et son assassinat en 1963 ; l'attribution à Martin Luther King du prix Nobel de la paix en 1964 ; les astronautes russes puis américains commençant la conquête de l'espace ; les marches pour les droits sociaux des Noirs américains. Tous ces faits et beaucoup d'autres ont marqué rapidement et profondément l'imaginaire de l'époque par leur visibilité répétée à la télévision qui était devenue, de façon définitive, un lieu de culture sociale incontournable. C'est dans ce contexte encore nouveau qu'on peut situer le voyage de Paul VI à l'ONU, qui fut pour le monde entier un événement médiatique. Et c'est ce qui donne une valeur emblématique à l'image de Paul VI, mise en valeur aussi bien à la télévision que dans les journaux, présentant son allocution à la tribune de l'Assemblée générale des Nations Unies, sous le regard attentif des trois dirigeants politiques qui siègent à la table de conférence située derrière lui et plus haut que lui. L'Église apparaît ainsi comme un partenaire venant contribuer à la mission d'une institution civile essentielle.

Désormais, la vie publique de l'Église catholique s'inscrit aussi dans une culture médiatique englobante. La visibilité dans les journaux et surtout à la télévision est devenue une composante essentielle de l'influence de l'Église. Et le jour où des événements négatifs surviennent dans l'Église, cette influence est directement touchée et quelquefois battue en brèche par la même visibilité. C'est un contexte nouveau, ambivalent, mais désormais permanent, à l'intérieur duquel l'Église, au Québec et au Canada, doit accepter d'évoluer et de parler au grand public sollicité par une multitude de discours. Mais l'Église doit aussi garder une constante volonté d'écouter avec bienveillance et de comprendre les points de vue que les médias apportent sur la réalité sociale, économique, politique, culturelle et religieuse d'un monde qui innove dans le temps et dans l'espace.

SECTION II

Vatican II Viewed by Other Christians / Vatican II vu par les autres chrétiens

Canadian Presbyterians and Vatican II: A Silent Revolution

Stuart Macdonald,
Knox College

Only one solution was offered—forget him. The romance needed to end. As the article in the 1958 denominational magazine the *Presbyterian Record* put it: "He is not the one and only person in this world who could fill your life with love. You could find somebody else to love and be loved by."[1] In the imagined scenario, it is a Presbyterian girl—intriguingly named "Mary"—who faced this dilemma. The reason for such a drastic proclamation is simple. The boy ("John") is Roman Catholic. This would be a "mixed marriage." In the world of pre–Vatican II Presbyterianism this was a very serious issue, one that required the exploration of a series of problems that were anticipated, all in the article entitled "Will Your Children Be Roman Catholic?"[2] "Mixed marriages" were only one of a series of tensions between Roman Catholics and Protestants in general, and Presbyterians specifically. At this time the chasm between the traditions of Catholic

[1] James M. Singer, "Will Your Children be Roman Catholic?" *Presbyterian Record*, February 1958, 15.

[2] Ibid.

and Protestant congregants was assumed, and one finds little evidence that anyone anticipated attitudes would change so much within a decade that the very suggestion that a marriage between a Protestant and a Roman Catholic faced insurmountable issues would seem silly. By 1966 Catholic and Protestant theological students would share the same classrooms. Clergy would officiate jointly at marriages. Worship would be held together. Such remarkable changes were beyond the Presbyterian imagination in 1958.

The Presbyterian reaction to Vatican II has not been a major topic of discussion or academic study. This corresponds with the larger reality that research and writing on the denomination and its antecedents has focused primarily on the periods from early settlement up to the conclusion of the debates around church union (1925). John Moir's general denominational history, *Enduring Witness*, first published in 1975 and subsequently briefly updated and republished (second edition, 1987; third edition, 2004) covers the post-1925 period, but a careful examination of Moir's references indicates how little other research the author was able to rely on. These were pioneering chapters. There was much to discuss, and it should be no surprise that Vatican II receives short, although perceptive, comment.[3] John Moir noted: "Officially the church [PCC] ignored that most remarkable of Roman councils ...."[4] This silence can lead one to assume that as nothing changed, and Presbyterians didn't notice, there was nothing to study. One topic that

---

3 John S. Moir, *Enduring Witness: A History of the Presbyterian Church in Canada* (Toronto: Presbyterian Publications, 1975). Vatican II is discussed on pages 258–59. The discussion is preceded by the work of the Committee on Inter-Church Relations followed by a discussion of the climate of criticism prevalent in Protestantism, both internationally and in Canada, during the early 1960s. Few other scholars have rushed into studying this period or this topic since Moir's original publication. It is very difficult to determine what has been written on the Canadian Presbyterian Church in the post–World War II period and even post-church union period. More articles are beginning to appear and certain topics have been investigated, but it remains a field of limited research. Two articles of note: Doug Du Charme, "Ecumenism in Canada: 'An Affection for Diversity,'" in *Papers, The Canadian Society of Presbyterian History* (Markham, Ont.: 1984–85), 25–41; and John A. Vissers, "Recovering the Reformation Doctrine of Revelation: The Theological Contribution of Walter Williamson Bryden to Post-Union Canadian Presbyterianism," in *Papers, The Canadian Society of Presbyterian History* (Markham, Ont.: 1987), 21–48. The current author has recently begun research and writing on the post–World War II period.

4 Moir, *Enduring Witness*, 3rd edition, 258.

has received study, thanks to the work of historian Peter Bush, has been the debate in the 1960s regarding the denomination's major Reformation creed, the 1647 Westminster Confession of Faith, and how Presbyterians chose to deal with the anti-papal references in that document.[5]

The argument of this paper will be that Presbyterians responded positively, although quietly, to the changes in the Roman Catholic Church during and after Vatican II. The silence in key committees can be explained by the tensions around Protestant ecumenism evident within the denomination at the time. We can, with a careful eye, note incredible changes in attitudes in a relatively short period of time. Anti-Catholicism moved from being an accepted feature of the Presbyterian Church's main culture to becoming a curious, anachronistic foible of those now seen as strangely bigoted. In order to explore this silent revolution, we need to begin by exploring the chasm that existed between Roman Catholics and Presbyterians prior to Vatican II. Next, we will look at the initial responses within the Presbyterian community to Vatican II. The strange silence of the Committee on Inter-Church Relations will be our third major area of discussion. Why did this committee, the committee responsible for ecumenism and which we would assume would have given the "official" response from the Presbyterian denomination, say nothing? After exploring this, we will look at other responses to Vatican II. John Moir's observation that "the rapprochement of Presbyterians and Catholics in Canada continued to grow steadily after Vatican II, although largely on an unofficial basis,"[6] is true. But as we shall see, this rapprochement began during Vatican II, and the denomination offered more support than has been recognized.

Solitudes in Tension: Presbyterians and Roman Catholics Prior to Vatican II

Throughout the 1950s and into the early 1960s when Vatican II began, divisions between Presbyterians and Roman Catholics were

[5] Peter G. Bush, "The Presbyterian Church in Canada and the Pope: One denomination's struggle with its confessional history," *Studies in Religion / Sciences Religieuses* 33:1 (2004): 105–15. Much of the article discusses the place of the Westminster Confession within The Presbyterian Church in Canada and that denomination's tradition of not changing the text of historical creeds. It is within this context that the events of the 1960s are placed.

[6] Moir, *Enduring Witness*, 258–59.

deep and real. As already noted, one of the issues that clearly divided the communities was that of "mixed marriages." One pamphlet produced by The Presbyterian Church in Canada in this period defined a "mixed marriage" as one in which each of the marriage partners made a commitment to practice their own faith.[7] This concern for "mixed marriages" was not new, and in voicing concerns Presbyterians stood with other Protestants in objecting to certain requirements, as well as doctrinal positions, of the Roman Catholic Church.[8] Occasionally distinct Presbyterian elements were brought to the discussion. A young people's pamphlet, "The Church of Jesus Christ," written in 1950, spoke directly to the issue of "mixed marriages" and quoted from Chapter 24 of the Westminster Confession:

> There is no doubt about the conclusion of the first part, is there?—"*should not* marry with infidels, Papists or other idolaters." And to take that as a law of life would be quite simple for us. But we choose rather to try to understand why it is better for us to marry *within* the Reformed Faith. That statement seems rather harsh to our more sensitive twentieth century souls, does it not? But this was framed in days when men and women and young people were giving their bodies to be burned for the sake of the Gospel. Then, it was, that young people knew the impossibility of living in harmony with those who followed men rather than God; who worshipped Mary rather than the Only Begotten Son, Jesus Christ. To their ears these words were not harsh—they were the confirmation of their soul's belief. Mixed marriages were absolutely unthinkable.
>
> Yet times have changed. Yes that is right. Never forget though—that the distinction between Roman Catholicism and Reformed Faith HAS NOT CHANGED.[9]

---

7 "Mixed Marriages," undated pamphlet, 1. Board of Evangelism and Social Action study papers, PCC Archives, 1982-1029-1-6.

8 The pre-1966 Presbyterian Church in Canada pamphlet, "Mixed Marriages," refers to additional resources, including a book by Dean Pike, *If You Marry Outside Your Faith*, and to the 1948 pamphlet "If I Marry a Roman Catholic," written by Leland Foster Wood and produced by the Commission on Marriage and the Home of the Federal Council of Churches of Christ in America. PCC archives, 1982-1029-1-6.

9 "The Church of Jesus Christ" (Young People's Society, Presbyterian Church in Canada [Toronto]: 1950), 108. PCC Archives, 1973-1018-1-10. [original emphasis]

Scripture is next quoted (Jesus' comments about fig trees not bearing olives, and figs not growing on thistles) before other, more modern analogies were used before concluding: "It is just as impossible for two souls to find harmony and peace in Christ who are so diametrically opposed in their ideas and beliefs concerning Christ and His Church."[10]

The pamphlet was obviously designed, as was much of this literature, to communicate the problem early enough so that no such Roman Catholic/Reformed romances would develop. Should such romances develop, there were other pamphlets and other advice, both specific to The Presbyterian Church in Canada and more generically Protestant, which could be used to deal with the perceived problem.[11]

Beyond the prohibition of the Westminster Confession of Faith, specific reasons were given about why "mixed marriages" were a bad idea. "Mixed marriages," it was argued, were more likely to fail.[12] Concerns were raised about Roman Catholic teaching around contraception and about the life of the mother in cases of difficult childbirth.[13] One issue that was always raised was the agreement that was required to raise the children as Roman Catholics. This annoyed Presbyterians. In the 1958 article "Will Your Children be Roman Catholic?" this scenario is played out. In the discussion with the imagined minister, Mary suggests that maybe she will sign the agreement to allow her children be raised as Roman Catholics. The pastor relates what he imagines will happen next. After the birth "John and his family will take your child and leave for the Roman Catholic Church to have your child baptized"—an event portrayed as only the beginning of a growing apart. Mary will not share in her child's religious instruction or first communion. There will be a "spiritual loneliness" for her, a separation between her and her husband, but even more so a growing alienation between her and her

10 Ibid., 108. Later in the pamphlet (109), marriage to someone outside the faith was also condemned.

11 A series of these pamphlets was discovered in the Arthur Gowland papers in a file entitled Roman Catholic Church. Arthur Gowland Papers, PCC Archives, 2007-5006 (uncatalogued; cataloguing has recently been completed).

12 "If I Marry a Roman Catholic" (New York: Federal Council of Churches, 1948), 4. PCC Archives, 2007-5006.

13 "If I Marry a Roman Catholic," 14–15; "Mixed Marriage," 4. PCC Archives, Board of Evangelism and Social Action, 1982-1029-1-64.

child. The child is portrayed as growing in resentment that Mary has not converted:

> While the Roman church does not directly teach a child to feel this way, it is able to make suggestions that lead a child to such conclusions. That your child should resent you and come to cut you out of his love would be a terrible reward for all your love.[14]

The portrait of alienation is painted starkly. Little hope is given that the child might ever accept Reformed Christianity, and instead it is posited the child is more likely to have "no real faith at all," which is seen as even more troubling. John's conversion to the Presbyterian Church is considered unlikely. Mary's conversion to Roman Catholicism is deftly dismissed. A "mixed marriage"—one in which each individual holds to his or her respective faith—was thus portrayed as an insurmountable problem for Presbyterians in this period. "Mixed marriages" were persuasively dismissed not only as undesirable but as untenable. The final piece of advice in the article suggests that the ministers know all and can skilfully help any young person avoid the problem: "Approach any romantic relationship with a Roman Catholic with extreme caution. If you should find yourself involved, go to your pastor and speak with him freely. Ask him for literature on the subject. Accept his help and advice in good faith."[15] The writer seems oblivious to the fact that these sentences make a mockery of the claim made throughout that Mary would be surrendering her "spiritual freedom" if she became Roman Catholic, and of the tenet "faith and its freedom" that is portrayed as so central to Reformed Christianity.[16] The chasm between the two traditions was perceived to be so deep and the stereotypes so strong that all that emerges in the literature about "mixed marriages" are caricatures and a dilemma with no resolution.

The Presbyterian community appealed to Protestant freedom in other contexts, indeed it was a major theme in the critique of Roman Catholicism in Canada. This was particularly on display in 1954 in the *Presbyterian Record* when the movie *Martin Luther* was banned

14 Singer, "Will Your Child," *Presbyterian Record*, February 1958, 15.

15 Ibid., 15.

16 Ibid., 14.

in Québec by the Quebec Board of Censors. The *Record* covered the controversy in two articles, one noting the decision (with the provocative title "The Film that Quebec Banned!") and a follow-up article describing what happened when congregations in Westmount decided to show the film. The articles were not simple news reports. The editor's opinion was clearly conveyed. The *Record* challenged the Quebec Board of Censors' explanation that it had in the past done similar things with other films deemed "offensive to various religious groups": "Nevertheless, films like *The Song of Bernadette*, *Going My Way* and *The Bells of St. Mary's*, and other definitely Roman Catholic films have been shown without question in the Province of Quebec."[17] At issue was not free speech—Presbyterians would gladly have banned any number of films they considered objectionable—but religious freedom, fairness, "national unity," and the power relationships between Roman Catholics and Protestants:

> Let us here remark that the action of the Quebec censors shows that the battle for religious freedom, and beyond that for freedom of conscience in all matters, is an unceasing battle. It is still our battle. Freedom cannot be taken for granted even in a democracy. Let us guard our freedom as new threats arise in our contemporary life.[18]

Several months later, while somewhat gleefully describing the showing of the film by the churches in Westmount, the *Record* commented that one result of the showings of the movie had been to "reveal that the Protestants in this majority Roman Catholic city cannot be pushed around."[19] The rhetoric of freedom versus oppression was clear, and the issue broadcast across Canada through the denominational magazine's pages.

The rhetoric of freedom and vigilance for any perceived slight or advantage given to the Roman Catholic Church was evident among Canadian Presbyterians in a variety of ways during this period. In 1957

---

17 "Westmount Churchgoers See Banned Film," *Presbyterian Record*, July–August 1955, 3. This comparison was first made in a slightly milder form a year previously in "The Film That Quebec Banned!," *Presbyterian Record*, February 1954, 3.

18 "The Film," 31.

19 "Westmount Churchgoers," 3.

the *Record* published Claris Edwin Silcox's article "Those Misleading K. of C. Ads!" Silcox believed that it was necessary to challenge some Knights of Columbus advertisements' assertion that Roman Catholics supported religious liberty. He reminded his readers that this was not the first time Presbyterians had to correct these kinds of advertisements, noting that the editor of the *Record* had written about this in 1949 and 1950 and that the first of these columns had been reprinted and circulated as a pamphlet. Silcox begged to differ with the advertisements' claims of support for religious liberty by Roman Catholics, and after asserting his case he suggested that his readers should "take these advertisements with plenty of salt."[20] Discussions related to education in the province of Ontario in 1963, arising out of the statements by Roman Catholic bishops on proposed changes in the separate school system, brought a swift response, both from committees and in the *Record*.[21] That same year the *Record* editorialized against "Income Tax Inequities," which it suggested gave Roman Catholic post-secondary institutions an advantage over Protestant institutions, because of the provisions for those in religious orders.[22] The Presbyterian Church in Canada was part of the Inter-Church Committee on Protestant–Roman Catholic Relations, a committee of Protestant churches (there were no Roman Catholic representatives) designed to both work on "good Protestant–Roman Catholic relationships" and "protect Protestant rights and interests."[23] The examples could be multiplied.[24] While The

20 Claris Edwin Silcox, "Those Misleading K. of C. Ads!," *Presbyterian Record*, September 1957, 17, 30–31. For more on Silcox, see John Young, "Reaction to Vatican II in The United Church of Canada," in this volume.

21 "Those Misleading K. of C. Ads!," 17.

22 *Presbyterian Record*, February 1963, 13.

23 "The Inter-Church Committee on Protestant–Roman Catholic Relations: What is it? What has it done?" Arthur Gowland papers, PCC archives 2007-5006. See the discussion in John Young, "Reaction to Vatican II in the United Church of Canada," in this volume.

24 Committee on Inter-Church Relations Report, Acts and Proceedings [A&P] 1959, 91–92 against RC separate schools on military bases. During the period of the council's meeting, the traditional comments and concerns of Presbyterians continued. An editorial in the Record in January of 1963 responded to comments made by various Roman Catholic bishops in Ontario about education and the place of religion within schools. "The Editor comments upon our Inheritance in Public Education," *Presbyterian Record*, January 1963, 17. The next month saw an editorial comment about injustices that favoured

Presbyterian Church in Canada generally avoided the more inflammatory anti-Catholic rhetoric of more extreme Protestants and there were some balanced portrayals,[25] a series of issues highlighted the continuing chasm that existed between these two Christian traditions in Canada. Solitudes they were; and the Presbyterian solitude was not shy about defending its perceived rights.

Early Presbyterian Responses to Vatican II

It was into such a context that word came that Pope John XXIII had called a church council. The March 1959 editorial page of the *Record* noted "The Pope's Proposal," highlighting that one duty of the council would be to study ecumenical relations between Roman Catholics and other Christians.[26] The *Record* was cautious, even skeptical, of the attention given to the announcement in "the secular press." It noted that the last ecumenical council in 1869 had, among other things, "contained the famous definition of papal supremacy" and also wondered "what all the fuss is about?" when so little was known about what specifically the council might do and what might be involved, other than invitations to Protestant and Orthodox Christians to be present as observers: "There is no indication that Protestant representatives will participate actively in any discussion at the so-called ecumenical council." The Presbyterian Church in Canada's denominational magazine placed itself clearly within the Protestant ecumenical movement by ending its brief editorial with a reference to the question posed by Dr. W. A. Visser't Hooft, the World Council of Churches' General Secretary, as to how ecumenical the council would, in reality, be. The *Record* concluded: "The world awaits the answer."[27]

Roman Catholics within the Income Tax Act within Canada. "Income tax Inequalities," *Presbyterian Record*, February 1963, 13.

25 Examples of more extreme positions can be found in *The Gospel Witness and Protestant Advocate*, several copies of which were found in the "Roman Catholic" file in the Arthur Gowland Papers. Arthur Gowland Papers, PCC Archives 2007-5006. A relatively balanced voice can be found in W. F. Butcher, "The Papacy Today," *Presbyterian Record*, December 1958, 8. At the time Butcher was a minister in Quebec City.

26 Editorial, "The Pope's Proposal," *Presbyterian Record*, March 1959, 2.

27 "The Pope's Proposal," 2.

Despite the caution, the first session of the council saw a spate of articles in the *Presbyterian Record* discussing Vatican II and even reporting news from it. While it is important to look at these articles, it is also worth noting that this amount of coverage was not repeated for any other session. It is also worth noting that between the announcement of Vatican II and these articles reporting on the council, Canadian Presbyterians celebrated a key anniversary: the four hundredth anniversary of the Reformation in Scotland (1560). A series of articles in 1960 reminded Canadian Presbyterians of their roots and the historical animosities between them and Roman Catholics.[28] It was within this context that Joseph McLelland, a professor at Presbyterian College, Montréal, addressed the subject with *Record* readers in his article "Questions about the Vatican Council," which appeared in October 1962.[29] McLelland offered an optimistic introduction to the council. One aspect of the council, relations with other Christians, was stressed by McLelland as a key feature of John XXIII's call for the council:

> The second Vatican council raises the most profound questions for Protestants, therefore, because of this bold and explicit call. We must not doubt its sincerity: a council which begins with invocation of the Holy Spirit is not to be taken lightly by any Christian! What we are invited to do is proceed to dialogue with the Church of Rome in an entirely new way. Indeed this has already begun, in many parts of the world (including Montreal), and is an exciting sign of the new things that Christ's Spirit can do with old enemies. Two questions in particular are raised by such dialogue, and these will no doubt be clarified by the council itself. One is the relationship between pope and bishops, the question of infallibility; the other is the question of councils in the church, the question of authority.[30]

---

28 In 1960 the *Presbyterian Record* published monthly articles from January through to October, all related to Reformation themes, including "Zwingli the Reformer" (October), "Europe and the Scottish Reformation" (January), and "What we Owe to the Scottish Reformation" (February).

29 Joseph McLelland, "Questions about the Vatican Council," *Presbyterian Record*, October 1962, 10–12. The *Record* usually appears early in the month of publication. The article was thus timed to appear in Presbyterian mailboxes just prior to the council's opening.

30 McLelland, "Questions," 11.

McLelland explored these two topics in a manner that was learned, direct, and yet hopeful. He did not use the traditional polarities of Protestant rhetoric (Bible versus Tradition, freedom versus tyranny, etc.) but instead offered a careful exploration of the issues dividing the Western Christian church in the mid-twentieth century. He was hopeful—assured by Hans Küng, whose book *The Council and Reunion*, he argued, "is a must for every Protestant"—that the Pope intended to "avoid merely controversial matters, including all speculation about the Virgin Mary," and quoted a pastoral letter from Dutch bishops to argue that there was more agreement on issues of authority and infallibility than many might assume.[31] It was this hopefulness that McLelland seemed intent on conveying to his readers, carefully placing all of the events within the larger frame of Christian history, stressing continuity up to the Council of Constance and the divisions since Trent that had only been enlarged by the First Vatican Council. The hope was that common ground could be found in a shared heritage—"a reformed churchman is anxious to hear the praise of God's glory in every church and cannot decide beforehand that a continuing reformation is denied the Church of Rome."[32] Indeed, McLelland noted that one's own "tradition" needed to first be examined and critiqued before he ended his article with a stirring quote from Pope John calling for prayers, including the prayers of those "not of this fold," for the council's success.[33]

McLelland's hopeful introduction to the council did not go unnoticed or unchallenged. Two letters to the editor appeared in the next issue (November) criticizing his position. Both correspondents relied on the more traditional themes of freedom, primacy of Scripture, and an almost permanent gulf between Protestants and Roman Catholics. One author concluded by arguing: "What we need today are more militant ministers, men with the convictions of Knox and Calvin, or the freedom so dearly bought by the blood of the martyrs will be irrevocably lost to us."[34] Apart from these two angry rebuttals, McLelland's optimistic ap-

31 Ibid., 11–12.

32 Ibid,, 12.

33 Ibid., 12.

34 *Presbyterian Record*, November 1962, 23–24.

praisal of the council created no major controversy.[35] In fact, interest in Vatican II was supplemented by selections in the "News" section of the magazine over the next months as the first session of the council met. In the same issue, October, it was noted that there would be three observers from the World Presbyterian Alliance in attendance.[36] A protest by the Free Church of Scotland (with which Canadian Presbyterians were not, generally, in sympathy) of visits to the Pope by the Queen, and other British officials, including a past moderator of the Church of Scotland (the Scottish church with much closer ties to the denomination) was noted. While reporting the protest, the *Record* managed to make it clear that this was an extreme position not worthy of much sympathy by including in this report the seeming unrelated piece of information that during another debate a Free Church committee member referred to the World Council of Churches as "one of the most serious menaces to the propagation of the Gospel in the world today."[37] Such a comment would have received little support from the majority of Canadian Presbyterians. In this way, the *Record* clearly conveyed what had become a cautious interest in what was happening at Vatican II that was further underscored by a distancing from extreme anti-Catholic posturing. Interest in the council was such that in the December issue, the *Record* had a special news feature, written by a "leading Italian Protestant."[38] The column included more commentary on the distinctiveness of Rome and of the challenges of Latin and of technology at the council than it

---

[35] One anticipates that letters to the editor will appear objecting to statements made in a denominational magazine. The number of published letters and responses can thus give some indication of the debate within the denomination. If there was major opposition, one would expect either an article to appear taking the other point of view, or for some action to be taken (an overture to General Assembly, a protest to one of the theological colleges, a motion at General Assembly or another church court, or some other action) that would make the displeasure more evident.

[36] "Vatican Council Observers from World Alliance," *Presbyterian Record*, October 1962, 22.

[37] "Free Church of Scotland Criticizes Recent Rome Visits," *Presbyterian Record*, October 1962, 26.

[38] "The Vatican Council," *Presbyterian Record*, December 1962, 23–24. Ironically, the "You were Asking?" column that appeared immediately at the end of the article addressed the question of "mixed marriages." The comments of Prof. A. L. Farris were judicious, simply noting the need for more effective education.

did a narrative of what occurred. What the commentator did suggest near the end was a brewing struggle between various factions:

> ... what some call the liberals and the conservatives, while others call them the nationalists and the internationalists. We may say simply that a group of cardinals, with a quota of bishops, all from central Europe, France and Germany in the lead, are standing against the curia (papal court), to try to transfer to the bishops some of the powers normally held by the pope. It is unfair and a little short to put it that way, but there is no better one.[39]

The commentator went on to speak of the strength of the curia, as well as the curiosity that it was from Europe, and not America, that the desire for change was coming.[40] What else the commentator might have said is, unfortunately, only speculation. There certainly were plans to publish further columns on the proceedings at the council. Indeed, the magazine introduced the column by noting "The first of a series of comments written exclusively for *The Record* by a leading Italian Protestant."[41]

While no more was heard about Vatican II from the special correspondent, news items in January and February of 1963 noted the work of the council. The closing of the first session was given thorough coverage (much more detailed than that given by the special correspondent). The report offered an objective summary of the conclusion of the council and the work that would proceed in the time before the next session.[42] In February a different kind of news item appeared. The *Record* printed a lengthy report (credited to the Religious News Service) from New York, outlining the positive shift in attitudes of Protestants and Catholics toward each other as a result of Vatican II. While detailing

39 "Vatican Council," 23–24.

40 Ibid., 24.

41 Ibid., 23.

42 "With Flurry of Discussion Council Session Closes," *Presbyterian Record*, January 1963, 25–26. No author is given for the column. The byline simply reads "Vatican City." While it is possible that this came from the "special correspondent," the change in approach and style is dramatically different. It is possible that the *Record* was able to reproduce a column that appeared elsewhere (although this is not indicated) or use another correspondent to provide this news.

some of the major events and challenges at the first session, the tone of optimism was strong:

> Father Sheerin (a Roman Catholic press representative present at the Council), asked whether council Fathers took any "definite steps" toward Christian reunion, said that by approaching the first chapter of a document on the liturgy, the council demonstrated that the church would be willing to take "serious acts" in that direction. "Every time a document was proposed for discussion," he said, "the bishops subjected it to an ecumenical test: Did this document help or hurt the cause of unity?"[43]

The mood of optimism, so evident in the above quote, was represented throughout the article. Given this coverage, the later silence of the *Record* becomes even more perplexing. Yet the reality remains that only this first session received extensive coverage in the *Record*'s "News" section. Whether it was the lack of a special correspondent, the recognition that denominational members were receiving news from other sources, or some other factor that led to this is not clear. Direct reports of Vatican II and comments upon the council ceased within the Presbyterian denominational magazine shortly after the first session ended.

Official Response: The Silence of the Inter-Church Relations Committee

While the early days of Vatican II were featured in the denominational magazine, references to the council do not appear in a major way in the yearly gatherings of The Presbyterian Church in Canada, the General Assembly. Looking back, this is a striking and puzzling omission, particularly when we search the reports and deliberations of the particular committee that one would assume would have responsibility in this area, the Committee on Inter-Church Relations. Yet in the period from 1959 through to the end of the 1960s, one looks in vain for any direct reference to Vatican II or to changes in the Roman Catholic Church from this committee. One assumes that this silence led John

[43] "Council Sifted Attitudes of Protestants, Catholics," *Presbyterian Record*, February 1963, 26–28.

Moir to make the previously quoted observation that the denomination said nothing official and seems to have missed the council. At the same time, when one looks closely at the reports of this committee and of reactions to them, it becomes clear that in the climate within the Presbyterian Church at the time, this committee could not have readily expanded its mandate to the point where it could have engaged the new ecumenical climate created by Vatican II. The committee was caught by the mythology of what had happened in "1925" (the creation of The United Church of Canada as a merger of Congregationalists, Methodists, and most Presbyterians), by the fears and ongoing struggle within the denomination on the meaning of ecumenism that paralyzed the Presbyterian Church at this particular moment. We need to look closely at the committee, its mandate, and its struggles to see why this committee—as odd as this may seem—was the last place where one would have been able to engage creatively in ecumenical outreach during this period.

In the yearly reports of the Committee on Inter-Church Relations to the General Assembly one can see the issues that dominated the committee's agenda throughout the decade. In 1961 the committee reported its work in clarifying "the position of Presbyterians with regard to relations with other communions" and stated that the committee's purpose was:

> to encourage study of the distinctive Presbyterian witness to Christian unity and the catholicity of the church and to clarify the thinking of our members about the true character of the Presbyterian position so that we may be faithful in making the witness to which God is calling us today.[44]

There was no bold vision of ecumenism here. This was a cautious position. Presbyterians began with themselves and who they were before reaching out. The committee met this purpose by relating to specific groups. These included the World Presbyterian Alliance (the precursor to the World Alliance of Reformed Churches), the World Council of Churches, the Canadian Council of Churches, and various other denominations that were usually referred to under the heading "Fraternal

[44] A&P, 1961, 361.

Relations." Two years later in 1963, the committee again discussed its mandate, this time talking about the importance of establishing "positive relations" with:

- other churches of the reformed faith
- churches of other denominations
- ecumenical agencies, such as the World Council of Churches and the Canadian Council of Churches
- confessional movements such as the World Presbyterian Alliance.[45]

Thus, just a few months prior to the opening sessions of Vatican II, the committee did not specifically mention the Roman Catholic communion, or include Roman Catholic–Presbyterian relations within its understanding of its mandate. It is important to see how this mandate was conceived because the committee was reluctant to step outside of its clearly defined tasks. Presbyterians (or at least the majority of them) were concerned that they be understood to be ecumenical. At the same time, the mythology had developed among those who continued as Presbyterians after church union in 1925 that it was friendly ecumenical discussions, begun innocently and informally, which had led to the split in the denomination. Ecumenism was thus, even with fellow Protestants, to be undertaken with great caution.

It was relationships with The United Church of Canada—and not issues related to changes brought about by Vatican II—that dominated the Inter-Church Relation Committee's agenda throughout the 1960s as it served as the official voice for Presbyterian ecumenism. For our purposes, however, what is enlightening about these discussions is that they show the concerns that dominated Presbyterians as they strove to be ecumenical in the 1960s. As a result of a minor dispute with the United Church over the establishment of a new congregation, a committee of representatives of both denominations was established to resolve the issue. The Inter-Church Relations Committee reported to the General Assembly in 1964 on this meeting. Yet, the first action

---

45 A&P, 1963, 386. This issue received considerable coverage as one of the notable events that had occurred at that year's General Assembly. *Presbyterian Record*, July–August 1963, 12.

of the Presbyterian representatives seems odd, displaying the extreme caution around ecumenicity:

> At this meeting, the chairman of our Inter-Church Relations Committee entered a caveat drawing to the attention of the assembled representatives of the action of the 89th General Assembly which specifically forbade any conversations between representatives of any other communion which might lead to the consideration of organic union. Our position was simply that the United Church had asked us to meet with them to discuss areas of tension, particularly, the matter of Rocky Mountain House, Alberta, and that we were quite prepared to do this, but not to discuss the matter of union at all. The United Church representatives agreed to meet with us on these terms, in fact insisted upon them, and negotiations are proceeding.[46]

This caveat demonstrates the tensions around ecumenism for Canadian Presbyterians.[47] The United Church of Canada again appeared on the committee's agenda as the United and Anglican communions discussed union. In 1967 the General Assembly allowed representatives to observe and consult with The United Church of Canada and Anglicans in their discussion in 1967 under very strict conditions—"but take no action which would commit our church to organic union without the consent of the Assembly"—but when the invitation was extended to the Presbyterians to take a more active role, they withdrew.[48] The relationship with the United Church (including the proposed union with the Anglicans) was a concern throughout the decade, one that overshadowed relations with the Roman Catholic Church, before, during, and after Vatican II.

The Inter-Church Relations Committee had reason to be cautious. Relations with other Protestant churches had been a major source of inter-denominational controversy in the period after World War II. The division, as John Moir has outlined, was between those who

---

46 A&P, 1964, 437.

47 A&P, 1964, 437. One of the ongoing issues was having two denominations, The Presbyterian Church in Canada and The United Church of Canada, each seeing themselves as a—or even the—Canadian "Presbyterian" voice at the World Presbyterian Alliance.

48 A&P, 1967, 53; A&P, committee report, 1969, 375.

favoured a broad ecumenism and those confessional conservatives who only wanted relations with communions who adhered to the Westminster Confession of Faith in a way similar to that of Canadian Presbyterians.[49] The former group found its voice in the Inter-Church Relations Committee. In the 1960s the confessional conservatives expressed their approach to ecumenism in a small independent journal known as *Presbyterian Comment. Presbyterian Comment* was edited by William Stanford Reid and represented the views of Reid and the confessional wing of the denomination on a variety of issues. Published three or four times a year, the journal reached several hundred people, with a maximum subscription list of about eight hundred.[50]

In *Presbyterian Comment* we see considerable commentary on Vatican II. Vatican II was addressed directly in the October 1964 issue. The juxtaposition of two brief articles, both by William Stanford Reid, is worth noting—"The Reformation Anniversary" appeared in one column and "Rome, Reunion and Religious Freedom" appeared in the other column of the same page. The latter discussed Vatican II directly. Reid argued that the Roman Catholic Church's position had not changed. One must still have "actually received Catholic baptism" to be saved. The debates within the Council on inter-church relations were cited, presented as evidence of a final position and one that had not changed. While Vatican II was referred to, what seems the main target of the brief column were Protestants who were open to ecumenism: "Troublous days lie ahead for those who stand by the work of the Reformation, if ecumenicalism has its way."[51] The column on the Reformation, ostensibly about the 447th anniversary of Luther's post-

49 Moir covers the divisions over ecumenism in the PCC, Enduring Witness, 3rd ed., 251–54, and refers to this as a "civil war." An example of the continuation of these tensions within the denomination is evident in an opinion piece featured in January 1966, M. C. Felderhof, "A Peculiar Attitude," *Presbyterian Record*, January 1966, 3. Felderhof's comments are the result of the decision of the Maritime Synod of the PCC not to participate in the Maritime Ecumenical Council. Relations with other Protestants who did not hold to Reformed confessional standards thus were reflected in a variety of ways in this period.

50 A. Donald MacLeod, "Putting in Its Place: Canadian Presbyterian Independent Journalism," *Channels*, Spring 2003, 17–22.

51 William Stanford Reid, "Rome, Reunion and Religious Freedom," *Presbyterian Comment*, October 1964, 3.

ing of his ninety-five theses at Wittenberg, made a similar point in an even more forceful manner. The anniversary must be celebrated, Reid argued, because if one forgot the principles of the Reformation it was too easy to abandon them and slip into a reunion, which would be on the terms of the Roman Catholic Church. He suggested:

> Today the Christian Church faces an apparently irresistible drive toward the establishment of an international super-church that will eventually include even the Church of Rome, which rejected the Reformers in the sixteenth century and has since moved farther from Scriptural teaching. This presents a serious danger.[52]

Vatican II was portrayed as changing nothing. It was Protestants who do not see this who posed the threat.

This idea that Vatican II changed nothing in regard to Protestant–Catholic relations appeared on other occasions in *Presbyterian Comment* as the journal continued to reflect (usually in a critical light) on the variety of changes it saw in the Church in the 1960s. In October 1965 Reid wrote about "Rome's New Face." He noted the fourth session of Vatican II, as well as the Pope's visit to the United Nations, but then asked whether or not there really had been change—"is it really a new face?"[53] A more positive evaluation of Vatican II was given by Louis de Groot, however, in a 1967 article entitled "Are We Ready for Reunion with Rome?" While generally positive, the article quickly returned to words of caution. De Groot listed all of the things that Protestants had come to associate with Roman theology—the place of Mary, saints, the place of tradition within the Roman Catholic tradition, papal infallibility, the Mass—and noted that as change had not occurred in any of these areas, it was far too early to think of reunification.[54] There was an optimistic tone, however, as he wrote of the changes that had occurred:

52 William Stanford Reid, "The Reformation Anniversary," *Presbyterian Comment*, October 1964, 3.

53 William Stanford Reid, "Rome's New Face," *Presbyterian Comment*, October 1965, 2.

54 L. Louis de Groot, "Are We Ready for Reunion with Rome?'" *Presbyterian Comment*, June 1967, 2.

Surely it is too much to say at this time that the walls which have separated Roman Catholics and Protestants have disappeared. There is still much that separates us from one another, but we can certainly say that a new day has dawned.[55]

The challenge now was for Protestants to turn again and look to Scripture to understand what it was they believed.[56] Thus, two opinions of Vatican II appeared in this small journal, one seeing some change (though urging caution) and the other, more frequently voiced opinion, seeing little change. One can see in these comments that Vatican II was taken seriously, even (and perhaps even especially) among confessional Presbyterians. At the same time, their caution on ecumenical dialogue must be taken into account when we consider the silence of the Inter-Church Relations Committee. Given the reality of an articulate vocal position in the denomination highly concerned with any ecumenical dialogue, let alone Roman Catholic, it is understandable why bold initiatives in expanding the committee's mandate or direct comments on events at Vatican II were unlikely.

Other "Official" Response

If the members of the Inter-Church Relations Committee proposed no motions we can see as a response to Vatican II, this is not true of other Presbyterians. Indeed, two overtures[57] came forward from various parts of Canada calling for the denomination to change its attitudes toward Roman Catholicism and also to change one of its most formative, indeed iconic, doctrinal statements—the Westminster Confession of Faith. In April 1964 a small northern presbytery, the Presbytery

55 De Groot, "Reunion with Rome?" 2.

56 Ibid., 2.

57 Within the system of Presbyterian polity there is a mechanism called an overture that allows congregations and presbyteries to ask the General Assembly (national church) to respond to a concern or changing situation. Overtures come from the periphery to the centre, are usually given to a committee for study and comment, and then the General Assembly as a whole decides whether or not it agrees with the response. Overtures also have a particular form. The problem is usually identified in a series of "whereas" statements. This must be followed by a suggestion of what one wishes the General Assembly to do with one's particular concerns, as well as a formal stated recognition that the Assembly may "do otherwise as the General Assembly in its wisdom may deem best."

of Temiskaming, passed an overture concerning the language of the Westminster Confession of Faith. Specifically, the presbytery, as respectful as it was of the Reformation heritage and the persecution at that time, noted that Chapter 5, section 6 of the Confession identified "the Pope as antichrist." This, the presbytery argued, could not be said of recent popes. Even more to the point, they conveyed their conviction "the present wording of the said article, besides failing to reflect the love of Jesus Christ, proposes an attitude of hatred, judgement and suspicion."[58] Noting that another Presbyterian church, the United Presbyterian Church U.S.A., had already reworded this section, the presbytery asked the General Assembly to change that wording to the one used by the United Presbyterian Church.[59] The overture was referred by the General Assembly to the appropriate committee, the Articles of Faith Committee (precursor to the Church Doctrine Committee), which reported to the 1965 General Assembly. The committee stated they were "sympathetic to the prayer of the overture in its concern over the harsh language" used for the Pope. The challenge was that this was a historic document and "its actual text ought not to be tampered with."[60] A different solution was suggested. The committee would prepare an "explanatory note" explaining the theology within the Confession and the concern regarding individual abuses of power that might happen and would "nevertheless make a serious attempt to assess the positive role of the papacy in recent decades."[61] This approach met with support from the Church.[62] At the next Assembly, the full text of the explanatory note was presented. The use of the term "anti-Christ" in reference to the Pope was placed in historical context. Recent popes were applauded for "a changed attitude from that of their predecessors in office," and particular reference was made to support for Biblical study and for a changed attitude to "the collegiality of bishops which at least consider-

---

58 A&P, 1964, 500–501.

59 A&P, 1964, 501.

60 A&P, 1965, 333.

61 Ibid.

62 The Record did receive one letter to the editor from Rev. H. Crump, Portage La Prairie, protesting the response to the overture, as it was reported in the *Record* in the issue covering the Assembly in 1965. *Presbyterian Record*, October 1965, 34.

ably widens the effective control of the church." Given these realities, "we must be willing to revise our attitudes concerning the papacy."[63]

What caused this interest in 1964? The timing, as well as the specific reference to collegiality, leads to the natural conclusion that this was, indeed a response, to Vatican II.[64] A second—and much more strongly worded—overture appeared in 1967. Seemingly not everyone agreed with the Articles of Faith Committee that adding explanatory notes was a sufficient response. The Presbytery of Sarnia forwarded a long overture, asking the General Assembly to "take action to amend for subscription purposes the Westminster Confession of Faith" by omitting four statements. What they seem to have been asking for was either the elimination of these statements, or, more likely, that those taking their ordination vows would be given some form of "liberty of conscience" on these so that they could disagree with them. In addition to Chapter 25, section 6 (which called the Pope "that antichrist, that man of sin, and son of perdition"), the presbytery objected to Chapter 22, section 7 (against celibacy and monastic vows); Chapter 24, section 3 (prohibiting marriage with "infidels, Papists, or other idolaters"); and Chapter 29, section 2 (against "that the Popish sacrifice of the mass").[65] The presbytery used strong language to challenge its own confessional standards, speaking of them as "derogatory references to other theological positions," "not essential," and "calculated to give offence to our Roman Catholic brethren." The opening two "whereas" statements certainly indicate what made Presbyterians in 1967 sensitive to language that had not seemed to bother them in 1957, 1947,

[63] A&P, 1966, 268.

[64] Bush, "Presbyterian Church and the Pope," 111. Bush effectively makes this argument, and this author concurs. One interesting question is the relationship between this overture and the actions of the Committee on Inter-Church Relations in asking the denomination in 1963 to think about ecumenism. Unintentionally, the committee may have encouraged the Presbytery of Temiskaming. Indeed, the committee's report notes several presbyteries that felt the position in the Westminster Confession needed to be altered. The committee also received one response questioning whether the denomination shouldn't withdraw from Protestant ecumenical activities such as the World Council of Churches and the Alliance of Reformed Churches. The divisions on ecumenism at this time within the denomination are again made very clear. While the committee may have stimulated the discussion, it did not move beyond its mandate.

[65] A&P, 1967, 421.

or earlier: first, "a spirit of ecumenism is beginning to pervade the Church of Jesus Christ"; and second, "we are discovering a new sense of brotherhood with our Roman Catholic brethren within the context of this movement."[66] That "new sense of brotherhood" was clearly reflective of the changes resulting from Vatican II. The response of the Articles of Faith Committee, though perhaps expected, would have been disappointing to the Presbytery of Sarnia. The committee again noted the Canadian Presbyterian practice of not altering historic creeds and advised against deletion. No explanatory note was proposed,[67] but the committee added this comment:

> Regarding our present-day attitude to the issues raised in the overture, we draw attention to the fact that the Church of Rome is herself currently re-thinking these matters, and we are watching with great interest the changes taking place in that Church (e.g. Hans Küng, "The Council, Reform and Reunion"). While we recognize the offensive nature of these statements and do not regard them as true, we nevertheless advise against making any definite judgment on these matters at this time.[68]

These are fascinating comments. They display awareness of the importance of the Council and of the changes that Vatican II brought. There is also a caution—but a caution that is difficult to read. What is it that one shouldn't make "definite judgement about"? Is it the changes themselves, or is it the "reunion" part of Küng's title? The answer is not at all clear. At the same time, it is clear what the committee has made a judgment on. They stated that the statements in the Westminster Confession were "offensive" and said they "do not regard them as true." Although unwilling to change an historic document, the Articles of Faith Committee was willing to state plainly that the Confession contained errors. It is difficult to imagine this being stated only a decade earlier.

It was also through an overture that we can discern the changes that Vatican II rapidly affected among Canadian Presbyterians. This

---

66 A&P, 1967, 421.

67 There was an ongoing parallel discussion regarding what it meant to "subscribe" to the Westminster Confession. As the overture inferred, subscription was the issue. This may have been why the committee chose not to prepare an explanatory note.

68 A&P, 1967, 241.

particular overture was received from the Synod (a provincial body) of Hamilton and London in 1967 and concerned the reality that questions were being received as to what to do when one received an invitation to participate in a joint worship service with Roman Catholics. This was, seemingly, a problem that had not been encountered before. In the rather formal language of an overture, the Synod noted that whereas "questions have arisen within this Synod pertaining to the possibility of invitations to our minister to attend and to add to certain rites of the Roman Catholic Church," and also as "there is uncertainty as to the possibility or desirability to accept such invitations," the Synod thought that there needed to be a common policy and asked that the General Assembly instruct the Committee on Inter-Church Relations to investigate the matter and report.[69] The Committee on Inter-Church Relation's response to this request came the next year. The response was simple. The committee rejected the idea that a national policy was needed. Instead, they suggested:

> There is no restriction on any Presbyterian minister taking part in the service of another communion. In any case he is under the discipline of the presbytery. Under the circumstances we can see no need to determine policy on a national scale.[70]

The committee's rejection of the need for a consistent national policy—which one anticipates would put restrictions on participation rather than encourage them—left the situation in the hands of the local regions throughout Canada and in individual consciences. By its silence, the committee allowed for great freedom in this area.

At this initial stage of research, it seems clear that two General Assembly committees dealt most directly with Vatican II. The Inter-Church Relations Committee, the one we would anticipate would have been most active, was largely silent on the issue. The words "Vatican II" never appeared, nor did the committee boldly expand its mandate to move into the area of Presbyterian–Roman Catholic dialogue. I have argued that this was unlikely to have happened, given the ongoing controversy about ecumenism within The Presbyterian Church in Canada,

69 A&P, 1967, 415.

70 A&P, 1968, 353.

and the near paranoia about "union" with other religious traditions. It was the Articles of Faith Committee, driven by two overtures from presbyteries, which dealt more directly with the effects of Vatican II. Again, bold action was not taken, in this case because of the tradition of not changing confessional standards that Canadian Presbyterians did (and continue to) hold to. The declaratory statement, however, and the comments of the committee in 1968, may be where we find the official response to Vatican II from Canadian Presbyterians. While not radical, these statements represent significant changes from what could have, or would have, been said even a decade before the council took place.[71]

Another indication of the important changes that Vatican II brought to Presbyterian relationships to Roman Catholics can be seen in an event that occurred during the 1967 General Assembly. A written protest was submitted by Rev. H. M. MacRury, taking to task "those responsible for inviting the papal delegate to bring greetings without prior consent of the general assembly."[72] The action of inviting a Roman Catholic representative to bring greetings was clearly unusual, and given what we have already seen concerning the tensions between the denominations, such a protest might have been expected. What happened next, however, indicates a changing attitude. Rather than support the protest, a motion to support the decision—a motion of commendation—was moved and passed by the Assembly. The vote was recorded (122 for the vote of commendation, 46 against, with some dissents recorded), allowing us to have a snapshot of support on such a key issue.[73] Like Vatican II itself, there were factions within Canadian Presbyterianism, but those open to the changes carried the day.

The responses of Canadian Presbyterians to Vatican II did not end here. The most dramatic changes can be seen not in official statements

---

71 The "Roman Catholic" file in the Arthur Gowland papers suggests that it might actually have been the Board of Evangelism and Social Action where much of the dialogue between Roman Catholics and Presbyterians may have taken place in this period. Arthur Gowland was the convenor of this board.

72 *Presbyterian Record*, July–August 1967, 13.

73 Ibid. It is also significant that the mover of the motion was the principal of one of the theological colleges, Principal J. S. Glen of Knox College, Toronto. Glen later became involved in the establishment of the ecumenical Toronto School of Theology, although he is generally perceived as a cautious participant in that bold venture.

but in changed behaviours and attitudes. Items appeared in the "News" section of the *Record*, noting these changes. In February 1966 it was reported that the choir of the Presbyterian Church of St. Andrew and St. Paul in Montréal had "accepted an invitation to sing Christmas music" at one of the city's Roman Catholic parishes. This "unusual opportunity for ecumenical friendship" was reported to have happened in "an atmosphere of warm welcome and cordial good will which made the event an unforgettable experience."[74] The same issue reported on a joint Presbyterian–Roman Catholic project in the United States to prepare a "common book of worship and Bible study."[75] Book reviews,[76] news items, and articles touching on change in the Church, including the Roman Catholic Church, all helped to make Presbyterians aware that old attitudes might need to give way. One such article, not directly linked to Vatican II but nevertheless speaking to the issues, featured an interview with Karl Barth, the dominant theologian for Reformed Christians in the early 1960s, discussing "The relationship between Rome and the churches of the reformation." Cautious, but open, Barth reserved his most critical comments for the German New Testament scholar Rudolph Bultmann, and for John A. T. Robinson, author of *Honest to God*.[77] This provides an important reminder to us, that the 1960s were a time of considerable turmoil and questioning within the Reformed tradition and Protestantism in general. Our understanding of

[74] "Presbyterian choir sings in a Roman Catholic Church,". *Presbyterian Record*, February 1966, 27.

[75] "Book for worship and study is Presbyterian-R.C. project," *Presbyterian Record*, February 1966, 31.

[76] Book reviews would include: William Klempa's review of *A Question of Conscience*, by Charles Davis, which appeared in the May 1968, *Presbyterian Record* (27–29), and Scarth Macdonell's review of James Kavanaugh's *A Modern Priest Looks at His Outdated Church*, which appeared July-August 1968 (28). Each of the reviewers moves beyond the criticisms made in the books of the Roman Catholic Church to comment on the challenge of reform within Protestantism.

[77] "The relationship between Rome and the churches of the Reformation: An interview with Karl Barth," *Presbyterian Record*, December 1965, 16–17. The article was a translation of the interview that was conducted by a Dutch minister. In the interview, Barth is cautious about Vatican II as he recognizes that the council had not completed its work. He noted that the reformers—he mentioned several times conversations he had with Hans Küng—are one group, and that differences in theology continued between Roman Catholics and Protestants. Barth also noted the divisions among Protestants.

the response to Vatican II has to take into account the reality that there was great turmoil within Protestantism during these years when Vatican II was meeting.[78] Much of that response was more subtle than direct, nevertheless a significant change in attitudes gradually developed. In 1972 The Presbyterian Church in Canada produced a new resource, "Marriage Guidelines," which was a study guide. "Mixed marriages" were no longer a major topic of concern. Instead, the discussion focused on "interfaith marriages." The change in the ecumenical climate was noted. The guide then went on to state: "Christian mixed marriages can be a source of real hope for the growing together of the churches."[79] Both marriages across Protestant denominations and Protestant–Roman Catholic marriages were discussed. The main issue seems to be working out how the various clergy might participate.[80] Another practical example of change comes from the Presbytery of East Toronto, as the presbytery joined with the Archbishop of Toronto in a joint ecumenical service opening the Flemingdon Park Catholic-Presbyterian Worship Centre in 1972. Both denominations began work in the Flemingdon Park area in 1967.[81] Again, it is difficult to imagine this happening a decade earlier. While certain tensions continued,[82] the shift in attitude is nonetheless significant.

---

78 The international discussions around Death of God theology, etc., are well covered in Patrick Allit, *Religion in America Since 1945: A History* (New York: Columbia, 2003), 72–79. In Canada, Pierre Berton, *The Comfortable Pew* (Toronto: McClelland and Stewart, 1965) and the compilation produced by The United Church of Canada, *Why the Sea Is Boiling Hot* (Toronto: Ryerson, 1965) reflect the self-questioning during this period.

79 "Marriage Guidelines," 6. PCC Archives, 1982-1029-1-6.

80 Ibid., 6.

81 Presbytery of East Toronto, worship bulletin from service, PCC Archives, 1993-3026.

82 An example would be the decision of the Canadian government to have an ambassador to Vatican City in the late 1960s. What is interesting is that in the brief prepared to Mitchell Sharp, the Minister of External Affairs, by the Inter-Church Committee on Protestant–Roman Catholic Relations, of which Presbyterians were part, it was noted that it was unfortunate that the government had raised such a difficult issue "at this time when a new spirit of understanding and friendship is growing between the Roman Catholic and other communions." Arthur Gowland Papers, PCC Archives 2007-5006.

Conclusion

This paper has argued that Presbyterians responded positively to Vatican II.[83] This response is not evident in some of the places where we might expect it—in particular within the recorded discussions or actions of the Inter-Church Relations Committee. Nonetheless, in other places a positive opening to change does occur. With all of the other challenges of the 1960s, Presbyterians still had time to notice the troublesome language of their confessional standards and raise the issue of changing it. Although it felt the language of an historical document couldn't be changed, in significant ways the Presbyterian Church in Canada distanced itself from this language. Issues that had divided the traditions—especially "mixed marriages"—ceased to be the problems they once were. Presbyterians started talking of Roman Catholics as their "brethren" (this was in the days before there was a sensitivity to using inclusive language). Anti-Catholic rhetoric, endemic among Presbyterians in the 1950s, became an oddity. These were dramatic changes and indicate the Presbyterian response to Vatican II.

---

83 As this is an initial survey of this subject, it is anticipated that as we study more fully the 1960s and 1970s more evidence will emerge that will either support or challenge the thesis of this paper. In particular, it seems that the real impact of Vatican II may have been in agencies of the denomination other than the Inter-Church Relations Committee, such as the General Board of Missions, and it is only as we look at their minutes and reports in other contexts that a fuller story will emerge. The impact of Vatican II on theological education has also been barely touched upon in this paper. Two other possible areas of enquiry are the way in which Women's Missionary Societies of the PCC responded in their publications to Vatican II, and how Canadian Presbyterians absorbed insights about Vatican II from sources outside of their own denominational publications (the Canadian media, international church publications, etc.).

Reaction to Vatican II in The United Church of Canada

John H. Young, Queen's School of Religion,
Queen's University

In the fall of 1954, The United Church of Canada's Commission on the Christian Faith published a sixty-four-page booklet entitled *What's the Difference? Protestant and Roman Catholic Beliefs Compared*. While the commission hoped "that this booklet will lead to a better understanding of both Protestantism and Roman Catholicism"[1] and asserted that "every attempt has been made to avoid an adverse and prejudiced attitude and to be fair and just in every judgment expressed,"[2] the document's doctrinal comparisons were certainly not designed to encourage the membership to visit a neighbourhood Roman Catholic parish. Not quite ten years later, in the winter of 1964, a picture of Gregory Baum graced the cover of *The United Church Observer*,[3] the denomination's national magazine. It had been preceded in the fall of 1962 by one of Pope John XXIII.[4] Explaining the changed perspective those examples suggest and examining the longer term effects of Vatican II on the United Church is the subject of this paper.

This essay will come at that task through an examination of three areas in succession: first, it will set the scene for a consideration of

---

1 Arthur G. Reynolds, *What's the Difference? Protestant and Roman Catholic Beliefs Compared* (Toronto: The United Church of Canada, 1954), 3.

2 Ibid.

3 *The United Church Observer*, February 1, 1964.

4 *The United Church Observer*, October 15, 1962.

United Church reaction to Vatican II by providing some sense of how the United Church viewed the Roman Catholic Church prior to Vatican II; second, the essay will look at how the United Church reacted to Vatican II as the council was taking place, primarily through an examination of how the council was covered in the denominational magazine and in committee or other official church reports; third, it will try to discern the effect that Vatican II had on the United Church. In this third area, the essay will explore several dimensions—almost immediately, a changed perspective on Roman Catholicism and a renewed commitment to ecumenism that was happening even before the council concluded in 1965; more slowly, though probably more noticeable in terms of what United Church congregants would have observed, some changes in the general liturgical ethos and worship patterns of the United Church, changes partly the result of increased Roman Catholic–Protestant interaction.

The United Church and Roman Catholicism Pre–Vatican II

Prior to Vatican II, the United Church viewed Roman Catholicism, and the Roman Catholic Church, with considerable suspicion. It was not that individual clergy at the parish level in various communities did not get along well, nor were there lacking instances of co-operation. The military chaplaincy, especially in wartime, and the Antigonish Movement in the Maritimes stand out as particular examples of such co-operation. But the *modus operandi* of many United Church clergy, and also of much of the denomination's leadership, was to view the Roman Catholic Church as a rival to be feared and to be challenged on the Canadian scene.

For example, when the United Church was formed in 1925 as a result of a union of Canadian Congregationalists, Methodists, and some Presbyterians, its doctrinal statement[5] declared, in the article on

[5] The doctrinal statement around which these three denominations came together was drafted between 1904 and 1908 as part of the negations toward this church union. There were very few changes made to that doctrinal statement between the completion of an initial draft in 1908 of the "Basis of Union" for the three denominations and the consummation of the union in 1925.

the Church, that "we acknowledge as a part, more or less pure, of this universal brotherhood, every particular church throughout the world which professes this faith in Jesus Christ and obedience to Him as divine Lord and Saviour."[6] While that statement acknowledging that every other denomination was a part, "more or less pure," of the Church represented a relatively charitable stance to Roman Catholicism and to some other denominations when it was drafted in the first decade of the twentieth century, the phrase "more or less pure" also damns with faint praise.

Fear and suspicion of Roman Catholicism had deep roots in the United Church. One major reason why some Methodist and Presbyterian leaders pushed hard for an ecclesiastical union of Methodists, Congregationalists, and Presbyterians during the early twentieth century was a perceived need to help "Canadianize" and "Christianize" the immigrants flooding in from Central and Eastern Europe to help settle the "empty" prairies during the first decade of the twentieth century. Neither the Methodists nor the Presbyterians, at that time two of the largest Protestant denominations in the country, believed that individually they had the resources to plant churches sufficient even to serve their members who had been moving into the prairies from eastern Canada or those from sister churches in Great Britain or the United States in increasing numbers since the late 1880s. They knew that they certainly lacked the additional resources needed to help "Canadianize" and "Christianize" these new immigrants from Central and Eastern Europe. "Canadianizing" and "Christianizing" meant having those immigrants adopt the conventional late nineteenth- and early twentieth-century Victorian values that marked White Anglo-Saxon Protestantism in this country. That Roman Catholic leaders in other parts of Canada viewed the West and the "Ruthenian Problem"—as these immigrants from the Ukraine and other parts of Eastern Europe were known—in somewhat similar terms (i.e., as persons who needed to be helped to acclimatize to Canada and to be brought into, or kept within, the ecclesiastical fold)[7] is immaterial. Roman Catholics and

---

6 The "Basis of Union," in *The Manual of The United Church of Canada*, 34th Revised Edition (Toronto: United Church Publishing House, 2007), 17.

7 See, for example, George Daly, *Catholic Problems in Western Canada* (Toronto:

mainline Protestants saw themselves as competitors, and the chasm between them was deep.

By the immediate post–World War II era, attitudes had not changed substantially. For example, in 1947, the United Church's General Council Executive and its three conferences on the prairies all engaged in ongoing opposition to the granting of a license for a French language radio station in Prince Albert, Saskatchewan.[8] It is hard to look at this particular example, among others, of such opposition without seeing language and an assumed religious affiliation being linked and, therefore, opposed. The great irony of this particular example is that during this same immediate post–World War II era, the United Church was endeavouring to strengthen its ministry among francophones in Québec.

Such attitudes lay behind the creation of the Committee on Protestant–Roman Catholic Relations in 1945. Composed of representatives of a number of denominations—the Anglican Church of Canada, the Baptist Federation of Canada, Christian Church (Disciples of Christ [in Canada]), the Evangelical United Brethren Church, The Presbyterian Church in Canada, the Salvation Army (in Canada), and The United Church of Canada—the committee met at least four times per year. The "Committee's sole objective was to discern the trend of Protestant-Roman Catholic tensions, to accumulate authentic information on points at issue and to assist the Churches in combating any threatened encroachment on Protestant liberty and rights."[9] The committee's members read and clipped articles from various Roman Catholic publications in order to be able to discern and counter any potential threats to the aforementioned liberty and rights. While the discussions and the decrees of Vatican II led to an entirely new objective for the Committee on Protestant–Roman Catholic Relations even before the last session of Vatican II had closed, the description of the committee's "sole objective" in the days of its creation indicates ever so tellingly

Macmillan Company of Canada, 1921).

[8] Editorial in *The United Church Observer*, July 15, 1947, 4.

[9] "Report of the Committee on Protestant-Roman Catholic Relations," *Record of Proceedings of the Twenty-First General Council* (Toronto: The United Church of Canada, 1964), 458.

how many mainline Canadian Protestants saw Roman Catholicism in the 1940s and 1950s.

The 1940s and 1950s saw the United Church either publish or circulate a number of pamphlets, all designed to help its members understand something about Roman Catholicism in order that, having such understanding, they would avoid so-called "mixed marriages" or anything else that might lead them from the United Church fold. To give but a sample from a longer list, following are the titles of some of those pamphlets: "What Protestants Believe and Why"; "Why Are We Protestants?'; "If I Marry a Roman Catholic"; Why Protestants Go to Church"; "When You Come Over: A Primer for New Protestants"; "The Mass or The Lord's Supper?"; "Mariolatry."

By far the best selling of such works was the much longer booklet noted at the beginning of this essay. *What's the Difference? Protestant and Roman Catholic Beliefs Compared* went through five printings and sold 140,000 copies in the first six months after its publication. The Commission on the Christian Faith, in publishing this booklet, noted its intention to be fair and fair-minded. The commission not only tried but also succeeded in producing a document less tendentious than much similar material published by a number of Protestant denominations, primarily in the United States, during the first half of the twentieth century. This particular work bore little resemblance to the virulently anti-Roman Catholic material published in the nineteenth century by Protestant writers and church leaders in both Canada and United States. That said, *What's the Difference? Protestant and Roman Catholic Beliefs Compared* certainly represented Roman Catholicism as the lesser choice a Christian could make. For example, after comparing classical Protestant and then Roman Catholic doctrine or teaching on a particular subject, the heading of the next section would outline why the Roman Catholic position was either wrong or incomplete. A document with a section or chapter entitled "What is wrong with the Roman Catholic teaching about salvation?"[10] was hardly going to enhance United Church–Roman Catholic relationships.

Finally, in this era, a major concern in the area of ecclesiastical allegiance that was reflected in such literature, in Church documents and

10 Reynolds, *What's the Difference*, 20.

reports, and in the denomination's magazine was mixed marriage. The subject was regularly addressed, always with a strong urging for those contemplating marriage to avoid such a thing. Church leaders saw it as a recipe for tension in a marriage (and in this era, given some of the existing attitudes, they were probably right), but they also saw it as a means by which they lost members.[11]

By the mid-1950s, there were increasing contacts and conversations between Roman Catholics and clergy from various Protestant denominations, particularly in some theological education venues and in major centres. There also existed, as there had for some time, individual members of the clergy or laity who had close relationships across that Protestant–Roman Catholic divide. Yet, a steady diet of the sort of literature, teaching, and anxieties noted above had had an effect and set a tone in terms of more general relations between the United Church and the Roman Catholic Church.

The United Church and Vatican II

How did the United Church react to Vatican II? Initially, the reaction was rather muted. While United Church leaders may have had their own personal thoughts about the decision of Pope John XXIII early in 1959 to call Vatican II, nothing formal appears to have been said nor did anything appear in the reports of the General Council committees where one would be most likely to find such a reference.

However, *The United Church Observer* (the denomination's national magazine, and a magazine that then, as now, was editorially independent) ran a guest editorial on the calling of Vatican II. In the guest editorial, which ran to a little over one page, Claris E. Silcox[12] expressed his pleasure that the Pope was planning to summon a conference at which Christian unity would be a major theme. While Silcox wondered

---

[11] For a much fuller discussion of the anxiety mainline Protestant felt about "mixed marriage," see the paper in this volume by Stuart Macdonald, "Canadian Presbyterians and Vatican II." United Church members, for the most part, held the same views as Presbyterians about the dangers and problems associated with a "mixed marriage."

[12] Claris E. Silcox came from a prominent Congregational–United Church family. He was well known in United Church circles as the author of *Church Union in Canada*, a 1933 work that still stands as one of the most comprehensive assessments of the events that led to the establishment of The United Church of Canada.

whether the Pope had in mind an ecumenical council of the Church or a more general conference of Christians from various Christian denominations, he thought that either could be valuable. Silcox himself believed that Christians needed to move toward some larger organic union, though he certainly did not see such a move as an objective for this forthcoming gathering. Interestingly, Silcox also assumed that whatever shape the gathering took, non-Roman Catholic Christians would be invited to come, whether as observers at a council or participants in a pan-Christian conference on Christian unity.[13]

This February 1959 editorial presaged the role *The United Church Observer* and its editor, the Rev. Al Forrest, would play in informing the United Church membership about Vatican II. Once Vatican II got underway, Al Forrest was to become, in the pages of *The United Church Observer*, a very positive voice concerning what was happening at Vatican II. Indeed, arguably more than any other individual in the United Church, Forrest, through articles and editorials in *The United Church Observer*, helped to foster a supportive atmosphere among the United Church's membership for a closer relationship between the United Church and the Roman Catholic Church.

However, that positive tone did not begin when Pope John XXIII issued the call for Vatican II. For example, the lead editorial in the same issue of *The United Church Observer* that contained Silcox's guest editorial, noted acerbically that the late Cardinal Stritch had refused to allow Roman Catholics to attend even as observers the 1954 gathering of the World Council of Churches.[14] The very next issue of *The United Church Observer*, under an editorial entitled "About an 'Infallible' Pope," expressed its disappointment that what had been hoped would be an ecumenical gathering "has turned out to be a General Council in Rome for 1,500 R.C. bishops and archbishops, to which some others may be invited as observers."[15] The editorial went on to speak in quite stereotypical terms about papal infallibility; if the editorial was not quite so stereotypically cutting about papal infallibility as United Church

13 *The United Church Observer*, February 15, 1959, 7.

14 Ibid., 6.

15 *The United Church Observer*, March 1, 1959, 7.

literature of a slightly earlier era, it certainly did not suggest that a major change in United Church attitudes toward Roman Catholicism would soon occur.

Later that same spring, however, *The United Church Observer* ran, in issues one month apart, an article reprinted from a Roman Catholic publication, *Information Magazine*, entitled "What Protestants Can Teach Catholics," followed up by "What Catholics Can Teach Protestants."[16] The latter four-page piece, again written by Claris E. Silcox, highlighted, in a thoughtful way, particular strengths of Roman Catholic organization or practice, strengths from which he believed United Church members in particular could learn much.

Beginning in 1961, a new attitude did set in, at least at *The United Church Observer*. One no longer sees from the editor or contributors, even irregularly, the earlier suspicion that had often seemed to accompany even a positive piece about Roman Catholicism. One particularly significant article that year was a version of an address Gregory Baum had delivered in Toronto, an article in which Baum signalled that Roman Catholic–Protestant relations were moving in a new direction.[17] The "newness" of *The United Church Observer*'s attitude became even more apparent in 1962. A coloured portrait of Pope John XXIII appeared on the cover of the October 15 issue of *The United Church Observer*, an issue dated just four days after the Second Vatican Council began. The issue included a four-page article by the American Presbyterian Robert McAfee Brown on the council and what Protestants might expect of it. Brown's article was a perspective on the council that sought to deal with some myths and misperceptions (e.g., because it had initially been called an "ecumenical" council, some Protestants had concluded that the Pope was inviting the heads of various Christian denominations to gather in a meeting with him). Brown made highly positive comments about the Roman Catholic Church; he also provided a realistic assessment of what non-Roman Catholics had reason to expect could come from the council.[18]

---

16 *The United Church Observer*, April 15, 1959, 14–15, 26; *The United Church Observer*, May 15, 1959, 14–15, 20–21.

17 *The United Church Observer*, November 1, 1961, 11–12, 23.

18 *The United Church Observer*, October 15, 1962, 15–17, 22.

A new attitude may have existed at *The United Church Observer* and among a growing number of United Church members. However, *The United Church Observer*'s decision to have a picture of Pope John XXIII on the cover of its October 15, 1962, issue sparked howls of protest from many subscribers. "If you must put a picture on the cover," one read, "surely there are many of our own churchmen who are worthy of a place. I am sure our Roman Catholic friends will be pleased with this kind of publicity."[19] Another wrote: "Until you can show me the picture of our United Church moderator on the cover of a Roman Catholic church paper, I ask you to please cancel my subscription."[20] And finally, "If you like the Pope's picture, hang it up in your office."[21] In turn, these critical letters brought forth responses from subscribers disgusted at what they regarded as the small-mindedness of those upset that *The United Church Observer* had put a picture of Pope John XXIII on the cover of one of its issues.[22]

One month later, the editor of *The United Church Observer*, the Rev. A. C. Forrest, wrote an enthusiastic account of the opening session and of Pope John XXIII's address. Forrest commented on the openness he experienced as a visitor at the proceedings, at the readiness of church officials to talk with the press. His recounted his understanding of John XXIII's address at the opening session. Forrest concluded his article by expressing thoughts that shaped how both *The United Church Observer* and, increasingly, United Church officials were viewing the Pope. After expressing reservations about some of the Pope's comments on Christian Unity, Forrest wrote: "However, despite such reservations, we believe that Protestants should continue to pray for the Vatican Council. And we should pray for the continuing health of Pope John XXIII, the best pope Protestants ever had."[23]

The *Observer* continued to report on events in Rome. The reconvening of Vatican II in the fall of 1963 got attention, as did the ending of that second session several months later. Forrest again wrote a major

---

19 *The United Church Observer*, November 15, 1962, 2.

20 *The United Church Observer*, December 1, 1962, 2.

21 Ibid.

22 *The United Church Observer*, January 1, 1963, 2.

23 *The United Church Observer*, November 15, 1962, 17.

piece reviewing the second session. While acknowledging that the pace of change might not be as rapid as some would like and the "measurable achievements of two sessions were not great,"[24] he quoted Archbishop (later Cardinal) George Flahiff of Winnipeg's point that what mattered was "the new mentality" present in the Roman Catholic Church. Forrest, while not denying the concerns that more liberal bishops and some Protestants had, continued to be enthusiastic about the council and what it represented.

By 1963 in the United Church, three things were happening in reaction to the Second Vatican Council. First, one was seeing an increasing number of special interdenominational worship services that now included Roman Catholics. And key United Church leaders made it a point to support them and to be part of them. When the United Church's General Council met in St. John's in September, 1964, it sent official formal greetings to the Second Vatican Council.[25]

Second, there was an increased interest by United Church members in what was happening in Vatican II. The trend continued throughout the remainder of the council's life. In addition to the articles in *The United Church Observer*, the annual reports of the Board of Evangelism and Social Service[26] began to give attention to the events of Vatican II. The board's annual report for 1963 devoted a few pages to Vatican II.[27] The board's annual report for the following year included reflections on Vatican II by two American Protestant academics who were

---

24 *The United Church Observer*, January 15, 1964, 15.

25 *Record of Proceedings of the Twenty-First General Council* (Toronto: The United Church of Canada, 1964), 54–55.

26 These annual reports, issued since the United Church had come into being, were widely read by United Church clergy and key lay leaders. The reports, which usually ran to approximately three hundred pages and were published in book form, consisted of relatively short articles; they would reflect upon the year prior to the date of publication (i.e., the report for 1963 concerned events in 1962 and included much material written during that year). The pieces included covered a wide variety of topics ranging from discussions of various aspects of sharing the gospel, to commentary on moral issues, to assessments of social issues in Canada, and to reflections on international events and developments. Some of the articles were written specifically for these annual reports, while others were culled from the popular press, church reports, or published works.

27 *Tel Star—Tell Peace! 38th Annual Report, 1963, Board of Evangelism and Social Service* (Toronto: The United Church Publishing House, 1963), 138–40.

official observers, and also excerpts from an English translation of the Constitution on the Sacred Liturgy.[28]

Third, interest in Roman Catholicism grew generally. United Church laypeople seemed particularly interested in knowing what Roman Catholics thought about certain traditional points of division. At the local congregational or parish level, 1963 and 1964 began to see increasing contact between Roman Catholic and United Church parishioners. *The United Church Observer* interviewed Archbishop (later Cardinal) Flahiff in 1963; in 1964, Gregory Baum was featured in a four-page cover story for one issue. At the magazine's invitation, a lay Roman Catholic woman wrote a two-page editorial piece for *The Observer* outlining her views about relationships with Christians of other denominations.[29] Perhaps most tellingly, in terms of this interest in knowing more about Roman Catholic thought, from December 1964 through March 1966, *The United Church Observer* had a regular column entitled "Protestants Query a Priest On ...". The columnist was the Rev. Walton Hannon from the Catholic Inquiry Forum in Montréal. The questions to which he responded every two weeks ranged from Roman Catholic attitudes about mixed marriage (still a very common theme in Roman Catholic–Protestant conversations) to various aspects of Roman Catholic teaching.

As the council progressed, *The United Church Observer* continued, through Al Forrest, to cover it. The magazine ran a four-page cover story as the fourth session began in the fall of 1965. For this issue, Pope Paul VI made the front cover, albeit he was pictured greeting key Protestant leaders who were present as observers at the Second Vatican Council. *The Observer* did another major story in conjunction with the conclusion of Vatican II. In this case, the writer was the Rev. R. H. N. Davidson, a United Church minister from Toronto who attended Vatican II as an official observer from the World Alliance of Reformed Churches. Davidson's assessment of the council captured well the more general United Church reaction to Vatican II. He commented on a number of the changes that Vatican II was ushering in, but the council's openness

---

28 *Breaking the Barriers: 39th Annual Report, 1964, Board of Evangelism and Social Service* (Toronto: The United Church Publishing House, 1964), 199–205.

29 *The United Church Observer*, September 15, 1964, 28–29.

to Christians of other traditions clearly moved him most. At the end of the article he wrote:

> The time has come to practise Christian love, not just preach it. Christians must learn to walk together by faith. Contrition and reform in the Roman Church must be matched by contrition and reform among us. The Vatican Council will make strenuous demands on all churches. Roman Catholic and Protestant alike must pray and labor that the seed sown by Vatican II may spring up and yield a mighty harvest of good grain.[30]

Effects of Vatican II on The United Church of Canada

In looking at the effects of Vatican II on The United Church of Canada, three things stand out. First, the Second Vatican Council changed fundamentally the way the United Church viewed the Roman Catholic Church. The council's Decree on Ecumenism was obviously one reason for this development. Perhaps even more crucial, though, was the initiative taken by Roman Catholic leaders like Cardinal Léger, as well as by local priests, in reaching out to work with other Christian communities. Cardinal Léger's address to the fourth Faith and Order Conference in Montréal in 1963 received high praise and extensive publicity. The United Church's Committee on Ecumenical Affairs called that address "unprecedented,"[31] and Canadian church historian John Webster Grant, in his review of this era, described it as the "first public sign of reconciliation"[32] in what had been a major divide in Canada. Differences and divisions remained, of course, but the atmosphere was different. While some United Church members retained their skepticism about Roman Catholicism, the litany of ecumenical services and co-operative events recounted in the pages of *The United Church Observer* made clear that many United Church clergy

30 *The United Church Observer*, January 1, 1966, 30.

31 *Record of Proceedings of the Twenty-Second General Council* (Toronto: The United Church of Canada, 1966), 530.

32 John Webster Grant, *The Church in the Canadian Era*, revised edition (Burlington, ON: Welch Publishing Company, Inc.,1988), 191.

and laity had begun to leave such prejudices behind. In that regard, lay members sometimes did so more quickly than the clergy. Roman Catholics seemed as anxious and open to attend United Church events as United Church folks were to have them.

By the mid-1960s, it was a given in many parts of Canada that Roman Catholics would be involved in ecumenical events such as The Week of Prayer for Christian Unity. But the United Church's interest in, and desire for, closer links with the Roman Catholic Church went deeper. A report to the United Church's General Council that met in 1966 revealed that during the previous two years it had become customary for the Roman Catholic bishop within whose diocese a United Church Conference was having its annual meeting to bring greetings on behalf of his particular diocese. In addition, bishops were being asked to come as theme speakers or presenters at such meetings.[33] Richard Davidson, in the article he wrote for *The United Church Observer* at the conclusion of Vatican II, had urged such contacts; in fact, Davidson went much further, urging that whenever a United Church minister was beginning a new ministry, the local Roman Catholic priest be invited to attend and to speak at the traditional reception that followed such a service.[34]

Davidson's advice may have been unnecessary. By 1963 one had already begun to see pictures in *The United Church Observer* from local congregational events where the local priest or members of a female religious order had attended. A *United Church Observer* story from 1965, "The Roman Catholic-Protestant Thaw: How it is Changing Your Church," described accurately the increased contact and co-operation that had been happening across the country during the several previous years. When after Cardinal Léger had left Montréal and gone to work in Africa, *The United Church Observer* featured him in a cover story, the magazine did not receive complaints in the fashion that had happened in 1962 when it had put John XXIII's picture on the cover. Many United Church members had come to view Cardinal Léger as a saintly figure worthy of admiration.

---

33 Ibid., 531–34.

34 *The United Church Observer*, January 1, 1966, 18.

But the changed view went beyond such exchanges at a local level or even the presence of Roman Catholics as theme speakers at United Church events. In 1964 the United Church's General Council had authorized a major study on ministry in the United Church entitled "The Ministry in the Twentieth Century." As the commission charged with preparing that report went about its work, it brought a number of resource persons to meet with the commission; among those were C. R. Fielding of Trinity College and Gregory Baum from St. Michael's College.[35] This pattern of consulting resource people from outside the United Church would be repeated for significant studies in future years.

Also indicative of the changed view United Church members held of Roman Catholicism was a more nuanced awareness of the tensions and differences that existed among Roman Catholics, both in Canada and abroad. In this fuller awareness, *The United Church Observer* again played a role. Al Forrest, in his articles on Vatican II for *The United Church Observer*, had talked about the tensions between "progressives" and "conservatives" at the council. However, in 1966 *The United Church Observer* ran a feature story on four of the figures involved in the publication of *Brief to the Bishops*.[36] Entitled "Catholic Radicals Speak Out," it featured an interview with Paul Harris, Mark MacGuigan, Jack Wilson, and Pat Hunt.[37] These four lay Roman Catholics would have helped not only to destroy old stereotypes but also to alert the magazine's readership to something of the range of view existing among Canada's Roman Catholic laity. The annual publication of the Board of Evangelism and Social Service, in its 1967 volume, included an article by Paul Harris looking at how Vatican II "updating" was going in the Roman Catholic Church in Canada. While raising a number of concerns, Harris was particularly critical of the "Catholic press" (i.e., church-related journals and newspapers), asserting that the "one exception to the dull Catholic newspaper fare in Canada is the *Western Catholic Reporter*, edited by a

---

35 *Record of Proceedings of the Twenty-Third General Council* (Toronto: The United Church of Canada, 1968), 221.

36 Paul T. Harris, ed., *Brief to the Bishops: Canadian Catholic Laymen Speak Their Minds* (Don Mills, ON: Longmans, Canada, 1965).

37 *The United Church Observer*, March 15, 1966, 19–22.

progressive layman, Doug Roche in Edmonton, Alberta."[38] This same board report contained a lengthy excerpt from a January 1967 story in the *Toronto Globe and Mail* on the decision of theologian Charles Davis to leave the Roman Catholic Church.[39] These two pieces, and others like them, when laid side by side with the enthusiastic coverage of Vatican II in *The United Church Observer* and in other church reports, sought to give members of the United Church a holistic view of the Roman Catholic Church. They provided such a view without exaggerating or playing to negative images of the Roman Catholic Church after the fashion of many of the pamphlets the United Church had either published or sold prior to Vatican II.

Second, the mid-1960s saw a burst of ecumenical fervour within the United Church, and Vatican II was a major contributing factor to that renewed commitment to ecumenism. The late 1940s and the 1950s had seen ecumenical activity flag in the United Church. The denomination had grown during this era, with both membership and financial support increasing significantly each year during the immediate post–World War II period. A kind of complacency, even a degree of self-righteousness had set in, as the United Church seemed, by most of the traditional statistical standards, to be doing well. Vatican II helped to kindle a more critical self-examination and, along with that examination, a renewed commitment to ecumenism.

Here, too, Al Forrest was prescient. In one of his articles on Vatican II for *The United Church Observer*, Forrest had observed that the kinds of reform and renewal in which the Roman Catholic Church was engaged at the council were leading other denominations to consider the ways in which they might need to change or to reform.[40] In the newly developing or strengthening relationships between the Roman Catholic Church and other denominations that followed the promulgation of the Decree on Ecumenism in 1964, ecumenical energy flourished, and it went beyond just Roman Catholic–United Church relations. Canadian church historian John Webster Grant implies that Vatican II, with its

---

38 *Canada and Its Future: 42nd Annual Report, 1967, Board of Evangelism and Social Service* (Toronto: The United Church Publishing House, 1967), 27.

39 Ibid., 28–32

40 *The United Church Observer*, January 15, 1964.

willingness to examine all aspects of the Roman Catholic Church, in its own way contributed to the renewed optimism of the mid-1960s that a union between the Anglican Church of Canada and The United Church of Canada might be achieved.[41]

It is not accidental that several ecumenical initiatives in theological education date from this time. If the roots of the Toronto School of Theology lie in collaboration around graduate degrees in the mid-1940s, it was during and after Vatican II that joint class sessions among the various colleges and other developments helped to create the conditions for the establishment of the Toronto School of Theology. The ecumenical fervour Vatican II helped to invigorate in Canada also led to the creation of the Atlantic School of Theology in Halifax.[42] Indeed, in 1968, the United Church's General Council passed a resolution to consolidate its theological colleges (reducing the number from nine to five) and to ensure that each of the five "move as quickly as possible into an ecumenical approach to theological education."[43] Ecumenical theological education became seen by many as the direction in which denominations in Canada needed to go.

Third, Vatican II had an effect upon the general worship life and ethos in the United Church. Greater contact with Roman Catholics, and therefore more direct awareness of Roman Catholic worship life and liturgy, led United Church clergy in particular, but also some of the laity, to begin to desire changes in United Church worship practices. Some of these changes had already begun to happen during the early 1960s as a result of greater awareness of other denominational traditions and also the liturgical renewal movement, but Vatican II gave such moves more energy.

Two areas of change stand out particularly. United Church clergy and members began, in the mid-to-late 1960s, to pay more attention to the Christian year. While particular congregations and individuals

---

41 Grant, *Church in the Canadian Era*, 193.

42 The Atlantic School of Theology, an organic union of Anglican, Roman Catholic, and United Church theological institutions in the city of Halifax, came into being in 1971 after several years of negotiations.

43 *Record of Proceedings of the Twenty-Third General Council* (Toronto: The United Church of Canada, 1968), 237; see also 81.

within the Church had already been observing the Christian year, most United Church members had followed the principles of an older Reformed tradition that saw Sunday as the key day and no one Sunday, with the possible exception of Easter, was to be valued over any other. Vatican II, and the resulting increased familiarity with Roman Catholic worship practices, led many in the United Church to have greater awareness of the seasons of the Christian year. The change began, particularly for many rural congregations, with the decision to have a service on Christmas Eve. While most urban United Church congregations had had such services for a number of years, many rural United Church congregations only introduced a Christmas Eve service in the late 1960s or the early 1970s.[44] A new or renewed appreciation of Advent, Lent, and Pentecost followed.

The other major change was that the United Church began to give much greater attention to the sacraments, most especially the sacrament of Holy Communion, or the Eucharist. This greater attention took several forms. Most noticeable was a gradual increase in the frequency of reception by United Church members. While there had always been United Church congregations where the sacrament of Holy Communion had been celebrated monthly, and a handful with yet greater frequency, the typical United Church pattern had been to have the sacrament of Holy Communion quarterly. After Vatican II, the number gradually began to increase, so that most United Church congregations came to have Holy Communion on six to eight Sundays per year, with some having a monthly pattern and a few offering the sacrament each Sunday.

New liturgies for the sacraments of baptism and Holy Communion, liturgies based on early Christian ones and therefore much more similar to liturgies in the Roman Catholic Church, were developed in the 1980s. Such new liturgies would probably have happened sooner but for the fact that a revision of the United Church liturgical materials was already well underway when Vatican II convened. So, that project continued apace, and the *Service Book for the Use of Ministers* was published in

---

44 For example, in the two-point parish I served from the mid-1980s until the early 1990s, my predecessor introduced the custom of a Christmas Eve service after he began to serve this parish in 1979.

1969. A new set of liturgies, with much greater resemblance to what a worshipper would have experienced in the Roman Catholic Church, would appear in the mid-1980s. While such liturgical development was a phenomenon across mainline Protestant denominations in the United States and Canada, greater exposure to Roman Catholic liturgy and liturgical practices helped to bring a greater and quicker degree of acceptance of such changes in the United Church.

Conclusion

Vatican II is an historical event where some influences were relatively clear almost immediately, while others became evident over time. The most significant change Vatican II brought to the United Church lay simply in the changed attitudes to Roman Catholicism that resulted among United Church ministers and laity, for from that particular change others followed. Suspicion of Roman Catholicism lingered in some circles, but it disappeared for most United Church members with remarkable speed. The old suspicions may have lingered more with clergy than with laity.[45] Perhaps the extent of the change is most evident in that, on those occasions when one does meet that old prejudice in a United Church member, one is genuinely startled by it, such is its rarity. Such an attitude seems a relic of a past era that can certainly be recalled, but recalled as a time that is blessedly passed.

45 I reflect here from, among other things, my own experience as a Theology student at the Atlantic School of Theology in the mid-1970s. Among laity, there was much enthusiasm for this combined Roman Catholic–Anglican–United Church enterprise. However, when I would meet United Church clergy, especially those who were then in their fifties or older, there would often be questions asked to try to determine if I was getting a good "United Church" education. It was also my sense, in the rural village in New Brunswick in which I grew up, that there was much enthusiasm for the ecumenical services that brought together the members of the Roman Catholic and United churches in the village, beginning in the early winter of 1966. In this particular case, the local Roman Catholic parish priest and the local United Church minister had excellent personal relationships and were strongly supportive of closer relationships between the two churches in the village. But it was also my sense that many of the laity in the village were more than ready to move on from the divisions and the attitudes of an earlier era. I still recall one elderly farmer in the village, a staunch member of the United Church, remarking after the first joint service in the Week of Prayer for Christian Unity: "We should have done this a long time ago."

"Hold onto Your Hats": Vatican II and *Aggiornamento* in the Anglican Church of Canada

Alan L. Hayes,
Wycliffe College

The Second Ecumenical Council of the Vatican had a profound impact on Canadian Anglicans in two general ways: it changed their ecumenical landscape forever, and it helped guide far-reaching changes in their denominational identity. As for the change in ecumenical landscape, Vatican II led Anglicans and Roman Catholics in Canada to cordial and close relationships with surprising speed. Within ten years of the opening session of Vatican II, the Canadian arms of the two communions were co-operating in such ventures as dialogue groups, local collaborations of various kinds, the Toronto School of Theology, and inter-church coalitions for social justice. As for the profound reshaping of Canadian Anglican identity that followed from Vatican II, this, too, was unexpected. In the early 1960s few Canadian Anglicans seem to have recognized that Vatican II might have serious implications for their own communion. They typically thought that Vatican II was a process by which Roman Catholics were finally becoming more like Anglicans: more acclimatized to modernity, liberalism, and secular critical thought; more *Protestant*. By the mid-1960s, however, they were realizing that Vatican II gave them a resource for renewal in their own church life, as they recognized the insufficiency of their received understandings of catholicity and catholicism, approaches to worship, and patterns of social and cultural engagement. Bishop George Luxton of the Anglican diocese of Huron, writing in the national denominational newspaper *Canadian Churchman* (*CC*) in February 1965, summarized what Vatican II was going to mean for Canadian Anglicans in a trenchant phrase: "Boys, hold onto your hats!"[1]

But although this outline of events is clear enough, the details are hard to retrieve. Few ordinary Canadian Anglicans recorded how they experienced Vatican II, if indeed they were even formulating views about it at the time; and any reflections that people did write, if they were preserved, would be found in far-flung places. So my modest historiographical approach has been simply to read through the *Canadian Churchman* for the years immediately before, during, and after the council, as well as the minutes and reports of the national denominational judicatory, General Synod, along with a few other documents, in search of the contemporary Canadian Anglican experiences of Vatican II.

Before Vatican II

Before Vatican II, relations between Anglicans and Roman Catholics in Canada were marked by suspicion and, frankly, disrespect. As Pope John XXIII announced Vatican II, Anglicans had completed their fourth consecutive century of general hostility to Roman Catholicism. The first century had been marked by King Henry VIII's repudiation of papal authority and the excommunication of Queen Elizabeth I by Pope Pius V. For many years, two annual events reminded Anglicans of their antagonism to Roman Catholicism. From the Restoration to the middle of the nineteenth century, they observed an annual thanksgiving, included in their *Book of Common Prayer*, for their deliverance from the Gunpowder Plot, a conspiracy of disaffected English Roman Catholics in 1605. This service of worship functioned as a liturgical declaration that the Church of England was "a church that stood opposed to, and by, Roman Catholicism."[2] (The popular celebration

1 *Canadian Churchman*, February 1965, 5. In the May 1965 *CC* Arnold Edinborough had already noted that Roman Catholic change predicted the upset of some familiar Anglican practice.

2 Charles Hefling, "The State Services," in *The Oxford Guide to the Book of Common*

of the foiling of the Gunpowder Plot, called Guy Fawkes Day, is still celebrated in a few places in English Canada.) Similarly, in Canada as elsewhere, the annual Orangemen's Day of July 12 celebrated a battle in County Louth, Ireland, in 1690, which secured a Protestant supremacy in Ireland. Parades and festivities and quite a bit of drinking were often accompanied by violence directed toward Roman Catholic buildings and persons.[3] From the 1830s, Anglican anti-Catholic feeling was partly mitigated but partly exacerbated by an Anglican Catholic movement usually connected particularly with the name John Henry Newman. This led to an institutionalized partisanship pitting high-church catholic Anglicans against low-church evangelical Anglicans (at least, that was the generally accepted typology). Party bitterness had declined by the 1950s, but there remained, at one end of the spectrum, a conservative evangelical group that loathed anything Roman, and at the other, a high-church group for whom an Anglican priest was simply a Roman Catholic priest who had failed his Latin.

In 1944 the House of Bishops of what was then still called the Church of England in Canada appointed representatives to an inter-Protestant group called the Committee on Protestant–Roman Catholic Relations.[4] It published reactions against perceived Roman Catholic slights and denigrations, distributed tracts intended for church pamphlet racks warning Protestants against Roman Catholic error, and registered frustration with the Roman Catholic Church on such issues as separate schools, missionary competition in northern Canada, mixed marriages, non-co-operation in social service and justice work, Canadian diplomatic recognition of the Vatican state, and religious accommodations of Roman Catholic military personnel. The committee was blind to the preconciliar theological ferment that in retrospect is so obvious to us; indeed it was blind to how diverse Roman Catholicism always was.

Prayer: A Worldwide Survey, ed. Charles Hefling and Cynthia Shattuck (Oxford and New York: Oxford University Press, 2006), 73.

3 My late colleague Michael Sheehan, who taught at the University of St. Michael's College, recalled that when he grew up in Ontario, his family annually left town on July 11 and returned on July 13; typically in the interval their house had been vandalized.

4 The reports of this committee to General Synod are included in the *General Synod Journal* for 1952, 1955, 1959, 1962, 1965, 1967. The reports of the Committee on Christian Unity and the Church Universal are also included in the *General Synod Journal*.

Instead it was prone to interpret Roman Catholicism through its conservative manifestations in Québec, in the repressions and vulgarities of what some Québec historians have come to call *la grande noirceur.* In 1949 the executive council of the Church of England in Canada appointed its own Committee on Protestant–Roman Catholic Relations, which was to work with the continuing inter-Protestant committee in common areas of grievance while also giving more specific attention to Anglican grievances. The most important specifically Anglican grievance of all was the invalidation of Anglican ordination by Pope Leo XIII in 1896 in *Apostolicae Curae*, one of the few papal bulls whose title was commonly known among religiously literate Anglicans. The committee commended a tract on *Apostolicae Curae* by a professor named George Lewis, which had originally been written in 1900, but which had recently been republished by the Anglican General Board of Religious Education.

In these pieces of anti-Catholic activity there was, however, more (or less) than met the eye. The chair of the Anglican committee was Frederick Wilkinson, the Anglican bishop of Toronto, and its secretary was Reginald Soward, the chancellor (lawyer) of the Anglican diocese of Toronto. Both were connected with Wycliffe College, which for many functioned as the standard-bearer of Protestant low-church evangelical Anglicanism. Wilkinson was a graduate and supporter of Wycliffe, and Soward was en route to the chair of its board of trustees. It seems likely that, in the contemporary context of Anglican partisanship, the committee's principal target was not Roman Catholicism, but Anglican Catholicism; that is, it had little thought of changing Roman Catholic minds, but it was warning Anglicans that the catholicizing tendencies of some of them would certainly lead to error. My impression that the committee represented only one viewpoint, and that a minority one, is confirmed by a motion in General Synod in 1952 by the Anglo-Catholic archbishop of Québec, Philip Carrington, "that the Committee be directed to fields in which friendly relation and co-operation with the Roman Catholic Church may be or has been effected."[5] A vigorous debate followed on the floor of General Synod, which resulted in a suc-

5 *General Synod Journal* 1952, 58.

cessful compromise motion recorded in the *General Synod Journal* to the effect that the executive council should re-examine the role of the committee. Moreover, in these years, many Anglicans, in Canada and elsewhere, were coming to regard their communion not as "Protestant," with its implication of "anti-Roman Catholic," or at least "not Roman Catholic," but rather as a kind of third race bridging the Roman Catholic and Protestant worlds. Indeed, General Synod decided in 1955 [GSJ 1955, 338] to review the name of the Committee on *Protestant*–Roman Catholic Relations, and before the next General Synod in 1959 the denominational executive had changed it to the Committee on *Anglican*-Roman Catholic Relations. Meanwhile, another, apparently rival, committee of General Synod, called the Committee on Christian Unity, had a commitment to improving ecumenical relations with the Roman Catholic Church. It's work in this respect, however, was overwhelmed by the more pressing agenda of seeking union with The United Church of Canada (which was to prove fruitless).

In 1959, when Pope John XXIII announced his intention to convene the Second Vatican Council, the Committee on Anglican–Roman Catholic Relations responded with initial skepticism. How could the Pope speak of an ecumenical council when Anglicans weren't invited as members? Wouldn't this council be a merely inward-looking one? Other Anglicans, however, were more optimistic, and in December 1960 their hope bloomed when for the first time since the Reformation an archbishop of Canterbury, the symbolic head of the Anglican communion, sat down in conversation with a pope. Formally, the meeting between Archbishop Geoffrey Fisher and Pope John XXIII was billed as a "visit of courtesy,"[6] but it was an historic event, and its cordiality symbolized the beginning of a new era for Anglican–Roman Catholic relations. The executive officer of the Anglican communion, Stephen Bayne, writing in the *Canadian Churchman*, rejoiced that after having lived so long "without any communication with the Roman Church, much less dialogue," Anglicans were seeing a friendship developing.[7] Because Canadian Anglicans generally had a strong sense of connection with

6 *CC*, January 1961, 1.

7 *CC*, February 1961, 5.

global Anglicanism, and with the Church of England in particular, this event captured their attention, even though it happened a long way away and involved no Canadians. Canadian Anglicans were therefore probably much more aware of Vatican II than other Canadian non-Catholic Christians, which had less residual nostalgia for the mother country and the British Empire, and more clearly Canadian identities.[8]

Major Anglican Interpreters

Over the next five years, during the preparations for and the sessions of Vatican II, three writers emerged as its primary interpreters and advocates for their fellow Canadian Anglicans. They reported on the council's activities, explained its significance, and corrected misinformation that they heard in conversation, or read in the daily media (or the *United Church Observer*).

The first of these three interpreters was Eugene Fairweather, the professor of theology at Trinity College, a medieval specialist with training from the Pontifical Institute of Medieval Studies in Toronto, where he was influenced by the eminent neo-Thomist scholar Étienne Gilson. He attended the third and fourth sessions of the council as one of the official Anglican observers appointed by the archbishop of Canterbury. One of the most distinguished intellectuals in the Anglican Church of Canada, Fairweather was influential not only in the academic halls of Toronto, but also as a speaker at church conferences and events (sometimes addressing audiences of several hundreds[9]), as an editor of the *Canadian Journal of Theology*, as a columnist for the Anglican newspaper for the diocese of Toronto (far and away the largest of the Canadian dioceses), and simply as a witty conversationalist.

A second Canadian interpreter of Vatican II to Anglicans was George W. B. Wheeler, a Wycliffe College graduate and rector of the modest Anglican parish of St. Crispin in the diocese of Toronto. The *Canadian Churchman* appointed him "special assignments editor," which allowed him to seek press credentials for admittance to Vatican II. Before being ordained he had taken an MA in medieval studies at

8 This insight was offered by a member of the audience during the discussion of an earlier version of this paper at the Vatican II conference at the University of St. Michael's College.

9 For an example, see *CC*, March 1965, 6.

the University of Toronto, so he, like Fairweather, had taken courses at the Pontifical Institute for Medieval Studies. One of his professors there was George Bernard Flahiff, CSB, who had become the Roman Catholic archbishop of Winnipeg; Flahiff graciously made arrangements for Wheeler in Rome. Wheeler attended the council on three occasions and wrote numerous interpretive columns for the *Canadian Churchman* beginning in 1962. Then, after the council in February 1966, he brought together a four-page spread in the *Canadian Churchman* with summaries and commentaries explaining the council's achievement. Like Fairweather, he was frequently invited to Anglican, United, and ecumenical church events to describe and interpret Vatican II.

The third interpreter, beginning a little later than Fairweather and Wheeler, was George Luxton, the Anglican bishop of Huron (this diocese covers western Ontario). A larger-than-life personality with strong views, a wry sense of humour, a very popular following in his diocese, and a considerable influence in the House of Bishops of the Anglican Church of Canada, he went to Rome during the fourth session of the council, secured an audience with the Pope, and came back inspired with a vision for church reform. Unlike many Anglican reformers of the 1960s, however, who were very liberal theologically, he preferred a mainstream doctrine, and Vatican II was particularly appealing to him as a model for a theologically orthodox but institutionally creative reform.

Fairweather, Wheeler, and Luxton had somewhat different but complementary interests. Fairweather was particularly attuned to the wider theological background of the council. Wheeler's purpose was to represent the institutional ethos of the Vatican II in a sympathetic way. Two examples can be given. When the Decree on Religious Liberty ran into procedural trouble at the end of the third session of Vatican II, and some smelled a conspiracy of conservatives, Wheeler explained that Anglicans of all people should understand that "procedure is procedure. The law is there not only to protect the majority from the minority, but the minority from the majority."[10] And when reports emerged from Vatican II of the sometimes sharp theological conflicts of its members,

[10] *CC*, January 1965, 12.

Wheeler reminded his Anglican readers of their own history of partisan churchmanship; Canadian Anglicans had only lately "agreed to live and let live about crucifixes, crossings, genuflections, and so on."[11] Finally, Luxton was most excited about the implications for Anglicans of the remarkable spirit of Vatican II: self-criticism, reform, outreach, and *aggiornamento.* "Surely a similar program should press strongly and creatively on the conscience of all Anglicans," he wrote.[12]

A New Spirit of Co-operation

What was most apparent to Canadian Anglicans was that Vatican II gave permission and encouragement to Roman Catholics on the national, diocesan, and local levels to think, plan, and co-operate ecumenically. Anglicans could recognize themselves as natural ecumenical partners for Roman Catholics since they shared Catholic creeds, many liturgical texts and ceremonies, an episcopal polity, a conciliar ethos, and various devotional traditions and sensibilities. As the council's Decree on Ecumenism would declare in 1964, of all the churches of the Reformation, the Anglican communion occupied a "special place" in respect of its partial continuance of "Catholic traditions and institutions." This affirmation made most Canadian Anglicans happy.

Encouraged by the council, ecumenical co-operation between Roman Catholics and Anglicans in Canada developed, at first episodically and then more systematically. In the early 1960s the *Canadian Churchman* began to publish stories, typically approving in tone, of local ecumenical initiatives involving the two communions. Roman Catholic clergy were reportedly taking part in Anglican worship services in London (Ontario), Hamilton, Kenora, Ottawa, and Kazabazua (Québec). At an ecumenical service at St. James Anglican Cathedral in Toronto, the preacher was Roman Catholic Archbishop Philip Pocock.[13] The Roman Catholic archbishop of Victoria, Remi De Roo, had given a gift *in person* to the Anglican archbishop of British Columbia on the

---

11 Ibid.

12 *CC*, February 1966, 6.

13 Report of the Committee on Anglican–Roman Catholic Relations, *General Synod Journal*, 1965.

occasion of the fiftieth anniversary of the latter's ordination.[14] A three-day conference of eighty Roman Catholic and Anglican clergy took place at St. Mark's Roman Catholic College at the University of British Columbia.[15] The biggest news of all, however, meriting generous front-page treatment in the *Canadian Churchman* for January 1964, was that a panel of Roman Catholic bishops had declared that *Apostolicae Curae* was judicial, not doctrinal, with the implication that it could be reversed. (As it happens, nothing has ever come of that overture, and among Anglicans this probably represents the single greatest disappointment in the council. According to one writer, *Apostolicae Curae* "hung like a dark spectre in the background" for Eugene Fairweather in his work on a new Canadian Anglican ordinal in the 1980s.[16])

It is also true, on the other hand, that despite the positive news, many Canadian Anglicans had doubts that the ecumenical momentum could be sustained. Some articles in the *Canadian Churchman* suggested that the status quo was still the default: Pope John XXIII was reaffirming the use of Latin in the liturgy;[17] reform was being stalled by dilatory procedures; draft documents were insufficiently progressive. There were worries that after the council its inspiringly open and progressive statements would simply be ignored and that the Church would lumber on as usual. Canadian Anglicans had their own reasons to be suspicious since they themselves were experiencing disappointment of the same kind. In 1963 they hosted a large international conference, the third (and, as it proved, the last) Anglican World Congress, that promised to reinvigorate and reorient Anglican world mission. (Cardinal P. E. Léger of Montréal and Archbishop Pocock of Toronto were noted as asking for the prayers of the faithful for this event; the latter appointed two observers who ranked as official guests, Gregory Baum and Aloysius Ambrozic.[18]) Over three thousand Anglican bishops, clergy, and lay-

---

14 *CC*, February 1963, 13.

15 *CC*, July–August 1963, 20.

16 David Holeton, "Eugene Fairweather's contribution to the Book of Alternative Services," *Liturgy Canada* 10, 1 (June 2003): 8.

17 *CC*, April 1962, 3.

18 *CC*, July–August 1963, 2; Émilien Lamirande, "Anglican World Congress and Ecumenism," *The Furrow* 14, 10 (October 1963): 617–623; 617, fn. 1; *The Ecumenist* 1, 1

people from around the world worshipped together in a nationally televised service in Maple Leaf Gardens and heard uplifting speeches, including one by the archbishop of Canterbury, Michael Ramsey, which was one of the most remarked and influential Anglican orations of the century. But while the event did launch organizational change in the upper reaches of the Anglican communion and in some national headquarters, ordinary Anglicans saw little come of it. A renewal in mission, an intensification of global Christian relationship, a commitment to the mutual interdependence of all Anglicans—these were promised, but they did not materialize.[19] So some Anglicans expected just as little from Vatican II. The interpreters Fairweather, Wheeler, and Luxton sometimes saw their task as persuading Canadian Anglicans that Vatican II really was far-reaching and irreversible. Thus Wheeler explained that in the Roman Catholic Church, "once policy has been definitely approved and promulgated, it is very hard for the individual Bishop to drag his feet entirely. This strength is absent in Anglicanism."[20]

The General Synod of the Anglican Church of Canada, which had the general pattern of meeting every three years, met in 1965 as Vatican II was concluding. The Canadian Conference of Catholic Bishops had invited the Anglican Church to appoint two bishops to join two of their own in dialogue, in a mutual commitment to further ecumenical understanding and co-operation. The Committee on Anglican–Roman Catholic Relations, the group that in the 1950s had played the attack dog, was now wagging its tail energetically. "Barriers of mistrust and prejudice which have seemed insuperable have begun to melt away," it reported to the Anglican General Synod. It gave several examples of ecumenical overtures by Roman Catholic bishops in Montréal, Toronto, and elsewhere, and it was pleased to report that informal discussions had begun with Roman Catholics on the issue of mixed marriages. It concluded, "The rapidity of change in this whole area has made us feel

(1962): 13, 15. Previous Anglican congresses were London (1908) and Minneapolis (1954).

19 The post-council commentary assembled by Wheeler for *CC*, February 1966, 8–9, included the following comment: "For many Anglicans, the 1963 Congress has already become a collection of books of speeches gathering dust."

20 *CC*, February 1965, 8.

that the present committee, both in its personnel and in its method of work, needs immediate and drastic revision." General Synod acted accordingly. It changed the membership of the committee to include five bishops, five priests, and five laypeople appointed by the primate, and it commissioned the committee to enable direct conversations between Anglicans and Roman Catholics.[21]

In the years following the council, the Anglican Church press reported evidence of further strong ecumenical momentum. In Sherbrooke, the archbishop invited the ecumenical ministerial association to a meal.[22] At St. Basil's Church, Toronto, on the campus of the University of St. Michael's College, Canada's first jointly approved solemnization of a marriage of an Anglican and a Roman Catholic was administered.[23] Archbishop Pocock of Toronto was quoted as stating that he knew of no doctrinal reasons why a woman could not be ordained a Roman Catholic priest.[24] In Winnipeg an Anglican and a Roman Catholic parish completed the joint purchase of a church in which costs would be shared half and half.[25] Roman Catholics, Anglicans, and several Protestant denominations were collaborating on the Christian pavilion at Expo '67 in Montréal. Gerald Emmett Carter, the bishop of London, Ontario, announced to the Anglican synod of Huron that he was about to convene an Anglican-style synod of clergy and laypeople, a unique event in North America.[26] Four Anglican couples joined the Montréal branch of the Roman Catholic Christian Family Movement.[27] The Jesuit superior general, Pedro Arrupe, visited Canada and spoke in favour of complete unity. The Canadian Council of Churches and the Canadian Conference of Catholic Bishops met in Montréal for an

---

21 See the reports of the committee in the *General Synod Journal* volumes for 1965 and 1967.

22 *CC*, March 1965, 7.

23 The Anglican officiant, John Rye, communicated the bride with the reserved sacrament from his church in Oakville; the Roman Catholic officiant, Michael Zolondek, CSB, communicated the groom with the reserved sacrament from St. Basil's. Both priests pronounced a blessing at the end. *CC*, June 1965, 3.

24 *CC*, March 1967, 8.

25 *CC*, June 1967, 15.

26 *CC*, June 1966, 17.

27 Bernard Daly's column in *CC*, June 1966, 2.

exploratory consultation.[28] By 1967 a formal Anglican–Roman Catholic dialogue group was meeting in Toronto, apparently enabled by the Anglican diocese and the Roman Catholic archdiocese. A national dialogue would begin five years later. In 1975 there began the National Anglican/Roman Catholic Bishops' Dialogue, which has been meeting annually in Canada since 1975.

The three primary Canadian Anglican interpreters of the council—Eugene Fairweather the observer; G. W. B. Wheeler, the religious journalist; and George Luxton, the episcopal visitor—continued to press the vision of the council and continued to make good use of the relationships they had cultivated with Canadian Roman Catholic bishops, staff members, clergy, and laypeople. Fairweather's friendships with Canadian participants in the council, and his lifelong ecumenical advocacy, are discussed by Michael Attridge elsewhere in this volume, but a particular contribution that deserves emphasis is his assistance in organizing the Congress on the Theology of the Renewal of the Church in August 1967 at the Pontifical Institute for Medieval Studies. The event involved 1,800 people directly, many others through broadcasts, and brought together a star-studded international cast of Roman Catholic, Protestant, Anglican, Orthodox, and Jewish theologians. "It is safe to say," Fairweather wrote in the *Christian Century* (with hidden pride since he failed to mention his own role), "that no Canadian church had ever mounted such an impressive demonstration of the vitality of the theological enterprise."[29] George Luxton, while in Rome during the council, built relationships with some of the Canadian Roman Catholic bishops and was mightily impressed with them personally: when he saw them at work on the Declaration on Religious Freedom, he found them to be a progressive, collegial, and strategically canny group.[30] Wheeler, too, maintained connections, and one supposes that it was through him that the *Canadian Churchman* appointed its first Roman Catholic columnist, Bernard Daly, the press officer for the Canadian Conference of Catholic Bishops (CCCB).

---

28 *CC*, June 1967, 7.

29 *Christian Century,* October 4, 1967, 1262.

30 *CC*, February 1966, 11.

Nevertheless, some complained that progress was insufficiently speedy. Bishop Luxton was unhappy that Vatican II did nothing to address the issue of Anglican orders. It was reported that a little girl who had been baptized in the Anglican Church was rebaptized by a Roman Catholic parish priest (the CCCB issued new directives as a result), and that if an Anglican who was about to marry a Roman Catholic was unwilling for the child to be raised in the Roman Catholic Church, the matter had to be remitted to Rome for consideration.[31]

Some positive events outside the country were being noted, however, and these buoyed the spirits of ecumenically minded Canadian Anglicans and Roman Catholics. The archbishop of Canterbury, Michael Ramsey, and the Pope met together for three days in March 1966. (Their meeting was marred slightly by three Anglicans demonstrating with signs accusing Ramsey of treason.[32]) Out of that meeting came the international Anglican–Roman Catholic International Commission (ARCIC), which by 1971 had issued the very significant Agreed Statement on Eucharistic Doctrine.[33] The Anglican General Synod invited comment on this ARCIC statement from the Canadian dioceses, which meant that the document was presented and discussed at many diocesan synods. In the summer of 1966, Richard Cardinal Cushing of Boston reportedly approved the use of the Oxford Annotated Bible, based on the Revised Standard Version with non-denominational commentary.[34] Later in 1966 Ramsey made his first tour of Canada and declared that from the Anglican side there were only three obstacles to unity with Roman Catholics, although they were big ones: the definition as core doctrine of the bodily assumption of the Blessed Virgin Mary, the teaching of papal infallibility, and the teaching that, as he put it, the Roman Catholic Church was the sole catholic church in the world.[35] In

---

31 "Report of the Committee on Anglican–Roman Catholic Relations," *General Synod Journal*, 1967, 280.

32 *CC*, April 1966, 1.

33 On the first ARCIC meetings and Eugene Fairweather's role, see *CC*, December 1966, 1, and February 1967, 3. ARCIC's "Agreed Statement on Eucharistic Doctrine," called the Windsor Statement, is available online in several places, including, accessed 5 January 2011, http://www.prounione.urbe.it/dia-int/arcic/doc/e_arcic_eucharist.html.

34 *CC*, July–August 1966, 16.

35 *CC*, October 1966, 1.

1967 the Anglican Centre was opened in Rome by the archbishop of Canterbury, with two cardinals (Bea and Willebrands) participating in the inaugural ceremonies. Informal consultations of Roman Catholic, Anglican, and Protestant liturgists were developing into more formal structures, such as the Consultation on Common Texts, which began in 1968.

As if to confirm the slogan "doctrine divides, while service unites," which is associated with the great ecumenical Christian Conference on Life and Work in Stockholm in 1925, the council's Decree on Ecumenism endorsed ecumenical co-operation in social teaching and activity. In consequence, Canadian Anglicans and Roman Catholics began joining together for the first time in social mission. In 1968 a workshop in Montréal called Christian Conscience and Poverty, originally conceived by Roman Catholic organizers, brought together Presbyterian, Lutheran, United Church of Canada, and Anglican workers as well—the distant origin of an anti-poverty group that in 1973 was constituted as PLURA, from the initials of the sponsoring denominations. More immediately, the Montréal workshop inspired some community-based ecumenical coalitions, generally short-lived, and it paved the way for numerous other national coalitions, including the Inter-Church Consultative Committee for Development and Relief (1970), the Inter-Church Committee on Development and Education (1972), Ten Days for World Development (1973), an advocacy group for global economic justice called GATT-Fly (1973), the Interchurch Fund for International Development (1973), the Taskforce on the Churches and Corporate Responsibility (1975), and the Inter-Church Project on Northern Development (1975). A key figure in the coalition movement was Romeo Maione, a former president of an international movement for social Catholicism called Young Christian Workers; he became the first executive director of the Canadian Catholic Organization for Development and Peace in 1967 and, in 1970, the director general of the non-governmental organizations division of the Canadian International Development Agency (CIDA).[36]

[36] Christopher Lind and Joe Mihevc, eds., *Coalitions for Justice* (Ottawa: Novalis, 1994).

One of the most important and far-reaching ecumenical initiatives of all for Canadian Anglicans and Roman Catholics came in the area of theological education, particularly in Toronto. The Decree on Ecumenism (*Unitatis Redintegratio*) of November 1964, encouraged dialogue with the Church's "separated brethren" and endorsed the teaching of sacred theology "with due regard for the ecumenical point of view."[37] St. Michael's College in Toronto, whose undergraduate program had long been federated with the Faculty of Arts and Science of the University of Toronto, was uniquely well positioned to connect its theological teaching with the Protestant colleges on campus. Administrators such as Father John Kelly, the president, and faculty members such as Father Gregory Baum, took up this challenge with enthusiasm. The Roman Catholic co-adjutor archbishop of Toronto, Philip Pocock, who carried considerable responsibility for the archdiocese during the infirmity of the ordinary, James Cardinal McGuigan, was also ecumenically committed.

In 1965 St. Michael's joined the Toronto Graduate School for Theological Studies (TGSTS), a consortium that administered two advanced theological degrees, the Master of Theology (Th.M.) and Doctor of Theology (Th.D.). The TGSTS, before St. Michael's joined it, comprised Trinity and Wycliffe Colleges (both Anglican), Knox College (Presbyterian), and Emmanuel College (United Church of Canada).[38] Three years later, Regis College, a Jesuit seminary, and St. Augustine's Seminary, sponsored by the Archdiocese of Toronto, participated with these other five schools (and others) in the Committee on Cooperation in Theological Education in Toronto, which recommended creating a Toronto School of Theology (TST). The TST, a consortium of these seven institutions, opened in September 1969, with co-operation not only at the advanced level but at the basic professional level as well. In other words, students training for the Anglican priesthood would be taught partly by Roman Catholic professors, and students training for

37 *Unitatis Redintegratio*, 10.

38 The experience of the TGSTS ended the vestiges of anti-Romanism at Wycliffe College, to which reference was made earlier. It was symbolic that a Wycliffe professor, Jakob Jocz, a committed ecumenist, was the head of the TGSTS when St. Michael's joined it.

the Roman Catholic priesthood would be taught partly by Anglican professors, along with Presbyterian and United Church professors. The experiment has flourished.

Thus by the early 1970s Vatican II, and its effects in the Roman Catholic world, had transformed the way in which Canadian Anglicans understood, experienced, and related to the Roman Catholic Church. For Canadian Anglicans, the journey from 1959 was breathtakingly speedy and dramatic. In 1959 they had known no formal relationship with the Roman Catholic Church; many viewed Roman Catholicism with suspicion; and many were skeptical that a so-called ecumenical council convened by the Pope would make much difference. By 1965 a typical Canadian Anglican felt an astonished admiration that the Roman Catholic Church had achieved such spectacular results in so short a time, and looked forward to further dialogue and co-operation. And by the early 1970s in Canada there were formal dialogues and collaborations that often included candid discussion of divisive issues and practices, coalitions for social justice, numerous instances of common activity at a local level, local discussions of a historic agreed theological statement promulgated at an international level, and co-operation in theological education and training for ordained ministry.

Impact on Anglican Identity

Not only did Vatican II make a huge impact on the external relations of the Anglican Church of Canada but it also profoundly influenced the denomination's sense of its own identity and mission. There is naturally a kind of logical connection between external relations and identity, but even so, the effect of Vatican II on Canadian Anglicanism was far greater than one might have predicted. Vatican II offered Anglicans a serious challenge toward *aggiornamento*, and a powerful model for it. That is why Bishop Luxton was warning Anglicans to hold onto their hats.

Vatican II came at a strategic time for Canadian Anglicans because they were coming to see that they would need to adapt to the post-Christendom Canada that was in gestation, but they remained dependent on theological and institutional patterns that had been forged in English Christendom. The Canadian Anglican ethos in the early 1960s has been accurately described as "very English, conservative, and stuffy."[39] The denomination's anglophilia, its attachment to the model of Christendom, its elitist reflexes, and its attachment to outworn traditions were evident in numerous ways: the Union Jacks in the churches, the state prayers at every service, the Tudor English of the *Book of Common Prayer*, the custom of singing "God Save the Queen" at the end of Sunday morning services, the loyal addresses to the Queen at synods, the loyal toasts to the Queen at dinner events, the premium placed on English accents in the pulpit, the seeming social prestige of Anglican bishops, the social reflex of asking Anglican clergy to say prayers on important civic occasions,[40] symbolic military connections such as annual parades and the laying up of regimental colours, the custom of referring to church dignitaries by title rather than by name, and the intense concern for such irrelevancies as what kind of clerical collar a priest wore, or whether at worship he wore a black scarf or coloured stole.

Vatican II was itself not one of the significant reasons why in the 1960s the Anglican Church of Canada had to begin relinquishing such an identity.[41] A great many more immediate motives for change were at work, including the erosion of Christendom, the independence of former British colonies, the challenge from the global south to northern missiological assumptions, the liberalization of Canadian immigration laws, union discussions with The United Church of Canada, secular theology, the critical turn in theological education, and the Quiet Revolution in Québec. But when, largely for these other reasons, the Anglican Church of Canada did face the need to reconstruct its identity,

---

[39] Thomas Millman, quoting a nameless "overseas visitor" in "Tradition in the Anglican Church of Canada," in *The Churches and the Canadian Experience*, ed. John Webster Grant (Toronto: Ryerson Press, 1963), 23.

[40] I have been told that as late as 1999, when the Air Canada Centre was dedicated, a call went out to the Anglican cathedral in Toronto to provide a cleric to say a prayer.

[41] For another view, see John Gibaut, "L'impact de Vatican II sur l'Eglise anglicane du Canada," in *L'Eglise canadienne et Vatican II*, ed. Gilles Routhier (Montréal: Fides, 1997), 359–372. He says that Anglican identity had been for so many centuries so intently focused on its difference from an unreformed Roman Catholicism that when Roman Catholicism reformed, Anglicans had to find a new identity. The evidence he presents in the article for this premise seems thin to me. I suspect that most Anglicans identified themselves more by their difference from the United Church: they were not so liberal, not so free-church, and not so nationalistically Canadian.

the liturgiology, missiology, and ecclesiology of Vatican II gave it its most powerful and convincing guidance.

Even while Vatican II was in session, Canadian Anglicans were recognizing that the council was challenging them towards critical self-examination. Our three Canadian Anglican interpreters, Fairweather, Wheeler, and Luxton, served once again as spokespeople and leaders in this development.

In one of his newspaper columns, Wheeler wrote that on the many occasions when he was invited to speak to an Anglican Church group on Vatican II, invariably someone would say, "Well, isn't it nice that the Roman Catholic Church is reforming and becoming like us." This attitude made him livid, he said, because of its "pious pride," and he launched into a critique of Anglican self-satisfaction: "We are smug about our Via Media. We are smug because we think that the Roman Catholic and United communions are becoming more like us every day." In fact, he more than hinted, many Anglicans were complacent only because they were trying to ignore the vital and insistent issues that Vatican II was tackling: the liturgy, Christianity and other religions, priestly training, the episcopacy, the apostolate of the laity, education, ecumenism, the authority of divine revelation.[42]

For his part, Luxton, in one of his columns, held up the Roman Catholic movement away from sixteenth-century liturgies as a model for Canadian Anglicans. Indeed, the Roman Catholic example in liturgical reform was becoming a widespread theme among Canadian Anglicans, especially the clerical intelligentsia who had long been on board with the Liturgical Movement. (An important example was an Anglican denominational official named Paul Gibson, who later staffed the national liturgical committee that produced the *Book of Alternative Services* in 1985; in 1966, in his first published book, he promoted liturgical change with explicit reference to Vatican II.[43]) Luxton also published a booklet called *Conversations in Rome*, a transcript of interviews with several of the ecumenical observers at Vatican II. He

---

42 *CC*, June 1965, 11.

43 For instance, he refers favourably to the Constitution on the Sacred Liturgy; *Say What You Mean and Do What You Say* (Toronto: [Department of Religious Education] Anglican Church of Canada, 1966), 21.

seems to have aggressively promoted this booklet in his own diocese, and it appears to have been widely distributed beyond. In his introduction, he wrote, "I offer it to my people with the prayer that we shall all be alert and responsive to this new life and thought. Our neighbours have much to teach us through their courage and foresight."[44]

One of Luxton's interviewees for *Conversations in Rome* was, naturally enough, Eugene Fairweather, who spoke of his particular enthusiasm for the council's "very clear direction" on the nature of Christian revelation, the place of Scripture, and the character of the Church. "This is going to be significant not only for Roman Catholics but for other Christians," he predicted.[45] Fairweather's enthusiasm for Vatican II contrasts tellingly with his relative disappointment in the Anglican Congress of 1963, whose proceedings he edited. "Very occasionally, a great conference produces a set of brilliant answers. Much more often, it ends by posing some good questions. The Toronto Congress was definitely a 'question' conference," he wrote. He was particularly unhappy with the intellectual level of the Anglican congress, which he thought displayed "a certain theological irresponsibility."[46] Fairweather, the most influential theologian in the Anglican Church of Canada, was not alone in recognizing that the inspiration for Anglican renewal had to come from Vatican II, not from Anglicans.

But *aggiornamento* in the Anglican Church of Canada would stall for a few years. One reason is that in the 1960s the denomination was immersed in internal bureaucratic reorganization of a conspicuously sterile character. Another is that many of its leaders were far more swayed by contemporary radical and secular theology than by the example of the renewal and reappropriation of orthodoxy as practiced at Vatican II. Still another is that a very large amount of institutional energy was being devoted to union discussions with The United Church

[44] George Huron [George Luxton, bishop of Huron], *Conversations in Rome, November, 1965: Vatican Council Observers Speaking with the Bishop of Huron* (London, ON: Bishop's Publication Fund, 1966), 2.

[45] Ibid., 38.

[46] E. R. Fairweather, ed., *Anglican Congress 1963: Report of Proceedings* (Toronto: Editorial Committee Anglican Congress, 1963), 3–4.

of Canada.[47] And, in all honesty, the primate of the day was not capable of giving imaginative theological leadership.

The year 1971 marks the real commitment of the Anglican Church of Canada to *aggiornamento*, as opposed to fixing and tidying, and it began perhaps the most intense period of change in its history. Vatican II and social Catholicism were its most prominent guides. I choose 1971 as the date because in that year that General Synod elected a new primate, Archbishop Ted Scott, who became the symbol, and perhaps the principal agent, of the changes that came to Canadian Anglicanism. His own background before becoming primate already represented many of the characteristics of the coming style of Canadian Anglicanism: he had been an ecumenical university chaplain, an advocate for woman church workers, and a participant in ministry with the First Nations; he came to be known for a radical social vision, a love of dialogue, a profoundly well-integrated Biblical theology, and an approachability summarized, and often caricatured, in his customary social opening, "Call me Ted." Anglican anglocentricity, elitism, insularity, establishmentarianism, conservatism, and patriarchy began to move off centre stage in 1971.

Many were the forces that maintained the profile of Vatican II during this period of Canadian Anglican reconstruction. Eugene Fairweather remained prominent, both directly and indirectly through the many clergy and bishops who had trained with him. The Roman Catholic presence in the Toronto School of Theology strongly influenced current and future Anglican leaders; in particular, Professor Gregory Baum of St. Michael's College, University of Toronto, was extremely active as a speaker at ecumenical events, a resource person for Anglican denominational committees, the editor of the periodical *The Ecumenist*, and a popular professor. Reinforcement came from some smaller theological centres, such as the Anglican studies program at Saint Paul University,

47 Gibaut, 366, believes that because of Vatican II the Anglican Church of Canada changed its principal dialogue partner from the United Church to the Roman Catholic Church. The evidence, however, is that Anglican leaders, seminary teachers, and synods remained well engaged, and probably *more* engaged, with the United Church until the Anglican bishops terminated discussions in 1975, which they did primarily not because they were enchanted by Vatican II but because the Plan of Union with the United Church would have weakened the episcopacy.

Ottawa, and the Atlantic School of Theology at Halifax, the latter of which originally had a much stronger Roman Catholic participation than it does now. The many ecumenical coalitions, dialogue groups, local partnerships, and events, such as have already been mentioned, were certainly formative. Canadian Anglicans were also well aware of the impact of the council on global Anglicanism. For instance, Canadian bishops meeting in 1968 with other Anglican bishops from around the world at the decennial Lambeth Conference in England heard the archbishop of Canterbury, Michael Ramsey, affirm the influence of the council "far beyond the boundaries of the Roman Catholic Church." Vatican II had shaken "the old complacency," he said in his sermon at the opening service, and it was stirring Anglicans to ask God "to show us what are things rightly shaken and the things not shaken which must remain."[48] The Conference recommended a joint commission, which eventually took shape as the Anglican–Roman Catholic International Commission.

The clearest and most important part of the reform of Canadian Anglicanism in the direction of Vatican II was the revision of its liturgy. Although the *Book of Common Prayer* of 1959 remained formally the standard, the vast majority of Anglican churches began using the *Book of Alternative Services (BAS)* after its publication and authorization in 1985. The first clear step toward the *BAS*, after the promulgation of Vatican II's Constitution on the Sacred Liturgy in December 1963, was the decision by the General Synod of the Anglican Church of Canada in 1965 to give diocesan bishops the authority to permit liturgical experimentation.[49] This was a dramatic step in a Church that for centuries had taken pride in the uniformity of its liturgical texts. What is sometimes called the era of the mimeographed liturgies followed. In 1971 General Synod mandated the project that became the *BAS*. The committee that produced it, staffed by Paul Gibson, included, for at least parts of its twelve years of work, Eugene Fairweather, a former student of his named William Crockett (a professor at the Vancouver School of Theology), and a sometime colleague named David Holeton,

---

48 http://anglicanhistory.org/amramsey/lambeth_opening1968.html (accessed 5 January 2011)

49 *CC*, Ocober 1965, 6; *General Synod Journal*, 1965, 119–120.

all strongly influenced by Vatican II. Their Liturgical Movement thinking, being neither quite Anglican high church nor Anglican low church, but in different ways attractive to both, undercut and helped to heal the historic controversies between the two great Anglican parties. For example, to begin with a little symbol of a larger ecclesiological difference, the high church had liked its clergy to preside at the Eucharist in an *ad orientem* position; the low church advocated what was called the north end position; but the Liturgical Movement asked the priest to take a basilical position, facing liturgical west, and now both Anglican factions could agree on this third position without either of them losing face. The Liturgical Movement's insistence on the full participation of the laity in the Eucharist struck evangelicals as an affirmation of the Protestant principle of the priesthood of all believers, while its insistence on a hierarchy of bishops, priests, deacons, and laity pleased the high church. The Liturgical Movement's preference for ceremonial simplicity pleased the Anglican low church, but its enthusiasm for a lavish expression of a very few important symbols, notably baptism, pleased the Anglican high church. Textually, too, the *BAS* paralleled Roman Catholic rites, most notably in its Eucharistic service.

John Gibaut has argued, paradoxically but plausibly, that even the ordination of women to the priesthood in the Anglican Church of Canada, which happened first in 1976, came as a result of Vatican II. The decision to ordain women, he maintains, was made primarily on the basis of an ecclesiology of "the whole people of God" and the sacramental primacy of baptism, which came to Canadian Anglicans from Vatican II.[50]

The reconceptualization of Canadian Anglicanism has not been an unmixed blessing. With the virtual loss of the prayer book tradition and lesser established markers of identity, and with an ever closer resemblance to a Vatican II Catholicism, Canadian Anglicanism (and, indeed, Anglicanism in many other places) lost its assurance of being distinctive and therefore struggled to find a reason to justify itself as *better*. A communion-wide identity crisis was identified in Stephen Sykes's *The Integrity of Anglicanism*[51] in 1978, which bluntly critiqued

50 Gibaut, "L'impact," 370.

51 Stephen W. Sykes, *The Integrity of Anglicanism* (London: Mowbray, 1978).

all existing rationales for a distinctive Anglicanism. (In the last two or three pages, it is true, the author came up with a rationale of his own, although it was easy to miss.) Sykes was invited to lead a discussion at a meeting of Anglican primates from around the world, and his book inspired conferences such as one at Renison College in Waterloo, Ontario, in 1981; it also initiated a succession of further books and articles on the same subject. More recently, a crisis of Anglican identity, most glaringly evident in disputes about the understanding of sexuality, has threatened to rupture the Anglican communion. Shaking off an outworn tradition has carried a cost.

A Conclusion

Reviewing this narrative, and recognizing the centrality of Toronto in it, I wonder whether I have been guilty of some geographical bias. Without denying that possibility, I also think that Toronto did provide a convergence of resources that was crucial to the effective and speedy reception of the wisdom of Vatican II by Anglicans. Toronto was the site of the headquarters of the Anglican Church of Canada, its two largest colleges, the editorial offices of its national newspaper, and the see of its largest diocese. Most of the Anglican population of Canada lived within a three-hour drive of Toronto. The Pontifical Institute of Medieval Studies in Toronto and St. Michael's College provided Canadian Anglican scholars, students, and leaders with their most accessible intellectual bridge to Roman Catholic theology (with Saint Paul University in Ottawa not far behind). The Roman Catholic coadjutor archbishop of Toronto, Philip Pocock, was unusually ecumenically committed. The first formal Anglican–Roman Catholic dialogue in Canada and the first solemnization of a mixed Anglican–Roman Catholic marriage happened in Toronto. The important international ecumenical theological conference of August 1967 was held in Toronto. The addition of St. Michael's College to the Toronto Graduate School of Theological Studies was one of the earliest, most symbolically important, most abiding, and intellectually most influential expressions of the ecumenical spirit of Vatican II. And the first Canadian members of the Anglican–Roman Catholic International Commission, Eugene Fairweather and John Keating, lived in Toronto. Thus, for Canadian

Anglicans, the influence of Vatican II was mediated primarily through Toronto and not least through the network that we know today as the Toronto School of Theology.

But whatever we may say about the specific role of Toronto in the process, it's clear that Vatican II dramatically changed the way Anglicans understood both Roman Catholicism and themselves. The council led directly to a desire for greater dialogue, ecumenical co-operation, and understanding. Many of its fruits, including its understanding of liturgy, the Eucharist, Christian mission, and the apostolate of the laity (or what Anglicans usually call lay ministry) as a consequence of baptism, were generally received by Canadian Anglicans into their own sense of Christian teaching. Vatican II provided a model for the Anglican Church of Canada as it left behind its "very English, conservative, and stuffy"[52] past and sought an effective presence in a post-Christendom Canada; and its example and teaching helped heal the historic low church–high church rift within Anglicanism. After Vatican II, and in large part in response to the vision it so effectively articulated, the Anglican Church of Canada entered an intense period of change symbolized by the primacy of Ted Scott from 1971 to 1986. After that, perhaps because it relied on Vatican II too much, or perhaps because it relied on Vatican II too little, the Anglican Church in Canada and globally experienced a gathering identity crisis that has recently challenged its unity.

52 Millman, 23.

SECTION III

Vatican II Viewed by the Theologians / Vatican II vu par les théologiens

Growing Awareness Regarding Vatican II in Canadian Theological Monographs and Journals (1959–1969)

Michael A. Fahey, SJ,
Boston College

On October 28, 1958, the College of Cardinals in conclave elected as Pope Angelo Giuseppe Roncalli, Patriarch of Venice, who assumed the name of John XXIII. Some three months later, on January 25, 1959, following a liturgy celebrated in Rome's basilica St. Paul Outside the Walls, the reigning Pope met with a small group of cardinals in the adjacent Benedictine monastery, and, totally unexpectedly, announced his resolve to hold a double celebration for the Roman Catholic Church. Speaking in Italian he promised a "*duplice celebrazione: di un Sinodo Diocesano per l'Urbe, e di un Concilio Ecumenico per la Chiesa universale.*"[1] It is that far-reaching decision to convene a

[1] *Acta Apostolicae Sedis* 51 (1959): 68. There is some controversy about the term that the Pope used in his announcement, whether it was "general council" or "ecumenical council." The official (and possibly "corrected") published text says "ecumenical council."

diocesan synod for Rome, but especially an ecumenical council, that we are commemorating in this collection, especially to consider how the council impacted the Canadian Christian community.

But, one may ask, has not research on this topic already been exhaustively explored? To a certain extent, yes. Especially for French-speaking Canada, thanks in large measure to Professor Gilles Routhier and his collaborators. Upon closer examination, however, I found several undiscovered nuggets, hopefully with a vein of gold, which merit further eyeing. To do so, I have restricted my search to a very particular scope, namely how French- and English-speaking Canadian theologians and their associates reacted in print during a ten-year period from the announcement of the forthcoming council (1959) to ten years later (1969), which falls during the first four postconciliar years. To accomplish this I have concentrated on works published either as books or journal articles during those years. This may sound very esoteric, and in a sense it is, but I am convinced that some insights emerge from this microscopic investigation.

I undertook this research in the Boston/Cambridge area, which is particularly rich in theological resources but a region that, not surprisingly, lacks certain Canadian materials, especially specialized periodicals. Thanks to the services of interlibrary loans, I was able to obtain the monographs I sought. And, of course, via Google and other Internet resources I was able to track down pertinent biographical and bibliographical data.

This essay has two prongs. First, an overview of this country's theologians who published during that ten-year window of opportunity. Surprisingly, outside of Canada, especially francophone Canada, several of these major figures are not well known or have been forgotten, partly because, with the passage of time, they were thereafter overshadowed by others who published in the subsequent decade, such as Jean-Marie Tillard, OP. I call to your attention especially to the works of Bernard Lambert, OP, Gregory Baum, René Latourelle, SJ, André Naud, and Eugene Fairweather. I provide a few words about Bernard Lonergan, SJ,

See Giuseppe Alberigo and Joseph Komonchak, eds., *History of Vatican II* (Maryknoll, NY: Orbis Books, 1995), 1:1, n. 2.

and Vatican II. I was tempted to include some vocal bishops who made an impact during this period by their pastoral letters, correspondence with the Pope, or eventually through interventions at the council: I have in mind ecclesiastics such as Paul-Émile Léger, G. Emmett Carter, George Flahiff, Remi De Roo, Paul-Émile Charbonneau, Antoine Hacault, and Maxim Hermaniuk. But I leave that for another occasion. Some persons I mention were editors or conveners of important congresses, such as Elmer O'Brien, SJ, and Lawrence Shook, CSB, I mention laypeople, who as journalists or administrators contributed with publications, but men who would not qualify as theologians: Bernard Daly, Paul T. Harris, as well as the proto-ecumenist Irénée Beaubien, SJ. And finally, I mention Gilles Routhier, who at a later date carefully studied the 1960s.[2]

Canadians Theologians and Their Helpers

Bernard Lambert, OP

One of the major figures who followed the council closely during its preparatory stages and during its subsequent sessions was the Canadian theologian Bernard Lambert, OP. Born on March 3, 1921, in Sainte-Anne-de-la-Pocatière, Québec, he entered the Dominicans in 1942 and pursued studies in philosophy and theology at the Couvent d'Études des Dominicains in Ottawa, followed by further studies at the Angelicum in Rome, where he was ordained priest in 1948. Thereafter he taught theology initially at the Dominican House of Studies in Ottawa. He spent several research stays at Union Theological Seminary (New York City) and at Fordham University during 1954 to 1958. In 1960,

[2] In this essay I will limit myself to works published by the theologians or to their contribution in academic journals, while at the same time aware that the survey could well be extended to other periodicals destined for a wider audience. I am thinking in particular of the Dominican publications *Maintenant* and *Communauté chrétienne*. One already finds numerous studies on the subject. See, for example, Maxime Allard, "Maintenant, symptôme pour comprendre le Québec de 1962," in *Modernité et religion au Québec*, ed. Robert Mager and Serge Cantin (Québec: Presses de l'Université Laval, 2009), 27–40; Gaëtan Baillargeon, "Les intellectuels québécois et Vatican II: de l'annonce du concile à son ouverture (1959–1962)," in *L'Église canadienne et Vatican II*, ed. Gilles Routhier (Montréal: Fides, 1997), 189–208; Gaëtan Baillargeon, "'De la cathédrale au chantier!' Les intellectuels québécois et Vatican II (1963–1966)," in *Vatican II au Canada: enracinement et réception*, ed. Gilles Routhier (Montréal: Fides, 2001), 273–292.

during the preparatory period of Vatican II, he worked at the World Council of Churches headquarters in Geneva, after which he travelled throughout the Balkans and the Middle East. In 1962 he published his massive *Le problème œcuménique*, which anticipated much of the spirit of the future conciliar decree *Unitatis Redintegratio*.[3] He was one of the few Canadians who published reactions to Vatican II between the first and second conciliar sessions, including a conference held at Université Laval in March 6, 1963.[4] He also published on May 15, 1964, between the second and third sessions, a major study with the provocative title *De Rome à Jérusalem* and containing thirty-nine short essays.[5]

According to the index of the *Acta* of Vatican II, Lambert was a *peritus* at the third and fourth sessions only, where he assisted Cardinal Maurice Roy, archbishop of Quebec City. But he was actively involved in a drafting committee for *Gaudium et Spes*.[6] In addition to his commentaries on *Gaudium et Spes* he also provided an early elucidation of *Lumen Gentium*.[7] At the conclusion of the council he oversaw the

---

3 Bernard Lambert, OP, *Le problème œcumenique*, 2 vols. L'Église en son temps, ed. Rémy Munsch (Paris: Centurion, 1962), translated into English as *Ecumenism: Theology and History*, trans. Lancelot C. Sheppard (New York: Herder & Herder, 1967). Also available in German and Spanish.

4 Bernard Lambert, OP, "Ancienne et nouvelle unité de l'Église," in *Études théologiques*, ed. Lorenzo Roy et al. (Québec: Presses de l'Université Laval, 1963), 93–119. An expanded version of these thoughts can be found in "Les deux démarches de la théologie," *Nouvelle revue théologique* 89 (mars 1967): 257–81.

5 Bernard Lambert, OP, *De Rome à Jérusalem: Itinéraire de Vatican II*, L'Église en son temps, ed. Rémy Munsch (Paris: Centurion, 1964). See especially the section: "Le rôle des théologiens au Concile," 206–16. Translated into German and Spanish.

6 Giovanni Turbanti, "La contribution canadienne à l'élaboration de *Gaudium et spes*," in *Vatican II au Canada: Enracinement et réception*, ed. Gilles Routhier (Québec: Fides, 2001), 387–426. See especially the section "La contribution du Père Lambert à la rédaction du troisième chapitre de la première partie," 417–20. Part three of *Gaudium et Spes* is devoted to "Humanity's Activity in the Universe," nos. 33–39. See Lambert's commentary: "La problématique générale de la Constitution pastorale," in *L'Église dans le monde de ce temps: Constitution pastorale "Gaudium et spes," Tome II: Commentaires*, ed. Yves Congar and M. Peuchmaud (Paris: Cerf, 1967), 131–70. Also, Lambert's "*Gaudium et Spes* and the Travail of Today's Ecclesial Conception," in *Church and Culture Since Vatican II: The Experience of North and Latin America*, ed. Joseph Gremillion (Notre Dame: University of Notre Dame, 1965), 31–52.

7 Bernard Lambert, OP, "La constitution [*Lumen gentium*] du point de vue catholique de l'œcuménisme," in *L'Église de Vatican II: Études autour de la Constitution conciliaire sur l'Église*, ed. Guilherme Baraúna (Paris: Cerf, 1966), 3.1263–77.

publication of a major collaborative study on the ecclesiology of Vatican II that extends to 567 pages. Some 103 pages (fourteen different essays) were written by Lambert himself. In all, the commentary contains fifty-eight essays by twenty-eight different authors.[8] In 1963 he was an official observer at the Fourth Conference of Faith and Order, held in the very Catholic city of Montréal. He participated at the international episcopal synods of 1969 and 1971. From 2002 on he was cared for at the health facility administered by the Dominican Sisters in Québec City, Le Pavillon Saint-Dominique. He died on April 10, 2004, at the age of eighty-three.[9]

It is curious that Lambert remains largely unknown outside of Québec and Canada. I venture to speculate that this is due in some measure to the fact that he was quickly overshadowed by his Dominican colleague Jean-Marie Tillard. Lambert was born in 1921, Tillard in 1927 (Tillard predeceased Lambert by four years). Both were active in Rome during the council; both were official *periti* at the third and fourth sessions. While in Rome, Tillard provided popular accounts of the council's proceedings for the Montréal newspaper *Le Devoir*. We are also fortunate to have a first-hand account by Tillard originally delivered at the conference held at Laval in October 1996.[10] Tillard's major publishing output came after the decade that I have chosen for this essay. During the earlier 1959–69 period, Tillard had published a work on the Lord's Supper, *L'Eucharistie: Pâques de l'Église* (Paris: Cerf, 1964). He contributed three articles to Lambert's edited *La nouvelle image de l'Église: Bilan du Concile Vatican II*. But much of Tillard's focus initially was on the theology of religious life. His first major ecclesiology, *L'Évêque de Rome*, did not appear until 1982 and was followed five years later by his pioneering study on the local church, *Église d'églises* (1987), which contributed to the growing importance of communion ecclesiology. Tillard became more widely known than Lambert through

[8] Bernard Lambert, OP, *La nouvelle image de l'Église: Bilan du Concile Vatican II* (Tours: Mame, 1967).

[9] See the lengthy obituary published in the Québec newspaper *Le Soleil*, 14 April 2004.

[10] See Tillard's "Souvenirs d'un expert canadien à Vatican II," in *L'Église canadienne et Vatican II*, Héritage et projet 58, ed. Gilles Routhier (Québec: Fides, 1997), 291–302.

his participation in two official international dialogues between the Roman Catholic Church and both with the Orthodox and with the Anglicans (ARCIC).

Gregory Baum

A second strong Canadian voice at the council was Gregory Baum, one of the few surviving *periti* of Vatican II, professor at the University of St. Michael's College's Institute of Christian Thought. He was made an Officer of the Order of Canada in 1990. He received honorary doctorates from five Canadian universities. During the council he served on the staff of Cardinal Augustin Bea's newly established Secretariat for Promoting Christian Unity (SPCU), now known as a Pontifical Council, which was also responsible for religious dialogue with Jews. Baum was an official *peritus* present at all four sessions of the council. He collaborated on Vatican II's text on non-Christian religions, *Nostra Aetate*, especially the chapter on the role of the Jews in salvation history, a chapter that bishops living in Arabic-speaking countries found problematic because of its possible political implications. Gilles Routhier persuaded Baum to record his recollections on his collaboration on that conciliar declaration even though he had not thought to save his personal archival material from that period.[11] While at St. Michael's, Baum founded the periodical *The Ecumenist*, which began in October 1962 continuing to the spring of 1991; in November–December 1993 it was given a second start initially by the Catholic publishing house Sheed & Ward. (I will comment more on this periodical in part two where I discuss theological journals.) Baum was editor of the publication from 1962 to 2004. He also published several books during and shortly after the council that touched especially on ecumenism.[12] In addition, he published in association with the editor of *America* magazine, Donald Campion, SJ, a hefty commentary on *Gaudium et Spes*.[13]

---

11 See his "Un souvenir de *Nostra aetate*," in *Vatican II au Canada*, ed. Routhier, 450–60.

12 Gregory Baum, *Progress and Perspectives: The Catholic Quest for Unity* (New York: Sheed & Ward, 1962), *The Credibility of the Church Today* (New York: Herder & Herder, 1968), and *Faith and Development: A Contemporary View* (New York: Paulist Press, 1969). See also Baum's *Amazing Church: A Catholic Theologian Remembers a Half-Century of Change* (Toronto: Novalis, 2005).

13 *De Ecclesia in mundo huius temporis: The Pastoral Constitution on the Church in the*

René Latourelle, SJ

Another Canadian theological voice during the council (also later created an Officer of the Order of Canada), then living in Rome where he taught fundamental theology for many years at the Gregorian University, was René Latourelle, SJ, born in Montréal in 1918. He was not an official *peritus* but collaborated closely. At the time of the council he was teaching a course on revelation at the Gregorian; in fact his Latin course notes were published privately but are available in various libraries.[14] Even before the promulgation of the council's Decree on Revelation (on which he collaborated closely), he published in French his major book on revelation.[15] Later, from the perspective of twenty-five years, he edited a major three-volume assessment of the council.[16]

André Naud

Another theologian whose contributions were important, albeit usually hidden, was André Naud. He served as redactor of various interventions of Cardinal Léger. He also served as a *peritus* at the second, third, and fourth sessions of the council. Naud worked to promote Catholic education in Québec. Only many years later did his bold views become public in his courageous work on "the uncertain magisterium."[17]

Modern World ... Commentary (New York: Paulist Press, 1968).

14 René Latourelle, SJ, *De revelatione. Pars dogmatica : schemata lectionum ad usum privatum auditorum* (Rome: Pontificia Universitas Gregoriana, 1961).

15 René Latourelle, SJ, *Théologie de la révélation* (Paris: Desclée de Brouwer, 1963), later translated into English, with a later commentary on *Dei Verbum*, namely *Theology of Revelation Including a Commentary on Dei Verbum* (Staten Island, NY: Alba, 1966). See his "L'Université Gregorienne et la *De Revelatione*," in *L'Église canadienne et Vatican II*, ed. Routhier, 319–33. One month after the promulgation of *Dei Verbum*, Latourelle published "La Révélation et sa transmission selon la Constitution *Dei Verbum*," *Gregorianum* 47 (1966): 5–40.

16 *Vatican II: Assessment and Perspectives: Twenty-five Years After (1962–1987)*, 3 vols., ed. René Latourelle (New York: Paulist Press, 1988–1989).

17 André Naud, *Le magistère incertain* (Montréal: Fides, 1987). At an October 1996 meeting of the Société canadienne d'histoire de l'Église çatholique, Naud gave an extensive, if modest, account of his involvement in the council. See Brigette Caulier and Gilles Routhier, eds., *Mémoires de Vatican II: Société canadienne d'histoire de l'Église catholique* (Québec: Fides, 1997), 39–71. This book also contains, besides a letter of Cardinal Léger to Pope John XXIII dated August 1962, the recollections of two Canadian bishops: Paul-Émile Charbonneau (23–38) and Antoine Hacault (73–92). See also Walter M. Abbott,

Eugene Fairweather

Also in this collection is Professor Michael Attridge's article about the Canadian Anglican delegate to Vatican II, Professor Eugene Fairweather (see Part II, Section II). Fairweather, together with Richard H. Davidson, a member of The United Church of Canada who had been appointed as a representative of the World Alliance of Reformed Churches, was actively and enthusiastically involved in the council. I will mention him later in connection with his writings in the *Canadian Journal of Theology* of which he was the editor during the conciliar years.

Bernard Lonergan, SJ

Although Bernard Lonergan is listed as an official *peritus* for the third and fourth sessions of Vatican II, in fact, his involvement in and commentaries on the council are negligible. Living in Rome at the time while teaching at the Gregorian University, he was prevented from participating in the preparatory or subsequent committee work of the council because of ill health. He followed the progress of the sessions from a distance and, in his own characteristic manner, judged its achievements against the background of his methodology as outlined in *Insight* and *Method in Theology*. Looking back on the conciliar years while at Boston College in 1981, he delivered a significant lecture that relates the council to the convictions of Chenu and to its role as a "pastoral" event.[18] Otherwise, I believe, he bequeathed no other written comments on Vatican II.

Gilles Routhier

Born in 1953, Gilles Routhier was only six years old when John XXIII announced the council. But he has been a valuable harvester of

---

Twelve Council Fathers (New York: Macmillan, 1963), which includes interviews with Paul-Émile Léger (1–21) and G. Emmett Carter (106–23). For brief recollections by Cardinal George Flahiff (recorded in May 1984), see "Recollections of a Council Father," in *The Church Renewed: The Documents of Vatican II Reconsidered*, ed. George P. Schner (Lanham, MD: University Press of America, 1986), 1–9.

18 Bernard J. F. Lonergan, "Pope John's Intention," in *A Third Collection: Papers by Bernard J. F. Lonergan, S.J.*, ed. Frederick E. Crowe, SJ (New York: Paulist Press, 1985), 224–38.

the council. Like the disciples in the Gospels, he has gathered up the loaves and fishes into baskets, out of which we have all been nourished. Following his graduate studies in Paris under the direction of Hervé Legrand, OP, Routhier produced a precious assemblage of studies recapturing the years before, during, and after the council. In 1993 his first major work appeared on the reception of Vatican II.[19] This work was later expanded with an essay on the impact of the council's announcement and preparation in Québec.[20] In October 1996 an international colloquium at Université Laval was organized by Routhier drawing upon European and North American collaborators.[21] A more modest meeting of the Société canadienne d'histoire de l'Église catholique published a series of recollections from the conciliar years.[22] Another major colloquium took place at Laval, August 23–25, 1999, part of the ongoing project *Vatican II et le Québec des années 1960*, containing twenty-five essays by various experts.[23] In the last several years, in 2004 and 2006, Routhier has published two collections, one of which gathers together earlier essays in sources difficult to access.[24]

Elmer O'Brien, SJ

In July 1964, after the first session of Vatican II, a conference was held at Loyola College, Montréal, which shortly thereafter merged

19 Gilles Routhier, *La réception d'un concile*, Cogitatio fidei 174 (Paris: Cerf, 1993).

20 Gilles Routhier, "L'annonce et la préparation de Vatican II: Réception et horizon d'attente au Québec," *Études d'histoire religieuse* 63 (1997): 25–44.

21 Routhier, ed., *L'Église canadienne et Vatican II*. A colloquium held at Québec, October 1996, Université Laval.

22 Brigette Caulier and Gilles Routhier, eds., *Mémoires de Vatican II*. This publication came out of an October 1996 meeting of the society. Besides the letter of Cardinal Léger to Pope John XXIII of August 1962, the volume contains recollections of two Canadian bishops, Paul-Émile Charbonneau (23–38) and Antoine Hacault (73–92), as well as those of theologian, adviser to Léger, André Naud (39–71).

23 Routhier, ed., *Vatican II au Canada*.

24 Gilles Routhier, ed., *Réceptions de Vatican II: Le concile au risque de l'histoire et des espaces humains*, Instrumenta Theologica 27 (Leuven: Peeters, 2004), and *Vatican II: Herméneutique et réception*, Héritage et projet 69 (Québec: Fides, 2006). The second book contains twelve articles by Routhier from 1997 to 2005. See especially "La réception de Vatican II au Canada" (269–318). For a general overview on the theology of reception, see Giuseppe Alberigo and J.-P. Jossua, eds., *La Réception de Vatican II* (Paris: Cerf, 1985). English translation: *The Reception of Vatican II*, trans. Matthew J. O'Connell (Washington: Catholic University of America, 1987).

with Sir George Williams University to become Concordia University. This workshop was hosted by the Loyola Professor Elmer O'Brien, SJ, to assess the achievements of the "decisive decade" (1954–64) in Catholic theological scholarship. Of the six presenters, three who gave an overview of research in their fields—Joseph Crehan (fundamental theology), Roland Murphy (Old Testament), and John J. Collins (New Testament)—made direct mention of the council that was in session. The other two and the editor—Walter Burghardt (patristics), John H. Miller (liturgy), and editor Elmer O'Brien (systematics)—made no reference to the council whatsoever.[25]

Lawrence K. Shook, CSB

A conference held at Toronto's St. Michael's College took place in August 1967 under the leadership of Basilian President and Professor Lawrence K. Shook (who served as a *peritus* at the fourth session only) under the theme "Theology of Renewal." It applied this theme both to "religious thought" and to "religious structures." Arguably, the symposium was the single most important Catholic academic conference held in Canada in the twentieth century. In volume 1, besides the European and US scholars giving papers, the following Canadians spoke: Bernard Lonergan, Paul-Émile Léger, Eugene Fairweather, Arthur Gibson, and two scholars working in Canada: Anton Pegis, Étienne Gilson; and in volume 2: Fernand Dumont, Roderick MacKenzie, and Jean-Marie Tillard.[26]

Before moving on to discussion of Canadian journal articles published between 1959 and 1969, I would like to pay tribute to several other persons who would clearly not describe themselves as professional theologians but who served the theological community in Canada behind the scenes during the decade under consideration. I have in mind the ecumenist Irénée Beaubien, SJ, and two book editors: Paul T. Harris and Bernard Daly.

---

[25] Elmer O'Brien, ed., *Theology in Transition: A Bibliographical Evaluation of the "Decisive Decade" 1954–1964* (New York: Herder, 1965).

[26] Lawrence K. Shook, ed., *Theology of Renewal*: vol. I: *Renewal of Religious Thought*; vol. II: *Renewal of Religious Structures,* introduction by Paul-Émile Léger (Montréal: Palm, 1968). A French version of these volumes is available. For a lengthy summary of this conference see "Ecumenism in Toronto, August 1967," *The Ecumenist* 5, no. 6 (September–October 1967) 81–93.

Irénée Beaubien, SJ

Irénée Beaubien, SJ, is the founder of the Centre canadien d'œcuménisme/Canadian Centre for Ecumenism in Montréal. Long before it was commonplace in Canada, he wrote on Church unity, first in French, *L'Unité chrétienne au Canada*[27] and then, adapted in English, as *Towards Christian Unity in Canada: A Catholic Approach.*[28] As early as 1958 Beaubien initiated innovative monthly dialogues between Protestant pastors and Catholic priests. In 1962 Cardinal Léger appointed him president of the new diocesan ecumenical commission of Montréal, and in 1963, he became director and founder of the ecumenical centre. That year he negotiated the choice of the Catholic city of Montréal as the venue for the Fourth Assembly of the Faith and Order committee of the World Council of Churches. Without the change in atmosphere that Vatican II had inaugurated, Montréal would never have been chosen. Beaubien was also instrumental in the establishment of the Christian Pavillon at Montréal's Expo 67. Appointed by Pope Paul VI in 1968 as "consultant of the Secretariat for Christian Unity" in Rome, he subsequently in the early 1970s visited thirty-three Canadian dioceses served by the National Ecumenical Office. In 1975 the Ecumenical Centre was integrated into the National Ecumenical Office and took as its legal name as the Canadian Centre for Ecumenism. On January 17, 2007, Beaubien was awarded the Prix Pionnier de l'œcuménisme (Pioneer of Ecumenism Award). For many years he was ably assisted at the centre by his late colleague Stéphane Valiquette, SJ, who had close ties with the Montréal Jewish community.

Paul T. Harris

Paul T. Harris, a prominent Catholic layman, served as director of public affairs with the federal government in Ottawa. He was a lay oblate of the Benedictine priory, Montréal, and he also served as director of the Catholic Information Centre, Toronto. During the council, he edited *Brief to the Bishops: Canadian Catholic Laymen Speak Their*

---

27 Irénée Beaubien, *L'Unité chrétienne au Canada* (Montréal: Palm, 1955).

28 Irénée Beaubien, *Towards Christian Unity in Canada: A Catholic Approach* (Montréal: Palm, 1956).

Minds.[29] This landmark publication contains responses of some thirty-four persons (seven of whom are women) collected in September 1964 between the second and third sessions of the council. It was highly original in content, articulating the laity's views on what their hierarchy should emphasize at the council. The book contained an introduction by Bishop Philip Pocock, coadjutor bishop of Toronto. Though, by contemporary standards, the book is quite mild in tone, it did break ground for more assertive input and sharing concerning council drafts still under consideration.

Bernard Daly

Bernard Daly was another important link in understanding the Canadian connection with Vatican II. He served in Ottawa as press secretary for the Canadian Conference of Catholic Bishops and was present in Rome during the four sessions of the council. It is not clear why he waited almost four decades before he published his account of what the Canadian delegates did during the council. Perhaps the title of his narrative (*Beyond Secrecy*) explains his sense that the information should remain secret at least during the lifetime of most of the participants. His account is not that of a theologian, but his powers of observation provide many interesting statistical and personal facts associated with the council.[30] For instance, he notes that during the first session of the council some eighty Canadian bishops came to Rome, checked into some nineteen hotels and religious houses, and joined with another 2,460 council fathers.[31] Unfortunately, there has never been a single volume published containing all the conciliar interventions by the Canadian bishops such as was published for the bishops of the United States.[32] Statistically over the four sessions there were some 105 Canadian bishops in attendance as opposed to 249 US bishops.

---

29 Paul T. Harris, *Brief to the Bishops: Canadian Catholic Laymen Speak Their Minds* (Toronto: Longman, 1965).

30 Bernard Daly, *Beyond Secrecy: The Untold Story of Canada and the Second Vatican Council* (Ottawa: Novalis, 2003). See also Daly's more recent work published in collaboration with his wife and the bishop of Victoria: Bernard Daly, Mae Daly, and Remi De Roo, *Even Greater Things: Hope and Challenge after Vatican II* (Toronto: Novalis, 1999).

31 Daly, *Beyond Secrecy*, 71.

32 Vincent A. Yzermans, ed., *American Participation in the Second Vatican Council*

Canadian Theological Journals (1959–1969)

In this second part, I examine Canadian theological journals that were being published between 1959 and 1969. Some journals may appear to be lacking in this examination, but this is possibly because they did not start publishing until later. This explains, for instance, the absence of *Église et théologie*, later known as *Theoforum*, which was begun only in 1970 at Saint Paul University, Ottawa. The same is true, for instance, of *Ecumenism/Œcuménisme*, published bilingually by the Canadian Centre for Ecumenism, but only beginning in 1981. The journals I have researched are: *Canadian Journal of Theology*, *Sciences ecclésiastiques*, *Laval théologique et philosophique*, *Studia Canonica*, *The Ecumenist*, *Relations*, and, by way of comparison for the same years, the flagship US Catholic journal, *Theological Studies*. In the cases of several journals there have been name changes during or after the time period studied. I have not addressed devotional publications, not because I consider them unimportant but simply because they do not lie within the scope of my research. At any rate, an excellent study of French-language devotional publications of that period has already been published.[33] My examination does not include secular newspapers (e.g., *Le Devoir*) or diocesan newspapers.[34] Professor Baillargeon has touched on the response of intellectuals to Vatican II but not specifically by consulting these journals.[35] In analyzing the contents of theological journals, I have found helpful the methodology used by Étienne Fouilloux, which he used in analyzing the Dominican journal of theology published in France.[36]

(New York: Sheed & Ward, 1967).

33 Marc Pelchat, "Les revues canadiennes-françaises de dévotion et le concile Vatican II (1959–1962)," in *L'Église canadienne et Vatican II*, ed. Routhier, 165–88.

34 Yves Therrien, "La couverture de Vatican II dans les quotidiens francophones du Canada (1959–1962)," in *L'Église canadienne et Vatican II*, ed. Routhier, 145–63. See also Jérôme Coutard, "La presse et le concile Vatican II: une histoire de représentations," in *Vatican II au Canada: Enracinement et réception*, ed. Routhier, 245–59.

35 Gaëtan Baillargeon, "'De la cathédrale au chantier': Les intellectuels québécois et Vatican II (1963-1966)," in *Vatican II au Canada: Enracinement et réception*, ed. Gilles Routhier (Québec: Fides, 2001), 273–92. This article is a follow-up of his essay "Les intellectuels québécois et Vatican II: de l'annonce du concile à son ouverture (1959-1962)," in *L'Église canadienne et Vatican II*, Héritage et projet 58, ed. Gilles Routhier (Québec: Fides, 1997), 189–207.

36 Étienne Fouilloux, "La Concile Vatican II dans la *Revue des sciences philosophiques et*

Canadian Journal of Theology

This prestigious journal with close connections to Anglican establishment Trinity College, University of Toronto, had a strong ecumenical thrust from its very beginning. The journal, which lasted until 1971, was eventually replaced by *Sciences Religieuses/Studies in Religion.* For my research I consulted volumes 5 (1959) through 16 (1970). The first three volumes that I read (1959, 1960, 1961), published after the council's announcement, did not make any mention of the forthcoming council. In fact, even Gregory Baum, publishing in volume 7 on "Roman Catholic Theology in Germany Today,"[37] makes no reference to the impending council. However, in the following year, 1962, even before the opening session, the Anglican theologian wrote an editorial entitled "The Second Vatican Council"[38] under his initials E. R. F., Eugene Rathbone Fairweather (1920–2002), professor at Trinity College for forty years, Keble Professor of Divinity, Faith and Order member, within the Toronto School of Theology. He argued that the coming council was "too big to ignore." He added: "... we know that all who support our work and share our aims will pray that God will use the Council to set forward the renewal and reintegration of his whole Church militant."[39]

Also, in that same volume, Université Laval professor of theology Gilles Langevin, SJ, explored material that he knew would play central importance at the forthcoming council, namely, "The Word of God and the Eucharist,"[40] but without alluding specifically to the council. Again, in the same volume, David Hay reviewed a new book just published

---

théologiques," Revue des sciences philosophiques et théologiques 92, no. 3 (juillet–septembre 2008): 677–90. See also Massimo Faggioli, "La recezione della collegialità del Vaticano II: le reviste teologiche 'romane' (1963–1970)," in *Réceptions de Vatican II: Le concile au risque de l'histoire et des espaces humains*, Instrumenta Theologica 27 (Leuven: Peeters, 2004), 19–47.

[37] Gregory Baum, "Roman Catholic Theology in Germany Today," *Canadian Journal of Theology* 7 (1961): 258–70.

[38] Eugene R. Fairweather, "The Second Vatican Council," *Canadian Journal of Theology* 8 (1962): 227–28.

[39] Ibid., 228.

[40] Gilles Langevin, "The Word of God and the Eucharist," *Canadian Journal of Theology* 8 (1962): 244–48.

jointly by Eugene Fairweather and Edward R. Hardy, *The Voice of the Church: The Ecumenical Council*,[41] as well as several other volumes on church unity. It is significant, some might say even ironic, that one of the earliest enthusiastic descriptions in a Canadian theological journal about the coming Vatican II was formulated first by a member of a sister church, namely by an Anglican theologian who would go on to become an official *peritus* at the council.[42]

Two years later, in 1964, following the death of John XXIII and the election of Paul VI, the journal's associate editor W. O. F. (W. O. Fennell) in his editorial "Ecumenism and the Second Vatican Council,"[43] written before the third session, expressed concern about whether John XXIII's original goal of the council would be pursued by his successor Paul VI. For the next three years there was no particular reference to Vatican II until volume 14 (1968) when H. L. Puxley reviewed *Vatican II: An Interfaith Appraisal*, edited by John H. Miller,[44] a work that recorded the talks at the International Theological Conference held at Notre Dame in 1966. In the following year there was a review of Karl Barth's *Ad Limina Apostolorum: An Appraisal of Vatican II* by Martin Rumscheidt, which he described as a jewel.[45] In the same volume there is an article by the US Jesuit Harvey Egan, SJ, "Towards a Theology of the Development of Dogma,"[46] which addressed a question frequently raised in connection with the council, namely whether dogma could indeed "develop."

Sciences ecclésiastiques

Sciences ecclésiastiques was founded in 1948, published initially three times a year by the Jesuits of Canada at their bilingual theologate,

---

41 Eugene Fairweather and Edward R. Hardy, *The Voice of the Church: The Ecumenical Council* (Greenwich, CT: Seabury, 1962).

42 For a brief account by Fairweather of Vatican II, see Bernard Pawley, ed., *The Second Vatican Council: Studies by Eight Anglican Observers* (London: Oxford University Press, 1967), 54–84.

43 W. O. Fennell, "Ecumenism and the Second Vatican Council," *Canadian Journal of Theology* 10 (1964): 221–22.

44 John H. Miller, ed., *Vatican II: An Interfaith Appraisal* (Notre Dame: University of Notre Dame, 1966).

45 *Canadian Journal of Theology* 15 (1969): 281–82.

46 Harvey Egan, SJ, "Towards a Theology of the Development of Dogma," *Canadian Journal of Theology* 15 (1969): 227–39.

L'Immaculée Conception in Montréal. Later, beginning with volume 20 (1968), it changed its name to *Science et Esprit* published by the Jesuits in Montréal and Trois-Rivières. In more recent times, under that new title, it is now published by the Dominicans of Ottawa.

In my research, I covered the years 1958 to 1971 (volumes 10 through 23). During the initial years of that period, no mention was made of the forthcoming council. The first article to appear about the ecumenical council was published in 1961 (volume 13) by an American Jesuit scholastic of the Byzantine Catholic Church, Robert F. Taft, SJ, prior to his ordination and doctoral studies on the Christian East at the Pontifical Oriental Institute in Rome. His article, entitled "The Neo-Orthodox View on Ecumenical Councils," outlined the thinking of theologians of the Russian Orthodox diaspora in Paris and New York, such as that of Alexander Schmemann, John Meyendorff, and others.[47]

During the years of the council the journal contained no articles analyzing the discussions or the texts. In volume 18 (1966) there is a book review by Marcel Grand'Maison, SJ,[48] of Michael Novak's book entitled *The Open Church: Vatican II, Act II*,[49] a work that focused especially on US participation in the council.

The first article that actually analyzes a text of Vatican II appears in 1967 in volume 19: a study by Jean-Marc Dufort, SJ, "Quelques aspects de la théologie de la vie religieuse selon Vatican II," which analyzes the council's Decree on the Adaptation and Renewal of Religious Life promulgated on October 25, 1965.[50] In the same volume there was also a brief report by Émilien Lamirande, OMI, on a congress held in Rome from September 26 to October 1, 1966: "Le Congrès International de Théologie," part of which is a section on Vatican II.[51]

---

47 Robert F. Taft, SJ, "The Neo-Orthodox View on Ecumenical Councils," *Sciences ecclésiastiques* 13 (1961): 437–44.

48 Marcel Grand'Maison, SJ, in *Sciences ecclésiastiques* 18 (1966): 314–15.

49 Michael Novak, *The Open Church: Vatican II, Act II* (London: Longman and Todd, 1964).

50 Jean-Marc Dufort, SJ, "Quelques aspects de la théologie de la vie religieuse selon Vatican II," *Sciences ecclésiastiques* 19 (1967): 111–20.

51 Émilien Lamirande, OMI, "Le Congrès International de Théologie," *Sciences ecclesiastiques* 19 (1967): 297–302.

In volume 20 (1968) under its new title *Science et Esprit*, there appeared a highly favourable article by Jean-Marc Dufort, SJ.[52] The essay concentrated on chapter seven of the Dogmatic Constitution on the Church entitled "The Eschatological Nature of the Pilgrim Church and Its Union with the Heavenly Church." In the following three years, 1969–71, there are no further articles on Vatican II. Because of the excellence of his study, Dufort had set a high standard for later commentaries on conciliar documents.

Laval théologique et philosophique

Laval théologique et philosophique was founded in 1945. Originally published twice a year, it later appeared three times a year. It always seemed to be more heavily devoted to philosophical articles. In volume 21 (1965), an article by Jean-Marie Tillard on the Church made no mention of Vatican II; nor did the articles on the same topic by L. Telmosse and Louis Pageau, which originally were talks given at Société canadienne de théologie in 1965. In volume 22 (1966), various talks given at 1965 meeting of the société, including ones by Julien Harvey, SJ, Émilien Lamirande, OMI, André Naud, Jean-Marie Levasseur, and Jean-Guy Pagé were published, but there is no mention at all of Vatican II. The first article that draws upon any document of Vatican II appears in volume 26 (1970), an essay by M. l'abbé Michel Gervais on revelation drawing upon *Dei Verbum*.[53]

Studia Canonica

Published by the Société canadienne de droit canonique in association with the Faculty of Canon Law at Saint Paul University, Ottawa, *Studia Canonica* was founded only in 1967. As with several US periodicals of canon law (such as *The Jurist*), it was actively involved in ecclesiological issues touched upon by texts of Vatican II. Its first four volumes contain a number of thorough analyses of conciliar texts.

Volume 1 (1967) published four articles, talks given at the 1966 meeting of the Canadian Canon Law Society: Valérien Bélanger (aux-

[52] Jean-Marc Dufort, SJ, "Histoire et théologie du VIIe chapitre de la Constitution '*Lumen gentium*,'" *Sciences et Esprit* 20 (1968): 77–94.

[53] M. l'abbé Michel Gervais, "La théologie fondamentale et la dogmatique de la Révélation," *Laval théologique et philosophique* 26 (1970): 223–32.

iliary bishop of Montréal), "Cette portion du peuple de Dieu … en particulier les religieux";[54] Alexander Carter (bishop of Sault-Sainte-Marie), "Bishop – Priest – Laïty Relationship in the Light of Vatican II";[55] Jacques Denis (from Sens, France), "L'Église diocésaine à la lumière de Vatican II";[56] and J. Maurice Théoret, "The Post-Conciliar Parish."[57]

Volume 2 from 1968 included "Episcopal Conferences and Collegiality" by Bernard Prince,[58] which was especially in relation to *Lumen Gentium,* and a lengthy article by Bernard Martin, "Le prêtre d'après le deuxième Concile de Vatican."[59]

Volumes 3 and 4 (1969 and 1970) had fewer studies on Vatican II than the other volumes, but did have two. Henri Grenier wrote about "Le droit canonique à la lumière de Vatican II"[60] and André Guay, OMI, published "From the Code of Canon Law to Vatican II."[61]

The Ecumenist

This publication, in some ways more of a high-level theological newsletter than a traditional journal, was founded by Gregory Baum, who was editor from 1962 to 2004. It was published as a bimonthly from October 1962 to the spring of 1991, when publication was suspended. In 1993 Sheed & Ward gave the periodical a "second chance." It is not possible here to list the many short but penetrating articles on various conciliar activities and texts that were offered. In its early years it also regularly published summaries of different episcopal documents.

---

54 Valérien Bélanger, "Cette portion du peuple de Dieu … en particulier les religieux," *Studia Canonica* 1 (1967): 1–19.

55 Alexander Carter, "Bishop – Priest – Laity Relationship in the Light of Vatican II," *Studia Canonica* 1 (1967): 79–95.

56 Jacques Denis, "L'Église diocésaine à la lumière de Vatican II," *Studia Canonica* 1 (1967): 179–90.

57 J. Maurice Théoret, "The Post-Conciliar Parish," *Studia Canonica* 1 (1967): 191–203.

58 Bernard Prince, "Episcopal Conferences and Collegiality," *Studia Canonica* 2 (1968): 125–32.

59 Bernard Martin, "Le prêtre d'après le deuxième Concile de Vatican," *Studia Canonica* 2 (1968): 133–83.

60 Henri Grenier, "Le droit canonique à la lumière de Vatican II," *Studia Canonica* 3 (1969): 239–49.

61 André Guay, OMI, "From the Code of Canon Law to Vatican II," *Studia Canonica* 4 (1970): 203–208.

Relations

Relations describes itself as "publié par un groupe de Pères de la Compagnie de Jésus" and is issued eleven times a year. I have not been able to consult all ten years envisaged 1959–69 (volumes 27–29) because not all the issues were available to me in Boston. But for the three years I was able to consult, 1967, 1968, and 1969, it is interesting to note that in the year 1967, shortly after the close of the council, four articles discussed Vatican II, two were on the laity, one on religious freedom, and another on pluralism in the Church. These are: René Latourelle, SJ, "Les laïcs, ferment de la société";[62] Robert Bernier, SJ, "Paradoxe de la déclaration conciliaire sur la liberté religieuse";[63] Robert Bernier, SJ, "Le pluralisme dans l'Église selon Vatican II";[64] and René Latourelle, SJ, "Laïcs théologiens."[65] However, in the following two years 1968, 1969, the focus shifted to encyclicals, especially *Humanae Vitae*, and the themes of coming international episcopal synods.

Some might argue that *Relations* does not strictly qualify as a theological journal but is rather a monthly periodical of *haute vulgarisation* discussing general cultural and ecclesiastical news. It certainly had a wider dissemination at least in Québec than the more academic journals. Jean-Claude Dupuis, who studied the periodical during Vatican II, has no hesitation to call it a "review."[66]

Theological Studies (USA)

It may be informative to briefly compare these Canadian publications with the premiere Catholic theological journal of the United States, to see if its record of discussion about the council differed from its Canadian counterparts at the same time. I reviewed volumes 20 through 30 (1959–69). For the most part, *Theological Studies* (*TS*) did not mention Vatican II in any of its articles, editorials, or book reviews

62 René Latourelle, SJ, "Les laïcs, ferment de la société," *Relations* 27 (1967): 3–5, 34–37.

63 Robert Bernier, SJ, "Paradoxe de la déclaration conciliaire sur la liberté religieuse," *Relations* 27 (1967): 38–40.

64 Robert Bernier, SJ, "Le pluralisme dans l'Église selon Vatican II," *Relations* 27 (1967): 96–99.

65 René Latourelle, SJ, "Laïcs théologiens," *Relations* 27 (1967): 309–12.

66 See Jean-Claude Dupuis, "La revue *Relations* et le Concile Vatican II," in *Les cahiers du Québec au XXe siècle*, Octobre 1996, 33–50.

until near the very end of the council. In volume 26 (1965) there is an article by Bernard Marthaler, OFMCap, of the Catholic University of America entitled "The Councils in History," a survey that mentions Vatican II only in passing.[67]

In volume 27 (1966) there are two articles on Vatican II, one by the non-Catholic, Princeton-based theologian Paul Ramsey, "The Vatican Council [II] on Modern War," which picks up various passages on moral issues related to warfare from *Gaudium et Spes*.[68] A lengthier article appeared by the *TS* editor, John Courtney Murray, on "The Issue of Church and State at Vatican Council II," discussing both *Gaudium et Spes* and *Dignitatis Humanae*.[69] In effect this article ended the Vatican ban on Murray's writings on religious freedom.

In volume 28 (1967), Canadian theologian Gregory Baum wrote "Vatican II's Constitution on Revelation: History and Interpretation."[70] In the same issue William H. Dodd, SJ, of the Bellarmine School of Theology, Chicago, wrote: "Toward a Theology of Priesthood," analyzing various Vatican II texts.[71] In volume 29 (1968) the journal, now under the editorship of Walter Burghardt, in a volume devoted to ecumenism, published an article by the German Methodist Manfred Hoffmann, professor at Emory University, Atlanta, entitled "Church and History in Vatican II's Constitution on the Church: A Protestant Perspective."[72]

In some ways Protestant colleagues seemed more excited at the time about Vatican II than their Catholic counterparts. Neither the editor nor most of the publishing authors expressed any excitement about the paradigmatic shifts that were underway at the council. Responses to the council were slow and measured.

---

67 Bernard Marthaler, OFMCap, "The Councils in History," *Theological Studies* 26 (1965): 393–406.

68 Paul Ramsey, "The Vatican Council [II] on Modern War," *Theological Studies* 27 (1966): 179–203.

69 John Courtney Murray, "The Issue of Church and State at Vatican Council II," *Theological Studies* 27 (1966): 580–606.

70 Gregory Baum, "Vatican II's Constitution on Revelation: History and Interpretation," *Theological Studies* 28 (1967): 51–75.

71 William H. Dodd, SJ, "Toward a Theology of Priesthood," *Theological Studies* 28 (1967): 683–705.

72 Manfred Hoffmann, "Church and History in Vatican II's Constitution on the Church: A Protestant Perspective," *Theological Studies* 29 (1968): 191–214.

Conclusion

What conclusions do I feel are warranted from my investigation within these restricted parameters?

First, I see confirmed a conclusion first outlined in Thomas S. Kuhn, *The Structure of Scientific Revolutions*,[73] that whenever a major paradigm shift is about to occur (such as in Catholicism at Vatican II), it is prepared for in advance by a minuscule number of researchers who proleptically and hesitatingly perceive the need for changes of attitudes or conversions of behaviour. Changes occur first in a very small nucleus of thinkers who anticipate what needs to be adjusted. In the case of the Catholic Church, only a few pioneer theologians, persons often held in suspicion and even silenced, prepared the way for the council by a process of *ressourcement*. If this teaches us anything for today, it is that we should be slow to dismiss out of hand theologians currently considered by officials as unorthodox or dissident.

Once Vatican II was announced and moved into its preparatory stage and actual sessions, commentaries in books and journals were slow to materialize. This is not surprising in the case of monographs and journal articles, since the time gap between incubation and birth is not insignificant. Still, at an earlier stage, one might have expected some references in editorials to what was in progress. At least the *Canadian Journal of Theology* met that expectation, as did the early publications of Bernard Lambert.

Even after conciliar constitutions, decrees, or declarations had been promulgated, there was a time gap before their publication, and the quality of the translations (at least into English) was quite inferior. It would be a long time before the *Acta* of the council were published, providing the interventions and corrected drafts that clarified certain seemingly innocent phrases or innovative terminology.

But shift in awareness even among most theologians did not happen at a fast pace. It took a while, after observing bishops disagreeing with other bishops or even with the Pope, before a larger number of persons realized that not every Vatican "official teaching" was immutable, and that inculturation would bear a variety of fruits. Nowhere was this more

[73] Thomas S. Kuhn, *The Structure of Scientific Revolutions* (Chicago: University of Chicago Press, 1962).

notable than in regard to church unity and the ecumenical agenda. Something new was occurring: non-Catholic observers and guests were being asked their views on draft statements. Although observers were not invited to step up to the council's microphone, they did speak out frankly at afternoon informal sessions.

One puzzlement today is why the high degree of amicable collaboration between bishops and theologians so prominent before and during the council gradually diminished to the point where it was replaced by a climate of suspicion and even hostility. What, if anything, did theologians do to merit this cooling of relationships to the point where the two groups seem often at odds? As this relationship became more chilly, relations among Catholic and Orthodox and Anglican and Protestant sisters and brothers warmed up, producing high-level consensus statements such as the Lima Report, the Porto Alegre Statement, and the Cyprus Report.

It does not seem disputable to conclude that French-speaking Canada's contributions to the preparation for and achievements of the council were more notable than those of their English-speaking counterparts. I attribute this to the superiority of their seminary education and their accessibility to the early renaissance of theology and pastoral renewal in France and Belgium. And this despite the secularizing tendencies simultaneously at work in the *révolution tranquille.*

In the last decade I have devoted many hours to researching the Belgian contribution to Vatican II.[74] Ironically, tiny bilingual Belgium's impact on the achievements of Vatican II was more significant than Canada's. This is related to the few members of the Belgian hierarchy (most of whom during the council lived together in Rome's Belgian College). It was much easier for the sixteen Belgian bishops housed together to confer and co-ordinate than it was for the 105 Canadian bishops spread out over some nineteen hotels and religious houses.

Still, all things considered, in retrospect, Canada, *a mare usque ad mare*, can be justly proud of its distinguished contributions to the Second Vatican Council before, during, and after.

---

[74] Doris Donnelly, Joseph Famerée, Mathijs Lamberigts, and Karim Schelkens, eds., *The Belgian Contribution to the Second Vatican Council*, Bibliotheca Ephermeridum Theologicae Lovaniensis, 216 (Leuven: Peeters, 2008), especially 685–701.

INSPIRATION AFTER *DEI VERBUM*

Andrea Spatafora,
Saint Paul University

The fiftieth anniversary of the calling of the Second Vatican Council by Pope John XXIII is an appropriate occasion to assess its impact on the Church and on its theology. This article will examine the developments in the Church's doctrine of inspiration since the council and will focus principally on the contribution of a Canadian exegete, Walter Vogels.[1] The study will begin with an overview of the origins and development of the concept of inspired Scripture up to Vatican II, followed by a brief presentation of the Dogmatic Constitution on Divine Revelation, *Dei Verbum*'s treatment of inspiration, and a brief survey of the work of Catholic theologians in the fifty years following the council.

The doctrine of the inspiration of the Scriptures is rooted in the mystery of the dual nature of the Bible as Word of God and as human writing. The notion of the inspired character of the Scriptures finds its origins in the early Jewish community that affirmed the divine origin of the Torah. This was gradually extended to the prophets and to the other writings, which were said to "soil the hands." Among the earliest Jewish writers to refer to the divine origin of the Scriptures are Philo of Alexandria and Josephus. The later Rabbinic tradition speaks of the pre-existence of the Scriptures, which were willed by God before creation and revealed to Moses.

[1] Walter Vogels, W.F., born in Belgium, has taught for over thirty years at Saint Paul University, Ottawa, where he is now professor emeritus.

There are no texts in the Old Testament that treat inspiration strictly speaking; that is, no passage addresses the question of the inspired nature of the Scriptures. Rather, many verses speak of the efficacy of God's word contained in the texts.[2] According to the Torah, Moses wrote down God's words on the stone tablets,[3] whereas in the prophetic writings, the authors often claim to speak God's words that have been revealed to them.[4] Although Ezra and Nehemiah, as well as 2 Maccabees, witness the written transmission of the divine words, there are no references to the inspired nature of the writings.[5]

In the New Testament there are two references to the inspired character of the Scriptures, namely 2 Timothy 3:16 and 2 Peter 1:20–21.[6] The text from 2 Timothy—"All Scripture is inspired by God (*theopneustos*) and is useful for teaching, for reproof, for correction, and for training in righteousness"[7]—is part of a final exhortation by the author (identified by the tradition as the apostle Paul) to his disciple inviting him to imitate his example. The term *theopneustos*—meaning "divinely inspired," literally "breathed by God," from the Greek words *theo*, "God," and *pneō*, "to breathe"—alludes to the *pneuma*, the Holy Spirit, who comes from God and renders the Scriptures useful for salvation. Since the Scriptures are inspired by God, they are useful for preaching and teaching; that is, they have the power to inspire God in the believers.[8] The passage does not attempt to delimit the list of inspired books; it

2 Isa. 55:10–11; Ps. 19.

3 Exod. 31:15; 34:27–28; Deut. 10:1–2,4; 27:3,8; 31:7–10.

4 Isa. 6:7; Jer. 1:9; 36:28,32; 51:60–62; Ezek. 2:8; 3:1,10–11; Hab. 2:2–3.

5 Ezra 7:12–26; Neh. 8:1; 2 Macc. 2:13–14 See Rinaldo Fabris, "In che senso la Sacra Scrittura è testimonianza dell'ispirazione?" in *Scrittura Ispirata. Atti del Simposio internazionale sull'ispirazione promosso dall'Ateneo Pontificio "Regina Apostolorum,"* ed. Antonio Izquierdo (Città del Vaticano: Libreria Editrice Vaticana, 2002), 52–57.

6 In both passages, the term Scripture may refer only to the Old Testament, the Bible of the first Christians, or it may include as well the earliest Christian writings that were to become the New Testament.

7 The Greek *pasa graphē theopneustos kai ōphelimos* can also be translated: "All Scripture inspired by God is useful."

8 See Fabris, "In che senso," 44. The term *theopneustos*, found nowhere else in the Bible, can have a passive meaning, "breathed by God" or "inspired," and an active meaning, "filled with God's breath or spirit" or "inspiring." Although most commentators translate the term in the passive sense, Walter Vogels privileges the active meaning, which constitutes an argument in favour of his linguistic model of inspiration.

does not speak of the inerrancy of Scripture nor does it provide a theory of inspiration.

The verses from 2 Peter—"First of all you must understand this, that no prophecy of Scripture is a matter of one's own interpretation, because no prophecy ever came by human will, but men and women moved by the Holy Spirit spoke from God"—are part of an exhortation by the author (identified by the tradition as the apostle Peter) to hold on not only to the apostolic witness but also to the prophetic word. The expression *pasa propheteia graphēs* is generally taken to refer to the entire body of Scripture in which is found the authentic prophetic word. Its proper interpretation must take into account its divine origin and, therefore, cannot result from private interpretation.[9]

In the Christian tradition there developed the consciousness that the Scriptures were God's words or those of the Holy Spirit.[10] The notion of God as the author of the Scriptures, first dated to Gregory the Great,[11] became an accepted theological idea in the medieval period and has appeared in official Church documents since the First Vatican Council.[12]

One of the earliest writers to reflect on the manner of inspiration was Philo, who proposed that the sacred authors were possessed by God and wrote down God's words while in an ecstatic state. This ecstatic or mantic notion of inspiration was never adopted by mainstream Christianity, which affirmed the independence of the human author. Throughout the history of the Church, the relationship between the divine author and the human authors has been understood in diverse ways. Various models of inspiration have been proposed. The earliest model is that of dictation. The model of prophetic inspiration was

---

9 See Fabris, "In che senso," 44–45.

10 See Tertullian, *Apologeticus pro Christianis*, 31; and Gregory of Nissa, *Contra Eunomium*, 7.

11 Gregory the Great, *Moralia*, præfatio, 1.

12 The attribution of God as author is found in the documents of the councils of Florence and of Trent, however, it would appear that in both cases, the expression refers to God as initiator of the covenant or of the economy of salvation. See Walter Vogels, "L'Écriture, inspirée et inspirante," in *Entendre la voix du Dieu vivant: interprétations et pratiques actuelles de la Bible*, ed. Jean Duhaime and Odette Mainville (Montréal: Médiaspaul, 1994), 4n.

adopted for the sacred authors: in the same way, the prophet received directly from God the words he spoke, so the authors of the biblical books wrote the words dictated by God.

Over the centuries, modifications were proposed to the dictation model. L. Lessius suggested that the biblical books, written without divine inspiration, were subsequently inspired or received approbation by the Holy Spirit. Lessius considered 2 Maccabees to be an example of this. He claimed that it was written by purely human activity and it was only later, when the Holy Spirit declared it free from error, that it became part of the canon. The theory of concomitant inspiration or assistance by the Spirit, developed by J. Bonfrerius, claimed that the Holy Spirit assisted the human authors so that the texts would be free of error. In the nineteenth century, J. B. Franzelin developed the model of formal inspiration that was adopted at Vatican I: Franzelin distinguished between the content and the form and proposed that God inspired the ideas while the human author chose the words and phrases. Franzelin's model did not enjoy much popularity and was supplanted by the model of instrumentality. This model, promoted by M.-J. Lagrange, was based on the work of the Church Fathers who used the images of the musical instrument, the pen of the scribe, and the members of the body to express how God uses the human authors as his instruments. Vatican II's document on divine revelation reaffirmed the Church's traditional teaching on the divine and human origins of Scripture, adopting implicitly this last model.[13]

Inspiration in *Dei Verbum*

The third chapter of *Dei Verbum* addresses briefly in three articles the question of the divine inspiration of Scripture and its interpretation.

---

13 For a more detailed summary of the models of inspiration, see Vogels, "L'Écriture, inspirée et inspirante," 269–78; "Three Possible Models of Inspiration," in *Scrittura Ispirata*, ed. Izquierdo, 64–69; Richard F. Smith, SJ, "Inspiration and Inerrancy," in *The Jerome Biblical Commentary*, ed. Raymond Brown, Joseph A. Fitzmyer, and Roland E. Murphy (Englewood Cliffs, NJ: Prentice Hall Inc., 1968), 505–506; Raymond F. Collins, "Inspiration," in *The New Jerome Biblical Commentary*, ed. Brown, Fitzmyer, and Murphy (London: Geoffrey Chapman, 1990), 1023–33. For a more detailed treatment, see, A. M. Artola, *De la revelación a la inspiración. Los origenes de la moderna teología católica sobre la inspiración bíblica*, Institución San Jeronimo 16 (Valencia: Ediciones Mensajero, 1983).

In number eleven, the council fathers affirm the relationship between revelation and inspiration: God's revelation is made known through the inspiration of the Holy Spirit and, consequently, all the books of the Old and New Testaments are sacred and canonical because they are written under the inspiration of the Holy Spirit. The document maintains a careful balance between the role of God and the role of the human writers: although God is the author of Sacred Scripture, the books of the Bible were also composed by men who used all their powers and faculties in order to include in them all that God intended. The council fathers, therefore, rejected the dictation model of inspiration. Although they avoided the use of the term "inerrancy," the council fathers also affirmed that since the Scriptures are inspired they teach without error all that is necessary for our salvation: the truth of the Bible is not concerned with historical or scientific exactitude but with transmitting the truth about God and his relationship with humanity.

The dual nature of the Scriptures impacts on their interpretation. Since they are human texts, the Scriptures must be submitted to scientific study that includes the literary genre, the historical and cultural context in which they were written, and the language used by the human authors. On the other hand, because the Scriptures have also God as their author, exegetes must also take into consideration the content and the unity of all the books of the Bible, as well as the Church's tradition and the rule of faith.[14] In other words, the ultimate goal of exegesis is to reveal God's Word and not simply to understand the historical and cultural elements in the texts.

Dei Verbum did not define inspiration, nor did it delve into the mode of inspiration:

> *Dei Verbum* also leaves some questions without complete answers. For example, although it asserts the doctrine of inspiration of the Scriptures, it does not describe how inspiration works. How do the divine author and the human authors interact in such a way that both are true authors? How does the Holy Spirit operate in this process? How does the Bible respect human literary qualities while embodying the divine message? These are the kinds of issues about inspiration that the constitution leaves open-ended.[15]

---

14 *DV*, 12.

15 Ronald D. Witherup, *Scripture: Dei Verbum, Rediscovering Vatican II* (New York:

Dei Verbum has opened the door for further investigation into the doctrine of inspiration. We now turn to an overview of the work done by Catholic scholars in the years since Vatican II.

An Overview of the Work of Catholic Scholars since *Dei Verbum*

In the years since the promulgation of *Dei Verbum*, there have been numerous studies on the biblical canon but fewer on the question of inspiration.[16] There have been, however, in the last few years two symposia, both of which took place in Rome. The first, held in 1999 on the interpretation of the Bible in the Church, was promoted by the Congregation for the Doctrine of the Faith, and it included two papers on biblical inspiration. The second, in 2001, promoted by the Pontificio Ateneo *Regina Apostolorum*, was dedicated entirely to the theme of inspired Scripture.[17]

In these symposia, the question of inspiration was examined from different perspectives: the biblical statements on inspiration,[18] the relationship of inspiration to the process of canonization,[19] its relationship

---

Paulist Press, 2006), 57. For a commentary on chapter three of *Dei Verbum*, see also, René Latourelle, *Comment Dieu se révèle au monde: lecture commentée de la Constitution de Vatican II sur la Parole de Dieu*, Collection Héritage et projet 60 (Québec: Fides, 1998), 47–57.

16 See Antonio María Artola and José Manuel Sánchez Caro, *Bibbia e Parola di Dio*, ed. Antonio Zani, Introduzione allo Studio della Bibbia 2 (Brescia: Paideia Editrice, 1994; Spanish original 1989); Lee Martin McDonald and James A. Sanders, eds., *The Canon Debate* (Peabody, MA: Hendrickson Publishers, 2002); Jaroslav Pelikan, *Whose Bible Is It? A History of the Scriptures Through the Ages* (New York: Viking, 2005); Craig C. Bartholomew, Scott Hahn, Robin Perry, Christopher Seitz, and Al Wolters, eds., *Canon and Biblical Interpretation*, Scripture and Hermeneutics Series 7 (Milton Keynes–Grand Rapids: Paternoster–Zondervan, 2006).

17 The proceedings of both symposia have been published. See Prosper Grech, Jean-Noël Aletti, Marc Ouellet, and Horacio Simian-Yofre, eds., *L'Interpretazione della Bibbia nella Chiesa. Atti del Simposio promosso dalla Congregazione per la Dottrina della Fede* (Città del Vaticano: Libreria Editrice del Vaticano, 2001), and Izquierdo, ed., *Scrittura Ispirata.*

18 Fabris, "In che senso," 41–60.

19 Michelangelo Tábet, "Ispirazione e canonicità dei Libri Sacri," in *Scrittura Ispirata*, ed. Izquierdo, 80–117; for an Orthodox perspective see, Petros Vassiliadis, "Inspiration, Canon and Authority of Scripture: An Orthodox Hermeneutical Perspective," in *Scrittura Ispirata*, ed. Izquierdo, 193–210.

with exegetical methods,[20] and its relationship with the sacred writings of other faiths.[21]

The Contribution of Walter Vogels

Among the scholars who participated in the latter symposium is Walter Vogels. His understanding of inspiration derives from his understanding of the nature of a book and in particular of a biblical book.[22] He sets the groundwork for his theory with an overview and critique of the classical modes of inspiration.

Vogels asserts that the traditional modes of inspiration mentioned above are all based on the understanding of a book as the work of an individual. According to this model, a book is written by one author who takes full responsibility for its contents. Furthermore, this understanding of authorship presupposes that the mode of written communication is similar to that of oral communication. As in the case of the listener, the reader's goal is to understand what the author intends to communicate. In other words, he or she seeks to discover the authorial intent behind the text. In accordance with this understanding, the books of the Bible have been traditionally attributed to individual writers, mostly prophets for the Old Testament and apostles for the New Testament. Consequently, inspiration is a gift given to the individual writers so that they might transmit God's Word. The original theory of the mode of inspiration was, as noted above, dictation. Vogels points out several difficulties with this theory: how do we explain the

20 Gianantonio Borgonovo, "Una proposta di rilettura dell'ispirazione biblica dopo gli apporti della Form- e Redaktionsgeschichte," in *L'Interpretazione della Bibbia*, ed. Grech, Aletti, Ouellet, and Simian-Yofre, 41–63; Antonio María Artola, "Los nuevos métodos de exégesis y la comprensión de la Inspiración bíblica," in *Scrittura Ispirata*, ed. Izquierdo, 132–66.

21 Angelo Amato, "Ispirazione biblica e « ispirazione » dei Libri Sacri delle altre religioni," in *Scrittura Ispirata*, ed. Izquierdo, 167–90.

22 Walter Vogels's writings on inspiration include several articles: "Inspiration in a Linguistic Mode," in *Biblical Theology Bulletin* 15 (1985): 87–93; the entry "Inspiration," in *Dictionnaire encyclopédique de la Bible*, eds. Pierre-Maurice Bogaert, Matthias Delcor, Edmond Jacob, Édouard Lipinski, Robert Martin-Achard, and Joseph Ponthot (Turnhout: Brepols, 1987), 614–17; "L'Écriture, inspirée et inspirante," in Duhaime and Mainville, *Entendre la voix du Dieu vivant*, 261–96; and "Three Possible Models of Inspiration," in *Scrittura Ispirata*, ed. Izquierdo, 61–79.

repetitions, contradictions, and errors in the biblical texts? This model privileges the role of God but reduces the human author to a simple scribe or secretary.[23]

As Walter Vogels has indicated, however, the other traditional modes of inspiration that were proposed as correctives to the dictation model also pose difficulties. The theory of subsequent inspiration or approbation claims that divine approbation was given after the final redaction of the book, but this subsequent divine approval remains difficult to verify.[24] The theory of concomitant inspiration protects the role of the human author but reduces God to a supervisor who prevents error from entering the text. Franzelin's theory of formal inspiration tries to understand the role of God and that of the human authors by differentiating between content and form, between idea and word, a distinction that is challenged by psychology and linguistics. In fact, there is no thought that is not expressed simultaneously in the form of a word. According to Vogels, of all classical models, that of instrumentality takes best into account the roles of God and the human authors. Nevertheless, like the other models, its difficulty lies in the fact that it also presupposes that the biblical texts are authored by individuals, a preconception that has been challenged by modern studies.[25]

Historical criticism has revealed that the biblical books have a complicated history of composition. Often various sources are at the origin of a book, sources that have been reinterpreted by subsequent generations before being used to give final shape to the biblical book. In some cases, these sources are of pagan origin, such as the Mesopotamian creation and flood myths. Identifying the sacred author is, therefore, not a simple task and it is not at all certain that the author to whom a particular book is ascribed is in fact the author. This raises questions as to who is inspired: is it the final redactor or does it include all those who have contributed to the composition of the text, with the exception of the authors of the profane sources? In this case, one can speak of the

23 Vogels, "Three Possible Models of Inspiration," 64–66.

24 B. D. Heneberg suggests that the approval by the Church to include a book in the canon is the sign of its inspired nature.

25 Vogels, "Three Possible Models of Inspiration," 66–69.

inspiration of the community, Israel, and the Church, rather than the inspiration of an individual author.[26]

Walter Vogels proposes a third model—a linguistic text model. According to him, the difficulty with both the individual author model and the community model is that both attempt to discover the authorial intent. The reason for the focus on authorial intent is that both models fail to make a distinction between oral and written communication. Authorial intent is identified in the one case with the individual author, in the other case with the historical context in which the various authors/redactors wrote.[27]

To understand the concept of inspiration, Vogels begins with recent studies on the nature of a text, namely the work of Paul Ricœur. Vogels shows how oral communication differs from written communication. In oral communication, the speaker and the listener are in immediate contact, even in the case of a telephone conversation. The speaker, for example, can verify with the listener if she or he has understood what has been said. In the case of a written text, there is no direct communication between the author and the reader; the text constitutes an object in itself and is an intermediary between the author and the reader.[28] Furthermore, the acts of writing and reading are not done simultaneously; in fact in the case of the biblical texts, they are separated by centuries. Written communication, therefore, consists of three elements, namely, the writer, the text, and the reader.

In writing a text, an author usually composes various drafts, each time making corrections, revisions, or additions, or eliminating text. At the end of the process, however, when the text is published, no further changes can be made and the text takes on an existence independent of the author. The reader may not necessarily understand everything that the author intended to write. As Vogels states, this is a common experience in letter writing—or e-mail communication—where the reader misunderstands the original message, the tone, or the intent.

---

26 Ibid., 69–73.

27 Ibid., 73.

28 "Inscription fixates a discourse and produces for us an autonomy of a text, not only vis-à-vis its author/speaker, but also vis-à-vis its immediate ostensive context and its addressee." John van den Hengel, *The Home of Meaning: the Hermeneutics of the Subject of Paul Ricœur* (Washington: University of America Press, 1982), 195–96.

The published text takes on an existence independent of the author. The text, however, is dormant or dead until someone reads it. The act of reading is done independently of the author; as Vogels says, the reader gives new life to the text or rewrites it. The act of reading, however, obeys the rules of the text itself: although various interpretations are possible, there are also certain interpretations that are excluded by the text. New meanings are possible because there are always new readers in different contexts or because a reader rereads a text from the perspective of a new context.

What are the implications of this understanding of the nature of a text for the question of inspiration? Walter Vogels notes that for both the individual and the communal models, inspiration is attached to the process of writing, hence with the person or persons who produce the text: the inspired author. The linguistic model, however, emphasizes the inspired text, and the inspired quality of the text influences both activities tied to it, writing and reading.[29]

Walter Vogels continues, therefore, that the biblical text is inspired because it is written under the inspiration of the Holy Spirit, that is, in all its process of formation. It is, however, also inspired because it is read by believers:

> And so secondly, the Bible as text has its unique privilege of inspiration because the faith community of readers, in which the same Spirit is at work, can identify with that Bible. A reading community sees in the Bible a revelation of God. She discovers the inspired character of the Bible, because the text reveals it to her and not because the author who is dead since centuries says that his text is inspired.[30]

As Vogels says, this is not to say that the text is inspired because the Synagogue or the Church has made a decision; rather

> the text itself, thanks to its unique production, has a quality which gives it the power to stimulate and to nourish the faith of readers since centuries. The same Spirit who was at work in the community which has created (written) the book, is equally at work

29 Vogels, "Three Possible Models of Inspiration," 75.

30 Ibid., 76.

> in the community which recreates (reads) that book. The Bible is the link between the community which has produced it and the community which reproduces it, both acting under the Spirit.[31]

As with the individual reader, the changing circumstances and conditions of the community allow it to discover new meanings. And it is only the believing community that can discover the limits of the text, the possible readings that it allows.

Conclusion

The contribution Walter Vogels has made to the understanding of inspiration is significant. Three points merit commentary. First, his approach, from the perspective of the nature of a written text, is unique. It is a helpful way to reflect on a unique literary corpus unlike other classical literature, to understand the mystery of Sacred Scripture as divine and human text. Second, he stresses the importance of the reader. Recently, the role of the reader in the interpretation of the text has been emphasized by reader-response theories. What is significant, however, in his work is the primacy of the faith community as reader. The Bible is first and foremost the book of the Church, and the Church is the first reader. In fact, his model relates to the Catholic Church's teaching on the roles of tradition and Scripture: tradition precedes Scripture and follows Scripture. Scripture is a moment in ongoing tradition that continually reads the Tradition and earlier texts in light of new situations. This is reflected in the Bible itself where the Bible interprets itself. The Bible is certainly read by individual readers, but those individuals are situated within a faith tradition and individual readings are guided by the Church's reading of the Scriptures.[32]

Finally, there is a connection between his understanding of inspiration and the role of the canon in the interpretation of the biblical texts. One of the aims of canonical criticism is to investigate

---

[31] Ibid., 76.

[32] "L'acte de lecture s'inclut ainsi dans une communauté lisante, qui, dans certaines conditions favorables, développe la sorte de normativité et de canonicité que nous reconnaissons aux grandes œuvres, celles qui n'ont jamais fini de se décontextualiser et de se recontextualiser dans les circonstances culturelles les plus variées." Paul Ricœur, *Temps et récit*, L'ordre philosophique (Paris: Éditions du Seuil, 1985), 3: 262.

how the canon is a hermeneutical key for interpreting the texts: older traditions or texts are reinterpreted and placed in new contexts by later writers. This is because the inspired and inspiring text brings forth new meanings. For a while, this process was incorporated into the biblical text itself; from the second century onward, this work has been done apart from the text.

Dei Verbum dealt very briefly with the concept of inspiration: it emphasized the roles of the divine and human authors and spoke of the truth of the Bible rather than its inerrancy. Vatican II, however, has opened the door for ongoing fruitful reflection, including the question of the mode of inspiration. The work of Walter Vogels is a significant contribution to that discourse and is an invitation to further study.

PART II

CANADIAN PARTICIPATION AT THE COUNCIL AND AFTERWARDS / PARTICIPATION CANADIENNE AU CONCILE ET APRÈS

SECTION I

The Activity of the Canadian Bishops / L'activité des évêques canadiens

Cardinal Paul-Émile Léger and the Establishment of the Mixed Commission on Revelation[1]

Karim Schelkens,
Katholieke Universiteit Leuven

This article investigates the role of one of Canada's most prominent voices at the Second Vatican Council, that of Cardinal Paul-Émile Léger, from material found in several archival collections.[2] In recent years, several publications have already documented

[1] The research conducted for this publication was made possible by the Fondation Gérard-Dion and is the result of a research stay at the Université Laval, Québec. I owe great thanks to Professor Gilles Routhier for his guidance in my research, as well as to canon Leo Declerck for his precious remarks on the manuscript.

[2] The present article is based upon research in several archives, kept in various centres:
1. Bibliothèque du Séminaire de Montréal (BSM): Archives cardinal Paul-Émile Léger, courtesy of the Fondation Jules et Paul-Émile Léger, Montréal. Inventoried by Pierre Lafontaine, *Inventaire des archives conciliaires du Fonds Paul-Émile Léger* (Montréal, 1995); Archives André Naud. Inventoried by Pierre Lafontaine, *Inventaire des archives conciliaires du fonds André Naud* (Cahiers de recherche sur Vatican II 1) (Québec, 1998); Archives Pierre Lafortune. Inventoried by Pierre Lafontaine, *Inventaire du fonds Pierre Lafortune* (Cahiers de recherche sur Vatican II 3) (Québec, 2005).

Léger's conciliar activities, making clear that Léger was—in the context of Vatican II—omnipresent.[3] Therefore, this contribution simply cannot

2. Archivio Segreto Vaticano (ASV), Rome: Vatican City.
3. University of Notre Dame Archives (UND), Hesburgh Library, Notre Dame, Indiana.
4. Centre Lumen Gentium (CLG), Université Catholique de Louvain, Louvain-la-Neuve: Archives Charles Moeller and Gustave Thils. Inventoried by Claude Soetens, *Concile Vatican II et Eglise contemporaine (Archives de Louvain-la-Neuve)*. I. *Inventaire des Fonds Ch. Moeller, G. Thils, Fr. Houtart* (Cahiers de la Revue théologique de Louvain 21) (Louvain-la-Neuve, 1989).
5. Center for the Study of the Second Vatican Council (CSVII), Katholieke Universiteit Leuven: Archives Emiel-Jozef De Smedt. Inventoried by Alois Greiler and Luc de Saeger, *Emiel-Jozef De Smedt, Papers Vatican II. Inventory* (Instrumenta Theologica 22) (Leuven, 1999); Archives Edward Schillebeeckx.
6. Archives of the Archdiocese of Mechelen-Brussels (AAM): Archives Leo-Joseph Suenens. See Leo Declerck and Eddy Louchez, *Inventaire des papiers conciliaires du cardinal L.J. Suenens* (Cahiers de la Revue théologique de Louvain 31) (Louvain-la-Neuve, 1998).
7. Istituto per le Scienze Religiose (ISR), Bologna: Archives Angelo Giuseppe Roncalli/John XXIII; Archives Giacomo Lercaro.
8. Archives de l'archidiocèse de Québec (AAQ): Archdiocese of Québec, Archives Crépeault.
9. Archives diocésaines de Sherbrooke (ADS): Diocese of Sherbrooke: Archives Georges Cabana.
10. Catholic University of Washington (CUA): Diary Joseph Clifford Fenton.
11. Archives of the Archdiocese of New York (AANY): Saint-Joseph Seminary, Dunwoodie, NY: Archives James Henry Griffiths.
12. Archives Deschâtelets (ADE), Oblates of Mary Immaculate, Ottawa: Archives Marcel Bélanger.
13. Archives of the Jesuit Province of Germany (AJPG), Munich: Archives Otto Semmelroth. Furthermore, references are often made to the official acts of Vatican II, published in the *Acta Synodalia Sacrosancti Concilii Œcumenici Vaticani II* (*AS*) and the *Acta et Documenta Concilio Œcumenico Vaticano II apparando. Series II. Praeparatoria* (*AD*).

[3] André Naud, "Le Cardinal Léger au Concile," *L'Église de Montréal* 109 (1991): 1086–87; André Naud, "Le cardinal Léger au Concile et la conduite de l'intelligence chrétienne," in *L'Église canadienne et Vatican II*, Héritage et projet 58, ed. Gilles Routhier (Montréal: Fides, 1997), 237–63; Gilles Routhier, "L'itinéraire d'un père conciliaire. Le cardinal Léger," *Cristianesimo nella Storia* 19, no. 1 (1998): 89–147; Riccardo Burigana and Gilles Routhier, "La conversion œcuménique du cardinal Léger et de l'église de Montréal au moment de Vatican II." Part I: "Les premiers ébranlements." Part II: "L'engagement résolu," *Science et Esprit* 52, no. 2–3 (2000): 171–91, 293–319; Gilles Routhier, "Léger et Suenens. Les relations difficiles de deux princes de l'Église," in *The Belgian Contribution to Vatican II*, Bibliotheca Ephemeridum Theologicae Lovaniensis 216, ed. Doris Donnelly, Joseph Famerée, Mathijs Lamberigts, and Karim Schelkens (Leuven, Peeters 2005). For a survey of more general literature on Léger, see Lafontaine, *Inventaire Léger*, 9. Also see the recent notice on him in Jean LeBlanc, *Dictionnaire biographique des évêques catholiques du Canada. Les diocèses catholiques canadiens des Églises latines et orientales et leurs évêques. Repères chronologiques et biographiques 1658-2002* (Montréal, Wilson & Lafleur 2002), 608–12.

study the full scope of Léger's actions, let alone the entire story of his involvement in the council's revelation debate, on which it will focus. On that debate too, much research has already been conducted.[4] It remains a *communis opinio* among Vatican II historians that particularly the November 1962 debate on the schema *De Fontibus Revelationis*, which ultimately led to the establishment of a mixed commission, and forced the Doctrinal Commission and the Secretariat for Christian Unity to join efforts, constitutes a landmark event of Vatican II history. Besides being a crucial step for the revelation debate, and a turning point for the first conciliar period, it was decisive for the council's entire further development. What I intend to do, based upon archival documentation, is to grasp the way in which the Montréal cardinal was involved in the revelation debate, keeping in mind several factors that have helped shape his interventions. While I had originally foreseen a paper that would include a study of Léger's role as president of subcommission five of the aforementioned Mixed Commission on Revelation, the abundance of source material has forced me to restrict myself to a study of his role up until the establishment of the mixed commission, and his involvement in bringing about the very decision to establish said commission.

The Central Preparatory Commission

In order to assess how Paul-Émile Léger dealt with the first period debate on the revelation schema, it is useful to take a few steps back. Specifically in Léger's case, this is revealing. Léger was involved, more than just informally, in various redactorial stages of the draft. So, a bit of preconciliar history is required.[5] As is evident from the Vatican

---

4 Umberto Betti, *La dottrina del Concilio Vaticano II sulla trasmissione della Rivelazione. Il Capitolo II della Costituzione dommatica Dei Verbum*, Spicilegium Pontificii Athenaei Antonianum 26 (Rome, 1985); Riccardo Burigana, "Progetto dogmatico del Vaticano II. La Commissione teologica preparatoria (1960–1962)," in *Verso il Concilio. Passaggi e problemi della preparazione conciliare*, Testi e Ricerche di Scienze Religiose (TRSR), Nuova Serie 11, ed. Giuseppe Alberigo and Alberto Melloni (Genova, Il Mulino 1993), 141–206; Riccardo Burigana, *La Bibbia nel Concilio. La redazione della costituzione 'Dei Verbum' del Vaticano II*, TRSR, Nuova Serie 21, (Bologna, Il Mulino 1998); Hanjo Sauer, *Erfahrung und Glaube. Die Begründung des pastoralen Prinzips durch die Offenbarungskonstitution des II. Vatikanischen Konzils*, Würzburger Studien zur Fundamentaltheologie 12 (Frankfurt am Main, Peter Lang 1993).

5 On this episode, see Burigana, *La Bibbia nel Concilio*, 80–866; and Karim Schelkens,

Archives, the *Schema De Fontibus* originates in the summer of 1960, when the Dutch Jesuit Sebastian Tromp only just appointed secretary to the Preparatory Theological Commission, drafted its very first version and gave it the title *Schema de Sacra Scriptura.*[6] That title is not altogether unimportant in order to understand the nature of what would become the schema *De Fontibus*. Without going into detail here, a closer look at the document's redaction history would reveal it as being first and foremost a draft on the Catholic Church's dealings with Scripture and with exegesis. In contrast to some other approaches, and quite justifiably, this scriptural preference is the lens that allows Léger his particular perspective on the text. In fact, the small core group of theologians who actually wrote the draft consisted almost entirely of biblical scholars. And it is interesting, yet not surprising therefore, that in the Central Preparatory Commission's discussion of it, the most salient and pertinent comments on the text come from Cardinal Augustin Bea, former rector of the Pontifical Biblical Institute that had recently been victimized by several professors of the Lateran University.[7] Also, Bea's critiques on the draft paid hardly any attention to the issue that later would be so controversial: that of the (in)sufficiency of Scripture with regard to tradition. But Bea's remarks are of interest for our story on Léger.

The Montréal cardinal was also a member of the Central Preparatory Commission (CC)[8] and took part in the discussions on several schemata in November 1961. He had been absent from the CC's first session in Rome, held in March 1961, so the discussions on the revelation draft

---

Catholic Theology of Revelation on the Eve of Vatican II. A Redaction History of the Schema De Fontibus Revelationis, Series in Church History 41 (Leiden and Boston, Brill Publishers 2010).

6 ASV: Conc. Vat. II, 736, 56: S. Tromp, Constitutio de Sacra Scriptura. Primum tentamen.

7 It should be noted though, that these attacks were hardly welcomed by TC Secretary Tromp, nor by the subcommission secretary, Salvatore Garofalo. See Anthony Dupont and Karim Schelkens, "Katholische Exegese vor dem Zweiten Vatikanischen Konzil (1960–1961)," *Zeitschrift für Katholische Theologie* 132, no. 1 (2010): 1-24.

8 BSM: Archives Léger, 10: John XXIII to Paul-Émile Léger, Letter of appointment to the Central Preparatory Commission, 15 June 1960. Léger already knew of the nomination beforehand, given the fact that he sent a letter of thanks to John XXIII already on June 8, 1960.

would be one of the first he attended, or to be more precise: his third intervention, after his initial votum on the participation of non-Catholic observers,[9] and a second intervention regarding the new profession of the faith[10] in which he had also followed Bea's advice.

On November 10, 1961, the members of the Central Preparatory Commission gathered to discuss the revelation draft, which had been introduced and defended by Cardinal Alfredo Ottaviani and the secretary, Sebastian Tromp, the day before. Tromp had made the finishing touches to the document on October 4 before sending it to the Vatican Polyglot Press. On October 14 an edition was printed and later distributed among the CC members.[11] Regulations provided for a voting round to be held at the end of debate on any given schema and a two-thirds majority required to declare a schema fit for council debate. This, however, wasn't quite the case for the schema on the sources of revelation. Although the draft had raised discussions within the previous plenary meetings of the Preparatory Theological Commission, the tone of discussion on November 9 and 10 was quite different.

When the final five-chaptered schema—with the first chapter on the relationship between Scripture and tradition; the second dealing with the issues of Scripture's inspiration, its inerrant nature, and its literary composition; the third and fourth chapters devoted to the Old and New Testaments; and the final chapter discussing the Church's relationship to the Scriptures—was introduced to the Central Commission, Ottaviani quickly argued that the foregoing draft resulted from serious study and debate among international scholars. Still, the atmosphere quickly turned against the schema, even though of all seventy-eight TC members present only nine actually raised their voices. Criticism mainly came from Cardinals Franz König, Julius Döpfner, and Bernard Alfrink, yet their interventions were very brief. As mentioned, it was mainly Cardinal Bea who disagreed with the schema[12]—quite scandalizing

---

9 *AD* II/1, 473. Compare BSM: Archives Lafortune 209.

10 See *AD* II/1, 517. Also see BSM: Archives Lafortune 210.

11 *AD* II/2.1, 523–62.

12 *AD* II/2.1, 546–49. On Bea's remarks, also see Antonino Indelicato, *Difendere la dottrina o annunciare l'evangelo. Il dibattito nella Commissione centrale preparatoria del Vaticano II*, Testi e ricerche di scienze religiose. Nuova Serie 8 (Genova: Il Mulino, 1992),

Tromp and Garofalo—and launched an elaborate and detailed attack of the draft, not once mentioning the draft's first chapter. Instead, Bea made a warm plea for exegetical freedom, fulminated against the condemning propositions in Articles 21 and 22 on the historicity of the Scriptures, and criticized the schema's viewpoints on scriptural infallibility. In contrast to this, Léger's response was very concise and harkened back to Cardinal Bea's intervention. In general it is interesting to see that Léger's final appreciation of the text was not fully disapproving, rather he voted *placet iuxta modum.*[13] And as for his main concerns, they are hardly in the field of revelation theology. Léger only touches upon two issues: the education of seminarians on dealing with Scripture and the relationships between theology and exegesis. Both issues deal only with the fifth chapter of *De Fontibus*, on the Church and the Scriptures.

To better understand Léger's interest at this juncture, we should point out that both elements were among the concerns that resulted out of the *Questionnaire en vue du IIème Concile du Vatican*. Léger had sent this question list to both the secular and regular clergy of his archdiocese on October 10, 1961,[14] a month before the Central Commission gathered. The reactions to the *enquête,*[15] particularly regarding its questions eight[16] and twelve,[17] explicitly display the Montréal clergy's sense of need for an open approach toward propagating the results of the Biblical Movement among priests and seminarians. In the analysis made at the level of the archdiocese, the possibility was therefore raised of improving the study program of the Montréal Seminary in this sense.

But let us return to the voting round of the Central Preparatory Commission. In the end,[18] only two *non placet* votes were uttered, and

---

86–90.

13 *AD* II/2.1, 557.

14 BSM: Archives Léger, 132–33 : Circular letter and seven-page questionnaire containing forty-nine questions.

15 See Pierre Lafontaine, "L'enquête préconciliaire de l'archidiocèse de Montréal, auprès du clergé. Portrait d'une Église," in *L'Église canadienne et Vatican II*, 80–98. An overview of the questionnaire is found as an appendix to this publication.

16 BSM: Archive Léger, 145.

17 BSM: Archive Léger, 149.

18 *AD* II, 2/1, 554–63.

a mere four members voted *placet* on the biblical schema. Four cardinals abstained, which implies that the sixty-eight remaining members voted *placet iuxta modum*—no less than fifty-one of them referring to Bea's remarks. So, notwithstanding the fact that he had some personal interest, Léger went with the stream, leaving us with a false impression that revelation theology wasn't very dear to his heart. The impression is not quite right, given Léger's apparent interest in another draft that also dealt with revelation theology, a text that, among others, harked back to *Humani Generis*'s sharp disapproval of the *Nouvelle théologie* movement. Roughly speaking, the schema *De Deposito Fidei* contained an overall view of revelation as a set of revealed propositions and further dealt with issues such as the debate on monogenism and the positions of Pierre Teilhard de Chardin, a topic on which Léger shared feelings with Henri de Lubac and had delivered a speech to the *Société Médicale de Montréal* on January 25, 1961.[19] And, in some contrast to the topic of the *De Fontibus*, Léger's archives do contain a good deal of material preparing his reaction to the *De Deposito* draft in the Central Commission.[20] His interest in it becomes even more tangible when one reads the well-known *supplique* he sent to John XXIII on September 11, 1962,[21] with the support of future council protagonists, such as Cardinals Joseph Frings, Julius Döpfner, Franz König, Leo-Joseph Suenens, Bernard Alfrink, and Achille Liénart. Still, to illustrate his minimal interest in the schema on the sources once again: Léger's letter to the Pope would discuss all of the first series of drafts from the Theological Commission, except *De Fontibus*.

---

19 Paul-Émile Léger, "Les Origines de l'homme," in *Trente textes du cardinal Léger qui ont marqué l'Église au Concile et au Québec*, Foi et liberté (Montréal: Fies, 1968), 5–27. See BSM: Archives Léger, Agenda Léger, 25 January 1961: Conférence aux médecins, Université.

20 BSM: Archives Léger, 1136–37. Here, too, Léger had reactions prepared by his theological advisors, see Archives Naud, 461–83;

21 BSM: Archives Léger: Letter from Léger to John XXIII, 11 September. Also Archives Lafortune, 211. The archives contain a full dossier on this, which has formed the basis for an elaborate article on the supplication by Gilles Routhier, "Les réactions du cardinal Léger à la préparation de Vatican II," *Revue d'histoire de l'église de France* 80 (1994): 281–302. The text of this letter to John XXIII was published in Brigitte Caulier and Gilles Routhier, eds., *Mémoires de Vatican II* (Montréal: Fides, 1997), 93–113. Also see AAM: Archives Suenens, 393–94.

Admittedly, up until this point, the result remains a bit shallow. However, Léger's preconciliar involvement with *De Fontibus* did not end with his succinct remark of November 1961. After the CC had voted upon the schema, it was transferred to the CC Subcommission on Amendments to be revised. The Subcommission on Amendments consisted of five cardinals: Carlo Confalonieri, Clemens Micara, Giuseppe Siri, Santiago Copello, and Léger. This subcommission was to revise the draft, in line with the reactions of the CC members. Given the attacks on the draft, one would expect some adaptations. However, procedure did not require the cardinals to revise the drafts themselves but allowed for the set up of a small *ad hoc* Revisions Commission that would consist of three persons belonging to the commission responsible for the schema. *Ergo* the Theological Commission got to revise its own text, and Ottaviani was to set up the *ad hoc* commission after he had received a report and a letter from Confalonieri on December 4, 1962.[22] The Revisions Commission consisted of Sebastian Tromp, Luigi Ciappi, and Salvatore Garofalo (president to the TC subcommission *De Fontibus*), and actually met just once. In preparation for their meeting, Tromp singlehandedly prepared a full report—which he discussed with Garofalo—and on January 3, 1962,[23] the Revisions Subcommission met with Cardinal Ottaviani.

The outcome of the meeting is quite revealing: they propose only minor adaptations in the text, and for the most part neglect Cardinal Bea's comments. Their argument was a juridical one, claiming that changes requested by just one member could not be accepted. This in fact neglected the reception of Bea's line of argument (with explicit references) by a vast majority of CC members. In the end, the report of this small group[24] turned out to be more a defense than a revision of the

[22] ASV: Conc. Vat. II, 744.176, Letter from Confalonieri to Alfredo Ottaviani: "Secondo le auguste disposizioni del Santo Padre, l'Eminenza Vostra è pregata di far esaminare le proposte stesse unitamente dal Segretario della Commissione, cui Ella presiede, dal Redattore dello Schema, cui gli emendamenti si riferiscono, e da un Esperto di Sua fiducia, con il compito di riferire quali degli emendamenti proposti siano da accogliere ed indicare i motivi di rigetto per quelle che non dovrebbero essere accettati."

[23] Alexandra von Teuffenbach, *Konzilstagebuch Sebastian Tromp s.j. Mit Erläuterungen und Akten aus der Arbeit der theologischen Kommission (1960–1962)*, 2 vols. (Rome: Editirice Gregoriana, 2006), 347.

[24] ASV: Conc. Vat. II, 745.182, Pontificia Commissio Theologica. Responsio ab

schema.[25] This report, and a slightly altered schema, *De Fontibus*, went back to Confalonieri, who contacted Léger and the other three cardinals on January 16, inviting them for what would be the first meeting of the Amendment Subcommission on January 22.[26]

Léger had already left for France four days prior to Confalonieri's invitation, and arrived at Leonardo da Vinci Airport on January 14 to take part in the CC debate on the schema *De Deposito*. On January 22 his agenda reads: "Sous-commission de emendationibus chez cardinal Micara." The report of the meeting in Micara's apartment is very concise, and as to the schema *De Fontibus*, the subcommission fully endorsed all decisions made by the Theological Commission.[27] A bit frustrated on this procedure, Yves Congar jotted down these words: "Le P. de Lubac me dit que la Commission centrale transmet ses remarques à une petite commission prise dans la nôtre, qui fait un peu ce qu'elle veut et fait entériner ses réponses ou modifications par un groupe de cinq cardinaux."[28]

So, my case has just become even worse: Léger took part in an important meeting but again he didn't seem to have taken great interest in the schema, nor did he take action against it. This is clear when

observationes factas in commissione centrali ad schema constitutionis de Fontibus Revelationis.

25 Burigana, *La Bibbia nel Concilio*, 83

26 *AD* II, 4/3.1. Letter from Confalonieri to Siri, Micara, Copello, and Léger, 16 January 1962: "Mi onoro rimettere all'Eminenza Vostra Reverendissima la relazione preparata per gli emendamenti da apportare agli schemi dei decreti discussi nella riunione plenaria della Pontificia Commissione Centrale dello scorso mese di novembre. Alla relazione sono allegati gli schemi che dovranno essere emendati. In essi l'Eminenza Vostra Rev. ma troverà già introdotte delle modifiche: si riferiscono agli emendamenti proposti dai Membri della Pont. Commissione Centrale ed accettati dalla Commissione che ha preparato lo schema. Il lavoro della nostro Sottocommissione verterà, perciò, soltanto sulle proposte che non sono state condivise dalle Commissioni che hanno proposto gli schemi. Sono quindi, a pregarLa di voler partecipare alla riunione che avrà luogo lunedì 22 alle ore 16.30 nella sala delle Congregazioni del Palazzo Apostolico."

27 *AD* II, 4/3.1, 98-107, Processus verbalis. Also see *AD* II, 4/3.1. Relazione (Vincenzo Fagiolo), 109–12, see 112: "VII – De Fontibus Revelationis. Le numerose osservazioni, che la Commissione Centrale aveva fatto su questo schema, sono state esaminate con particolare attenzione dalla Commissione ridotta teologica. Il testo originario, quindi è stato in più punti modificato. In altri non ha subíto modifiche, nonostante i rilievi mossi da qualche Membro della Commissione Centrale."

28 Yves Congar, *Mon Journal du Concile*, ed. Éric Mahieu, 2 vols. (Paris: Cerf, 2002), Vol. 1: March 5, 1962, 89.

one reads the report of the Amendments Subcommission, which states bluntly: "Non è quindi da rimproverare alla Commissione Teologica —come qualche Membro della Commissione Centrale sembra aver fatto—di poca sensibilità verso gli studiosi e di aver redatto una schema poco positive."[29]

We might conclude that when Henry F. Davis of Canada's Department of External Affairs informs Canada's Prime Minister on September 4, 1962, that "Cardinal Léger has been extremely active" in the conciliar preparations, this may well be true in a number of cases, yet it is hardly the case for our topic.[30] As for the schema itself, it was sent to the Vatican Presses again,[31] now to be distributed among the council fathers in July 1962, as a part of the first series of drafts.[32]

The Council's Revelation Debate and Léger's Intervention

Four months later, after the distribution of the text, the council began debating the draft on the sources of revelation. And, immediately on the first day of the debate, November 14, 1962, Paul-Émile Léger was among those to take the stand and comment on this draft with which he was all too familiar.[33] In considerable contrast to his earlier, and some-

---

[29] See *AD* II, 4/3.1,100: "La Sottocommissione ha infine osservato che lo schema, attesa la delicatezza della materia, è da conservare nell'impostazione ad esso data dalla Commissione Teologica, la quale per necessità ha dovuto prendere posizioni precise e di condanna di errori, a tutela della Fede. Non è quindi da rimproverare alla Commissione Teologica – come qualche Membro della Commissione Centrale sembra aver fatto – di poca sensibilità verso gli studiosi e di aver redatto una schema poco positivo. Dovendo il Concilio sopratutto e innanzitutto difendere la Fede, non si può essere indulgente verso gli errori."

[30] Letter from Davis to John George Diefenbaker, Archives Department of External Affairs, Ottawa, 4 September 1962.

[31] ASV: Conc. Vat. II, Diary Tromp, 6 February 1962: "Mane colloquium cum Mgr. Fagiolo, secret. S.C. Cardinalium de revisione. Approbatus est textus revisus Professionis fidei; approbatus quoque textus de Const. de Fontibus, de quo secretarius mihi adhuc proponit duo parva dubia quae solvuntur. Auctore Exc.mo Principi mense Octobri Patribus proponentur Const. de Fontibus, de Ordine Morali, de Deposito pure Custodiendo. [...] In genere laudatur labor Comm. Theol."

[32] BSM: Archives Léger, 934: Schemata Constitutionum et Decretorum de quibus disceptabitur in Concilii sessionibus. Series prima, 1962, 9–22.

[33] See his speech in *AS* I/1, 41–42. The original version of it contained in BSM: Archives Léger, 1019, and a French version of it is found in 1020.

what unaffected attitude, he began to take an opinionated and noted stance,[34] immediately demanding that the entire schema be rejected. Léger explained that where the Church had been hoping for a positive appreciation of the Biblical Movement, the schema laid out before the council fathers was of hardly any use to the contemporary situation. Léger's intervention listed four major reasons for his rejection.[35] First, the draft tended to judge, with all too much certainty, issues that were still subject to vivid theological debate, such as the precise nature of the relationship between Scripture and tradition. Next, the cardinal claimed that the mistrust with which the schema treated the Scriptures and contemporary Catholic exegetes was harmful to the Church for various reasons, not in the least because it was precisely through their efforts that the Church reached a better understanding of its principle source. Third, Léger pointed out that it went against the very intentions of the council, and against the spirit of *aggiornamento* proposed by John XXIII, to write conciliar drafts based on a fear of errors. Nothing, he claimed, is more dangerous to Catholicism than this kind of negativist hold which reduces many Catholics to passive subjects. At the time, Léger said, the Church was in need of a positive discourse, and he added a final warning against the risk of letting one theological school prevail over a variety of theological opinions in the Church, as well as pointing to the need for openness toward other denominations. Within the cardinal's response is what one might call a turnabout.

---

[34] For instance, immediately the next day his name figured prominently among those of other major council protagonists such as Liénart, König, Frings, Bea, Alfrink, and Suenens in an article in *Il Messaggero*, 15 November 1962. The article was given the title "Otto cardinali sono contrari ad uno schema di Ottaviani."

[35] BSM: Archives Léger, 1048. The communication office of Canadian Catholic Bishops Conference rendered Léger's speech as follows:

> The whole schema needs revising. It contains some good articles but its mentality is no help to the church.
> It is imprudent to decide or even speak with such certitude on questions disputed among experts, e.g. the relation between Scripture and tradition.
> The church will suffer if biblical theology is handicapped. There is a danger that the schema may unjustly create diffidence among exegetes.
> The schema is based on fear of error. That is its mentality. But, though errors must be repelled, the church should be able to speak serenely on any subject. The positive approach pleases both Catholics and non-Catholics.
> The opinion it advances is only one of the opinions present in the church and the different schools do not themselves talk in terms of conflict.

So, the question should be raised: What constituted the background for Léger's change of tone and clearly outlined opinion? Naturally, the cardinal's reaction can only be fully understood within the context of the opening days of Vatican II and by considering the importance of the revelation debate during that era. This in itself is quite a complex matter and I will only sketch some elements and events here. Then, I will look at the immediate preparation of Léger's intervention and how this interplays with the events of the time.

In the tumultuous atmosphere of the opening days of the council, Léger figured among those prelates highly concerned with safeguarding the council's conciliar nature and was involved in several efforts at once. Léger simultaneously supported the well-known claim that *concilium episcoporum est*[36] and laid a constant stress on the need for better communication with contemporary society, which becomes quite clear in some personal notes he jotted down upon his arrival in Rome on October 7, 1962.[37] In those days, Léger was corresponding with Marie-Dominique Chenu regarding a message from the council fathers to the world.[38] Also the cardinal kept in constant touch with several council protagonists to be, and only days before the scheduled first general session—devoted to voting the commission members into the new conciliar commissions—Léger was involved in obtaining the notorious postponement of that vote. Behind the scenes, his agenda shows him meeting Cardinals Bea, Döpfner, and Suenens. As he records in his notes:

> Nous nous entendons alors pour que chaque épiscopat put présenter une liste de membres qualifiés en vue des élections de la première session, afin que la liste préparée par le secrétariat générale ne fut pas imposée à cette multitude de pères qui, ne se connaissant pas entre eux, se seraient ralliés à cette liste 'préfabriqué.' Il fallait donc déjouér la manœuvre et agir en vitesse.[39]

36 Mathijs Lamberigts and Alois Greiler, "'Concilium episcoporum est.' The Interventions of Liénart and Frings Revisited," *Ephemerides Theologicae Lovanienses* 73 (1997): 54–71.

37 On Léger's activities in Rome during the month of October 1962, see Gilles Routhier, "Note de recherche. Un tournant de Vatican II," *SCHEC. Études d'histoire religieuse* 64 (1998): 71–79.

38 See correspondence and several initial text drafts in Archives Léger, 483–86.

39 BSM: Archives Léger 17, Cahiers de notes sur les débuts du Concile, 2.

On October 12 Léger again met several cardinals to impress upon them the importance of postponing the elections, and he reflected: "la cause me semblait gagnée."[40] Léger's precise role remained yet to be determined, but nevertheless the interventions of Frings and Liénart during the October 13 session resulted in the postponement of the vote. Only three days later would the council fathers actually vote for commission members. Then, on October 20, Canadian Bishop Marcel Bélanger would copy the result in his diary: "Parmi les élus, je note : Card. Léger et Mgr Roy dans la Commission sur la Foi, Mgr Lemieux dans celle de la Liturgie, Mgr Pocock dans la Discipline du Clergé."[41]

Even though Léger did not mention *De Fontibus*, we should still keep in mind the importance of his September letter to the Pope here, which André Naud dubbed Léger's "programme d'attitude" for the council. In this warm but altogether urgent plea for an *Ecclesia semper reformanda*, Léger stressed the need to avoid having the council crushed under the weight of the Roman curia. Now, at the opening of the council, he stuck with that. While Léger's letter was sent to the Pope only on September 11, it had already been drafted in Montréal in August and Léger circulated it for about a month among several members of the College of Cardinals, asking for their support. Léger's letter, strongly underlining the need for the adaptation of theology to the modern world, would be endorsed by John XXIII's highly influential opening address at the council, *Gaudet Mater Ecclesia*, given on October 11, 1962. Also, even though Léger's letter never actually mentioned the schema *De Fontibus*, it does give a strong sense of Léger's mindset as early as August 1962 with regard to the coming conciliar agenda. August is

---

40 BSM: Archive Léger 17, Cahiers de notes sur les débuts du Concile, 3.

41 ADE: Archives Bélanger, Journal de Concile, 20 October 1962. Also see ASV: Conc. Vat. II, Diary S. Tromp, 20 Oct. 1962: "Sabbato: *In Vat. incipiunt discussiones de Liturgia. Mittuntur Secretario* Generali *Observationes* Episcoporum spectantes *ad Const. Liturgicam.* Communicantur *nomina Membrorum Commissionis de Fide et Moribus, electorum ab Episcopis Concilii.* Ordo est secundum numerum maiorem vel minorem suffragiorum, quae acceperunt. Asteriscus (*) indicat Episcopum iam membrum fuisse Commissionis Theologicae. *Jos. Schröffer, Ep. Eichstätt • Gabr. Garrone, Arch. Toulouse • Fr. Card. König, Arch. Wien • Joh. van Dodewaard, Ep. Haarlem • *Alfr. Scherer, Arch. Porto Alegre • P. Card. Léger, Arch. Montréal Can. • Erm. Florit, Arch. Firenze • Joh. Dearden, Arch. Detroit. • Andr. Charue, Episc. Namur • *Joh. Wright, Episc. Pittsburgh • M. McGrath, Ep. aux. Panama • *Jac. Griffiths, Ep. aux. N. York • *M. Roy, Arch. Québec, Canada • Santos C. Rufino Arch. Manilla [sic] • Franc. Šeper, Arch. Zagreb •*Joh. Peruzzo Arch. Agrigento"

precisely the month in which he gathered his theological advisors, Pierre Lafortune and André Naud—only weeks after the latter returned from Japan—to draft comments on the first series of schemata, including the one on the sources of revelation. Here then, we have the background for Léger's November 14 speech.

André Naud and Pierre Lafortune—who would later become conciliar *periti* on account of Léger[42]—joined forces, and, mainly on the basis of drafts that had already been prepared by Pierre Lafortune in June 1962, they developed a substantial *Votum Generale* on the schema.[43] Léger, Naud, and Lafortune redacted critical reactions on all chapters, except, somewhat surprisingly, the fifth one. They critiqued the way the relationship between tradition and Scripture was defined, especially noting how the chapter on inspiration and inerrancy caricatured contemporary biblical scholarship. They raised doubts about the passages regarding the authorship of the Old Testament and of the Gospels as displayed in the schema. Foremost, they refuted the suspicious attitude toward Catholic exegetes that had shaped the condemnations in the fourth chapter, making reference to *Divino Afflante Spiritu*.

In fact, the basic sense of the entire collection of reactions is one defending the rights of Catholic exegetes against attacks and restrictions from above. Altogether, the collection takes up about nine pages, which are very much in line with criticisms made by many of Léger's European and North American contemporaries—some renowned, others less-known theologians—on the eve of the council debate. Just a few of those similarly concerned with the schema included Paul-Émile Crépeault,[44] Gregory Baum,[45] Karl Rahner,[46] Edward Schillebeeckx,[47]

---

[42] BSM: Archives Léger, 337: Letter from Léger to Angelo Dell'Acqua, 19 October 1962, proposes Lafortune as *peritus*. See the actual nomination letter in BSM: Archives Lafortune, 221.

[43] This document, as well as some draft versions of it, is kept in BSM: Archives Léger, 1032–38. While in the inventory the title *Votum generale* is only applied to n. 1032, this is in fact the main title for documents 1032–26, which all together constitute one single project. Also see the documents contained in BSM: Archives Lafortune, 352–56.

[44] AAQ: 21CM, Vol. 10A: Paul-Émile Crépeault, *Constitutio de Fontibus Revelationis. Animadversiones*, 1p.

[45] BSM: Archives Léger, 1042.

[46] BSM: Archives Léger, 1046: [Karl Rahner], De *revelatione Dei et hominis in Jesu Christo facta*.

[47] BSM: Archives Léger, 1060: [Edward Schillebeeckx], *Iudicium generale de schemate I*

René Laurentin,[48] and Charles Moeller.[49] Their reactions, as well as those of others, would somehow arrive at Léger's desk between August and November 14, 1962. During this period there is much correspondence on the revelation debate. Still, most of the material only served the cardinal indirectly, by strengthening and supporting his convictions. This fact becomes clear, but not so much from reading the nine pages of text produced together with his experts and criticizing the schema in great detail. Rather a brief comparison between the one-and-a-half page introduction to the *Votum Generale*, written in August, and the November intervention says it all. The *Votum*'s introductory note would simply become the basis for Léger's speech, and the differences between the two texts are only very minor.

There were two other influences on Léger at this period, and these should be pointed out. First, the aforementioned debate between the Lateran University and the Pontifical Biblical Institute had been dragging on—actually since the mid 1950s—featuring often unfair attacks on the Jesuits of the latter institute.[50] Eventually, this debate resulted in a teaching prohibition for two Jesuit professors, Stanislas Lyonnet and Max Zerwick. Apparently, Léger had followed the controversy closely and sympathized with Lyonnet when he was rendered suspicious before the Holy Office. It is partly in his defense that Léger's November speech contains a warm defense of Catholic biblical scholarship rather than focusing on dogmatic issues. Second, during the final draft stage, Léger took the collection of reactions to the schema to one expert for consultation. Only days before taking the stand in St. Peter's Basilica, Léger had the *Votum Generale* reread by the Lyon-Fourvière Jesuit, Henri de Lubac.

De Lubac received the entire Montréal *Votum* only on October 10 and responded to it the next day in a letter to Léger. Léger sent Pierre

---

De fontibus Revelationis.

48 BSM: Archives Léger, 1062: René Laurentin, *Histoire du schéma De fontibus*, Archives Léger, 1062. Also see Archives Léger, 615: René Laurentin, Animadversiones in schemata voluminis I.

49 BSM: Archives Léger, 1064: *Remarques générales sur le schema I.* See also Archives Léger, 620: Sur la rédaction des deux premiers schémata.

50 On this matter, see Maurice Gilbert, *L'Institut Biblique Pontifical. Un siècle d'histoire* (Rome: Pontificio Istituto Biblico, 2009), 158–71.

Primeau to retrieve de Lubac's letter immediately,[51] an indication that the cardinal was quite eager to know his opinion. De Lubac's reaction was a positive one. He judged the *Votum* to be excellent in its entirety, although he, too, noted that its main interest was not so much with doctrinal issues. He wrote, "Peut-être le souci de défendre la bonne exégèse et les bons exégètes a-t-il empêché de mieux voir un autre aspect des choses, à savoir, les graves déficits doctrinaux de cette Constitution." In the end, he also noted some problems with the quality of the Latin[52] in his version.

If anything, this reconstruction of events makes clear at least one thing: Léger already made his turn toward an open stance long before the conciliar atmosphere formed. The constant proliferation of replacement drafts, and the overall sentiment of rejection toward the work of the preconciliar Theological Commission in general, only strengthened his convictions.

As a consequence, the spot in which Léger found himself with regard to the *De Fontibus* debate was both comfortable and squarely in the centre of the council majority. He had already taken a similarly position during the liturgy debate.[53] On the other hand, he found himself a bit isolated, for even though his *prise de position* was not altogether unexpected,[54] it did not put him on the same track as some

51 Henri de Lubac, *Carnets du Concile*, ed. Loïc Figoureux, 2 Vols. (Paris: Cerf, 2007), Vol. 1, 254. "J'ai rédigé quelques observations sur le Votum du cardinal Léger. Un théologien canadien, l'abbé Primeau, secrétaire de l'archevêque de Saint-Boniface, Mgr. Maurice Baudoux, vient les chercher."

52 BSM: Archives Léger, 1047: H. de Lubac, Remarques sur le votum generale, 11 November 1962: "Dans l'ensemble, ce votum paraît excellent. Il y aurait d'autres observations à faire sur cette constitution; mais on ne peut tout dire. [...] Sur le votum generale lui-même, je ne vois qu'une remarque à présente. Peut-être, à l'art. 19, est-il imprudent de dire que, pour tous, les quatre auteurs (Matt., Mc., Luc., Jo.) sont seulement « auctores principales evangeliorum ». D'autre part, il serait bon de revoir le latin, pas toujours très correct, et parfois trop calqué sur le français pour être intelligible à tous."

53 Léger offered no less than three interventions in the liturgy debate, thereby becoming a well-known voice to many of the council fathers. See his speeches on October 23 (*AS* I/1, 371), October 29 (*AS* I/1, 602), and November 7 (*AS* I/2, 334). For background infomation, see Mathijs Lamberigts, "The Liturgy Debate," in *History of Vatican II*, ed. Giuseppe Alberigo and Joseph A. Komonchak, *The Formation of the Council's Identity: First Period and Intersession, October 1962–September 1963*, 5 Vols. (Maryknoll and Leuven, 1997), 119, Vol. II.

54 Archives Deschâtelets: Journal Bélanger, 14 November 1962: "C'est ensuite au card.

of his Canadian colleagues in the episcopate. When Hermaniuk wrote in his diary that the clash between minority and majority "provoked quite an unpleasant reaction in a great number of bishops,"[55] the same is true for the Canadian episcopate. Léger was not the only Canadian involved in the debate. Apart from him, five other Canadian bishops prepared interventions on the revelation debate: the aforementioned Maxim Hermaniuk, Greek-Catholic Metropolitan of Winnipeg; Bishop J. M. O'Neil, Havre-de-Grace; Maurice Roy, Archbishop of Québec; Patrick Jacob Skinner, St. John's Diocese, Newfoundland; and then Georges Cabana, from Léger's neighbouring diocese of Sherbrooke. Although I mentioned Cabana last, he was the only one to intervene before the decision fell to end the debate and to establish a new Mixed Commission on Revelation on November 21. Hermaniuk orally intervened later on the 21st (though he had been in the *De Fontibus* subcommission and shared Léger's negative appreciation),[56] and the three other Canadians—Skinner, O'Neil, and Roy—only handed in written interventions. Furthermore, the arguments offered by Skinner and O'Neil[57] were sound echoes of what Cabana had already expressed a day before.[58] All of them seem to have agreed that the schema was perfectly fit as it was, not only because of its sound doctrinal value, but moreover because it avoided false irenicism and therefore met the expectations of the other denominations perfectly when it came to true ecumenism.[59]

There is more to be said. Léger not only acted in contrast to several other Canadian bishops but the day before his intervention he had

Léger d'exprimer son avis. On s'attendait à sa prise de position: Tota constitutio praesens est recognoscenda (réviser)."

55 Archives Metropolitan, See, Winnipeg, Diary Maxim Hermaniuk, 14 November 1962.

56 Archives Hermaniuk, Diary Hermaniuk, 21 November 1962.

57 *AS* I/3, 360. Also see CLG: Archives Moeller, 141, for the version written on 19 November 1962.

58 ADS: Archives Cabana, P44/262.5, contains the document's initial draft. Also see, on his intervention, *La Documentation Catholique* (1962): 1590.

59 This type of attitude was making reference to a clause in Pius XII's encyclical *Humani Generis*, which sounded: "nec denique putent falso 'irenismo' indulgentes, ad Ecclesiae sinum dissidentes et errantes feliciter reduci posse, nisi integra veritas in Ecclesia vigens, absque ulla corruptione detractationeque sincere omnibus tradatur." See *Acta Apostolicae Sedis* 42 (1950): 578.

made his intentions very clear during a preliminary meeting of the newly established Doctrinal Commission. This November 13 meeting was hastily scheduled by Ottaviani and Tromp in order to align their commission members and have them defend *De Fontibus*, up for debate the next day. They did not quite succeed since an increasingly hostile atmosphere had taken hold,[60] an atmosphere in which the Holy Office, in particular, was to become anxious and forced to defend itself.[61] The atmosphere was also one in which contradictions came to a head, and the debate of the November 13 evening meeting brought to the surface a host of problems with the schema. Also, this was the first meeting of the new conciliar *Commissio de Doctrina Fidei et Morum*, which had been reconstituted at the beginning of the council, and it became evident that two parties were likely to emerge, the members of which

---

60 Congar, *Mon Journal du Concile*, Vol. I, 182, on November 5, 1962: "Le climat général fait beaucoup. Aujourd'hui, c'est le climat du concile: climat pastoral, climat de liberté, climat de dialogue, climat d'ouverture. Alors, c'était le climat du 'Saint-Office' et des chaires de collèges romains. On était neutralisé par un code tacite mais puissant, par une pression sociale très forte et contre laquelle on ne réagissait pas jusqu'au point où il eût fallu tout mettre en question." More elaborate information on the general atmosphere is found in Burigana, *La Bibbia nel Concilio*, 105–31.

61 The very fact that the first meeting of the Conciliar Doctrinal Commission, gathered by Ottaviani on the eve of the council's revelation debate, was an exceptional meeting testifies to this. See Leo Declerck and Claude Soetens, *Carnets conciliaires de l'évêque de Namur A.M. Charue*, Cahiers de la revue théologique de Louvain 32 (Louvain-la-Neuve: Peeters, 2000), 46. On November 13, 1962, Charue wrote: "17h. Séance de la commission doctrinale à Ste. Marthe [...] Le card. Ottaviani prononce quelques paroles, dans lesquelles déjà on sent de l'amertume. Il parle d'une théologie moderne, qui est un danger pour l'Église et dit que Mgr. Parente donnera des preuves d'un travail de sape accompli par des gens qui veulent substituer un nouveau schéma à celui de la commission." Charue further adds, on page 47: "Intervention énergique du card. Léger et de Mgr Garrone qui déclarent être là pour servir l'Église et la liberté, pas le schéma; qu'ils préféreraient sinon démissionner." Compare ASV: Conc. Vat. II, 788: Relatio Secretarii Commissionis Conciliaris DFM, 4-5: "Die 12 nov. ad Secretarium novae Commissionis de doctrina fidei et morum pervenerunt duo Schemata, non a Commissione praeparatoria theologica elaborata, sed ab extraneis: Unum erat Schema abbreviatum in quo per modum unius agitur De fontibus Revelationis [...] Illud Schema inter Plures Patres Concilii distribuendum curaverunt Praesides Conferentiarium Episcopalium Austriae, Belgii, Galliae, Germaniae et Neerlandicae. Die 13 Nov. in hospitio S. Marthae hora 17-19, habita est prima sessio Commissionis. [...] Maxime autem nocuit controversia acris circa Institutum Biblicum, in qua ab ambabus partibus litigantibus discussio Schematis alicuius conciliaris, praevalenter biblici, arrepta est, ut suam positionem defenderent. Sic factum est, ut Schema De fontibus Revelationis consideratum fuit tanquam opus curiale S. Officii contra Institutum Biblicum et non, sicuti est, ut fructus Commissionis Theologicae, quae processit sine ira et studio."

would increasingly side with the "left" or the "right."[62] Almost all of those present at that meeting were impressed with the attitude and role of Cardinal Léger. Be it said that Léger did not at all address the content of the schema there,[63] but—once more, faithful to his September letter to the Pope—aimed at the more general underlying issue: the freedom of the council. The Montréal cardinal strongly rejected the idea of being obliged to defend the schemata. To quote the personal notes of Bishop James Henry Griffiths, auxiliary from New York: "Léger says he does not want to be regarded as a heretic, but wishes to preserve any liberty of speaking in the Council. He shall resign from the Commission if this is to affect his freedom of speaking in Council."[64]

Washington theologian Joseph Clifford Fenton voiced similar views to those of Bishop Griffiths. In his diaries, he writes that "Léger is furious [...] Léger is the first to speak out against Ottaviani. He said that he would rather resign." Quite cynically, Fenton adds: "I wish he would."[65]

Background: Léger and the Holy Office

Léger refused to have his hands tied by the Holy Office. Freedom of speech is one issue that returns in almost all reports. Another one that struck me when reading various reports of the meeting is his heartfelt complaint that he felt like a suspect at an inquisition meeting rather than a member of a conciliar commission. Let me quote Edward Schillebeeckx's council diary on the occasion: "Suddenly, Cardinal Léger can no longer take it, and bursts out in anger. In such atmosphere of pressure and suspicion I can no longer function, and resign from the commission."[66] Tromp's personal notes, held in the Vatican Archives,

---

62 Philippe Levillain, "La discussion du schéma De fontibus," in *Les églises comme institutions politiques*, ed. Leo Moulin (Brussels: Institut belge de science politique, 1978), 73-94.

63 BSM: Archives Léger, 19, Cahiers de notes sur les 19-24èmes congrégations générales. See his notes on the meeting of November 13.

64 Both are quoted from AANY: Archives Griffiths: Council Notes, E-9, Small green notebook, 2–3.

65 CUA: Diary Fenton, 13 November 1962.

66 CVII: Archives Schillebeeckx, Council Notes, 13 November.

have Léger literally using the word "tribunal."[67] Of course, Léger stood his ground and defended what he had already pled for with John XXIII, but the background to his outcry is larger and more complex than that, because Léger was indeed under suspicion by the Holy Office at the time the council opened.

For some years already, members of *Via, Veritas, Vita*,[68] the Canadian branch of the France-based movement *La Cité Catholique*, had been raising suspicions against him. This intransigent movement of members, founded by Jean Ousset in 1946, had spread itself in Argentina and French-speaking Canada since the 1950s, and from 1961 it regularly attacked Léger in periodicals such as *Verbe*[69] and *Itinéraires*. The critical group was quite close to Léger geographically, as well, because at the beginning of the 1960s it had moved its *Siège de direction internationale* to the Rue Sainte Famille, in Québec City. Not too long before the November 13 meeting, Léger had openly complained that the movement's members were also acting against him via the Holy Office. This, of course, clarifies that, for the Montréal archbishop, his actions against the schema *De Fontibus* and against the Holy Office's secretary, Ottaviani, had a double agenda. It also gives further cachet to Léger's ongoing contacts with John XXIII. In fact, on October 18, 1962, a month after his September plea and right after the opening events of the council and postponement of the election, Léger wrote another letter to the Pope[70] seeking support against the accusations and insinuations of the Holy Office and the attacks of *La Cité Catholique*. And, as will become apparent, this interweaving of his personal defense against Rome with his combatting *De Fontibus* would have crucial consequences.

In the days that followed, the council debates confirmed what had already been anticipated at the first meeting of the conciliar *Commissio*

---

67 ASV: Conc. Vat. II, Diary Tromp: "Emus Léger dicit se velle libere loqui in Concilio, etiamsi contradicat antiquae Commissionis Theologicae. Commissionis de fide et moribus non esse Tribunal, sed adiutorium Ecclesiae." Tromp adds to it: "Emus Léger dicit se audivisse accusationes et insinuationes. Qui non habet spiritum scholasticum est haereticus!"

68 BSM: Archives Léger, 32–37, contains reports on these attacks and correspondence with P. Justin, Montréal, on the matter.

69 In this context, it is not insignificant to point out that Cardinal Ottaviani had close ties with the organization and published in their periodicals on a regular basis.

70 BSM: Archives Léger, 474, Letter from Léger to John XXIII, 18 October 1962.

de Doctrina Fidei et Morum. Opinions on the schema became more and more focused and divided: members either gave it their unqualified support or they rejected it completely; only a few voices sought their place in the centre of that continuum. One of the most important speeches in the series of meetings was delivered on November 19 by Belgian Bishop Emiel-Joseph De Smedt, in the name of the Secretariat for Christian Unity (based on a *nota* from Gustave Thils). This speech has often been said to have shaped the debate to a significant degree and also determined the schema's ultimate demise.[71] Still, it was not the only decisive element in play. On November 20, when the impasse was seemingly complete, the council presidency organized an early voting round, with Cardinal Ernesto Ruffini asking the fathers to vote on whether the debate had to be interrupted. This was a rather tricky way of putting things since a positive vote (*placet*) would signal the end of the debate, whereas a negative vote (*non placet*) would have meant its continuation. Defeat appeared to be final.

The outcome of the vote was well known: the text was given just a little short of a two-thirds majority of positive votes, thus implying that the discussion would have to be continued even though only 822 fathers had indicated the need to do so. The division between the council fathers was abundantly clear, with a majority of 1,368 fathers who wanted the schema to be rejected.[72] The situation was unbearable

[71] AJPG: Diary Otto Semmelroth, 19 November 1962: "Heute morgen muß es in der Generalkongregation recht massiv zugegangen sein. Bischof De Smedt von Brügge hat die Interessen und Anliegen des Sekretariaten für die Einheit der Christen sehr wirksam vertreten. Er hat mit recht starken Geschossen gegen die Theologische Kommission geschossen und betont, daß diese es dem Einheitssekretariat unmöglich gemacht habe, Kontakt mit ihr zu nehmen. Er muß dann starken Beifall bekommen haben." De Smedt's intervention (originals in CSVII: Archives De Smedt, 576) was based upon a text by Thils (CSVII: Archives De Smedt, 578). See Mauro Velati, "Le Secrétariat pour l'Unité des Chrétiens et l'origine du décret sur l'œcuménisme (1962–1963)," in *Les commissions conciliaires à Vatican II*, Instrumenta Theologica 18, ed. Mathijs Lamberigts (Leuven: Peeters, 1996), 181–204, and *AS* I/3, 184–87: "Loquor nomine secretariatus ad christianorum unitatem fovendam. In discussione schematis De fontibus revelationis, multis Patres ostenderunt sollicitudinem vere œcumenicam. [...] Problema est hoc: Quid requiritur in aliqua doctrina et in stylo alicuius schematis ut revera inservire possit ad meliorem dialogum inter catholicos et non-catholicos obtinendum? [...] Noster secretariatus suum adiutorium obtulit commissioni theologicae, sed commissio, propter rationes de quibus mihi non est iudicandum, noluit. Proposuimus constitutionem subcommissionis mixtae; sed commissio theologica respondit: non, non volumus."

[72] *AS* I/3, 254–55: "Audiant omnes! Cum, praeter spem habitus sit exitus suffragationis,

and stirred several types of reactions. For one, the Bologna Cardinal Giacomo Lercaro drafted a letter to the substitute of Vatican State Secretary Angelo Dell'Acqua. In the letter Lercaro addressed the council's checkmate position from a procedural angle. He argued that the vote should be declared invalid, because the presidency's formulation "*con opportuna delicatezza*" went against council regulations, offering a vote with a negative object.[73] He added a second argument, namely the fact that the vote did not have the text itself as its object but that it decided only on the issue of whether or not the debate should be continued. Notwithstanding these excellent arguments, it was Léger's way of dealing with the situation that was more likely to be successful. Let us, again, look at how the Montréal cardinal fits into all of this.

Léger and John XXIII: The November 20 Audience

Again, two different issues coincide. On the evening of the vote proposed by Ruffini, John XXIII received the Canadian bishops in an audience, in which Léger was appointed as their spokesman. The interesting element here is that after the collective audience,[74] Léger stayed on with the Pope for a private audience in the papal library. That private audience is, by nature, poorly documented. Even so, several sources—among them the agendas and letters of John XXIII[75]—make it possible to reconstruct its content. Apparently, two major subjects

---

hiç idem exitus communicatur statim ex mandato em.mi praesidis. Praesentes votantes: 2209. Tulerunt votum Placet: quod significat esse interrumpendam discussionem totius schematis: 1368. Tulerunt votum non Placet: scilicet esse continuandam discussionem: 822. Vota nulla: 19. Maioritas quae requirebatur, maioritas 2/3 partium, erat 1473. Cum igitur Placet non attigerit hanc maioritatem, non potest possidere, quapropter, de mandato praesidis, continuabitur discussio de schemate revelationis."

73 ISR: Archives Lercaro, Letter from Lercaro to Dell'Acqua, 21 November 1962: "Infatto il Regolamento non prende votazioni che abbiano un oggetto negativo."

74 The audience was reported in *L'Osservatore Romano*, 268 (22 November 1962): 1. Also see on this occasion, the article by Gilles Routhier, "L'itinéraire d'un père conciliaire. Le cardinal Léger," *Cristianesimo nella Storia* 19 (1998): 11.

75 Angele Giuseppe Roncalli/Giovanni XXIII, *Pater amabilis. Agende del pontefice, 1958–1963*, ed. Mauro Velati, Edizioni nazionale dei diari di A.G. Roncalli 7 (Bologna: Il Mulino, 2007), 458–59: "Specialmente solenne il ricev. alla Clementina dei Vescovi del Canada col Card. McGuigan, e card. Léger. Questo era un po'afflitto : Ma poi vedendoci soli in biblioteca cercai di consolarlo come si merita."

were discussed in the meeting between John XXIII and Paul-Émile Léger on November 20, 1962. First of all, Léger had asked for the conversation in order to talk about the aforementioned suspicions raised against him, still seeking papal support for his cause. Yet, the events of that day—and the fact that in Léger's mind his role in the revelation debate was closely linked to his personal issues with Ottaviani—led the conversation to the subject of the Pope's opening discourse, the role of safeguarding the council's liberty, and the general stalemate due to Ruffini's proposal for the vote. This, of course, led to the second subject, a discussion of Léger's interventions, both in the November 13 commission meeting and at the council.[76] Apparently, the cardinal, taking comfort in the Pope's confidence, seized the occasion to suggest a way out of the conciliar impasse. Léger's idea was that a new commission be founded, combining several cardinals, including Ottaviani and Bea, but also adding Achille Liénart, Michael Browne, Albert Meyer, Joseph Frings, and Marcel Lefebvre. Such a composition would allow a watchful eye to be kept on the way the schemata were being redacted and to keep them from being entirely in the hands of the curia. At that instant, Léger was the right man in the right place, it appears.

The next day, the Pope sent Léger a short handwritten note[77] and a pectoral cross. But this was hardly the most important consequence of their late-evening conversation. For on the morning of November 21, 1962, Monsignor Pericle Felici presented to the council assembly, which was continuing the debate, a message from the Pope that went: "Augustus Pontifex benigne statuit rem speciali Commissioni examinandam committere, quam component quidam Em. Patres Cardinales atque sodales, sive Commissionis theologicae, sive Secretariatus ad unitatem christianorum fovendam."

So, not only was the debate ended, but also a new mixed commission consisting of members from both the Doctrinal Commission and the Secretariat for Unity was to be set up. This decision was crucial, not only for the revelation debate but also for the further development of

---

[76] BSM: Archives Léger, 19, Cahiers de Notes sur les 19–24 congrégations générales.

[77] The letter, found in BSM: Archives Léger, 39 (and as yet not consultable in the Léger archives) was published in Giovanni XXIII, *Lettere 1958–1963*, ed. Loris F. Capovilla (Rome: San Paolo, 1978), 434–35.

the entire council, and it clearly underlined John XXIII's ongoing efforts for the Church's *aggiornamento*. Apparently, the decision itself was made right after Léger left, and when the Pope called Amleto Cicognani, his secretary of state, to communicate the news, it was written down in a document signed *ex audientia.*[78] Of course, in many minds, and certainly among the Canadians, Léger's personality was almost immediately linked to this. Just to illustrate this, the following quotation from the council diary of Bélanger proves worthwhile:

> Tout ce qui vient de se passer me laisse plus ou moins inquiet, je l'avoue. Ce n'est pas la décision même qui m'inquiète. Franchement, je crois que tôt ou tard il aurait fallu en venir là, vu que, l'opposition n'ayant pas désarmé hier à la suite du vote – j'ai su qu'une délégation, dont le card. Léger, était allée chez le St-Père hier après-midi pour faire des représentations.[79]

As for Léger himself, he seems to have kept things rather quiet, even when we find him writing a letter to Charles Moeller on that November 21, admitting, "J'ai vu le St-Père longuement hier soir et je lui ai parlé en toute franchise," and adding with much enthusiasm that an historical act had just taken place.[80]

Just four days later, the mixed commission would have its first meeting. All of the aforementioned cardinals were invited, as well as a good number of bishops from both groups. But, as André-Marie Charue, the bishop of Namur, observed with some surprise in his personal notes, there was no talk of Léger's membership as yet. Léger, too, must have wondered why his name did not yet figure on the list of cardinals that was published on the front page of *L'Osservatore Romano* on November 25.[81] His absence was clearly felt during the November 25 meeting, for

---

78 ISR: Archives Roncalli, 54.

79 ADE: Archives Bélanger, Journal de Concile, 21 November.

80 CLG: Archives Moeller, 3033: Letter from Léger to Charles Moeller: "Le fait historique a eu lieu ce matin. Au début de la séance, le secrétaire général nous a communiqué la décision prise par le saint-père à la suite du vote d'hier: le schéma théologique ne sera plus discuté au Concile. Il sera totalement remanié par une nouvelle commission dont les membres ne sont pas encore connus."

81 *L'Osservatore Romano*, 271 (25 November 1962): 1. The names mentioned were: Liénart, Frings, Ruffini, Quiroga y Palacios, Lefebvre, and Meyer. To that one should add the names of Bea and Ottaviani as commission presidents.

two days later—at the second commission meeting—we note his presence. Better still, while that meeting saw the appointment of Bea and Ottaviani as presidents, it also established five subcommissions—one for each chapter of the *De Fontibus* draft to be revised—and this time, Léger was appointed to preside over Subcommission V. This commission, which, besides Léger,[82] consisted of bishops Hermann Volk, James Henry Griffiths, Aniceto Fernandez, and Hart, would ultimately be responsible for the subject of the Church's dealing with the Scriptures in general, yet was also to redefine the relationship between theologians, biblical scholars, and the magisterium. This was a perfect fit for a cardinal whose main interest in the discussion on the schema had circled precisely around these topics.

Conclusion

The role of Cardinal Léger with regard to the schema *De Fontibus*, and its transfer into a mixed commission, is, to say the least, a captivating one. The cardinal's developed from a largely uninterested position to that of one of the key players in the debate. Several reasons can be given for this, such as the fact that—rather than the schema *De Deposito Fidei*, which had taken much of his interest, yet would never appear on the conciliar agenda—the *De Fontibus* discussion had become a hot topic. Still then, Léger's involvement hardly plays on the level of theological debate or content. Even when he makes several pertinent remarks in his November 14 intervention, his agenda is always more complex than that. It is the cardinal's conflicted personal situation that urges him to act strongly, for he never fights the schema *De Fontibus* as a mere theological text but rather as a representation of the Holy Office, which at the time was acting against his person. His personal dignity and his conciliar involvement are strongly interwoven, and it is this interconnectedness that leads him to seek support with John XXIII.

---

82 Other accounts of this meeting note that Cardinal Quiroga y Palacios was appointed as head of the subcommission, yet based on the fact that notes by Griffiths on December 3 refer to the addition of a Spanish cardinal, we can conclude that these accounts are wrong in putting the appointment on that date. This is confirmed by a document entitled: Membra Subcommissionum in CSVII: Archives De Smedt, 586, and serves as a correction on Sauer, *Erfahrung und Glaube*, 225–56. See also CUA: Diary Fenton, 27 November.

The Lesser of Two Evils? Archbishop Philip Pocock, Vatican II, and the Birth Control Controversy

Peter Meehan,
Seneca College

On the afternoon of Wednesday, October 21, 1964, during the third session of the Second Vatican Council, Philip Pocock, the coadjutor archbishop of Toronto, was enjoying a rare moment of personal time. He was getting a haircut. He later recalled that tumultuous afternoon, sitting in the barbershop of the Hotel de la Ville on the Via Sistina, ten minutes from the Vatican: "That barbershop had a telephone in every chair. The telephone rang and it was for me. I was talking to some reporter in Toronto while the barber was clipping my hair around the back."[1] The call, from a reporter with *The Toronto Star*, would bring the most shocking news of Pocock's life: that he was making headlines at home in Canada's national newspaper, *The Globe and Mail*, as the first Catholic prelate to support use of the birth control pill!

Written by staff reporter Warren Gerrard, the article referenced confidential instructions given by Pocock at a clergy retreat at St. Augustine's Seminary the previous June. It explained, in part, that when

1 *The City*, September 1978.

their advice was sought in the confessional, Pocock had given Toronto priests permission to approve post-partum use of the pill for a period of sixteen to eighteen months in order for mothers to be able to regulate their menstrual cycles. Citing confirmation from the director of Toronto's Catholic Information Centre, Paulist Father Frank Stone, who was, ironically, a licensed pharmacist, Gerrard heightened the drama of his story by quoting the remarks of Dr. Elliott Rivo, assistant to the Catholic inventor of "the pill," Dr. John Rock. To Rivo's knowledge the approval was the first ever given by a representative of the Church.[2]

Pocock was not the first Catholic bishop to enter the mounting public debate over artificial birth control. A year earlier William Bekkers, the bishop of Hertogenbosch, Holland, bluntly stated on national television that the problem required more intensive study, a position supported months later by a joint statement of his national bishops conference, agreeing that the Church "has no immediately appropriate answers ready that meet all situations."[3] However, the ensuing storm caused by Philip Pocock's involvement in the debate over the pill in 1964, at the height of its controversy, adds a unique perspective to the Canadian Catholic historiography of the birth control debate in the 1960s. Understanding that the subject had been deliberately kept from the council's agenda at the Pope's discretion, scholarly attention has largely focused on "The Winnipeg Statement," the 1968 pastoral directive of the Canadian bishops, prompted by the release of Pope Paul VI's "birth control encyclical," *Humanae Vitae,* the same year. Its focus on the need for Catholics to take recourse to their *informed consciences* in regard to artificial birth control reflected the disappointment of many Canadian bishops with the encyclical's lack of sensitivity to a matter of their mounting pastoral concern. While Pocock has been acknowledged as a supporting player at the meeting of the Canadian Catholic Conference in August 1968 that produced the Winnipeg Statement,[4]

---

2 *Globe and Mail,* 20 October 1964, and *Toronto Telegram,* 20 October 1964.

3 Cited in Robert McClory, *Turning Point: The Inside Story of the Papal Birth Control Commission, and How Humanae Vitae Changed the Life of Patty Crowley and the Future of the Church* (New York: Crossroad, 1995), 27.

4 Michael W. and Douglas R. Letson, *My Father's Business: A Biography of His Eminence G. Emmett Cardinal Carter* (Toronto: MacMillan of Canada, 1990), 106.

consideration has not been given as yet to his effort to render a pastoral solution to the question of artificial birth control four years *before* the release of *Humanae Vitae*. Off-handedly dismissing his *in camera* remarks at the time as "normal moral theology … I simply gave clergy a required clarification—required because of the newness of the pill," Pocock's entry into the birth control debate in 1964 reflected the essence of his desire that the council would offer "… the presentation of a new and more intelligible image of the Church to the world."[5] Unprepared for the tumult that would be raised in the *aula* later that fall, where birth control was not a topic *of* the council but very much a topic *at* the council,[6] Pocock, despite his considerable enthusiasm for a new spirit of *aggiornamento* in the Church, would sustain injuries to his reputation in Rome from which he would never fully recover.

Over the course of his more than fifty years in religious life, service and compassion remained central to Philip Pocock's priestly vocation. In a journal he began in the summer of 1926, the same year he would present himself to Bishop Michael Fallon as a candidate for the diocesan priesthood in London, Ontario, he pleaded, "Lord, make me kind and merciful in the confessional—not soft or cruel … cold knowledge and mere learning will never warm my heart with love for God, nor will it touch the hearts of others and inspire them to amend their lives."[7] On retiring as the archbishop of Toronto in 1978, he described his vocation in much the same way, asking to be remembered for his conviction: "To know God and make God known, to love God and make God loved by others."[8]

Despite a powerful desire to serve as a parish priest, Pocock was given only brief parochial appointments following his ordination on June 14, 1930.[9] Recalled for graduate studies in 1931 by the new bishop

---

5 *Toronto Star*, 21 October 1964 and *BC Catholic*, 29 October 1964; Archives of the Roman Catholic Archdiocese of Toronto (ARCAT), Pocock Papers, PO DA 19.09, Carter to Pocock, 1 September 1962.

6 Other topics included discussion of clerical celibacy and reform *of* the Roman curia. See John W. O'Malley, *What Happened at Vatican II* (Cambridge, MA: The Belknap Press of Harvard University Press, 2008), 6.

7 ARCAT, Pocock Papers, PO AA 13.01, Personal Journal, undated, 1926.

8 *The City*, September 1978.

9 *Ontario Catholic Directory*, 1931, 1932.

of London, Thomas Kidd, he earned a licentiate in canon law (JCL) in 1931 from the Catholic University of America and his doctorate (JCD), magna cum laude, from the Pontifical Angelicum University in Rome in 1934.[10] Returning that summer to assignments on the faculty at St. Peter's Seminary and on the local diocesan marriage tribunal, Pocock quickly established himself as the rising star in the diocese.[11] His classes in canon law and moral theology gained for him a reputation as one of the most engaging seminary professors in English Canada, and his work in the London curia saw him widely sought out for the soundness and sensitivity of his canonical opinions and judgments.[12] In order to satisfy his yearning for pastoral work, he also served as the diocese's founding Director of Lay Retreats, from which he was soon acknowledged throughout the province as a leader in spiritual direction for the laity.[13]

By the end of World War II, Pocock's ascent in the Church was swift and sure. Designated in 1943 as the first English secretary of the Canadian Catholic Conference,[14] the needs of the Church in western

---

[10] Archives of the Catholic University of America (ACUA), General Catalogue, 1931–1932, Commencement Program, 43rd Commencement, CUA, 15 June 1932.

[11] Diocese of London Archives (DLA), Deceased Priest Files, "Pocock, Philip F.," Pocock to Rev. J. C. Kelly, 16 May 1934. Pocock's dissertation was published by *The Catholic Record*, three weeks after his return from Rome. See Philip F. Pocock, *The Defender of the Matrimonial Bond* (London, ON: The Catholic Record, 1934) and DLA, Deceased Priest Files, "Pocock, Philip F.," Kidd to Pocock, 7 January 1935.

[12] Interview with Rev. Bernard Dunn, Diocese of Saskatoon, 31 May 2007; ARCAT, Pocock Papers, PO NT 31.03, Pocock, Philip F., "Some Principles on Paedagogy," undated; *Prairie Messenger*, 14 October 1951—Pocock testimonial by Francis J. Leddy; ARCAT, Pocock Papers, PO NT 31.02, Teaching Notes, undated; DLA, File—Kidd Papers, JTK 3, "St. Peter's Seminary," Rev. J. C. Kelly to Pocock, 31 March 1943; DLA, Kidd Papers, JTK 3, "Report of the Sacra Paenitentiara Apostolica, 23 December 1942," and Kelly to Pocock, 8 February 1943; Jean Michel to Kelly, 8 February 1943; Kelly to Kidd—Report on the Case of Jean Michel," 9 February 1943; Kelly to Pocock, 15 February 1943; DLA, File—Kidd Papers, JTK 3, "St. Peter's Seminary," Kelly to Pocock, 31 March 1943.

[13] *Catholic Record*, 15 April 1944; DLA, Kidd Papers, JTK 4, Box 5, "Clergy Conference," Bishop Kidd conference notes, 27 October 1937; *Catholic Record*, 17 July 1937. On June 26, 1939, Pocock was invited to give a keynote address on lay retreats for the thirty-thousand people gathered for the Holy Names Society Rally at Toronto's Varsity Stadium. See *Catholic Record*, 1, 11 July 1939; DLA, File—Kidd Papers, JTK 3, "St. Peter's Seminary," Rev. J. C. Kelly to Pocock, 31 March 1943.

[14] ARCAT, SS8003, Kidd to McGuigan, 21 December 1943; SS8004, McGuigan to Kidd, 21 December 1943; SS8005, McGuigan to Villeneuve, 28 December 1943.

Canada intervened before he could take up the posting, and he was made second bishop of the far-flung diocese of Saskatoon, Saskatchewan, early the next year. The youngest member of the Canadian hierarchy at only thirty-seven, he immediately turned his considerable energies and organizational skills to building up the diocese still reeling from the after-effects of the Depression and World War II. Reconstituting or creating a host of initiatives, including the parish-level organization of the Confraternity of Christian Doctrine, a provincial radio program, *The Catholic Hour of the Prairies*, and his Herculean organizational effort behind the first province-wide Family Rosary Crusade, he sought to engage the faithful with a three-pronged approach emphasizing catechesis, faith development, and proto-ecumenical engagement with Protestants.[15]

With his 1951 appointment as coadjutor to Alfred Sinnott, the archbishop of Winnipeg, it is clear that Pocock's ecclesiology was beginning to shift with the progressive winds bringing the Church on course to the Second Vatican Council. His reading of the prophetic theologians of the 1940s and 1950s, such as Karl Rahner, SJ, Jean Daniélou, SJ, Marie-Dominique Chenu, OP, Henri-Marie de Lubac, SJ, and Yves Congar, OP, appealed to his sense for the richness of human experiences and contributions as opposed the traditional neoscholastic vision of the Church as a perfect society transcending "the fluctuations of time and the relativity of culture."[16] He openly disdained the "psychology of de-

[15] Saskatoon Diocese Archives (SDA), BDC, "Maurice Baudoux," (3) 02, Pocock to Baudoux 16 November 1944, and Baudoux to Religious Superiors, 20 December 1944; *Prairie Messenger*, 27 July 1944; SDA, BDC, "Maurice Baudoux," (3) 01, Antoniutti to Pocock, 15 July, 28 September 1944; SDA, BSK Diocesan Circulars, (2) 2, Pocock to Clergy, 30 December 1944; SDA, "Catechesis," (1) 52 (c), Pocock—Rosary Hall Notes, 28 December 1950 and Memorandum to Clergy, 30 December 1944; *Prairie Messenger*, 18 September 1947; SDA, Main Collection (2) 2 Diocesan Bulletin, No. 4, 30 October 1947; *Prairie Messenger*, 23 September 1948; *Regina Leader-Post*, 2 October 1948; SDA, "C.W.L.," (1) 58 (c), "Minutes of the Second Annual Convention of the Saskatchewan Provincial Council - Catholic Women's League of Canada," 7–8 September 1948; *Catholic Register*, 28 June 1969; *Prairie Messenger*, 30 September and 18 November 1948; SDA, BSK (2) 2, Pocock to Clergy, 23 November 1948; SDA, BSK (2) 2, Pocock to Clergy, 15 December 1948. *Prairie Messenger*, 30 September and 18 November 1948; SDA, BSK (2) 2, Pocock to Clergy, 23 November 1948; SDA, BSK (2) 2, Pocock to Clergy, 15 December 1948.

[16] See ARCAT, Pocock Papers, PO NT 20.04, "The Lay Apostolate" by Karl Rahner, SJ, *Theology Digest*, February 1957; a selection of other readings in Pocock's collection may

fense," that had taken hold among Catholics, and its resulting "ghetto" mentality.[17] As an early proponent of the "lay priesthood," he embraced an inclusive understanding of the Church in which the faithful were invited to partake in the "royal priesthood" of Christ.[18] Heralding this vision as the featured homilist to the thirty-five thousand souls gathered at Toronto's Exhibition Park on October 2, 1955, for the Rosary Sunday Holy Hour, Pocock's words were met with rapturous applause.[19] Three years later, during his term as president of the Canadian Catholic Conference, Pocock brought this inclusive spirit to the sixth annual Social Life Conference held in his Archdiocese of Winnipeg. With the program fixed on the question of Catholic leadership and social questions, Pocock confirmed his place at the forefront of Canada's English-speaking hierarchy, calling on the faithful to "learn how to become leaders with Christ, how to share His life, His convictions, and His dynamic personality. Such a project calls for humble minds, strong hearts, and wills submissive to the guidance of the Holy Spirit."[20]

As a moral theologian and as a bishop who openly described himself as a "liberal progressive,"[21] it is unthinkable that Pocock could have avoided the question of contraception. Already by 1961, the year he was appointed coadjutor to the archbishop of Toronto, Cardinal James McGuigan, the sea change taking place in the Church's attitude to birth regulation was making it a major pastoral concern. While Pius XI's 1931 encyclical, *Casti Connubii*, reaffirmed procreation as the primary end

---

be found in ARCAT, Pocock Papers, PO PB 02.01-.05. See also Daniel Donovan, *The Church as Idea and Fact* (Wilmington, DE: Michael Glazier Inc., 1988), 28.

17 ARCAT, Pocock Papers, PO NT 20.03, Speech Notes—Grand Forks, December 1952; See also PO NT 46.53a and b, speech notes, undated, "Bishops Reding and Brian Hennessy," and "Speech Notes - Catholic Foundation of Manitoba," 16 March 1979.

18 Revised Standard Version of the Bible, 1 Pet. 2:9, "But you are a chosen race, a royal priesthood, a holy nation, a people for his own possession, that you may proclaim the excellencies of him who called you out of darkness into his marvelous light."

19 See also ARCAT, Pocock Papers, PO NT 33.07, Speech Notes, Rosary Sunday, 2 October 1925, and *Catholic Register*, 1, 8 October 1955. See also ARCAT, Pocock Papers, PO NT 46.53a and b, speech notes, undated, "Bishops Reding and Brian Hennessy," and "Speech Notes - Catholic Foundation of Manitoba," 16 March 1979. See also Interview with Msgr. Ken Robitaille, 11 March 2007.

20 *Catholic Register*, 15 November 1958.

21 ARCAT, Pocock Papers, PO CO 02.144c, Pocock to Sullivan, 3 January 1963.

of marriage, his successor began to steer Catholicism along a markedly different course. Pius XII's approval of the sympto-thermal ovulation or "rhythm" method of birth control in 1951 was the first acknowledgement by the Church of a licit option for the faithful to put limits on their fecundity.[22] The public revelation of hormonal contraceptives in the mid-1950s led the Pope to speculate on September 12, 1958, that indirect sterilization by virtue of contraceptives would be permissible according to the principle of "double effect," that is, when the pill was prescribed for other medical reasons.[23]

Following the first session of the council, mounting public concern over the question encouraged Pope John XXIII to create the Pontifical Commission for the Study of Population, Family and Births in March of 1963. Composed of six men, including three laymen and three priests, with backgrounds in medicine, sociology, demography, and moral theology, the Pope desired that their recommendations would be included in a definitive statement from the council. By the time the next Pope, Paul VI, finally revealed the commission's existence to the world a year later, he had expanded its membership but stipulated that its deliberations were to be completely distinct from the work of the council.[24]

For the faithful, the announcement of the papal commission only worsened the sense of moral ambiguity surrounding the question of artificial birth control: for many, what had for so long been considered wrong was now possibly right. Building on the successful release of Dr. Rock's *The Time Has Come: A Catholic Doctor's Proposals to End the Battle Over Birth Control*, a flood of highly touted new releases in 1964—including *Contraception and Natural Law* by Germain Grisez, *Contraception and Catholics* by Louis Dupré, and *What Modern Catholics Think About Birth Control and the Experience of Marriage* by

22 Noonan, John T., *Contraception: A History of its Treatment by the Catholic Theologians and Canonists* (Cambridge, MA: Harvard University Press, 1965), 426, 445–46.

23 Ibid., 461, 468.

24 Paul VI announced the commission's existence on June 23, 1964. It held six official meetings. After April 1964, its membership was expanded to fifteen for the third meeting in June 1964, which for the first time included the participation of married couples. For the fourth and fifth meetings, in March 1965 and April 1966 respectively, there were fifty-eight and seventy-two invited. McClory, *Turning Point*, 2.

Michael Novak—ensured that the matter was front and centre in the court of lay-Catholic opinion.[25] Of particular interest to Pocock would have been the release that fall of an edited collection, *Contraception and Holiness*, including a contribution from the man who would emerge as Pocock's most trusted advisor at this time, Gregory Baum.

An Augustinian priest and associate professor at the Centre of Ecumenical Studies at St. Michael's College in Toronto, Baum was in the process of forging his international reputation in the field of ecumenism, leading to his appointment in 1960 as a *peritus* or theological advisor to the council's Secretariat for Christian Unity. In his contribution, entitled "Can the Church Change Her Position on Birth Control?" he admonished: "If married people who seek to live as Christians and try to be faithful to the demands of the Gospel, tell us that the dividing line which the Gospel cuts across their sexual existence does not always exclude the use of contraceptives, we must take their conviction very seriously."[26]

While Baum insists that their relationship was purely consultative, and that he never served in any formal capacity for Pocock, their correspondence suggests that Baum exercised a significant influence on him at the council.[27] Marked with a deep sense of frustration from his time as a consultor to the Preparatory Commission on Discipline of Clergy and the Christian People, whose prefects and administrators he found to be dictatorial and poorly organized,[28] Pocock appears to have

---

[25] Rock observed that the formation of Catholic conscience on the matter of artificial contraception was a synthesis of "papal pronouncements" and the "humble and reverent application of common sense." See John Rock M.D., *The Time Has Come: A Catholic Doctor's Proposals to End the Battle Over Birth Control* (New York: Alfred A. Knopf, 1963), xiv.

[26] *Commonweal*, 5 June 1964. See also Thomas D. Robert's, SJ, *Contraception and Holiness* (New York: Herder and Herder, 1964), 329.

[27] Interview with Gregory Baum, 16 January 2009. See also ARCAT, Pocock Papers, PO VA 13.05a, Baum to Pocock, 20 November 1961; 13.05b, Baum to Pocock, sub secreto, undated; 10.05, Baum to Pocock, 10 July 1963.

[28] Pocock found the preconciliar commission to be highly disorganized and lacking a progressive vision. ARCAT, Pocock Papers, PO VA 03.01b, Tardini to Pocock, 8 May 1961; PO VA 03 06, 07 and 08, Rev. C. Berutti to Pocock, 11 September and 20 November 1961, Pocock to Rev. C. Bender, 18 September 1961, and Bender to Pocock 9 October 1961; PO VA 09, Bender to Pocock, 20 November 1961; PO VA 03.11a and b, Very Rev. G. Moehler to Pocock, 3 March 1962, and Pocock to Moehler, 13 March 1962.

invested little of himself into its work.[29] Rather, through his growing association with Baum, whose theological insights and vibrant ecumenical imagination spoke to both Pocock's mind and heart, Pocock sought to realize his full pastoral vision at the council. Showing him off at lunches and dinners with the likes of Emmett Carter, the bishop of London, and Jesuit philosopher Bernard Lonergan,[30] Pocock was moved to create the impression that Baum was his *peritus*.[31]

Nowhere was Baum's influence on Pocock at the council clearer than in the discussions surrounding the need for a statement condemning hatred and discrimination of the Jews as a "deicide people." As archbishop of Winnipeg, Pocock had encouraged co-operation between the local Church and the city's Jewish community. He continued these efforts in Toronto, engaging leading Jews, such as politicians Phil Givens and Alan Grossman and the senior rabbi of Holy Blossom Synagogue, Gunther Plaut, in discussion of the council's vision for enhanced Jewish-Christian relations.[32] This culminated in Pocock's only intervention at the council, *De Judaeis*, on September 28, 1964, only weeks before the birth control story would break.[33] Composed by Baum, the speech

---

[29] Immediately following the end of the first session, Pocock noted his frustration with having already cast 102 ballots on the schemata concerning distribution of clergy and benefices: "I have nothing specific to suggest. However, in both cases I believe that it will be impossible to do more than to set down general guiding principles" to fellow commissioner and Opus Dei Secretary General Archbishop Alvaro del Portillo. See ARCAT, Pocock Papers, PO VA 03.16, Pocock to del Portillo, 3 January 1963. Ultimately this commission would recommend the eradication of benefices, or ecclesiastical offices, which, since the middle ages, had come with fixed incomes. O'Malley, *What Happened*, 231.

[30] Floyd Anderson, ed., *Council Daybook: Vatican II: Session 1* (Washington DC: National Catholic Welfare Conference, 1965), 85. Pocock's favourite restaurant was Alfredo's in the Via della Scroffa. See ARCAT, Pocock Papers, PO AA 13.03, Council Journal, 14 November 1962 and 18 February 1963.

[31] ARCAT, Pocock Papers, PO AA 13.003, Council Journal, 23 November 1962; PO DS 09d, Pocock to Baggio, 11 July 1962; Interview with Gregory Baum, 16 January 2009. In a letter to Pocock during the summer of 1963, Baum wrote to Pocock to discuss his attendance at a meeting of theologians appointed by the Canadian bishops at the council. See ARCAT, Pocock Papers, PO VA 10.05, Baum to Pocock, 10 July 1963.

[32] ARCAT, Pocock Papers, PO SU 51.12, Pocock to Durocher, 24 April 1963 and PO DS 67.08, Pocock to Pignedoli, 12 April 1965.

[33] Bishop Alex Carter recalled the tense mood in the *aula* in the days before Pocock's intervention, where a group distributed anti-Semitic propaganda among the council fathers. See Alex Carter, *A Canadian Bishop's Memoirs* (North Bay: Tomiko Publications,

roundly dismissed historical characterizations of the Jews as abuses of "truth and charity," and won fulsome praise from Grossman for its "important implications in both the Christian and Hebrew world communities."[34]

Pocock's public involvement in the birth control debate, as with his efforts on behalf of Jewish-Catholic relations, must be understood as an extension of his pastoral sensibilities as an archbishop of the Catholic Church. Taking the question of contraception directly to a panel of Catholic physicians in Toronto in March of 1964,[35] Pocock was determined to offer guidance regarding a problem that he knew was, for many of the faithful, a source of increasing frustration and heartache. His response that summer to a woman in the archdiocese who referred to the pill as "not worthy of God's plan" exposes the depth of his pastoral sympathies:

> Not infrequently situations arise which cause a good Catholic wife and mother to ask herself if God does not wish her to exercise discretion in bringing more children into the world. Suppose she is the mother of four or five small children, some of whom are mentally deficient, and she is married to an unemployed, alcoholic husband who appears regularly to insist on his rights. Would she be guilty of sin if she suggested to her husband that he might restrict his approaches to non fertile periods? Some very devout Catholic mothers do have problems similar to this; and this is the question which moralists must answer.[36]

1994), 176. Composed late in 1963 and presented to the Canadian hierarchy that December, Pocock noted that his intervention had received the support of thirty-eight Canadian bishops. ARCAT, Pocock Papers, PO SU 51.001-026; PO VA 13.04 b and c, Pocock to Cicognani, 24 January 1964. ARCAT, Pocock Papers, PO VA 04.13, Baum to Pocock, 30 May 1963; Interview with Gregory Baum, 16 January 2009.

34 Anderson, *Council Daybook 3*, 69–70, and ARCAT, Pocock Papers, PO VA 13.04d, "ITALCABLE," Grossman to Pocock, 30 September 1964. That the intervention was composed by Baum is attested to in the council diary of Rev. Eugene Fairweather, an observer appointed by the Anglican Church of Canada, who noted on Thursday, October 8, 1964, "I walked home to the 'Castello' with Gregory Baum, who admitted that he had drafted Archbishop Pocock's speech *De Judaeis*." University of Trinity College Archives (UTCA), Diary of Eugene R. Fairweather, "Diary I," file 987-0012-019 (07), 80. I am grateful to Prof. Michael Attridge of the Faculty of Theology, University of St. Michael's College, for this reference.

35 *Toronto Star*, 21 October 1964.

36 ARCAT, Pocock Papers, PO SU 03.09a and b, Blanche Boyden to Pocock, 24 June

Following his meeting at St. Augustine's Seminary, Pocock's circular letter of June 8, sent in confidence "To priests commissioned to care for the souls in the Archdiocese of Toronto," laid out the essentials of his pastoral directive. Explicitly stating that that the pill, "as a direct contraceptive, cannot presently be considered a morally acceptable method of birth regulation," he addressed the perception of questionable moral certitude surrounding the question:

> While knowing that a single bishop, or even a conference of bishops, cannot claim to speak on behalf of the Church, I wish nevertheless, as your bishop, to provide you, insofar as I am able, with some guidance on these questions. Changing conditions are making it increasingly difficult for the large family to be recognized as an ideal by the Christian conscience of many married people. The urban home with its restricted living quarters, the early age at which many young people marry, the need of providing a higher level of education in this modern age, are general factors which make some family planning a necessity for parents in the average or low income brackets. Unemployment, the frail physical or emotional health of one of the parents, hereditary disease and other special factors, create situations in which it might well be rash to bring more children into the world. We must understand these problems with which many married couples are faced. We must not merely insist that "God will provide"; for in a multitude of cases it would be imprudent for parents to go on having children.[37]

Following the "double effect" logic of Pius XII, Pocock allowed that use of the pill could be considered lawful for the purpose of regulating a woman's menstrual cycle even though the result would cause temporary sterility. Contrary to the newspaper report, Pocock did not speculate on the exact time frame involved, broadly referring to its use only during the lactation period, and additionally clarifying that where a mother could not nurse her child, the directive was "sufficiently probable to be followed." Additionally, he suggested priests guide penitents to the *internal forum* of penance *outside* of the confessional, where the Church teaches that the private needs of the individual can be addressed ac-

---

1964, and Pocock to Boyden 9 July 1964.

37 ARCAT, Pocock Papers, PO CP04.34a, Pocock to Clergy, 8 June 1964.

cording to the dictates of their informed Catholic conscience. He even offered exact wording to be used by confessors: "The Church has not approved the use of the pill to prevent conception. Some theologians are, however, asking whether it might not be used in a situation such as yours. You must form your own conscience on this matter, asking the Holy Spirit for light to do what is right."[38] In what would ultimately be his critical miscalculation, Pocock's normal practice with inquiries to the question was to forward copies of the article "Theology and the Pill" by the renowned German Redemptorist Bernard Häring, on which his position was clearly grounded.[39]

Professor of Moral and Social Theology at the Alfonsian Academy and the Lateran University in Rome, Häring's emphasis on a "personalist" theology, described in the years before Vatican II as the "restless-heart-toward-God" model, stressed the place of the informed conscience in helping individuals "to gain the right vision, to assess the main perspectives, and to present those truths and values which should bear upon decisions to be made before God."[40] As secretary to the subcommittee charged with producing perhaps the most challenging schema of the council, number 13 on the Church in the Modern World, Häring understood the papal directive and was careful to avoid specific reference to artificial birth control. Released *sub secreto* in the spring of 1964 to the members of the Mixed Commission of Theology and Lay Associations,[41] the first draft outlined the uniquely human concerns of married and family life and sought a "proper equilibrium between the principles of the Gospel and the practical lives of men."[42] Häring's influence was clear in Article 21 entitled "The Dignity of Marriage and the

---

38 ARCAT, Pocock Papers, PO CP04.34a, Pocock to Clergy, 8 June 1964.

39 ARCAT, Pocock Papers, PO SU 03.04, Jacques Tousignant, SJ, to Pocock, 21 June 1964, and Bernard Häring, CSsR, "Theology and the Pill," *Catholic Herald*, 29 May 1964. See also PO SU 03.22b, Fulton to Mrs. R. Laprairie, 21 October 1964; 03.24, Fulton to Tagliaferri, 22 October 1964, and PO SU 03.37a, P. A. McKay to Pocock, 28 October 1964; *Canadian Register*, 31 October 1964.

40 Robert J. Smith, *Conscience and Catholicism: The Nature and Function of Conscience in Contemporary Roman Catholic Moral Theology* (New York: University Press of America, 1998), 73, 75.

41 Noonan, *Contraception*, 503.

42 Anderson, *Council Daybook 3*, 163.

Family," which linked love and procreation but rejected the traditional view of marriage, rooted in natural law, as having primary and secondary goals. It also avoided an outright condemnation of contraception, permitting parents "full and conscious responsibility" to determine the number of their children.[43]

Despite his cautious avoidance of the question in his schema, Häring saw the critical function of the council was to restore the place of the laity in the Church and could not avoid discerning the moral theology of artificial birth control at this time.[44] Appointed to the newly expanded Papal Commission on Births for its second meeting, also *sub secreto*, at the Pio Latino in Rome, April 3–5, he disagreed with the perception of the pill as "intrinsically evil" and reiterated his opposition to the contention that procreation was the primary end of marriage.[45] Ultimately, as part of a rancorous debate in the English press mere weeks later, Häring allowed these very private opinions to reach a broad public audience. Prompted by the musings of the retired archbishop of Bombay, Jesuit Thomas D. Roberts, who saw no rational arguments against artificial contraception and who opined, despite the papal directive, that the council was the proper place to discuss the matter,[46] the conservative English hierarchy went on the offensive. Led by the archbishop of Westminster, Cardinal John Heenan, their joint response of May 7, 1964, declared that while "the Council may well be called upon to give guidance" in regard to the use of the pill, they declared, "contraception itself, however, is not an open question for it is against the law of God."[47] Asked for his opinion on the matter two days later, Häring broadly rejected the tone of the pastoral letter,

---

43 Noonan, *Contraception*, 503, 508; O'Malley, *What Happened*, 236.

44 Bernard Häring, CSsR, *Road to Renewal: Perspective of Vatican II* (Montréal: Palm Publishers, 1966), 120.

45 McClory, *Turning Point*, 47, 49.

46 The article appeared in the independent English Christian newsletter *Search* and in London's *The Times*, April 1964, cited in Leo Pyle, *The Pill and Birth Regulation: Documentation of the Catholic Debate* (London: Dartman, Longman and Todd, 1964), 85, and McClory, *Turning Point*, 50. Roberts composed the introduction to *Contraception and Holiness* released later that fall.

47 *Universe*, 7 May 1964, cited in Pyle, *The Pill and Birth Regulation*, 95.

suggesting that theologians should not condemn an act as mortally sinful unless absolutely certain:

> What we must consider is this—does the pill offend the dignity of marital intercourse, could it destroy the purity of conjugal love? The danger is that the pill may be taken as an escape from responsibility. But there are good reasons for believing it might help a couple to avoid greater dangers to chastity, to fidelity and to family unity. I feel that most confessors and moralists would say that the pill is, at least, the lesser of two evils.[48]

With accusations and demands for clarification from Heenan and a host of English clerics in the ensuing weeks, Häring was moved to form his clearest statement on the matter to date.[49] Published in the *Catholic Herald*, May 29, 1964, "Theology and the Pill" offered a circumspect analysis of the birth control debate within the Church, condemning the "anti-baby" mentality of some contraceptive advocates, while sympathizing with the various challenges faced by the faithful who were living out the "theology of parenthood." He allowed latitude for the use of "personal conviction and personal conscience" in rendering decisions on the use of artificial contraception during the period of the Church's discernment, while cautioning "… it is too soon yet for married people to conclude from current discussions that the pill is a positively acceptable form of birth-regulation, raising no difficulties or problems from the moral point of view. We must have patience and await further developments in weighing all of the pros and cons."[50]

With Häring's draft schema scheduled for official introduction that fall, birth control soon became the dominant *non-topic* in the *aula*. Two days before the Pocock story broke in Canada, the Council Presidium was offered a petition requesting a re-examination of the Church's position signed by 182 fathers from twelve European and North American countries.[51] In the days after October 21, a barrage of interventions from

---

48 *Manchester Guardian*, 9 May 1964 cited in Pyle, *The Pill and Birth Regulation*, 152.

49 *The Guardian*, 9, 14, 22 May 1964 and *The Catholic Herald*, 29 May 1964 cited in Pyle, *The Pill and Birth Regulation*, 150–57.

50 "Theology and the Pill," *The Guardian*, 29 May 1964.

51 *Globe and Mail*, 20 October 1964.

progressive cardinals including Léger of Canada, Alfrink of Holland, and Reuss of Germany, all addressing the efficacy of Christian marriage as less than subtle code for birth control, prompted repeated reminders from conservatives that the topic was not to be discussed.[52] Finally, it was the speech made on October 30 by perhaps the most progressive voice at the council, Cardinal Leo Suenens of Malines, Belgium, which brought the matter to its critical mass. Asking that the cloak of secrecy be lifted in the Church's deliberation of artificial birth control, he boldly called on the Pope to publicly disclose the names of the members of his pontifical commission.[53]

Despite the chaos raised by the birth control question at the council, Pocock could not have known the scope of the imbroglio soon to envelop him at home and abroad. In the next issue of the *National Catholic Reporter*, Jesuit sociologist John L. Thomas hailed Pocock as a Catholic defender of contraception, agreeing that, pending a definitive statement from the Church, "a confessor cannot forbid anyone who says his own conscience tells him it is all right."[54] For the next year and a half Pocock was assailed by a host of magazines, newspapers, and clergy from Sydney, Nova Scotia, to Mineral Wells, Texas, all of them hungry for an elaboration of his thoughts on the contentious matter of contraception.[55] A Parisian medical journal even encouraged Pocock to write an article detailing his role as an ecclesiastical champion of artificial birth control.[56] Yet, while the Church universal clamoured for

52 These included Bishop Emilio Guano of Italy, Cardinal Gregorio Agagianian, Prefect of the Congregation for the Propagation of the Faith and Cardinal John F. Deardon of Detroit. See Anderson, *Council Daybook 3*, 164; O'Malley, *What Happened*, 237; Daly, *Beyond Secrecy*, 180.

53 O'Malley, *What Happened*, 238.

54 *National Catholic Reporter*, 28 October 1964.

55 ARCAT, Pocock Papers, PO SU 03.31a, Orlando Lucero, SJ, Gonzaga University, to Fulton, unspecified date, October 1964; PO SU 03.29, K. M. Chrysler, *US News and World Report* to Pocock, 30 November, 1964; PO SU 03.04a, Rev. Angus MacLeod, Diocesan Director of Family Life Bureau, Sydney, Nova Scotia, to Pocock, 20 January 1965; PO SU 03.05a and b, Rev. Leo Sexsmith CSsR, St. Peter's Parish, St. John, New Brunswick, to Pocock, 1 February 1965, and Pocock to Sexsmith, 8 February 1965; PO CO 05.07, Pocock to Most Rev. J. F. Whealon, Auxiliary Bishop of Cleveland, 5 February 1965; PO SU 03.06a, Rev. John Barbernittz, Mineral Wells, Texas, to Pocock, 8 February 1965.

56 ARCAT, Pocock Papers, PO SU 03.36a, Marcel Tauber, Atlantic Press, Paris, to Pocock, 30 October 1964.

more discussion of the question, it was soon to be eminently clear that the Pope did not. On November 7 Cardinal Suenens rose abruptly in the *aula* during discussion of the Church's missionary efforts to clarify the "misunderstanding in public opinion" that had resulted from his challenge to the Pope a week earlier.[57] More tellingly, before the last session of the council, Bernard Häring was quietly replaced on the drafting committee for *Gaudium et Spes* by Pierre Haubtmann of the Institut Catholique de Paris.[58]

Taking the long-view to Philip Pocock's fate—always a prelate but never a prince of the Church—the conventional wisdom of the local church in Toronto points to his critical involvement in the birth control question in 1964. With a glass ceiling henceforth fixed squarely over his further ascent in the Church, Pocock would never receive the cardinal's red hat that now presumably comes with the See of Toronto.[59] That they went to his friends and successors in the Sees of Winnipeg (George Flahiff, 1969) and Toronto (Emmett Carter, 1979) is perhaps better explained by their cultivated Roman alliances than by the damage done to Pocock through his growing reputation among his brothers in the Canadian hierarchy as "Phil the Pill."[60]

---

57 Suenens's speech took place on November 7, 1964. See Anderson, *Council Daybook* 3, 237, and O'Malley, *What Happened*, 237–38.

58 O'Malley, *What Happened*, 238.

59 Starting with James McGuigan in 1946, and with the notable exception of Pocock, the archbishop of Toronto has been (and is likely to become!) a member of the College of Cardinals.

60 See Platt, *Gentle Eminence*, 133, and Higgins and Letson, *My Father's Business*, 67. While Higgins and Letson point to the significant relationship between Carter and the apostolic delegate to Canada, Sebastiano Baggio, later prefect of the Congregation for Bishops, Pocock's relationship with the man characterized as "the bishop maker" was more uneven. Two days after arranging to pay for a new suit for Baggio, who was being reassigned as papal nuncio to Brazil, Pocock accused him of not grasping the linguistic makeup of the Canadian Church by virtue of his recommendation of only French-Canadian bishops and priests to the postconciliar commissions. See ARCAT, Pocock Papers, PO DS 66.14a, Pocock to Baggio, 19 June 1964; Platt, 133. ARCAT, Pocock Papers, PO DS 66.28a and b, Baggio to Pocock, 16 June 1964, Pocock to Baggio, 17 June 1964. That September he challenged Baggio's successor, Sergio Pignedoli, for the "political" decision to appoint Toronto uranium magnate Steve Roman as a lay auditor for the third session of the council, describing him as a "good Catholic," but one who "... has taken no part in Catholic Action at any level." ARCAT, Pocock Papers, PO VA 04.18c, Pocock to Pignedoli, 27 September 1964. Pocock and Carter suggested Francis Leddy, recently made first president of the University of Windsor. See ARCAT, Pocock Papers, PO VA 04.18, Carter

Examining the length and breadth of Pocock's life, including fifty-four years as a priest and forty years as a bishop of the Catholic Church, it is clear, however, that admission to the Sacred College was not the defining ambition of his life. His was foremost a pastoral vocation, and by the time of his retirement in 1978, to his first calling as an archbishop-in-residence at St. Mary's Parish in Brampton, Ontario, his efforts in a host of areas not covered in this paper underscored his desire to be a "people's bishop." His broad-band implementation of the council's various directives and decrees, including reactivation of the permanent diaconate, the creation of the Toronto Senate of Priests, and the lay-directed Archdiocesan Pastoral Council, set the standard for conciliar conformity in the dioceses of English-speaking Canada. Ironically, the matter of birth control would also find its way back into Pocock's pastoral objectives. His withdrawal of Catholic Charities from the United Way in 1976 over its association with Planned Parenthood resulted in his creation of ShareLife, which continues today as the major fundraising arm of the Archdiocese of Toronto.

A rare feature interview in Toronto's *The City* magazine in 1978 offered Pocock perhaps his final opportunity to identify the legacy of his many years of faithful service to the Church. Interestingly, the reporter assigned to cover this story was Warren Gerrard, who had broken the birth control story years earlier. Asked to speculate on why he had not been made a cardinal, Pocock's response was one of quiet resignation and humility: "I was not called."[61]

---

to Pignedoli, 28 September 1964. Angelina Nicora, the wife of council historian Giuseppe Alberigo, shared this concern for political appointees among the laity, noting at the time: "We have always had reason to shake our heads at the choice of lay people to sit in the Council. It is a lay Curia, whose members are chosen for their situation in life rather than for any real competence that might on rare occasions make them capable of collaboration. In the end, the hierarchy does not want competent lay people." See Alberigo, Giuseppe ed. *History of Vatican II – Vol. II: The Formation of the Council's Identity, First Period and Intercession October 1962 – September 1963* (Maryknoll: Orbis, 1997), 72.

[61] *The City*, September 1978.

The Council Diary of Metropolitan Maxim Hermaniuk and Turning Points in the History of the Catholic Church: An Interpretation

Peter Galadza,
Saint Paul University

Allow me to begin on a note of thanks to the organizers of the conference upon which this collection is based. If not for the conference I would have remained ignorant of certain important moments in the history of my own Church, the Ukrainian Catholic.[1] Before outlining how I plan to structure my analysis of the Council Diaries of Metropolitan Archbishop Maxim Hermaniuk, allow me to

[1] For a concise history and overview of the current state of the Ukrainian Catholic Church see Ken Perry, ed., *The Blackwell Companion to Eastern Christianity* (Malden, MA: Blackwell, 2007), 291–318. Hermaniuk, of course, was a member of this Eastern Catholic Church, which is also known as the Ukrainian Greek Catholic (or Greco-Catholic) Church. Until the 1950s the older term "Ruthenian" was used instead of "Ukrainian." Also, instead of "Greek Catholic" one sometimes finds "Byzantine Catholic." For an overview of the Ukrainian Catholic Church in relation to the decrees and events of Vatican II, see Peter Galadza, "The Reception of the Second Vatican Council by Greco-Catholics in Ukraine," *Communio: International Catholic Review* 27 (2000): 312–39.The research for the present paper was made possible by the Centre for the Study of the Second Vatican Council, Katholieke Universiteit Leuven, which has made possible access to the English language translation of the council diary of Metropolitan Maxim Hermaniuk. This publication of the diary is forthcoming.

share some facts that illustrate this ignorance, and then, more importantly, suggest the significance of this lack of knowledge. I do so only to indicate that in some parts of the Church "the state of the question" regarding Archbishop Hermaniuk[2] and Vatican II has involved more of a question mark than anything resembling a "state."

Until 1992, when I started working at the Sheptytsky Institute of Eastern Christian Studies and occasionally encountering Hermaniuk, I had never heard—or at least I do not recall anyone referring to him—as the "Canadian father of collegiality."[3] In fact, until then I do not recall hearing anyone speak of his prominence at Vatican II. I am certainly not proud of this ignorance, but in view of the fact that in 1976 I had taken a full-semester graduate course at St. Michael's College entitled "Vatican II and the Eastern Churches," taught by a Ukrainian Catholic professor and attended by seven other Ukrainian Catholic students, my ignorance is significant. In the seminar, students presented papers on a wide range of topics, but "Hermaniuk and Collegiality" was not among them. Recently I asked a well-informed Ukrainian Catholic colleague of mine whether he had been aware of Hermaniuk's status as a father of collegiality. He replied that until the 1980s, when he encountered a Roman Catholic bishop who had been at Vatican II, he, too, had never heard of Hermaniuk's stature at the council.

How can one explain this? Without any desire to justify my earlier ignorance, I think this lack of knowledge about Hermaniuk's role at the council points to elements of a hermeneutic for understanding both Hermaniuk's own work as well as other dimensions of Vatican II.

---

2 Born in Western Ukraine to the family of a cantor in 1911 (then part of the Austro-Hungarian Empire), Hermaniuk entered the Redemptorist Minor Seminary in his native land in 1927 and was subsequently sent to Belgium for studies. Ordained to the presbyterate in 1938, he wrote a doctoral dissertation on the Gospel Parables in the thought of Clement of Alexandria and became a *Maître agrégé*. In 1948 he was transferred to Canada, ordained bishop in 1951, and made the first metropolitan archbishop of the Ukrainian Catholic Church in Canada in 1956, with his see in Winnipeg. He died in Winnipeg in 1996. To Hermaniuk's credit, he was and remained to his dying day the Sheptytsky Institute's most important episcopal patron.

3 Bernard M. Daly, "Maxim Hermaniuk: Canadian Father of Collegiality at Vatican II … and After," in Gilles Routhier, ed., *Vatican II au Canada : enracinement et réception : actes du colloque organisé par la Faculté de théologie et de sciences religieuses et le CIEQ dans le cadre du projet de recherche "Vatican II et le Québec des années 1960," 23 et 24 août 1999* (Montréal: Fides, 2001), 427.

More specifically, it demonstrates how in history and interpretation, context frequently *is* text. To illustrate this, let me begin with the following paradoxes:

1. In spite of the fact that Hermaniuk's theological output at Vatican II was the most prominent and creative of any Ukrainian Catholic theologian, including Patriarch Josyf Slipyj,[4] Hermaniuk never published anything of significance after the council.[5]
2. In spite of Hermaniuk's profound concern for ecumenism and his ecumenical contacts, as attested by his council diary, his eparchy (diocese) remained an ecumenical backwater.
3. In spite of Hermaniuk's distaste for scholastic paradigms and methods—again, as attested by his council diary—his eparchy never progressed beyond a pre-Vatican II scholastic ethos in its liturgical life.[6]
4. And finally, in spite of his council diary's reference to support for optional celibacy, Hermaniuk's eparchy was among the last to begin ordaining Canadian-born married candidates to the priesthood—more than thirty years after the council. In fact, during Hermaniuk's tenure as archbishop, the Winnipeg Archeparchy retained a strong emphasis on mandatory celibacy.

I shall return to all of these points later, but by now it should be obvious that Hermaniuk's dynamic thinking on various topics remained unrealized desiderata. Thus, after the council, his ideas—unlike those of the Melkites,[7] for example—continued to lack ecclesial context, which helps explain the ignorance surrounding his work at Vatican II.

---

[4] For a study of this towering Ukrainian Catholic churchman, see Jaroslav Pelikan, *Confessor Between East and West: A Portrait of Ukrainian Cardinal Josyf Slipyj* (Grand Rapids, MI: William B. Eerdmans Publishing Company, 1990).

[5] In fact, besides his doctoral dissertation, his only book was a collection of newspaper articles: Максим митрополит Германюк, *Наші Завдання: Збірка Статтей* [Our tasks: a collection of articles] (Вінніпеґ: Поступ, 1960). However, Hermaniuk did have the distinction of being the founding editor of the theological journal *Logos*.

[6] All of my assertions are based on personal experience in parishes of the Winnipeg Archeparchy and familiarity with the archeparchial newspaper during and immediately after Hermaniuk's episcopate. However, before writing this article, I consulted with several knowledgeable priests of the archeparchy to ensure that my impressions were correct.

[7] See, for example, Saba Shofany, *The Melkites at the Vatican Council II: Contribution of*

Incidentally, the fact that Roman Catholics—rather than Eastern Catholics—have been more attuned to Hermaniuk's work demonstrates that while, to his credit, he had managed through hard work to climb the heights of Catholic officialdom, he nonetheless had not descended to the depths—and breadth—of his own Church's realities. This poses the question about the relationship between "the centre" and "the periphery" in Catholicism, and the fact that the two can remain somewhat disconnected, even in the case of extremely fine people like Hermaniuk.

In what follows I hope to review the contents of the Metropolitan's council diary in light of the question "Vatican II: A Turning Point in the History of the Catholic Church?" My analysis will proceed according to the following order: 1. the question of collegiality, 2. ecumenism, and 3. Eastern Catholic, more particularly Ukrainian Catholic, realities. In doing so, I hope to focus on aspects of the question that have not been as prominent in the public record. Thus I will not summarize Hermaniuk's interventions at the council. In fact, even my review of Hermaniuk's diary will be very selective, as the diary is scheduled for publication and there is no need to outline what will be available to all in due course.

However, let me convey—if ever so summarily—the general character of the diary. Hermaniuk's first entry, dated October 3, 1960, alludes to his frustration at not being able to attend the first meeting of the Pre-Conciliar Theological Commission to which he had been appointed the previous July.[8] Hermaniuk provides no reason for his inability to attend, but he does note how difficult it is to prepare for work in the commission without access to an adequate theological library or contact with other theologians who could discuss the materials with him. In today's age of instant communication and Internet libraries it is important to appreciate the hurdles that previous generations had to overcome. The very last entry is dated December 8, 1965, that is, the

the Melkite Prelates to Vatican Council II on the Renewal of Moral Theology (Bloomington, IN: Authorhouse, 2005).

8 Because Hermaniuk's diary remains in manuscript form but will soon be published, it seems that the best way to cite it is to refer to entry dates. This approach also commends itself as the entries are usually no longer than a page.

council's closing day. It concludes with the words, "The Council has ended, but the problems raised by it await resolution." As I will note below, in some instances Hermaniuk had hardly an inkling of those problems.

As for content and tone, the diary is not sensational. In other words, it is bereft of highly confidential or emotionally charged material. Also, it is characterized by discretion, modesty, and kindness. One must presume that Hermaniuk expected it to be circulated some day, and he obviously believed that such virtues should be associated with one's reputation even after death. In essence, then, we do not find an inner, or private, Hermaniuk pouring his soul into a text that should only be published posthumously. In particular, with regards to authority figures, Hermaniuk displays no passive aggression whatsoever. In fact, the same deference for authority that characterized Hermaniuk's public persona characterizes his diary as well.

Collegiality

Bernard Daly concludes his superb article, "Maxim Hermaniuk: Canadian Father of Collegiality at Vatican II ... and After," with the words "Collegiality is a Vatican II teaching that has yet to be truly received in the Catholic Church. Maxim Hermaniuk's vision is still to be made real."[9] Hermaniuk's council diary reveals that the archbishop had no idea how difficult it would be to make it real. The following quotations demonstrate a naïve euphoria that persisted even after Paul VI's unfortunate *Nota Praevia* of September 15, 1965.[10]

To begin with, the entry for September 30 of the previous year reads:

> The Council adopted the teaching on the collegiality of bishops. This is the most significant moment of the Council. Some of the expert theologians said that, after this voting, the Council has effectively ended. Thanks be to God, that this teaching was adopted

---

9 Daly, "Maxim Hermaniuk," 439.

10 The text can be found in Norman P. Tanner, ed., *Decrees of the Ecumenical Councils, vol. 2* (London and Washington: Sheed and Ward and Georgetown University Press, 1990), 899–900.

with such a great majority. That will make it easier for the Apostolic See to put it into practice.

A similar tone is struck in the following entry:

> November 21, 1964 will remain a historic day in the history of the Church of Christ forever. This is the day of the solemn proclamation by Pope Paul VI of the collegiality of the episcopate. In the future, now the entire episcopate, delegated with a certain number of representatives, will together with the Pope, decide on all significant matters in the Church of Christ. In this lies the distinct meaning of today's promulgated constitution *On the Church.*

And as noted above, even the *Nota Praevia* was interpreted in the most positive light. For September, 15, 1965, under the heading "Synod of Bishops: A Great Historic Day" (with the latter phrase underlined), we read:

> The Holy Father Paul VI is present at the Holy Mass. After the Holy Mass, the Secretary of the Council, Archbishop Felici, reads the Apostolic letter—*Motu proprio Apostolica sollicitudo*, by which the Holy Father calls into existence the *Permanent Synod of Bishops* [underlined in the original]—with the mission of helping the Holy Father in leading the Universal Church. This is putting into practice *episcopal collegiality*" [underlined in the original].

Lest anyone, however, think that Hermaniuk was alone in his naïveté, note the next sentences in his diary: "The Fathers of the Council welcomed the decision with loud applause. All were overjoyed, that in the end bishops will occupy their proper place in leading the whole Church of Christ."

Curiously enough, Hermaniuk's suspicions remained dormant even when several weeks later Paul VI reserved the question of celibacy to himself, thereby removing it from conciliar discussion. Nowhere in the diary is there even a hint that "the entire episcopate, delegated with a certain number of representatives," actually *will not* "together with the Pope, decide all significant matters in the Church of Christ."

Is it possible that Hermaniuk was hoping that Paul VI would eventually bring the issue of celibacy to a permanent synod where bishops would have a deliberative voice in the matter? The diary gives no hint of this, but the possibility may help explain Hermaniuk's lack of concern. The question of optional celibacy, incidentally, is important in this context as Hermaniuk had actually prepared an intervention on the topic—arguing for the merits of both a married and celibate clergy.[11] But after the announcement of the papal reservation, he had to settle for forwarding his text by registered mail to the Pope's office.[12]

Such facts and the subsequent history of collegiality's non-implementation demonstrate that for Vatican II to truly have been a turning point in the history of the Catholic Church, simply augmenting Vatican I would have been insufficient. What actually was needed was a reinterpretation of *Pastor Aeternus* to effectively return Peter to the apostolic college.

Before concluding this section on collegiality, note that as consistent and insistent as Hermaniuk had been regarding shared governance in the Church, he apparently never became as explicit as the Melkite patriarch regarding the importance of episcopal conferences. Maximos IV specifically argued for the election of bishops by the episcopal conferences to (a truly effective) permanent, or apostolic, synod.[13] Hermaniuk had always been vaguer regarding participation in such conferences by anyone below the rank of cardinal.

Ecumenism

Few people today will recall that Archbishop Hermaniuk was elected (November 29, 1963) by the council fathers to the Pontifical Council for the Promotion of Christian Unity by a vote of 1,641.[14] The vote revealed a broad consensus among bishops from different continents who recognized Hermaniuk's commitment to, and competence in, the area of ecumenism.

The commitment was sincere. Already during his first private meeting with Cardinal Bea on September 29, 1961, Hermaniuk had stressed the need to invite Orthodox and Protestant observers to the council.

---

[11] See the entry for 12 October 1965.

[12] 16 October 1965.

[13] See Thomas E. Bird, *Patriarch Maximos IV Saygh*, *The Men Who Make the Council*, No. 6 (Notre Dame, IN: University of Notre Dame Press, 1964), 14–27.

[14] The number is mentioned by Hermaniuk himself in the entry for that date.

And in his very first intervention in the Pre-Conciliar Theological Commission on March 6, 1962, Hermaniuk asserted that infallibility should be presented in a way that would "correspond more to the mentality of the Eastern [Orthodox] Churches." His formula, "The subject of ecclesiastical infallibility resides in the college of bishops under the authority of the Roman Pontiff" (with further nuancing), was, according to Hermaniuk, supported immediately by the Leuven delegates and the Germans, along with Yves Congar. But, as Hermaniuk notes in his diary, "Cardinal Ottaviani delegated the matter to a sub-commission for further study."[15]

Incidentally, throughout the diary it is obvious that Hermaniuk personally admires and, in turn, is supported by, the so-called "progressives" of the council. The archbishop expresses appreciation for the views of Rahner, Schillebeeckx, and Häring, not to mention the "progressive bishops" of the council.[16]

Returning to ecumenism, Hermaniuk's diary reveals how passionate he was in Rome about forging ecumenical contacts, especially with the Greek Orthodox and representatives of Constantinople.[17] It also reveals that Vatican II really was a turning point for him personally. Imagine the following: Hermaniuk had been in Winnipeg since 1951, from around the same time as his Ukrainian Orthodox counterpart, Metropolitan Ilarion Ohienko. But it was only on March 16, 1963, that he and Ohienko finally met for a private meeting to discuss ecclesial issues.[18] To Hermaniuk's credit, it was he who initiated the exchange, hoping to convince Ohienko to accept an invitation to observe the council, and, again to his credit, when Ohienko insisted that Hermaniuk travel to his residence—no doubt in order to avoid the impression that Ohienko was seeking out a Catholic authority—he readily acquiesced.

Ohienko, unlike his American Ukrainian Orthodox colleague Archbishop, later Metropolitan, Mstyslav Skrypnyk, never did accept the invitation to be an observer, causing Hermaniuk to note: "I really

---

15 All of this is mentioned in the entry for 6 March 1962.

16 See the entries for 28 September 1961, 4 October 1963, 25 October 1964, and 17 September 1965.

17 See the entries for 16 and 20 November and 1 December 1965.

18 See the entry for that date.

regret that Metropolitan Ilarion did not have the courage to lead the Ukrainian Orthodox Church to the ecumenical arena of the Council in Rome and in this way to open her eyes to the full reality of the Church of Christ under the leadership of St. Peter's successor."[19]

To understand this quotation, one must realize that, according to Hermaniuk, Ohienko was personally in favour of accepting the invitation, but felt constrained by strong opposition from his clergy and faithful, many of whom were former Ukrainian Catholics who had become Orthodox in part because of their less than edifying experience of "the leadership of St. Peter's successor." But even Ohienko, according to Hermaniuk, found it difficult to "hide his instinctive intolerance towards Rome."[20] (The sentiment, no doubt, had been bolstered in the late 1930s when Ohienko witnessed more than 130 Orthodox churches in Volynia, Western Ukraine, burned or confiscated by Roman Catholics without any intervention from Rome.)[21]

Hermaniuk's passion for ecumenism, did, however, have its limits. Apparently he never once met the Moscow patriarchate's observers at the council. Initially this was due to his resentment over the fact that they were able to travel to Rome while the primate of the Ukrainian Greco-Catholic Church, Metropolitan Josyf Slipyj, languished in the Gulag.[22] Even after Slipyj's release, there is no reference to any meetings with the Russian Orthodox observers but rather a continued criticism of their presence. Abstracting from the observers' personal merits or the advisability of meeting even one's opponent, today one feels greater sympathy for Hermaniuk's aversion to Vitaly Borovoj and Vladimir Kotljarov—even if it did reveal a diplomatic insouciance. Post-Soviet archival discoveries demonstrate what Hermaniuk knew instinctively: their participation had been a decision of the Politburo itself.[23]

---

19 Entry for 6 August 1963.

20 Entry for 4 April 1963.

21 For the facts surrounding this tragic period in East–West relations, see the courageous report by Andrei Sheptytsky in Cyrille Korolevskij, *Métropolite André Szeptyckyj - 1865–1944* (Rome: Stoudion, 1964), 212–18.

22 See the entry for 21 October 1962.

23 See A. Melloni, ed., *Vatican II in Moscow (1959–1965): Acts of the Colloquium on the History of Vatican II Moscow, March 30–April 2, 1995* (Leuven: Bibliotheek van de Faculteit Godgeleerdheid, 1997), 69.

As a transition from ecumenism to our next section, on Eastern Catholicism, allow me to draw attention to another postconciliar problem that Hermaniuk could not have fully imagined: the conflict between the council's passion for reunion with the Orthodox and its stress on the integrity of the Eastern Catholic churches. Under October 13, 1965, Hermaniuk writes:

> After the meeting of the Secretariat for Christian Unity [*sic*], I had a short discussion with His Eminence Cardinal Bea concerning the Ukrainian Patriarchate. Cardinal Bea told me: The Holy Father is against the creation of the Ukrainian Catholic Patriarchate, since it would be against the ecumenical movement—against Moscow.

Those two sentences succinctly summarize the whole dilemma created by two of the council's equally central, but unfortunately equally conflicting "goods" (*bona*)—a dilemma that continues to the present. The problem is how to valorize the existence and vitality of the previously objectified—nay, repressed—Eastern Catholic churches, while also effecting rapprochement with Orthodox churches that desire the very elimination of Eastern Catholicism.

Ironically, Eastern Catholics experienced Vatican II as a turning point in that the Roman Curia no longer managed them as tools for "the conversion of the dissidents," but rather came to manipulate them as expendable pawns for the mollification of certain Orthodox. Only after the fall of Communism did this begin to change—and then only in the Eastern Bloc. (In the West, one notes a different dynamic, which I have discussed elsewhere.)[24]

Eastern Catholicism and Ukrainian Greco-Catholicism in Particular

Let me begin this section on Eastern Catholicism and Ukrainian Greco-Catholicism in particular by noting what I consider to be one of the most curious omissions from Hermaniuk's council diary. I do so because the omission helps explain dimensions of Hermaniuk's

---

24 See my contribution in Stephanie Mahieu and Vlad Naumescu, eds., *Churches In-between: Greek Catholic Churches in Post-Socialist Europe* (Berlin: Max Planck Institute for Social Anthropology, 2008), 143–53.

thinking and acting, as well as that of many Eastern Catholics to the present day.

It is my contention that for Eastern Catholics *the* most significant turning point at Vatican II was its thrice-repeated definition[25] of ecclesial "particularity," that is, the declaration that a "particular" church (nowadays, usually—if unfortunately—designated an "ecclesia *sui iuris*") is constituted by a distinctive theology, liturgy, spirituality, and canon law. (Before Vatican II, these churches were only "Rites"—thus, constituted by distinct, albeit Latinized, worship.)

For whatever reason, Hermaniuk makes no mention of this momentous change anywhere in his diary and, I would argue, understood its importance only belatedly.[26] Thus, throughout most of his life, Hermaniuk conceived of his own Church's particularity in predominantly ethnic terms (not even bolstering the pre-Vatican II approbation of *liturgical* distinctiveness). The first time I ever heard Hermaniuk speak—in 1985—I was surprised by his insistence that "there is no Ukrainian Church without the Ukrainian nation; there is no Ukrainian nation without the Ukrainian language; ergo, there is no Ukrainian Church without the Ukrainian language."[27] I was even more surprised when I subsequently learned that he had been repeating this syllogism among Ukrainian Catholics for decades.

Of course, the trauma of two world wars and repeated denials of Ukrainian statehood, not to mention genocide and other horrors, could excuse such logic among secular Ukrainians. But the inability of Church leaders to transcend it has fostered the decline of many a Ukrainian Catholic parish. This last point illustrates how Eastern Catholics have facilitated their own demise.[28]

---

25 *Lumen Gentium* 23, *Unitatis Redintegratio* 17, and *Orientalium Ecclesiarum* 5.

26 In the entry for 28 November 1964, Hermaniuk expresses dissatisfaction with the text of the conciliar Decree on the Eastern Churches (*Orientalium Ecclesiarum*). He notes that it could have been a much better document. Typically, however, he leaves it at that, and we are left wondering about how he would have changed it.

27 Speech at eparchial assembly, St. Nicholas Ukrainian Catholic Cathedral auditorium, Chicago, Illinois, October 1985.

28 On this problem, see Peter Galadza, "The Structure of the Eastern Churches: Bonded with Human Blood or Baptismal Water?" *Pro Ecclesia* 17 (2008): 373–86.

Let me now turn to an unresolved issue, signaled by Hermaniuk, which casts light on the Vatican's role in weakening Eastern Catholicism. Throughout the diary, Hermaniuk bemoans the inability of the Ukrainian Catholic Episcopal Conference to work together.[29] The conference, which during the council gathered almost twenty bishops from all over the world every Thursday evening, was plagued by acrimonious bickering and boycotts. But only once in the diary does Hermaniuk faintly hint at one of the roots of the problem, and even then, he does so only by expressing gratitude for the unidentified perpetrator's shift in approach.[30] What I have in mind is that both before and during—not to mention after—Vatican II, the Congregation for the Eastern Churches was notorious for dividing the Ukrainian Catholic episcopate in order to promote curial agendas. Thus, the antipathy between the Basilian and non-Basilian hierarchs was exploited by the congregation to prevent joint action on issues such as the creation of a patriarchate, or more generally, autonomy in governance. The reference above to Hermaniuk's appreciation for the perpetrator's positive gesture relates to the fact that after a string of boycotts by the Basilian bishops A. Senyshyn, A. Horniak, and J. Martynec, the three finally appear at a Thursday meeting, and, as Hermaniuk, writes (September 23, 1965): "It looks as if the Basilian bishops have received a directive to participate finally in the work of our Bishops' Conference." "But," continues Hermaniuk,"the harm done is hard to rectify."

Of course, such "directives" could have been issued more often. In other words, the papacy could indeed have used its authority *ad aedificationem ecclesiae*. But it did not, and in fact the Vatican's bestowal of a papal honour ("assistant to the papal throne") on Metropolitan Ambrose Senyshyn, the leader of the obstructionists, is mentioned by Hermaniuk (May 9, 1964) with a certain pain.

Allow me to conclude this section of my paper with a reference to a part of the diary that is particularly revelatory, especially in view of history's very different course. Most of us are aware that Patriarch Josyf Slipyj ended up being associated with strong anti-Sovietism,

---

29 See, for example, the entries for 10 October and 22 November 1964, and 6 December 1965.

30 See the entry for 23 September 1965.

while Cardinal Jan Willebrands became his nemesis, renowned for his conciliatory stance toward the USSR. Hermaniuk's diary reveals that when eight months after Slipyj's release from Siberia Slipyj insisted on attending the celebration of the anniversary of the Bolshevik Revolution at the Soviet Embassy in Rome, it was Willebrands who tried to dissuade him. But Slipyj went after all.[31] For those surprised by Slipyj's decision, it is important to note that after his release from the Gulag, Slipyj sincerely—if naïvely—imagined that the Soviets might allow him to return to Ukraine to shepherd his flock. Thus he, unlike Hermaniuk, was willing to meet with the Russian Orthodox observers on several occasions, and as a Soviet citizen show goodwill toward its government.

Conclusion

To end where I began, for an entire generation of Eastern Catholics, the work of Maxim Hermaniuk at Vatican II has remained something of a mustard seed. However, the beauty of memory, generated by conferences such as the one for which this essay was prepared, is that such seeds receive watering. I have no doubt that, inspired and encouraged by the thought of Hermaniuk, future generations of Ukrainian Catholics will create the kinds of contexts that will finally enable his texts to thrive.

---

[31] See the entry for 20 November 1963.

Canada's Ukrainian Catholics and Vatican II: A Guide for the Future or Struggling with the Past?

Myroslaw Tataryn,
St. Jerome's University

The question of the reception of Vatican II by Ukrainian Catholics in Canada is a particularly vexing one because it is not a well-trodden path and has eluded critical inquiry. Thus it remains a question that will involve not just academic study but also personal bias or, more diplomatically put, context. The current author, for example, does not come to the study as a researcher of Vatican II but rather as someone who has been perplexed by the difference in religious cultures among Ukrainian Catholics in eastern and western Canada. One of the main differences in these cultures relates to varying understandings or reception of Vatican II.

The initial intent of this study was to review the three major Ukrainian Catholic weeklies in Canada in the 1960s: *Ukrainski Visti / Ukrainian News* in Edmonton, *Postup/Progress* in Winnipeg, and *Nasha Meta / Our Aim* in Toronto. All weeklies were published in Ukrainian. In quickly reviewing the papers it became apparent and of note that it was in fact the Toronto eparchial (diocesan) paper, *Nasha Meta*, that had the most coverage of the preparation for the council and then of the council itself. The other papers took a more, so to speak, apophatic approach to the preconciliar phase and the council's early days. In fact, I was astounded by how much coverage *Nasha Meta* gave to the council and to its themes. As a result, my focus shifted to my own eparchy, Toronto, where, I have come to conclude, the council had its first and most significant impact on Ukrainian Catholics in Canada. I have read the diocesan paper for the years 1961 until 1966 and also analyzed a series of pamphlet-style publications (also published in eastern Canada) commenting on the council. I have isolated particular themes reflected in those years, significant authors whose reflections dominate the discussion, and as a result suggest that there were two events that became pivotal in the reception of Vatican II by Ukrainian Catholics in eastern Canada: the first was the arrival in Rome of Metropolitan Josyf Slipyj in February 1963, and the second a clandestine meeting of thirteen Ukrainian Catholic priests in Winnipeg on November 1 and 2, 1965.

Preconciliar Themes

One of *Nasha Meta*'s correspondents wrote in January of 1962, under the banner "Participating in an epochal program," an extensive report on the monumental events scheduled for that year and looking toward the council. These events included a Ukrainian Eucharistic Congress and what was called the "First Provincial Synod of the Ukrainian Catholic Province of Winnipeg." The latter in fact gave rise to a "Conference of Ukrainian Bishops" from around the world (outside Eastern Europe) in June of 1962. The article also touched on two themes that would be intertwined in the process of understanding and appropriating Vatican II: the project of renewing Church unity and that of opposing "militant atheism." The theme of Church unity was dominant throughout the paper's coverage in this period. However, the understanding of what that meant must be made clear: it was unambiguously understood within the very specific Ukrainian context.

In a telling article in March of 1962, an active layman, who in the 1980s would become *Nasha Meta*'s editor, wrote that the purpose of the Ukrainian Church itself was to "convert the East and build a single, national Church."[1] His article was entitled "About those who left

1 All texts from the newspaper are translated from the Ukrainian by the author.

Byzantium, but have not arrived in Rome" and referred to the Ukrainian Orthodox.[2] It was recognized that this theme of Church unity was one of importance to most church leaders. A long and very positive article examined John XXIII's encyclical *Aeterna Dei Sapientia*, in February 1962.[3] The encyclical commemorating the 150th anniversary of the death of Pope Leo I spoke of the upcoming council as one aimed at building Church unity—a goal embodied in the work of Leo I. The article also made certain to emphasize that the See of Peter was the visible and actual hub around which that unity was to be built. Recognizing the need for Church unity, according to reports in the paper, went beyond the Catholic world, however. In both February and March of that year articles appeared speaking of the ecumenical patriarch's concern for a renewal of Church unity. Again the presentation was positive and lacking any triumphalist note. The commemoration by the head of the Ukrainian Autocephalous Orthodox Church in the United States, Metropolitan Mstyslav, of the sixty-ninth birthday of the Ukrainian Catholic primate, Josyf Slipyj, imprisoned in a Soviet camp at the time, became the occasion not of a simple mention but of a front-page report using the metropolitan's prayerful commemoration to demonstrate his ecumenical spirit.[4]

This perceived broad consensus on the need for Church unity was placed within a very particular context: in reporting on the perspective of the Ecumenical Patriarch, the anonymous author wrote: "the matter of Christian unity, for which both East and West have striven and which is a necessary goal for all Christians, is of paramount importance in our age when we are confronted by the aggressive advance against faith in God and Christ's Church of soulless materialism and militant atheism."[5] Even the opening of the council resulted in a story in the October 13th edition stating that John XXIII had called the council at this time of battle between "God's world and the world of atheism,"

---

2 M. Poroniuk, *Nasha Meta*, March 17, 1962.

3 "Shche odyn zaklyk do jednosty [One more call for unity]," *Nasha Meta*, February 3, 1962.

4 M. Poroniuk, *Nasha Meta*, March 17, 1962.

5 "Vselens'kyj Patriarkh na shljakhu do tsekovnoji jednosty [The Ecumenical Patriarch on the road to church unity]," *Nasha Meta*, March 31, 1962.

and it is this battle that forces Catholics to recognize the value of the notion of "separated brethren"—for "the notion … does not allow us to look at them as non-Christians, but rather calls on us and demands of us true Christians to assist them to augment that which is lacking in their Christianity."[6] Thus in most of the presentations of the need to work for Christian unity this theme had two other elements: the need for the Ukrainian Church to restore unity with the Ukrainian Orthodox and the need for the entire Church to build unity in order to more effectively combat communism. These elements are interwoven in most of the reporting, with one significant exception: a series of articles by Father Meletij Solowy, OSBM.

Voices

His is the first voice to which my attention was drawn in reading *Nasha Meta*. Solowy was a Ukrainian Catholic priest and scholar, member of the Order of St. Basil the Great (OSBM). Meletij Solowy's articles on ecumenism were published regularly throughout 1962. His interventions are clearly scholarly and motivated by a clear embrace of the best of the ecumenical spirit. In fact in September of 1962 the paper serialized Solowy's commentary on papers presented by Orthodox theologian John Meyendorff the past July at a conference at Marquette University. Solowy suggests that Meyendorff's ecclesiology was very compatible with current Catholic thought, his approach was not at all polemical, and his analysis eminently objective. Solowy's analysis concluded with the assertion:

> It would be desirable for contemporary Ukrainian Orthodox in the emigration to familiarize themselves with the ecumenical movement in the non-Ukrainian Orthodox world. Following the example of Prof. Meyendorff, Ukrainians could commence an "ecumenical dialogue" and thus end an unnecessary and harmful politics of ecclesiastical particularism and "brilliant isolation."[7]

[6] I. S., "Pochavsja Vselens'kyj Sobor [The Ecumenical Council has begun]," *Nasha Meta*, October 13, 1962.

[7] "Problema tserkovnoji jednosty v pravoslavnomu nasvitlenju [The problem of church unity from the Orthodox perspective]," *Nasha Meta*, September 29, 1962.

Solowy wrote about the late-1950s work of a Ukrainian Orthodox priest, Mykhailo Kozarijchuk. Solowy presented Kozarijchuk as someone whose perspective on Catholic–Orthodox unity paralleled in many ways the 1930s and 40s work of Metropolitan Andrey Sheptytsky. Solowy remarked that both men recognized that there were no significant dogmatic reasons that impeded unity; that the first task, however, was for the Ukrainian Orthodox to rediscover their unity and recognize historical and political circumstances as the actual cause for Ukrainian Christian division.[8] Solowy's work stands in *Nasha Meta* as an academic counterpoint to the more dominant agenda tying work for unity with the struggle against Communism. His influence was widespread given his published works on liturgy and his being editor of the Ukrainian Basilian magazine *Svitlo* from 1954–58 and again from 1975–80. However, his broad ecumenical vision is not one that finds systematic support within the Ukrainian Catholic community until much later.

The somewhat remarkable insertion of a clearly academic voice into the paper, more usually dominated by popularizing voices, was, I would suggest, a characteristic of another voice of note. This voice was largely unidentified in the newspaper and it is of the editor, Father Peter Chomyn, who edited *Nasha Meta* from 1950 until 1980. Father Chomyn was an important figure not just because of his editorial role but also because of his connections to pre-war Ukraine, his academic training, and his personal connection to the soon-to-be-freed Metropolitan Josyf Slipyj. Father Chomyn was ordained in 1923 in L'viv, currently Ukraine, and within a year was appointed to assist at one of the most prestigious parishes in L'viv, the Holy Transfiguration. While assisting there he served as the secretary of the L'viv seminary, of which Slipyj was rector, and was editor of the journal *Nyva*—both from 1929 until 1939. The journal was the voice of the Society of Saint Andrew, an organization of diocesan clergy who were regarded as promoters of the more Eastern traditions of the Ukrainian Catholic Church. Upon his arrival in Canada in 1950 Chomyn was appointed by Bishop Isidore (Borecky) of Toronto as editor of the diocesan paper and assistant in St. Nicholas parish in Toronto (again a prestigious appointment). In

8 *Nasha Meta*, October 13, 1962.

the 1970s Father Chomyn was a founding member of the group of diocesan priests in Canada that revived the Society of Saint Andrew, and for four years once more published *Nyva*. Father Chomyn's at times broader perspective was apparent in his editorial greeting of the opening of the council, published in the October 13th edition. In this editorial he did not emphasize an anti-Communist agenda, but rather placed the council in the context of a positive and forward-looking horizon. Chomyn wrote:

> The Ecumenical Council is gathering at a time when around the world various intellectual and social revolutions have taken place and the Church stands in the midst of the expectations which have been generated at this turbulent time. The Church is expected to present a way forward clearly and powerfully. In order to take command of these revolutionary movements and to actualize the Church's renewal the Head of Christ's Church has called the hierarchy together in Council. This Council's first and primary goal will be to assess the state of the Church, make precise its current goals, update its canons, its liturgy, its attitude to the world. The Church must clarify its approach to contemporary technology, to nuclear technology and to a humanity divided into two blocs: free and dictatorial.
>
> In addition the Council has a formidable and holy purpose: to lead us to the unity of the divided and varied Christian world.[9]

Chomyn's perspective does not completely avoid an anti-Communist view but seems to recognize that the ecumenical agenda is not a tool in the battle with Communism but rather stands alone as a fundamental Christian imperative. In early 1963, rather providentially, Chomyn picked up the theme of the absence of anyone at the council from the persecuted Church in Ukraine, the Orthodox presence at the council, and reflected upon the work of the Secretariat for Christian Unity. With the release from the Soviet camps of the Ukrainian Catholic Primate Josyf Slipyj and his arrival in Rome on February 10, 1963, after eighteen years of Soviet incarceration, Chomyn turned the newspaper more and

9 P. Chomyn, *Nasha Meta*, October 13, 1962.

more to Slipyj and Slipyj's developing agenda for the Ukrainian Catholic Church. But more of that in a moment.

A third voice of note, which also reflected a broader perspective was that of Father Myroslav Marusyn, then secretary to the Apostolic Visitator for Ukrainian Catholics in Western Europe, Bishop Ivan Buchko. Marusyn was the regular correspondent for *Nasha Meta* from the council and in many ways demonstrated an insider's perspective, given his ongoing role in the Church's bureaucracy. Marusyn's career was totally that of an insider's insider. He was ordained in 1948 and completed his doctoral studies in Rome in 1951. Immediately thereafter he became Buchko's secretary and remained so until 1972. In 1963 he added the role of secretary to Slipyj, which he also concluded rather tumultuously in 1972. In that year he was appointed Buchko's successor and ordained to the episcopate in 1974. From 1977 until 1982 he also served on the Commission for the Codification of Oriental Canon Law. In 1982 he was named archbishop and secretary of the Congregation for Oriental Churches. In 2001 he retired. Marusyn's commentaries in the newspaper were quite varied. He offered many ongoing reports of people and events. However, he also supplied a number of significant interventions. Prior to the council's opening, he offered a number of reflections on the significance of the council for providing an arena to raise the issue of the persecuted Church in the Soviet Union. He joined others who lamented the absence of Metropolitan Slipyj at the opening of the council. In November of 1962 he reported on the international attention that focused on the Ukrainian Catholic bishops attending the council and then the "great interest in Metropolitan and Confessor of the Faith, Josyf."[10] During the first session, Marusyn also reported on the liturgical discussions and the significant conciliar role of Melkite Patriarch Maximos. In 1963 the newspaper serialized a number of articles by Marusyn: on the historic role of Ukrainian bishops at ecumenical councils; on the doctrinal statements of ecumenical councils; under the title "Metropolitan Josyf Slipyj: teacher and pastor. The Great Absentee" (but published soon after Slipyj's release in February 1963) an article about Slipyj and his theological importance; an article as-

10 "Vselens'kyj Sobor [The Ecumenical Council]," *Nasha Meta*, November 10, 1962.

sessing the state of relations with the Orthodox; and finally, published toward the end of the year, a review of the first session including a rather confused explanation of the rejection of the schema on revelation in which he emphasized the very positive nature of the schema and wondered why some bishops opposed it.[11] This series of articles was more scholarly in character and provided insights into major questions of the day. However, surprisingly given Marusyn's presence in Rome, the article on relations with the Orthodox was less irenic than the earlier work of Solowy and concluded with an appeal to Orthodox bishops, priests, and laity to follow the lead of "the heroic ... great hierarchs," who entered into union at the Council of Florence.[12] Marusyn's voice in the newspaper was extremely strong and significant during the council's first session, but with the arrival of Slipyj in February 1963 and the pause between the first two sessions, the presence of this voice diminished.

The fourth voice is one that is heard on the pages of *Nasha Meta* initially in October 1962. It is a voice that was also often heard academically in Canada: the voice of Petro Bilaniuk, then a professor at St. Michael's College, University of Toronto, and to his great dismay not ordained a priest until 1981. His is the only lay voice among those I am mentioning. Bilaniuk's public lecture of October 1962 was serialized in the newspaper throughout the final three months of that year. The article was an overview of the ecclesiology and history of ecumenical councils and contained this prophetic statement: "It is one thing to successfully conduct an Ecumenical Council and a completely other matter to implement its decisions in the life of the Church."[13] Bilaniuk's place among these voices is not because of his role on the pages of the diocesan newspaper, however. Rather it is due to the role he came to play in the events of 1965 and 1966. Most clearly, Bilaniuk became the intellectual spearhead in Canada for Slipyj's "Easternizing" agenda.

---

[11] "Vselens'kyj Sobor [The Ecumenical Council]," *Nasha Meta*, August 31, 1963.

[12] "Vselens'kyj Sobor is pravoslavni tserkvy skhodu [The Ecumenical council and the Orthodox Churches of the east]," *Nasha Meta*, June 8, 1963..

[13] "Shcho take Vselens'kyj Sobor? [What is an Ecumenical council?]," *Nasha Meta*, November 17, 1962.

Events

As mentioned earlier, on February 10, 1963, then Metropolitan of L'viv and titled Confessor of the Faith Josyf Slipyj was freed from the Soviet gulag thanks to the combined intervention of Pope John XXIII and President John F. Kennedy. His liberation was startling and completely unexpected. However, as Jaroslav Pelikan noted in his biography of Slipyj, he came to the West with a "detailed agenda" for his Church, "which he almost immediately set about implementing, from the full-blown schema for the Ukrainian Catholic University to the idea of the patriarchate," which suggests that during his captivity "he was planning and dreaming about the needs of his church."[14] At the age of seventy, rather than establishing a new home of comfort in the Vatican, he commenced a whirlwind agenda that transformed his Church and in so doing radically affected how the council would be received. That agenda, and the person of "The Metropolitan and Confessor," became the staple feature on the pages of *Nasha Meta* for years to come, not surprising when one recalls that the editor had been Slipyj's secretary at the L'viv seminary before the war. Most significantly, commencing in May of 1963, the newspaper regularly published Slipyj's talks, homilies, and other items that Chomyn perceived of value to all his readers. As a result, Slipyj's agenda was well known in the Eparchy of Toronto, and not surprisingly this eparchy soon came to be seen as the most supportive of that agenda. However, Slipyj's arrival, though greeted exuberantly by the Ukrainian hierarchs, soon came to be a source of debate and confrontation.

Slipyj's primary vision for his Church was its need to build unity. In his eyes Ukrainian Catholics worldwide needed to recognize their common heritage and common faith experience. In addition, he felt this unity needed to serve the persecuted Church, which one day he said would be free and need assistance from the Church in the West. This theme was already evident in a homily he gave to the Ukrainian Basilian community three weeks after his arrival in Rome. In the homily he called upon the Basilians to be ever prepared for the challenges posed by the needs of the faithful in Eastern Europe:

---

[14] Jaroslav Pelikan, *Confessor Between East and West: A Potrait of Ukrainian Cardinal Josyf Slipyj* (Grand Rapids, MI: Eerdmans, 1990), 169–70.

> there you will find different barriers, a very different culture, another social organization; you will find different technologies and a very different psychology. You will come up against "many enemies", devastated Churches, a materialistic society, militant atheism, you will be greeted by aggressive attitudes against the Church and religion and against all that is holy. But you will also find people in whom the spark of God remains, in whom the spirit of God is alive. You will find people of faith as were the first Christian communities. You will see long prayers, significant self-denial, you will find prostrations and severe fasting, in other words, heroic efforts of Christian love. All this is mixed together. Your responsibility will be to rectify the situation, raise and strengthen the good, weed out evil and assist the development of holiness so that the life of the Church may flourish once again as it had once done in our land.[15]

Slipyj also embraced the ecumenical theme; in a homily a few weeks later, he stated that unity in the Catholic Church means overcoming national, political, and even religious barriers—he unequivocally stated that Christians are all united by a common faith and a "common call to prayer on Sunday"[16] in the same homily in which he spoke of the importance of "priesthood" in human history beginning with the priesthood in "Assyria, Babylon and Egypt." He underlined that in many religions and civilizations priests were the "creators of culture, artists of the human psyche and technology, learning and literature."[17] In a talk delivered at the Greek College of St. Athanasius, Slipyj spoke about the need to dedicate oneself to the unity of the Church, a unity that he said must be built on ascesis and learning.[18] Slipyj, who has often been painted as a obstructionist toward Vatican Ostpolitik, commended Pope John XXIII's *Pacem in Terris* for being able to get beyond the political confrontation of the two superpowers.[19] But he took every opportunity

---

15 *Nasha Meta*, June 29, 1963.

16 *Nasha Meta*, August 3, 1963.

17 *Nasha Meta*, August 10, 1963.

18 *Nasha Meta*, August 31, 1963.

19 Pelikan, *East and West*, 183.

to remind Paul VI of the need to speak up for the persecuted Church.[20] Under Slipyj's direction the so-called Conference of Ukrainian Bishops began to evolve its nomenclature, which by 1969 had come to be the Synod of Bishops of the Ukrainian Catholic Church: a title that was not welcomed by the Vatican. In late 1963 and then until his death in 1984 the debate with the Vatican over titles would become a central feature on the pages of *Nasha Meta* and the primary prism through which Vatican II would be read.

On October 11, 1963, Slipyj made what was to become an historic intervention at the council, from the perspective of Ukrainian Catholics, when he called upon the council to raise the dignity of his Church to that of a patriarchate as a clear sign of support for the silenced suffering Church. The intervention was probably premised on the draft of the Decree on the Eastern Catholic Churches, which allowed for an ecumenical council to erect a patriarchate (as could the Pope). Slipyj's speech was reported to have been greeted with widespread support but official inaction. On December 23, 1963, and welcomed quite widely by Ukrainian Catholics, Pope Paul VI approved the term Major Archbishop for use by Slipyj. He received this honour as a sign of caring and distinction for the persecuted Church.[21] But in his letter of thanks to the Pope, he made it clear that, "This is a historic act and the first step toward the Ukrainian patriarchate, which will undoubtedly have great and salutary consequences for the development of our church in the future."[22] The Ukrainian bishops twice unanimously approved an official letter to the Pope requesting the elevated status for Slipyj and their Church.[23] On January 25, 1965, Pope Paul VI appointed Slipyj cardinal, but not patriarch.

Slipyj's agenda was stalled but not abandoned. However, internal opposition was developing. This opposition mainly developed from two sources: Metropolitan of Philadelphia Ambrose Senyshyn and the

---

20 "Majemo papu! [We have a Pope!]," *Nasha Meta*, June 29, 1963 and "Papa Pavlo VI vidviduje mytropolyta-ispovidnyka druhyj raz [Pope Paul VI visits the Metropolitan-Confessor a Second Time]," *Nasha Meta*, July 13, 1963.

21 Letter to Paul VI on 4 January 1964 in Pelikan, *East and West*, 195.

22 Pelikan, *East and West*, 195.

23 10 October 1963, and 17 September 1964.

male Basilian Order, the latter being a very strong and influential force in western Canada. The causes for this latter tension seem to have been two-fold: Slipyj resented the autonomy from episcopal influence that the Basilians had grown to cherish in the post–World War II environment, and he was particularly disturbed by innovations initiated by many Basilians, who were regarded by Slipyj as further undesirable (although now "conciliar") Latinizations. In his interventions at the council in 1964, he continued the theme begun by his predecessor, Metropolitan Sheptytsky: his Church's contribution to the Universal Church and ecumenism lay in maintaining its historic, although often tarnished, Eastern traditions, a theme that he repeatedly demonstrated was echoed in the Decree on the Eastern Churches. It was this "Easternness" that Slipyj regarded as both the guarantee of the unity of his Church and its ability to extend an embrace of Christian unity to the Orthodox world. This latter agenda placed him in conflict with some North American bishops, most significantly the aforementioned Ambrose Senyshyn.

In the years 1964–65 Ambrose Senyshyn and Bishop of Chicago Jaroslav Gabro authorized the introduction of the Gregorian calendar. Similarly, although less formally, the calendar was introduced in many western Canadian parishes by the Basilian fathers and eventually by the Redemptorist priests, as well. Slipyj was becoming increasingly concerned about what he called "deritualization" and "denationalization." Sociologists will tell us that these changes should not have been seen as exceptional: initially immigrant communities became settled and "normalized" within their new homeland and wished to increasingly adapt themselves to the norms of the dominant culture. But for Slipyj this "evolution" was a threat to the unity of his flock and to the very existence of his Church. Increasingly Slipyj was being regarded not as a promoter of a living legacy and viable identity but rather as a culturally dislocated defender of the past.

Not as a challenge to Slipyj, but at least for some perceived as a challenge to his supporters and his agenda, thirteen Ukrainian Catholic priests in Canada met in Winnipeg on November 1 and 2, 1965. The priests came from all the eparchies in Canada: three from Toronto, four from Winnipeg, five from Saskatoon, and one from Edmonton. All but one were Canadian born. At the conclusion of their clandestine meeting they issued an open letter to the Ukrainian Bishops of Canada—it was, according to a number of the participants,[24] not a challenge to Slipyj, but rather a challenge to Metropolitan Maxim Hermaniuk, who they felt was not implementing the positions he was presenting at the council. The open letter called on the bishops to present a more favourable picture of the Ukrainian Church to the Canadian public and renew the Church, by: introducing the wholesale use of English in the liturgy; allowing for the formal introduction of the Gregorian calendar; allowing the introduction of liturgical innovations (read experimentation); developing a Ukrainian Catholic school system; establishing a seminary in Canada; establishing an English-language Ukrainian Catholic press in Canada; and finally presenting a leadership that would implement the full reforms of Vatican II.

In Canada a significant split had come out into the open between those who would read Vatican II through the agenda of Josyf Slipyj and the Decree on the Eastern Catholic Churches and those who would attempt to move the Church in the direction of what they regarded as the council's agenda to modernize and update the Church according to the demands of Western society. The result in Canada was decades of tension mainly (but not exclusively) between the Eparchy of Toronto and the Church in western Canada. Maxim Hermaniuk was not perceived by the modernizing group as a supporter in spite of his relationship with Slipyj being often tense. In the end, Hermaniuk found himself often isolated and not embraced as a viable interpreter of the council by either constituency. In western Canada, the Basilian fathers maintained their dominance, while in the east, Bishop Borecky's embrace of Slipyj's agenda and the powerful pen of Petro Bilaniuk provided ample stimulus to ensure that the work of Vatican II was almost completely narrowed to the Decree on the Eastern Catholic Churches. As a result, the Easternization of the Church was most dramatic in the Eparchy of Toronto, while western Canada resisted it for decades. For example, the attire of Bishop Borecky was transformed virtually overnight, whereas for the other bishops it was more gradual. The erection of traditional Church edifices was much more common in eastern Canada than in the

24 Expressed by them directly to the author.

west. Most churches in the east were built immediately with iconostases (icon screens) whereas in the west a concerted effort to have churches erect icon screens had to wait for the celebration of the Millennium of Christianity in 1988!

Conclusion

In my opening I referred to the path I embarked upon as one that was not well trodden. It is, I hope, however, one that will soon see other travellers. It contains a remarkable story: one that begins with a breadth of possibilities, a spectacular cause for celebration (the arrival of Slipyj in Rome) but then an unfortunate denouement—the struggle over ecclesiastical structure and identity—and one that sidetracked the larger agenda of the reception of the fullness of Vatican II. It could be a tragic story, and yet perhaps it is a story with a silver lining: with the arrival of new immigrants to North America from Poland, the former Yugoslavia, and the former Soviet Union, the fact that the Church maintained more of its traditional character has meant that these people have found and continue to find an ecclesial home here that may not have otherwise sustained itself, had the events of 1963 not transpired as they did. However, the reception of Vatican II remains as an ongoing project, but with the fall of the Soviet Union a project for the entire worldwide Ukrainian Greek Catholic Church, not just its Canadian branch.

Experimenting Creatively with Being Church in the Modern World: The Social Affairs Commission of the Canadian Conference of Catholic Bishops, 1965–1984[1]

Peter E. Baltutis,
University of St. Michael's College

Promulgated on the last day of the Second Vatican Council, December 7, 1965, "The Pastoral Constitution on the Church in the Modern World"[2] articulated the council fathers' desire that religion should not only affect a Catholic's private life but it should also influence their cultural, social, and political engagement with the world. Beginning with the principle that all human beings have an in-

1 The author would like to thank Michael Attridge for welcoming this research into the *Vatican II in Canada* colloquium; the participants of the Toronto colloquium for their insightful comments on the original presentation; William F. Ryan, SJ, who was interviewed several times during this investigation; the General Secretariat of the Canadian Conference of Catholic Bishops (CCCB) and Archivist Brigitte Pollock, who granted the author full access to the CCCB Archives; and the Social Science and Humanities Research Council of Canada (SSHRC) for funding this project.

2 Vatican Council II, "Pastoral Constitution on the Church in the Modern World" (*Gaudium et Spes*), in *Vatican Council II: A Completely Revised Translation in Inclusive Language*, ed. Austin Flannery, OP (New York: Costello Publishing Company, 1996), 163–282.

herent dignity since they were created in the image of God,[3] *Gaudium et Spes* (the constitution's Latin title) argued that humans can only attain their full potential by participating in community.[4] In promoting the common good of the human race (solidarity), as well as allowing individuals to pursue their own vocation (human rights), the Church challenged all Christians to work for more humane and just conditions in all areas of life (not only political freedoms, but justice in the economic, cultural, and social fields, as well.)[5] *Gaudium et Spes* served as a benchmark document in modern Catholic social teaching because it presented a more explicitly developed theological basis for the Church's social engagement in the world than is found in earlier papal encyclicals, and it promoted social justice as integral to the Church's mission. This prophetic document had a profound resonance throughout the global Church as it spoke on behalf of the world's bishops.

This paper seeks to answer this fundamental question: what was the influence of *Gaudium et Spes* on the theology and praxis of Catholic social justice in Canada? There are numerous ways that one can approach this question, but I have limited the scope of this research to addressing the formal response of the institutional Church as articulated in the initiatives of the Canadian Conference of Catholic Bishops (CCCB).[6] The CCCB is not a national church headquarters, but it is a unique forum for Canada's bishops to process their experiences on the life of the Church. Within the CCCB, a permanent Social Affairs Commission (comprised of several bishops and a full-time staff of animators) is mandated to engage in broad consultations, research, and ecumenical collaboration for the purpose of implementing the vision of *Gaudium et Spes* of "being Church" in the modern world. Through creative experimentation, this commission helped establish a new paradigm for understanding and practicing Catholic social justice in Canada during the two decades directly following Vatican II.

---

3 Vatican II, *Gaudium et Spes*, #11-22, 173–88.

4 Vatican II, *Gaudium et Spes*, #23-32, 188–98.

5 David Hollenbach, SJ, "Commentary on *Gaudium et spes*," in *Modern Catholic Social Teaching: Commentaries and Interpretations*, ed. Kenneth R. Himes (Washington, DC: Georgetown University Press, 2005), 266–91.

6 The Canadian Catholic Conference (CCC) was founded in 1943 but was not officially recognized by the Holy See until 1948. In 1977 the name of this group was formally changed to the Canadian Conference of Catholic Bishops (CCCB).

The origins of modern Catholic social teaching date back to 1891 when Pope Leo XIII issued the encyclical *Rerum Novarum*, which addressed pressing social questions raised by the Industrial Revolution.[7] Using this document as a catalyst for social action, several independent Catholic grassroots movements sprang up throughout various regions of Canada. Catholics in Québec founded their own labour school (the *École Sociale Populaire*), organized a religious-based labour union (the *Confédération des travailleurs catholiques du Canada*), built a widespread network of credit unions (*caisses populaires*), and established a branch of the European-based Catholic Action Movement for youth (*Jeunesse ouvrière catholique*).[8] In English-speaking regions, the pioneering bishop to apply papal social teaching to a Canadian context was Archbishop Neil McNeil of Toronto (1912–34).[9] Collaborating with McNeil were Henry Somerville, who publicized social Catholicism as editor and columnist of the *The Catholic Register*,[10] and Catherine de Hueck Doherty, who combated economic injustice and Communism through her Friendship House movement.[11] In the Maritimes, Moses Coady and Jimmy Tompkins initiated the Antigonish Movement by organizing an effective program of adult education and community

[7] "*Rerum Novarum*: The Condition of Labor (Leo XIII, 1891)," in *Catholic Social Thought: The Documentary Heritage*, ed. David J. O'Brien and Thomas A. Shannon (Maryknoll, NY: Orbis Books, 1992), 14–39.

[8] Oscar Cole Arnal, "From Reaction to Radicalism: The Changing Face of Quebec's Catholic Church toward the Working Class (1920–1990)," *Historical Papers: Canadian Society of Church History* (1991): 33–46; and Roberto Perin, "French-Speaking Canada from 1840," in *A Concise History of Christianity of Canada*, ed. Terrence Murphy and Roberto Perin (Toronto: Oxford University Press, 1996), 207–208, 236–37, 253.

[9] Peter Ernest Baltutis, "'To Enlarge Our Hearts and To Widen Our Horizon': Archbishop Neil McNeil and Social Catholicism in the Roman Catholic Archdiocese of Toronto, 1912–1934" (MA thesis, University of St. Michael's College, 2006).

[10] For the most current assessment of Henry Somerville, see Joseph Sinasac, *Fateful Passages: The Life of Henry Somerville, Catholic Journalist* (Ottawa: Novalis, 2003). For a more scholarly account, see Jeanne Ruth Merifield Beck, "Henry Somerville and the Development of Catholic Social Thought in Canada: Somerville's Role in the Archdiocese of Toronto, 1915–1943" (PhD dissertation, McMaster University, 1977).

[11] For an autobiographical account, see Catherine de Hueck Doherty, *Fragments of My Life* (Notre Dame, IN: Ave Maria Press, 1979). For historical assessments, see Jeanne R. Beck, "Contrasting Approaches to Social Action: Henry Somerville, the Educator, and Catherine de Hueck, the Activist," in *Catholics at the "Gathering Place": Historical Essays on the Archdiocese of Toronto, 1841–1991*, ed. Mark George McGowan and Brian P. Clarke (Toronto: Canadian Catholic Historical Association, 1993), 213–32.

economic development through co-operatives and credit unions.[12] Equally important to the work of Coady and Tompkins in Atlantic Canada were the ministries of female religious congregations, such as the Sisters of St. Martha.[13] Finally, Catholic social action spread across the prairies and western Canada by the innovative work of religious orders, such as the Sisters of Service[14] and the Redemptorists.[15]

While various regional Catholic social justice initiatives took place prior to World War II, there were no national campaigns at this time. This changed in 1943 when the Canadian bishops established the Canadian Catholic Conference (CCC) to be a permanent organization with working commissions that would meet between annual plenary sessions.[16] In 1948 the CCC established a permanent Social Action Department staffed by two directors, one for each linguistic region of Canada. During the 1950s, much of their work was devoted to organizing annual conferences on Catholic social teaching. Québec had been hosting popular *Semaines sociales du Canada* since 1920, and in 1953 this model was adapted to English Canada as the Catholic Social Life Conferences.[17] These popular annual meetings attracted bishops, clergy, religious, and laity from across the country and provided a national forum for social concerns. Out of these gatherings developed Social Action Sunday in the English-speaking dioceses of Canada in 1956.[18]

---

12 For an autobiographical account, see Moses Coady, *Masters of Their Own Destiny* (New York: Harper, 1939). For historical assessments, see Anne Alexander, *The Antigonish Movement: Moses Coady and Adult Education Today* (Toronto: Thompson Educational Publishing, 1997); and James Lotz and Michael R. Welton, *Father Jimmy: Life and Times of Jimmy Tompkins* (Wreck Cove, Cape Breton Island: Breton Books, 1997).

13 Heidi Macdonald, "Doing More with Less: The Sisters of St. Martha (PEI) Diminish the Impact of the Great Depression," *Acadiensis* XXXIII, no. 1 (Fall 2003): 21–46; and James Cameron, *"And Martha Served": History of the Sisters of St. Martha, Angonish, Nova Scotia* (Halifax: Nimbus, 2000).

14 Jeanne R. Beck, *To Do and To Endure: The Life of Catherine Donnelly, Sister of Service* (Toronto: Dundurn Press, 1997).

15 Paul Laverdure, *Redemption and Renewal: The Redemptorists of English Canada, 1834–1994* (Toronto: Dundurn Press, 1996).

16 Bernard Daly, *Remembering for Tomorrow: A History of the Canadian Conference of Catholic Bishops, 1943–1993* (Ottawa: Canadian Conference of Catholic Bishops, 1995), 20–21.

17 Brian F. Hogan, "Salted With Fire: Studies in Catholic Social Thought and Action in Ontario, 1931–1961" (PhD dissertation, University of Toronto, 1986) 240–46.

18 Brian F. Hogan, "The Institute of Social Action and Social Catholicism in Canada in

Also in 1956, the Social Affairs Office inaugurated a series of annual Labour Day Messages, whereby the bishops addressed pressing social issues.[19]

Collectively, these preconciliar Labour Day Messages—written by the Social Affairs Office and approved by the Canadian bishops—articulated an underlying theology to the CCC national social action program. According to these statements, injustice was perceived narrowly as having spiritual causes and the bishops' suggested remedy was personal conversion. The 1958 Labour Day Message stated that all economic problems, such as labour-management relations, were linked to global economic warfare centred on the "struggle between total control by a godless state [USSR] on the one hand, and various combinations of free enterprise and democracy on the other."[20] In these statements, the Canadian bishops opposed Communism not on political or economic grounds but rather as a religious ideology. This social analysis conflated military, economic, and political issues with religious ones. The result is that the Labour Day Messages presented their audience with only two alternatives: Christian faith, freedom, and capitalism on the one hand and atheism, repression, and Communism on the other.[21] This dualistic approach by the Canadian bishops sanctified the socio-economic status quo of capitalism and democracy and attributed any injustice to atheism and Communism.

The Labour Day Messages also reveal the ethical methodology of the preconciliar period. The solution to social problems, the bishops argued, began with a disciplined study of the Church's social doctrine, which was rooted in natural law reasoning. Thus, the ethical task was a deductive exercise, moving from timeless moral principles to specific historical applications. While the bishops noted accurately enough the

---

the 1950s," *CCHA Hostorical Studies* 54 (1987): 129–44.

19 The texts of the Labour Day Messages are available in E. F. Sheridan ed., *Do Justice! The Social Teaching of the Canadian Catholic Bishops, 1945–1986* (Sherbrook, QC: Édition Paulines; Toronto: Jesuit Centre for Social Faith and Justice, 1987).

20 Social Action Department, Canadian Catholic Conference, "Unemployment: Part of Economic Warfare, Labour Day Message—1958," in Sheridan, *Do Justice!* 76.

21 Lee Cormie, "Revolutions in Canadian Catholic Social Teaching," in *Church and Canadian Culture*, ed. Robert E. VanderVennen (Lanham, MD: University Press of America, 1991), 60.

major social issues of the day, there was no substantive analysis or mention of statistics or social science sources.[22] There were few references made to scripture in the CCC statements, rather nearly all references were to Vatican statements. Furthermore, suggestions were general and represented religious rather than social discourse.[23] Recommendations included: sobriety and restraint, practice of good citizenship, and reverence for spiritual values. In other words, religious conversion was seen as the answer to the social question. Taken as a whole, the social Catholicism of this period existed in a one-way relationship to the world. It saw itself as having much to give and little to receive.[24]

In contrast to the triumphalist approach of preconciliar period, *Gaudium et Spes* introduced several revolutionary shifts in how the Church approached social justice. Most notably, it expanded the scope of the Church's social concern from being limited exclusively to the problems of industrialization to a discussion of social problems that affected the whole human race (such as world peace, poverty, and political oppression).[25] Equally important, there were significant shifts in methodology. The council fathers abandoned the exclusive appeal to "natural law" for a more theologically and scripturally informed approach to social justice.[26] The deductive approach of applying ethical principles was exchanged for a more historically conscious and inductive understanding of ethics.[27] This put far greater emphasis on the person as subject and, thus, on freedom, equality, and participation as central goods in social life. Finally, "Church in the Modern World" shifted from a primarily hierarchical understanding of ecclesiology to one that also emphasized the pilgrim character of the journey of the people of God in this world.[28] Succinctly stated, "[t]he hierarchical

---

[22] Ibid., 66.

[23] Sheridan, "Introduction," *Do Justice!* 36.

[24] Robert Martin McKeon, "The Canadian Catholic Social Justice Paradigm: Birth, Growth, Decline and Crisis" (PhD dissertation, University of St. Michael's College, 2003), 36.

[25] William Ryan, "A Developing World: A Developing Church," *Social Thought,* 1 October 1967, 9.

[26] Charles E. Curran, *Catholic Social Teaching, 1891–Present: A Historical, Theological, and Ethical Analysis* (Washington, DC: Georgetown University Press, 2002), 21–52.

[27] Ibid., 53–100.

[28] Ibid., 101–21.

teaching office has changed from an authoritative source of eternal and natural law applied to human problems to a dialogue partner that has something to contribute to the world but can also learn from the world."[29] In promulgating *Gaudium et Spes*, Vatican II affirmed that the Church and humanity experience the same earthly situation and need to work together for the mutual benefit of both.[30]

The enthusiastic embrace of *Gaudium et Spes* by Canadian bishops is not surprising since more of them spoke in the plenary sessions on this council document than on any other. In fact, Cardinals Paul-Émile Léger of Montréal and Maurice Roy of Québec, as well as Québec theologian Bernard Lambert, were heavily involved in finalizing the text.[31] Furthermore, in preparing for conciliar debate on this proposed document, the Canadian bishops became aware that only bishops of larger dioceses had ready access to competent theological expertise to help them prepare adequate interventions. For that reason, in 1964, the CCC administrative board reorganized itself into "a dynamic and top-quality secretariat, oriented towards study and research, equipped to give specialized and competent services promptly, able to discern social changes, and to observe and analyze all problems of interest to the Church."[32] The principal instrument of this new-look secretariat would be the greatly enhanced Social Affairs Office, which would serve as a common resource for all Canadian bishops who were dealing with the complex issues associated with promoting meaningful relationships between the Church and society. To fulfill its dynamic new role of assisting the bishops with "reading the signs of the times," the Social Affairs Office hired professionally trained social scientists to its staff, such as the Harvard-trained Jesuit economist Bill Ryan, who served as co-director in 1964.

Once the council ended, the newly empowered Social Affairs Office organized national institutes for priests on the significance of *Gaudium*

---

29 Ibid., 106.

30 Vatican II, *Gaudium et spes*, #40-45, 206-217.

31 Bernard Daly, *Beyond Secrecy: The Untold Story of Canada and the Second Vatican Council* (Ottawa: Novalis, 2003), 197–98.

32 Archives of the Canadian Conference of Catholic Bishops (ACCCB), Meeting Minutes, CCCB Administrative Board, 14 February 1964, Vol. 3, No. 35, 296.

et Spes. The English section invited over forty priests (representing every English-speaking diocese in Canada) to Guelph for an intensive study of the pastoral constitution facilitated by Jean-Marie Tillard, who had served as a *peritus* (theological advisor) to the Canadian bishops at the council.[33] As a follow-up, co-directors Jack Shea and Bill Ryan conducted nationwide tours that instructed priests, religious orders, and parish groups throughout English Canada on the importance of *Gaudium et Spes*. Their French counterparts Charles Mathieu and Jean-Guy Hamelin carried out similar programs throughout Québec and French-speaking communities across Canada.[34] Invoking *Gaudium et Spes*'s call for dialogue between clergy and laity, these meetings were also designed for the Social Affairs staff to solicit constructive suggestions for evaluating their work in the light of Vatican II. At a national meeting in 1967, a group of sixty bishops, clergy, and laity, were asked if "Catholic Social Doctrine has had a significant influence on English Canadian society?" Since the overwhelming majority answered with a clear no,[35] Social Affairs developed three new approaches in its work.

First, in the words of the Bill Ryan, "the most profound change that has taken place in the Canadian Bishops' National Conference since Vatican II has been the growing tendency to study more and to consult the experts for help to read 'the signs of the times' before moving into action."[36] One expression of this priority for consultation was, from 1966 through 1972, the French Social Affairs Office established the *Conseil national d'action sociale* (CNAS).[37] Acknowledging that social justice work is a ministry involving the whole church, CNAS was a consultative body of influential union leaders, businessmen, and lawyers. Due to the important role that this group played in the development of Labour Day Messages, the CNAS was hailed as a "tangible expression

---

33 ACCCB, Report of the Social Action Department (English Section), Canadian Catholic Conference, to the Archbishops and Bishops of Canada, 1966.

34 ACCCB, Special Report Inventory and Evaluation, Presented by the Social Action Department to Members of the Board, 4–7 March 1969.

35 Ryan, "A Developing World: A Developing Church," 11–12.

36 Ibid., 11.

37 ACCCB, Special Report Inventory and Evaluation, Presented by the Social Action Department to Members of the Board, 4–7 March 1969.

of the co-operation of members of the people of God who are working together to help the Church to accomplish even better its mission in the modern world."[38]

Another new approach was that the Canadian church's social justice initiatives took on a more international perspective on social problems. Beginning in 1959, a national program of pastoral action was established that sent thousands of Canadian bishops, priests, religious, and laity to minister in Latin America.[39] These missionaries became observers and participants in the struggles for justice and the new concepts of liberation theology. Many of them became strong advocates for social change upon their return to Canada. In 1965–67 members of the Social Affairs Office helped found the Canadian Catholic Organization for Development and Peace (CCODP).[40] From the beginning, CCODP had the twin goals of financial support of Third World peoples within a partnership relationship and the education of Catholics and all Canadians about the causes of global inequality and injustice. Furthermore, in 1967 when Pope Paul VI created the Pontifical Council for Justice and Peace, Cardinal Roy of Québec was named the first president of the council, serving from 1967 to 1975. With Cardinal Roy's support, the Canadian Social Affairs staff built strong bonds with the Pontifical Council and actively participated in broadly based international conferences of the Committee on Society, Development and Peace (SODEPAX)—the new experimental social justice initiative of the World Council of Churches and the Vatican secretariat.[41]

The third new approach was ecumenical collaboration and interchurch co-operation on social issues. In 1965 the Social Action staff of the CCC joined with other Christian denominations, nongovernmental

---

38 Daly, *Remembering for Tomorrow*, 59.

39 Daly, *Remembering for Tomorrow*, 47–49; Alexander Carter, *Alex Carter: A Canadian Bishop's Memoirs* (North Bay: Tomiko, 1994), 150–56; Bob Ogle, *North/South Calling: An Autobiography* (Saskatoon, SK: Fifth House; Ottawa: Novalis, 1987).

40 Jack Panozzo, "Two Bishops Remember," in *Journey of Solidarity: The Story of Development and Peace*, ed. Susan Eaton, Gabrielle Lachance, Fabien Labœuf, and Eileen McCarthy (Ottawa: Novalis, 1992), 31–35.

41 William F. Ryan, "Personal Recollections and Reflections on the Implementations of the Second Vatican Council by the Canadian Conference of Catholic Bishops (1964–1990)," *CCHA Historical Studies* 73 (2007): 52.

organizations, business leaders, politicians, and other popular groups to conduct a national conference entitled "A Health Charter for Canada."[42] Bishop Remi De Roo of Victoria believed that this so-called "Medicare Coalition" and the publicity that it received "no doubt contributed to the growing public support for publicly administered health care insurance in Canada."[43] In a 1967 report to the Canadian bishops, the Social Affairs Office described this model of interchurch collaboration as

> the single most important item among our ongoing activities ... [they are] a forum for frank and able theological and practical discussion in the social action field ... it provides "church focus" in social problems independent of any one group—labour, management, or government—and as such is well-placed to assure an open educational forum on problems of current concern as was evident in the National Conference on Health Services in Canada. Eventually, it may provide a channel to voice the common concern of the Christian Churches on urgent social problems and overcome the present weakness of separate statements.[44]

A very public ecumenical collaboration was the partnership of seven churches in a shared Christian Pavilion at Expo, the 1967 Montréal World's Fair.[45] The following year, in 1968, the Social Action Office joined eleven other denominations, federal and provincial governments, and community organizations for a conference in Montréal to address "Poverty at Home and Abroad." Out of this widely acclaimed public conference evolved the National Coalition for Development, an ongoing partnership of churches, labour, business, and community

---

42 ACCCB, "Evaluation of Present Work of the Social Action Dept. (C.C.C.) and Recommended Future Orientation of its Work" (1966–67).

43 Remi De Roo, "Culture, Gospel Values, and the Canadian Economy: The Church Enters Public Dialogue," in *The Church and Culture Since Vatican II: The Experience of North and Latin America*, ed. Joseph Gremillion (Notre Dame, IN: Notre Dame Press, 1985), 121.

44 ACCCB, "Evaluation of Present Work of the Social Action Dept. (C.C.C.) and Recommended Future Orientation of its Work" (1966–67).

45 A fascinating study of the Christian Pavilion at Expo 67, detailing how a "Christian Canada" was being replaced by an officially "interfaith" country, is found in Gregory Miedema, *For Canada's Sake: Public Religion, Centennial Celebrations, and the Re-making of Canada in the 1960s* (Montréal and Kingston: McGill-Queen's University Press, 2005).

organizations.[46] This coalition prepared a detailed strategy for common action involving financial resources, community animation, and political action.[47]

As these overlapping themes of consultation, international perspective, and ecumenical collaboration took root, Canadian social justice was given a fundamentally new orientation. The large Catholic Social Life Conferences were discontinued in favour of open forums that looked to the outside world and to other Christians to read the "signs of the times." This was a conscious shift away from helping only Catholics and moving toward serving all members of society.[48] Important changes are also evident in the postconciliar Labour Day Messages. The annual bishops' statements now followed the *Gaudium et Spes* methodology of using an inductive approach of starting with the study of lived situations of injustice and then proceeding to a moral analysis.

Due to its extensive missionary work in the region, the Canadian Church took great interest in the 1968 conference of Latin America and the Caribbean bishops in Medellín, Colombia. Donal Dorr described this episcopal conference as "a turning point in the life of the Latin American Church—and indeed of the Catholic Church as a whole."[49] The documents produced at this conference noted that "development" strategies emulated Western capitalism and engendered an unhealthy dependency. Instead of characterizing the situation in Latin America as "underdevelopment," they described the situation as exploitation, as "institutionalized violence" against the poor, and a "sinful situation." The Medellín documents called for "liberation," similar to the Exodus account. They also concluded that the Church itself was in need of transformation to become the Church of the poor.[50]

---

46 Joe Gunn and Monica Lambton, *Calling Out the Prophetic Tradition: A Jubilee of Social Teaching from the Canadian Conference of Catholic Bishops* (Ottawa: Canadian Conference of Catholic Bishops, 1999), 18.

47 Strategy Committee Report to Canadian Council of Churches, Canadian Catholic Conference and All Concerned Canadians, *Poverty & Conscience—A Christian Response and Towards a Coalition for Development: Recommendation; A Unified strategy for the 1970's; Priority Steps in 1969* (Toronto, 1969).

48 Ryan, "A Developing World: A Developing Church," 12–16.

49 Donal Dorr, *Option for the Poor: A Hundred Years of Vatican Social Teaching, Revised Edition* (Maryknoll, NY: Orbis, 1992), 206.

50 Ibid., 206–11.

Similarities between the Medellín documents and the Canadian bishops' statements in succeeding years are remarkable. The 1969 Labour Day Message, "New Powers," stated that poverty had a political as well as an economic dimension. "[N]ew power refers to the ever-increasing will of the powerless, the deprived and forgotten to have a public voice, to express their dissatisfactions, to make known their longings and aspirations, to dialogue with the present holders of power."[51] These statements described this new power in biblical language, as a "contemporary form of that 'hunger and thirst for justice' of which the Gospel speaks."[52] The bishops acknowledged that the claiming of new power by those previously without it can lead to "contestation and conflict," but this was acceptable. This understanding of social conflict contrasts with the harmony of preconciliar social Catholicism. In that same year, the bishops concretized this understanding of the new power in their support of Native Peoples' efforts to obtain sufficient resources to negotiate their future effectively with the Canadian government.[53] In a 1970 ecumenical brief to the Senate Committee on Poverty, the CCC emphasized that the word "liberation" is more helpful than "development." Here, the bishops also mentioned that existing social systems tend "to perpetuate inequities" and that "[j]ustice demands nothing less than the creation by the people of new social structures in harmony with human fulfillment."[54]

While the Canadian bishops were not participants at Medellín, they were heavily involved at the Third International Synod of Bishops in 1971 that focused on the issue of social justice. The Canadian bishops made this synod a focal point for their activities and underwent extensive preparatory work. The Social Action Offices prepared a special dossier entitled "Justice in Canada"[55] that provided the background

---

[51] Episcopal Commission for Social Action, "Labour Day Message—1969: New Power," in Sheridan, *Do Justice!* 175.

[52] Episcopal Commission for Social Action, "New Power," 177.

[53] Canadian Catholic Conference, "Brief to the Federal Government: Indians in Canada," 28 November 1969, in Sheridan, *Do Justice!* 180–81.

[54] The Executive Committees of the Canadian Catholic Conference and the Canadian Council of Churches, "A Brief to the Special Senate Committee on Poverty," 11 June 1970, in Sheridan, *Do Justice!* 184–85.

[55] ACCCB, Patrick Kerans, Janet Somerville, and Grant Maxwell, "Justice in Canada Dossier."

notes for the Canadian bishops. In ten workshops and a full committee session, more than seventy bishops reviewed and amended the final twenty-five policy stands on justice that the Canadian delegates were to present at the synod.[56] Also to prepare for the synod, twenty-two bishops representing North and Latin America gathered in Mexico City to discuss the problems and challenges facing the two continents. Bill Ryan was asked by the American and Canadian Bishops Conferences to prepare, in co-operation with American theologian Joseph Komonchak, a working paper for the 1971 Inter-American Bishops Meeting entitled "Liberation of Men and Nations—The Role of the Church in the Americas." This document describes the vision that the Canadian bishops were striving to achieve: "God summons the Church to be a social prophet and catalyst—protesting every injustice, offering reasons to hope and motives to serve."[57] Interestingly, the Canadian and Latin American bishops strongly endorsed the statement, while the US bishops were divided and withheld support.[58]

Once at the synod, the Canadian bishops played an influential role. The intervention of Bishop Alexander Carter of Sault Ste Marie on the potential abuse of multinational corporations earned him an invitation to the United Nations Conference on Trade and Development.[59] Similarly, the intervention by Cardinal George Bernard Flahiff of Winnipeg on the role of education in social justice received warm personal approval from Pope Paul VI and influenced the final synod statement.[60] The document produced by this synod, "Justice in the World," has become one of the most quoted in modern Catholic social teaching.

---

56 ACCCB, Social Action Office (English Sector), "The Demands of Justice—Commitments to Action," October–November 1971.

57 William Ryan and Joseph Komonchak, "The Liberation of Men and Nations: The Role of the Church in the Americas," *Social Thought*, 1 July 1971.

58 Ryan, "Personal Recollections and Reflections on the Implementations of the Second Vatican Council by the Canadian Conference of Catholic Bishops (1964–1990)," 53.

59 Alexander Carter, "Synod Presentation: Super-States and Multi-National Corporations in a Developing World Community," 20 October 1971, in Sheridan, *Do Justice*! 222–25; Alexander Carter, *Alex Carter*, 219–24.

60 George Flahiff, "Synod Presentation: Christian Formation for Justice," 20 October 1971, in Sheridan, *Do Justice*! 218–21; P. Wallace Platt, *Gentle Eminence: A Life of Cardinal Flahiff* (Montréal and Kingston: McGill-Queen's University Press 1999), 136–37.

> Action on behalf of justice and participation in the transformation of the world fully appear to us as a constitutive dimension of the preaching of the Gospel, or in other words, of the Church's mission for the redemption of the human race and its liberation from every oppressive situation.[61]

This phrase placed social justice at the centre of the Catholic faith. The 1972 statement of the Canadian bishops' "Sharing National Income" showed the influence of "Justice in the World": "The riches of Canada are unequally shared. This inequality, which keeps so many people poor, is a social sin."[62] Without espousing any particular program, the bishops invited Canadians to accept the social goal of an equitable redistribution of income. Also their 1972 Labour Day Message insisted that the disparities of poverty and wealth did not come because of fate. The problem, the text stressed, "is the abuse of power, the coercion of the weak by the powerful—internationally, nationally, and locally."[63] Throughout the 1970s, the Canadian bishops increasingly called for not only spiritual conversion but also for political and structural "liberation."

The year 1973 marked a turning point for the social justice work of the CCC as the two Social Affairs Offices, English and French, became one bilingual Social Affairs Commission. Also from 1973 onward, ecumenical social justice collaboration became an increasingly important priority of the Canadian bishops. "In the spirit of ecumenism, Church leaders saw that it was possible to do things together that may have been impossible to do alone."[64] The bishops' social teachings reflected the substantial research being done by interchurch coalitions, which became a critical source of empirical evidence of social disparity and injustice in Canada and elsewhere. At the same time, the coalitions developed as new channels through which Catholic social teaching became more widely known by members of other Christian denomi-

---

61 Synod of Bishops, "Justice in the World," in O'Brien and Shannon, 289.

62 Assembly of the Canadian Catholic Conference, "Sharing National Income," 21 April 1972, in Sheridan, *Do Justice!* 229.

63 Episcopal Commission for Social Action, "Labour Day Message—1972: Simplicity and Sharing," in Sheridan, *Do Justice!* 234.

64 Christopher Lind and Joseph Mihevc, eds., *Coalitions for Justice: the Story of Canada's Interchurch Coalitions* (Ottawa: Novalis, 1994), 11.

nations. According to Tony Clarke, co-director of the Social Affairs Commission at this time, the formation of interchurch social justice coalitions was the most significant development during the 1970s.[65]

In 1973 several interchurch coalitions were formed with a mandate for research, education, and action on major policy issues, both national and international in scope. Staff from the Anglican, Lutheran, Presbyterian, and United churches joined with the Social Affairs Commission in forming GATT-Fly, an interchurch research coalition on international trade issues and their impact on the poor.[66] Focused on poverty in Canada, these major Christian denominations also formed PLURA (an acronym made up of the first initials of each of the founding churches—Presbyterian, Lutheran, United, Roman Catholic and Anglican), a national agency that committed money for local anti-poverty projects and self-help initiatives.[67] The Inter-Church Committee on Chile lobbied the Canadian government to denounce the military coup of General Pinochet. Later, this group enlarged its scope to become the Inter-Church Coalition on Human Rights in Latin America.[68] The Canadian bishops were also part of ecumenical delegations at the key United Nations Conferences on Trade and Development (on new Economic Order in Chile, on Population in Bucharest, on Food in Rome, on the Environment in Stockholm, on Housing in Vancouver, and others), where they co-operated with and monitored the initiatives of the Canadian government.[69] Eventually, there would be more than a dozen of these interchurch coalitions—a uniquely Canadian model of ecumenical co-operation to achieve social justice.[70]

In 1977 the Social Affairs Commission reorganized its entire program around a three-year pastoral action plan that would encourage

[65] Tony Clarke, *Behind the Mitre: the Moral Leadership Crisis in the Canadian Catholic Church* (Toronto: HarperCollins, 1995), 13.

[66] Dennis Howlett, "The Ecumenical Coalition for Economic Justice," in Lind and Mihevc, *Coalitions for Justice*, 99–116.

[67] Mary Boyd, "PLURA," in Lind and Mihevc, *Coalitions for Justice*, 134–41.

[68] Bill Fairbairn, "The Inter-Church Committee on Human Rights in Latin America," in Lind and Mihevc, *Coalitions for Justice*, 169–74.

[69] Ryan, "Personal Recollections and Reflections on the Implementations of the Second Vatican Council by the Canadian Conference of Catholic Bishops (1964–1990)," 51.

[70] Daly, *Remembering for Tomorrow*, 63.

"more members of the Catholic community to become more actively involved in creating a socio-economic order based on justice."[71] This plan was launched with the 1977 statement, "A Society to Be Transformed," which was approved by all the Canadian bishops in a plenary assembly. Canadians were told that "in the name of the Gospel, all Christians must involve themselves in transforming our ways of living and our social and economic structures."[72] This statement contained a critical social analysis that described Canadian capitalism as a "woeful system," and expressed openness to the use of Marxist-based tools of social analysis.[73] The importance that the Canadian episcopal conference gave to social issues during this period is illustrated by the fact that during the mid-1970s through the mid-1980s there were eight bishops on the Social Affairs Commission itself (chaired by Bishop Remi De Roo of Victoria, 1975–77 and 1980–85) and seven staff positions facilitating their initiatives.

By 1982 over 1.5 million Canadians were unemployed (13 per cent of the work force).[74] To address this situation, the Social Affairs Commission issued the statement "Ethical Reflections on the Economic Crisis." This statement rooted its analysis in two gospel principles: "preferential option for the poor, afflicted and oppressed" and "special dignity and value of human work."[75] These principles called for policies that included certain ethical priorities: "The needs of the poor have priority over the wants of the rich; that the rights of workers are more important than the maximization of profits; that the participation of marginalized groups has precedence over the preservation of a system which excludes them."[76] The commission argued that the structures of

[71] This plan of action is outlined in ACCCB, Report of the Episcopal Commission for Social Affairs to the Plenary Assembly of Canadian Bishops, 28 November–2 December 1977. And further details are provided in ACCCB, Report of the Episcopal Commission for Social Affairs to the Plenary Assembly of Canadian Bishops, 19–23 November 1979.

[72] Canadian Conference of Catholic Bishops, "A Society to be transformed," 1 December 1977, in Sheridan, *Do Justice!* 327.

[73] CCCB, "A Society to be transformed," 330–32.

[74] Clarke, *Behind the Mitre*, 41–43.

[75] Episcopal Commission for Social Affairs, "Ethical Reflections on the Economic Crisis," 22 December 1982, in Sheridan, *Do Justice!* 399–400.

[76] Ibid., 400.

the current economic crisis revealed "a deepening moral crisis" in which capital was valued at the expense of labour, which violated the ethical priority of people over profit articulated by John Paul II in his 1981 social encyclical, *Laborem Exercens*.[77] "Ethical Reflections" presented specific proposals including giving primary attention to unemployment rather than inflation, more labour intensive industries, and increased worker and community ownership of industry. The bishops concluded by stating that this search for alternative economic strategies was a core religious concern: "the cries of the poor and powerless are the voice of Christ, the Lord of History, in our midst."[78]

On the morning that "Ethical Reflections" was published in the *Toronto Star* (January 31, 1982), Cardinal Emmett Carter, Archbishop of Toronto called a news conference to distance himself from the statement for two reasons: the process within the CCCB that led to approval of the statement and the overtly radical content of its economic and ethical analysis.[79] Carter's charge that proper consultation procedures had not been followed in the release of the statement, thus implying that it was a statement of the Social Affairs Commission and not of the Canadian bishops, was refuted by Archbishop Henri Légaré, OMI, of Grouard-McLennan, president of the CCCB.[80] Légaré maintained at the time, and for many years afterward, that in authorizing the release of "Ethical Reflections" he had fully respected the CCCB's code of procedures for texts that contained no new policies. According to the Social Affairs Commission, "Ethical Reflections" did not constitute any new policies but was actually a reaffirmation of previous CCCB statements going back to 1976.[81]

While there had been strong disagreements among the Canadian bishops over previous Social Affairs statements in the past,[82] they had

---

77 Ibid., 402–403.

78 Ibid., 405–408.

79 Michael W. Higgins and Douglas R. Letson, *My Father's Business: A Biography of His Eminence G. Emmett Cardinal Carter* (Toronto: Macmillan, 1990), 213–19; Clarke, *Behind the Mitre*, 61–64.

80 Daly, *Remembering for Tomorrow*, 69.

81 ACCCB, "Ethical Reflections on the Economic Crisis: A Continuation of the Social Teachings of the Canadian Bishops," January 1983.

82 Clarke, *Behind the Mitre*, 22–26.

always taken place behind closed doors. Carter's unprecedented public critique of the document sparked a media circus. While previous CCCB statements received only minor media coverage, "Ethical Reflections" became the front-page news item of most Canadian newspapers for several days. The statement also received international coverage in *The New York Times*, *Washington Post*, *Los Angeles Times*, *Time*, and *Newsweek*.[83] Carter subsequently created additional interest in the statement by establishing his own independent public hearing process on "Ethical Reflections" in June 1983. Chaired by Dr. George Ignatieff, chancellor of the University of Toronto, these well-publicized hearings received over one hundred written briefs that ultimately confirmed the general thrust of the bishops' statement, namely that the high rate of unemployment was unacceptable—"immoral" in the bishops' words—and was, indeed, Canada's most pressing problem.[84] According to De Roo, no other Church document in Canadian history ever created an equivalent reaction.[85] Over the course of the following year, members of the Social Affairs Commission were enveloped in the need to respond to an avalanche of speaking engagements related to "Ethical Reflections." Bishop De Roo described this period as challenging yet euphoric: "I have never been told by so many people, many of them professed atheists, alienated Catholics, humanists, and members of other world faiths, that our pastoral statement revealed to them a different Church than the one they had known: a Church of compassion and hope; a Church that proclaims the 'good news.'"[86] Although the Social Affairs Commission recognized some valid criticisms regarding the lack of analysis of the possible detrimental effects of a more self-sufficient Canadian economy on countries of the global South, "Ethical Reflections" served as a major catalyst for the new dialogue between the Church and the modern world.

During Pope John Paul II's visit to Canada in 1984, he strongly endorsed the Canadian bishops' ongoing social teaching and practice

---

83 Ibid., 53–77.

84 Hearing Panel on "Ethical Reflections on the Economic Crisis," *Canada's Unemployed: The Crisis of our Times* (Toronto: Archdiocese of Toronto, 1983).

85 De Roo, "Culture, Gospel Values," 115.

86 Ibid.

of social ecumenism. In Flat Rock, NL, the Holy Father mentioned how he was aware that the Canadian bishops had "frequently deplored" the human costs of unemployment. "I join with them … to work together to find appropriate solutions … including restructuring of the economy, so that human needs be put before mere financial gain."[87] While in Toronto, the heartland of Canada's industrial and technological development, the Pope recalled that "the needs of the poor must take priority over the desires of the rich; the rights of workers over the maximization of profits; the preservation of the environment over uncontrolled industrial expansion; production to meet social needs over production for military purposes."[88] In Edmonton, speaking on international development and reflecting on Matthew 25, the Pope warned:

> in the light of Christ's words, this poor South will judge the rich North. And the poor people and poor nations—poor in different ways, not only lacking in food, but also deprived of freedom and other human rights—will judge those people who take these goods away from them, amassing to themselves the imperialistic monopoly of economic and political supremacy at the expense of others.[89]

In giving his public papal blessing to the social justice initiatives of the Canadian bishops, John Paul II's visit served as a capstone to a remarkable chapter in Canadian Church history.

While the Canadian bishops successfully stimulated public debate on social justice issues during the early 1980s (both in Canada and abroad), by the end of the decade the CCCB was conspicuously silent on major justice issues, local social action offices were closed, and interchurch social justice coalitions were downsized due to financial cutbacks.[90] How did things unravel so quickly? There is no single cause,

87 John Paul II, "The Primacy of Man in the Factors of Production," address to the fishermen at the port of Flatrock in Newfoundland, 12 September 1984, in *Canada: Celebrating Our Faith* (Boston: Daughters of St. Paul, 1985), 112.

88 John Paul II, "The Restoration of Christian Unity is of Crucial Importance to Evangelization," address given at an ecumenical meeting with the representatives of other Christian churches, 14 September 1984, in *Canada: Celebrating Our Faith*, 200.

89 John Paul II, "The Poor South will Judge the Rich North," homily given at Edmonton Airport, 17 September 1984, in *Canada: Celebrating Our* Faith, 273.

90 McKeon, "Social Justice Paradigm," 72–91.

but several factors contributed to a de-emphasizing of social justice by the bishops. During the 1980s, the Vatican became increasingly critical of the liberation theology, which was a major source of theological inspiration for the Canadian bishops.[91] Equally important, after 1983 John Paul II's social teaching called for injustice to be addressed in a non-conflictual manner "from above," which was interpreted as a retreat from earlier papal social encyclicals that envisioned social change coming from popular movements (from below).[92] Within Canada, controversy over "Ethical Reflections" raised questions about the consultation and approval process within the CCCB for Social Affairs statements, as well as their content. In 1985 the bishops elected Bishop Paul John O'Byrne of Calgary to take over the chair of the Social Affairs Commission from the high-profile Bishop De Roo. Many saw this move as a rejection by the bishops themselves of the direction the commission had taken in its recent statements.[93] Along with De Roo's removal, another major blow to the social justice thrust of the Canadian bishops was the tragic death in 1987 of Adolphe Proulx, the prophetic bishop of Gatineau-Hull, who provided strong moral leadership to the Social Affairs Commission.[94] From 1986–89 the CCCB underwent a major review and restructuring initiative that shifted much of the justice agenda of the Social Affairs Commission to the four regional episcopal conferences and local dioceses. The resultant cutbacks in funding and staffing at the Social Affairs Commission, combined with the Canadian bishops not issuing any public statements on social justice between 1988 and 1993, "sent a dispiriting message to all in the faith and justice movement across the country."[95] While the intention of the bishops was to empower local communities, the transition of leadership was happening during a period of large-scale closing of diocesan social justice offices. Without direction from the CCCB or diocesan offices, the nationwide social justice movement quickly lost its momentum.[96]

91 Christian Smith, *The Emergence of Liberation Theology: Radical Religion and Social Movement Theory* (Chicago: University of Chicago Press, 1991), 222–26.

92 Dorr, 332, 376.

93 Clarke, *Behind the Mitre*, 103–106.

94 Clarke, *Behind the Mitre*, 122–24.

95 McKeon, "Social Justice Paradigm," 164.

96 Ibid., 87–90.

Simultaneously, the widely publicized scandal of child sexual abuse in church institutions seriously undercut the ability of church leaders to address issues of injustice. Church leadership, responding to the fallout of the abuse scandal, was forced to divert significant human and financial resources from virtually every other church activity throughout the 1990s.[97] During the decade of the 1990s and into the new millennium, social justice issues were no longer an episcopal priority of the Canadian bishops.

A final point to consider is that while the Canadian bishops were able to compile an impressive body of episcopal social teachings, the Social Affairs Commission was never able to successfully connect these exemplary statements with the social consciousness among lay Catholics in the pew.[98] Bill Ryan concludes that "the bishops have to bear major responsibility for the present lack of social faith consciousness among the laity and even among priests, because, for the most part, they did not personally teach nor actively encourage their priests to teach the very pastoral social teaching they voted, often unanimously and enthusiastically."[99] The division between the bishops' statements and inability to effectively integrate these social justice teachings into the faith formation of clergy and laity became especially pronounced after 1984. In the training of future priests, social justice was no longer part of seminary formation. In a 1985 survey of North American Catholic seminarians, 65 per cent agreed with the statement, "Salvation is total liberation from both individual and collective sin, from injustice and inhuman conditions here and now"; in 1995 the number of Canadian seminarians in agreement with this same statement dropped to 26.9 per cent.[100] Nor were the bishops regularly visible in promoting or defending this social teaching with Catholic political, business, and education leaders, who by this very teaching, are supposed to be the vanguard of the Church in the modern world. This disconnect, especially after

---

97 Ibid., 91.

98 Bishops commented on this failure on the occasion of the CCCB's fiftieth anniversary celebration. See Daly, *Remembering for Tomorrow*, 171.

99 Ryan, "Personal Recollections," 61.

100 Martin Rovers, *Who's in the Seminary? Roman Catholic Seminarians Today* (Ottawa: Novalis, 1996), 38.

1984, remains an "Achilles heel" in the Canadian bishops' otherwise remarkable social teachings.

In conclusion, Vatican II introduced significant shifts in the overall methodology and content of Catholic social teaching. From 1965–84, the Canadian bishops took this new theology seriously and made social justice a priority for being Church in the modern world. Animating this multi-dimensional national program was the Social Affairs Commission. The intensity of the commission's work is evident by the two-volume compilation of 153 statements issued on behalf of Canada's bishops between 1945 and 1990, edited by Edward Sheridan (of which only ten were issued pre–Vatican II). After *Gaudium et Spes*, these statements changed from a deductive and moralizing approach to employing a methodology that looked in detail at a situation, judged it in the light of the Gospel or other Church teachings, and suggested appropriate action that should be taken.

Enhanced by the hiring of more professional staff, the Social Affairs Commission moved from working primarily within Catholic organizations to becoming active participants in a wide variety of ecumenical initiatives. By the mid-1970s, many of these issue-focused, ad hoc collaborations were institutionalized in a network of national interchurch coalitions.[101] With this ecumenical perspective, the concerns of the CCCB expanded to include the socio-economic and cultural development for all peoples, marginalization, problems of world poverty, and human rights worldwide.

Most radically, the Canadian bishops developed "the growing insight that it is the dominant ideology and the economic mechanisms of Canadian and world orders which create and maintain the injustice under which a majority of mankind labours."[102] They cultivated a critical analysis of human suffering that gave greater attention to economic, political, and social structures than individuals. Thus, injustice was no longer seen primarily as the result of individual selfishness to which the Church responded with a call of personal conversion. Rather, injustice was primarily the result of unjust economic systems, which required a

101 McKeon, "Social Justice Paradigm," 93.

102 Sheridan, "Introduction," *Do Justice!* 37.

structural analysis and institutional transformation.[103] This is more than a shift in details. "It represents a shift in the kind of social teaching, a different experience of God, a different understanding of the world, and a different conception of the mission of the church, a different starting point and method, and a different kind of authority."[104] This change in ethical methodology began with Canadian participation at Vatican II but was further developed by insights from Latin American liberation theologians, heavy Canadian involvement at the 1971 World Synod of Bishops, and participation in ecumenical social-justice coalitions. Yet, as significant as this new paradigm of social justice was for the Canadian bishops, the effectiveness and permanence of these episcopal teachings would be jeopardized by the inability to integrate these teachings into the faith formation of the Catholic community.

---

103 Gregory Baum, *Compassion and Solidarity: The Church for Others* (CBC Massey Lecture Series) (Concord, ON: Anansi Press, 1987), 58–59.

104 Cormie, "Revolutions in Canadian Catholic Social Teaching," 58.

Le synode extraordinaire de 1985 : l'expérience canadienne

Jacques Racine,
Université Laval

Le 25 janvier 1985, en la fête de la Conversion de Paul, lors de l'octave de prière pour l'unité des chrétiens, Jean-Paul II annonce la tenue d'un synode extraordinaire des évêques qui sera célébré du 25 novembre au 8 décembre de l'année en cours. Il y convoque les patriarches, quelques évêques des Églises orientales et les présidents de toutes les conférences épiscopales. Il affirme :

Le but de cette initiative est non seulement de commémorer le concile Vatican II vingt ans après sa clôture, mais aussi et surtout de :

- Revivre en quelque manière cette atmosphère extraordinaire de communion ecclésiale qui caractérise les Assises œcuméniques, dans le partage réciproque des souffrances et des joies, des luttes et des espérances, qui sont propres au Corps du Christ dans les diverses parties de la terre ;
- Échanger et approfondir des expériences et des informations sur l'application du Concile au niveau de l'Église universelle et des Églises particulières ;
- Favoriser l'approfondissement ultérieur et l'insertion constante de Vatican II dans la vie de l'Église, à la lumière aussi des exigences nouvelles[1].

1 *Synode extraordinaire. Célébration de Vatican II*, Paris, Cerf, 1986, p. 36.

Jean-Paul II termine son annonce par la phrase suivante : « L'Église d'aujourd'hui veut poursuivre son chemin vers le troisième millénaire de l'histoire, au milieu des hommes et avec eux, participant à leurs espérances et à leurs attentes, suivant la voie tracée par Vatican II, et à l'écoute de "ce que l'Esprit dit aux Églises" (Ap 2, 7.11.17.29)[2]. »

Le 1er avril 1985, le secrétaire général du synode des évêques envoie un questionnaire aux présidents des conférences épiscopales, leur demandant de faire parvenir leurs réponses avant le 1er septembre. Quatre questions portent sur des considérations générales traitant de la réception du concile, de ses bienfaits, des erreurs dans l'interprétation, des difficultés rencontrées dans l'interprétation et l'application des constitutions et des décrets. Neuf questions particulières visent l'interprétation des constitutions et des décrets de Vatican II et leur mise en pratique.

L'annonce de la convocation du synode extraordinaire est reçue comme une bonne nouvelle par l'épiscopat canadien, même si ce dernier sort à peine d'une année faste marquée par la visite réussie de Jean-Paul II au Canada. L'épiscopat est fier du visage de l'Église qu'il a présenté au Pape et au monde, de la participation des croyants en grand nombre, de l'accueil des médias de masse, de la concordance de vue qui semble être partagée avec le Vatican. Il sort d'une vaste expérience de collaboration entre diocèses, provinces, autorités civiles de tout niveau. Il a pu compter sur l'appui sans faille de bénévoles, religieux, prêtres, laïcs. Malgré les brefs délais, il est prêt à se lancer dans l'aventure du synode, à prendre la parole et à s'impliquer.

Mon exposé, sans doute influencé par ma participation au synode comme personne-ressource de la délégation canadienne, se divisera en trois parties : la préparation de l'Église canadienne au synode, la participation de la délégation canadienne au synode, le bilan à court et à long terme du synode. L'analyse de cet évènement mettra en lumière une certaine réception de Vatican II par l'Église du Canada.

La préparation de l'Église canadienne

Deux grandes étapes ont marqué la préparation de la Conférence des évêques catholiques du Canada (CECC) au synode : la réponse au

2 *Ibid.*, p. 37.

questionnaire du Secrétariat du synode, entre le 1er avril et le début de septembre, et l'Assemblée plénière de la CECC tenue du 21 au 25 octobre 1985. Cette deuxième étape a été la plus significative.

La réponse au questionnaire du Secrétariat a été effectuée à partir d'une consultation réalisée auprès des diocèses. Le peu de temps alloué et la période de l'année visée ont fait qu'elle a pris des formes variées, selon le modèle d'organisation de chaque diocèse et la disponibilité de ses ressources. Dans certains cas, l'évêque s'est excusé de ne pas avoir eu le temps de favoriser une réelle participation et a lui-même répondu au questionnaire.

Quand est arrivé le temps de faire une synthèse de ces rapports, on a constaté, malgré certaines constantes, la grande diversité des situations et des analyses, surtout lorsqu'il était question de mentionner les difficultés rencontrées dans l'application du concile ou encore de traiter de l'interprétation de certains décrets. On pouvait quelquefois retrouver des affirmations contradictoires.

Un premier document synthèse a pu être produit pendant l'été à partir des résumés francophone et anglophone[3]. Il cherchait à rester proche des formulations utilisées par leurs auteurs. Parmi les bienfaits du concile, on notait, par ordre de priorité : le vent de fraîcheur qui circulait, le rôle des conférences épiscopales, la libération du laïcat, la reconnaissance de l'Église comme Peuple de Dieu, les exigences de la justice sociale, l'engagement avec le monde, l'œcuménisme, la liberté religieuse, les relations avec les juifs, l'intérêt pour la Bible, le rôle des femmes dans l'Église, les mouvements de spiritualité, la reconnaissance de la liberté de conscience, le diaconat permanent.

À la question portant sur les abus et les erreurs qui s'étaient introduits dans l'interprétation et l'application du concile, le document indiquait par ordre de priorité : l'Église-institution n'a pas réussi à céder certains de ses pouvoirs ; les synodes n'ont pas d'autorité réelle ; l'inculturation souhaitée n'est pas respectée ; peu de place est accordée à la création en liturgie. On signale aussi, avec moins d'insistance, la confusion sur le rôle des prêtres et le peu de poids des laïcs, les difficultés d'adaptation du clergé et des religieux, le manque de préparation du clergé et sa précipitation dans l'action, une fausse interprétation de

[3] La synthèse ici présentée est réalisée à partir de mes archives personnelles.

la liberté de conscience et de la liberté, la disparition des dévotions populaires, la difficile compréhension du rôle des théologiens.

Le questionnaire demandait d'indiquer quelles étaient les difficultés rencontrées par rapport aux nouvelles exigences résultant de l'évolution des mentalités. Les réponses colligées dans le document sont les suivantes, par ordre de priorité : les avancées de la technologie de l'information et des communications ; l'évolution culturelle ; la place et le rôle des femmes dans l'Église ; la possession tranquille de la vérité qui bloque le dialogue avec le monde ; l'absence de respect du principe de subsidiarité de la Curie par rapport à l'Église locale ; la naissance de nombreuses sectes et le développement des sciences occultes ; l'absence de pastorale adaptée aux athées et aux indifférents ; le lien entre célibat et prêtrise, en donnant comme exemple la situation des Inuits ; l'individualisme ; la mise en question de la famille ; le mariage interconfessionnel qui favorise la non-pratique de la religion.

À la dernière question générale, qui demandait quelles mesures devraient être prises à la suite du synode pour faire avancer les choses selon l'esprit et la lettre du concile Vatican II, on retrouvait les énoncés suivants : exprimer l'ecclésiologie de Vatican II telle que présente dans *Lumen gentium* et *Gaudium et spes* ; confirmer le processus initié par Vatican II ; voir le positif dans le monde d'aujourd'hui, sans naïveté ; établir un véritable dialogue avec le monde, dans le respect des mentalités ; restaurer la collégialité ; affirmer une unité qui respecte les besoins et les coutumes locales.

Les réponses aux questions particulières sont aussi intéressantes, mais elles sont moins pertinentes pour notre propos.

Cette première synthèse a été retravaillée par la CECC et a fait l'objet d'un envoi à Rome. Elle s'est retrouvée dans le journal *Le Devoir*, d'abord sous la forme d'un résumé, le 16 octobre 1985, puis *in extenso*, le lendemain 17 octobre, un mois après que les autorités vaticanes aient interdit aux conférences épiscopales de divulguer le fruit de leurs travaux. Il faut rappeler que cette interdiction était venue après que les conférences épiscopales de France, d'Angleterre et des États-Unis, entre autres, aient rendu publics leurs rapports[4].

---

[4] Marie LAURIER, « Le Synode extraordinaire de Rome étudiera les 20 ans de vie conciliaire », *Le Devoir* (23 novembre 1985).

Une assemblée plénière de la CECC avait été prévue du 21 au 25 octobre 1985. Deux thèmes étaient à l'ordre du jour : « Le concile et l'avenir » et « Les points à présenter au synode extraordinaire ». C'est là véritablement que s'établira la position de la délégation canadienne au sein du synode.

Pour préparer cette rencontre, les évêques avaient entre leurs mains des textes qui présentaient les vues des organismes suivants sur ces deux thèmes :

- Assemblée des évêques de l'Atlantique ;
- Assemblée des évêques du Québec ;
- Conférence des évêques catholiques de l'Ontario ;
- Conférence catholique de l'Ouest ;
- Diocèses du Nord canadien ;
- Conférence religieuse canadienne ;
- Conseil canadien des Églises ;
- Conférence des organismes laïques catholiques du Canada, représentant une trentaine d'organismes.

Parmi les observateurs à l'assemblée, on notait :

- Trois invités des autres Églises ;
- Cinq délégués de la Conférence religieuse canadienne, dont trois femmes ;
- Deux délégués des organismes laïques du Canada ;
- Deux représentants du clergé francophone ;
- Deux représentants du clergé anglophone ;
- Deux secrétaires généraux des assemblées d'évêques (Québec et Ontario) ;
- Deux représentants des Œuvres pontificales missionnaires.

Pour favoriser les échanges sur le concile et l'avenir de l'Église, deux panels avaient été organisés. Le premier panel était constitué de cinq évêques qui traitaient du concile et de sa dynamique. Conformément à l'invitation du secrétariat général du synode, ce panel s'est attardé surtout aux quatre grandes constitutions de Vatican II[5].

---

[5] Les résumés qui suivent ont été faits à partir des textes écrits des panellistes remis par la CECC aux participants à l'Assemblée.

D'entrée de jeu, cependant, Mgr Alexander Carter traita de l'impact de Vatican II sur les évêques, de l'esprit de Vatican II, du climat de liberté qui y régnait, de la redécouverte de la collégialité. Il indiqua cinq approches nouvelles acceptées par le concile : la légitime diversité dans l'Église, l'inculturation, l'option préférentielle pour les pauvres, le besoin urgent d'enseigner et de pratiquer la justice sociale, ainsi que l'acceptation profondément nouvelle de la liberté de conscience.

Mgr Joseph-Aurèle Plourde présenta l'histoire de la constitution *Lumen gentium*. Rappelant la mise au rancart des textes préparés par la Curie et la prise en charge de la rédaction par les évêques, il évoqua le premier schéma présenté et les critiques qu'il a entraînées, le second schéma, la décision d'intervertir les chapitres 2 et 3 et la signification de ce choix. La présentation de l'Église comme Peuple de Dieu était le point dominant de son exposé.

Mgr William E. Power rappela que l'origine de la constitution *Gaudium et spes* était liée à l'intervention du Cardinal Suenens, qui évoqua le besoin d'un document s'adressant à l'Église *ad extra*. Il expliqua pourquoi un tel document ne pouvait que donner de grandes orientations quant à la conduite des sociétés dans un monde constamment en mutation. Le travail d'analyse reste toujours à faire, le monde nouveau est toujours en train de naître, l'Esprit du Seigneur est à l'œuvre dans les événements. L'Église est toujours appelée au discernement et au respect de la dignité de chaque personne.

Mgr Jean-Marie Fortier présenta la constitution *Sacrosanctum concilium* en rappelant d'abord l'histoire du mouvement liturgique, puis les longues discussions sur l'usage de la langue vernaculaire, mais il insista surtout sur la qualité des grands principes qui y sont affirmés : le caractère pastoral et catéchétique de la liturgie, la mise en valeur de la parole de Dieu, le respect des diversités et l'utilisation de la langue du pays.

Mgr Hermaniuk, dont on se serait attendu qu'il traite de la quatrième constitution *Dei Verbum*, surprit un peu tout le monde en présentant une réflexion sur *Lumen gentium*, qui avait toutes les apparences d'une proposition formelle. Comme expression de la collégialité, il exprima le besoin de la mise sur pied d'un synode permanent d'évêques, composé de membres élus par les délégués du présent synode et de membres désignés par le pape. Ce synode aurait eu le pouvoir législatif de régler avec le Saint-Père, et sous son autorité, toutes les questions dans la vie de l'Église qui étaient décidées par le Saint-Père avec la Curie. Cette dernière ne conserverait qu'un pouvoir exécutif.

Le second panel de l'Assemblée portait sur « Le concile et ses réalisations au Canada ». Le premier conférencier était le père Julien Harvey, jésuite, directeur de la revue *Relations.* Dans son introduction, il affirma : « Nous ne pouvons rien immobiliser, ni le monde, ni l'Église, ni l'interprétation du Concile. » Par la suite, il jeta un regard sur l'évolution du monde depuis 20 ans et expliqua le passage de l'État-providence au libéralisme qui provoquait un retour aux lois de la jungle, avec ses conséquences pénibles pour les personnes. Il rappela que le concile s'était déroulé dans une période plutôt calme de l'histoire et que, depuis lors, de nombreux problèmes s'étaient posés, dont le terrorisme, la prolifération des armes nucléaires, etc. Il exprima son accord avec la synthèse des travaux préparatoires au synode élaborée par la CECC, en soulignant particulièrement la question de la collégialité et son extension à tous les niveaux de la vie de l'Église. Il invita le synode à ne pas se refermer sur les problèmes internes de l'Église. Il souhaitait que l'Église canadienne soit l'Église des pauvres. Elle ne pouvait suivre le monde dans le néolibéralisme.

La seconde conférencière était madame Jean Forest, de l'Alberta, une laïque engagée qui connaissait bien la réalité canadienne. Après avoir fait écho à la diversité des opinions qu'elle entendait, elle prit personnellement position en affirmant que bon nombre des problèmes évoqués dans l'institution étaient liés à l'évolution de la société et non au concile. Pour elle, l'Église est le Peuple de Dieu, conscient de la dignité humaine, uni dans l'amour, appelé à servir toute l'humanité et à s'ouvrir aux autres religions ; les principes de collégialité et de subsidiarité devraient constituer le fondement des relations envers les diverses congrégations religieuses et le Saint-Siège. À la fin de son exposé, elle souleva la question de la place des femmes dans l'Église.

Riches de l'ensemble des rapports, des exposés, des discussions et de leurs propres expériences, les évêques se réunirent ensuite à huis clos pour déterminer les priorités qu'ils retenaient et qui devraient guider la délégation canadienne. Ils retinrent cinq thèmes, que l'on retrouve dans le Rapport officiel de l'Église canadienne publié dans le livre sur le synode extraordinaire, aux éditions du Cerf :

- La collégialité, en soulignant particulièrement le rôle du synode des évêques et des conférences épiscopales ;
- Une théologie des Églises particulières qui tient compte de l'Église diocésaine, mais aussi des Églises régionales ou nationales. Sous ce thème, les évêques soulèvent la question de l'application du principe de subsidiarité à l'Église ;
- Les ministères au sein d'une Église communion et tout entière ministérielle qui favorise la participation de beaucoup d'hommes et de femmes dans l'animation même des communautés chrétiennes ;
- La formation de la conscience et la compréhension du magistère. « Il serait encore utile de mettre en rapport les enseignements sur la conscience personnelle et sur le magistère et d'en mieux faire voir les exigences pour une conciliation nécessaire[6]. »
- L'Église, sacrement du salut au milieu des hommes. « Si l'Église s'intéresse à elle-même, c'est pour mieux correspondre à l'action de l'Esprit qui la sanctifie et pour mieux collaborer à la mission du Fils[7]. »

La préparation au synode est révélatrice de la réception de Vatican II par une importante majorité d'évêques du Canada et de leurs attentes à l'égard du synode extraordinaire.

La participation de la délégation de l'Église canadienne

La délégation canadienne au synode était formée de Mgr Bernard Hubert, élu président de la CECC lors de l'Assemblée générale et ainsi désigné *ex officio* président de la délégation canadienne, de Mgr James Hayes, vice-président de la CECC, désigné personnellement par le Pape, et de Mgr Maxim Hermaniuk, à titre de métropolite des Ukrainiens catholiques et membre de droit du synode.

---

6 *Synode extraordinaire. Célébration de Vatican II*, p. 177.

7 *Ibid.*, p. 178.

Le père William Ryan, secrétaire général anglophone de la CECC, Jacques Binet, agent de presse, et moi-même, à titre de personne ressource, accompagnions la délégation.

Pour traiter de la participation de cette délégation aux travaux du synode, je procéderai en deux temps. J'analyserai d'abord les six textes que la délégation présenta au synode ; dans un second temps, je traiterai d'autres aspects de cette participation.

Les textes de la délégation

Mgr Hubert intervint dans l'Assemblée synodale dès le 26 novembre pour suggérer un autre mode d'organisation du synode, qui permettrait de mieux travailler les questions complexes qui se posaient au monde et à la mission de l'Église et qui favoriserait la participation à cette démarche de tous les autres évêques et des baptisés intéressés, en pleine collégialité et coresponsabilité. Les deux semaines du synode seraient utilisées, d'une part, pour préparer un message pastoral aux fidèles et aux gens de bonne volonté afin d'y manifester l'unanimité des évêques à poursuivre le travail amorcé à Vatican II et, d'autre part, pour identifier les problèmes de ce temps que le synode désirerait aborder dans une prochaine session de travail qui aurait lieu, dans un an ou plus, pour donner suite aux travaux réalisés dans les Églises particulières[8].

Cette intervention reçut, l'après-midi même, l'appui de la délégation suisse[9]. Mais il n'en fut plus question par la suite. C'est même la seule intervention faite par un membre du synode à ne pas être reproduite le lendemain par l'*Osservatore romano*. Elle avait été égarée, a-t-on dit, et on ne l'a retrouvée qu'après le synode[10].

Le 27 novembre, Mgr Hayes s'adressa aux Pères synodaux en traitant de l'Église, communion de communautés. Évoquant la lettre *Ecclesiam suam* de Paul VI sur le dialogue et le respect de la liberté et de la dignité de chaque être humain considéré comme sujet de sa propre histoire, il fit le point sur la situation de l'œcuménisme au Canada et sur les progrès réalisés. Il interpela le synode sur la question de l'intercommunion

---

[8] *Ibid.*, p. 397-399.

[9] *Ibid.*, p. 284. Il ne s'agit pas de l'intervention même, mais cette référence au Rapport de la délégation nous indique bien une identité de vue.

[10] AFP, « Un soupçon d'autocensure », *Le Droit* (30 novembre 1985).

qui, pour lui, était liée à la reconnaissance formelle du baptême dans les autres Églises et du droit qui en découlait. Dans le même contexte, il évoqua la nécessité de la collégialité, « expression privilégiée de la communion et condition indispensable de la marche vers l'unité des chrétiens ». Il conclut ainsi son exposé : « L'Église, communion d'un peuple qui tire son unité de la Trinité, peut se percevoir concrètement comme une communion de communautés, dans le respect des personnes considérées comme sujets responsables et des cultures perçues comme expressions de la démarche des peuples pour assurer la promotion de la femme et de l'homme à chaque époque[11]. » Au cœur de son texte, il établit aussi les liens entre collégialité, coresponsabilité et reconnaissance de l'autorité de l'évêque. Pour ce faire, il fit appel à la juste notion de subsidiarité.

Le 25 novembre, Mgr Hermaniuk reprit à l'Assemblée synodale le message qu'il avait présenté à la CECC sur le synode permanent des évêques sous forme d'une proposition. Il souligna que l'acceptation de celle-ci pourrait aider à résoudre certains problèmes très importants dans le dialogue avec d'autres Églises chrétiennes, comme l'Église orthodoxe d'Orient, l'Église anglicane, etc.[12]. L'attention aux motivations sous-tendant une telle proposition était nécessaire pour ne pas croire que son auteur ne se préoccupait que du pouvoir des évêques.

Les trois autres interventions des évêques canadiens furent des textes écrits déposés au secrétariat du synode. Ils circulèrent dans les délégations et auprès des journalistes. Ils cherchaient à répondre au second objectif du synode tel qu'énoncé par Jean-Paul II : « permettre aux pères synodaux d'échanger et d'approfondir des expériences touchant l'application du Concile au niveau de l'Église universelle et des Églises particulières ». Chaque texte faisait part d'une expérience que l'Église du Canada avait faite, dans la continuité du concile, des bienfaits qui en avaient résulté et des questions qu'elle soulevait. Ils reprenaient, dans une recherche de dialogue, les points retenus par la CECC ou soulignés par des groupes importants tels que les religieux.

---

11 James Hayes, « L'Église, communion de communautés », *L'Église canadienne* (19 décembre 1985), p. 230.

12 *Synode extraordinaire. Célébration de Vatican II*, p. 394-397.

Le 29 novembre, Mgr Hubert déposa un texte sur les ministères dans une Église-communion. Il soulignait le fait que de nombreux laïcs et religieux s'étaient mis au service des communautés chrétiennes, qu'ils avaient acquis une formation et exerçaient un véritable ministère qu'il restait bien souvent à qualifier. Ces ministères exercés dans les faits par un grand nombre de femmes devraient être reconnus de quelque façon. Il terminait sa présentation par deux questions : quels ministères, pour quelle Église ? Quel type d'articulation des ministères dans une Église-communion pour accomplir la meilleure réalisation possible de la mission confiée par le Christ à son Église[13] ?

Le 2 décembre, l'évêque de St-Jean-Longueuil rendit public un texte sur les pratiques de justice dans le monde, appelant à une prise de parole du synode en ce domaine pour remettre en lumière une affirmation du synode sur la justice qui n'avait pas toujours été gardée en mémoire ecclésiale : « Le combat pour la justice et la participation à la transformation du monde apparaissent pleinement comme une dimension constitutive de la prédication de l'Évangile[14]. » À partir des engagements des évêques canadiens dans la mouvance d'*Octogesima adveniens*, Mgr Hubert rappela les difficultés de chercher avec les personnes de bonne volonté les solutions praticables pour changer le monde, et cela, souvent au cœur de situations conflictuelles. Il invita les pères synodaux à « affirmer, entre autres, la volonté des chrétiens de participer à la construction du monde en donnant priorité à deux problèmes des plus urgents : la dette du tiers-monde et la menace de conflit nucléaire[15] ».

L'intervention écrite des évêques canadiens sur la vie religieuse fut déposée par Mgr Hayes le 3 décembre. Ce dernier y faisait état de l'implication des religieuses et des religieux dans le ministère pastoral et de leur profond engagement dans les questions de justice et de paix. Il soulignait la qualité des relations entre la Conférence religieuse canadienne et la CECC. Il terminait par deux souhaits qu'il transmettait

---

[13] Bernard Hubert, « Les ministères dans une Église-communion », *L'Église canadienne* (19 décembre 1985), p. 231-232.

[14] Bernard Hubert, « Les pratiques de justice au cœur du monde », *L'Église canadienne* (19 décembre 1985), p. 233-234.

[15] *Ibid.*, p. 234.

au synode de la part des religieux et religieuses du Canada : que la vie religieuse soit mieux comprise par le clergé et que les décisions sur l'orientation et la vie des congrégations ne soient pas prises uniquement par des hommes.

En conclusion, on peut affirmer que les textes présentés par la délégation canadienne représentent bien la position de l'Église canadienne telle qu'elle s'était exprimée dans les différentes étapes de la préparation au synode. Ils nous disent beaucoup sur la réception du concile Vatican II par cette Église, mais aussi sur son style d'organisation, sur son authenticité et sur son attention à la société et à la culture dans lesquelles elle s'insère. Les évêques se considéraient comme responsables d'une mission à réaliser dans un monde différent, en changement constant et rapide. Selon eux, les problèmes qu'ils rencontraient n'étaient pas liés à Vatican II, et encore moins causés par celui-ci.

Les autres aspects de la participation de la délégation canadienne au synode

En 1985, la CECC a déjà une longue pratique de participation aux synodes et un sens de l'organisation à l'américaine. Elle envoie à Rome une délégation importante et lui assure des conditions que l'on ne retrouve pas dans beaucoup de pays. Les délégués canadiens ont tout ce qu'il faut pour travailler, pour recevoir des invités et pour communiquer avec la presse ; ils le font sans répit, mais dans un climat exceptionnel de coresponsabilité, d'entraide et de fraternité entre évêques et collaborateurs.

Outre la participation aux différentes activités du synode, la délégation doit procéder à l'analyse des textes des autres délégués, préparer ses propres interventions, échanger sur le déroulement quotidien des évènements, exercer son appréciation des documents ou projets de message qui circulent. Mais en même temps, il lui faut rencontrer d'autres délégations pour partager des expériences pratiques ou encore pour discuter de ce qui se passe au synode même et échanger sur le contenu éventuel du message final. Ainsi, régulièrement le midi, elle recevait à dîner à la maison Del Clero où nous habitions. Je me rappelle de rencontres très instructives avec les délégués d'Australie et de Nouvelle-Zélande sur leurs liens avec les Églises de Chine, ou encore avec les délégués du

Brésil ou des États-Unis sur le développement, la pauvreté et l'économie. Enfin, les entrevues avec la presse étaient très nombreuses, puisque les interventions des évêques canadiens touchaient des questions pratiques et soulevaient des problèmes qui rejoignaient les gens.

Je suis resté avec l'impression que, pour certains personnages, ces activités de la délégation et particulièrement ses liens avec la presse ont dérangé, tout comme certains aspects de ses interventions. Cela s'est exprimé clairement lors de la première intervention de Mgr Hubert. Mais nous avons aussi compris que le seul fait de soulever directement ou indirectement la question de la situation des femmes en Église était mal perçue et gênait.

Dans le groupe des évêques de langue française (un des *circuli minores*) auquel il participait, Mgr Hubert a été pris à partie de façon assez directe. Il admit à une journaliste que cela avait « donné lieu à une dynamique assez difficile[16] ». Il dut se débattre avec le cardinal Hamer sur deux questions auxquelles tenait l'épiscopat canadien : le statut des conférences épiscopales et le principe de subsidiarité. Il faut dire que le Cardinal avait établi sa position sur ces questions à la session des cardinaux qui avait immédiatement précédé le synode[17]. Son discours avait été largement diffusé pendant le synode des évêques. Il portait sur la signification ecclésiologique de la Curie romaine, sur l'absence de fondements théologiques des conférences épiscopales et sur l'inutilité du principe de subsidiarité en ecclésiologie. Il a certainement eu son effet dans le groupe de langue française où siégeaient le Cardinal et Mgr Hubert. Le reporter du groupe écrivit : « Une conviction quasi unanime s'est manifestée pour dire que l'appel généralisé et indifférencié au principe de subsidiarité semble bien être une fausse piste… Toutefois, un membre du cercle demande que l'on reste ouvert au principe de subsidiarité par rapport à la vie de l'Église qui est à la fois mystère, communion et société[18]. » Nous avons toutes les raisons de croire qu'il s'agissait là de Mgr Hubert et qu'il était fort isolé.

---

[16] Danièle Blain, « Une lutte sourde mais violente oppose les différentes tendances à la plénière du Synode », *Le Devoir*, 5 décembre 1985.

[17] *Synode extraordinaire. Célébration de Vatican II*, p. 598-604.

[18] *Ibid.*, p. 523.

Comme j'ai pu le constater lors d'un souper avec la délégation française, les rapports avec le cardinal Lustiger étaient aussi tendus et concernaient entre autres l'orientation du message final du synode, dont la première version, rédigée par ce dernier, avait été fortement critiquée. Ce projet portait un regard pessimiste sur l'homme et sur le monde et présentait une théologie de la Croix qui laissait peu de place à la présence agissante de l'Esprit.

Malgré ces tensions, après deux semaines d'échanges et de célébrations, tous en ressortirent heureux, vivifiés par la rencontre des autres, enrichis d'une forte expérience spirituelle de communion et encouragés par l'attitude de Jean-Paul II. Le cardinal Daneels, dans son rapport final, écrivit : « Ce synode a été pour nous une occasion d'expérimenter une nouvelle fois la communion dans l'unique Esprit, dans l'unique foi et espérance et dans l'unique Église catholique, non moins que dans la commune volonté de faire passer le Concile dans la praxis et dans la vie de l'Église[19]. »

Je ferai une analyse complémentaire de ce synode en comparant le bilan officiel de Mgr Hubert aux attentes de l'assemblée générale de la CECC en 1985. Je terminerai par quelques observations personnelles, plus de vingt ans après cet évènement.

Le bilan

Il m'apparaît important, au point de départ, de revenir sur le rapport que Mgr Hubert avait préparé pour la CECC et qui a été publié dans un livre intitulé *Le Concile revisité*, publié aux Éditions Paulines[20]. On y trouve l'évaluation officielle et publique de l'acteur principal de la délégation canadienne, président de la Conférence des évêques, dans les semaines qui suivent immédiatement le synode. Que dit-il ?

D'entrée de jeu, il affirme que l'affrontement annoncé par les médias entre les conservateurs et les progressistes n'a pas eu lieu. « Le Synode est un évènement spirituel qui a pleinement confirmé les orientations de Vatican II », écrit-il. Dans un second temps, cependant, il rappelle les questions majeures qui n'ont été ni soulevées ni débattues au synode :

---

[19] *Ibid.*, p. 549.

[20] Gaëtan Baillargeon (dir.), *Le Concile revisité. Réflexions sur le Concile et l'après-Concile*, Montréal, Éd. Paulines et Médiaspaul, 1986.

- L'articulation des deux ecclésiologies sous-jacentes au texte de *Lumen gentium* : l'une plus communautaire, l'autre plus cléricale ;
- La question du ministère, qui est pourtant primordiale pour l'Église ;
- La mission de l'Église dans le monde ;
- Les relations des conférences épiscopales avec la Curie romaine[21] ;
- Le contenu du projet d'un nouveau catéchisme qui avait été avancé avant le synode dans les milieux romains.

Mgr Hubert considère comme des acquis du synode l'expérience de collégialité vécue et le discours conclusif de Jean-Paul II, qui demande que désormais les synodes soient préparés en intégrant sérieusement les membres du Peuple de Dieu sur le sujet à traiter. Il en conclut que le synode sera de moins en moins consultatif et qu'il ira vers sa maturité. En terminant, Mgr Hubert invite la CECC à poursuivre des études sur la collégialité et le principe de subsidiarité, à consolider ses liens avec les conférences épiscopales des États-Unis, des pays d'Amérique latine et des Antilles et à collaborer avec le Conseil canadien des Églises.

Ce rapport reflète bien l'homme : son espérance et sa foi vive, mais aussi sa capacité d'analyse critique et franche ainsi que son désir d'influencer l'avenir par des engagements pratiques. S'il accepte que tout ne se soit pas déroulé comme souhaité, il regarde en avant et met son espoir dans le Pape, dont l'écoute et les discours de convocation et de conclusion du synode semblent lui donner le ton juste et la confirmation souhaitée de pouvoir poursuivre les orientations que l'Église canadienne s'est données.

Je ne sais quel jugement Mgr Hubert porterait aujourd'hui sur les fruits de ce synode ; à mon avis, il est toutefois permis de penser qu'il serait fort déçu relativement aux attentes qu'il avait formulées sur des sujets tels que la collégialité, la mission de l'Église dans le monde, l'attention aux grands problèmes de ce temps, la coresponsabilité, les ministères, les relations avec la Curie, la reconnaissance de l'Église

[21] On renvoie pour étude la question du statut des conférences épiscopales et l'application du principe de subsidiarité à l'Église.

particulière, le rôle du synode et la question de la présence des femmes dans l'Église.

Pour ma part, je considère que ce synode a provoqué une distance certaine entre l'épiscopat canadien et la Curie romaine qui a cherché à le mettre au pas, et cela, dès le synode.

Je suis toujours resté embarrassé par la convocation stratégique d'une réunion des cardinaux immédiatement avant le synode des évêques, d'autant plus que cette rencontre avait comme principal objectif de traiter de la Curie romaine, de son organisation et de ses relations avec les évêques, thème que les Conférences épiscopales voulaient étudier au synode, considérant pour plusieurs que la Curie n'avait pas pris le tournant souhaité par le concile.

Tout en reconnaissant la liberté de chaque cardinal et sa capacité de se faire une opinion propre, la session des cardinaux sur le thème qui était à l'ordre du jour et le discours du cardinal Hamer qui a été coulé auprès des membres du synode me conduisent à l'hypothèse qu'il y a eu une certaine tentative de noyautage du synode, afin d'orienter les discussions au sein des groupes linguistiques.

Plus sérieux encore, on note un décalage important entre la formulation du second objectif présenté dans la convocation du synode par Jean-Paul II et son interprétation par Mgr Schotte dans le texte où celui-ci divulguait l'organisation du synode. Jean-Paul II invite à « échanger et approfondir des expériences et des informations sur l'application du Concile au niveau de l'Église universelle et des Églises particulières[22] », ce que la délégation canadienne fera dans ses interventions. Mgr Schotte parle plutôt d'« échanger et approfondir les expériences et les informations sur l'application du Concile[23] ». Il résume cet objectif en y accolant le terme « vérifier ». Il néglige la référence à l'Église universelle et aux Églises particulières, ce qui permettra de fixer l'attention sur les seules Églises particulières.

De même, quand on relit le questionnaire envoyé aux Églises pour la préparation du synode, on n'y retrouve pas la même préoccupation relative aux défis des exigences nouvelles, la même confiance à ce que

---

22 *Synode extraordinaire. Célébration de Vatican II*, p. 36.

23 *Ibid.*, p. 43.

l'Esprit dit aux Églises. Le second objectif est perçu en termes de vérification quant à la justesse de l'interprétation des Églises particulières plus que d'échange et d'approfondissement quant à leurs expériences et leurs défis. Cet objectif a même pu être perçu comme une vérification de la vérité et de la justesse du concile par un synode. Dans son rapport terminal au synode, le cardinal Daneels écrit : « Nous avons vérifié que le concile Vatican II est une expression légitime et valable, et une interprétation du dépôt de la foi, tel qu'il est contenu dans l'Écriture sainte et dans la tradition vivante de l'Église. » Joseph Komonchak, dans l'introduction au livre publié par les Éditions du Cerf sur les textes du synode, attire notre attention sur le caractère étrange de cette déclaration d'un synode qui juge un concile[24].

À vrai dire, la seule façon d'éviter des débats exigeants au synode a été de mettre l'accent sur la célébration du concile, de reporter à plus tard les questions qui auraient mis en question l'organisation de l'Église, de ne pas reprendre le débat sur l'articulation entre le chapitre 2 et le chapitre 3, en insistant sur le chapitre 1 de *Lumen gentium* qui ne fait pas problème : l'Église comme mystère et don. On a de plus évité de discuter des questions trop complexes du siècle.

Au fil du temps, on sait cependant que la notion de Peuple de Dieu, jugée si importante par beaucoup d'épiscopats et par les fidèles, a été critiquée et peu à peu abandonnée par celui qui est aujourd'hui Benoît XVI, que la collégialité et l'institution synodale n'ont pas progressé dans le sens attendu par de nombreuses délégations, que les conférences épiscopales ont été mises au pas comme le souhaitait le cardinal Ratzinger[25], que la compréhension d'une Église au cœur du monde est mise en question, comme manifestant un trop grand optimisme.

En conclusion, je crois que l'Église canadienne a pris au sérieux le concile Vatican II et les orientations initiales données au synode par Jean-Paul II, mais qu'elle n'a pas pris assez au sérieux l'opposition et les critiques de certains. Attentive au Peuple de Dieu et à l'évolution de la société dans ses diverses dimensions, elle s'est mise à la tâche. Elle a

---

24 J. Komonchak, « Introduction », *Synode extraordinaire. Célébration de Vatican II*, Paris, Cerf, 1986, p. 12, note 5.

25 Joseph Ratzinger, Vittorio Messori, *Entretien sur la foi*, France, Fayard, 1985, p. 65-72.

fait siennes les grandes orientations données par Jean XXIII, Paul VI et Jean-Paul II dans *Pacem in terris*, *Ecclesiam suam*, *Populum progressio*, *Redemptor Hominis* et *Laborem exercens*. Au nom de la liberté de conscience promue par le concile, elle a suggéré une certaine interprétation d'*Humanae vitae*, en s'appuyant sur la réflexion faite au sein des mouvements familiaux catholiques depuis des années. Elle a essayé de se situer au cœur d'une société en évolution rapide en participant, à sa façon, à son devenir. Jusqu'à ce synode de 1985, elle a cherché à réaliser au Canada l'*aggiornamento* appelé par Jean XXIII et à traduire dans la réalité canadienne les grandes inspirations conciliaires. Elle a rencontré deux difficultés : l'importance des changements amorcés par le concile Vatican II et l'accélération de l'histoire du Québec et du Canada au cours des 20 années qui ont suivi le concile. C'est cette seconde difficulté qui a posé les plus grands défis, défis toujours présents, qui invitent sans cesse au discernement, à l'accueil de l'Esprit, à une certaine humilité ; défis qui imposent collaboration, écoute, dialogue, mais aussi interpellation évangélique et recherche de vérité.

Selon la grille de lecture utilisée par Benoît XVI pour évaluer deux interprétations du concile qui se sont cristallisées, l'une favorisant une herméneutique de la discontinuité et de la rupture, l'autre une interprétation du renouveau dans la continuité ; l'une provoquant la confusion, l'autre portant des fruits[26], on peut penser que l'Église canadienne, au moment du synode, était considérée par la Curie comme se situant trop du côté de la rupture et de la discontinuité, trop du côté des défis posés par sa présence à un monde en pleine évolution, pas assez du côté de la continuité. Prenant au sérieux l'invitation faite par Jean-Paul II aux présidents des conférences épiscopales et le travail préparatoire de la CECC qui s'est associé des prêtres, des religieuses et religieux, des laïcs, la délégation canadienne est peut-être apparue à certains comme trop « grégaire », trop « ouverte au monde », trop « managériale », pas assez « romaine malgré tout »[27].

---

26 Cardinal Bertone, « Vatican II, clef pour comprendre le pontificat [de Benoît XVI] », ZENIT.org, 29 janvier 2009.

27 Tous ces termes sont utilisés par le cardinal Ratzinger pour parler des conférences épiscopales ou des évêques qui ont été nommés peu de temps après Vatican II. Voir Joseph Ratzinger, *Entretien sur la foi*, 1985, p. 70,73,75.

SECTION II

Experiencing the Council / L'expérience du concile

Marcel Bélanger : itinéraire d'un expert canadien à Vatican II

Philippe J. Roy,
Université Laval

Marcel Bélanger et son journal conciliaire

Marcel Bélanger[1] naquit à Valleyfield le 6 novembre 1908. Fils d'Alfred Bélanger, entrepreneur, et de Florida Desjardins, il fit ses études primaires dans sa ville natale entre 1914 et 1920, et ses études secondaires au Collège de Valleyfield, où il obtint un baccalauréat ès arts en 1928. Cette année-là, il entra au noviciat des Oblats de Marie Immaculée de Ville-La-Salle. Après sa profession, le 2 août 1929, il poursuivit ses études au Scolasticat Saint-Joseph, à Ottawa, jusqu'en 1932. Entre-temps, en 1930, il avait obtenu une licence

[1] Pour composer la biographie de Marcel Bélanger, nous avons travaillé à partir de l'entrée qui a été faite sur lui par Gaston Carrière dans le *Dictionnaire biographique des Oblats de Marie Immaculée au Canada,* version informatique (Ottawa, Archives Deschâtelets, 2005), d'une notice nécrologique composée en février 1975 par l'un de ses confrères et ancien recteur de l'Université d'Ottawa, le frère Rodrigue Normandin, de son journal conciliaire en cours de publication, ainsi que de la revue des Oblats, *Études oblates,* dans laquelle se trouvent plusieurs articles du père Bélanger.

en philosophie et, en 1932, un baccalauréat en théologie. Lorsqu'il eut prononcé ses vœux perpétuels, le 8 septembre 1932, son autorité provinciale l'envoya poursuivre sa formation à Rome. Il étudia tout d'abord à l'*Angelicum*, université dominicaine qui se développa sous Léon XIII, lorsque celui-ci fit de la doctrine de Thomas d'Aquin la base du renouveau théologique de l'Église et le fondement de la formation du clergé[2]. En 1934, il y obtint une licence en théologie. L'année suivante, il suivit sa scolarité de doctorat à la Grégorienne, avant de rentrer au Canada. Entre-temps, le 16 juillet 1933, il avait été ordonné prêtre par le cardinal Francesco Marchetto Selvaggiani.

Marcel Bélanger fut profondément marqué par son séjour romain, comme en témoigne l'un de ses confrères, Rodrigue Normandin, dans la notice nécrologique qu'il lui consacra :

> Qu'on le veuille ou non, la vie romaine marque son homme. En outre n'était-il pas alors de règle que l'étudiant entrât docilement et de plein gré dans le sillage de ses maîtres ? [...] je demeure convaincu que notre confrère a reçu de ses études à Rome une impulsion qui se fera sentir tout le reste de sa vie[3].

De son passage à Rome et à la Grégorienne, Marcel Bélanger garda en effet un attachement particulier pour la mariologie et une grande déférence envers le thomisme. Le frère Rodrigue Normandin l'atteste d'ailleurs lorsqu'il présente les écrits de son confrère :

> On reconnaît dans ces deux articles[4], tout comme dans les autres nombreux écrits du père Bélanger, l'homme formé à l'école de saint Thomas d'Aquin, en pleine possession d'un système de pensée dont la valeur essentielle ne pouvait, dans son esprit, faire l'objet du moindre doute. Là, on retrouve aussi l'intellectuel qui, de ses maîtres de l'Université grégorienne (1934-1935), a pleinement

2 Encyclique *Aeterni Patris*, 4 août 1879.

3 Rodrigue Normandin, « Marcel Bélanger, Missionnaire des Oblats de Marie Immaculée 1908-1972 », Province Saint-Joseph, Notices nécrologiques, Ottawa, 2 février 1975, CD-Rom *Notices biographiques des Oblats du Canada*, Archives Deschâtelets, 2008.

4 Marcel Bélanger, « *Assumpta est Maria in Caelum* », *Revue de l'Université d'Ottawa*, section spéciale, 1951 : p. 137-150 ; « Introduction à l'étude de la Maternité spirituelle », Journées d'études — Université de Sherbrooke, 19-20 octobre 1956, Ottawa, Éditions de l'Université d'Ottawa, 1958, p. 1-42.

assimilé les leçons sur la méthodologie de la recherche en histoire et en théologie et dont il a lui-même fait profiter les étudiants de la Faculté de Théologie[5].

Rodrigue Normandin va plus loin :

> Une autre donnée s'impose ici parce qu'elle aide à juger équitablement les positions doctrinales du père Bélanger, aussi bien dans son enseignement que dans ses écrits. C'est un fait avéré que l'orientation nettement tracée des études philosophiques et théologiques se voulait d'une fidélité absolue au thomisme le plus authentique et d'une rigoureuse orthodoxie. Que ce soit par le contact direct avec la Somme théologique, que ce soit indirectement par la pratique assidue des commentateurs les plus autorisés, saint Thomas d'Aquin était LE maître incontesté tant chez les professeurs que chez les étudiants[6].

Ce séjour à Rome fit également de Marcel Bélanger un catholique très conservateur, très romain, de cette romanité que le pape Pie XI définissait comme « la perfection de la catholicité[7] » et que son successeur, Pie XII, considérait comme une vertu sacerdotale[8]. Une étude historique et une définition conceptuelle claire seraient à faire sur cette notion de romanité, mais l'on peut déjà considérer qu'elle est une des principales caractéristiques et une clef de compréhension essentielle du catholicisme intransigeant. Celui-ci naquit au XVIIIe siècle de la réaction catholique à la Révolution française, il se renforça au siècle suivant chez les ultramontains, qui défendirent l'infaillibilité pontificale lors du premier concile du Vatican, et on le retrouva parmi les représentants de la minorité lors du concile Vatican II.

De retour au Canada, Marcel Bélanger fut assigné au Scolasticat Saint-Joseph jusqu'en 1952. En même temps, il enseigna à la Faculté de théologie de l'Université d'Ottawa, où il termina son doctorat en 1938. Il eut une activité universitaire considérable : de 1940 à 1947, il fut se-

---

5 Rodrigue NORMANDIN, *op. cit.*, p. 3-4.

6 Rodrigue NORMANDIN, *op. cit.*, p. 6.

7 Pie XI, audience du 19 avril 1923 au Séminaire français de Rome, cité dans J.-B. FREY, *Le Saint-Siège et le Séminaire français de Rome*, Rome, Librairie Vaticane, 1935, p. 109.

8 Pie XII, « Allocution de Sa Sainteté Pie XII à de jeunes prêtres espagnols, 21/03/1957 », *La Documentation catholique*, n° 1250 (28 mars 1957), p. 524-525.

crétaire de la Faculté de théologie et, de 1947 à 1952, il en fut le doyen. En 1952, il devint le premier vice-recteur de l'Université, charge qu'il garda jusqu'en 1964. Pendant ce temps, il fut également directeur de la *Revue de l'Université d'Ottawa* (1953-1958), régent de la Faculté de droit civil (1953-1959) et vice-supérieur de l'Université (1958-1964). En plus de toutes ces charges universitaires, il fut directeur des *Semaines missionnaires du Canada* (1934), secrétaire de la section théologique de la *Société thomiste de l'Université d'Ottawa* (1944), fondateur et cheville ouvrière pendant plus de vingt ans de la *Société canadienne d'Études mariales*, association dont il garda le fardeau de secrétaire jusqu'en 1971. Mariologue chevronné, il était aussi membre de l'Académie mariale internationale de Rome (1952-1972). Son intérêt pour la Vierge trouva toute sa satisfaction lors de la proclamation du dogme de l'Assomption par le pape Pie XII le 1er novembre 1950. Il assista d'ailleurs à la déclaration solennelle à Rome, et l'article qu'il écrivit à son retour témoigne de son allégresse[9].

En 1965, lorsque les composantes ecclésiastiques de l'Université d'Ottawa furent séparées des composantes séculières et que fut fondée l'Université Saint-Paul, il en devint le premier vice-recteur (1965-1967), en même temps que supérieur de la résidence des professeurs oblats de l'Université d'Ottawa (1964-1967). Il joua un grand rôle dans l'érection des édifices de l'Université Saint-Paul. Il mourut à Ottawa, le 8 septembre 1972. Simultanément à toutes ses charges et aux nombreux travaux parallèles qu'elles pouvaient occasionner, Marcel Bélanger laissa de nombreux articles de théologie, surtout en mariologie, dont plusieurs furent publiés dans la revue *Études oblates*.

Ce qui doit retenir particulièrement notre attention ici, c'est son activité et son itinéraire au concile Vatican II. Entre 1960 et 1962, il fut effectivement nommé consulteur de la Commission pontificale de

[9] Marcel BÉLANGER, « Définition de l'Assomption et notre bonheur », *La Bannière de Marie-Immaculée*, 1952, p. 72-89. Il commence ainsi son article : « L'inoubliable fête ! Ce matin-là, juché sur la colonnade du Bernin dont les bras interminables n'arrivaient plus à enserrer la foule qui se pressait jusque dans les rues conduisant à la Place de Saint-Pierre, j'eus la faveur de participer, comme ces milliers de pèlerins privilégiés, à ce qu'on a si justement appelé la plus triomphale des fêtes mariales. *Exaltata est* ! C'était autant qu'on peut l'imaginer l'exaltation de la Mère, écho magnifique ici-bas, après vingt siècles de foi et de prière, de la glorieuse Assomption de Marie au ciel » (p. 72).

théologie pour la préparation du concile, puis expert au concile pour la première session. Il ne semble pas qu'il ait assisté aux autres séances, probablement pour des raisons de santé, car il souffrait d'une grave maladie depuis 1947. Durant la première session, il tint quotidiennement son journal, remplissant ainsi deux cahiers, le premier de 115 pages et le second de 67 pages, d'une écriture fine, serrée et régulière. Dans ce journal, l'opinion de Marcel Bélanger est quelquefois, mais rarement, explicite. La lecture de ses notes intimes laisse deviner un catholique très conservateur, un expert qui admire la pensée des leaders de la minorité, comme Ottaviani, Ruffini, Siri, Lefebvre, etc. Cependant, il est sans *a priori* contre les leaders de la majorité. Lorsqu'il en blâme un, il ne s'en prend pas à sa personne, mais il décompose plutôt son argumentation et sa démonstration pour montrer en quoi, selon lui, elle est déficiente.

Dans ce journal, Marcel Bélanger présente au jour le jour le contenu de chacune des interventions en Congrégation générale. Ce type d'exercice pourrait être rébarbatif à la lecture, mais l'oblat sait dégager les idées fortes de chacun des exposés, et la lecture de son journal présente une synthèse intéressante des interventions *in aula* de la première session. En nous basant sur ce journal, nous présenterons donc l'itinéraire de Marcel Bélanger au concile Vatican II, en nous attardant sur les aspects qui le préoccupaient davantage pendant cette première période conciliaire, c'est-à-dire les schémas *De fontibus* sur la nature de la Révélation (*Dei Verbum*) et *De Ecclesia* sur l'Église (*Lumen gentium*). Nous nous pencherons également sur les discussions formelles et informelles autour de la question mariale, qui préoccupait beaucoup le mariologue Bélanger. Enfin, en conclusion, nous présenterons les angoisses d'un expert de la minorité, mal à l'aise par rapport au tournant conciliaire.

1. Marcel Bélanger et le schéma *De fontibus*. Au milieu de la querelle entre le Latran et l'Institut Biblique

Le concile s'est ouvert alors que sévissait à Rome une dispute théologique très intense entre l'Université du Latran et l'Institut Biblique[10].

---

[10] Voir à ce sujet l'article d'Anthony Dupont et Karim Schelkens, « *Scupoli vintandi.* The Historical-Critical Exegesis Controversy Between the Lateran and the Biblicum (1960-1961) », *Bijdragen, International Journal in Philosophy and Theology*, vol. 69, n° 1

Étant donné que les enjeux de cette querelle sont fondamentaux pour expliquer le parcours du schéma *De fontibus* et qu'elle permet de mettre en perspective la pensée de Marcel Bélanger, il nous semble nécessaire d'en expliquer très brièvement les positions respectives. Mais pour y parvenir, il faut revenir à la période préconciliaire.

À partir des années 1950, des rumeurs contre l'Institut Biblique circulaient à Rome, rumeurs qui prirent une tournure plus concrète lorsque le recteur reçut du cardinal Pizzardo[11], le 27 janvier 1955, un *pro-memoria* dans lequel le Biblique était accusé « de propager des idées d'avant-garde (*avanzate*) de la critique moderne du protestantisme libéral et de mettre en doute la foi en Dieu et en la rétribution future dans l'Ancien Testament[12] ». L'auteur de ce pamphlet n'était nul autre que Mgr Antonino Romeo, secrétaire de la Congrégation des séminaires et universités et professeur à l'Université du Latran. Romeo revint à la charge deux ans plus tard, dans une lettre datée du 23 décembre 1957, dans laquelle il s'élevait contre l'*Introduction à la Bible* parue sous la direction d'André Robert et d'André Feuillet : « Je sais parfaitement bien que deux pieux religieux de l'Institut Biblique Pontifical sont responsables de cet incroyable volume, qui est une bouffonnerie comme jamais jusqu'à présent il ne s'en est produit dans le champ de l'exégèse catholique[13]. »

En décembre 1960, Antonino Romeo récidiva, cette fois contre un article du jésuite espagnol Alonso Schökel, « Dove va l'esegesi cattolica[14] ? », paru dans *La Civiltà Cattolica* et réimprimé en tiré à part par l'Institut Biblique. Dans ce texte, l'auteur tâchait de démontrer

---

(2008), p. 18-51. Voir également la contribution de Riccardo Burigana, « Tradizioni Inconciliabili ? La "querelle" tra l'Università Lateranense e l'Istituto Biblico nella preparazione del Vaticano II », dans Philippe Chenaux (éd.), *L'Università del Laterano e la preparazione del concilio Vaticano II, Atti del Convego Internazionale di Studi (Città del Vaticano, 27 gennaio 2000)*, Rome, Pontificia Università Lateranense MURSIA, 2001, p. 51-66.

11 Préfet de la Congrégation des séminaires et universités, Grand Chancelier de l'Institut.

12 Maurice Gilbert, *L'Institut Biblique Pontifical. Un siècle d'histoire (1909-2009)*, Rome, Editrice Pontificio Istituto Biblico, 2009, p. 158.

13 Cité dans Maurice Gilbert, *L'Institut Biblique Pontifical*, *op. cit.*, p. 159.

14 Alonso Schökel, « Dove va l'esegesi cattolica ? », *La Civiltà Cattolica*, III, n° 2645 (3 septembre 1960), p. 449-460. Cet article fut réimprimé comme tiré à part par l'Institut Biblique.

que l'exégèse était en mouvement depuis le début du XXe siècle et que le magistère encourageait les biblistes à aller de l'avant. Dans la revue du Latran, *Divinitas*, Romeo lui reprocha de faire peu de cas de la Tradition[15]. Cet article mit le feu aux poudres et le Biblicum répondit aux accusations de Romeo dans sa revue *Verbum Domini*[16]. Entre-temps, le cardinal Ernesto Ruffini dénonça « un spirito ipercritico » qualifié d'hérétique et de moderniste dans un texte intitulé « Generi letterari e ipotesi di lavoro nei recenti studi biblici[17] », tandis qu'un autre professeur du Latran, Francesco Spadafora, publiait dans la revue *Palestra del Clero*, le 15 septembre 1961, un article intitulé « Un documento notevole per l'esegesi cattolica[18] », dans lequel il s'en prenait à toute nouveauté en matière d'exégèse et louait l'article de Romeo. Une attaque appelait une contre-attaque, si bien que le Saint-Office lui-même s'en mêla[19], appuyant sans réserve Romeo qui accusait l'Institut Biblique de faire passer dans le monde catholique la théologie protestante sur la Tradition. Mais laissons là les aspects événementiels de cette querelle, notre objectif n'est pas d'en présenter un historique détaillé, mais seulement de mentionner qu'au-delà des idées et des hommes cette polémique était relayée par les organes de diffusion des établissements d'enseignement respectifs, en particulier les revues *Divinitas* pour le Latran et *Verbum Domini* pour l'Institut Biblique. À la veille du concile Vatican II, l'Institut Biblique était donc dans la ligne de mire des courants conservateurs, et plus particulièrement de l'Université du Latran.

---

15 Antonino ROMEO, « L'enciclica "Divino afflante Spiritu" e le "Opiniones Novæ" », *Divinitas*, nº 4 (1960), p. 387-456.

16 Pontificium Institutum Biblicum, « Pontificium Institutum Biblicum et Recens Libellus R. mi D. ni A Romeo », *Verbum Domini*, nº 39 (1961), p. 3-17.

17 Ernesto RUFFINI, « Generi letterari e ipotesi di lavoro nei recenti studi biblici », *L'Osservatore Romano* (24 août 1961), p. 1. Ruffini disait : « Parlare di ipotesi di lavoro, che nel caso nostro sono palliate negazioni della storicità, a riguardo per es. dell'Annunciazione dell'Archangelo Gabriele a Maria Santissima (*Luc.* 1, 26-38) e della promessa del primato a San Pietro (*Matth.* 16, 17-19) fatte derivare da imitazioni di precedenti esemplari o da maturazioni posteriori del pensiero cristiano, è capovolgere l'esegesi cattolica e un attentato ereticale contro verità ritenute sempre – a cominciare dai primi Patri della Chiesa – corrispondenti a realtà storiche. »

18 Francesco SPADAFORA, « Un documento notevole per l'esegesi cattolica », *Palestra del Clero*, nº 40 (15 septembre 1961), p. 969-981.

19 *Acta Apostolicae Sedis*, 51 (1961), 507.

Aussi n'est-il pas étonnant de voir combien leurs réponses respectives à la consultation préconciliaire étaient différentes lorsqu'ils abordèrent la question de l'Écriture.

Dans ses *vota* répondant à la consultation préconciliaire, l'Université du Latran accordait une place très importante aux études bibliques[20]. Les auteurs du texte demandaient à ce que le concile promeuve les études en théologie biblique, comme le concile de Trente l'avait fait pour les travaux sur l'Écriture en général. Ils souhaitaient également que le concile résolve la question de l'interprétation des neuf premiers chapitres de la Genèse (en créant une Commission qui rédigerait un texte biblico-théologique sur le sujet), que soit imposé un cours sur l'Écriture à tous les étudiants en théologie, que l'inerrance absolue de la Bible soit définie et, enfin, qu'une édition catholique de l'Ancien Testament soit réalisée. Les auteurs insistaient sur l'inerrance absolue de la Bible.

Ces demandes étaient loin de celles de l'Institut Biblique, qui semblaient provenir d'un univers totalement différent. Pour le Biblicum[21], qui avait divisé ses *vota* en deux parties, doctrinale et disciplinaire, le concile devait être le lieu où discuter et confronter les résultats des études contemporaines, et non pas l'occasion de confirmer la doctrine traditionnelle et de formuler des condamnations à l'encontre de ceux qui cherchaient des voies nouvelles dans le champ de l'exégèse[22]. D'un point de vue doctrinal, l'Institut Biblique demandait que le concile ne fasse pas le choix entre une école plutôt qu'une autre, mais qu'il explique la relation entre l'Écriture sainte et la Tradition, et qu'il les présente comme deux canaux distincts, comme deux fonds de la même Révélation. Le Biblicum demandait également que le concile explique le rôle de la foi dans le processus de salut, le rôle effectif de Dieu dans les Écritures saintes et dans la sanctification des chrétiens. L'Institut invitait également le concile à déclarer qu'il était incorrect de chercher

20 *Acta et Documenta*, IV, 1/1, 171-442. Voir en particulier les *vota* de T. Garcia, 189-194, ceux de F. Spadafora, 263-270, et ceux de C. Zedda, 274-275.

21 *Acta et Documenta*, IV, 1/1, 123-136.

22 Riccardo Burigana, « Tradizioni Inconciliabili ? La "querelle" tra l'Università Lateranense e l'Istituto Biblico nella preparazione del Vaticano II », *L'Università del Laterano...*, p. 56.

dans l'Écriture le fondement ultime de l'antisémitisme. Mais le point sur lequel le Biblicum insistait le plus, c'était l'historicité des évangiles, pour laquelle l'Institut demandait à ce que le concile confirme les articles de foi qui devaient diriger l'interprétation des Écritures. Anthony Dupont et Karim Schelkens résument très bien cette proposition :

> According to the Biblicum there are three articles to be considered : a) Christian faith is based on divine intervention in historical circumstances, especially in the incarnation, life, death and resurrection of Jesus Christ ; b) Revelation was not complete prior to the apostolic period ; c) Given that the four gospels are inspired, they possess infallibility in a manner that can be reconciled with their historicity[23].

Ce *votum* suggérait également que les interprètes catholiques des Écritures saintes puissent déterminer le type d'historicité des évangiles, sous l'autorité du magistère. En d'autres termes, il appelait tout simplement à une approche historico-critique des Écritures.

Ainsi, pour résumer les positions respectives, le Biblicum cherchait le point de départ et le but de toute réflexion en exégèse dans les Écritures saintes, tandis que le Latran les cherchait plutôt dans la Tradition. Fondamentalement, la querelle reposait sur un conflit entre exégèse et dogme : tandis que l'un se préoccupait de raffiner ses instruments méthodologiques, l'autre estimait que ces méthodes étaient nuisibles à l'enseignement révélé de l'Église.

Les positions étant exposées, il convient maintenant de considérer un autre aspect. Il faut effectivement souligner que, dans la préparation des schémas préconciliaires, il revenait à la Commission de théologie de préparer un texte sur le fondement de la Révélation. Or, cette commission était dirigée par Ottaviani et composée des têtes pensantes suivantes : Sebastiano Tromp, Luigi Ciappi, Charles Balić, Rosaire Gagnebet, Salvatore Garofalo et Franz Hürth. Avec une telle composition, il n'est pas étonnant que la Commission ait pris fait et cause pour la position du Latran et que le texte préparé et présenté en Congrégation générale le 14 novembre 1962, le *De fontibus*, soit

---

23 Anthony Dupont et Karim Schelkens, « *Scupoli vintandi*. The Historical-Critical Exegesis Controversy Between the Lateran and the Biblicum (1960-1961) », *Bijdragen, International...*, p. 23.

une condamnation des études bibliques contemporaines, présentées comme le vecteur de théories dangereuses. Cependant, ce schéma fut critiqué et, quelques jours plus tard, le 20 novembre, il fut repoussé et ultérieurement remplacé par un autre qui avait été rédigé dans un esprit totalement différent.

Ainsi donc, à l'ouverture du concile, la querelle entre le Latran et l'Institut Biblique suscita une grande attention, d'autant plus que le duel était entretenu par des passes d'armes de toutes sortes, en particulier par des échanges d'attaques et de contre-attaques au moyen de brochures et de pamphlets distribués aux Pères conciliaires[24].

Au milieu de tout cela, quelle était la position de Marcel Bélanger et quel fut son cheminement ? Tout d'abord, il semble ne s'être jamais préoccupé de cette querelle avant son arrivée à Rome. Ce n'est que le 14 octobre 1962 qu'il lit l'article de Mgr Romeo contre le père Alfonso. Son commentaire est le suivant : « Charge formidable ! » Ainsi, de nature, de psychologie et d'éducation, il est plutôt attiré par les positions conservatrices, mais ce qu'il ajoute montre qu'il n'a pourtant aucun parti pris : « Mais, qu'en penser, surtout après la réponse que l'Institut Biblique lui-même a jugé devoir faire à l'accusateur[25] ? » Bélanger est donc un homme qui tente de se situer au-delà de la querelle. Il se déplace même pour entendre les adversaires de son système de pensée, car avant la discussion du schéma, de nombreux *periti* exposaient leur point de vue sur les schémas des Commissions préparatoires. Ainsi, le 24 octobre, il va écouter le jésuite Xavier Léon-Dufour à Saint-Louis des Français qui fait une conférence sur « L'historicité des évangiles »[26]. Après avoir présenté la communication du père jésuite, il écrit :

> Je comprends que de pareilles propositions puissent alerter certains personnages mal préparés à adhérer et que ces derniers ripostent farouchement pour « sauver » la foi. On retrouve ici

[24] À ce sujet, voir Maurice GILBERT, *L'Institut biblique pontifical. Un siècle d'histoire (1909-2009)*, p. 167-171.

[25] Archives Deschâtelets (AD), *Journal conciliaire de Marcel Bélanger*, 1er cahier (14 octobre 1962), p. 5.

[26] *Ibid.*, 1er cahier (24 octobre 1962), p. 14.

l'opposition classique entre penseurs, les uns d'avant-garde, les autres sur la réserve et inquiets[27].

Il écrit cette remarque au moment même où Francesco Spadafora fait circuler une brochure contre l'enseignement de l'Institut Biblique[28]. Bélanger commente ainsi la querelle :

> Jusqu'ici, je n'ai pu arriver à trouver la note juste. Je crains que le groupe du Latran ne se méprenne et n'exagère plus ou moins. D'autre part, j'avoue que des théories semblables à celles que je viens d'entendre de la bouche du P. Léon-Dufour sont loin de me rassurer sur l'équilibre de jugement et même sur la pleine orthodoxie des bons Pères de l'Institut Biblique[29].

C'était donc un homme conservateur, mais qui cherchait objectivement à se situer par rapport au débat, dans un climat général où les sympathies allaient de plus en plus vers l'Institut Biblique et les thèses « nouvelles ». Deux jours après avoir entendu Xavier Léon-Dufour, il va écouter Yves Congar au Séminaire Français dans un exposé sur la Tradition. Marcel Bélanger présente objectivement le contenu de la conférence du dominicain, mais termine son commentaire en soulignant que celui-ci critique le *De fontibus* comme étant le reflet d'un professeur manquant de personnalité[30], ce avec quoi il n'est pas vraiment d'accord. Marcel Bélanger, comme tous les conservateurs, comme les autres membres de la Curie et de la minorité, est très attaché aux schémas préparatoires, comme en témoigne son commentaire à la sortie d'un entretien avec le père Général des O.M.I., le père Deschâtelets, le 18 octobre :

> La réaction du Général devant les réactionnaires du Concile m'a un peu surpris et surtout causé beaucoup de satisfaction. Le T.R. Père commence à réaliser qu'on va un peu loin, et surtout qu'on a trop souvent une attitude purement négative en critiquant sans merci les schémas préparés par les Commissions qui fonctionnaient

27 *Ibid.*, p. 14-15.

28 Francesco Spadafora, *Razionalismo, Exegesi cattolica e Magistero*, voir Maurice Gilbert, *L'Institut biblique pontifical. Un siècle d'histoire (1909-2009)*, p. 168.

29 AD, *Journal conciliaire de Marcel Bélanger*, p. 15.

30 *Ibid.*, 1er cahier (26 octobre), p. 16-17.

depuis deux ans. Je l'ai approuvé sans restriction, en ajoutant que certaine attitude de la part de plusieurs évêques à l'endroit du Saint-Siège et de sa politique soi-disant centralisatrice allait à l'encontre de la nature même du gouvernement de l'Église et s'avérerait plus tard nuisible aux évêques eux-mêmes. Une fois engagé dans une voie démocratique, jusqu'où n'irait-on pas[31] ?

Par ce commentaire, on voit vraiment que Bélanger était un homme de la minorité, un homme formé à l'école « romaine » des années 1930. Plus tard, le 27 octobre, il réagit à un exposé du père de Lubac contre le schéma *De Doctrina Fidei et Morum* : « Une chose me frappe : pourquoi des gens, qui furent membres de la Commission préparatoire, n'ont-ils pas tenu jadis le langage démolisseur qu'ils tiennent aujourd'hui[32] ? » Le 12 novembre, peu de temps avant que ne commence véritablement le débat sur le schéma doctrinal, Bélanger va de nouveau écouter une conférence du père Congar au Collège Pio Latina. Dans cette allocution, le dominicain affirme qu'il faut renvoyer les schémas préparatoires. Au *De fontibus*, il reproche ses considérations sur les « deux sources » de la Révélation. Pour lui, il n'y a qu'une seule source : l'Évangile, car le mot « source » désigne l'« origine première ». Cette fois, Marcel Bélanger commente : « Je ne puis accepter cette argumentation, qui donne au mot "source" un sens tout à fait différent de ce que les théologiens lui assignent communément. » Marcel Bélanger se rallie en effet à la position théologique tenue par les théologiens romains avant Vatican II, qui affirment que la Révélation se trouve contenue dans deux sources : l'Écriture et la Tradition. Pour Marcel Bélanger, « les objections du P. Congar portent tout simplement à faux ici ». De plus, Bélanger désapprouve une deuxième raison évoquée par le père Congar, à savoir le souci de ne pas heurter inutilement les non-catholiques pour lesquels il n'y a qu'une source, l'Écriture : « J'ai bien l'impression que cette deuxième raison est vraiment celle qui commande la position de Congar[33]. »

---

31 *Ibid.*, 1er cahier (18 octobre), p. 8.

32 *Ibid.*, 1er cahier (27 octobre), p. 18.

33 *Ibid.*, 1er cahier (12 novembre), p. 36-40.

Comme les autres membres de la minorité, Marcel Bélanger s'insurge contre les schémas de remplacement qui circulent sous le manteau. « Tout ceci me paraît peu de bonne guerre. Je note que les "periti" opposants comptent d'anciens consulteurs de la Commission Préparatoire de Théologie. Serait-ce du sabotage ? » Il continue en écrivant : « [...] j'ai l'impression qu'il y a bien du monde fourvoyé dans cette affaire et qu'en ce moment on est victime d'un certain emballement plutôt irréfléchi. Mais va-t-on se ressaisir ? [...] » Il considère « qu'on ne rend pas justice, ni à la Curie en général, ni à la Commission Préparatoire qui a travaillé des mois durant pour préparer le schéma actuel. On croirait qu'en tout ceci, il y a pas mal de sentiment mêlé aux raisons objectives qu'on peut avoir. » Au final, tout comme le père Deschâtelets, il trouve « que l'opposition excède dans ses affirmations et ses procédés[34] ».

Mais comment Marcel Bélanger interprète-t-il le tollé presque général des Pères contre le schéma en Congrégation générale dès le premier jour ? En effet, il est tout de suite évident que seuls la Curie et les évêques italiens appuient le schéma. Presque tous les autres évêques s'y opposent. Tout d'abord, Marcel Bélanger estime qu'il y a alors deux visions du catholicisme. Ceux qui se montrent en faveur d'une ouverture et d'un accueil pour les non-catholiques, qui pensent en termes de pastorale et non de dogmatique, et ceux qui, en revanche, insistent sur l'aspect doctrinal et sur la nécessité d'une formulation claire et ferme des vérités chrétiennes. Il considère au final que les deux mentalités ont du bon, mais qu'à s'affronter comme elles le font, elles pèchent toutes les deux par excès et qu'« il faudrait une synthèse et un dosage équilibré des deux aspects. L'Esprit souffle vers les préoccupations pastorales, c'est sûr. Mais il ne sacrifie rien de la vérité ni de ses droits[35]. » On a ici un autre aspect fondamental de la théologie scolastique et « romaine » du catholicisme préconciliaire : les droits de la vérité, qui seule peut en posséder. Cependant, depuis la Révolution française, de nombreux théologiens libéraux n'admettaient pas que la vérité puisse avoir le moindre droit. Ils estimaient que seuls les hommes pouvaient en posséder. Or, à l'aube du concile, la majorité des évêques étaient de cet avis.

---

[34] *Ibid.*, 1er cahier (13 novembre), p. 43-44.

[35] *Ibid.*, 1er cahier (14 novembre), p. 59.

Si Marcel Bélanger pouvait concéder que les rivaux avaient chacun des torts, il estimait cependant que « les adversaires du schéma obéissent au moins autant que les autres, sinon plus, à des motifs sentimentaux, à des préjugés. Ils affirment gratuitement beaucoup de choses, quelques-unes même en matière doctrinale. Des mises au point s'imposent[36]. » Marcel Bélanger est d'avis qu'il faut prendre « garde de trop décrier le mode scolastique du schéma, en un temps qui plus que tout autre souffre de l'absence de philosophie[37] ».

Alors que les adversaires du schéma lui reprochent un caractère trop professoral et scolastique, un manque de souffle pastoral, la rigidité excessive de certaines affirmations, le danger de rendre la vérité incompréhensible aux chrétiens non catholiques, l'omission du problème du salut avant la Révélation et des non-baptisés depuis, le peu d'encouragements donnés au travail scientifique en théologie et en exégèse, les protagonistes de leur côté font valoir qu'il n'y a pas d'action pastorale possible sans une exposition claire de la doctrine et qu'il ne peut y avoir d'offense faite aux frères séparés dans l'exposition de la vérité, puisque qu'ils la recherchent. Tout en se rangeant du côté de cette minorité qui affirme le devoir du concile de garder intègre la doctrine et de l'appliquer, et qui fait valoir la préparation sérieuse du schéma, Marcel Bélanger juge « que certains adversaires du schéma éprouvent le besoin de préciser davantage la portée de leurs critiques[38] ». Cependant, plus les jours passent, plus le schéma perd du terrain. « Mais il n'y a lieu ni de s'attrister ni de se réjouir, écrit-il. Il n'y a qu'à attendre le sort qui lui sera fait en finale par le vote des Pères. Et ce vote exprimera ce que l'Esprit veut dans les circonstances, indépendamment des préférences de chacun[39]. » En même temps, il dénonce « les allégations équivoques, parfois fausses, des opposants ». Il n'admet pas qu'on s'attaque à la doctrine des « deux sources de la Révélation[40] ». Pour lui, c'est une doctrine certaine et non une opinion discutable. Il s'exclame à ce propos :

---

36 *Ibidem.*

37 *Ibid.*, 1er cahier (16 novembre), p. 64.

38 *Ibid.*, 1er cahier (16 novembre), p. 66.

39 *Ibid.*, 1er cahier (17 novembre), p. 74.

40 *Ibidem.*

> Franchement, je crains que trop d'Excellences et même d'Éminences ne se laissent en ce moment impressionner par des gens dont le métier consiste trop souvent à tout remettre en question. Quelqu'un ne se lèvera-t-il pas pour dire : halte-là et rappeler aux Pères qu'ils sont les gardiens par excellence de la foi[41] ?

L'opposition de certains Pères à la doctrine traditionnelle des deux sources l'angoisse particulièrement :

> D'ailleurs, toute cette opposition à la doctritionnelle [doctrine traditionnelle] des deux sources contenant la Révélation devient inquiétante. Bon gré mal gré, une question se pose : quels sont les vrais mobiles qui animent les opposants ? Bien sûr, personne ne veut découvrir son jeu dans le camp des opposants ; et c'est plutôt gênant pour les autres de les mettre en demeure de parler[42].

Il écrit craindre que ce soit « uniquement un motif d'œcuménisme qui pousse tant de gens ici à faire le silence sur les deux sources, à ignorer la Tradition tout spécialement et à n'employer qu'un mot de nature à plaire et à donner satisfaction aux non-catholiques : l'Évangile ». Il continue en se demandant : « N'est-ce pas là tomber dans ce que Pie XII a qualifié de "faux irénisme" ? de complaisance exagérée et entretenue aux dépens de la vérité[43] ? »

Il ne souhaite donc pas que soit changé un iota à la doctrine contenue dans le schéma, mais il convient cependant qu'il faudrait le travailler « pour donner à la présentation de cette doctrine une tournure plus ouverte, plus pastorale, plus sympathique[44] ». Le 20 novembre, jour où a lieu un vote pour savoir s'il faut interrompre l'étude du *De fontibus*, le résultat des suffrages montre que 1 368 Pères sont pour l'interruption des discussions sur le schéma et 825 contre. Les deux tiers requis n'étant pas atteints ni par l'un ni par l'autre des partis, il est annoncé que les discussions devront continuer le lendemain[45]. Ce jour-là, non sans un brin de malice, Marcel Bélanger laisse poindre son contentement :

---

41 *Ibid.*, p. 75.

42 *Ibid.*, p. 76.

43 *Ibid.*, p. 76.

44 *Ibid.*, p. 75.

45 AS I/III, p. 254-255.

> Pour ma part, je suis surtout satisfait de voir que les adversaires du schéma n'ont pas remporté la victoire escomptée. Depuis l'ouverture du Concile, et même dans les jours précédents, ces gens n'ont cessé de déblatérer à qui mieux mieux contre le schéma. Ils ont même mené dans les coulisses une campagne orchestrée pour dissuader les évêques de voter en faveur du schéma, multipliant les conférences en ce sens, démontrant l'incongruité, pour ne pas dire l'inanité du schéma. Je trouve bon que ces gens reçoivent en passant la douche d'eau froide qu'ils méritaient[46].

Mais le lendemain, 21 novembre, il est annoncé aux Pères que bien que les deux tiers requis n'aient pas été atteints, le Saint-Père accorde que soit formée une Commission spéciale chargée de réviser le schéma avant qu'on en poursuive l'examen. Bien qu'il trouve la décision de Jean XXIII opportune, « en même temps que souverainement sage[47] » — car il semble impossible pour les Pères de s'entendre sur ce schéma —, Marcel Bélanger ne cesse d'être inquiet :

> [...] il est à craindre que les adversaires du schéma, non pas tant il est vrai les évêques que les doctrinaires, ne donnent à la décision pontificale un sens qu'elle n'a pas dans les circonstances et ne l'utilisent à leurs fins propres. Je crains que ces gens ne chantent victoire contre les promoteurs du schéma et ne produisent cette décision pontificale, qui n'a pourtant qu'un sens disciplinaire, comme l'approbation suprême tant recherchée à leurs façons de penser et de voir en matière de doctrine proprement dite[48].

De façon plus précise, il se méfie de ceux qu'il appelle les œcuménistes. Il craint tout d'abord qu'ils ne se disent approuvés par le Saint-Père « dans leur propension manifeste à édulcorer, pour fins de rapprochement avec les frères séparés, la doctrine catholique et à taire tout ce qui dans cette doctrine serait, à leur jugement, un obstacle au dit rapprochement ». Ensuite, il redoute qu'ils se croient autorisés à faire échec à la doctrine traditionnelle de la Tradition et à lui apposer une autre interprétation. Il conclut : « La tactique de ces "novateurs" me

46 *Ibid.*, 1er cahier (20 novembre), p. 91.

47 *Ibid.*, 1er cahier (21 novembre), p. 98.

48 *Ibid.*, p. 96-97.

paraît se ramener à ceci : faire accréditer, comme opinion défendable en théologie, leur nouvelle notion de la Tradition et, du même coup, rabaisser à l'état de pure opinion la doctrine qui, sur ce sujet, était depuis longtemps la seule reçue en théologie[49]. » Il estime avoir trouvé un aveu explicite de son appréhension dans un article paru dans le journal *Il tempo*, le 21 novembre. Dans cet article, l'assomptionniste français Georges Tavard écrit que l'Église doit se baser sur l'Écriture comme le font les protestants, de façon à faciliter le dialogue :

> Si l'on se base plutôt sur la seconde école [celle qui dit que toute la vérité se trouve contenue dans l'Écriture], qui, sans refuser quoi que ce soit à la Tradition, se fonde sur l'Écriture tout comme le font les protestants, pour autant se trouve rendu aisé le commencement d'un dialogue avec nos frères séparés[50].

Pour Marcel Bélanger : « Et voilà ! Mes soupçons étaient bien fondés. [...] quand l'œcuménisme en est rendu à ce point, on peut craindre qu'il ne soit lui-même conduit par un faux irénisme et qu'il ne soit prêt à faire les concessions doctrinales les plus surprenantes pour obtenir le dialogue. » Il termine sa réflexion en disant : « Et dire que les Pères du Concile se sont en majorité prononcés pour le rejet du présent schéma sous des prétextes complètement différents : forme aride, scolastique, pas assez pastorale, etc. Puissent-ils n'avoir pas à se repentir ! Puissent-ils découvrir toute la vérité, un jour[51] ! » On le voit ici, une des appréhensions de Marcel Bélanger était l'œcuménisme, tout comme pour les membres de la minorité en général.

2. Le *De Ecclesia*

Le *De Ecclesia* fut un autre schéma contre lequel se manifesta la minorité, et il est particulièrement intéressant d'étudier la position de Marcel Bélanger à ce propos. Pendant sa préparation, l'opposition entre la Commission théologique et le Secrétariat pour l'unité avait été plus virulente encore que pour le *De fontibus*. Les divergences au sujet de la nature de l'Église touchaient les points essentiels du schéma. Aussi n'est-

49 *Ibid.*, p. 97.

50 *Ibid.*, p. 99-100.

51 *Ibid.*, p. 100.

il pas étonnant qu'avant même que le texte ne soit discuté dans l'*aula* à partir du 1er décembre, certains *periti* donnaient déjà des conférences pour ou contre le schéma. Ainsi, le 29 octobre, les pères Daniélou, Gagnebet et Lécuyer font chacun un exposé sur l'épiscopat à la Maison Générale des O.M.I.[52]. Marcel Bélanger note que le père Gagnebet (conservateur) expose en termes clairs la teneur du chapitre « De Episcopalis » du schéma (encore à venir) sur l'Église :

> Le Père souligne mieux que ses deux confrères la primauté du Pape dans le corps épiscopal, les deux autres affichant un penchant manifeste à insister sur le rôle et les pouvoirs des évêques en face, pour ainsi dire, du Pontife Romain. Cette manière de faire plaît manifestement à l'assemblée. Elle est d'ailleurs dans l'air, partout. Mais je n'arrive pas à m'y rallier. Même considérés collégialement, les évêques n'ont de personnalité authentique et de pouvoirs authentifiés que s'ils se maintiennent en union de pensée avec le Saint-Père et que s'ils acceptent sa supériorité. Même les fameuses « Conférences épiscopales » ne vaudront qu'à ces conditions[53].

Quelques semaines plus tard, le 16 novembre, Marcel Bélanger va entendre Hans Küng à la *Sala traspontina* dans une conférence sur la Primauté pontificale et l'épiscopat. Marcel Bélanger note à son sujet : « Encore jeune — 35 ans environ —, l'orateur affiche une liberté de parole à peine croyable pour délimiter [?] la Primauté et proclamer les droits des évêques. » Bélanger admet qu'une certaine décentralisation de la Curie romaine au profit de l'administration locale ou diocésaine est importante, mais il estime que l'orateur est parfois « caustique et heureux de ridiculiser le pouvoir central[54] ». Il continue :

> Une chose m'étonne un peu dans la bouche d'un catholique : à l'heure qu'il est, l'Église s'apprêterait à procéder aux réformes que demandait précisément Luther. Alors ? L'Église aurait-elle été dans l'erreur en s'opposant à Luther ? Enfin, au pur point de vue théologique, je ne suis pas prêt à endosser une affirmation comme celle-ci : l'opinion d'une juridiction épiscopale dérivant du Pape est

52 *Ibid.*, 1er cahier (29 octobre), p. 20.

53 *Ibidem.*

54 *Ibid.*, 1er cahier (16 novembre), p. 66.

insoutenable historiquement et inacceptable œcuméniquement. Aussi, Vatican II devrait-il s'abstenir de revenir sur cette question, que le Concile de Trente n'a pas voulu trancher et que Vatican I a laissée tout simplement dans l'ombre. Pourtant, l'orateur sait mieux que moi que des considérations sociales – la guerre – et non doctrinales n'ont pas permis à Vatican I de considérer ce point. Aussi, je trouve un peu forte pareille façon d'argumenter[55].

Le 1er décembre, lorsque s'ouvre dans l'*aula* l'examen du schéma *De Ecclesia*, le cardinal Ottaviani est très bref et quelque peu ironique dans la présentation d'usage à tout nouveau schéma. Tout d'abord, il ne reste que cinq congrégations générales avant la clôture de la première session. Et puis, comme Marcel Bélanger, il sait que le schéma est perdu d'avance. L'oblat commente ainsi la présentation du cardinal : « En la circonstance, cette présentation se fait sur un ton nouveau : le schéma était déjà jugé et condamné avant même qu'il fût distribué. On disait comme au Prétoire : Tolle, Tolle. À quoi bon alors s'éterniser en présentations[56] ? » Ce jour-là, Marcel Bélanger s'élève contre l'exposé de Mgr De Smedt qui se prononce sévèrement contre le *De Ecclesia*. Que dit-il ? Tout d'abord, qu'il n'y a aucune trace d'œcuménisme dans le schéma ; ensuite, qu'on y trouve au contraire du triomphalisme (un style ampoulé et naïf où l'on parle trop d'une Église qui « milite » et pas assez du « pusillus grex ») et du cléricalisme (une présentation surannée d'une hiérarchie à trois degrés — pape, évêques, clercs — et du peuple situé au-dessous). Mgr De Smedt se demande pourquoi tant rabâcher cela, alors que l'on sait pertinemment que dans la Patrie toute cette hiérarchie disparaîtra et que seul demeurera le peuple des fidèles. Enfin, l'évêque de Bruges dénonce le juridisme du schéma : au lieu de considérations sur l'organisation et les pouvoirs de l'Église, il pense qu'il vaut mieux présenter l'Église comme une « mère » tout occupée de ses enfants[57]. Évidemment, ce type de discours ne pouvait plaire à la minorité, et la réaction de Marcel Bélanger est symptomatique :

---

55 *Ibid.*, p. 67.

56 *Ibid.*, 2e cahier (1er décembre), p. 27.

57 *Ibid.*, p. 32.

> J'avoue que tout cela sent la mise en scène et constitue un démenti vivant opposé aux allégations de l'orateur. Je le dis d'autant plus librement que maints évêques m'ont confié avoir eu une impression semblable à la mienne. À ce train, le bon évêque va brûler sa poudre en peu de temps et obtenir le résultat qu'il mérite avec ses descentes enflammées, ponctuées, contre l'esprit encore régnant, Dieu merci[58].

Ce jour-là, il se montre en revanche favorable à l'intervention de Marcel Lefebvre qui, voyant qu'une conciliation serait difficile entre les promoteurs de pastorale et les promoteurs de doctrine, propose de faire sur chaque sujet important deux exposés d'allure différente : l'un à l'usage des fidèles, l'autre pour les évêques et les théologiens[59]. De même, il se montre en parfait accord avec Mgr Carli qui fait « un heureux contrepoids à ses prédécesseurs immédiats[60] ». Voyons ce que dit Mgr Carli, car cela nous aidera à mieux cerner la vision de Bélanger. Tout d'abord, il regrette que le concile entame l'examen d'un schéma aussi important sans que les Pères aient eu suffisamment de temps pour l'étudier. Ensuite, il fait plusieurs remarques sur l'œcuménisme, en se plaignant de son envahissement excessif au concile dont il n'est pas la fin[61]. Il estime également que la préoccupation de l'unité ne doit pas trop influencer les travaux conciliaires :

> La règle de nos travaux, écrit-il, devrait être l'affirmation de la doctrine sans craindre de toucher à tous les sujets. On dirait que, pour certains, il ne faut parler ni de la Tradition ni de la Ste Vierge à cause des protestants ; ni de la primauté pontificale, à cause des Orientaux ; ni de l'athéisme, pour ne pas paraître faire de la politique ; ni même de l'ordre moral, pour ne pas indisposer l'homme moderne[62].

Marcel Bélanger surenchérit : « La remarque, en plus d'être fondée, me paraît des plus opportunes. Un œcuménisme intempérant constitue

---

58 *Ibid.*, p. 32-33.

59 *Ibid.*, p. 33.

60 *Ibid.*, p. 34.

61 AS I/IV, p. 158-161.

62 AD, *Journal conciliaire de Marcel Bélanger*, 2e cahier (1er décembre), p. 34.

une menace sérieuse pour l'orthodoxie ou du moins pour une affirmation courageuse de la vérité intégrale[63]. »

3. Les déceptions mariologiques de Marcel Bélanger

Marcel Bélanger est très dévot envers la Vierge. Il est un mariologue connu et respecté. Pour lui, « l'attitude filiale envers Marie constitue l'un des traits les plus caractéristiques du catholicisme[64] ». Il est cependant un mariologue traditionnel, l'un de ceux qui ne tiennent pas compte des aspects œcuméniques de la mariologie contemporaine, comme en témoigne la phrase suivante, tirée de son article « Introduction à l'étude de la Maternité spirituelle » : « Le catholique a toujours vigoureusement rejeté l'opinion dissidente, en particulier celle des protestants pour qui il ne saurait être question de rôle sotériologique propre à la Sainte Vierge[65]. » Au regard de son intérêt pour le sujet et de ces citations, il n'est pas étonnant de le voir se soucier du schéma *De Beata Virgine*, qui ne devait pas être discuté lors de la première session, mais qui préoccupait déjà les esprits, divisés entre les maximalistes et les minimalistes. Les maximalistes étaient ceux qui visaient à obtenir de nouvelles définitions dogmatiques, tandis que les minimalistes cherchaient à diminuer, par souci œcuménique, la portée des dogmes déjà définis (p. ex., l'Immaculée Conception et l'Assomption). Ainsi, le 27 novembre, Marcel Bélanger s'insurge contre un article paru dans *Il tempo* intitulé « Divergences de vues au Concile à propos des dogmes concernant la Madone ». Dans cet article, l'auteur présente le schéma *De Beata Virgine* comme étant d'inspiration maximaliste et visant à obtenir une ou des proclamations dogmatiques. Bélanger estime « qu'une présentation des choses comme celle-ci est non seulement insidieuse, mais nettement injuste ». Il se demande : « Aurait-on, par cet article, voulu porter [illisible] d'un prochain débat et préparer, en conséquence, l'opinion chez les Pères comme on l'a fait à propos de la doctrine des "Sources" ? On le saura mieux bientôt[66]. » Ainsi, pour Bélanger :

---

63 *Ibidem.*

64 Marcel Bélanger, « Introduction à l'étude de la Maternité spirituelle », p. 1.

65 *Ibid.*, p. 2.

66 AD, *Journal conciliaire de Marcel Bélanger*, 2e cahier (27 novembre), p. 13.

> Il n'est pas vrai que le schéma « De Beata Virgine » soit d'inspiration maximaliste et vise à obtenir une ou des proclamations dogmatiques. Pas un point doctrinal qui, dans ce schéma, ne s'appuie sur les sources les plus autorisées, sur les documents pontificaux en particulier : les notes sont là, pour le démontrer. Peut-être jugerait-on que les Pontifes romains ont exagéré et qu'il faut maintenant abandonner leurs positions ? On en verra peut-être de belles[67] !

Le 29 novembre, le cardinal Ottaviani demande à ce que soit abordé le schéma *De Beata Virgine* après le schéma sur l'unité de l'Église. Cela lui est refusé[68]. Marcel Bélanger commente :

> [...] quand on sait que les pressions contre le schéma de B.M.V. s'exercent déjà, on peut se demander si le conseil de Présidence n'a pas épousé en définitive le point de vue des opposants [...] Encore une fois, l'opposition triomphe avant que la cause ne soit entendue. C'est l'histoire du schéma « De Fontibus Rev » qui commence à se répéter. Le cas est jugé d'avance ; et, en attendant que le procès ne s'institue, les opposants auront encore plus de temps qu'ils ne semblaient pouvoir avoir normalement pour fourbir leurs armes. Il devient manifeste que la marche du Concile est boiteuse en ce sens qu'un seul parti a l'audience des puissants. Par bonheur, aucune mesure définitive n'a été prise jusqu'ici[69].

Ce jour-là, l'opinion de Hans Küng, rapportée dans le journal *La Croix*, le fait de nouveau réagir. Hans Küng estime en effet qu'« il serait dangereux qu'à l'occasion de la discussion prochaine sur un texte de la *Vierge Marie* de nouveaux dogmes mariaux soient envisagés, ce qui serait un nouvel obstacle au rapprochement avec les autres chrétiens et ferait perdre au Concile son caractère œcuménique[70] ». Bélanger s'insurge :

> Pourquoi cet épouvantail imaginé de toutes pièces ? Qui songe à obtenir de nouvelles définitions ? N'a-t-on pas en mains le texte du schéma sur la Ste Vierge ? J'avoue retrouver ici la tactique qui

---

67 *Ibidem.*

68 AS I/III, 691-692.

69 AD, *Journal conciliaire de Marcel Bélanger*, 2e cahier (30 novembre), p. 20-21.

70 Cité par Marcel BÉLANGER, *Ibid.*, p. 24.

> a si bien réussi aux opposants du schéma « De Fontibus ». On produit ou on fabrique des fantômes, puis on leur donne la chasse en ameutant les Pères du Concile. Reste à savoir si le procédé va produire des résultats dans le sens espéré par ces gens[71].

Comme Marcel Bélanger n'assiste pas aux autres sessions conciliaires, nous perdons le fil de son cheminement à propos de ce schéma. Cependant, diverses sources nous permettent de savoir ce qu'il pensait de l'évolution de la mariologie post-conciliaire, car il s'en ouvrit à quelques confrères. Ainsi, dans le journal *Le Droit* du 8 décembre 1972 (trois mois après la mort du père Bélanger), le père André Guay écrivait :

> [...] la diminution, après le Concile, chez un certain nombre de prêtres et de religieux, de la dévotion, du culte et de la confiance envers la Vierge Marie fut-elle pour lui une douleur profonde. D'autant plus qu'à titre de membre de la Commission théologique conciliaire il avait participé à l'élaboration de la Constitution sur l'Église. Il en savait par cœur, pourrait-on dire, le chapitre 8, qui traite du rôle de Marie dans le mystère du Christ et de l'Église. Il n'arrivait pas à comprendre que tant de gens qui se réclament à grands cris du Concile puissent faire silence total sur ce point précis et passer outre aux directives sacrées de ce même Concile[72].

Marcel Bélanger ne cachait pas son émoi devant un phénomène semblable qu'il percevait au sein même de sa congrégation. Dans un article intitulé « Pour un renouveau authentique », il s'adressait ainsi à ses confrères :

> N'est-il pas étrange et en même temps symptomatique que la Vierge Marie, sans être sortie complètement de notre champ de vision, soit quand même passée à l'arrière-plan de nos préoccupations spirituelles avec une facilité et presque une soudaineté déconcertante ? C'est entendu : je me reporte ici à un phénomène dont l'ampleur déborde largement ce qu'il nous a été donné de constater chez nous. Est-ce à dire, pour autant, que nous sommes nous-mêmes sortis indemnes de l'aventure, demandons même, exempts de toute faiblesse regrettable[73] ?

---

71 AD, *Journal conciliaire de Marcel Bélanger,* 2e cahier (30 novembre), p. 24.

72 André Guay, *Le Droit* (8 décembre 1972).

73 Marcel Bélanger, « Pour un renouveau authentique », *Études oblates,* vol. 31, no 3

L'angoisse théologique d'un conservateur

Après avoir présenté le cheminement de Marcel Bélanger pendant le concile, après avoir constaté ses réactions de conservateur, essayons de voir rapidement comment il a vécu intimement le concile. En effet, bien des aspects de celui-ci allaient contre ses convictions profondes de catholique conservateur et intransigeant. Deux sources principales nous permettent d'appréhender quelque peu cet aspect : la notice de Rodrigue Normandin et l'article de Marcel Bélanger « Pour un renouveau authentique », paru dans la revue *Études oblates* à l'été 1972. Cet écrit est considéré par ses confrères comme son testament spirituel. Dans cet article, Marcel Bélanger est très critique à l'égard du catholicisme contemporain.

Tout d'abord, Rodrigue Normandin parle de son confrère en ces termes :

> Affligé dans son corps [à cause de sa maladie], le père Bélanger ne le fut pas moins dans son âme, inquiète et écartelée à ses heures. Écartèlement que provoquèrent des situations concrètes apparemment incompatibles avec ses plus fermes convictions de théologien plus traditionnel qu'innovateur et avec les obligations de la vie religieuse oblate telle qu'il la concevait selon les engagements pris et telle que, sans ménagement pour lui-même, il s'est toujours efforcé de la vivre[74].

Selon le père Normandin, Marcel Bélanger ressentait de l'« inquiétude sur l'orientation des œuvres avec lesquelles il avait partie liée et sur l'esprit qui doit les animer[75] ». Mais à quoi tenaient exactement cette inquiétude, cette angoisse ? C'est dans son article « Pour un renouveau authentique[76] » que l'on peut trouver la réponse. Dans ce texte, où il « sollicite la permission d'exposer sans détour la réalité nouvelle, de la dénoncer même, surtout en ce à quoi elle tient comme en sa portée plus

(juillet-septembre 1972), p. 238.

74 Rodrigue Normandin, « Marcel Bélanger, Missionnaire des Oblats de Marie Immaculée 1908-1972 », p. 12.

75 *Ibid.*, p. 12.

76 Marcel Bélanger, « Pour un renouveau authentique », p. 225-241.

ou moins nocive[77] », il parle de ce qu'il appelle la « tourmente actuelle[78] » dans l'Église et dans sa communauté, laquelle traverse, selon lui, de « graves difficultés en même temps que de pénibles incertitudes[79] ». Mais ces difficultés ne sont pas propres à l'Église ni à sa communauté ; il considère que la société tout entière est malade :

> Bien entendu, à l'origine de ce bouleversement spirituel, nous ne sommes pas les seuls ni les premiers responsables, historiquement du moins. Somme toute, c'est d'un mal qui afflige présentement la société entière que nous souffrons, à vrai dire, surtout par contrecoup[80].

Marcel Bélanger s'en prend toutefois aux autorités ecclésiastiques qu'il accuse d'avoir suspendu, « depuis quelques années, des messages ou rappels adressés périodiquement jadis aux communautés en matière de vie spirituelle[81] ». Il estime que « notre regard de foi n'a plus la limpidité ni la force de pénétration qui le caractérisaient[82] ». Quant à sa communauté, il considère qu'elle a été emportée « par une vague qui déferle de tous côtés[83] ». Il s'interroge donc sur la provenance de cette conjoncture ecclésiale nouvelle, et la réponse ne tarde pas : pour lui, cette situation vient d'une fausse interprétation de l'*aggiornamento* conciliaire, d'une sécularisation à outrance, de certaines capitulations de l'Église, ainsi que de certaines complicités :

> Un peu partout dans l'Église post-conciliaire une fausse interprétation de l'*aggiornamento*, de la mise à jour ou du rajeunissement si l'on veut, a très tôt accrédité une surprenante dévalorisation et la mise en veilleuse plus ou moins empressée de formes d'apostolat parmi les plus répandues et de moyens de salut parmi les sacrements eux-mêmes. Avec quoi sont venues se combiner de l'extérieur les fâcheuses pressions d'une sécularisation à outrance pouvant aller jusqu'à la désacralisation, sans parler de plusieurs

---

77 *Ibid.*, p. 226.

78 *Ibid.*, p. 226.

79 *Ibid.*, p. 225.

80 *Ibid.*, p. 226.

81 *Ibid.*, p. 227.

82 *Ibid.*, p. 227.

83 *Ibid.*, p. 229.

> capitulations trop faciles au-dedans, encore moins de regrettables complicités. Il en est résulté chez nous, en même temps qu'une perte d'assurance en nous-mêmes et de confiance en l'Église nouvelle [...][84].

Ce qu'il pourfend ouvertement dans l'Église issue de Vatican II, c'est son humanisme qu'il juge incompatible avec la doctrine traditionnelle. Aussi n'est-il pas étonnant de le voir s'insurger contre les clercs qui

> [...] osent prétendre du haut d'une chaire ou dans un écrit quelconque que le temps est désormais venu pour le prêtre de s'intéresser à l'homme tout juste pour lui-même, [...] et non plus comme auparavant à sa destinée éternelle ainsi qu'à sa condition spirituelle de membre du Peuple de Dieu, là j'avoue ne pas retrouver en aucun de ces nouveaux pasteurs les traits d'un fils authentique, d'un fils aimant de l'Église, préoccupé d'elle par-dessus tout[85].

Plus loin, il juge que cette attitude est « gnostique » et qu'elle va contre l'Église et contre son enseignement, contre *Mater et Ecclesia, Pacem in terris, Gaudium et spes, Populum progressio* et contre le Message de Paul VI pour la Journée missionnaire mondiale (octobre 1970). Il estime que cette nouvelle façon d'appréhender le catholicisme va contre « l'enseignement intégral » du magistère, et que ce serait « renverser singulièrement la vapeur que de restreindre la mission de l'Église et la tâche des gens d'Église à la pure restauration sociale de l'homme, sans une attention, non seulement égale, mais prédominante, accordée au spirituel[86] ».

Face à cette situation, devant les jeunes dont l'Église a du mal à se faire entendre, devant les chrétiens qui prennent de plus en plus leurs distances à l'égard de la religion, « devant tant de confrères du sacerdoce, quelquefois même de l'épiscopat, désemparés eux-mêmes, prêts à l'aventure, acceptant mal parfois, discutant même trop ouvertement l'autorité d'un Magistère et d'un Gouvernement suprême [...][87] », Bélanger s'interroge avec inquiétude :

---

[84] *Ibid.*, p. 228.

[85] *Ibid.*, p. 230-231.

[86] *Ibid.*, p. 231.

[87] *Ibid.*, p. 233.

> […] dans quelle mesure allons-nous tenir bon ? L'équipement spirituel et apostolique dont nous disposons ou que nous cherchons à nous donner autorise-t-il un espoir vraiment fondé ? […] allons-nous perdre contenance à notre tour et, faute du ressort voulu au-dedans, en un mot, faute de la foi nécessaire, allons-nous plier bagage l'un après l'autre[88] ?

Une autre source d'inquiétude et d'angoisse pour ce religieux viscéralement « romain », c'est le manque d'attachement au magistère de l'Église :

> Pour le déclarer tout net, je trouve d'abord effarante et positivement désastreuse la facilité de jour en jour croissante avec laquelle le croyant comme tel en prend à sa guise avec les données objectives de la foi, définies ou non. En outre, je trouve scandaleuse et souverainement dommageable l'attitude d'affrontement que prend plus d'un clerc en face du Magistère ainsi que l'attitude d'indifférence, on dirait presque de brigandage intellectuel, qu'adoptent parfois ces mêmes gens à l'égard du dépôt de la foi, en le réduisant comme bon leur semble[89].

Il appelait donc à une « soumission empressée et sans réserve au Magistère », même si, « en nos temps un individualisme plus ou moins émancipé dispute au Magistère son ascendant sur l'esprit du croyant[90] ».

Marcel Bélanger était donc un homme déconcerté, décontenancé et mal à l'aise dans l'Église post-conciliaire qui ne correspondait plus à celle dans laquelle il avait été formé. Cependant, contrairement aux traditionnalistes, bien qu'il ait les mêmes préoccupations (infaillibilité pontificale, nature et portée de la Collégialité épiscopale, liberté religieuse, etc.), bien qu'il fasse exactement les mêmes constats, il ne remit jamais en cause le concile.

Les dernières années de sa vie furent incontestablement une période de torture morale, intellectuelle et spirituelle, comme en témoigne Rodrigue Normandin :

---

88 *Ibid.*, p. 233.

89 *Ibid.*, p. 235.

90 *Ibid.*, p. 235-237.

Ainsi tenaillé de tout son être, le père Bélanger trouvait refuge dans le Christ Rédempteur et dans Marie [...]. C'est à eux qu'il se confia quand la coupe menaça de déborder. Un matin, dans la chapelle rustique de la maison de vacances, un confrère l'entendit priant à haute voix : « Mon Dieu, suppliait-il, venez donc me chercher[91]. »

[91] Rodrigue NORMANDIN, « Marcel Bélanger, Missionnaire des Oblats de Marie Immaculée 1908-1972 », p. 13.

"A Great Historic Day": The Conciliar Diaries of Metropolitan Maxim Hermaniuk

Jaroslav Z. Skira,
Regis College

This essay will broadly examine some of the late Metropolitan Maxim Hermaniuk (1911–96) of Winnipeg's contributions to the preparatory stages and sessions of the Second Vatican Council[1] through his comments on his experiences on the Preparatory Theological Commission, the Secretariat for Christian Unity, and in actual council debates. This research is largely based on selected passages of his unpublished council diaries and his work on two conciliar pastoral letters of the Synod of the Ukrainian Catholic Bishops.[2] In these diaries the late metropolitan dealt with a number of themes, such as relations with the Orthodox churches, interreligious dialogue,

[1] Hermaniuk is indexed twenty times in *Acta* (*AS*) of the council as giving a speech or writing a scripta/letter. *Acta Acta synodalia Sacrosancti Concilii Œcumenici Vaticani II* (Vatican City: Typis polyglottis Vaticanis, 1970). The following is the breakdown (9 speeches; 10 scriptae; 1 *relatio*): *De ecclesia* – 3 speeches, 3 scriptae; *De œcumenismo* – 1 speech, 1 scripta, 1 *relatio* (plus *De ecclesia unitate* – 1 speech); *De ecclesia in mundo huius temporis* – 1 speech, 1 scripta; *De sacra liturgia* – 2 scriptae; *De fontibus revelationis* – 1 speech; *De ecclesiis orientabilis* – 1 speech; *De activite missionali ecclesiae* – 1 scripta; *De libertate religiosa* – 1 scripta; *General congregations* – 1 speech, 1 scripta. The Index to *AS* neglects to include *AS* I/2, pp. 236–237.

[2] When referring to or quoting Hermaniuk's diary entries, I cite the dates of the entries in the footnotes. The diaries are currently being translated from the Ukrainian and annotated, by myself and others, toward publication.

sobornicity and synodality, the laity and liturgical reform, and judged the council's establishment of a permanent synod of bishops as "a great historic day." This latter event encapsulates two main meta-themes that run through the diary: collegiality and ecumenism. For ecumenism, I will specifically touch upon Hermaniuk's comments and contributions in the realm of relations with the Orthodox churches (such as the Ukrainian and Russian Orthodox). And in terms of collegiality, there are really two main areas on which one can focus: the permanent synod of bishops and the autocephaly and synodality of the Ukrainian Church. The three times that Hermaniuk uses the phrases "a historic day," or the once-used "great historic day," encompass, in one way or another, all of these preceding themes.

The Context

In order to appreciate some of the motivations and preoccupations of Hermaniuk at the council, one must first understand the context in which Hermaniuk and all of the Ukrainian Catholic bishops at Vatican II were living: all were from émigré communities. At the beginning of the council there was not a single Ukrainian Catholic bishop present at the council from Ukraine. The reason was simple: Ukraine was under the rule of a Communist Soviet regime, a regime that had forcibly liquidated the Ukrainian Catholic Church in a pseudo-sobor of 1946 and then announced its "return" to Orthodoxy (under the jurisdiction of the Russian Orthodox Church).[3] As part of this union, the Church was declared illegal, and many of faithful, clergy, and bishops were arrested,

---

[3] This has been documented in many places. See *Хресною дорогою: функціонування і спроби ліквідації Української Греко-Католицької Церкви в умовах СРСР у 1939–1941 та 1944–1946 роках: збірник документів і матеріалів*, Ред. Михайло Гайковський (Львів: Міціонер, 2006) [*Way of the Cross: The Functioning and Attempts to Liquidate the Ukrainian Greco-Catholic Church under the USSR in 1939–1941 and 1944–1946: A Collection of Documents and Materials*], and Bohdan Bociurkiw, *The Ukrainian Greek Catholic Church and the Soviet State (1939–1950)* (Toronto: Canadian Institute of Ukrainian Studies, 1996). The anniversary of this event is, regrettably, still celebrated by the Moscow Patriarchate and some Ukrainian Orthodox churches. See for example, *The Lvov Church Council: Documents and Materials, 1946–1981* (Moscow: Moscow Patriarchate, 1983); and "The Address of the Ukrainian Orthodox Church (Moscow Patriarchate) on the Occasion of the 60th Anniversary of the L'viv Sobor," in *Religious Information Service of Ukraine*, 9 March 2006, accessed 14 January 2011, http://www.old.risu.org.ua/eng/resources/reldocs/mp_60years_lvivsobor46.

murdered, or sent into exile (to the now infamous Siberia). A central figure epitomizing this Church's persecution was the Metropolitan of L'viv-Halych Josyf Slipyj.

Slipyj was arrested in 1945 by the Soviets and eventually ended up in Siberia, spending roughly seventeen years there. He was not present at the opening of the council and is often mentioned in Hermaniuk's preconciliar and early conciliar diaries. For example, while in Rome for the Preparatory Theological Commission, Hermaniuk writes of his praying at the tomb of St. Peter (in St. Peter's Basilica)—the apostle martyred for his faith—for Slipyj.[4] The parallel between the two should be mildly obvious. The issue of the persecuted Church, and of Slipyj, is again recounted by Hermaniuk in a 1961 audience he had with Pope John XXIII. In this audience, Hermaniuk raised a number of points that would be prophetic of the nature of his participation at the council. His summary of the meeting was thus:

1. The invitation [of non-Catholic observers at Vatican II should] in some form show a solidarity of faith against atheistic communism, by the representatives of all who profess one God (Jews, Muslims) ...;
2. The invitation, in some form, of Orthodox and Protestants to the Council;
3. The first provincial Synod of the Archeparchy of Winnipeg;
4. The persecution of the Church in Ukraine and the martyrdom of our nation, especially the great Metropolitan J. Slipyj.[5]

Hermaniuk later lamented that not present at the opening of the council was the "Great Absent One"—referring to Slipyj.[6] It would not be until February 1963 that Slipyj would be released from the Soviet gulag. "The Common Pastoral Letter of the Synod of Bishops of the Ukrainian Catholic Church" in 1962 is likewise replete with references to the persecution of the Ukrainian Catholic Church in Ukraine under the Soviets.[7]

---

[4] 19 September 1961.

[5] 30 September 1961.

[6] 11 October 1962.

[7] This text originally appeared (in Ukrainian) in Maxim Hermaniuk, *The Spirit of the Second Vatican Ecumenical Council; and, The Pastoral Letter of the Ukrainian Catholic*

Religious Liberty

It may not be all that surprising to know that at least four of Hermaniuk's nineteen speeches or letters at the council touch upon the issues of militant atheism, Communism, the persecution of Christians, and religious freedom. Hermaniuk's first intervention at the council was his 1962 proposal for an emendation to a letter from the council fathers to the world,[8] which suggested that the letter mention social and political injustices, and refer to the "Church of Silence."[9] In the third period, March of 1964, Hermaniuk commented on the proposed text for *De Libertate Religiosa*, of which he chaired a subcommission, as making "a very good impression. Its acceptance and proclamation by the Council will become one of the most significant decisions of the Council."[10] Six months later he added: "The debate on religious freedom finished successfully. The Council, with a great majority, supports the proposed text .... This is a very significant event for the future relations of the Church with all non-Catholic Churches and non-Christian religions. This is a critical turning point in the Church's life."[11] However, the next day he lamented:

> Why can't the Council step forward with the same might against the persecution of the Church behind the Iron Curtain—especially in Ukraine?—Why can't the Council condemn the savage genocide perpetrated by the Muscovite communists against the Ukrainian nation?
>
> One may find many different answers to this question. But the best response—probably would be the fact that the time of God's justice in that matter has not yet come.[12]

Hierarchy on the Occasion of the XXI Ecumenical Council, Rome, November 21, 1962 (Winnipeg: Postup, 1963), 18–30, esp. 24.

8 The letter was *Nuntios ad universos homines mittendus*, *AS* I/1, 230–32. Hermaniuk's emendations are found in his diary entry of 20 October 1962.

9 *AS* I/1, 241. The "church of silence" refers to all those churches persecuted by the Soviet Communist government.

10 5 March 1964.

11 28 September 1964. See *AS* III/2, 567–607 for these deliberations.

12 29 September 1964. This is written also within the context of the discussions on Judaism and Islam.

Nevertheless, on November 19, 1964, on the topic of the cessation of debate on *De Libertate Religiosa*, we see him describe this as an "historic day" because he felt that opposition to the decree had caused the debate to be postponed to the fourth session.

Orthodox Observers at the Council

One of the points noted by Hermaniuk, at the above mentioned audience with the Pope, was the presence at the council of Orthodox observers. On numerous occasions in his council diary he mentions both the presence and the absence of certain Orthodox observers at the council. What is clear is that Hermaniuk wanted to reach out to the Orthodox. He had a number of meetings, in the intercessory periods, with Metropolitan Ilarion Ohienko, the Ukrainian Orthodox metropolitan of Canada. This Orthodox hierarch seemed to be open to attending the council, though in the end his church synod ruled against it. Hermaniuk found this very regrettable. In his 1962 article, "The Spirit of the Second Ecumenical Vatican Council," Hermaniuk wrote:

> The Ukrainian Orthodox Churches in the free world, divided and at odds with each other, regrettably, have not endeavoured up to now to show any serious sign of a sincere desire to be involved in this ecumenical activity of the Christian world so that, together with other Christian nations, to work together for the attainment of the full unity of all Christians, and hence, in the first place, for the full unity of our great Ukrainian nation.[13]

In their Common Pastoral Letter of 1962, published during the first session of the council, the Ukrainian Catholic bishops went to great lengths in publicly lamenting the absence of the Ukrainian Orthodox observers and encouraging their participation.[14] Hermaniuk also made other personal entreaties in Rome to secure other Ukrainian Orthodox bishops and clergy as council observers. In some cases he succeeded in his entreaties, such as when he arranged for Archbishop Mstyslav Skrypnyk (Ukrainian Orthodox Church in America)—who received

---

[13] Hermaniuk, "The Spirit of the Second Vatican Ecumenical Council," in *The Spirit of the Second Vatican Ecumenical Council*, 16. Translation mine.

[14] Ibid., 25–28.

the blessing of the Patriarch of Constantinople, Athenagoras—to attend the council.[15]

By his own accounts, Hermaniuk also seemed to have a cordial relationship with Archimandrite Andrew Scrima, the personal representative of the Ecumenical Patriarch. He gives a report in his diary about a conversation he had with Scrima about synodality and the fact that Scrima wanted a copy of his *relatio* on the apostolic college and on the nullification of the anathemas of 1054. Hermaniuk indicates that he felt some of the members of the commission (the Secretariat for Christian Unity) were not pleased with this suggestion for the *relatio* (on the first part of the third chapter of the Decree on Ecumenism), nevertheless, it was included in the final text.[16] This *relatio* was read just after the discussions On the Apostolate of the Laity, when the moderator of the council, Cardinal Suenens from Belgium, called on Hermaniuk to read the report:

> My report made a very nice impression, especially the presentation of the excommunications of Cardinal Humbert (a papal legate) against Patriarch Cerularius and his adherents, where Cardinal Humbert accused them of all heresies known at that time in Christ's Church, while, in reality, this whole conflict ... was not about any dogma. As an example of this, which one can cite is the lack of a correct understating of the Christian East .... At the time of the same congregation, the personal representative of the Patriarchate of Constantinople at the Council Fr. Archimandrite Scrima, with emotion declared to me, that this in his opinion—is the highest degree of the ecumenical spirit of this Council.[17]

On September 14, 1965, Scrima mentioned to Hermaniuk that the Patriarch would like to show up at this last period of the council and that he "would like to reach the point so that Rome and Constantinople annul the decrees of excommunication and return to the conditions from before 1054." The significance of this, of course, is that the anathemas were indeed nullified at the conclusion of the council by

15 For example, 24 October and 23 November 1963.

16 23 September 1964.

17 7 October 1964. See *AS* III/4, 10–13.

Pope Paul VI and Patriarch Athenagoras (through his representative Metropolitan Meliton).[18] This, taken as a whole, would lead one to the conclusion that Hermaniuk had a sincere desire for a formal rapprochement between the Catholic Church and the Orthodox East.

The Eastern Catholic Churches and Ecumenism

One also sees Hermaniuk's contributions to the council in the decrees On Ecumenism and On the Eastern Churches, both showing again his concern for relations with the Orthodox. Hermaniuk contributed at least four speeches or letters, though in a few places in his council diary he expresses disappointment with the results of the schemata. At the start of voting on the Decree on the Eastern Churches, he wrote:

> This surely is a nice success. However, there were also many Fathers of the Council, who, sincerely wishing well for the Eastern Churches, would rather prefer, that the Commission for preparing this schema, supplemented by some new members-Orientalists, rework this schema anew and insert into it all of what was said in benefit of the Eastern Churches during the last debates. Then the schema would be more comprehensive, more ecumenical and more acceptable for the Orthodox Churches.[19]

Hermaniuk again expresses his mixed feelings with the text the following month:

> New in the church is also the promulgation, today, of a separate conciliar decree On the Oriental [Eastern] churches.[20] This decree, though it is not as it could've been, and this on account of the division among the Eastern patriarchs themselves, is nevertheless a great achievement for the Christian East. Unfortunately, as it seems, the Eastern representatives of the Commission, who

18 7 December 1965. See *AS* IV/7, 52–54 for the text of the speech. The encounter between Hermaniuk and Scrima was similarly recounted in Chris Guly, "Interview: Hermaniuk reflects on career in Catholic Church," in *The Ukrainian Weekly*, LV/30 (July 26, 1987), 4.

19 20 October 1964.

20 *Decretum Orientalium Ecclesiarum*, promulgated by Paul VI on November 21, 1964.

developed this decree, were not at the height of their duties—with a small exception—Patriarch Maximos IV.[21]

Nevertheless, Hermaniuk thought that these decrees would ensure that the Eastern churches develop theologically, liturgically, and spiritually according to their own traditions, and be able to govern themselves according to their own Eastern synodal structures.

Directory of Ecumenical Practices

Perhaps being inspired by the newfound openness of the council to the East, and movements in the direction of ecumenical relations with the Orthodox and other churches, Hermaniuk took upon himself the task of preparing a "Directory of Ecumenical Practices" for the Ukrainian Catholics.[22] This coincided with his participation on a subcommission, *De Directorio*, of the Secretariat for Christian Unity and its work on developing a *Directorium de Motu Œcumenico*.[23] The directory also coincided with Hermaniuk's earlier exchanges on *communicatio in sacris* in the subcommisisons (in the development of the Decree on Ecumenism).[24] Hermaniuk's directory is remarkable from a number of different perspectives. Its basic thrust is that the faithful may share in the sacraments of the "brethren of the divided churches," as long as this is done in "good faith" or where there is a "spiritual need." Clergy and the laity may also participate in the worship services of the "separated" Christians, the only exception being the "active concelebration" of the clergy of both the Catholic and separated churches in the Divine Liturgy, "which is the highest manifestation of the unity of Christ's Church."[25] Despite Hermaniuk's presentation of this directory to his fellow Ukrainian bishops on a number of occasions, he was disappointed with their critique of the document: "Unfortunately, only [one bishop] fully supported it, and the others, almost unanimously decided that a separate subcommission develop a more detailed draft and limit

21 21 November 1964.

22 15 October 1965.

23 The directory was completed in 1967.

24 For example, see the entries for 4 March 1964 and 15 May 1965.

25 See sections II.1 and III.A.1.d., for example, in this proposed directory.

our ecumenical practices to a minimum."[26] About a later meeting of a Conference of Ukrainian Catholic Bishops, at which the directory was also discussed, he writes:

> Unfortunately, the Directory on Ecumenical Practices ratified at that meeting, in its second part concerning the participation of Catholics and Orthodox in various liturgical and prayer functions, has no clear principle—it is rather limited to some general unclear principle and enumeration of: requiems, the consecration of a cultural home, the prayer service for the unity of the churches and the blessing of a monument. About the rest—it is as if it is not allowed—but why? [27]

The reference in this diary here to the "Catholic and Orthodox" is perhaps a clue to whom Hermaniuk had in mind when he composed his draft. In an undated draft of this directory in the Archeparchial Archives (which must be a draft rejected by the bishops since its is quite comprehensive in its regulations concerning *communicatio in sacris*), Hermaniuk refers to "Catholics" (which would include the Ukrainians) and "brothers of the separated churches," seemingly meaning that the latter are all those not in communion with Rome. However, at the end of the document there is a note: "Attention: It is desired, in conformity with the Decree on the Eastern Churches, n.29, that each bishop ratify this Directory of Ecumenical Practices with the ecclesiastical representatives of the separated churches (Orthodox) in his territory."[28] Based on this latter caveat and his diary entries, one wonders if it is reasonable to conclude that this directory was intended to only deal with the relations between the Orthodox, and not other "separated Christians."

The Russian Problem

At this juncture I shall raise the issue of the Russian Orthodox observers at the council. The two Russians who are mentioned most

---

[26] 15 November 1965.

[27] 1 December 1965.

[28] Archives of the Ukrainian Catholic Archeparchy of Winnipeg, Box 17, 1-MH, "Directory of Ecumenical Practices in the Ukrainian Catholic Church," 7. Translation and emphasis mine.

frequently are Vitaly Borovoj and Vladimir Kotlijarov. At first one is struck by a perceived contradiction in the manner in which Hermaniuk treated these two representatives. For despite Hermaniuk's obvious ecumenical and cordial relations with the Orthodox, and his desire for the council to reflect more of the traditions of the Christian East, he objected to the presence of Russian Orthodox observers at the council. On October 17, 1962, he wrote to the Holy Office, on behalf of the Ukrainians, a letter protesting the presence of the Russian observers. He subsequently began preparing a letter to present to all the council fathers, voicing such an objection.[29] The intrigue continued through to the end of October, as Hermaniuk reports:

> Most Rev. G. Bukatko informs me by telephone that His Excellency Scapinelli, from the Oriental Congregation, was at Most Rev. I. Bučko's tonight and informed him that the Holy Father wishes that we, the Ukrainian bishops, not take any actions regarding the presence of the two Russian "observers" at the Council. This means someone has accused us and now our action is paralyzed.[30] It's a real pity! Shameful![31]

Things reach a critical point on November 21, 1962, when an article appeared in *Il Giornale d'Italia*, purporting to contain a declaration by Ukrainian bishops about the churches behind the Iron Curtain.[32] This controversy arose contemporaneous to the council's discussions on the schema *De Ecclesiae Unitate.* In his diaries, despite meticulous details about many of the other key events at Vatican II, Hermaniuk is noticeably silent about the origin and appearance of the text, neither

---

29 18 October 1962.

30 In the notes of Mgr. Willebrands on the events of October 23–27, 1962 (Archive Willebrands, Archdiocese of Utrecht), on October 25 he indicates that he and Cardinal Bea knew of the intention of the Ukrainian bishops to publicly protest the presence of the Russian observers.

31 27 October 1962.

32 See F. Pucci, "Una solenne e drammatica dichiarizione sulla 'Chiesa del silenzio': Invocata da 15 Vescovi ucraini al Concilio sulla libertà per i sacerdoti detenuti oltrecortina" ["A solemn and dramatic declaration on the "Silent Church": Invoked by 15 Ukrainian bishops at the Council regarding freedom for the priests detained behind the Iron Curtain"], in *Il Giornale d'Italia*, 21 November 1962.

affirming nor denying its contents.[33] Eventually the issue died away,[34] perhaps fatefully, since this was literally on the eve of the negotiations for Slipyj's release.

Hermaniuk and the other Ukrainian bishops were quite wary and disturbed by the Vatican's *Ostpolitik* [Eastern Policy], or non-confrontational approach to the Soviet government and Russian Orthodox Church, which they thought should instead lead to an explicit condemnation of Soviet Communism. Part of the Vatican's *Ostpolitik* did result in the release of Slipyj from Soviet prisons, though under the condition that Slipyj not be allowed to return to Ukraine and not talk about his release. During the preparations for the Common Pastoral Letter from the Ukrainian bishops at Vatican II, Hermaniuk confided in his diary, "It was hard for me to sense what … Slipyj would sign and what he couldn't."[35] To further add to the complexity of this issue, it seems that Slipyj himself had engaged in a similar *Ostpolitik*. Hermaniuk recounted in his diary entries on November 14 and 20 of 1963 that Slipyj had asked Cardinal Willebrands to accompany him to the Soviet embassy for a celebration of the Communist Revolution, which Slipyj eventually attended. Hermaniuk, though quite critical of the Russians, Rome's dealings with the Soviet Union, and the hostile stand some Ukrainian bishops had taken toward Slipyj on account of this, did not himself in the diary pass any negative judgment on Slipyj in this regard. He simply reported the occurrence of this event.

The Apostolic College

The second main meta-theme that is also prominent in the diary is Hermaniuk's desire to see the Catholic Church adopt a more collegial system of governance, one more akin to the synodal structures of the Christian East. One of his first interventions in the preparatory phase of the council era called for the establishment of the "apostolic college of bishops."[36] He recounts:

---

[33] A general statement of the Ukrainian episcopate was eventually published in *Il Giornale d'Italia* (November 1962). However, in a 1987 interview, Hermaniuk admitted that indeed the Ukrainian bishops printed this letter. See Guly, "Interview: Hermaniuk reflects," 4.

[34] 6 December 1962.

[35] 19 November 1963.

[36] For some of this analysis, I am indebted to Bernard Daly, "Maxim Hermaniuk:

> 9:30—further consultations of the Theological Commission. At the end, an examination of the constitution *De Magisterio Ecclesiae*, I made a motion that the issue of the primacy and infallibility of the Roman Pope be presented in such a way that it would correspond more to the mentality of the Eastern Churches, namely:
>
> The subject of ecclesiastical infallibility resides in the college of bishops under the authority of the Roman Pontiff. This infallibility is exercised in a twofold mode:
>
> 1. Ordinary: through the authentic ordinary magisterium;
>
> 2. Extraordinary: a) In a collegial way—within an ecumenical council; b) In a principal way—by the Roman Pontiff in his capacity as head of the apostolic college.[37]

Hermaniuk repeats this proposal on October 1, 1963:

> During the congregation in the discussion upon the schema *De ecclesia—in genere*—I brought up the plan of establishing a so-called "Apostolic Synod" under the leadership of the Holy Father, which effectively would be representative of the entire episcopacy directing—under the leadership of the Holy Father—the entire universal Church .
>
> My speech, in general—was very well received by the Fathers of the Council, both Eastern and Western. Many of the Fathers personally expressed their sincere congratulations to me on this occasion.[38]

Hermaniuk wrote that Yves Congar was in favour of his suggestion, though Congar notes in his own diary that he saw Hermaniuk afterwards and offered to refine a few things in Hermaniuk's formulation in order to achieve his desired meaning.[39]

The Father of Collegiality at Vatican II ... and After," in *Vatican II au Canada*, ed. Gilles Routhier (Québec: Fides, 2001), 427–39.

37 6 March 1962.

38 1 October 1963.

39 Yves Congar, *Mon journal du concile* (Paris: Cerf, 2002), 91.

One of the very few times (out of twenty-eight times in total) that Hermaniuk underlines text in his diary is in connection with the establishment of the Synod of Bishops, a date Hermaniuk calls "A great historic day." This was through the promulgation of the *motu proprio*—*Apostolica Sollicitudo*.[40] Hermaniuk writes:

> The Holy Father calls into existence the Permanent Synod of Bishops[41]—with the mission of helping the Holy Father in leading the Universal Church. This is putting into practice episcopal collegiality. The Fathers of the Council welcomed the decision with loud applause. All were overjoyed, that in the end bishops will occupy their proper place in the leadership of the whole Church of Christ.[42]

Out of all the speeches that Hermaniuk had at the council, he mentions episcopal collegiality quite frequently.[43]

The 1965 Common Pastoral Letter of the Ukrainian Bishops, which we know was drafted to a large degree by Hermaniuk and which reflects many of the preoccupations noted in his council diary, refers to the Synod of Bishops in the following way:

> The form of collegial governance of the Church of the entire Catholic episcopate under the leadership of the Roman Pontiff, the successor of St. Peter, which is one of the greatest new decisions of this Council. It opens before the members of the ecclesial hierarchy enormous opportunities in the act of the renewal of Christian life: of primary interest are the needs of the Universal Church, the exchange of ideas of the bishops of the various peoples and nations and closer organized cooperation. Such common work by the episcopate in the renewal of the Church should be manifest, for example: in an appropriate distribution of priestly resources; in the practical division of eparchies, parishes and mission territories; in better mutual assistance in the building of new churches, educational and pedagogical institutes, and particularly in the spiritual

---

40 *Apostolica Sollicitudo*, published in *AS* IV/1, 19–24. Cf. *AS* IV/1, 140–42.

41 Emphasis in original.

42 15 September 1965. Emphasis in original.

43 *AS* I/3, 716; *AS* I/4, 512; *AS* II/1, 370, 372; *AS* II/2, 782.

> and material assistance to those brethren who suffer persecution for the sake of Christ and are victims of human evil.[44]

One can see here the great hopes that Hermaniuk had in the collegial governance of the Church, which in turn he hoped would have positive ecumenical results, especially with the Orthodox. However, by all accounts, Hermaniuk's assessment of this act was perhaps overstated, as will be shown by what follows.

The Extraordinary Synod of Bishops (1985)

Hermaniuk had great hopes for the establishment of the Synod of Bishops. Later in his career he had a chance to reflect on the latter days of the council and voice his disappointment in the trajectory of developments resulting from the council. For example, in 1985, in his presentation to the Extraordinary Synod of Bishops in Rome, Hermaniuk once again repeated his belief that the Dogmatic Constitution on the Church was one of the "most important documents of Vatican II."[45]

He cited the establishment of the Synod of Bishops as a collegial meeting to discuss issues in the Church, from evangelization to social justice, the family, and sacraments,[46] but the language he used implies that he lamented that these gatherings had only an "advisory character" and had become a "kind of international study days of the Catholic bishops."[47] For Hermaniuk, this college of bishops was only a first step in the "true collegial government of the church," which now needed to move beyond its advisory character and exercise "legislative" powers: "Then, and only then, one may speak of the real and true collegial government of the Church by the college of bishops." In the same speech he continued, "Now, 20 years after Vatican II, it is a good time to cor-

---

[44] "The Common Pastoral Letter of the Synod of Bishops of the Ukrainian Catholic Church Present at the Closing of the Fourth Session of the Second Vatican Ecumenical Council in Rome," in *Blahovisnyk* 1/1 (1965): 3–24. Translation mine.

[45] Maxim Hermaniuk, "Dogmatic Constitution on the Church 'Lumen Gentium': Twenty Years after Vatican II," in *Twenty Years Later: Study Texts from the Extraordinary Synod of Bishops 1985* (Ottawa: Canadian Conference of Catholic Bishops, 1986), 20.

[46] Ibid.

[47] Ibid.

rect the existing structure of the Synod of Bishops."[48] He proposed the establishment of a "Permanent Synod of Bishops" (elected by the current synod, with some papal appointments), which would have legislative powers, and he advocated for a diminished capacity for the curia. The final point of his address is worth repeating since it encompasses many of the key themes in Hermaniuk's council diary. Hermaniuk believed that such a change in the constitution of the Synod of Bishops could have a great influence:

- on the real and true participation of the whole college of bishops in the whole life of the church;
- it may help solve some very important problems in the ecumenical dialogue with other Christians, such as: Eastern Orthodox, Anglican and other Christian Churches and communities;
- such legislative responsibility of the college of bishops in the government of the church may assist the bishops very much in their active participation with the Holy Father and under his authority in the care and government of the universal church.[49]

He ended his speech, typical of his petitions in his council diaries,[50] with a prayer that God "help this Extraordinary Synod" arrive at the "right solution to this very important problem."[51]

Synodality and Autocephaly in Canada and Ukraine

The comments Hermaniuk made on his desire for synodality and collegiality are not simply made in the context of the Second Vatican Council but also with regard to some contemporaneous movements in the life of the Ukrainian Catholic Church in Canada. After a number of years of existence as an exarchate, and with the increase in faithful, the Apostolic See eventually subdivided the Canadian Church into three smaller exarchates in 1948, with further subdivisions in 1951.[52] As the

---

48 Ibid., 21.

49 Ibid., 22.

50 For example, see 17 September 1961, 13 August 1962, and 25 September 1964.

51 Hermaniuk, "Dogmatic Constitution on the Church," 22.

52 With these requests of the Ukrainian hierarchy in Canada was also the request that

Ukrainian Church continued to grow and expand, on November 3, 1956, Pope Pius XII, in the apostolic constitution *Hanc Apostolicam*, erected an ecclesiastical province for the Ukrainians and appointed Hermaniuk as the first metropolitan of the Apostolic See of Winnipeg.[53] In 1960, during the first Metropolitan Conference (March 31, 1960), the bishops began preparations for a provincial synod, which took place on May 2, 1962. Hermaniuk had planned to present the acts and decrees of the synod to the Apostolic See in 1963. Hermaniuk sought to establish a synodal order in Canada in line with the canon law at the time, but with the advent of Vatican II, much of what he had worked for in the confines of a pre-VII ecclesiology soon became irrelevant. This new constitution of the synod, though ratified by his synod, was not promulgated by Rome, though it was used for a time by the Ukrainian Catholic Church in Canada.

Significant for Hermaniuk's ecclesiology was not only collegiality but also the autocephaly of the Ukrainian Church. In fact, one of the first affirmations of the dignity or identity of the Ukrainian Catholic Church comes in Hermaniuk's objection to Rome that Slipyj's name was listed in the official directory as being under "Russia" and not "Ukraine."[54] Apart from his precision in recording the clerical ranks of those he met, one sees a gradual shift in the language that Hermaniuk uses to describe the Ukrainian Church and its bishops. In the early years of the council, he refers to the gatherings of bishops as conferences and synods, but by the end of the council, there is a slow evolution to writing about this Church as a patriarchate. His hope, and that of other Ukrainian bishops, was that Vatican II's decree On the Eastern Churches would elevate the See of L'viv-Halych to that of a patriarchate.

In 1964 the Ukrainian Synod of Bishops formally discussed the erection of a L'viv-Halych patriarchate, arguing that "it was necessary in order to preserve ritual unity and ecclesial discipline and to co-ordinate

---

the nomenclature of this Church be changed from "Ruthenian" to "Ukrainian."

53 Much of this work has been well documented in David Motiuk, *Eastern Christians in the New World: An Historical and Canonical Study of the Ukrainian Catholic Church in Canada* (Ottawa: Metropolitan Andrey Sheptytsky Institute of Eastern Christian Studies, 2005), 46–51.

54 16 October 1962.

missionary work."[55] In his council diary, Hermaniuk recorded a number of personal interventions with curial prelates and bishops toward the establishment of a patriarchate.[56] All of this gave rise to the patriarchal movement in the Ukrainian Catholic Church, which still continues today. And although the Ukrainian Catholic Church is still considered a major archiepiscopal church, with all the rights and privileges of a patriarchate, its faithful refer to its major archbishop today, as they did to Slipyj in the wake of Vatican II, as "His Beatitude," an ecclesiastical title reserved for Eastern patriarchs. What does all of this have to do with Vatican II? Well, it shows Hermaniuk's desire for a sense of collegiality and synodality for his own Church, as well as for that of the entire Catholic Church.

Related to Hermaniuk's desires for collegiality and synodality is the issue of the tensions among some of the Ukrainian Catholic bishops during the Vatican II years. Hermaniuk complained repeatedly in the early to mid-days of the council that the conferences of the Ukrainian Catholic bishops were marked by inefficiency and dissent. On November 19, 1964, he writes: "5 p.m.—Conference of our episcopate. It was unpleasant, as usual." In contrast, Hermaniuk admires the orderliness and efficiency of the Canadian Roman Catholic bishops: "I really admired the way how orderly the Canadian Latin Bishops decided these important and complicated matters; how far still is this for us Ukrainians? God grant, that some of our bishops finally realize their real tasks and proceed finally to positive, creative work ...."[57] Part of this tension emerges between Hermaniuk and his colleagues versus a number of Ukrainian Catholic Basilian bishops. Hermaniuk singles out Metropolitan Senyshyn of Philadelphia as the chief antagonist of these disruptions. These tensions were manifested most acutely in discussions about the establishment of a Ukrainian Catholic Church patriarchate, and in the critique of the person of Slipyj. In reading the diary, one is left wondering if this instability in the Ukrainian hierarchy was primarily the result of a lack of a clear system of governance (syno-

[55] Motiuk, *Eastern Christians in the New World*, 89.

[56] For example, 11 October 1963 (in session), 27 February 1964 (with Cardinal Bea), and 9 August 1964 (with Archbishops Baudoux and Flahiff).

[57] 26 September 1964.

dality, collegiality, or primacy), of differing visions of ecclesiology, or of personal conflicts—but we have no definitive record by Hermaniuk indicating which one.

Conclusion

I know that more could be said about Metropolitan Hermaniuk's participation at the council, and his coterminous ministry for his Church in Canada. Here I could possibly cite his support of liturgical reform in the Church, particularly his insistence on using a "living language" of Ukrainian (which was normal for that historical period) for his Church in Canada, and even allowing for the possibility of using English in parts of the services. During this conciliar period, one can read in his diary about the establishment of a liturgical commission for his metropolia, which had as its goal the revision and translation of the various service books. On a number of occasions during the gatherings of Ukrainian bishops during the council in Rome, he could not understand the need of some to retain the Old Church Slavonic language. Thus, he also found it odd that some Roman Catholic bishops still insisted on using Latin in their worship services rather than a "living language."[58]

One could also mention his disappointment at the discussions about Judaism and Islam, and at how certain fathers of the council were undermining the possibility of relations and positive statements about other faiths. In this connection, on October 24, 1965, Hermaniuk reported on a certain visitor he personally received in Rome: Kurt Lewin, author of *A Journey Through Illusions*,[59] whose rabbi father was killed by the Nazis, though his own life was saved through the efforts of Metropolitan Andrey Sheptytsky and his brother, Ihumen Klementij Sheptytsky.

His diary is also replete with references to the laity and catechesis (particularly of youth), and to the importance of the inclusion of the laity in the life of the Church in terms of spreading the Gospel. However, the 1965 Common Pastoral Letter of the Ukrainian bishops,

---

58 23 October 1962.

59 Kurt Lewin, *A Journey Through Illusions* (Santa Barbara, CA: Fithian Press, 1994).

unlike *Lumen Gentium* (which opens with sections on the mystery of the Church and then proceeds to a discussion on the people of God), opens with paragraphs about the hierarchical structure of the Church and only later deals with the laity. A synopsis of the text is as follows:

> Christ the Eternal Pastor, in instituting his Church, desired that the Apostles and their successors, that is the bishops, be pastors in his Church until the end of time .... In carrying out this pastoral office in the Church priests assist the bishops, who are, together with them, participants of Christ's priesthood, and are seen as their leading co-workers and assistants. On a lower rank of the hierarchy stand the deacons .... Other members of the People of God are members of the monastic state, ... [and] laypersons, who are incorporated in Christ through their Baptism, who share in the priestly, prophetic and royal service of Christ, and carry out their part of the mission of the entire Christian people.[60]

In Hermaniuk's defence, the text does mention "the priesthood of all believers," and the final Letter may be not of his own accord since the text was critiqued and amended by others in his episcopal conference.

From what I discussed above, one can discern certain areas that reflect Hermaniuk's primary preoccupations at the council, most notably on ecumenism and collegiality. In many ways, one can see that he was not simply receiving the teachings of the council but was in fact shaping their formulation. However, the question remains regarding the reception of Vatican II in the wider Ukrainian Catholic Church in Canada, in Ukraine, and elsewhere abroad. In other words, to what degree was Hermaniuk's assessment correct when he wrote of these events as "historic days"? His last entry at the conclusion of the council is this: "The Council has ended, but the problems raised by it await resolution."[61]

---

[60] "Common Pastoral Letter of the Synod of Bishops of the Ukrainian Catholic Church," 1.A. Translation mine.

[61] 8 December 1965.

A Canadian Anglican at Vatican II: The Activity of Eugene R. Fairweather

Michael Attridge,
University of St. Michael's College

It is difficult to imagine how Eugene Fairweather must have felt when he received the letter from England the week before Christmas in 1963. Signed by Canon John R. Satterthwaite, secretary to the Archbishop of Canterbury, Michael Ramsey, the letter asked Fairweather if he would be "willing to be appointed one of the three Anglican Observers for the next session" of the Vatican Council in Rome.[1] "The Archbishop," its author wrote, "is keen to send observers who are theologically-minded, and I know he would be grateful if you were able to consider going."[2] According to Satterthwaite, this invitation was still informal since, according to Anglican protocol, the Archbishop of Canterbury would have to seek first the approval of the Anglican primate of Canada.

Eugene Rathbone Fairweather was born in Ottawa on November 2, 1920.[3] Soon thereafter, his family moved to Montréal, where he was

---

1 Satterthwaite to Fairweather, 20 December 1963, Fairweather Archives, University of Trinity College, Toronto Canada, 978-0012/019 (06).

2 Ibid.

3 Cf. Biographical Sketch of Fairweather at the Front of the Fairweather Finding Aid, University of Trinity College, Toronto Canada; Howard W. Buchner, "Fairweather at Trinity," *Toronto Journal of Theology* 3, no. 1 (1987): 138–41; and, Robert D. Crouse, "In Memoriam, Eugene Rathbone Fairweather 1920-2002," *Anglican Theological Review* 85,

raised—as one biographer wrote "in Anglo-Catholic piety"[4]—and where he received his early education. Fairweather earned his BA from McGill University in 1941. In September that same year, he moved to Toronto to begin divinity studies at Trinity College and an MA in philosophy at the University of Toronto. In 1943 he completed both degrees and was ordained an Anglican priest the following year. In 1944 he began teaching at Trinity, first as a tutor (1944), then as a lecturer (1946). In 1947 he left the college to pursue advanced studies in theology under the mentorship of Paul Tillich at Union Theological Seminary in New York City, where he earned the degrees Master of Sacred Theology (STM) and Doctor of Theology (ThD). In 1949, at only twenty-nine years of age, he returned to Trinity as Associate Professor of Theology and Ethics and remained there until he retired in 1987.

Fairweather was already a well-known and well-respected theologian throughout North America when that letter arrived from Palace Court in December 1963. He had been a regular contributor to the *Canadian Churchman*—now known as the *Anglican Journal*—as well as the Montréal-based publication the *Anglican Outlook*, a "semi-official organ"[5] of the Anglican Fellowship for Social Action. From 1954 to 1955 he served as president of the Canadian Society of Biblical Studies and from 1957 to 1958 president of the Canadian Theological Society. In 1960 he founded, edited, and was a frequent contributor to the *Canadian Journal of Theology*, which eventually became the *Toronto Journal of Theology*.[6] Having earned a reputation in the United States, Fairweather delivered the Bishop Paddock Lecture at the General Theological Seminary in New York City in 1956, and in 1963 he gave the Hale Memorial Lectures at Seabury-Western Theological Seminary in Evanston, Illinois.

Fairweather had also gained international experience as an ecumenist. In 1951 the Anglican primate of Canada invited him to participate in the World Council of Churches, Commission on Faith and

---

no. 1 (Winter 2003): 3–5.

4 Crouse, "In Memoriam," 3–5.

5 Stephen F. Hopkins, "The Anglican Fellowship for Social Action," (MA thesis, University of St. Michael's College, 1982), 9.

6 Crouse, "In Memoriam," 3.

Order's World Conference in Lund, Sweden, the following year. There, Fairweather contributed to the formulation of what would become known as the "Lund Principle"—that is, that the churches, wherever possible should do together all that can be done together, and do separately only that which must be done separately. It is clear that this would shape Fairweather's ecumenical outlook in the years to follow. Equally important at Lund were the contacts he made. According to Canadian Anglican Bishop John Baycroft, Lund was the place where Fairweather first formed friendships with other international theologians and discovered that a great deal of theological progress could be made during short and infrequent meetings because of a climate of affection, trust, and respect among the participants.[7] At Lund, Fairweather met and befriended Michael Ramsey, who at the time was Regius Chair of Divinity at Cambridge. Ramsey would later become the Archbishop of Canterbury when Fairweather was invited to be an observer at the council.

Fairweather responded quickly to Satterthwaite's letter and agreed to be appointed as an observer. Shortly thereafter he received a letter from Michael Ramsey himself, who had been in touch with the Canadian primate. Fairweather would be an official observer at the upcoming third session of the Second Vatican Council. His appointment was for the entire session; however, Fairweather had already indicated that he would not be able to attend for the entire time. There were matters to attend to at Trinity College, and he was involved in "Stage Three" of the Anglican–United Church union agreement in November of that year.[8] According to letters of correspondence in his archives, Fairweather arrived in Rome on September 9, 1964, for the opening ceremonies on Monday, September 14. However, he had to return to Canada on October 18—a month before the session closed on November 20.[9]

---

[7] John Baycroft, "Pontifex: A Brief Biographical Note on Some of the Contributions of Canon Eugene Fairweather to the Canadian Church," *Toronto Journal of Theology* 3, no. 1 (1987): 130.

[8] Diary of Eugene R. Fairweather, "Diary I," file 987-0012-019 (07), 85.

[9] Satterthwaite, Ramsey, Fairweather, 7 January 1964, 5 February 1964, 17 February 1964, 19 February 1964, and 24 March 1964, Fairweather Archives University of Trinity College, Toronto Canada, 978-0012/019 (06).

It is worth mentioning at this point that Fairweather attended not only the third session in fall 1964 but also the fourth and final session in 1965. His initial invitation, however, did not include the 1965 session since, at the time, it was not certain there would be a fourth session.

I should mention something about my sources for this analysis. Most of the details of Fairweather's activity at the council come from unpublished material in his archives at the University of Trinity College in Toronto, Canada. We are especially fortunate to have two of his council diaries, both of which are legible and easy to read. Unfortunately, however, there were originally three diaries and the second one is missing. The first one covers the period from the time he arrived in Rome in September 1964 until almost the time he returned to Canada the following month; it ends in mid-sentence on October 14, 1964, four days before his departure. The third one begins, also in mid-sentence, the following year on October 11, 1965, which means the second one would presumably have had the details of the last few days of his stay in 1964 and the first four weeks of his activity in 1965. The three diaries would indeed have painted a more complete picture of Fairweather's council experience, however, the two we have available still provide much detail.

Fairweather's accommodations were arranged by the Vatican's Secretariat for Christian Unity.[10] He would stay in the same place as most of the other ecumenical observers—in the Pensione Castel Sant'Angelo on the Piazza Adriana, no. 12—a fifteen-minute walk from St. Peter's Basilica. Room and board was £3 per day, which included three meals. The Church of England had been covering the expenses of all Anglican observers, except those from the United States. The Archbishop of Canterbury did, however, ask the Canadian primate if the Church in Canada would finance Fairweather's time in Rome.

The idea to have ecumenical "observers" at the council goes back to the early days of its planning. As early as August 1959, Pope John XXIII is said to have welcomed the presence of non-Catholic observers.[11] Two months later in a press conference, Vatican Secretary of State

---

10 Thomas Stransky to Fairweather, 3 August 1964, Fairweather Archives, University of Trinity College, Toronto Canada, 978-0012/019 (06).

11 A. Wenger, *Vatican II: Volume I: The First Session* (Westminster, MD: Newman Press, 1966), 141–42.

Domenico Tardini said that the matter was under consideration, but it was probable that non-Catholic observers would be welcome if they were interested.[12] The matter was settled the following year by Pope John, who confirmed that indeed non-Catholics would be called upon to assist at the great meeting of the Church, and the newly established Secretariat for Christian Unity would be responsible for liaising with them.[13]

In the summer of 1964 Fairweather received an information sheet from the secretariat's Monsignor Jan Willebrands, apprising him of various details for the upcoming session.[14] "General Congregations" would be held in St. Peter's Basilica every morning, Monday to Friday, from 9:30–12:30 p.m., preceded by Mass at 9 a.m. Afternoons and evenings were free except Tuesday afternoons, when the Secretariat for Christian Unity would hold special meetings with observers and guests. Observers would have access to confidential information and documentation; for the most part it would be the same as the material distributed to the fathers (bishops and religious superiors) and the theologians of the council. The observers, however, would not be permitted to speak or to vote at the discussions and sessions of the council.[15]

The place where the observers sat in the basilica was at the front, near the bronze statue of St. Peter. According to Fairweather, the Orthodox, Anglicans, and Old Catholics were grouped together in one section in front of the statue of St. Longinus, and the rest of the observers were seated just around the corner.[16] Presumably, they were categorized according to Reformation and non-Reformation churches. As one of Fairweather's fellow Anglican observers, Howard Root, said to him: "they do think about these things; one doesn't always know what, but they do think."[17]

12 *Acta et documenta Concilio œcumenico Vaticano II apparando; Series prima* (Vatican: Typis Polyglottis Vaticanis, 1960–61), vol. I, 154.

13 Ibid., 8.

14 SPCU Information Sheet, No. 1.

15 SPCU Rules and Regulations, June 1964.

16 Diary of Eugene R. Fairweather, "Diary I," file 987-0012-019 (07), 16.

17 Ibid.

These were premium seats positioned close to the council presidents and moderators and immediately next to the secretaries. According to another Anglican observer, the view was "splendid" and they "were far more integrated into the proceedings than were many hundreds of bishops."[18] Moreover, the observers held a certain distinction. Whenever the Pope would visit the Council Hall he would always pause for a moment to greet them.[19] This was also Fairweather's experience, even from the beginning of his arrival in Rome. During the Pope's opening speech of the third session, his address to the observers was the only part for which he showed enthusiasm. He wrote: "The Pope delivered his allocution [this morning] from a chair placed in front of the papal altar. He read his text in a level (almost flat) voice, except for the third section, in which his emotion was evident." In this section, he addressed the observers "and through us to our churches. .... [His] concern for Christian Unity appeared here, both in the text and in the obvious feeling with which he read it, smiling repeatedly towards us—[even] as he had when he was carried past us before Mass."[20]

The hours spent in the observers' booth were not always spent in total silence listening to the council fathers. There were also occasions for conversation and even a bit of humour. Fairweather tells the story of an exchange that happened one day during the voting on collegiality. As an official was rushing past the observers' tribune with the tally from the IBM machine, one of the mentors assigned to the observers, Monsignor Arrighi, asked: "How is it going?" The official replied, "It is going well, I suppose, if you like the new Church. I do not." Arrighi laughed and said: "Oh! I understand, you are an Old Catholic. There are already two of you in the observers' box!"[21]

Fairweather seems to have been well equipped, linguistically, to function during his time in Rome. The observers were provided with interpreters who translated the council speeches, which were delivered mostly in Latin. Fairweather, though, seems not to have used them;

---

[18] John Moorman, *Vatican Observed: An Anglican Impression of Vatican II* (London: Darton, Longman & Todd, 1967), 20.

[19] Ibid.

[20] Diary of Eugene R. Fairweather, "Diary I," file 987-0012-019 (07), 1–2.

[21] Ibid., 35.

he appears to have had some facility with the Latin language. When the English Benedictine abbot Christopher Butler spoke, Fairweather described his Latin as "intelligible" and his pronunciation "delightfully Oxonian." On the other hand, he noted, with amusement, that their interpreter was not able to follow all of the speeches. "Some accents" of the fathers, he wrote, "are close to unintelligible to Anglo-Saxon ears." In addition to Latin, and of course English, Fairweather was most likely fluent in French. He describes encountering a French tourist one evening at dusk when he was standing atop one of Rome's seven hills. During their conversation she kept repeating: "Rome est plus belle que Paris."[22]

Within days of arriving in Rome, Fairweather slipped into the rhythm of a council observer's life: daily Mass and general congregations; weekly Tuesday meetings with the Secretariat for Christian Unity; frequent gatherings organized by the observers themselves. There were also excursions, receptions, dinner parties, and many opportunities for people to meet, develop relationships, and to discuss the council and its theology.

Liturgy was clearly important to Fairweather and he attended daily Mass at St. Peter's almost without exception. Each morning he wrote a line or two in his diary describing the celebration. Often they were uneventful and the description was simple: "The Mass of the Holy Ghost was said in *aula* by the Archbishop of Quebec (Maurice Roy)."[23] Occasionally they revealed disappointment:

> The *caerimoniarius* was unusually sloppy; at the collect we had a long wait while he leafed through the missal and found the wrong one (which was followed in due course by the wrong offertory and post-communion prayers). He also gave the celebrant the preamble to the wrong *oratio fidelium*. Cardinal Meouchi managed at one point to knock his chair off the patriarchs' dais, thereby attracting considerable attention from the servers and singers. All in all, things were a bit confused.[24]

---

22 Diary of Eugene R. Fairweather, "Diary III," file 987-0012-019 (07), 254.

23 Diary of Eugene R. Fairweather, "Diary I," file 987-0012-019 (07), 28.

24 Diary of Eugene R. Fairweather, "Diary III," file 987-0012-019 (07), 216.

On the whole, however, Fairweather was pleased with the council Masses, describing them as "dignified and reverent."[25] One of his favourite experiences was of an Eastern liturgy, celebrated near the end of the council in 1965 by the Ukrainian Cardinal Josyf Slipyj. "Slipyj as a celebrant," he wrote, "was magnificent, and the overall impression was one of splendour and what one might call liturgical gusto! ... I doubt that I had ever felt the distinctive impact of the Byzantium Liturgy so sharply." Every Sunday morning Fairweather would attend Mass at the Anglican All Saints Church at 8 a.m. Occasionally he would then go to Mass later in the morning at one of the Catholic churches. Liturgy was clearly important to him and an important part of his time in Rome.

The weekly Tuesday meetings organized by the Secretariat for Christian Unity were opportunities for observers to interact with bishops and theologians of the council and to discuss the conciliar texts. Usually there was some expert present who would speak about a schema currently under discussion by the council, and observers could ask questions and offer criticism. For example, in the afternoon of his second day in Rome, Fairweather heard Charles Moeller from Leuven, Belgium, deliver a "lucid report" on Chapters VII and VIII of the document on the Church, which Moeller himself had been directly involved in writing. In response, one of the observers, Kristen Skydsgaard, a Danish Lutheran, was able to point out to Moeller that the document neglected the importance of the "world" in the "account of the destiny of the Church."[26] Occasionally, at these weekly gatherings, tempers would flare. At a meeting in which Mary was discussed, Fairweather recounts that a Greek Orthodox observer, Nikos Nissiotis, was "provoked to wrath" by a sympathetic speech from another Greek Orthodox observer, Andrew Scrima. Nissiotis, says Fairweather, "poured it all out on the Roman Church beginning with observations on the 'Maria for definition'" and finishing with his "Filioque speech."[27] The French Dominican theologian Yves Congar, one of most influential experts at Vatican II, was often on hand to discuss topics of ecumenism, missionary activity, life and ministry of priests, etc. The Tuesday

25 Diary of Eugene R. Fairweather, "Diary I," file 987-0012-019 (07), 71.

26 Ibid., 6–7.

27 Diary of Eugene R. Fairweather, "Diary I," file 987-0012-019 (07), 31.

meetings were not just for information sharing with no measureable impact beyond. One of Fairweather's colleagues, Anglican observer John Moorman, tells the story of how Skydsgaard criticized the document on the Church during one of the Tuesday gatherings. Six days later, one of the observers said to Moorman as they were entering the Council Hall: "Do you remember Skydsgaard's speech at the meeting last week?" "Well, you're going to hear it again this morning. Cardinal Meyer has heard about it and is going to make the same points."[28]

Occasional audiences with the Pope were also a part of the observer's experience, and their reception was as friendly as the one received in the Council Hall. Two weeks after the opening of the third session, the Pope hosted the group in the Sistine Chapel. He addressed them, Fairweather writes, "in a most friendly way," thanking them and their churches for their presence and interest. After a prayer together, Paul VI went around speaking to each in turn and presenting them with a "specially bound" copy of A. Merk's Greek-Latin New Testament; only one hundred copies of which were produced in this binding.[29] The experience was a good one, concluded Fairweather, "and the Pope's good will in the matter of ecumenism [was] more strongly established."[30]

By the end of the council in 1965, the audiences were even more personal. Three weeks before the council's closing, the Anglican observers had their own meeting with Pope Paul; this time not in the Sistine Chapel but in his private library. The Pope sat at his desk while the five Anglicans formed a semicircle in front of him. As they relaxed, the conversation, describes Fairweather, which was conducted in a mixture of Italian, French, and English, was friendly, even though he found Pope Paul "really very shy." This time the Pope presented them with a single copy of a new facsimile edition of Codex Vaticanus to be given to the Archbishop of Canterbury. Pope Paul asked about Canon Bernard Pawley, an Anglican observer who was present at all four sessions and for three of them was the Archbishop of Canterbury's official representative. The Pope had met Pawley many times before. He also asked about Pawley's family, especially the children. "Then he looked

28 Moorman, *Vatican Observed*, 28.

29 The book is in Fairweather's archive.

30 Diary of Eugene R. Fairweather, "Diary I," file 987-0012-019 (07), 54–56.

rather thoughtful, rummaged in his desk drawer and pulled out two envelopes of Vatican stamps for the youngsters."[31] The gesture was well received.

According to Fairweather's diary, the Anglican observers (a small number: seven in 1964 and ten in 1965) were in regular contact with one another. There's nothing to suggest that they had "official" weekly meetings, but Fairweather mentions that they did meet as an Anglican "caucus." Individuals would prepare position papers on behalf of all the Anglican observers on variety of topics covered at the council; sometimes these would be on entire documents and other times on individual chapters or particular issues. For example, John Lawrence of England, who was appointed for the fourth session, prepared a memorandum on missionary activity, which was then sent to Bishop Willebrands at the Secretariat for Unity.[32] Fairweather himself prepared at least three of these papers. During the fourth session, at the time when the document on the Church in the modern world was being discussed, he wrote a paper on the controversial topic of birth control.[33] Again, in the same session, he prepared one on religious freedom for Canadian Archbishop Maurice Baudoux of St. Boniface, Manitoba.[34] The third was a text prepared by him after the episode involving Nissiotis at the weekly Tuesday meeting. He writes: "Bishop Willebrands and other members of the Secretariat had been so taken aback by the vehemence of Nissiotis's somewhat inconsistent attack on Roman Catholic Mariology, and so discouraged by what seemed to be a widespread failure among the observers to appreciate what the 'moderates' had achieved, that Pawley and others felt a statement from the Anglican side was highly desirable, and I agreed to draft something."[35] There is no indication that the secretariat had invited these papers. But he and the other Anglicans felt that the substance of the chapter on Mary, although not entirely in agreement with their theology, could at least be interpreted by Anglicans in an acceptable way. They thought it important that the secretariat

31 Diary of Eugene R. Fairweather, "Diary III," file 987-0012-019 (07), 263–65.

32 Ibid., 211.

33 Ibid.

34 Ibid., 226.

35 Diary of Eugene R. Fairweather, "Diary I," file 987-0012-019 (07), 45–46.

know that not all observers held the same views; in other words, as he wrote in his diary, to avoid "guilt by association."[36]

The Anglican observers also gathered regularly at the home of Canon Bernard Pawley for dinner. They were social occasions, and the guests invited were often bishops and archbishops and other dignitaries. Fairweather attended his first a week after he arrived in Rome. The guests were Cardinal Suenens and Bishop De Smedt, both from Belgium and both high profile, outspoken figures at the council. Also present was the rector of the Belgian College. According to Fairweather they spoke about many things both pertaining and not to the council and that "the Anglican post-mortem decided" the evening was "well spent."[37] Two weeks later two bishops from India, the coadjutor of Delhi and the archbishop of Bhopal, were the honoured guests.[38] On another occasion the company was Cardinal Alfrink, Bishop Willebrands, and Father Frans Thijssen, all from the Netherlands.

For Fairweather, one of the most important of these dinners must have been the one with the Canadian Catholic hierarchy, which included Cardinal Léger of Montréal, Archbishop Pocock of Toronto, and Bishop De Roo of Victoria. Fairweather's presence at the third session was a novelty for the Canadian hierarchy. For the first two sessions there had been no Canadian observer, no one with whom the Canadian bishops could consult for an ecumenical perspective. Shortly after arriving in Rome he wrote in his diary about a coffee he had had with Archbishop Johnson of Vancouver. "The Canadian bishops," he said, "seem glad to have a Canadian observer at last, and I hope (as I think they do) that our shared experience here will help the ecumenical work in Canada."[39]

Fairweather met Léger and Pocock that evening at the Canadian College and accompanied them to Pawley's home. As he arrived at the college he found both of them waiting in the front hall. "Both," he said, "were wearing black suits, with pectoral crosses tidily tucked into vest pockets. The Cardinal, however, was distinguished by a pair

---

36 Ibid., 23.

37 Ibid., 27–28.

38 Ibid., 72–73.

39 Ibid., 39.

of bright red socks!"[40] Bishop De Roo met them at Pawley's house and the conversation flowed. Fairweather sat beside Léger and they "talked at length about Canadian politics, with special reference to Quebec." Léger said that he thought the newly elected prime minister, Lester Pearson, understood Canada's constitutional problems well but "lacked the force to put his knowledge into effect." The solution, he thought, rested with the provincial governments of Ontario and Québec, which should take a stronger lead in resolving the constitutional problems.[41] Fairweather was obviously impressed with the Cardinal's political savvy. When the conversation turned to the changes that had been happening in Québec society in the 1960s, he wrote: "... I think [Léger] has (as one would expect) great insight into the nature of the Quebec revolution. He insists, for example, on the radically altered relation between Church, society and culture in contemporary Quebec."[42] As the evening ended the conversation turned to the council. Bishop De Roo expressed what seemed to be a concern over how quickly things were moving, which he feared was the result of "the convergence of two tendencies." On the one hand many of the fathers were getting fed up with routine of the council and with having to be absent from their dioceses. On the other hand, many of the conservatives in the curia who were unhappy with the rapid and radical changes, and who were fearful of what else might change, were anxious as Fairweather wrote, to get the council "off their necks."[43]

Fairweather's contact with the Canadian bishops at Vatican II was frequent and his relations with them seem to have been quite good. Within a week of arriving in Rome he mentions chatting with Bishop De Roo, Bishop Carter of London, and Archbishop Baudoux outside of the tribune, after the morning session.[44] Weeks later he mentions discussing the Marian text with Archbishop Pocock; the latter expressing the opinion that there was still insufficient biblical material in the text for it to be valued ecumenically.[45] On one occasion, he and Bishop

40 Ibid., 50–51.

41 Ibid., 51.

42 Ibid., 51–52.

43 Ibid., 52.

44 Ibid., 18.

45 Ibid., 39-40.

Carter talked about the topic of celibacy, which had come up because of the discussion on priestly life and ministry.[46] On another occasion he ran into Archbishop Flahiff of Winnipeg and Father Laurence Shook walking together, and the three had a "brief exchange of views" about the document on the Jews.[47] As one can see the topics were varied and often coincided with whichever council text was currently being discussed. The conversation though always appears to have had substance and overall there is a strong sense in Fairweather's diaries that these encounters were meaningful.

Cardinal Léger, of course, was known to be one of the leaders at Vatican II, not just among the Canadians but among all the bishops. His influence at the council has been well documented, most notably by Professor Gilles Routhier. In his first council diary, Fairweather praises Léger over and again: "An excellent speech was made [today] by Cardinal Leger, who urged a new approach to the bishops' pastoral duties … taking account of the independent mentality of the modern scientific [mind]"[48]; "Cardinal Leger gave another excellent speech … [on religious liberty] … (It seems to me that so far no one has spoken on such a consistently high level.)"[49]; "The session [this morning] was devoted to [the text on the Jews] … Cardinal Leger made another good speech (his fourth this session)"[50]; "The discussion [on Revelation] continued [this morning]. Cardinal Leger made a fine speech (the best of the morning, I think)"[51]; and, " [This morning on the ministry and life of priests] … Cardinal Leger urged the inculcation of a priestly spirituality more integrally related to the duties of the pastoral ministry … [Fairweather concluded] (If every Father's thought and enunciation were as clear as Leger's, the general congregations would be an enjoyable experience.)."[52]

46 Diary of Eugene R. Fairweather, "Diary III," file 987-0012-019 (07), 204.

47 Ibid., 236.

48 Diary of Eugene R. Fairweather, "Diary I," file 987-0012-019 (07), 25.

49 Ibid., 34.

50 Ibid., 49.

51 Ibid., 57.

52 Diary of Eugene R. Fairweather, "Diary III," file 987-0012-019 (07), 210.

Fairweather's praise of the Canadian bishops goes beyond his admiration of Léger. And a picture emerges from his diaries of a hierarchy who were active, organized, and among the leaders of change at Vatican II. In some places his comments are simple passing remarks like: "Archbishop Flahiff of Winnipeg spoke well" this morning on the revelation text;[53] or "[Cardinal] Roy made the most useful contribution" of the three presentations this morning on celibacy;[54] or Bishop De Roo made a good speech on the priest and the mission of Christ—probably the best of the morning.[55] In other places, the comments are more detailed and Canadian bishops are seen as united in their attempt to bring about change. In the third session, during the discussion of the text on the laity, Bishops De Roo and Charbonneau raised serious criticisms in the Council Hall, saying that the revised schema was marked by "clericalism," "juridicalism," and "paternalism." The following day when the conversation continued on the laity, Bishop Carter of Sault Ste. Marie said that the document had been "'born in sin'—the sin of clericalism—and urged that it be drastically revised under the guidance of lay experts." Later in the day, Archbishop Baudoux said to Fairweather that the Canadian bishops were "well organized to make their anticlericalist point."[56] Another "excellent speech" was made the day after by Bishop Power of Antigonish, who spoke about the apostolic formation of the laity and proposed "several definite points for revision."[57] In the midst of this debate, Fairweather wrote that he was pleased to see "the Canadian bishops giving such consistently progressive leadership when they speak."[58]

The activity of the Canadian bishops though was not restricted to what was said in the Council Hall, which is recorded in the official published acts of the council. According to Fairweather they were also busy behind the scenes. Fairweather tells the story of a "confidential meeting" of the Canadian bishops on October 11, 1964, to discuss

53 Diary of Eugene R. Fairweather, "Diary I," file 987-0012-019 (07), 60.

54 Diary of Eugene R. Fairweather, "Diary III," file 987-0012-019 (07), 216–17.

55 Ibid., 224.

56 Diary of Eugene R. Fairweather, "Diary I," file 987-0012-019 (07), 82–83.

57 Ibid., 87.

58 Ibid., 77–78.

"an urgent matter that had unexpectedly arisen."[59] The next morning, Bishop De Roo told Fairweather that the meeting had been to discuss the future of two of the council's declarations—the one on religious liberty and the one on the Jews.[60] Attempts had been made by a conservative minority to try to keep these documents off the floor of the council. The Canadian bishops were not the only ones concerned. Fairweather describes the atmosphere in the general congregation that morning as "restless." He noted that Cardinal Suenens was absent from the moderators' table and that Cardinal Léger did not appear to be his usual self.[61] Later, Canadian theologian Gregory Baum said that "unspecified cardinals had approached the Pope" on the issue the night before.[62] Presumably Cardinal Léger had been one of them. The next day, Bishop De Roo told Fairweather that the atmosphere had cleared. Bishop Carter said that some of the bishops had threatened to withdraw from the council in protest against curial interference with its business and refusal to accept its judgment.[63] The Pope had accepted the protest of the progressive cardinals and promised that the declarations would not be interfered with by the curial conservatives.[64]

It is difficult to measure exactly the extent to which the Canadians were able to influence the outcome of this event (and others), but the story illustrates at least several things: the Canadian episcopacy was on the side of change; they were in regular contact with one another; and, they were actively following the outcome of this crisis. Their contributions to the progress of the council did not go unnoticed. In the fourth session someone noted to Fairweather how liberal and efficient the Canadian hierarchy was in comparison with the American. The comment reminded Fairweather of another one made just a few days before by American Lutheran observer Warren Quanbeck, who said that the German and Canadian hierarchies seemed outstanding in their effectiveness.[65]

---

59 Ibid., 85.

60 Ibid., 87.

61 Ibid., 88.

62 Ibid., 89.

63 Ibid., 95.

64 Ibid., 98.

65 Diary of Eugene R. Fairweather, "Diary III," file 987-0012-019 (07), 273–74.

The closing weeks of the council in 1965 were a time for people to plan next steps and consider how best to implement the work achieved over the past four years. According to his diary, Fairweather was involved in the planning of a number of these. He and the other Anglicans met with a Benedictine abbot who was establishing an Anglican studies institute in Trier, Germany. They encouraged the abbot to send his faculty, not just to Oxford and Cambridge but to the United States and Canada where they might also gain experience with what Fairweather called the "non-established" Anglican churches.[66] At the same time as they were encouraging this initiative, Fairweather and the others were assisting with the plans for a new Anglican Centre in Rome. Among other things, the centre would have a good Anglican library; a chapel, which would be a place for prayer for Christian unity; and a resource centre for the surrounding Roman universities to offer courses on Anglicanism.[67] The centre still exists today.

A third initiative, the one that would have the greatest impact globally on Anglican–Roman Catholic relations, was the beginning the Anglican–Roman Catholic International Commission (ARCIC). I already mentioned earlier the audience that the Anglican observers had had with Pope Paul VI three weeks before the closing of Vatican II. At this meeting it is clear that both parties were already thinking about next steps for Anglican–Roman Catholic relations. The Pope asked the observers about when they thought Michael Ramsey would visit him in Rome. They also discussed the prospects of an Anglican–Roman Catholic dialogue, something the Anglican delegation assured him they very much wanted.[68] The Pope expressed concern over how the Church of England and the other Anglican churches would collaborate in such a project given that their ecclesiological structure means that authority rests not centrally but locally in the Anglican churches throughout the world. One of the observers from England, John Lawrence, assured him that their structure resembled that of Orthodoxy. Later, Bishop Willebrands quipped to Fairweather that that may not have

66 Ibid., 235–36.

67 Ibid., 270–71.

68 Ibid., 265.

been the best analogy. After all, he said, in his experience—unlike the Orthodox—Anglican primates and metropolitans could usually work together with one another when necessary!

This meeting proved seminal. Months later, the Archbishop of Canterbury indeed met with Paul VI in Rome for several days. At the end of their meeting they agreed to sponsor a dialogue between the two churches. This was the beginning of what would become the Anglican/Roman Catholic International Commission, whose goal remains to this day, unity between Anglicans and Roman Catholics. Fairweather was a member of the international commission for many years. It is difficult to know if he was aware at the time of what they were building.

How was it that Eugene Fairweather was chosen to be an observer at Vatican II? Was the invitation initiated by the Church of England, which saw that it had representatives from around the world, including the United States, but no one from Canada? Or was it through Michael Ramsey himself, who had met and developed a friendship with Fairweather a decade or so earlier? Or was it through the Canadian bishops, who were anxious to have a Canadian observer with whom they could test theological ideas? Did they suggest his name? At this point, we don't know. We do know that he was already a well-established Canadian theologian, engaged in international ecumenical work, by the time his invitation arrived in late 1963. Moreover we know that his theological formation and ecumenical experience would have served him well at the council.

Fairweather clearly took his time in Rome seriously. He attended almost every general congregation and public session, every daily liturgy, every weekly observer's meeting. He attended social functions, accepted invitations to speak, and had frequent contact and consultation with the Canadian hierarchy, mostly anglophone.

He prepared position papers on a variety of topics from an Anglican perspective for the Secretariat for Christian Unity as well as the Canadian bishops. The bishops had brought with them their Catholic theological experts: André Naud, Bernard Lambert, Jean-Marie Tillard, Pierre Lafortune, Gregory Baum, etc. Given the amount of contact and apparent consultation that Fairweather had had with the Canadian bishops, one wonders whether it would not be appropriate to consider him their non-Catholic ecumenical expert. It would be interesting to see whether any of the ideas in his papers were incorporated by the bishops in their own interventions at the council.

Regardless, his zeal for Christian unity grew during his time in Rome. He described his experience as the council as "enjoyable," and he found the climate "open and hopeful."[69] Fairweather's enthusiasm encouraged the establishment of an Anglican institute, the Anglican Centre in Rome, and he helped initiate the international dialogue between Anglicans and Roman Catholics. He felt a sense of responsibility to do what he could to promote ecumenism. He wrote in his diary: "The movements to which the Council is giving so strong an impetus may well have quite unpredictable effects on the ecumenical situation in the next few decades ... without knowing just what to expect, Anglicans and others must do their best to keep the dialogue going effectively for the benefit of [everyone]."[70]

Indeed, he did do his best to keep the dialogue going. Upon his return from Rome he was almost immediately appointed to the Anglican–Roman Catholic International Commission, on which he stayed for fifteen years until 1981. In Canada he worked hard to have the results of the international dialogue received from coast to coast, primarily through his involvement in the Canadian, Anglican–Roman Catholic dialogue. Fairweather was also involved internationally on the Anglican-Orthodox dialogue and the World Council of Churches' Commission on Faith and Order. In Canada, in addition, he was a "key Anglican participant" in the plan to unite The United Church of Canada and the Anglican Church of Canada in the 1970s. According to Canadian Anglican Bishop John Baycroft, all of this activity and more earned Fairweather the title "Pontifex," that is, bridge-builder.[71]

Eugene Fairweather died in Halifax, Nova Scotia, in 2002 in his eighty-second year. Biographers and chroniclers of his achievements scarcely give a line or two of attention to Fairweather's time at Vatican II. After two sessions at the council, though, developing a network of

---

69 Diary of Eugene R. Fairweather, "Diary I," file 987-0012-019 (07), 85.

70 Ibid., 97.

71 Baycroft, "Pontifex", 133.

international contacts, discussing theology, building personal relations with the Canadian hierarchy, witnessing the most significant changes the Roman Catholic Church had undergone in centuries, Vatican II was obviously a pivotal time for Fairweather. The evidence for this is found in his conciliar diary.

Vatican Council II: A Turning Point in the Church's History

Gregory Baum,
McGill University

After the Second Vatican Council (1962–65), Catholic theologians discussed among themselves how to interpret the doctrinal evolution that had taken place. They all felt that in response to the conditions of modernity, the Church, in fidelity to the Gospel, had reinterpreted its teaching in a certain discontinuity with the past. During a discussion at the board of directors of the review *Concilium*, Hans Küng made a brilliant suggestion that became the topic of a learned symposium in 1984[1] and has subsequently been widely accepted in the field of religious studies.

The Swiss theologian adapted for his use in theology the idea of "paradigm shift," introduced by Thomas Kuhn to interpret the changes of explanatory models in the evolution of the natural sciences. Küng argued that when the inherited form of Catholicism was no longer able to respond to the challenges of modern society, thoughtful Catholics became restless: they searched for new answers, reread Scripture and tradition, engaged in dialogue with modern thought, and had new religious experiences. They were gripped by a new perception of Catholicism, a new sense of its meaning and power in today's world. What occurred in them, Küng argued, was a paradigm shift, which was

1 Hans Küng and David Tracy, eds., *Paradigm Change in Theology* (Edinburgh: T. & T. Clark, 1989).

subsequently endorsed by the Second Vatican Council. The substance of faith remains identical, but the form of Catholicism has changed. The council produced a creative reinterpretation of the Church's teaching and practice, faithful to their divine origin, which allowed it to communicate the Gospel to today's troubled world.

Since Hans Küng made the proposal over forty years ago, the idea of paradigm shift has been widely accepted in the field of theology and religious studies to render an account of the changes experienced by religious traditions as they enter into radically altered historical circumstances. Küng himself has applied this idea in his major historical studies of Christianity,[2] Judaism,[3] and Islam.[4] Asian scholars have also tested to what extent this idea helps them to understand the shifts and changes in the development of their own religious traditions.[5]

The meaning of paradigm shift in the history of the sciences is not the same as its meaning in ecclesiology. A paradigm shift in the sciences is produced by researchers who discover that the inherited theory no longer explains the experimental findings, while the paradigm shift in the Christian Church is a gift of the Spirit: it is something that happens, provoked by new questions, sustained by religious experience, and clarified by theological thought.

According to Thomas Kuhn, the proposal of a new paradigm in the natural sciences provokes the opposition of scientists still attached to the inherited theory. The emergence of a new paradigm of Catholicism has had a similar effect: it has provoked an opposition among Catholics—bishops, priests, and laity—attached to the Catholicism of yesterday. In the second part of my presentation, I will offer some reflections on the conservative opposition in the Church.

Paradigm Shift at the Vatican Council

In the first part of my presentation, I wish to illustrate the paradigm shift that has taken place at Vatican II by giving three examples of

2 Hans Küng, *Christianity: Essence, History and Future* (New York: Continuum, 1996).

3 Hans Küng, *Judaism: Between Yesterday and Tomorrow* (New York: Crossroad, 1992).

4 Hans Küng, *Der Islam: Geschichte, Gegenwart und Zukunft* (München: Pieper, 2004).

5 Patrick Ghanapragmasam and Elisabeth Schüssler Fiorenza, eds. *Negotiating Borders: Theological Explorations in the Global Era* (Delhi: ISPCK, 2008).

startling doctrinal developments. First, the Church defined its relationship to outsiders in terms of dialogue and co-operation. Second, the Church recognized the commitment to social justice as an imperative of the Gospel and hence part of the spiritual life. And third, the Church acknowledged the need to reinterpret its teaching in response to the historical conditions of the present. In the second part of my presentation, I shall turn to the resistance in the Church to these doctrinal changes and the confusion this has created even in the ecclesiastical magisterium.

Dialogue and Co-operation with Outsiders

At the Vatican Council the Church redefined its relationship to outsiders, to dissident Christians, Jews, and members of other religions. In the past non-Catholic Christians, called schismatics and heretics, were regarded as total outsiders, deprived of grace and walking in darkness. In his 1928 encyclical, *Mortalium Animos*, Pius XI still condemned the ecumenical movement initiated by Protestants and Anglicans. He wrote that if the dissident Christians are eager to promote Christian unity, they should become Catholics and start to obey him.[6] In his 1943 encyclical, *Mystici Corporis Christi*, Pius XII still insisted that non-Catholic Christians live lives deprived of the Holy Spirit.[7] Yet, Vatican II's Decree on Ecumenism (*Unitatis Redintegratio*) affirms that, by their faith and their baptism, dissident Christians are incorporated in Christ's mystical body and share with Catholics a spiritual communion, even though an imperfect one. This new teaching, we note, had a prehistory. Prior to the council, a number of Catholic theologians engaged in dialogue with non-Catholic Christians, experienced spiritual communion with them, and produced theological arguments in favour of the Church's participation in the ecumenical movement.

Second, in its Declaration on the Relation of the Church to Non-Christian Religions (*Nostra Aetate*), the Second Vatican Council purified

6 Pius XI, encyclical *Mortalium Animos* (1928), no. 7, accessed 15 October 2009, http://www.vatican.va/holy_father/pius_xi/encyclicals/documents/hf_p-xi_enc_19280106_mortalium-animos_en.html.

7 Pius XII, encyclical *Mystici Corporis Christi* (1943), no. 22, accessed 15 October 2009, http://www.vatican.va/holy_father/pius_xii/encyclicals/documents/hf_p-xii_enc_29061943_mystici-corporis-christi_en.html.

the Christian tradition of the religious rhetoric that produced contempt for Jews and Judaism. Recalling the teaching of St. Paul that God does not repent of his promises and that the Jews remain God's first-loved people, the council declared that God's ancient covenant with the people of Israel remains intact and is a source of grace for them today. Implicit in this declaration is that an organized effort to convert Jews to Christianity is no longer appropriate. Again, the new teaching has a prehistory. In response to the Holocaust, circles of Catholics and Protestants, listening to their Jewish friends, recognized with regret and repentance the anti-Jewish rhetoric that was part of the Christian tradition.[8] They advocated the purification of Christian preaching and offered biblical and theological arguments for respecting post-biblical Judaism.

Third, there were the pagans or infidels. In his apostolic letter of 1919, *Maximum Illud*, Benedict XV still claimed that the infidels "lived in ignorance of God, and thus, bound by the chains of their blind and violent desires, are enslaved in the most hideous of all forms of slavery, the service of Satan."[9] What a leap to the conciliar declaration, *Nostra Aetate*, which honours the world religions, recognizes that the Church shares many truths and values with them, and recommends that Catholics engage in interreligious dialogue and co-operation—for mutual enrichment and the promotion of the common good.

The new conciliar teaching on outsiders demanded important changes in the Church's public worship, in particular the universal prayers offered on Good Friday for the salvation of non-Catholic Christians, Jews, and members of the world religions. In the post-conciliar liturgy, the insulting words of these prayers were replaced by terms expressing respect.[10]

Fourth, at the Second Vatican Council the Church redefined its relation to the world. Consider this opening sentence of the Pastoral

---

8 Christian Rutishauser, "The 1947 Seelisberg Conference," *Studies in Christian-Jewish Relations* 2 (2008), issue 2, art. 6, accessed 15 October 2009, http://escholarship.bc.edu/scjr/.

9 Benedict XV, encyclical *Maximum Illud* (1919), no. 13, accessed 15 October 2009, http://www.svdcuria.org/public/mission/docs/encycl/mi-en.htm.

10 Gilles Routhier, "Adopter la liturgie romaine antérieure à la réforme de 1970, " *Cahier de spiritualité ignatienne* (mai-juin 2008): 97–108.

Constitution on the Church in the Modern World (*Gaudium et Spes*):

> The joys and the hopes, the griefs and the anxieties of the men and women of this age, especially those who are poor or in any way afflicted, these are the joys and hopes, the griefs and anxieties of the followers of Christ.[11]

It would be hard to find a similar sentence in Catholic theological texts prior to the twentieth century. That Catholics are meant to extend their solidarity to all human beings is a spiritual realization that occurred only after World War II, in part as a reaction to the relative silence of the Church during the Holocaust and in part, after the collapse of Western colonialism, as an expression of fidelity to the formerly colonized populations. According to the council, the Holy Spirit summons the Church to universal solidarity, beginning with the poor and afflicted.

According to the Second Vatican Council, the Holy Spirit is present in people, wherever they are, calling them to seek the truth and love peace and justice. The offer of God's grace is universal, as *Gaudium et Spes* affirms:

> Since Christ died for all humans, and since the ultimate vocation of humans is one and divine, we ought to believe that the Holy Spirit in a manner known only to God offers to every person the possibility of being associated with the paschal mystery.[12]

That God is present in the world, sustaining people's efforts to know the truth, do good to their neighbour, and build a just society was strongly emphasized after the council by Pope John Paul II. Here is a famous quotation from his encyclical *Redemptoris Missio*.

> The Holy Spirit manifests himself in a special way in the Church and in her members. Yet his presence and activity are universal, limited neither by space nor time .... The Spirit is at the very source of the human person's existential and religious question-

---

[11] Second Vatican Council, Pastoral Constitution on the Church in the Modern World *Gaudium et Spes*, (1965), [*GS*], art. 1, accessed 2 January 2011, http://www.vatican.va/archive/hist_councils/ii_vatican_council/documents/vat-ii_cons_19651207_gaudium-et-spes_en.html.

[12] Ibid., art. 22.

ing which is occasioned not only by contingent situations, but by the very structure of its being. The Spirit's presence and activity affects not only individuals but also society and history, peoples, cultures and religions. Indeed, the Holy Spirit is at the origin of the noble ideals and undertakings which benefit humanity in its journey through history.[13]

In the sinful world of injustice, arrogance, and superficiality, the Spirit is graciously present, summoning people to create a civilization of peace and justice. The task of the Church is here to discern where the Spirit is at work, thank God for the divine presence, and support the endeavours that serve the common good.

Social Justice, an Imperative of the Gospel

Proposed by the council and emphasized by subsequent ecclesiastical documents is a new teaching dealing with the political meaning of the Gospel, i.e., the divine summons to social justice. Prior to the council, in line with the scholastic tradition, the Church distinguished between the "natural" order, to which people in the world belonged, and the "supernatural" order, to which Catholics were elevated by faith and divine grace. In writing their encyclicals on social justice addressed to men and women of good will, the popes drew their arguments, not from Scripture but from the theory of natural law. The encyclicals did not invoke the love of God and neighbour; they appealed instead to people's natural virtue of justice. According to the scholastic tradition, commitment to justice belongs properly speaking to the natural order; it is not an imperative of the Gospel. As a consequence, the supernatural or spiritual life remained indifferent to issues of social justice. The love of God and the quest of holiness tended to be otherworldly. The spiritual literature used in monasteries and convents, and the books of piety written for lay people, never referred to the social injustices such as wars, conquest, colonialism, exploitation, and unemployment. In those days, the life guided by the Holy Spirit was conceived as quite separate from society.

---

13 John Paul II, encyclical *Redemptoris missio* (1990), no. 28, accessed 15 October 2009, http://www.vatican.va/holy_father/john_paul_ii/encyclicals/documents/hf_jp-ii_enc_07121990_redemptoris-missio_en.html.

An important theological development in the twentieth century questioned the distinction between the natural and the supernatural spheres of life. Thinkers like Karl Rahner and Henri de Lubac revived an ancient theological tradition, based on the Prologue to John's Gospel, according to which God's eternal Word, incarnate in Jesus, addresses the whole of humanity and each individual person. Secular life is not as secular as it looks—for men and women everywhere are summoned by the Holy Spirit to a conversion of the heart, making them seek the truth and do the good. This theological insight was confirmed by the Second Vatican Council.

Abandoning the idea of the two spheres, John XXIII invoked rational ethical arguments as well as the Christian message in *Pacem in Terris* (1963). Promoting peace, social justice, and human rights is now seen as obedience to the Gospel and not simply as a demand of a rational ethic. The subsequent popes adopted the same practice: they presented their teaching on peace and justice as an imperative of the Gospel. John Paul II was quite specific: "spreading the social teaching of the Church pertains to its evangelizing mission and is an essential part of the Christian message."[14] His statement in the encyclical *Laborem Exercens* is even stronger.

> The Catholic Church is firmly committed to the cause (of workers and the poor), for she considers it her mission, her service, a proof of her fidelity to Christ, so that she can truly be the 'Church of the poor' the 'poor' appearing under various forms, in various places, at various times.[15]

Preferential solidarity with the poor—also called "the option for the poor"—in the name of Jesus Christ was widely received in the post-conciliar Church. It found expression in the pastoral statements of the Canadian bishops made in the 1970s and early 80s. Here is one quotation:

---

[14] John Paul II, encyclical *Centesimus Annus* (1991), no. 5, accessed 15 October 2009, http://www.vatican.va/holy_father/john_paul_ii/encyclicals/documents/hf_jp-ii_enc_01051991_centesimus-annus_en.html.

[15] John Paul II, encyclical *Laborem Exercens* (1981), no. 8, accessed 15 October 2009, http://www.vatican.va/holy_father/john_paul_ii/encyclicals/documents/hf_jp-ii_enc_14091981_laborem-exercens_en.html.

> As Christians, we are called to follow Jesus by identifying with the victims of injustice, by analyzing the dominant attitudes and structures that cause human suffering and by actively supporting the poor and oppressed in their struggle to transform society.[16]

Thanks to a remarkable evolution in the Church's understanding of the Gospel, we recognize that implicit in Christian faith is not only an impulse to the love of neighbour but also a summons to solidarity with the poor. Christian spirituality is no longer conceived as politically neutral: it now includes a yearning for the emancipation of the disadvantaged and excluded. This deeper understanding of faith has even been sensed by men and women dedicated to the contemplative life. I am thinking of Madeleine Delbrêl (1904–64) in France and Thomas Merton (1915–68) in the United States, both of whom experienced in their union with God a summons to speak out for justice in society.

The Need of Doctrinal Reinterpretation

The Second Vatican Council recognized that if the Christian message is to be understood and retain its relevance in today's society, it must be reread and adapted as a response to people's problems and questions. Since the appropriate conciliar texts are not well known, I will cite them at some length.

> From the beginning of her history the Church has learned to express the message of Christ with the help of the ideas and terminology of various philosophers, and has tried to clarify it with their wisdom. Her purpose has been to adapt the Gospel to the grasp of all as well as to the needs of the learned .... Indeed this accommodated preaching of the revealed Word ought to remain the law of all evangelization. For thus the ability to express Christ's message in its own way is developed in each nation. At the same time there is fostered a living exchange between the Church and the diverse cultures of people. To promote such an exchange, especially in our days, the Church requires the special help of those who live in the world, are versed in different institutions and specialties, and grasp their innermost significance in the eyes of

[16] E. F. Sheridan, ed., *Do Justice: The Social Teaching of the Canadian Bishops* (Sherbrooke, QC: Éditions Paulines, 1987), 399–400.

> both believers and unbelievers. With the help of the Holy Spirit, it is the task of the entire People of God, especially pastors and theologians, to hear, distinguish and interpret the many voices of our age, and to judge them in the light of the divine Word, so that revealed truth can become more deeply penetrated, better understood and set forth to greater advantage.[17]

Elsewhere, *Gaudium et Spes* affirms:

> Recent studies and findings of science, history and philosophy raise new questions which effect human lives and demand new theological investigations. Within the requirements and methods proper to theology, theologians are invited to seek continually for more suitable ways of communicating doctrine to the men and women of their times; for the deposit or the truths of faith are one thing and the manner in which they are enunciated, in the same meaning and understanding, is another. In pastoral care, sufficient use must be made not only of theological principles, but also of the findings of the secular sciences, especially of psychology and sociology, so that the faithful may be brought to a more adequate and mature life of faith ....
>
> May the faithful live in close union with the other people of their time and may they strive to understand perfectly their way of thinking and judging, as expressed in their culture. Let them blend new sciences and theories and the understanding of the most recent discoveries with Christian morality and the teaching of Christian doctrine, so that their religious culture and morality may keep pace with scientific knowledge and with the constantly progressing technology. Thus they will be able to interpret and evaluate all things in a truly Christian spirit.[18]

These texts taken from *Gaudium et Spes* clearly show that the Church wants theology to be in dialogue with the cultural and scientific self-understanding of contemporary society and to adapt, interpret, or reformulate the Christian doctrine as the saving message for people of the present time. In previous ecclesiastical statements, doctrinal devel-

---

17 *GS*, art. 44.

18 *GS*, art. 62.

opment was always presented as the passage from the implicit to the explicit. These statements did not acknowledge that the Church's entry into a new cultural conditions calls for a rethinking and a reformulation of the divine message, leaving intact the substance of the faith. *Gaudium et Spes* recognizes that at the present time the Church must be open to shifts in the interpretation of its divine message.

The three examples I have chosen demonstrate that at the Second Vatican Council the Catholic Church redefined its presence and mission in the world. In obedience to Jesus Christ and with the assistance of the Holy Spirit, the Church is able to reinterpret its teaching and change its pastoral practice. The Church now sees itself in dialogue with other churches, with Judaism and the world religions, fostering a movement toward mutual understanding, co-operation, and reconciliation. The Church is also summoned by the Gospel to stand against the structures of injustice and exclusion in the local societies and the entire world.

I could have given other examples of the doctrinal evolution introduced by the Second Vatican Council, yet the three examples I have chosen are sufficient to show that what has taken place in the Catholic Church is a paradigm shift. What has been projected is a new form of Catholicism, leaving intact the substance of faith, which is God's self-revelation in Jesus Christ as understood in the Catholic tradition, but responding creatively to the challenges of the present.

Continued Attachment to the Older Paradigm

The older paradigm, the Catholicism of yesterday, did not disappear altogether at the Second Vatican Council. To obtain the approval of the overwhelming majority of the bishops, the conciliar documents that offer the new teaching also include texts that reflect the older paradigm. There are texts that still present the Church as destined to gather in all dissident Christians and convert all non-Christians to the Christian faith. There are still texts that see the Church's mission in society as a spiritual one, located above social and political conflicts. There were also moments when the wish of the majority of bishops to introduce a new perspective was frustrated by the decisions of Pope Paul VI to protect the traditional teaching. For instance, the Pope decided to correct the position of the council on collegiality, thus effectively reaffirming the inherited pontifical centralism.[19] Paul VI also forbad the council to debate the Church's sexual ethics, even though the bishops wanted to raise serious questions in regard to it.[20] While a new form of Catholicism emerged at the Council, it did so in an institutional context marked by ambiguity.

Thomas Kuhn's account of the conflict of paradigms in the history of the social sciences sheds a certain light on what has happened in the Church after the council. Opponents of the new paradigm, deeply attached to the Catholicism of yesterday, created centres and networks that advocate a conservative reading of the conciliar documents and resist the consistent application of the new paradigm. Among these opponents are lay people, priests, bishops, cardinals, and popes. The unresolved conflict between the old and new paradigms has created a certain confusion in the Church.

Dialogue or proclamation?

The first example of this confusion is the Church's official teaching regarding religious pluralism. John Paul II and Cardinal Joseph Ratzinger had different approaches to the world religions: the former emphasized dialogue, while the latter stressed proclamation. Over the years I have followed this lack of unanimity in a series of articles.[21] After the prayer for peace at Assisi in 1984, to which John Paul II had invited representatives of the world religions, Cardinal Ratzinger published an article that criticized the assembly, arguing that Catholics may not pray with members of other religions. The cardinal held that interreligious dialogue, while approved by the Second Vatican Council, was not without danger since it might promote relativism among Catholics.

In the Instruction of the Congregation for the Doctrine of the Faith, *Dominus Iesus*,[22] published in his name in the year 2000, the cardinal

---

19 John W. O'Malley, *What Happened at Vatican II* (Cambridge, MA: The Belknap Press, 2008), 244–46.

20 Ibid., 236–38.

21 Gregory Baum, *Signs of the Times* (Toronto: Novalis, 2007), 122–34; also "Proclamation or Dialogue? Unresolved Questions in Pope Benedict's Teaching," *The Ecumenist* 44 (Winter 2007): 1–4; and "Benedict's Jerusalem Message on Religious Liberty," *The Ecumenist* 46 (Summer 2009): 1–4.

22 Accessed 15 October 2009, www.vatican.va/roman_curia/congregations/cfaith/

claimed that religious pluralism exists only "in fact," but not "in principle," for there exists only one true religion. Since interreligious dialogue brackets the truth-question, the cardinal regarded it as problematic. For the Catholic participants, he laid down, interreligious dialogue is part of the Church's evangelizing mission.

John Paul II continued to tell Jews and Muslims that they and Catholics believed in the same God and that the Church respected their religious tradition. The back-and-forth between dialogue and proclamation continued as Cardinal Ratzinger became Benedict XVI. At Regensburg, Germany, in 2006,[23] Pope Benedict tried to show that Catholics and Muslims do not worship the same God, for which he was severely criticized by Muslim and Christian scholars. A few months later, however, on his visit to Turkey, he adopted the position taken by John Paul II, acknowledging that Catholic and Muslims do worship the same God and recognizing the urgent need for interreligious dialogue.[24] Benedict XVI even said that Catholics and Muslims have a common mission to give witness to God in an increasingly secular world. Yet a year later, in 2007, the Congregation of the Doctrine of Faith published a Doctrinal Note on Some Aspects of Evangelization,[25] repeating the points made in *Dominus Iesus*, claiming that interreligious dialogue had undermined the Church's evangelizing mission and that Catholics who engage in such dialogue must remember that its ultimate purpose is the conversion of the world to the Christian faith. Yet when Pope Benedict addressed a gathering of Christians, Jews, and Muslims in Jerusalem in June 2009,[26] he paid no attention to the doctrinal note. He acknowledged with gratitude that the believers in the three Abrahamic

documents/rc_con_cfaith_doc_20000806_dominus-iesus_en.html.

23 Accessed 15 October 2009, http://www.vatican.va/holy_father/benedict_xvi/speeches/2006/september/documents/hf_ben-xvi_spe_20060912_university-regensburg_en.html.

24 Accessed 15 October 2009, http://www.vatican.va/holy_father/benedict_xvi/speeches/2006/november/documents/hf_ben-xvi_spe_20061128_pres-religious-affairs_en.html.

25 Accessed 15 October 2009, http://www.vatican.va/roman_curia/congregations/cfaith/documents/rc_con_cfaith_doc_20071203_nota-evangelizzazione_en.html.

26 Accessed 15 October 2009, http://www.vatican.va/holy_father/benedict_xvi/speeches/2009/may/documents/hf_ben-xvi_spe_20090511_dialogo-interreligioso_en.html.

traditions hold many common truths about God, God's creation, and humanity's ethical vocation. He even offered a theological justification for interreligious dialogue and emphasized its importance at the present historical moment. Will the Pope change his mind again? On this issue the magisterium is presently inconsistent.

In Jerusalem Benedict also addressed the two chief rabbis who were increasingly afraid, especially after the instruction *Dominus Iesus*, that the Church was changing its mind and again wanted to convert Jews to Christianity. Pope Benedict said to them, "Today I have the opportunity to repeat that the Catholic Church is irrevocably committed to the path chosen at the Second Vatican Council for a genuine and lasting reconciliation between Christians and Jews."[27] But is this definitive?

In 2002 a group of Catholic and Jewish scholars in the US published a document in two sections called "Reflections on Covenant and Mission"[28] that was well received by the American bishops. The Catholic section interpreted *Nostra Aetate* and subsequent Vatican statements on the Jews to say that God's covenant with the Jews remains valid and that the mission to convert the Jews has thus lost its theological legitimacy. Yet conservative Catholic circles in the US opposed this conclusion. Challenged by them, the American bishops decided to publish a statement on June 18, 2009, declaring that Jesus Christ is the saviour of humanity, including the Jews, and that Catholics in dialogue with them may not hide this message from them.[29] When Catholic and Jewish scholars expressed their dismay over this notice, a group of five Catholic bishops published a statement on October 2, 2009, in which they confirm the teaching of the Second Vatican Council, honour present-day Jewish covenantal life as a vital witness to God's saving will, and declare that Catholic-Jewish dialogue is not and will never be a disguise for inviting Jews to believe in Jesus, even if Catholics believe that he, their Lord, is the universal saviour.[30]

---

27 Accessed 15 October 2009, http://www.vatican.va/holy_father/benedict_xvi/speeches/2009/may/documents/hf_ben-xvi_spe_20090512_rabbini_en.html.

28 For the Catholics section of this document see *The Ecumenist* 39 (Spring 2002): 3–6; and for the Jewish section *The Ecumenist* 40 (Fall 2003): 6–10.

29 Jerry Filteau, "Catholic-Jewish Text Under Scrutiny," *National Catholic Reporter*, 10 July 2009, Nation, 11.

30 Accessed 15 October 2009,.http://www.uscatholic.org/news/2009/10/us-bishops-

It is not perfectly clear at this time what the Catholic Church is telling the Jews. Is it "Find in your Jewish tradition the resources for sanctifying your life?" Or is it "Find in your Jewish tradition divine hints that you should become Christian?" At this time, the magisterium is incoherent.

Questioning God's Presence in the World

On God's presence in the world, the old and new paradigms continue to be in conflict. There has always been a difference between John Paul II's and Cardinal Ratzinger's attitudes toward the modern world.[31] Both of them lament the domination of techno-scientific rationality, the decline of ethical reason, and the all-pervasive relativism. Yet John Paul II also gratefully recognized the emancipatory movements in modern society, the struggles for humans rights, just social conditions, peaceful relations, and environmental respect. As we saw in the above-quoted paragraph from his encyclical *Redemptoris Missio*, he attributed these endeavours to God's gracious presence in history. Inspired by the council, John Paul II recognized two faces of the modern world, the dark face produced by human sin and the bright face produced with God's help by people who love justice and peace. Yet Cardinal Ratzinger saw almost exclusively the dark face of modernity. For him, God's redemptive presence was confined to the Church.

I am grateful that in his encyclical of 2009, *Caritas in Veritate*, Benedict XVI offers a radical analysis of the dark face of contemporary society: the dehumanizing impact of ethical relativism and the damaging effects of neoliberal capitalism on the economic and cultural conditions of people in the South and the North. Yet the encyclical does not acknowledge the bright face of modernity, i.e., the masses of people engaged in institutional networks supporting social justice, ecological responsibility, the cessation of war, the demilitarization of society, and the struggle for an alternative globalization serving the common good of humanity. The encyclical follows the preconciliar paradigm that saw the Church as the graced community, the walled garden, surrounded by unbelievers caught in sin and error, waiting in darkness for their

clarify-statement-catholic-jewish-dialogue.

31 Gregory Baum, "The Cardinal and the Pope (II)," *The Ecumenist* 42 (Fall 2005): 16–19.

saviour. The encyclical acknowledges that secular people and followers of the world religions often work for peace and justice, and it urges Catholics to co-operate with them,[32] yet *Caritas in Veritate* does not recognize with John Paul II that their dedication is initiated by the Holy Spirit acting in their hearts. Benedict XVI's inability to recognize God's presence in the world has an effect on the entire Church.

Questioning the Option for the Poor

According to the Second Vatican Council, the commitment to social justice is an imperative of the Gospel. What precisely this commitment means has subsequently been explored by bishops' conferences in Latin America and other parts, including Canada. This commitment is the will to look at society from the perspective of its victims and to offer public support for their struggles for emancipation. This has been called "the option for the poor." Here is a quotation from the statement, "Ethical Reflections on the Economic Crisis," made by the Canadian bishops in 1982.

> As Christians, we are called to follow Jesus by identifying with the victims of injustice, by analyzing the dominant attitudes and structures that cause human suffering, and by actively supporting the poor and oppressed in their struggle to transform society.[33]

At the present time, the option for the poor is being challenged by several currents in the Church's official teaching. There is Cardinal Ratzinger's decades-old campaign against liberation theology that denounces it for relying on Marxist principles and privileging the perspective of the poor and excluded. There is the Pope's warning addressed to missionaries in the global South not to fall prey to political ideologies nor to join partisan movements.[34] Then there is the oft-repeated reminder that Jesus was not a political leader but a religious

---

32 Benedict XVI, encyclical *Caritas in Veritate* (2009), no. 55, accessed 2 January 2011, http://www.vatican.va/holy_father/benedict_xvi/encyclicals/documents/hf_ben-xvi_enc_20090629_caritas-in-veritate_en.html.

33 Canadian Bishops, "Ethical Reflections on the Economic Crisis (1982)," in *Do Justice: The Social Teaching of the Canadian Bishops*, ed. E. F. Sheridan (Sherbrooke, QC: Éditions Paulines), 399–400.

34 Benedict XVI, encyclical *Deus Caritas Est* (2005) # 31b, 33. See Gregory Baum, "Benedict XVI's First Encyclical," *The Ecumenist* 43 (Spring 2006): 11–14, 12.

one. In his book *Jesus of Nazareth*,[35] Benedict argues throughout that Jesus preached a purely religious message devoid of political meaning.[36] The Christians of the second and third centuries, he reports, venerated Jesus as saviour, man of prayer, and philosopher. Benedict never mentions that in the New Testament Jesus is also a prophet in the tradition of Israel. Jesus was condemned by the Sanhedrin, Benedict argues, because his claim to divinity was regarded as blasphemy, and not—as most exegetes claim today—because his prophetic message produced social unrest among the people, something the Sanhedrin, subservient to the Roman Empire, wanted to forestall at all costs. To strengthen his non-political interpretation of the Christian message, Benedict even reminds his readers that St. Paul wanted slaves and slave owners to love one another as brothers, not to challenge the system of slavery.

At the same time, Benedict does hold that Christians must stand up for justice in society. But if the Gospel summons believers to work for justice, how, we may ask, can one still argue that the Gospel is purely religious, devoid of political meaning? Benedict replies to this question. He argues that normally, in most situations, Catholics committed to justice arrive at different political viewpoints: they may become conservative, liberal, socialist, or green. Benedict welcomes this political pluralism in the Catholic community. Yet there are some unusual circumstances, he argues, when Catholics ought to speak to society in a single voice, when the commitment to justice demands resistance to a great evil. Then the Gospel has in fact political meaning. The Pope probably thinks here of the Catholic resistance in Communist countries, or against apartheid in South Africa, or in societies subject to oppression or dictatorship. These are exceptional cases. Normally, and in most cases, Benedict argues, Catholics committed to justice arrive at different political options.

Addressing the Latin American Bishops Conference at Aparecida, Brazil,[37] the Pope acknowledged that to overcome the misery and ex-

---

35 Benedict XVI, *Jesus of Nazareth* (New York: Doubleday, 2007).

36 See Gregory Baum, "Reflections on Pope Benedict's *Jesus of Nazareth*," *The Ecumenist* 44 (Summer 2007): 1–5.

37 Inaugural Session of the Fifth General Conference of the Bishops of Latin America, Aparecida, Brazil, March 13, 2007, accessed 15 October 2009, www.vatican.va/holy_father/

clusion of the masses, structural changes are necessary, yet there is not a single way of achieving this. In other words, since Latin Americans are politically divided, the Church should not identify itself with any political movement. The option for the poor, it would seem, is no longer appropriate.

No New Perspective on Women and Sexuality

Despite the call of the Second Vatican Council for dialogue with contemporary culture, philosophical thought, and the natural and social sciences, the teaching of the Vatican has so far refused to question its traditional teaching on women and human sexuality. The Church's readiness to enter the new paradigm and change its teaching on social issues is not matched by a similar openness in regard to issues involving women and sexual ethics.

The recent ecclesiastical documents on these issues reflect a preconciliar attitude: they have been produced without attention to the teaching of other Christian churches. They defend the traditional Catholic teaching on sexuality against a secular cultural trend that regards sex as sport or entertainment, totally unaware that there are Christian churches that reflect on sexuality in biblical and ethical terms and arrive at different moral norms. Not recognizing that the Christian conscience is divided on many of these issues, the magisterium does not reply to the question raised by many Catholics: "Why is the sexual ethics of their Church so different from that of their Protestant neighbour?"

How can one explain the difference between Catholic and Protestant teaching on these issues? It is well known that conservative Evangelicals tend to agree with Catholic sexual teaching, yet they follow a literalist reading of the Bible that the Catholic Church normally rejects. The question for which Catholics want an answer is why their Church's teaching on women and sexuality differs from that of the Anglican and the major Protestant churches.

Can this difference be explained by the sociology of knowledge? It could be argued that in the Protestant churches the official teaching is produced by a process that involves men and women, young and old

---

benedict_xvi/homilies/2007/documents/hf_ben-xvi_hom_20070513_conference-brazil_en.html.

people, married and single people, and straight and gay people, while in the Catholic Church these decisions are all made by a small number of old bachelors. Yet this is only part of the story. What is special about the Catholic Church is that it must offer its ethical teaching to Catholics living in different cultures all across the globe, while the Protestant and Anglican churches are organized nationally, each with the authority to interpret Christian ethics for its own society, i.e., for people sharing the same culture. Since most people beyond the Western world live in traditional societies, the popes and their advisers believe that they must continue to defend the traditional teaching on women and sexuality. Catholics in Western societies have, to a large extent, decided to take the magisterium on these issues with a grain of salt. I for one find the Anglican teaching on women and sexuality more faithful to Scripture and more convincing than the official Catholic teaching.

Conclusion

I conclude from the study of the conciliar texts that the Second Vatican Council has produced a paradigm shift in the Catholic tradition. The Church has become more critical and, at the same time, more open to the world. The Church has become more critical because it has taken on a prophetic role and denounces injustice and inequality; and it has become more open because it now recognizes God's redemptive action in the world, summoning people to struggle for the humanization and pacification of humanity. At the same time, a conservative movement sponsored by the Vatican itself remains attached to the old paradigm, overlooks the bolds texts of the conciliar documents, and tries to restore the Catholicism of yesterday. The Second Vatican Council may suffer neglect for a certain time, but as an ecumenical council it cannot be invalidated. It is a turning point that cannot be reversed. It is bound to reveal its power in the future.

Théologiens à Vatican II. Notes et carnets, témoins de l'expérience vécue à la Commission doctrinale[1]

Léo Laberge,
Université Saint-Paul

Les sessions de Vatican II nous renvoient aux années 1962-1965. L'annonce du concile et sa préparation, par ailleurs, incluent les années 1960-1962. Si les participants directs ont disparu pour la plupart, la mémoire du concile se retrouve dans une multitude de documents tant officiels que privés, parmi lesquels les notes personnelles des Pères du concile et des autres participants, tels les théologiens et les conseillers des évêques, qui deviennent accessibles dans des archives ici et là dans le monde, tout particulièrement en Europe et en Amérique.

On dispose, bien sûr, des 23 volumes des *Acta et Documenta Concilio Œcumenico Vaticano II Apparando*, ainsi que des 31 volumes des *Acta Synodalia Sacrosancti Concilii Œcumenici Vaticani II*, mais on doit admettre que la consultation n'en est pas toujours facile. En ce qui concerne le détail des travaux des Commissions avant et durant le concile, de nombreux documents tirés des archives personnelles de

[1] Pour alléger, je me contenterai des abréviations suivantes : CT renvoie à la Commission théologique durant la période préconciliaire, alors que CFM renvoie à la *Commissio de doctrina fidei et morum* (ou Commission doctrinale, à partir de la première session du concile).

Pères du concile ou de théologiens deviennent peu à peu accessibles. Bien qu'une partie de ces documents ait été publiée dans les *Acta Synodalia*, en tant que documents soumis au concile, il reste encore beaucoup de textes et de notes qui dorment dans les Archives du concile au Vatican.

Qu'il s'agisse de rapports officiels ou de notes personnelles, la publication progressive de tels textes nous permet de mieux comprendre les enjeux de Vatican II.

Comme l'indique le sous-titre de cette contribution, il sera ici question de Vatican II à partir du témoignage de certains théologiens[2]. En guise de préliminaire, une première partie traitera de ma base documentaire ainsi que de la manière de l'utiliser. La deuxième examinera surtout la phase préparatoire du concile : choix des membres de la CT, méthode de travail. Une troisième partie, que j'intitule « Galerie de portraits », vise à présenter quelques-uns de ces théologiens sur scène, peut-on dire : comment ils agissent et comment on les perçoit.

1. Base documentaire

Je me limiterai aux ouvrages suivants, qui ouvrent bien des fenêtres sur les travaux et les jours, de même que sur le caractère des personnes rencontrées au concile : 1) Yves Congar (1904-1995), *Mon Journal du Concile*[3] (plus de 1200 pages), publié en 2002. Vu le caractère délicat de certaines notes, Congar avait imposé un embargo de publication jusqu'en 2000. 2) Henri de Lubac (1896-1991), *Carnets du Concile*[4] (1200 pages), publié en 2007. Le père de Lubac avait précisé : « Ces pages ne doivent pas être publiées », mais le provincial de France des jésuites et le président de l'Association internationale Cardinal Henri de Lubac ont cru bon de passer outre au vœu exprimé par de Lubac[5].

2 Théologiens, au masculin, vu le très petit nombre de femmes invitées au concile et, encore, non à titre de théologiennes.

3 Yves CONGAR, *Mon Journal du Concile*, présenté et annoté par Éric MATHIEU, Paris, Les Éditions du Cerf, 2002, t. I : LXVII + 595 p. ; t. II : 632 p. [Sera cité CONGAR I ou II, suivi de l'indication des pages.]

4 Henri DE LUBAC, *Carnets du Concile*, introduit et annoté par Loïc FIGOUREUX, Paris, Les Éditions du Cerf, 2007, t. I : L + 567 p. ; t. II : 569 p. [Sera cité DE LUBAC I ou II, et pages.]

5 Voir DE LUBAC I, p. VII-VIII.

3) Gérard Philips (1899-1972), *Carnets conciliaires de Mgr Gérard Philips*, publiés en 2006 (texte original flamand de notes de retraite, avec traduction française et notes)[6]. 4) Sebastian Tromp, s.j., *Diarium/Konzilstagebuch*, vol. I, publié en 2006[7]. Cette première tranche ne couvre que la période qui va du 6 juin 1960 au 11 octobre 1962, soit tout juste avant la première session du concile. On prévoit au moins cinq volumes pour publier la totalité des notes de Tromp. Le texte original est en latin, avec traduction en allemand. L'introduction et les notes critiques sont en allemand.

Comment utiliser ces notes ? Les remarques de Mgr Philips sont extraites de ses cahiers de réflexion spirituelle rédigés lors de retraites. Il s'agit donc d'un retour sur son activité et ses rencontres pour en signaler l'impact dans sa vie. À ce titre, c'est un document précieux pour comprendre ce qui motivait la vie et l'activité de Mgr Philips durant les travaux conciliaires. Notes précieuses, il va sans dire, même si elles sont rédigées avec un certain retard dans le temps. Ce théologien est un prêtre conscient de sa responsabilité dans l'Église, soucieux de vivre en union à Dieu dans l'accomplissement d'une tâche presque surhumaine, étant donné ce qu'on attendait de lui. La fin du concile le trouve physiquement épuisé, victime d'une crise cardiaque.

Les notes du P. Tromp suivent au jour le jour le détail des rencontres avec les personnes, donnent le calendrier des activités de la Commission de théologie ainsi que des sous-commissions, fournissent en résumé la synthèse des thèmes discutés. En annexe[8], on trouve, par exemple,

---

[6] [Gérard PHILIPS], *Carnets conciliaires de Mgr Gérard Philips, secrétaire adjoint de la Commission doctrinale*. Texte néerlandais avec traduction française et commentaires par Karim SCHELKENS. Avec une introduction par Leo DECLERCK. Leuven, Maurits Sabbebibliotheek, Faculteit Godgeleerdheid / Uitgeverij Peeters, 2006, XXVII + 180 p. [Sera cité PHILIPS, et pages.]

[7] Sebastiani TROMP, *Diarium* Secretarii Commissionis Theologicae Concilii Vaticani II, adiunctis Documentis variis, ad fidem manuscriptorum edidit, introductione generali, commentario mulitiplici, notis, indicibus illustravit Alexandra von TEUFFENBACH, versionem germanicam confecit Bruno WEGENER, Vol. I/1 et I/2 : Commissio Praeparatoria (1960-1962) — Sebastian TROMP, S.J., *Konzilstagebuch* mit Erläuterungen und Akten aus der Arbeit der Theologischen Kommission II. Vatikanisches Konzil, herausgegeben von Alexandra von TEUFFENBACH. Band I/1 und I/2 (1960-1962). Rom, Editrice Pontificia Università Gregoriana, 2006, [V p., dont photo du P. Tromp] et 965 p. en pagination continue. [Sera cité TROMP I, et pages.]

[8] TROMP, Vol. I/2, soit à partir de la p. 577.

les procès-verbaux des réunions générales de la Commission, les dates de réunions des commissions et sous-commissions. C'est un précieux instrument pour l'étude, car il s'agit de notes écrites à la plume au fil des jours et qui indiquent tout ce qui concerne la Commission et ses réunions de travail. La lecture peut en être aride, mais ces notes ont été rédigées avec le souci de rendre service à quiconque voudrait par la suite faire des recherches sur les textes de la Commission[9]. Ces notes permettent d'établir le calendrier des rencontres des groupes de discussion et de repérer facilement qui est intervenu lors de ces multiples rencontres.

Les textes du P. Congar et du P. de Lubac nous montrent les réactions de deux grands théologiens, qui font partie de la Commission de théologie dès sa constitution au milieu de 1960. Tous deux arrivent à Rome avec crainte, car ils ont souffert de leur mise à l'écart comme théologiens par les interventions romaines, tout particulièrement du Saint-Office, autour des années 1950. Les interdictions de publier, puis les censures préalables aux publications entretiennent chez eux le soupçon d'être surveillés, de rester toujours suspects d'hétérodoxie possible. Tous deux souffrent aussi dans leur corps, le P. de Lubac éprouvant de fortes migraines depuis la première Grande Guerre et le P. Congar, déjà pris par la maladie qui peu à peu le réduira à l'immobilité. Il n'est que de suivre les notes du P. Congar sur ses déplacements dans Rome où, souvent, il doit s'arrêter car il ne peut plus marcher ou encore sur le fait qu'il ne peut écrire qu'avec peine, tant ses mains lui font mal. On peut aussi constater à quel point il souffre d'insomnie. Le courage, la détermination d'œuvrer de toutes ses forces pour le bien de l'Église n'en sont que plus admirables chez Congar qui rédige son *Journal du Concile*, conscient de la valeur de ses notes pour l'histoire. L'œcuménisme lui tient tellement à cœur qu'il vaut la peine de suivre ses annotations sur ses rencontres avec les représentants des autres Églises au concile. Cela vaut aussi pour ses réflexions, ses conférences, ses interventions pour faire avancer la cause de l'œcuménisme. « Je marche pour que l'Église

9 « Sciat lector me hoc diarium scripsisse haud raro multis aliis laboribus occupatum. Est medium pro illis qui indagant de actis Comm. Doctrinalis. Si sunt errores grammaticales et stilistici [*sic*], immo forsitan reales, eos corrigent et eos tegant mantello amoris », 31 mars 1966 (Tromp I, p. 46).

avance ! » écrit-il en exergue de son journal[10]. Relativement bref pour la période préparatoire[11], de même que pour les périodes entre les sessions conciliaires (une centaine de pages pour chacune), ses notes comptent entre 147 et 208 pages pour chacune des quatre sessions conciliaires[12]. C'est le point de vue, la réaction à chaud d'un théologien qui accomplit sa mission de service de l'Église, en répondant aux questions de qui vient le consulter, Père du concile, théologien ou laïc. Il prépare des esquisses d'interventions pour les évêques, donne des exposés doctrinaux ici et là dans Rome, participe aux réunions officielles comme aux réunions de groupes choisis, groupes d'influence (lobbies), ou tout simplement pour suggérer des corrections ou pour fournir des pistes de recherche.

Les carnets du P. de Lubac consacrent 100 pages à la période préparatoire au concile et plus de 400 pages à la première session du concile[13]. Dans le second tome, la couverture des trois sessions suivantes est plus limitée, ce qui vaut aussi pour les périodes entre les sessions[14]. La couverture très détaillée de la première session montre un P. de Lubac attentif à suivre les délibérations *in aula* ; il est intéressant de voir comment il réagit à ce qui se passe à St-Pierre et comment il prépare ses interventions et ses entretiens avec évêques et théologiens. On peut aussi comparer ce que note des délibérations à St-Pierre le P. Congar.

L'ordre chronologique de ces carnets, les tables des noms de personnes comme les notes ajoutées par les éditeurs nous permettent de glaner bien des renseignements utiles, mais cela ne remplace pas une lecture suivie qui, seule, permet de retrouver le cadre des événements, pour y restituer sentiments et affects profonds.

Que de Lubac et Congar, à la fin de leur vie, aient été nommés cardinaux ne fait que souligner qu'on est passé, à Rome, de la suspicion à la reconnaissance pour le travail accompli par ces théologiens. Ils avaient su gagner la confiance et des autres théologiens et, tout particulièrement, du pape Paul VI.

---

10 Voir Congar I, p. 3, avec la note 1. Citation de s. Thérèse de Lisieux (« Je marche pour un missionnaire »), adaptée par Congar.

11 Congar I, p. 3-104.

12 Voici les références pour les quatre sessions elles-mêmes : Congar I, p. 104-311 ; 401-589 ; II, p. 131-288 ; 387-534.

13 de Lubac I, p. 105-522.

14 de Lubac II, p. 7-58 (2e session), p. 112-343 (3e session) et p. 400-483 (4e session).

Pour une bonne utilisation de ces notes, il est important de les comparer, pour corriger les détails qui peuvent contenir des erreurs ou manquer de nuances dans les appréciations données. Les notes ajoutées par les éditeurs permettent de mieux identifier les participants, soit par des notices biographiques, soit par les tables en fin de volume. On fera bien de s'y référer. Bien sûr, il restera à tirer profit des ouvrages plus nettement historiques, pour compléter le tableau, mais aussi pour élaguer de ces textes ce qui est plutôt anecdotique, approximatif ou trop étroitement personnel.

2. Choix des participants et méthode de travail de la Commission

Jean XXIII avait pris tout le monde par surprise en annonçant la tenue d'un concile. Personne n'avait d'expérience concrète sur la façon d'organiser et de tenir de telles assises. Il fallait donc improviser avec les moyens du bord, et c'est là une des sources de nombreux malaises, car on demanda aux diverses congrégations romaines de voir à faire enquête puis à colliger les remarques envoyées du monde entier à Rome, en vue de préparer des textes pour le concile. En ce qui concerne les questions de foi et de morale (les questions théologiques), cela revint à la Suprême Congrégation du Saint-Office, un titre qui en dit long sur son emprise à la Curie romaine. Comme on peut le constater encore de nos jours, la Congrégation pour la doctrine de la foi conserve toujours un droit de regard sur bien des questions, même après la transformation du Saint-Office.

Le manque d'expérience sur la tenue de conciles a conduit à improviser, car on n'avait pas prévu d'étapes bien marquées conduisant de l'annonce du concile par Jean XXIII à la tenue du concile. Ce sera aussi le lot de bien des interventions durant les sessions conciliaires elles-mêmes. Qu'on songe aux interventions de la Commission centrale ou encore aux interventions qui ont fait rejeter les textes préparés par la CT. Il y a donc eu des groupes de pression tant par les pouvoirs en place que par les pouvoirs qui se taillaient une place au concile, d'où des affrontements, d'où aussi des interprétations *a posteriori* qui demandent d'être appréciées à leur juste mesure. Des théologiens habitués à travailler en cercle fermé, choisis comme membres ou consulteurs du Saint-Office à cause de la sûreté d'une orthodoxie conçue de façon plutôt étroite, mais aussi parce que vivant à Rome et enseignant dans des institutions romaines, étaient davantage portés à examiner et à juger en fonction d'une procédure ancienne où la loi du secret permettait d'intervenir sans toujours avoir à justifier leurs prises de position. Sans trop y réfléchir, cette politique du secret, qui pouvait faciliter le travail initial, a provoqué des mésententes, suscité rivalités et suspicions, ce qui a conduit à créer des blocs d'influence qui s'opposaient, sans toujours se comprendre. Sur un autre plan, la presse et les autres médias ont démontré que la politique du secret fonctionnait mal ; il fallait admettre que le secret et l'improvisation ne pouvaient, à la longue, que causer des problèmes[15].

À l'inexpérience, au secret, il faut ajouter l'incertitude des moyens financiers qui obligea le Vatican à compter sur les moyens du bord plutôt que sur une organisation indépendante et efficace. La conséquence en fut que les premières réunions des commissions se tinrent surtout entre théologiens déjà présents à Rome, ce qui ne put que faire croire aux non-romains qu'on se préoccupait assez peu de leur avis. On n'avait pas prévu que les non-romains auraient dû participer aux réunions, ce qui impliquait de couvrir leurs frais de déplacement. De plus, pour fonctionner efficacement, il aurait fallu mieux pourvoir en personnel les organismes œuvrant pour le concile[16].

---

15 Voir CONGAR I, p. 19 (juillet 1960) : « On me demande le secret, sauf avec les membres de la commission. Or ce secret m'apparaît bien, à certains égards, utile, car l'indiscrétion de la presse ou de l'opinion est catastrophique. Mais aussi un moyen d'atomiser et de neutraliser toute opposition. Il nous réduit pratiquement à l'état d'hommes n'ayant de relations que directement avec Rome, mais pas entre eux : c'est la destruction pratique de la catholicité horizontale, au profit de la seule verticale. Et aussi, à supposer que nous soyons consultés et que nous ayons réagi : nos réactions, demeurées secrètes, sont reçues à Rome, qui peut les passer sous silence et n'en tenir aucun compte impunément. » Voir les remarques de PHILIPS, p. 84, alors qu'il prépare un texte parallèle, au début du concile : « Ce travail est soi-disant secret. Je suis gêné de ne pouvoir parler de cette affaire à mes anciens collègues, les théologiens. Ma situation est délicate : j'ai travaillé au schéma officiel et je propose maintenant de le modifier [...]. Je prévois que l'affaire s'ébruitera à un moment donné et que je serai mis dans une situation très inconfortable. Mais je ne puis refuser ce service demandé par l'épiscopat belge. » Voir TROMP I, p. 825.

16 Un exemple : à la CT, le travail de secrétariat était assuré par du personnel prêté, à temps partiel, par le Saint-Office. Ce n'est qu'en janvier 1961, soit plus de six mois après sa création, que la CT réussit à engager une personne à temps plein (Léo Laberge, o.m.i.),

Une des difficultés majeures dans la méthode de travail vient du fait qu'une fois qu'une ébauche de texte était rédigée, il était concrètement impossible de s'en départir. La discussion portant sur un texte donné, on ne pouvait qu'introduire des corrections mineures, des amendements, sans qu'une vue d'ensemble ait la chance de prévaloir. Ainsi en est-on venu à une impasse, dont la conclusion fut que les textes préparés furent rejetés en session conciliaire, pour être remplacés par des textes préparés en marge des activités officielles[17].

Les premiers membres et consulteurs de la CT venaient du Saint-Office, et ce sont eux qui devaient proposer des noms pour compléter la liste[18]. Parmi les premiers noms suggérés, il faut remarquer ceux des P. Congar et de Lubac à la CT, mais aussi celui de Mgr Marcel Lefebvre, à la Commission centrale. À ce sujet, on peut souligner la remarque du P. Franz Hürth, s.j., en date du 30 juin 1960, qui suggère que la nomination et du P. Congar et du P. de Lubac clouerait le bec à leurs nombreux opposants[19]. Par contre, l'opposition de Mgr Marcel Lefebvre et, surtout, les motifs allégués par lui montrent bien que son entêtement et la pauvreté de sa théologie ne datent pas de l'après-concile. C'est en tant que membre de la Commission centrale que Mgr Lefebvre, le 18 juin 1961, écrit pour montrer son étonnement du fait que les P. de Lubac et Congar étaient membres d'une commission préparatoire[20].

---

pour y travailler au secrétariat. De fait, le P. Michel Leclercq, o.m.i., du Saint-Office, finit par être, lui aussi, au service de la CT durant les années 1961 et 1962.

17 Voir, pour novembre 1962, les remarques de Philips, p. 85-90, à propos du rejet du texte de la CT par le concile, de même que du travail de Mgr Philips sur un nouveau texte qu'il prépare à la demande de plusieurs évêques et, à propos de quoi, on le considère comme « un transfuge et un traître » (p. 86).

18 Voir Tromp I, p. 793-818 (p. 793-806, pour les premières listes).

19 Le P. Hürth, à propos de la nomination possible du P. Congar, note ce qui suit : « non in omnibus traditionalis scientiae theol. sectator ; sed eius nominatio pluribus opponentibus os clauderet » ; au sujet du P. de Lubac, il conclut en ces termes : « Valet quod supra de P. Congar monitum est » (Tromp I, p. 803-804).

20 Dans cette lettre, Lefebvre manifeste son « étonnement au sujet de la nomination de certains conseillers des Commissions préparatoires. / Le faisant, je me suis fait l'interprète de nombre d'évêques et de prêtres qui m'en avaient parlé : / En effet, les noms des Pères de Lubac et Congard [*sic*] sont à juste titre des noms qui évoquent des oppositions à la pensée de l'Église et en particulier à "Humani Generis". Comment ces théologiens d'esprit moderniste ont pu être désignés, nous nous le demandons? /Le Père de Lubac frisa le Pélagianisme et a bien eu quelques divergences avec le Saint-Office, si je ne me trompe. Le Père Congard [*sic*] dans son ouvrage "Essai sur une théologie du laïcat" enseigne des erreurs manifestes » (Tromp I, p. 815).

Les premières ébauches de textes ont été préparées à la fin de 1960 par les théologiens présents à Rome, ce qui ne pouvait que créer très tôt l'impression que les autres théologiens passaient comme figurants, comme le note avec amertume le P. Congar, dans son journal, le 17 novembre 1962[21]. La suite des événements, surtout durant le concile, montre que les « non-romains » ont joué un rôle déterminant, ce qui ne peut être attribué à la seule victoire d'un camp sur l'autre. Au milieu des tensions internes dues au caractère des personnes en présence, il faut souligner le sens de la mission ecclésiale qui motivait les meilleurs de ces théologiens[22].

On a souvent noté, pour l'Église au XXe siècle, l'influence du sérieux et de l'approfondissement portés aux études bibliques, la liturgie mieux connue et mieux vécue, ainsi que la meilleure connaissance des sources de la pensée chrétienne, tout spécialement chez les Pères de l'Église. Comme on le sait, cela ne s'est pas fait sans peine et sans incompréhension ni suspicion de la part de qui restait à l'écart du mouvement, tout en s'appuyant sur ses propres certitudes réaffirmées, mais guère soumises à examen sérieux. Si on ajoute à une activité d'enseignement bien remplie le besoin de donner *sub secreto* un avis sur l'orthodoxie d'écrits qu'on n'a guère le temps d'examiner en profondeur ou qu'on juge forcément à partir d'un résumé tendancieux, à partir d'une théologie traditionnelle axée sur des thèses qui cherchent de simples appuis littéraires tirés de l'Écriture, des Pères et de la raison, on obtient un squelette de notions à défendre et non pas une théologie qui s'enrichit par l'apport d'un enracinement dans l'histoire. On comprend que les P. de Lubac et Congar, dont les écrits avaient été jugés et censurés par ceux-là mêmes qu'ils rencontraient pour la préparation du concile, se sentent mal à l'aise[23].

---

21 Voir CONGAR I, p. 233-234.

22 Voir, par exemple, CONGAR I, p. 20-21 (juillet 1960) ; CONGAR II, p. 510-511 (7 décembre 1965) ; PHILIPS, p. 95 (texte du 10 avril 1963) : « Je ne dois pas penser à l'avenir, mais bien faire ce qui est indiqué continuellement par les événements, dans la conviction que tout se terminera bien, comme le veut ou le permet le Seigneur. Nous ne devons pas désirer être plus intelligent que Lui. Encore une fois : l'*oculus simplex* de l'Évangile et l'écoute réceptive de ce que l'Esprit dit aux Églises » ; voir aussi p. 107. Des remarques similaires pourraient être cueillies dans les écrits du P. de Lubac et chez d'autres théologiens.

23 Cela vaut aussi pour leurs relations tant avec le Maître général des dominicains qu'avec le Père général des jésuites. Voir les références aux noms suivants dans les index :

Au-delà des personnes, il y a l'incompatibilité des approches théologiques. Les débats sur l'Église et le rôle du pape, les discussions sur la liberté religieuse et l'œcuménisme, sans oublier en 1961-1962 les disputes à propos des nombreux textes de la CT, en témoignent nettement. On ne peut certes pas mettre tous les « romains » dans le même camp, ni du reste tous les « non-romains » dans un autre camp, comme on le verra plus loin, dans la présentation de notre galerie de portraits de théologiens[24].

Le temps qui passe, les rencontres qui se multiplient, tout cela contribue à des échanges qui amènent un changement de climat, comme le note le P. Congar[25]. Si la présence de Mgr Philips à la CFM finit par lui donner le rôle principal, pratiquement à la place du P. Tromp, on doit noter que son influence s'exerce dès le début des séances de la CT. Philips et Tromp, en dehors des sessions, peuvent communiquer dans leur langue maternelle ; ils se connaissent et savent respecter leur différence d'approche dans la tenue des débats. On a beaucoup parlé de l'expérience de Mgr Philips, fin connaisseur des procédures parlementaires au Sénat de Belgique, ce qui lui a certes servi. Il faut ajouter à cette compétence le profond respect qu'il manifeste aux personnes qu'il rencontre. Il tâche de les comprendre, en tirant le meilleur parti des suggestions proposées, car il est convaincu que tous et chacun cherchent à rendre les textes meilleurs et susceptibles d'être acceptés par les Pères

Michael Browne, o.p. ; Emmanuel Suarez, o.p. ; Jean-Baptiste Janssens, s.j.

24 Voir Congar I, p. 21-23 (lors d'une rencontre entre Congar et de Lubac à Lyon, le 6 septembre 1960) ; Congar I, p. 47-49 (rencontre Congar-Philips à Louvain en mars 1961) ; de Lubac I, p. 34-36 (19 et 20 septembre 1961) ; voir Philips, p. 86-87 (en référence à novembre 1962) et p. 114-115 (14 novembre 1963) ; je me permets de citer ces quelques lignes à la p. 114 : « Les tensions et les oppositions entre la Curie et surtout le Saint-Office, d'un côté, et la majorité du Concile, de l'autre côté sont intenses. / À la base de ces conflits se trouve aussi l'opposition entre la théologie juridique notionnelle et une théologie de la révélation ouverte qui tient compte du travail scientifique moderne. / Ou autrement dit : la conception angoissée qui veut à tout prix conserver les positions établies, et la tendance qui veut apporter le message évangélique aux hommes » ; voir aussi p. 123-124 (2 août 1964). Le 24 mai 1965, après ses réflexions sur *Lumen gentium* et l'éventualité de devoir aller résider à Rome, il conclut ainsi : « Dommage que nous ne soyons pas plus vertueux : nous découvririons plus facilement la vérité » (Philips, p. 142).

25 Voir Congar II, p. 57 (15 mars 1964) : « Le climat de la Commission théologique a changé. En mieux. Cela tient, je crois : 1°) au fait qu'on se connaît [...] ; 2°) Mgr Philips, qui a la confiance de tout le monde [...] ; 3°) les nouveaux membres. Ils sont tous très bien. Ils sont entrés dans le travail [...]. »

du concile. Plus que de la diplomatie ou une habileté conciliatrice, on a là l'accomplissement de ce que Philips perçoit comme une mission pour le Christ dans l'Église. Ses notes de retraite en témoignent avec la sincérité de qui sait qu'il risque d'y laisser sa santé[26].

Lors de la phase préparatoire du concile (1961-1962), la CT a tenu quatre réunions plénières : le 27 octobre 1960, du 13 au 16 février 1961, du 18 au 30 septembre 1961 et du 1er au 10 mars 1962. Si la première comprend en majorité des « romains », on doit souligner la présence de Mgr Philips à ces assises qui présentent les premières ébauches des projets de constitution. Pour ces quatre rencontres, on dispose des notes et des rapports du secrétaire, le P. Tromp[27].

La première visite à Rome, tant du P. de Lubac que du P. Congar, dans le cadre des réunions de la CT, semble être celle du 15 novembre 1960, alors qu'ils participent à une rencontre ordinaire de la CT. Les 15 et 16 novembre, ils prennent contact avec d'autres membres de la commission, dont le cardinal Ottaviani et le P. Tromp[28]. À la session de février 1961, le P. de Lubac est présent, mais ses Carnets ne permettent guère de voir ce qu'il en pense ; il en retient une mention négative concernant Teilhard de Chardin, dont il sera question plus loin[29]. Faute de rappel et d'invitation explicite, le P. Congar était absent, ce qui le conduit à fournir un commentaire plutôt dur. Il a appris la tenue de la session dans une lettre du P. de Lubac. Je crois qu'il y a eu là un malentendu, attribuable pour une bonne part à un secrétariat trop peu fourni en personnel[30]. Pour la session de septembre 1961, on dispose de remarques du P. de Lubac et du P. Congar[31].

---

26 Philips, p. 94-96 (à propos du 28 février 1963) ; p. 99 (note rédigée le 11 avril 1963) ; p. 107 (bas de page) ; p. 115 (14 novembre 1963) ; p. 126 (10 août 1964) ; p. 144 (24 mai 1965) ; p. 155-156 (1 novembre 1965).

27 Voir Tromp I, p. 579-587 (« Verbalia ») et p. 673-675 (« Relatio ») pour la session d'octobre 1960 ; p. 588-635 et p. 680-688 (« Relatio ») pour la session de février 1961 ; p. 692-723 (« Relatio ») pour la session de septembre 1961 ; p. 730-747 (« Relatio ») pour la session de mars 1962.

28 Voir Tromp I, p. 115, 117 ; de Lubac I, p. 13-16 ; Congar I, p. 33-42.

29 Voir de Lubac I, p. 50-51.

30 Voir Congar I, p. 46-47.

31 Voir de Lubac I, p. 33-58 ; Congar I, p. 60-79.

La quatrième session générale de la CT s'est tenue du 1er au 10 mars 1962, pour mettre au point les textes à imprimer en vue du concile. On pourra enrichir le rapport (la « Relatio ») du P. Tromp par les observations qu'en donnent le P. Congar et le P. de Lubac[32]. Malgré les divergences de fond sur l'approche théologique des uns et des autres, on peut noter, chez le P. Congar, le sentiment qu'il y a progrès. Par exemple : « Le climat est bien différent de ce qu'il était il y a un an. Les consulteurs parlent comme les autres, c'est une discussion libre et fructueuse. [...] en intervenant directement, on arrive souvent, et sans grande difficulté, à faire passer son idée. Je le fais sur plusieurs points[33]. »

La lecture des carnets et journaux du concile permet de dresser un tableau parfois peu flatteur des personnes et des idées qui s'affrontent en cette période de préparation au concile. Il vaudrait la peine de reprendre par tranches, selon une segmentation chronologique, les textes et les discussions qu'ils provoquent. Il est clair que les théologiens les plus actifs dans ces débats savent qu'ils ont une mission à accomplir en Église; c'est pourquoi ils interviennent. Cela vaut certes pour Congar et de Lubac, mais aussi, il ne faut pas l'oublier, pour le P. Tromp et le card. Ottaviani, comme le soulignent ces carnets. Le cardinal était un juriste plutôt qu'un théologien ; il était presque aveugle, ce qui aurait dû le mettre à l'écart, mais il était doué d'une mémoire si vive qu'on oubliait qu'il comptait plus sur ce qu'il entendait que sur ce qu'il voyait. Cela lui permettait aussi d'ignorer telle ou telle demande d'intervention[34].

Une fois le concile commencé, le travail des commissions, en particulier celui de la CFM, est nécessairement axé sur ce qui se discute *in aula*. En conséquence, la CFM reçoit copie des interventions orales comme des interventions remises uniquement par écrit. Durant les

32 Tromp I, p. 730-747 ; Congar I, p. 86-97 ; de Lubac I, p. 59-83.

33 Congar I, p. 86-87.

34 Voir Congar I, p. 37-38 (15 novembre 1960), un texte qui montre le malaise manifeste entre Congar et le cardinal. Le 15 mars 1964, après avoir signalé l'amélioration des conditions à la CFM, le P. Congar note ceci : « Quant au cardinal Ottaviani, il semble qu'il ait pris son parti de certaines choses. Peut-être aussi lui a-t-on fait la leçon en haut lieu. Peut-être est-il objectivement en confiance avec Mgr Philips et en voyant qu'on ne cherche pas la victoire d'une école comme telle... » (Congar I, p. 57). Le P. de Lubac souligne la présence d'esprit du cardinal, dans sa façon de présider les rencontres (de Lubac I, p. 36). Comme exemple cocasse concernant la sélection des intervenants par le card. Ottaviani, voir de Lubac II, p. 80 (4 juin 1964).

années 1963-1965, en plus des nombreuses réunions en commission et en sous-commission, il faut organiser la documentation reçue, la recopier en suivant l'ordre des textes discutés. Puis, avec l'aide des théologiens, la CFM mettra cela sur fiches pour une consultation plus aisée. Dans son rapport du 30 octobre 1963, Mgr Philips note que, à partir des interventions lors de la première session, la CFM a préparé une liste de propositions et corrections de 143 pages grand format, sans interlignes ; sur les interventions lors de la deuxième session, on comptait alors un dossier de 1 800 fiches, composées à partir de près de 400 interventions *in aula*. La commission était alors subdivisée en 7 sous-commissions, plus une sous-commission de supervision générale[35]. En 1963, au secrétariat, mon travail a consisté, pour une bonne part, à réorganiser cette documentation et à la remettre sous forme de polycopies aux participants des sous-commissions de la CFM pour qu'on en tienne compte. Vu que ces textes ont ensuite été remis aux Pères conciliaires pour étude, une bonne part de ce travail a été imprimée dans les *Acta Synodalia* (le tout sous couvert d'anonymat). La méthode de travail de la CFM fut bientôt suivie par d'autres commissions du concile. La fameuse loi du secret permettait de parler librement entre membres des commissions, mais empêchait, au début du moins, d'en parler à d'autres[36].

3. Galerie de portraits

Pour cette partie de mon exposé, je compte présenter deux par deux un certain nombre des membres[37] de la commission, dans le seul but d'illustrer certaines tendances en présence. Par le fait même, on voit le côté bien humain de ces théologiens, avec leurs traits de caractère.

---

35 Voir « De labore Commissionis Doctrinalis Hucusque Peracto, d. 29 m. oct. 1963 », 4 p., voir p. 1-2 [LL 4610-4611].

36 Voir Congar I, p. 36 ; II, p. 32-33, 43. À quelques reprises, le P. de Lubac note sa gêne de ne pouvoir parler librement à des confrères sur des questions discutées à la CT ou à la CFM (voir de Lubac I, p. 7, 14, 36, 50, 58). Voir aussi, plus haut, la note 15 (pour Congar et Philips).

37 Je ne tiendrai pas compte ici de la distinction officielle entre membres et consulteurs.

Sébastien Tromp et Gérard Philips

Inutile ici d'expliquer comment peu à peu Mgr Philips prend la place du P. Tromp, le secrétaire de la commission (l'histoire en est bien connue). Professeur consulté par Pie XII, consulteur du Saint-Office à qui on avait jadis confié des missions délicates aux résultats controversés, le P. Tromp n'hésitait pas à se prononcer parfois rudement, lorsqu'il était question de foi et de convictions personnelles. Il gardait alors son ton professoral et il savait défendre ses thèses[38]. Mgr Philips était professeur de théologie, mais avec le tempérament d'un conciliateur, habitué de la procédure parlementaire. Il faut admirer, chez Philips, l'attention aux autres et tout particulièrement le soin qu'il prit pour n'humilier personne. Malgré les difficultés rencontrées, il réussit à garder un contact correct avec le P. Tromp qui, par ailleurs, sut le reconnaître[39]. Si la position de Philips était délicate, il sut s'acquitter de sa tâche avec maestria : les discussions en commission, la réélaboration des textes, les formules obtenues à la suite de pourparlers et de consultations, tout cela exigea doigté, assurance et sens de l'organisation. À ce sujet, on peut lire bien des remarques chez Congar et de Lubac[40].

Rosaire Gagnebet et Carlo Colombo

Bien que d'orientation théologique différente, les deux savent gagner la confiance de leurs interlocuteurs. Gagnebet, dominicain de l'Angelicum, connaît le milieu romain où il est bien accepté. Au début, le choix de secrétaire à la CT devait se faire entre Tromp et Gagnebet[41]. Par la suite, lorsqu'il fut question de nommer un secrétaire adjoint, le choix devait se faire entre Mgr Philips, qui obtint 16 voix contre 6 au

---

38 Voir Congar I, p. 69, 84, 351 ; II, p. 10, 315 ; de Lubac II, p. 291.

39 Voir Philips, p. 88-89, 100. Sur le travail de la commission et des sous-commissions, voir p. 114-115.

40 Congar II, p. 220 (22 octobre 1964 : « Il [Philips] pacifie et clarifie tout » ; voir p. 283-284 et 359 (Congar y cite un propos du P. de Lubac). À la fin du concile, Congar note, le 7 novembre 1965 : « Mgr Philips est parti au train de 14 h, assez peiné de partir, mais serein. On lui doit tant et tant! Jamais, sans lui, la commission n'aurait fonctionné comme elle a fonctionné, ni n'aurait donné les beaux textes qu'elle a donnés. Il n'est pas seul à avoir mis au monde ces textes, mais il en est pourtant le père » (Congar II, p. 465) ; voir, déjà, la remarque du 25 novembre 1963 : Congar I, p. 567.

41 Voir Tromp I, p. 761.

P. Gagnebet[42]. Colombo était professeur de théologie à Milan. Modéré et accueillant, on perçoit chez lui une ouverture d'esprit qui explique que le cardinal Montini de Milan lui faisait confiance (son nom ne figurait pas sur les premières listes de noms)[43]. Il est nommé le 13 août 1960, probablement sur la recommandation du cardinal Montini[44]. Congar découvre assez tôt la qualité de ses interventions[45]. À partir de la deuxième session du concile, on sait que Mgr Colombo a ses entrées chez Paul VI, qui tient à le rencontrer. Des messages ou de simples suggestions peuvent ainsi être transmis de part et d'autre. Par les journaux et notes de nos théologiens, on voit que la discussion avance, sans qu'intervienne une décision venue d'en haut de façon autoritaire, mais on tient compte des observations transmises. Par Mgr Colombo, on apprend aussi comment Paul VI suit les travaux du concile[46]. Le P. Congar sait avoir recours à Mgr Colombo pour faire passer certaines suggestions personnelles qui donnent des résultats concrets[47]. Le P. de Lubac note le 10 novembre 1964 que d'aucuns manifestent « sinon de l'hostilité, du moins une certaine réserve et un *a priori* critique à l'égard de Paul VI. [...] On s'impatiente contre Mgr C. Colombo, dont quelques-uns estiment le rôle indiscret. Tout cela n'est pas de très bon augure[48]. » Mgr Philips, lui aussi, est en bons termes avec Colombo : « Parmi les

---

42 Voir Philips, p. 116 ; Congar I, p. 582 ; de Lubac II, p. 57. Sur la place des Belges, voir la remarque de Congar I, p. 582, et de Lubac II, p. 370.

43 Voir Tromp I, p. 793-810.

44 Tromp I, p. 814 ; voir p. 287. Le 24 septembre 1961, le P. de Lubac note : « D'après le Père Congar, c'est Mgr Montini qui a réussi à imposer don Carlo Colombo, du grand Séminaire de Milan, à la commission théologique. On sent bien en effet qu'il ne fait pas partie du sérail » (de Lubac I, p. 39).

45 Congar I, p. 83 (23 novembre 1961) : « Ce sont les P. Lécuyer, Mgr Philips et Mgr Colombo qui, avec finesse, douceur, obtiennent la meilleure audience pour les bonnes idées ou qui, sans en avoir l'air, assouplissent les formules jusqu'à les rendre inoffensives. On leur doit beaucoup. »

46 Voir Congar II, p. 28, 29, 178-179, 411, 495.

47 Voir Congar II, p. 243, 267, 269, 389, 514. Après le concile, le 28 septembre 1966, Congar note que Paul VI souhaite rencontrer des théologiens, en dehors d'audiences formelles (Congar II, p. 538). Dans II, p. 110-114, Congar parle de sa visite chez Paul VI, le 8 juin 1964.

48 De Lubac II, p. 290 ; voir aussi II, p. 338-339. Le P. de Lubac note des visites de Colombo à Paul VI, p. 362, 388, 399 : par une lettre de Daniélou, de Lubac (10 septembre 1965) apprend que Paul VI désire le rencontrer, ce qui aura lieu le 5 décembre 1965.

Italiens, seul C. Colombo semble ouvert aux nouvelles perspectives[49]. » En novembre 1964, Mgr Philips relate en détail les tractations entre lui et Paul VI par l'intermédiaire de Mgr Colombo[50].

Le P. Gagnebet, pour sa part, est moins connu. Conscient de sa mission de théologien vivant à Rome, il intervient parfois assez rudement, par exemple en novembre 1962, à propos du texte parallèle présenté par Mgr Philips, à la demande d'évêques belges[51]. Par la suite, il se présente comme bon interlocuteur et comme personne avenante, qui respecte les autres et cherche à les rejoindre[52]. On voit le P. Congar lui accorder peu à peu pleine confiance[53]. Le P. de Lubac le trouve aimable, mais conscient de son importance[54].

Piolanti et Lattanzi, de l'Université du Latran

Piolanti était recteur et Lattanzi, doyen de la Faculté de théologie. Je me garderai bien d'en faire des épouvantails, mais ils donnent de la théologie une image peu agréable.

On connaît le rôle du Latran dans la campagne contre le Biblicum[55]. On soupçonne là-dessous une rivalité entre institutions, en vue de voir l'Université du Latran recevoir une reconnaissance pour son enseignement plus « orthodoxe » de l'Écriture Sainte[56]. Le 20 décembre 1960, le P. Tromp note que Lattanzi a envoyé aux P. Gagnebet et Tromp une lettre peu amène regrettant qu'on ne lui ait pas confié la rédaction du premier

---

49 Philips, p. 89.

50 Philips, p. 134-138.

51 Philips, p. 86-87 et la note 32, p. 159.

52 Philips, p. 88, 109.

53 Congar I, p. 39-40 ; II, p. 81. D'après Tromp, la première impression de Congar sur Gagnebet aurait été plutôt négative, lors de la visite de Congar à Tromp le 16 novembre 1960 : « Putat Patrem Gagnebet esse mentis nimis arctae » (Tromp, I, p. 117).

54 De Lubac I, p. 80 : « Le Père Gagnebet, à son tour, se montre aimable [...]. (J'ai remarqué, au cours des séances, qu'il a un aplomb, une assurance, une conscience de son rôle de "grand théologien", extraordinaires) » ; voir I, p. 125, 151, mais aussi II, p. 69 ; pour finir sur un ton positif, voir II, p. 426.

55 À partir d'un article de Mgr Antonino Romeo, « L'enciclica "Divino afflante Spiritu" e le "Opiniones Novae" », *Divinitas*, 4 (1960), p. 387-456. Voir, par exemple, Congar I, p. 49-51 ; de Lubac I, p. 26-32.

56 Voir de Lubac I, p. 27.

chapitre sur l'Église, car cela revenait au Latran[57] ! Verbomoteurs, les deux théologiens du Latran indisposent leurs confrères, car plus souvent qu'à leur tour ils coupent la parole aux autres et Piolanti, par sa voix forte, enterre les autres. De plus, il ne se gêne pas pour déblatérer contre les autres théologiens jugés ni plus ni moins hérétiques[58]. En somme, ce n'était que recherche de pouvoir et d'influence par des moyens peu acceptables. On doit ajouter que la réputation et l'influence de nos deux héros n'a fait que décliner par la suite.

René Laurentin et Jean Daniélou : les journalistes au concile

L'abbé Laurentin doit sans doute sa nomination à la CT au fait qu'il est mariologue et que le P. Balić se construisait de bons appuis en prévision des discussions sur la Vierge Marie[59]. On sait, par ailleurs, que Laurentin, durant le concile, est journaliste pour *Le Figaro*[60]. C'est Balić, encore une fois, qui pourra se vanter d'avoir fait nommer Laurentin comme *peritus* au concile[61]. Quant au P. Daniélou, son rôle officiel commence avec la première session du concile en octobre 1962, ce qui n'exclut en rien sa présence et son influence auprès de plusieurs intervenants avant et durant le concile. L'un et l'autre sont habiles pour

---

[57] Voir TROMP I, p. 343, 347 et 359 : Tromp retire son propre texte. Voir CONGAR I, p. 86, 93-94. Je cite I, p. 351 (11 mars 1963) : « Les types les plus ennuyeux sont, pour le fond, le cardinal Browne, mais qui reste très humble et très honnête — et, extérieurement, Dhanis et Lattanzi. »

[58] Voir CONGAR I (novembre 1960), p. 26-27 : « À la séance de rentrée, Mgr Piolanti a déclaré : de même que l'église S. Jean du Latran est la première de toutes les églises, de même l'université du Latran doit être la première des universités. / Mais ça ne se décrète pas. Pas plus qu'on ne peut nommer un poète par décret consulaire. » Voir aussi I, p. 49-50, 91, 176, 515-516 (Congar y note l'intervention de Paul VI faisant la leçon au Latran, le 31 octobre 1963). Jugement sévère, là aussi, du P. de Lubac : DE LUBAC I, 22, 27, 31-32, 45 (27 septembre 1961) : « Mgr Garofalo avait fait, au nom de l'exégèse, une longue intervention embrouillée, qui s'était prolongée en duel avec Mgr Piolanti. Flots d'éloquence et gestes théâtraux de Piolanti, qu'on ne parvenait pas à faire taire. Beaucoup s'amusaient de ce duel. La scène était en effet comique. Plusieurs avaient la simplicité de penser que c'était quand même une belle bataille théologique. » Voir aussi les p. 52-53, 55, 197-198, 289-290 ; II, p. 9 (intervention de Paul VI) et p. 412.

[59] TROMP I, p. 796, 799 et 809 (juin-juillet 1960).

[60] Voir, par exemple, CONGAR II, p. 471, et la note de l'éditeur dans CONGAR I, p. 18, note 3 ou DE LUBAC I, p. 65, note 2.

[61] Voir de LUBAC I, p. 238.

recueillir renseignements et nouvelles ; on les sent omniprésents, prêts à fournir des notes à droite et à gauche, ce qui ne manquera pas de susciter méfiance ou gêne[62].

Apprenant la nomination de Laurentin, Congar note à son propos : « me fait craindre qu'on ne projette des doctrines mariales[63] ». Toutefois, en septembre 1961, Congar reconnaît les qualités de Laurentin : « La discussion est d'abord assez rude. Heureusement, Laurentin est courageux, mesuré et informé[64]. » Mais la façon d'agir de Laurentin peut exaspérer les gens. Le 3 novembre 1962, au milieu d'un petit groupe de théologiens d'évêques, Congar répond aux questions durant deux heures. Il remarque : « Laurentin prend des notes, questionne, fait répéter pour mieux noter : prépare-t-il un livre[65] ? » Tout cela suscite contre lui certaines préventions, comme il l'indique à Congar le 2 juin 1964[66]. Par ailleurs, le P. de Lubac reproche à Laurentin d'avoir publié dans *Le Figaro* du 9 décembre 1963 « un article tendancieux et malheureux » à propos d'une fête en l'honneur du P. Congar le 8 décembre au Saulchoir[67].

Le P. Daniélou s'attire, lui aussi, des manifestations de méfiance vu son style et sa nervosité légendaire. Sa notion de propriété intellectuelle paraît jouir d'une interprétation très large (est-ce dû à une habitude d'échange de travaux dans la Société de Jésus ?). Le P. Congar, le 23 fé-

---

62 Voir CONGAR I, p. 330.

63 CONGAR I, p. 18. Voir aussi I, p. 22. À la p. 27, Congar a cette bonne remarque, à propos des développements mariologiques : « Le mieux — et ce serait la tendance du P. Tromp — serait de faire une déclaration synthétique liant Marie au Christ et à l'Église. » Voir aussi les remarques au sujet de Laurentin, I, p. 557, et II, p. 51-52 (Congar note que Mgr Philips est exaspéré).

64 CONGAR I, p. 67 ; voir aussi p. 73.

65 CONGAR I, p. 180 ; voir II, p. 143 : « Pendant la conversation, une fois de plus Laurentin tire son carnet et prend des notes. Il ne se rend pas compte à quel point il est pénible ainsi. » Voir II, p. 471, 497-498. Congar (10 octobre 1962 : I, p. 105) écrit : « Je reçois une visite de Laurentin qui me paraît être devenu impossible, très mouche du coche, arrangeant des trucs, sautant sur tout ce qu'il peut utiliser, tout ce dont il peut faire son profit. Si je ne le connaissais pas, je dirais : intrigant. » Voir encore I, p. 188, 190, 258, 322.

66 Voir CONGAR II, p. 89, 93-94.

67 Voir DE LUBAC II, p. 59 : « D'une part, l'optique de tout l'article est d'un "provincialisme" français outrageant. D'autre part, il parle du concile comme si celui-ci avait ratifié, pris à son compte, tout le mouvement français "d'avant-garde" » (toute cette page est à lire). Voir, de plus, II, p. 464-465. Le P. de Lubac émet une appréciation plus favorable dans II, p. 409-410.

vrier 1963, reçoit de la part de Mgr Léon-Arthur Elchinger un certain nombre de remarques sur ce qui se passe à Rome durant l'intersession. À la suite de quatre observations de Mgr Elchinger, Congar écrit que Mgr Elchinger a « vu le P. Daniélou pendant deux heures, mais sans cesse dérangé par le téléphone. Daniélou, me dit-il, travaille comme un journaliste. Beaucoup se plaignent de lui. De plus, il arrange les textes à sa façon […]. De fait, il a arrangé et coupé mes textes [c'est Congar qui s'exprime] ; il en a publié un sous mon nom (avec Holstein) que je n'ai jamais envoyé ; il a raccourci celui du P. Lécuyer à sa façon. Laurentin était aussi très monté sur ce point[68]. » Ailleurs, on note à plusieurs reprises chez Congar des signes d'impatience devant Daniélou[69]. Il sait toutefois reconnaître la qualité de son travail : « Daniélou est vraiment extraordinaire. Il va vite, trop vite, mais il a un don exceptionnel de présence et d'aller à l'essentiel[70]. » Selon le P. de Lubac, Mgr McGrath hésite à inviter Daniélou à l'Université Notre Dame (pour 1966), « le trouvant quelquefois trop rapide dans sa réflexion théologique[71] ». Chez Mgr Philips aussi, on rencontre les traits déjà notés par d'autres à propos de Daniélou. Par exemple : « Il [Daniélou] m'envoie aussi des textes qui emploient en partie les miens[72] » ; « Daniélou est souvent agité et un peu confus ; il passe d'une chose à l'autre. » C'est le côté humain des grands hommes !

Philippe Delhaye et Ermenegildo Lio

Les deux font partie de la CT dès les débuts et s'occupent de théologie morale. Le chanoine Delhaye, alors professeur à Lille, donnait aussi des cours à Montréal, ce qui peut expliquer que le cardinal Léger l'ait

---

68 Congar I, p. 328-329.

69 Voir Congar I, p. 151, 317 ; je cite, p. 157 : « Daniélou, qui prépare d'autres schémas et refait un peu tout le concile […] » ; voir I, p. 181, à propos des textes Daniélou-Rahner (jugement de Congar à nuancer ; de Lubac I, p. 114, fait mention, lui aussi, de la possibilité d'une fusion de texte Daniélou-Rahner) ; au sujet d'une rédaction de texte Rahner-Ratzinger, voir Congar I, p. 201-204. Autres remarques sur Daniélou : Congar I, p. 459 ; II, p. 312, 434-435, 440. Rapportant un propos de Rahner (16 octobre 1965) : « Rahner me dit : Daniélou me tape sur les nerfs au plus haut point, par sa façon de reprendre une minute après, comme sienne, une idée qu'on a exprimée et qu'il avait d'abord écartée… »

70 Congar I, p. 298. Voir I, p. 332-334 et 368-369.

71 De Lubac II, p. 387.

72 Philips, p. 91-92 ; voir p. 93, pour la citation suivante.

choisi comme conseiller. D'une grande susceptibilité, il se sent souvent incompris ou mis de côté, ce qui peut faire comprendre certains commentaires plutôt acerbes de sa part[73]. On sait que la morale était et est restée un sujet délicat ; on sait que les textes sur la question venaient surtout de moralistes peu influencés par les renouveaux, tant biblique que patristique. Le P. Franz Hürth, s.j., n'avait plus la force et l'acuité intellectuelle pour animer la discussion et le P. Bernard Häring, c.ss.r., ne faisait pas partie des premiers rédacteurs de textes, même si, très tôt, son influence fut marquante[74]. Assez rapidement, le P. Congar prend ses distances par rapport au chanoine Delhaye : « Il y a, dans ses réactions, un facteur personnel et passionné vraiment gênant. J'ai l'impression que nous ne sommes pas tout à fait au même diapason[75]. » Le P. de Lubac, en septembre 1961, fait état des âpres discussions au sujet de la morale, selon ce que lui en dit Delhaye[76]. Le P. de Lubac introduit ces propos par le détail suivant : « Le Chanoine Ph. Delhaye, vu ces jours derniers, est fort mécontent (c'est son habitude). »

Le P. Lio, franciscain, professeur à l'Antonianum, « l'un des principaux auteurs des schémas moraux de la commission théologique préparatoire », comme le note le P. de Lubac[77], illustre assez bien les tendances dites romaines. Le 24 octobre 1962, il publie un article dans l'*Osservatore Romano* et écrit, entre autres choses : « Négliger la doctrine *de fide et de moribus*, qui a demandé un si gros travail au cours de la préparation du concile, ce serait non seulement faillir aux promesses données par le pape… mais ce serait de plus faillir à ce que le monde attend aujourd'hui. » À quoi le P. de Lubac joint la remarque suivante : « Quelqu'un me fait remarquer que le travail du P. Lio est faible et que

73 Voir Tromp I, p. 261, à propos de textes qu'il n'aurait pas reçus. Voir Congar I, p. 64 : frustré qu'on n'ait pas tenu compte de ses remarques, Delhaye « se retire sous sa tente et grogne à part lui » ; I, p. 66 : à propos de Mgr Janssen, du chanoine Delhaye et du P. de Lubac : « Ils sont découragés et aigris. On n'a tenu et on ne tient aucun compte de leur avis. Tout se passe entre Romains. »

74 Voir Congar I, p. 79 (28 septembre 1961) : « Le P. Häring parle au nom d'une large expérience pastorale, catéchétique. Il prend les choses très tragiquement. Mais je suis de son sentiment pour le fond » ; de Lubac I, p. 79 (10 mars 1962) : « Le Père Häring, homme bon, évangélique, qui voit, peut-être à l'excès, les défauts du milieu romain. »

75 Congar I, p. 74.

76 De Lubac I, p. 40-41. La citation se trouve à la p. 40.

77 De Lubac I, p. 237. L'article de Lio est cité d'après ce qu'en rapporte le P. de Lubac.

le monde ne l'attend pas particulièrement[78]. » En 1964, le P. Lio avait encore l'oreille du cardinal Ottaviani, comme le note de Lubac. À propos de mariage et de famille, le P. Häring avait expliqué le sens et l'ordre d'un texte à ce sujet. Je cite de Lubac : « Ottaviani : Interrogeons le P. Lio. — Lio (qui se trouve là pour la première fois) : Nous avons eu de très longues discussions, les avis n'étaient pas concordants, et voici que le schéma nous propose uniquement les conceptions du P. Häring : or il ne tient pas compte de l'ordre objectif : il parle seulement de l'amour[79]. » Le P. Congar, quant à lui, notait le 2 mars 1963 que le P. Lio essayait constamment de réintroduire des points de vue déjà mis de côté[80]. On comprend que la conciliation n'était pas facile et que, pour répondre aux exigences des uns et des autres, les textes donneront l'image réelle de compromis sur lesquels il sera tentant de revenir par après !

Charles Balić et Karl Rahner

On a là deux personnalités fortes, imposantes, aux caractères bien tranchés. Balić, éditeur de Duns Scot, est mieux connu pour son activité dans le domaine de la mariologie. Bon organisateur, il fait flèche de tout bois ; charmeur, il peut embrigader toutes les forces disponibles pour promouvoir sa cause. Il fait nommer des mariologues à la CT ; il intervient auprès des évêques et des cardinaux. On peut dire que, par réaction, il a obligé les évêques et les théologiens à se prémunir d'un minimum de prudence face aux exagérations en ce domaine. Pour contrer le zèle du P. Balić, qui prônait une mariologie envahissante, les théologiens, puis les Pères du concile ont dû répondre aux questions et aux objections que soulevaient cette surenchère concernant la piété mariale et la réflexion théologique qui l'accompagnait[81]. Bien sûr, le

---

78 De Lubac I., p. 238. Voir la remarque du P. de Lubac au sujet d'un autre article de Lio, de décembre 1962 : de Lubac I, p. 529.

79 De Lubac II, p. 100-101. Voir Congar II, p. 110, sur cette discussion du 6 juin 1964.

80 Congar I, p. 332 : « [Lio] veut ramener tous les textes des schémas officiels. » Voir la remarque du P. Louis-Joseph Lebret rapportée par Congar II, p. 315 (3 février 1965) : « Le P. Lebret me dit : Nous avons, dans notre sous-commission (économie) un Père franciscain qui bloque tout! Il s'appelle Lio… »

81 Le 30 septembre 1964, Philips avait discuté longuement à St-Pierre avec Balić sur le texte concernant la Vierge Marie. Philips fait allusion au besoin de renvoyer le texte en commission ; il fait aussi état de la prudence demandée par Paul VI (Philips, p. 131).

P. Congar perçoit clairement les manœuvres de Balić et il s'en méfie quelque peu[82]. Quant à la réflexion en concile sur la Vierge Marie, Congar ne prend pas la chose à la légère : « Je vis là le drame qui accompagne toute ma vie : la nécessité de lutter, au nom de l'Évangile et de la foi apostolique, contre un développement, une prolifération méditerranéenne et irlandaise, d'une mariologie qui ne procède pas de la Révélation, mais à l'appui des textes pontificaux[83]. » Balić voulait un texte à part pour la Vierge Marie ; on optera, en fin de compte, pour un huitième chapitre de *Lumen gentium*. Par ailleurs, Balić et d'autres romains craignent toujours qu'on enlève au pouvoir du pape pour en donner aux évêques[84]. L'opposition entre Congar et Balić devient si forte que certains propos de Balić sur le P. Congar, tels que rapportés par le P. Henri-Marie Féret, forcent Congar à riposter par une lettre à Balić[85]. Comme le franciscain a le don d'exaspérer le dominicain, Congar ne se gêne pas pour introduire des remarques caustiques sur le mariologue[86].

Pour sa part, le P. de Lubac évoque bien les difficultés survenues dans l'élaboration de ce qui deviendra le chapitre 8 de *Lumen gentium*[87]. Le 30 octobre 1962, de Lubac note : « Le P. Balić, OFM, continue de me battre froid, depuis que j'ai marqué quelques réticences devant ses projets mariologiques trop amples[88]. » Plus modéré que Congar dans son appréciation du franciscain, de Lubac le juge cependant

---

82 Congar I, p. 17 (juillet 1960) : « Balić, qui ne pense qu'à superexalter Marie pour faire avancer la "cause [de béatification]" de Scot ». Voir, pour les 21 et 22 septembre 1961, les séances parfois orageuses à propos du chapitre sur la Vierge Marie, dans Congar I, p. 64-67.

83 Congar I, p. 66-67. Sur tout cela, voir l'appréciation plus nuancée de Congar, le 1er février 1964 : II, p. 12-13. Pour la suite des discussions (et les sautes d'humeur de Congar à propos de Balić), voir Congar I, p. 83, 89, 451-452, 482 ; II, p. 14-15, où Congar s'explique ; voir aussi II, p. 52, 201.

84 Voir Congar I, p. 333 ; II, p. 92.

85 Congar I, p. 486 (20 octobre 1963).

86 Congar I, p. 66 : « notre camelot dalmate » ; II, p. 90 : « Balić (qui vend des tapis ou des bretelles! Bateleur de foire!!!) » ; II, p. 92 : « Balić nous donne un magnifique numéro de cirque » ; II, p. 175 : « Balić est plus batteleur [*sic*] de foire que jamais. »

87 De Lubac I, p. 76-77 ; I, p. 382 ; II, p. 63-68.

88 De Lubac I, p. 191 ; voir p. 200.

parfois ridicule[89]. Il ose même lui adresser des reproches à la fin des interventions *in aula*, le 17 septembre 1964. Je cite de Lubac : « Il me dira, vers la fin, d'un air de triomphe : "Ah ! La Sainte Vierge se défend bien, aujourd'hui !" Je lui réponds en posant ma main sur son bras : "Père Balić, ne parlez pas ainsi, c'est mal. Personne ici n'a attaqué la Sainte Vierge ; tout le monde la défend." Il ne paraît pas content[90]. » Bien que les notes du P. Tromp ne couvrent que les années 1960-1962, on peut signaler sa remarque inscrite le 25 mai 1961, après une séance de la sous-commission sur l'Église ; il constate que le P. Balić intervient tout le temps, défendant le pour et le contre. C'est la confusion. Selon une remarque du P. Gagnebet, deux heures perdues[91].

La nomination du P. Karl Rahner à la CT n'est pas venue tout de suite. Dans la liste des membres et consulteurs des commissions préparatoires, son nom figure dans la liste publiée le 25 novembre 1961 à la Commission de la discipline des sacrements. De fait, sa nomination avait été refusée pour la CT, comme on peut le voir dans la correspondance et les notes publiées en annexe au journal du P. Tromp[92]. À l'Arbresle (6-9 avril 1961), Congar rencontre le P. Rahner ; il fournit les détails suivants : « Il a contre lui le card. Ottaviani, qui résumait récemment sa position sur la Messe, en ces termes : pour Rahner, une messe pieuse est préférable à cent messes non pieuses… Il y a donc barrage contre lui. Mais le card. König et deux ou trois autres évêques ont insisté pour qu'on le nomme à une commission du concile. On vient de le nommer consulteur à celle des Sacrements… il voit là une dérision[93]. »

---

89 Voir DE LUBAC I, p. 112 ; II, p. 76-77.

90 DE LUBAC II, p. 121-122.

91 TROMP I, p. 223. Voir les notes de PHILIPS, p. 93, 116, 131.

92 TROMP I, p. 816-818. Entre le 14 octobre et le 11 décembre 1960, il y a eu, selon Tromp, les interventions du P. Josef A. Jungmann, s.j., et de Mgr Josef Höfer pour faire nommer Rahner à la CT. Le P. Tromp clôt ce dossier par ces mots écrits à la suite d'une lettre de Mgr Höfer (6 déc. 1960) : « 11 Dec. Responsum dedi Em[inentissimum] Card[inalem] petitioni satisfacere non posse, meque post decisionem Em[inentissimi] ulterius insistere non posse / Seb. Tromp sj. » Voir aussi TROMP I, p. 133 + 135 (rencontre avec Höfer le 15 déc. 1960) et p. 199 (23 mars 1961) : « Audio R. Patrem Car. Rahner SJ fuisse nominatum membrum Commissionis de Sacramentis ».

93 CONGAR I, p. 54 ; voir DE LUBAC I, p. 23-24, qui, le 20 novembre 1960, note « que plusieurs s'étonnaient de l'absence du P. Karl Rahner à la commission ; il [Michel Leclercq] m'a répondu qu'il y avait eu un barrage » ; I, p. 94-95, de Lubac note, le 8 octobre 1962, que

Rahner fera partie de la commission doctrinale (CFM) dès le début du concile ; son travail tant à la CFM que pour de nombreux évêques, spécialement les évêques allemands, aura une influence considérable[94]. Il a trouvé en Jean XXIII un défenseur ; Paul VI lui manifestera, lui aussi, sa confiance[95]. Si le style de Rahner en allemand donne des textes difficiles à lire, on a remarqué, parfois avec humour, que ses exposés en latin étaient brefs et précis, ce qu'il reconnaissait comme favorisé par le fait de devoir s'exprimer en une langue étrangère. Ses interventions à la CFM sont parfois source d'impatience chez Congar[96]. Mgr Philips perçoit les difficultés que peuvent rencontrer ceux qui affrontent le P. Rahner[97]. Pour nuancer le jugement porté par Congar, il vaut la peine d'ajouter cette remarque faite après le concile, lors d'une rencontre du Secrétariat pour les non-croyants, le 24 septembre 1966 : « Rahner, dès qu'il parle, a UNE PLÉNITUDE de pensée, d'HUMANITÉ de parole, de courage et de loyauté. C'est vraiment un seigneur[98]. »

---

la censure préalable du Saint-Office concernant la publication d'écrits par Rahner vient d'être levée ; voir aussi I, p. 106, selon quoi Jean XXIII « se serait fâché très fort contre la mesure prise par le St-Office au sujet du P. Karl Rahner ».

94 Voir DE LUBAC I, p. 234-235, 264, 324-327. De Lubac (I, p. 521) cite un article de la revue américaine *Time* (14 décembre 1962) qui voit en Rahner « le plus profond théologien d'aujourd'hui. L'article est assez bien documenté ». À la p. 528 (12 janvier 1963), de Lubac (p. 528) note qu'à une demande du card. Ottaviani « de chasser de Rome Karl Rahner », Jean XXIII aurait répondu « qu'il ne voulait pas attenter aux droits des évêques ; il en profita pour montrer à Ottaviani le témoignage de trois cardinaux en faveur de Rahner ». Mais les opposants ne désarmaient pas : selon Congar (I, p. 287, note du 2 décembre 1962), « le P. Rahner devait faire une conférence à la Capranica, mais cette conférence a été interdite par le Vicariat ».

95 Voir DE LUBAC II, p. 17 : « Avant-hier [soit le 8 novembre 1963], Paul VI, recevant en hommage de la maison Herder les volumes du *Lexikon für Kathol. Theologie*, a fait l'éloge du P. Karl Rahner. »

96 Voir CONGAR I, p. 382 ; je cite ce passage de la p. 479 (16 octobre 1963) : « Rahner, comme toujours, accapare le dialogue. Il est merveilleux, mais ne se rend pas compte que là où il est, il n'y a plus place pour autre chose » ; voir ce que note DE LUBAC II, p. 78 (4 juin 1964) : « Il [Congar] est volontiers critique et dédaigneux pour les interventions de Rahner. »

97 PHILIPS, p. 83 : « Rahner est aigri et narquois, mais pas réellement extrémiste » ; p. 93 : « Rahner est très méticuleux, mais au fond très orthodoxe et prêt à la concertation ; il me propose de m'aider au maximum. »

98 CONGAR II, p. 532. Voir aussi la p. 537 : « Exposé très plein de Rahner, dans un latin magnifique et donné avec une conviction humaine totale. »

Concernant les interventions de Congar et de Rahner, le P. de Lubac rapporte un fait assez cocasse (4 juin 1964), lors des réunions de la CFM : « Mgr Henriquez demande qu'on interroge les PP. Rahner et Congar. Mais Ottaviani lève la séance. Après 5 minutes de pause, on se remet au travail. Un peu plus tard, le card. König demande que Rahner soit interrogé : Ottaviani passera outre. Nous dirons entre nous, en plaisantant, qu'on a trouvé le bon moyen pour accélérer la marche de la commission : aux noms de Rahner ou de Congar, Ottaviani passe au n° suivant[99]. » Convaincu, d'allure sévère, Rahner en impose : c'est un combattant sérieux dont il fallait tenir compte.

P. Édouard Dhanis, s.j., et Mgr Gabriel Garrone

Je vous les présente sans les mettre en parallèle ni vouloir les comparer.

Le P. Édouard Dhanis, professeur, puis recteur de la Grégorienne, était peut-être un homme timoré, dont le rôle durant le concile n'est pas toujours limpide, ce qui gêne beaucoup le P. de Lubac, qui en souffre, mais qui ose tout de même affronter son confrère.

Dès son arrivée à Rome, le P. de Lubac essaie d'entrer en contact avec le P. Dhanis. La distance entre les deux ne fera que grandir, car le P. Dhanis évite de répondre clairement. La campagne d'Antonino Romeo contre le Biblicum évoque chez le P. de Lubac l'acharnement contre Fournière, dont il fut victime, ce qui ne le rassure guère. Devant les réticences de Dhanis à répondre, de Lubac rédige une lettre qu'il décide par la suite de ne pas livrer[100]. Par ailleurs, leur théologie ne s'alimente pas aux mêmes sources, comme on peut le constater par les appréciations du P. de Lubac sur les écrits de son confrère[101].

Le P. de Lubac prenait à cœur la défense de la mémoire du P. Teilhard de Chardin (cette histoire est bien connue). Qu'on se serve du concile pour donner le coup de grâce en condamnant Teilhard, cela, le P. de Lubac ne pouvait l'accepter, même si on procédait par simple allusion. La rencontre des P. de Lubac et Dhanis à la commission de

---

99 De Lubac II, p. 80. Voir la p. 88. Les discussions ne sont pas toujours calmes : voir de Lubac II, p. 424.

100 De Lubac I, p. 26-31 (février 1961).

101 De Lubac I, p. 21, 34-37.

théologie fut grevée de malentendus que de Lubac voulait dissiper, mais que Dhanis entretenait par son refus de répondre aux demandes du P. de Lubac. Le P. Congar, qui rend visite au P. de Lubac à la Grégorienne, le 28 septembre 1961, résume bien le nœud de l'histoire : « Il est très ennuyé, très écrasé. Il est certain que le P. Dhanis a introduit, dans le *De Deposito*, un nº 22 contre lui, de Lubac. Le P. de Lubac y retrouve en effet EXACTEMENT ce que le P. Dhanis lui a imputé dans les ennuis que le P. de L. a eux [lire *eus*] depuis 1950[102]. » Congar poursuit : « Celui-ci [de Lubac] est convaincu que le P. Dhanis profite du concile et du rôle assez considérable qu'il y joue pour justifier ses attaques contre de Lubac et Teilhard de Chardin. [...] Le P. de Lubac a vu le P. Dhanis et lui a demandé qui il visait par ceux "*qui sentiunt...*" Dhanis a refusé de lui répondre et, comme de Lubac insistait, Dhanis lui a dit : J'ai mes raisons[103]. » Le texte visé est celui du *De Deposito Fidei*[104] qui ne fait pas référence explicite à Teilhard[105]. Si, à tout prendre, ce nº 22, discuté en septembre 1961, ne fait pas mention explicite de Teilhard, il reste que dès la session de février 1961, il était bel et bien question de Teilhard[106], dans le schéma *De Deposito Fidei pure custodiendo*, au ch. 3 : *De Deo creatore et de evolutione mundi*. En effet, ce texte, qui porte la date du 18 janvier 1961, a été rédigé par le P. Dhanis : ce projet de constitution ne laisse aucun doute, car le texte des p. 10-12 est suivi d'une *Explicatio*, aux p. 12-17, qui cite de nombreux textes de Teilhard de Chardin en français[107].

Comme le P. de Lubac se sent pris à partie dans des textes rédigés par le P. Dhanis et discutés lors de la session de septembre 1961, la discussion est serrée, comme on peut le voir dans les *Carnets* du

---

102 CONGAR I, p. 77-78.

103 CONGAR I, p. 78. Voir DE LUBAC I, p. 40 (qui raconte avec davantage de détails).

104 Texte sous la cote C.T. 7/61 : 56, au ch. 4, *De Revelatione et Fide*, nº 22, p. 14-15 [LL 1186-1187].

105 Voir DE LUBAC I, p. 37. Il en sera de nouveau question un peu plus bas. (À la fin de la note 5 [note des éditeurs], la fin doit se lire ainsi : « impares esse ad res divinas *significandas modo simpliciter vero, etsi utique incompleto et imperfecto* »).

106 Voir TROMP I, p. 604, 631-632.

107 Texte qui porte la cote « C.T. 20/60 » et comprend 17 pages [LL 211-218, pour les p. 10-17]. C'est à la préparation de ce texte que fait allusion le P. Tromp dans sa note du 16 décembre 1960 : TROMP I, p. 135.

P. de Lubac[108]. Devant l'insistance du P. de Lubac à demander un entretien avec Dhanis, celui-ci se dérobe toujours. Le 28 septembre 1961, alors que le ton monte entre les deux, le P. Tromp, qui passe, est accosté par Dhanis qui lui annonce que de Lubac l'a injurié. Je cite de Lubac :

> Le P. Tromp est éberlué ; brave homme, il nous dit à peu près : « Vous me semblez être tous les deux émus ; mais enfin, vous êtes frères dans le Christ. » Sur quoi, je dis : « Précisément, mon Père, je proposais au P. Dhanis un entretien fraternel, mais depuis que je suis arrivé ici, il se dérobe. Est-ce qu'un consulteur de la commission théologique ne peut pas s'entretenir avec un membre de la même commission, afin de s'éclairer sur le texte que ce membre a rédigé[109] ? »

À la suite de cet incident, le P. de Lubac rédige une lettre d'explication qu'il envoie au P. Tromp le 28 septembre 1961[110]. Le 30 septembre, le P. Tromp, dans sa réponse par lettre, assure le P. de Lubac que personne n'a pensé, à la CT, à l'inclure dans ceux qui « s'éloigneraient dangereusement de la vérité[111] ». On peut ajouter que le texte du schéma *De Deposito Fidei* imprimé à la fin de 1961, au ch. 3 (*De Deo creatore et evolutione mundi*), visait à mots couverts, au n° 14, des expressions teilhardiennes[112]. Heureusement, ces textes ne survivront pas.

Avec le recul qui s'impose, on peut juger exagérées l'attitude et l'insistance du P. de Lubac, mais on comprend qu'il s'est senti sous surveillance doctrinale, et son honnêteté foncière exigeait plus de clarté de la part de qui pouvait le considérer suspect d'hétérodoxie. Il faut noter que le P. Dhanis s'opposera à ce que le P. de Lubac soit invité à donner une conférence à la Grégorienne[113], refus renouvelé en 1963, alors que Dhanis est devenu recteur[114]. Le 1er novembre 1963, de Lubac se contente de noter ce qui suit : « Un journal du soir nous apprend la

---

108 De Lubac I, p. 39-52.

109 De Lubac I, p. 49-50.

110 On en trouvera le texte dans la note 1 (de Lubac I), p. 50-51. Voir la réaction du P. Tromp dans de Lubac I, p. 54-55.

111 Voir le texte latin de la lettre de Tromp dans de Lubac I, p. 56, à la note 3, ainsi que la réponse du P. de Lubac (p. 56-57, note 3).

112 *Quaestiones théologicae*, Typis polyglottis Vaticanis – MCMLXI, p. 10 [LL 1306].

113 Voir de Lubac I, p. 84.

114 Voir de Lubac II, p. 17.

nomination du P. Édouard Dhanis comme consulteur du Saint-Office », sans ajouter aucun commentaire[115]. Le P. Congar signale cette nouvelle cueillie dans le *Quotidiano* : « J'y vois aussi que le P. Dhanis a été nommé consulteur au "Saint-Office" : j'avais prévu cela dès 1960, à le voir dans la commission théologique préparatoire[116]. » On confiera d'autres missions « délicates » au P. Dhanis dans les années qui suivent le concile !

De son côté, Mgr Philips, qui cherchait le consensus et la bonne entente, se reprochera d'avoir réagi peut-être trop fortement contre Dhanis, le 28 février 1963 :

> Je ne crois pas avoir perdu le nord pendant ces trois premières semaines. Si, j'ai été irrité un instant[117], non quand Schauf a fait des difficultés et que j'ai dû le remettre fermement à sa place, mais quand Dhanis a proposé une interprétation des textes sortis de leur contexte en les qualifiant pratiquement d'hérésies. Objectivement c'était inacceptable et blessant, mais je n'aurais pas dû l'interrompre. Ma réaction n'était pas bien grave, mais elle était déplacée[118].

Le P. de Lubac n'était donc pas le seul à constater que le P. Dhanis forçait la note.

Mgr Gabriel Garrone est un homme bon, sans prétention, qui cherche la bonne entente et joue un rôle de conciliateur dans la commission dont il fait partie. Il ne joue pas au grand théologien, ce qu'il n'est pas, mais sans doute apprend-il beaucoup sur le plan personnel de ces rencontres, ce qui, après le concile, amènera le pape Paul VI à lui confier un poste de direction à la Congrégation des séminaires et universités.

Comparant certains groupes de théologiens et d'évêques, Mgr Philips note en 1963 : « des Allemands semblent souffrir d'une sorte de complexe [d'*infériorité*] : leurs évêques, y compris les Autrichiens et les Suisses, sont peu nombreux. Mais ils ont la "*Wissenschaft*" […]. Les Français en général sont plus nuancés. Garrone est même prévenant et bon[119]. »

---

115 De Lubac II, p. 8.

116 Congar I, p. 516.

117 Texte original : « Wel een ogenblik geprikkeld… » (Philips, p. 17-18).

118 Philips, p. 95.

119 Philips, p. 83.

Au tout début du concile, Congar se plaint du peu de relations entre les évêques français et leurs théologiens, contrairement à la bonne organisation des Espagnols, des Allemands et des Hollandais[120]. Congar se montre même quelque peu méprisant envers Mgr Garrone : « Mgr Garrone est soucieux de panache et d'inviter tout le monde, mais il n'y a pas de séance de travail[121]. » Lorsque le schéma Rahner-Ratzinger est présenté par les Allemands « au nom des présidents des conférences épiscopales d'Autriche, Allemagne, Hollande, Belgique et France », Congar constate que le cardinal Liénart a donné son accord « sans rien demander aux évêques français, pas même à Mgr Garrone qui est leur tête théologique[122] ». De son côté, Daniélou prépare un texte sans avertir Mgr Garrone[123]. Déçu, Congar se laisse aller à des jugements sévères au sujet du style des évêques français, Garrone inclus[124]. Devenu en mars 1963 « expert de Mgr Garrone à la sous-commission *De Ecclesia*[125] », Congar apprend à mieux le connaître et à collaborer avec lui[126]. En février 1965, il porte sur Mgr Garrone un jugement nuancé et favorable. Il note, chez Garrone, « une sérénité, un optimisme et une assurance sans problème. Il a le don de prendre "philosophiquement" les choses et d'éliminer l'inquiétude à mesure que, pense-t-il, les problèmes sont réglés et le travail fait. C'est une force. Cela lui permet d'aborder successivement, sans inquiétude, les problèmes. Ce sur quoi il s'est fait une conviction est pour lui acquis, réglé, assuré. Il passe alors à autre chose calmement et sans revenir sur ce qui est acquis[127]. »

Lorsqu'il apprend, le 3 février 1966, que Mgr Garrone est nommé pro-préfet de la Congrégation des séminaires et universités, le P. Congar manifeste sa joie : « Génériquement, c'est le premier signe notable d'une

---

120 Voir Congar I, p. 176.

121 Congar I, p. 176 (31 octobre 1962). Même grief le 7 novembre 1962 (Congar I, p. 193).

122 Congar I, p. 203

123 Congar I, p. 204.

124 Voici, par exemple, ce qu'il dit de Garrone le 19 novembre 1962 (I, p. 239) : « pathétique, homilétique, sentimental, vague ».

125 Congar I, p. 332.

126 Congar I, p. 437-438 ; le 19 novembre 1963, Congar, à propos d'une intervention de Garrone *in aula*, remarque (I, p. 547) : « Très beau texte, donné de façon très intérieure et religieuse, mais d'un ton un peu pleurard » ; voir aussi II, p. 324.

127 Congar II, p. 328.

internationalisation de la Curie. Et ceci dans le sens du concile. Il semble que le Saint-Père veuille faire appliquer le concile par les hommes qui y ont été actifs [...]. Je vois depuis longtemps qu'un des problèmes majeurs de l'après-concile sera de garder la coopération organique — qui seule a permis et fait le concile — entre évêques et théologiens[128]. »

De son côté, le P. de Lubac constate qu'il y a peu de collaboration entre évêques et théologiens de France[129]. À la deuxième session (fin de 1963) et par après, il reste toujours quelque peu distant de Mgr Garrone. À Mgr Collini qui lui demande s'il voit Mgr Garrone, de Lubac répond « que Mgr Garrone est très aimable quand je le rencontre, que nous causons volontiers, mais que la confiance ne se commande pas[130] ».

De 1945 à 1960, il est certain que les relations entre évêques et théologiens, en France, n'étaient pas au beau fixe. Contrairement à d'autres pays, la France ne réussit pas, lors du concile, à inspirer le regroupement des forces intellectuelles ni à susciter une bonne organisation des intervenants. Le résultat en est le peu d'influence des évêques français comme corps épiscopal au concile. Congar et de Lubac en ressentent les effets et ils ne se gênent pas pour en parler[131].

Au tout début de son *Journal du Concile*, le P. Congar était plutôt pessimiste[132]. Peu à peu, toutefois, il gagne en confiance et comprend que sa mission est d'œuvrer pour l'Église, tout spécialement pour l'unité des chrétiens. Malgré un état de santé déplorable, il fournira un travail surhumain et exercera une influence difficile à mesurer. De

---

128 Congar II (5 février 1966), p. 518. Le 5 mars 1966, il ajoutait : « c'est un homme indépendant, qui sait voir l'essentiel parmi les détails, et s'y tenir ; il est doué d'une grande faculté de travail et d'un calme étranger à tout énervement » (II, p. 519).

129 Voir, par exemple, pour le 29 octobre 1962, de Lubac I, p. 190 : « Depuis notre arrivée à Rome, Mgr Garrone ne m'a pas fait signe. » Le 8 novembre 1962 (I, p. 237), de Lubac note : « Le P. Congar a écrit aujourd'hui à Mgr Garrone pour lui dire son étonnement de ce que l'épiscopat français semble vouloir ignorer les théologiens nommés experts par le Saint-Siège. » Voir aussi de Lubac I, p. 247.

130 De Lubac II (26 novembre 1963), p. 47. Le P. de Lubac conclut les notes de ce jour par ces mots (II, p. 48) : « Tous les évêques français que je rencontre sont aimables ; quelques-uns, confiants, mais je n'ai aucune liaison avec leur travail collectif, leurs assemblées, leur représentant [Mgr Garrone] à la commission théologique. » Voir encore de Lubac II, p. 63 et p. 211 (15 octobre 1964).

131 Voir Congar II (10 octobre 1964), p. 191 ; de Lubac I (8 octobre 1962), p. 97 ; de Lubac II (16 octobre 1964), p. 220.

132 Qu'on relise, pour s'en convaincre, les pages de Congar I, p. 3-23.

suspect, il deviendra grand théologien du concile. Ce qu'on remarque chez Congar, il faut aussi le signaler pour de Lubac, Philips et bien d'autres. Leur engagement dans le travail du concile répond à ce qu'ils perçoivent comme une mission, une réponse à un appel du Christ pour la vie de l'Église.

Paul-Émile Léger (1904-1991) et Maurice Roy (1905-1985), deux archevêques québécois membres de la CFM

Les deux ont joué un rôle important durant et après le concile, mais de façon bien différente. En 1961-1962, le cardinal Léger est membre de la Commission centrale, dont les travaux se terminent à l'ouverture du concile. Le cardinal Léger est alors nommé à la CFM. Quant à Mgr Roy, il est nommé le 26 février 1961 à la CT, et il est membre de la CFM durant le concile[133].

Les deux avaient été professeurs de séminaire, Léger à Issy-les-Moulineaux, au Japon et à Montréal, Roy à Québec. L'abbé Maurice Roy est aumônier militaire avec les troupes canadiennes en Europe de 1940 à 1945 et devient le premier vicaire aux armées pour le Canada (1946-1981), évêque de Trois-Rivières (1946-1947), puis archevêque de Québec (1947-1982 ; cardinal en 1965). Mgr Paul-Émile Léger, de 1947 à 1950, est à Rome, recteur du Collège canadien, d'où il revient comme archevêque de Montréal (1950-1968 ; cardinal en 1953) ; à la fin de 1967, il remet sa démission comme archevêque de Montréal, après dix-sept ans à ce poste. Roy est archevêque de Québec de 1947 à 1982, soit durant près de 35 ans.

Il est difficile de trouver deux personnages plus contrastés. Par tempérament surtout, ils sont aux antipodes l'un de l'autre. Léger est impulsif, bon orateur, de qui on peut attendre des déclarations qui peuvent étonner : il a du flair et sait toucher son auditoire. Sensible, il reste isolé, sujet à subir les contrecoups d'une notoriété qui le propulse à l'avant-scène. Roy est pondéré, d'une prudence qui le fait agir lentement, au point qu'on lui reproche ses silences, mais, somme toute, on doit reconnaître sa sagesse, car il n'est pas naïf. Une fois les décisions prises, on le verra les défendre avec calme et simplicité ; on ne le voit pas

---

133 Voir TROMP II, p. 813-814 : lettre du card. Ottaviani au card. Tardini 14 févr. 1961 ; voir p. 854 : présentation de Mgr Roy à la sous-commission *De Ordine sociali*, 20 avril 1961.

changer de cours ou revenir en arrière. Il n'est pas l'homme des grandes foules, mais celui des contacts personnels et sur qui on peut compter au fil du temps. Son expérience d'aumônier militaire lui a appris à réagir calmement, même au milieu des crises les plus graves[134].

Le rôle du cardinal Léger au concile est bien connu, celui de Mgr Roy sans doute moins. Léger a su s'entourer de théologiens qui l'ont aidé à préparer bien des interventions *in aula*, par exemple ses théologiens de Montréal, Pierre Lafortune et André Naud, sans oublier Philippe Delhaye, Charles Moeller et bien d'autres. De plus, évêques et théologiens, comme aussi les divers groupes d'influence, ont recours au cardinal pour qu'il porte leur message (notes et réactions) aux assises conciliaires. Avec les cardinaux Frings, Liénart, Döpfner, Alfrink, il compte parmi les « strong voices for the majority[135] ».

Dans le *Journal* du P. Congar, comme dans les *Carnets* du P. de Lubac, il est intéressant de suivre l'évolution du jugement que l'un et l'autre sont amenés à porter sur le cardinal Léger[136]. Le 7 novembre 1962, le P. Congar note ce qui suit : « Cardinal Léger : une fois de plus, très écouté. Il exprime certainement la pensée la plus générale des Pères. Je pense qu'il devrait être un des dirigeants du concile[137]. » Deux jours plus tard, après une heure d'entretien avec le cardinal au Collège canadien, le P. Congar déchante : « L'homme n'a pas l'allure que je me représentais d'après ses interventions. Autant celles-ci sont calmes, autant l'homme est nerveux [...] J'avais pensé, pour l'avoir entendu, qu'il pourrait être une tête du concile. Je le crois moins après l'avoir vu : 1) il est trop impulsif ; 2) il est trop seul et le restera trop. Par goût et par choix répondant à ses goûts. Il suit son chemin sans s'inquiéter

---

134 Le 11 juillet 1972, il s'exprimait ainsi en réponse à des journalistes : « Nous vivons une période dure, cruelle pour tous ceux qui ont des responsabilités... Je me sens aujourd'hui plus de mordant, d'audace que j'en avais au début. À la guerre, on n'avait pas de problèmes avec les soldats quand il y avait des batailles : tout le monde était heureux. C'est en arrière, quand il n'y avait plus rien à faire que ça allait mal! » Texte repris et publié dans *Pastorale-Québec*, 84 (1972), p. 385.

135 John W. O'Malley, *What Happened at Vatican II*, Cambridge, MA, London, The Belknap Press of Harvard University Press, 2008, p. 117.

136 Consulter l'Index des noms de personnes de leurs ouvrages.

137 Congar I, p. 192. Voir aussi I, p. 161.

de l'accord des autres[138]. » Congar note qu'il a rencontré un homme pessimiste, dramatique[139]. C'est bien là le drame de ce personnage haut en couleur qui est arrivé à Montréal en 1950 avec tous les honneurs d'un « prince » de l'Église, au moment même où de grands bouleversements étaient amorcés au Québec et, tout spécialement, dans sa ville de Montréal. Impulsif ? La suite de sa vie le démontre bien : il quitte Montréal pour aller chez les lépreux et donne comme motif la crise religieuse de son milieu montréalais, tout comme le désir de mettre en pratique le souhait du concile d'aller vers les plus abandonnés[140]. De retour d'Afrique, après un bref essai de travail en paroisse (1974-1975), il se retire pour s'occuper de ses œuvres de charité du Dahomey et du Cameroun. Homme de communication, il répond aux invitations qui lui sont faites de se présenter à la radio et à la télévision. C'est alors qu'il peut, d'une certaine manière, témoigner des changements dans l'Église et dans la société du Québec.

À la CT, comme à la CFM, ainsi qu'au concile, les interventions de Mgr Roy ne sont pas limitées aux questions sociales, bien qu'on l'ait choisi pour sa compétence en ce domaine. Lors de sessions générales de la CFM, en 1961-1962, le président se fait parfois remplacer par Mgr Roy[141]. En 1964, à la CFM comme en session conciliaire, c'est Mgr Roy qui donne le rapport sur le chapitre concernant la Vierge Marie, comme le notent Congar et de Lubac[142]. Comme les évêques canadiens, en général, favorisent une mariologie de type maximaliste, c'est à dessein et pour contrer cette tendance que, selon Congar, Mgr Roy fait venir à Rome en octobre 1963 le P. Jean-Marie Roger Tillard[143]. Il vaut la peine de citer encore une fois le P. Congar (11 septembre 1964) : « Delhaye me dit que Mgr Roy, non seulement a comme théologiens le

---

138 Congar I, p. 197.

139 Congar I, p. 198, 199, 208. Voir aussi les p. 341-343. Le 17 novembre 1962, de Lubac note ce que lui rapporte le cardinal Léger d'une réunion houleuse à la CFM le 13 novembre : de Lubac I, p. 317-319 ; voir aussi I, p. 458, et II, p. 380.

140 Voir *Doc. Cath.* 64 (1967), c. 2170-2171 ; *Doc. Cath.* 89 (1992), p. 46-47 : « On ne peut connaître le Tiers Monde, ou le comprendre sans être "dedans". C'était le prix à payer, et j'ai voulu le payer. »

141 Voir, par exemple, Tromp II, p. 707, 740.

142 Voir Congar II, p. 104 et 138 ; de Lubac II, p. 238, 260.

143 Voir Congar I, p. 436.

P. Lambert et un laïc (de Koninck), mais qu'il apporte un rapport fait par ce dernier en faveur de la pilule contraceptive[144]... » En novembre 1965, lorsqu'il est question du mariage dans une sous-commission de la CFM, une lettre de la Secrétairerie d'État sème l'émoi. Les cardinaux Léger et Roy se seraient alors présentés chez le pape Paul VI avec un couple mexicain[145]. On devine la suite, vu ce qui advint après le concile. Je laisse à qui peut consulter les archives des cardinaux Léger et Roy de confirmer, d'infirmer ou de compléter ces renseignements. Il reste qu'en tout cela, le cardinal Roy sait écouter et faire entendre sa voix. On ne peut que spéculer sur ce qui serait advenu si Paul VI avait accepté la discussion par les Pères du concile des questions de morale conjugale, par exemple.

Après le concile, de 1966 à 1981, en tant qu'archevêque de Québec, le cardinal Roy sera témoin des changements rapides, parfois violents, qui surviennent au Québec. Sur le plan ecclésial, il reste calme, prudent : il est parfois bon de montrer aux autorités (tant civiles qu'ecclésiastiques) qu'on est soucieux de ce qui se passe, mais qu'il vaut mieux ne rien casser ; c'est ainsi que le cardinal Roy a réussi à conserver la confiance même des personnes qui n'étaient pas toujours d'accord sur son style d'administration. Par ailleurs, la confiance qui semble se vivre entre le pape et lui l'amène à exercer son influence au-delà de son archidiocèse. En juillet 1966, il est nommé président du Comité provisoire pour l'application de *Apostolicam actuositatem* 26 et de *Lumen gentium* 90[146], ce qui, en 1967, le fait nommer président du Conseil des laïcs et président de la Commission pontificale d'études « Justice et Paix »[147], poste qu'il occupera de 1967 à 1976. Une déclaration faite au congrès des laïcs, le 14 octobre 1967, attire l'attention : il s'était adressé à un groupe d'évêques

---

144 CONGAR II, p. 126. Il s'agit du P. Bernard Lambert, o.p., connu pour ses travaux sur l'œcuménisme, et du professeur Charles de Koninck, père de famille et philosophe bien connu. On sait comment, par la suite, Paul VI se réservera l'examen des questions concernant la sexualité ; on sait tout aussi bien ce qui advint dans l'Église après *Humanae Vitae*. Le cardinal Léger, pour sa part, demandait un renouveau de la morale (voir DE LUBAC II, p. 305, note du 14 novembre 1964).

145 Je renvoie à CONGAR II, p. 489.

146 L'*Osservatore Romano* du 8 juillet 1966 : voir *Documentation catholique*, 63 (1966), c. 1440.

147 L'*Oss. Romano* des 11-12 janvier 1967 : voir *DC*, 64 (1967), c. 197-198.

le 11 octobre, recommandant aux évêques (et aux théologiens) de laisser parler les laïcs, au lieu d'intervenir en leur nom ou encore de corriger certains de leurs propos[148]. On se rappellera que la Lettre apostolique de Paul VI, *Octogesima adveniens*, du 14 mai 1971, qui évoque le rôle de l'Église dans les questions sociales depuis *Rerum Novarum*, est adressée au cardinal Roy, en tant que président de « Justice et Paix »[149].

En ces cardinaux du Québec, on peut signaler la détermination à prendre au sérieux ce qu'implique la vie en Église depuis Vatican II. Leur engagement plénier envers le Christ et dans l'Église ne peut être mis en doute. Leur approche est toutefois bien différente, car par toute leur personne et par leur histoire, comme par leur tempérament, ils témoignent de la variété des grands serviteurs de l'Église[150].

En guise de conclusion

Si les textes du concile ressemblent trop souvent à des textes résultant de compromis, il vaut la peine d'essayer de comprendre ce que cela signifie. La consultation de notes personnelles de théologiens, d'évêques et de non-participants qui suivaient les événements peut nous apprendre beaucoup sur la teneur du texte final, celui qui nous est transmis pour la vie de l'Église, une Église qui ne fait que commencer, dans le long terme, à vivre et à étudier le concile. Là aussi, la tradition vit le processus bien connu : ce qui nous a été transmis, nous devons le connaître et

---

148 Voir *DC*, 64 (1967), c. 1837-1838. Je cite deux extraits de ces notes : « Si les évêques ou les prêtres prennent trop souvent la parole, on risque que le carrefour ne devienne une discussion entre théologiens… car les théologiens peuvent parler très longtemps. […] En un mot, j'ai demandé aux évêques et aux prêtres de laisser toute initiative aux laïcs et de garder à ce Congrès son caractère de rencontre du laïcat. »

149 Voir *Acta Apostolicae Sedis*, 63 (1971), p. 401-441 ; pour la traduction en français, voir *DC*, 68 (1971), p. 502-513.

150 Je me permets, pour le cardinal Roy, de rappeler les témoignages d'estime et de reconnaissance manifestés lors de son vingt-cinquième anniversaire comme archevêque de Québec en 1972. À ce sujet, voir *Pastorale-Québec*, 84 (1972), p. 309-313 ; 384-385 (propos du cardinal Maurice Roy à des journalistes et un commentaire de Claude Ryan, directeur du *Devoir*, le 27 juillet 1972). Ryan conclut ses notes par ces mots : « Il faut, de nos jours, un homme qui ne parle pas trop souvent, qui n'élève pas inutilement la voix, qui ne donne aucun signe d'anxiété maladive. Tel est peut-être le charisme de ce serviteur modeste de l'unité et de la concorde que demeure dans notre milieu le cardinal Roy. » Voir aussi les textes publiés à l'occasion du décès du cardinal Roy : *Pastorale Québec*, 97 (1985), p. 402-413 ; voir, entre autres, l'article de Denis Duval, « L'éminent et insaisissable prélat », p. 412.

en vivre pour pouvoir à notre tour, par ce que nous vivons et croyons, être en mesure de le transmettre. Sinon, on se sert de textes du concile pour pousser quelques marottes ou encore pour réinterpréter à notre sauce ce qui aujourd'hui et ici même contribue à nous satisfaire. La vie de l'Église ne peut se concevoir comme si Vatican II n'avait pas eu lieu. Avant de songer à un Vatican III, ou à tout autre concile, il est important, pour nous et pour notre vie en Église, de « recevoir » Vatican II, pour en cueillir tous les fruits. À notre tour d'avancer et de dire avec Congar : « Je marche pour que l'Église avance[151] ! » et, avec Mgr Philips : « J'ai essayé de servir la Vérité qui est Notre Seigneur Jésus Christ, y compris avec mes manquements[152]. » « J'espère avoir accompli mon travail avec honnêteté. *Sed Dominus est qui judicat*[153]. »

---

151 Congar I, p. 3.

152 Philips, p. 124.

153 Philips, p. 156. Ce sont là les derniers mots des notes de Mgr Philips, le 1er novembre 1965, après la crise cardiaque qui l'empêche d'assister à la fin de la session.

PART III

RÉCEPTION DE VATICAN II DANS LA VIE DE L'ÉGLISE / VATICAN II IS RECEIVED BY THE CHURCH

SECTION I

Liturgy and Catechesis / Liturgie et catéchèse

The St. Lawrence Flows into Lake Ontario: Tides of Liturgical Renewal

Darren J. Dias,
University of St. Michael's College

Introduction

The liturgical renewal movement in Canada in the years prior to Vatican II seemed to flow from the French-language Church to the English-language Church. This movement is evident in the Canadian Dominican province in the 1950s and 1960s. The Province of St. Dominic of Canada was the foundation of the Paris province (France) principally present in French-speaking Canada. Its ties to the French-speaking Dominicans in Europe were most evident in its program of study: in 1950, 15 per cent of Canadian students were pursuing advanced degrees in centres such as Le Huy, Louvain, and the Saulchoir, where they were immersed in the ressourcement theology and the renewal movement.

This essay focuses on a particular aspect of the liturgical renewal movement, known in French as *la pastorale liturgique*. It will take a genealogical approach that looks at this single concept and how it was expressed in several concrete instantiations in the Dominican province of Canada and in the writings and ministry of Canadian Dominican liturgist Claude Poirier from the early 1950s until the end of the Second Vatican Council in 1965. *La pastorale liturgique* seems to be an option of the French theological academy for which there is no English-language equivalent. English renditions, such as "pastoral liturgy" or "practical liturgy," do not capture the scholarly rigor and methodological implications of the French concept, reducing it to a liturgical "how to." Moreover, *la pastorale* is not limited to liturgy but extends to other areas of theology and ministry: hence, *la pastorale* of youth ministry, of education, of parish administration, etc. *La pastorale* is the noun modified by *liturgique*. The concept of *la pastorale* is best translated as "pastoral practice"[1] rendering *la pastorale liturgique* to "pastoral practice of liturgy" in English.

This genealogy of the pastoral practice of liturgy in the Dominican province of Canada is divided into four sections. The first section explores the orientations that made certain initiatives possible in the province—specifically, the establishment of the Institut de pastorale des Dominicains in Montréal in 1960. The next section examines the concept of *la pastorale liturgique* as it is articulated in the writings of Claude Poirier. A third section surveys *la pastorale liturgique* as it was instantiated at St. Dominic's Parish in the Archdiocese of Toronto, where Poirier was pastor from 1963 to 1975. Finally, the conclusion briefly sketches the significance of a genealogy of *la pastorale liturgique* for Vatican II scholarship.

Early Career

Claude Poirier took the Dominican habit on August 3, 1945. Early in his studies his interest and ability in liturgy were recognized in his appointment as sub-cantor of the Priory of Saint-Jean Baptiste d'Ottawa in 1946. He was ordained to the presbyterate in 1951 and shortly thereafter appointed cantor, the friar responsible with oversight of the liturgical life of the community. He completed his lectorate[2] in theology

---

1 I am indebted to my colleague Mary Ellen Sheehan, IHM, for her help in finding this suitable English term.

2 The lectorate was a degree internal to the Order of Preachers.

in 1953 writing "Le rôle de l'office divin dans la vie du Frere Precheur" (The Role of the Divine Office in the Life of the Friar Preacher). He then completed another degree in liturgy at Notre Dame University under the direction of the French Oratorian Louis Bouyer in 1957. His thesis, entitled "L'aspirant au catholicisme et son initiation à la vie de l'Église" (The Aspirant to Catholicism and his Initiation into the Life of the Church), drew upon the adult catechumenate program that he had established at the Parish of St-Jean-Baptiste in 1954 and directed until 1960.

The Priory of St. Jean-Baptiste housed a high number of students[3] and young priests who welcomed the liturgical renewal, making changes in the liturgy easier, though not always without resistance. Younger friars were eager to devour the latest editions of *La Maison Dieu* and *L'art Sacré*, and implement the ideas about which they were reading.[4] Reflecting on his time as cantor in Ottawa, Poirier remarks,

> The liturgical life of the Church after the encyclical Mediator Dei of Pius XII (1947) was in full ferment. The 50s marked the beginning of the liturgical calendar reform and of simplified rubrics governing the celebration of the divine office; the reform of Holy Week celebrations; the new discipline of Eucharistic fast and the appearance of afternoon and evening Mass; the wider use of the vernacular in the celebration of the sacraments and of the Eucharist; the acknowledgement of the role of religious popular song … a rich variety of vernacular psalms and hymns. Within this framework of fervor the Ottawa Priory experienced renewed liturgical impulse.[5]

Since the bilingual *Rituale* had been approved for use in Canada on February 12, 1955,[6] Poirier began the practice of "doubling" at the

---

[3] Statistical information is available in the annual *Catologus* of the province; more than half the community was comprised of students.

[4] I am indebted to the many friars I interviewed to discover the atmosphere of the priory in the 1950s, in particular, Pierre Metivier, OP, who became master of ceremonies at Saint-Jean-Baptiste while Poirier was cantor; Philippe LeBlanc, OP, who was assigned to Toronto with Poirier; and Denis Gagnon, OP, liturgist at the *Institut de pastoral*.

[5] Claude Poirier, *Curriculum Vitae* (Unpublished autobiographical material), 3.

[6] L. Binkhof, OFM, "Chronicle of the Liturgical Movement," in *Liturgy in Development*, trans. H. J. J. Vaughan (Westminster, MD: The Newman Press, 1965), 61.

conventual Mass, proclaiming the texts in the vernacular while the celebrant read them *soto voce* in Latin. While this permitted practice, like that of an adult catechumenate, became more common as the council drew nearer, it was certainly rare in the mid-1950s.

Between 1950 and 1960 Poirier organized Holy Week liturgical encounters with hundreds of students from classical colleges in Ontario and Québec. The reintroduction of the Easter Vigil in 1952 and the further revisions to Holy Week in 1955 provided an opportunity not only to celebrate a more biblically and historically oriented liturgy but also to explain the meaning of the liturgy and the liturgical renovations to students so that they might better appropriate their meaning and participate in the liturgy. The purpose of the encounter, writes Poirier, was not merely aimed at liturgical "participation" but entering into the experience of the mystery of faith—the death and resurrection of Jesus Christ—consciously and intelligently.[7] Intelligence of the faith necessary for "intelligent participation" draws on liturgy and the Bible, "Two inseparable realities; for the liturgy, to introduce us into the very heart of the Christian mystery, constantly draws on inspired texts: it interprets and constitutes a Christian reading of the bible."[8]

L'institut de Pastorale

In 1956 the Apostolic Constitution *Sedes Sapientiae* gave further impetus to some of the pastoral initiatives that were already unfolding in the Dominican province. The constitution demanded the "pastoral preparation" of religious priests "for the dutiful performance of his apostolic ministry."[9] In addition to the traditional philosophical and theological course of study required for priestly formation, a "pastoral curriculum"[10] suited to the charism of each institute that would include such subjects as "psychology, pedagogy, education, catechesis, social

---

7 Claude (Albert) Poirier, "Le Triduum pascal chez les Dominicains," *La Revue Dominicaine* (n.p, n.d.), 303.

8 Ibid., 299. "Deux réalités inséparables: car la liturgie, pour nous introduire au cœur même du mystère chrétien, recourt constamment au texte inspiré: elle l'interprète et constitue une lecture chrétienne de la bible."

9 *The Apostolic Consitution Sedes Sapientiae and the General Statutes* (Washington: The Catholic Universtiy of America Press, 1957), 25.

10 Ibid., art. 9.

science, pastoral theology" was deemed necessary.[11] *Sedes* suggests that the curriculum begin early in formation and, upon completion of the traditional course of study, culminate in a pastoral year with an apprenticeship and one hundred days of classes in order to complete the necessary "theoretical and practical knowledge of pastoral theology."[12] The final proposal of *Sedes* commends a "school of special pastoral stûdy be practically and formally organized to complete also the religious and priestly formation."[13]

The establishment of a "school of special pastoral study" is exactly what the Dominican province did in 1960. This was an opportune time to respond to the exigencies of *Sedes* and, in the words of its founders, confirm the "path that the province was already on."[14] The so-called École de pastorale et prédication had been in operation under the direction of Dominicans R.-M. Hébert and T.-M. Milot in Québec City and moved to Montmorency in 1955. Its purpose was to teach young Dominicans to preach.[15] Hébert and Milot were receiving requests from both secular and religious clergy for something similar for them.[16] In the diocese of Québec the Centre de culture populaire was interested in supporting clergy involved in pastoral ministry and putting into place the pastoral practice of the liturgical renewal.[17] This group was particularly concerned with the participation of the faithful in Sunday mass and the diffusion of information regarding liturgical matters such as the restoration of the Paschal Vigil.[18] While the group lasted but a few years, it greatly influenced the Dominicans who would establish the Institut de Pastorale des Dominicains.[19] Another major influence in the

---

[11] Ibid., art. 13.

[12] Ibid., art. 42.2.2 and 48.1.

[13] Ibid., 53.2.2.

[14] R.-M. Hébert and T.-M. Landry, "Mémoire sur L'Établissement de L'École de Pastorale et de Prédication de la province Saint-Dominique de l'Ordre des Frères-Prêcheurs" (Montréal: May 1958), 7.

[15] Ibid., 5.

[16] Ibid., 7.

[17] Gilles-M. Bélanger, OP, "Au service du clergé, D'une École d'éloquence à un Institut de pastorale," *Communauté Chrétienne* 12, no. 70 (1973): 308. "... mise en œuvre d'une pastorale liturgique renouvelée."

[18] Ibid.

[19] Ibid.

approach of the new *institut* was to be the burgeoning method of adult education that was gaining popularity and momentum in secular institutions, though largely ignored by clerical and theological institutions where the more traditional magisterial style of teaching held sway.

In 1958 a proposal was made[20] to transform the École de pastorale et de prédication into an Institut superieur de Pastorale et de parole publique and to move it from Québec to Montréal. Such an institute would respond to the need for pastoral formation using praxis-based pedagogical methods. Pastoral theology, the history of *la pastorale*, technical sciences, pedagogy, psychology, sociology, media, catechism, encyclicals, and the history of the local church would comprise the curriculum. Further, special evening sessions would be offered for those who could benefit from an institute of continuing education. The institute would not be set up like a religious house of studies but like a university, with university-level expectations, so that it could eventually be affiliated with the University of Montreal. The faculty would team-teach an integrated curriculum to students already involved in some form of ministry.

In 1960 the Institut de Pastorale des Dominicains opened its doors to students from ten different religious communities.[21] Its invited professors included the noted sociologist Fernand Dumont, Claude Ryan from Catholic Action, and Bishop Paul-Émile Charbonneau. Its prospectus addressed itself to "all priests already engaged in ministry, to religious men and women and to laypeople who seek either an initiation to new forms of pastoral action or a deepening of the resources for their pastoral service."[22] It was to be a site of continuing education, a place of contact for those in active ministry, formed by "the reality of pastoral practice in all its diversity."[23] This aspect was also a response

---

20 The friars behind this proposal were R.-M. Hebert, T.-M. Landy, L.-M. Regis, and J.-M. Parent.

21 According to the first year registration, these included the Dominicans, Viatorians, Franciscans, and Spiritans.

22 Bélanger, "Service du clergé," 311. "… à tous les prêtres déjà engagés dans le ministère, aux religieux, aux religieuses, et aux laïcs qui recherchent soit une initiation aux formes rajeunies de l'action pastorale, soit une approfondissement des sources de leur service pastoral."

23 Ibid., 313. "… la réalité pastorale en toute sa diversité."

to the Provincial Chapter of the Dominicans of 1959 that demanded "that the liturgical movement that presently animates the church interest more the preachers and priests in parish ministry, and that they inform themselves of all that pertains to the pastoral practice of liturgy. May we sense in our priests who are called to celebrate Mass before the faithful a concern that favors their participation."[24]

In its first year the *institut* offered courses in preaching; pastoral practice of the Word, of worship, of the ecclesial community; psychology; sociology; education; professional ethics; and public speaking. [25] The *pastorale du culte* (pastoral practice of worship), consisting of sections on baptism, confirmation, the profession of faith, mass, homily, penance, marriage, liturgy of the sick, liturgy for the dead, celebrations of the word, chant, the liturgical year and holy week, was team-taught by André Gignac, OP, and Claude Poirier. Both would become key figures in the development of liturgically and catechetically literate, committed, post–Vatican II communities in Montréal and Toronto respectively.[26]

The Institut de Pastorale was housed in the newly erected Priory of St. Albert the Great. In addition to the *institut*, the complex contained a community of eighty-six friars, a conventual chapel that served the population of professors and religious on the new campus of the University of Montréal. St. Albert also was home to three journals: *Maintenant*, a journal of culture and current affairs that claimed to have no particular agenda except providing space for conversation;[27] *Communauté chrétienne*, a journal of pastoral theology of the *institut*; and later the liturgical journal, *Liturgie et Vie Chrétienne*.[28]

In the August 7th letter containing Poirier's new assignation to St. Albert, Prior Provincial Thomas-Marie Rondeau describes his desire to unite the role of rector of the conventual church with that of cantor for the sake of unity between "choir and church."[29] He claimed that this

24 Actes du Chapitres, 1959, Section 3, no. 27. Dominican Archives, Montréal.

25 From its course catalogue.

26 Gignac at La Communauté chrétienne St. Albert le Grand, and Poirier at St. Dominic's.

27 Henri-M. Bradet, editorial, *Maintenant* 1 (1962): 1.

28 This journal was founded by the canons of Mary Immaculate but transferred to the Dominicans at St. Albert.

29 Thomas-Marie Rondeau to Claude (Albert) Poirier, 7 August 1960, Dominican Archives, Montréal. "D'abord pour l'unité de la liturgie, au chœur et à l'église.—Unité

unity would be furthered through Poirier's ministry: teaching at the *institut* and overseeing the actual practice of the liturgical life of the Dominican and larger worshipping community. This unity of choir, worshipping community, and pastoral theology would serve as an example for students at the *institut*. In a phrase that shaped Poirier's outlook on the pastoral practice of liturgy,[30] Rondeau says that a capable individual must have oversight of the liturgical life of the community if

> we [Dominicans] wish to establish such a [unified] liturgy, to have liturgical offices that do not only succeed but that will clearly be a teaching as well as incentive to better understand the liturgy and to better participate in the prayer of the Church.[31]

In addition to teaching the entire section of *la pastorale du culte* with Gignac, Poirier gave a conference roughly every month of the academic year of 1960 on such topics as: "Catechism and the Mass" for the priests of the Diocese of Sherbrooke, "Liturgy and the Laity" for the students of Marianopolis Women's College, "In what way can a liturgical spirit transform Sunday preaching" for a congress of Dominican preachers, and "Active Participation: Why?" for the seminarians at the University of Ottawa. He participated in monthly ecumenical meetings with the professors of McGill Divinity School. Poirier became a regular homilist on the CBFT TV Mass. In 1962 he participated in the annual session of the Centre de pastorale liturgique de Paris in Angers and in an ecumenical encounter at the Abbey of Chevretogne. Between 1960 and the summer of 1963, Poirier wrote over thirty articles in a variety of journals[32] on diverse aspects of *la pastorale liturgique*.

également entre l'enseignment donné à l'Institut de pastorale, où vous devez professer vous-même, at la pratique qui se fera à l'église, laquelle nécessairement servira d'example et de modèle pour les étudiants de l'Institut tant étrangers que dominicains."

30 *Notice Nécrologique: Fr. Claude (Albert) Poirier, OP 1925–2005*, 5.

31 Rondeau to Poirier, "Ensuite si nous nous voulons instaurer une telle liturgie, avoir des offices non seulement réussis mais qui soient en definitive un enseignement autant qu'une intite [*sic*] à mieux comprendre la liturgie et à participer advantage à la prière de l'Eglise, si nous voulons en arriver là, dis-je, il faut quelqu'un de compétent."

32 For example, *Liturgie et Vie Chretienne, Service de L'homilétique, Maintenant, The Canadian Journal of Theology, Revue Dominicain* and *Communauté Chretienne*.

La pastorale liturgique in Poirier's Writings

Poirier's articles give us a sense of the complexity of *la pastorale liturgique*. The idea that the liturgy was not only to succeed (visually or organizationally) but to be both a teaching and an incentive to better understand and participate in the liturgy remains a central concept throughout his work. Methodologically, it is in "doing" liturgy, in the act of liturgical worship, that meaning is consumed, produced, and appropriated by the contemporary worshipping community, and by doing liturgy, new questions arise out of its lived experience.

The 1947 papal encyclical, *Mediator Dei*, was a watershed document for the liturgical renewal. Its dimensions of interiority and understanding are particularly important in the development of *la pastorale liturgique*. Article 23 states, "The worship rendered by the Church to God, must be, in its entirety, interior as well as exterior."[33] Later, in Article 26, "God cannot be honored worthily unless the mind and heart turn to Him in the quest of the perfect life, and that the worship rendered to God by the Church … is the most efficacious means of achieving sanctity."[34] The encyclical distinguishes between "objective piety" as the "effective reality of sanctifying grace, on the action of God in the sacraments and in the Mass" and "subjective or personal piety."[35] *La pastorale liturgique* acknowledges the historical development of liturgy and the potential to change and revise certain exterior forms of worship. What remains essential is that participation in the liturgy is dependent upon some act of understanding of its meaning, transforming mere participation into "intelligent participation" and then commitment.

As early as 1956 Poirier lamented that the liturgical renewal underway was relatively unknown in parishes.[36] Priests and laity remained ignorant of this important movement. Moreover, he warned that changes brought by the renewal, such as the dialogue Mass and the use

---

33 *Mediator Dei*, encyclical of Pope Pius XII On the Sacred Liturgy, art. 23, accessed 3 January 2011, http://www.vatican.va/holy_father/pius_xii/encyclicals/documents/hf_p-xii_enc_20111947_mediator-dei_en.html.

34 Ibid., art. 26.

35 Ibid., art. 28.

36 Claude (Albert) Poirier, "Le renouveau liturgique en paroisse," *Liturgie et Vie Chretienne* 3 (1956): 4.

of missals, not become routines that would encourage new forms of passivity. Thus, he writes, changes must not be "imposed superficially" but through a "progressive liturgical education of the faithful."[37] The aim of *la pastorale liturgique* is to understand the meaning of participation, not to participate thoughtlessly. Echoing *Mediator Dei*, Poirier writes, "It is not the material participation in the cult that is important to achieve, but the *interior* participation, that favors a participation in voice and action."[38] External forms must have a correlative interior dimension: baptism without faith and belief is a meaningless gesture[39] just as penance without conversion is empty.[40]

The interior dimension that makes faith intelligible is cultivated in the habit of liturgical participation and on the communal interpretation of Scripture. Through the liturgical celebration the faithful were exposed to the Word;[41] hence, the importance of being able to understand the Word proclaimed in the vernacular. Poirier recognized that the practice of the celebrant reading the biblical texts in a low voice while a lector proclaimed the texts in the vernacular was not ideal but advisable until such a time as official authorization to proclaim the scriptural texts was given.[42] He asserts that this practice has resulted in a "veritable discovery of the Bible" on the part of the faithful who would otherwise remain largely unexposed to Scripture.[43] Furthermore, the Word proclaimed has a communal and participatory function both in its hearing that draws the assembly together and then in the response that it elicits.

The proclamation of the Word was to be complemented by a preaching aimed at presenting the Word as an actual reality addressed

---

37 Ibid.

38 Ibid., 5.

39 Claude (Albert) Poirier, "The Sacrament of Baptism and the Word," *Canadian Journal of Theology* IX (1963) 2: 76.

40 Claude (Albert) Poirier, "Carême et le sacrament de penitence," *Communauté chrétienne* 2 (1962): 90.

41 Andre Gignac and Claude Poirier, "La lecture dans l'assemblée liturgique" *Communauté chrétienne* 7 (1963): 61.

42 Claude (Albert) Poirier, "L'usage de la langue vivante dans la liturgie du triduum pascal," *Communauté chrétienne* 8 (1963): 119. The Directoire pastoral de la messe of the Archdiocese of Montréal permitted the practice.

43 Ibid.

to the assembled community.[44] Poirier suggested employing biblically inspired vocabulary and not technical theological language because biblical concepts resonate with lived experience,[45] and preaching must take lived experience into account.[46] Poirier reminded clergy that they were both ministers of sacrament and Word such that the homily must be regarded neither as an interruption of the Mass nor merely an "hors d'œuvre" for the Eucharist. The homily serves to "prolong the liturgy of the Word, and to prepare the Eucharistic response of the Church assembled."[47] Thus, contrary to a common practice of the time, Poirier admonishes those priests who interrupt the liturgy with parish announcements instead of scriptural and kerygmatic preaching.[48]

While good preaching encourages intelligent participation, on its own it is insufficient. Poirier highlights the centrality of catechesis in *la pastorale liturgique*. Liturgical catechism, he says, is not informational; it is not the transmission of liturgical facts but the liberation of "the profound sense of the Eucharistic celebration" so as to enter more consciously into the liturgical action.[49] Throughout his articles in the period 1960–63 Poirier repeats several strategies to facilitate a *prise de conscience*, an "appropriation," of the liturgical renewal. First, he claims liturgical innovation and even good preaching cannot have a durable effect if not accompanied by preparation and structures that facilitate liturgical literacy.[50] Even a proliferation of papal and diocesan documents

---

44 Claude (Albert) Poirier, "L'homélie dominicale, fonction liturgique," *Liturgie et Vie Chrétienne* 23 (1961): 25.

45 Claude (Albert) Poirier, "Prédication dominicale: fidélité à l'évangile ou réponse aux besoin des gens?" *Communauté chrétienne* 7 (1963): 36.

46 Ibid.

47 Claude (Albert) Poirier, "Le prône" *Liturgie et Vie Chrétienne* 35 (1963): 36. "Puisque l'homélie n'interrompt pas la messe, mais prolonge la liturgie de la Parole, et prépare la réponse eucharistique de l'Église assemblée, présidé par le prêtre, n'est-on pas amené à souhaiter que la proclamation de l'évangile soit *immédiatement* suivi de son commentaire homilétique?"

48 Ibid.

49 Claude (Albert) Poirier, "La Catéchèse de la messe," *Revue Eucharistique du Clergé* (February 1961): 66. "Livrer le sens profond de la célébration non pas dans un but d'information, mais afin de faire entrer de façon consciente dans l'action liturgique."

50 Claude (Albert) Poirier, "Le renouveau liturgique en paroisse," *Liturgie et Vie Chrétienne* 3 (1956): 8.

will not effect this "prise de conscience." For example, in a 1962 article Poirier lamented the fact that the clergy of Montréal had not taken the diocesan Directoire de la messe seriously enough to implement it; he chided those clergy for not acting as proper delegates of the bishop who desired its implementation. Structurally, Poirier advised that parishes establish training programs and liturgical councils and for parishes of a certain territory to work together to implement good liturgical practices for the sake of consistency and unity.[51] In this co-operative effort, he predicted, some parishes could play a leading role.[52]

A second strategy made the Sunday Mass a site for catechism and faith education through a commentator. Sunday Mass was recognized as being the only time that the majority of Catholics were exposed to Word and Sacrament. A commentator could help the assembly to understand both the Scripture and the liturgical action with some explanatory remarks before the epistle, invitatory, and preface. Through a non-intrusive explanation of the liturgical action, the assembly was invited to intelligently participate.

Another catechetical tool was to explain the meaning of the liturgy through explicit comparison with experiences of everyday living. For example, Poirier argued that Eucharist needed to be related to table fellowship, the meal, if its meaning was to be grasped. Illustrative examples could only be drawn from the lived experience of the faithful. These strategies that facilitate a *prise de conscience* of the liturgical renewal would be concretely implemented when Poirier became pastor of St. Dominic's in 1963.

Poirier also emphasized the role of music and youth in achieving some of the aims of *la pastorale liturgique*. Good liturgical music, writes Poirier, not only cultivates spirituality but also serves the liturgy by complementing the readings and the collects of the day.[53] Liturgical music is fluid and involves choir and congregation in responses and hymns at affective, aesthetic, and spiritual levels. Music should be scripturally sound, thoughtful, and well rehearsed if it is to encourage

---

51 Claude (Albert) Poirier, "Le Directoire de la messe, initiative diocésaine" *Communauté chrétienne* 3 (1962): 157–60.

52 Ibid., 159.

53 Poirier, "Le chant aux messe dominicales," *Liturgie et Vie Chrétienne* 7/8 (1957): 92.

participation. Another strategy involved the inclusion of the youth in the liturgy. Poirier posited that the youth were open to new forms of song and worship; moreover, they would build the community of the future.[54]

In February 1962 the community of St. Albert experienced a commotion over an article that appeared in the periodical *Maintenant* entitled "*Le 'racket' des lampions*" and written by Prior of St. Albert Marcel-Marie Desmarais, arguably one of the most popular preachers in French Canada. In the article, Desmarais, hiding behind a literary fiction, attacked both the faculty of the *institut* and the rector of the conventual church, chiding both as cerebral intellectuals who dismissed the affective and emotional, who preached ideas and not morality, who were contemptuous of the uneducated and the simple, ignorant of the tangible supports of prayer and the circumstances of the material world.[55] Desmarais's article was clearly directed toward the movement of *la pastorale liturgique* at St. Albert: the faculty of the *institut* and those responsible for the conventual liturgies. Poirier himself had preached every Sunday Mass of 1960, and in 1961 a select few, such as Frs. Benoît Pruche, Simon Pierre, Jacques Tellier, and Benoît Lacroix, shared in these duties.[56] Desmarais's article prompted an angry response from the director of the Office national de liturgie published in *Le Devoir*;[57] it was suspected by some that the faculty of the *institut* had a hand in the response. The article reflected a certain malaise on the part of some of the renewal movement. Poirier responds privately to these attacks in a letter to the prior provincial in February of 1962, defending the *pastorale liturgique* at St. Albert and reminding the provincial that the renewal movement was not unique to St. Albert but a "movement of the Church which one does not actually have the right to oppose."[58]

---

54 Claude (Albert) Poirier, "Congrès national du Centre de Pastorale Liturgique (Angers)," *Communauté Chrétienne* 5 (1962), 350.

55 *Notice Nécrologique,* 5.

56 Ibid.

57 Ibid.

58 Claude Poirier, Letter to Thomas-M. Rondeau, OP, 19 February 1962. "Mentionnons aussi le mouvement général de renouveau lui-même qui est un mouvement d'Église et auquel on n'a pas le droit de s'opposer actuellement."

This incident is a reminder that the pastoral practice of the liturgy was met with resistance and even hostility.

The malaise with the new pastoral program of the Dominican province is also evinced in the removal of responsibility for the pastoral year from the Institut de Pastorale and its director, and the creation of an École de Pastorale under the direct responsibility of the regent of studies of the province in 1963.[59] This in spite of the fact that the provincial chapter of that same year highlighted the importance of the Institut de Pastorale and pledged continued support.[60]

La pastorale liturgique in St. Dominic's

During Holy Week 1963, the pastor of St. Dominic's Parish in the Archdiocese of Toronto died suddenly. As the parish needed an English-speaking pastor, Poirier assumed this ministry in April 1963. Poirier's move to parish ministry is significant because, as George Devine comments, the twentieth-century liturgical movement was not a "grass-roots phenomenon" but generated by cognoscenti in monasteries, abbeys, priories, and seminaries; religious who could combine a "life of liturgical and theological scholarship with a life of communal liturgical celebration."[61] Its leaders were neither bishops nor pastors "but ... the liturgical experts were professors in seminaries and colleges. Their impact was in the classroom, lecture hall, the occasional retreat or speaking engagement, and perhaps in publication among their scholarly peers. But they were not in a position to directly influence the course of liturgical attitudes or actions in the parishes and dioceses of America."[62] Poirier's arrival at St. Dominic's directly influenced the course of liturgical attitudes and action in the parish, and later in the Archdiocese of Toronto.

Shortly after his arrival at St. Dominic's, Poirier announces in the June 23, 1963, bulletin that "The Scriptural readings of the Epistle and Gospel—which contain a wealth of teaching for all of us—will be read in

59 Andre Gignac to Claude Poirier, 1 August 1963, Dominican Archives, Montréal.

60 Actes du Chapitre, 1963, no. 19, Dominican Archives, Montréal.

61 George Devine, *Liturgical Renewal: An Agonizing Reappraisal* (New York: Alba House, 1973), 25.

62 Ibid.

the vernacular at every daily Mass" although it was not until March 15, 1964, that the Canadian bishops permitted the vernacular Scripture reading at all Masses. At that time Poirier told the parish, "For some time now at St. Dominic's, the Scripture lessons have been read to you in English, while the celebrant read the text privately at the altar [in Latin]. Now the Canadian Bishops have agreed that at all Masses attended by the faithful ... epistle and Gospel are to be proclaimed only in the vernacular."

The week of July 7, 1963, Poirier refers to an article in the July 6 *Canadian Register* claiming that the laity was not responding to the liturgical movement by "participating actively." Poirier referred to Archbishop Pocock's instructions that since people were not aware of the liturgical action at the altar, the priest was to speak the Mass parts slowly and distinctively and that both the Epistle and Gospel be read in the vernacular. He goes on to quote the archbishop, "the liturgical movement has appeared as a sign of God's providential dispositions for the present day, a movement of the Holy Spirit in the Church intended to open to the faithful of our time the spiritual riches available through their active participation in the liturgical life."[63]

In the June 30, 1963, bulletin Poirier applied his principle that liturgy can only be truly understood by drawing on the lived experience of the faithful. He describes the communion rail as a table, an extension of the altar, and the communion rail cloth as a tablecloth such that one should place one's folded hands on the cloth like at the table, not under it, when receiving Communion: "Since at Mass, we celebrate a meal, should not the normal way at home teach us the normal way in church?"[64] He asks that parents explain the significance of the meal for understanding the Eucharist to their children. The practice of placing one's hands on top of the altar cloth for the reception of Communion anticipated the change to the diocesan rule that came in November of the following year.

On September 29, 1963, St. Dominic's resumed the High Mass after summer hiatus; however, Poirier warns:

---

[63] Bulletin of the week of July, 7, 1963. Archive of St. Dominic's Parish, Mississauga, ON. The following dates refer the the weekly bulletin.

[64] 30 June 1963.

> Active participation in the Mass, which our Archbishop has been promoting for over a year, is not intended for the Low Mass only. It is urgent that we become concerned with taking active part also in the High Mass: remaining silent at High Mass and becoming again mere spectators, offers indeed very little interest for people who have experienced active participation. … Congregational singing is in order at High Mass and it will begin next Sunday, with the singing of the simple responses … by all.

In the summer of 1964 he informed the parish that beginning on January 1, 1965, there would be widespread use of the vernacular in the Mass and sacraments. Latin would only be retained for the prayers at the foot of the altar and the Eucharistic Prayer. Suitable sung responses in the vernacular would become available.[65] While the sacraments of Confession, Communion to the Sick, Nuptial Blessing, and Confirmation were in English by January 1965, the translation of the missal had been delayed. On the first Sunday of Lent 1965, St. Dominic's celebrated its first Mass in English (with the exception of the Preface and Canon, which had yet to be translated). On that day, however, Poirier also had the altar removed from the wall and brought forward and to preside facing the assembly. After the creed, the "most traditional and ancient" prayers of the faithful to which people responded were added, while a commentator directed the responses and explained the ritual. Responses were facilitated by printed inserts for the dialogue in English. According to Poirier, changes in the Dominican rite permitted the celebrant to preside over the introductory rites and the liturgy of the Word from the chair and not the altar and to omit the last Gospel.[66]

Poirier declared that the day the Mass was permitted in the vernacular, and facing the people was a "day of great joy." After the first Mass facing the people he commented in the bulletin, "there is far better communication between the priest and faithful." Poirier felt it was no longer "his" Mass but the "people's" Mass. Seeing the assembly at prayer, he felt "moved by your attention and piety and he felt sustained by your prayer." Poirier goes on to say that "He will be grateful for any

65 26 July 1964.

66 21 February and 7 March 1965.

remark you may see fit to make [about his presiding]. If his manner is not what you, as God's people, have a right to expect, he will try to improve it, so that his every word and gesture are becoming and truthful in this greatest of celebrations."[67]

As early as June 23, 1963, Poirier informs the parish that announcements "will no longer interrupt Mass (after the Gospel)." He explains that "... preaching itself does not interrupt the Mass. The sermon is part of Mass: it follows the Gospel and should always be closely connected with it. The Word of God is first proclaimed (Epistle, Gospel), then it is presented to God's people, who are made to realize that this message is addressed to them on this day, and it concerns them."[68]

Poirier was concerned with cultivating a sense of ownership of the parish on the part of the parishioners. Shortly after arriving, he removed the "seat money baskets" that were placed at the end of the pews that served as a repository for donations. He writes to the parishioners: "The Church is your house, the house of all baptized Christians who meet to worship together, and for this no admission fee ought to be asked of you."[69] In the following bulletin he assured the parish that in spite of the removal of the baskets, the collection amount remained the same. For its 1964 parish census Poirier decided that lay members of the parish would be involved in collecting data and visiting other parishioners. Poirier writes, "We see many advantages to associating the laity with this work as the Parish list should concern all .... Here is a wonderful opportunity for people to share in the pastoral effort of the Parish, to meet one another and to realize that the Church is not just a handful of clergymen. You are the Church"[70] This ecclesiological position is also reflected in the liturgical posture of the assembly that he encouraged: standing as a genuine prayerful posture that expresses "vigilance, activity, deference, worship" and dignity. He states, "As baptized members of Christ's Body, we can stand before God in confidence and faith."[71]

---

67 7 March 1965.

68 23 June 1963.

69 Ibid.

70 8 December 1963.

71 18 August 1963.

The bulletins reveal Poirier's adult faith education programs, support of lectures and study days of the liturgy, establishing a book rack and ordering copies of magazines like *Commonweal* free for parishioners. He was vigilant in explaining any liturgical changes, and what they meant. From time to time he quoted from Vatican II documents or from pastoral letters regarding the council. For example, at the end November of 1965, he quotes from a letter of Pocock on the end of the council as the beginning of a new era : "The mighty task of bringing to life the Council in our communities and in the lives of the faithful now begins and success depends on a continued outpouring of the Spirit of God and our cooperation."[72]

In a 1991 brief history of St. Dominic's prepared by two longtime parishioners it is recorded that during Vatican II there were "3 main preoccupations: liturgy, faith education and contribution to the larger community, especially in the area of ecumenical dialogue."[73] They remember the liturgical changes lead by Poirier that began "small" and were "always accompanied by careful explanation." The pastor was eager to know how people experienced the changes, asking them to be patient during this transformative period. Although some parishioners left because of the pace of the changes, more people began enrolling in the parish.[74] Through faith education and sacramental preparation the parish applied "the insights of the Council to our understanding of ourselves as a people trying to live the Gospel."[75] In his message to the parish on the occasion of its twenty-fifth anniversary, Poirier writes, "The years after Vatican II were years when we had to reflect seriously on the true nature of the Church, accept new orientations, cope with many changes, become creative, find new ways of building community. They were not easy years for everyone."[76] Poirier later reflects specifically on the liturgical changes at St. Dominic's: "Our people quickly and

---

72 28 November 1965.

73 Edna Clough and Winnie Crowe, "History of St. Dominic's" (Written for St. Dominic's Parish, Mississauga, 1991), 2.

74 I am grateful to Winnie Crowe and her niece, Eilleen Burgess, both lifelong and active parishioners of St. Dominic's, for sharing their memories and archive with me.

75 Interview with Winnie Crowe. January 22, 2009.

76 Claude Poirier, "St. Dominic's 25th Anniversary," newsletter.

generously accepted the comparatively rapid rhythm of the changes that were being implemented. There was an effort to prepare the way with a catechesis that one expected adequate."[77] He goes on to claim, "The new legislation could only be an encouragement to pursue the work already begun."[78]

Poirier's work at St. Dominic's parish continued through a period of rapid growth and pastoral creativity in the decade following the council. The implementation of the council brought with it intensified liturgical activity, renovations, and an active pastoral team that included Dominican sisters. Seven years after his arrival in the seven-hundred-person parish, there were thirty-one catechism teachers and thirteen classes for public-school children on Saturday mornings. His pastoral achievement was significant and even a model for the Church of Toronto. Thus, in 1975, he was invited by Archbishop Pocock to assume the positions of house liturgist at St. Augustine's Seminary, liturgy professor within the Toronto School of Theology, and director of liturgy for the Archdiocese of Toronto. Pocock writes that Poirier's appointment would help "priests and people to celebrate good liturgy."[79] With the encouragement and support of Pocock and Rev. Brian Clough, Poirier established the Pastoral Center for Liturgy in 1977 and served as its director for many years, publishing the bulletin *Fragments* to serve those involved in the pastoral practice of liturgy across North America.

Conclusion

A genealogy of the pastoral practice of liturgy in the Dominican province of Canada in the era of Vatican II illustrates its importance as a *prise de conscience* of the liturgical renewal that was taking root and expanding, particularly in the French-speaking Church, and slowly flowing down the St. Lawrence into Lake Ontario. *La pastorale liturgique* was part of a larger movement, not without a disruptive element, to promote the "intelligent participation" of all baptized Catholics in the life of the Church, beginning with the source and summit of ec-

77 *Notice Nécrologique*, 7.

78 Ibid.

79 Archbishop Philip Pocock to Claude Poirier, 21 April 1976, Dominican Archives, Montréal.

clesial life, the liturgy. For Poirier the liturgy was indeed "a teaching and an incentive for better participation," with cognitive and existential dimensions—better understanding and the appropriation of meaning respectively—that coalesced into *la pastorale liturgique*.

La pastorale liturgique that was operative in the Dominican province before the council seems amazingly current; for example, the pastoral curriculum and adult-education method of the *institut* aimed at the "intelligent participation" of the baptized. The biblical and historical dimensions of the liturgy; the consumption, production, and appropriation of liturgical meaning; and the intelligent participation of the assembly are as central today as they were in the years immediately preceding and during Vatican Council II. Poirier's pastoral concerns were equally current: full, active, and conscious participation of the faithful, fostering a sense of ownership of the Church; education of the faith; and good preaching. The practitioners of *la pastorale liturgique*, such as Claude Poirier, did not primarily prepare the people of God for the liturgical-ecclesial changes to come but for the reception of those changes already underway. Instead of igniting *la pastorale liturgique*, the Second Vatican Council finally confirmed the movement and gave it further impetus and encouragement to continue and develop the work already begun.

La réception de Vatican II dans la formation catéchétique au Québec

Raymond Brodeur,
Université Laval

Cette recherche s'inscrit dans l'œuvre novatrice entreprise depuis quelques années par Gilles Routhier autour de l'herméneutique relative à l'événement et aux productions de Vatican II. L'angle de travail privilégié ici traite des apports de Vatican II sur le développement de la catéchèse et, de manière plus précise, sur ce qui touche à la formation d'une nouvelle génération de catéchètes. Cette étude contient d'emblée de nombreuses vertus, car elle concerne à la fois la façon de concevoir la mission première de l'Église, la formulation des contenus théologiques, les aspects anthropologiques, sociologiques et psychologiques inhérents aux personnes destinataires des activités catéchétiques et aux communautés engagées dans cette intervention. La formation catéchétique ne peut pas faire l'économie des enjeux proprement pédagogiques reliés à la pédagogie de la foi et aux stratégies pédagogiques ou andragogiques. À cela, on peut encore ajouter les questions d'ordre plus proprement épistémologique : de quoi parle-t-on au juste quand on traite de la formation catéchétique ? Dans cet ordre d'idée, on est également justifié de chercher à discerner ce qui relève de la catéchèse par rapport à ce qui relève de l'enseignement religieux, ou de l'enseignement de la religion, ou encore de la culture et de l'éthique religieuse.

Il n'est évidemment pas question ici, dans le cadre de ce chapitre, de faire, même sommairement, un résumé des bouleversements et des transformations qui caractérisent, depuis un siècle, l'enseignement religieux de type catéchétique, tant en France qu'au Québec. Mon propos consistera plutôt à mettre en perspective l'influence directe de l'événement et de certains textes de Vatican II à partir de ce qu'on retrouve dans les notes de certains cours dispensés à l'Institut de catéchèse de l'Université Laval de Québec depuis l'année de sa fondation, en 1962[1], jusqu'en 1970. Deux corpus de textes principaux ont été retenus pour la présente recherche : une série de 125 mémoires de licence produits entre 1964 et 1973 dans le cadre du programme de licence en catéchèse[2] et une série de documents dactylographiés comprenant des conférences et des notes de cours donnés entre 1964 et 1970[3].

L'enseignement de Vatican II à l'Institut de catéchèse

Une grande partie des enseignements offerts à l'Institut de catéchèse depuis l'année 1962-1963 a été dispensée par des professeurs invités provenant de Montréal, Ottawa, Paris et Bruxelles[4]. L'allure infléchie par Jean XXIII, puis par Paul VI, à cette célébration et à ses travaux les inspire et les stimule grandement. Dans son cours donné en 1964, le dominicain André Gignac, liturgiste, évoque l'appétit soulevé par ce concile :

> Depuis six ans, nous vivons un événement qui, dans la pensée de Jean XXIII et de Paul VI, a pour but de redonner à l'Église ses traits originels. Je pense que si telle est la volonté de tout un Concile, nous pouvons quand même, nous aussi, nous référer au

1 L'Institut de catéchèse de l'Université Laval fut créé par le Conseil universitaire en décembre 2001. Son premier directeur fut Jacques Laforest.

2 Ces mémoires sont disponibles à la bibliothèque de l'Université Laval.

3 Ces documents sont regroupés dans un ensemble d'archives constitué par une ancienne étudiante, puis professeure dans cet Institut, madame Renée Dubeau-Legentil. Le fond Dubeau-Legentil est actuellement en dépôt dans nos bureaux de recherche à la Faculté de théologie et de sciences religieuses.

4 Dans son mémoire de licence intitulé « Le sens de Dieu et le sens du péché », écrit en 1970, Denis Cossette donne systématiquement, au fil de son texte, le nom de presque tous les professeurs, tant québécois qu'européens, qu'il a rencontrés durant sa formation.

passé, pour en tirer profit, nous éclairer et nous aider à mieux comprendre ce qu'est la liturgie[5].

Cette volonté de retour aux traits « originels » de l'Église et de la foi est davantage une revendication à retrouver ce qui constitue, non pas tant une origine chronologique de l'Église que sa spécificité originelle dans ce qu'elle peut avoir de plus vraie, dégagée des formes et des traces de divers contextes historiques et culturels. Cette même volonté de retrouver l'originalité profonde de l'Église, et de la vie de foi qui la caractérise, se retrouve chez plusieurs enseignants. Dans son ouvrage intitulé *Introduction à la catéchèse*, publié en 1966, le directeur de l'Institut, Jacques Laforest, estime que « l'échec du renouveau méthodologique force [...] les catéchètes à réfléchir plus en profondeur sur la nature de la catéchèse. [...] Au fait, est-ce qu'il en a toujours été ainsi ? Les apôtres par exemple, ils devaient s'y connaître en catéchèse... comment procédaient-ils[6] ? »

Ce projet de retour aux sources définit également le cœur même de l'enseignement de Jean Daniélou, spécialiste de la patristique. Dans une conférence d'abord présentée à Lyon, puis à Québec, en 1970, il dit : « C'est en revenant ainsi aux origines, en ressaisissant dans leur premier mouvement ce qu'ont été à la fois les rapprochements et les séparations que nous pouvons le mieux, par la racine même, peut-on dire, reprendre et ressaisir ce qui s'est ensuite perdu. » Il conclut en ces termes : « Et c'est en ce sens, je pense, que nous devons être reconnaissants à ceux qui ici travaillent à cette tâche et voir précisément en eux et saluer en eux des serviteurs très efficaces bien que très cachés de ce renouveau de l'Église qui en notre temps est quelque chose de si essentiel[7]. »

Dans ce mouvement même d'aspiration pour revenir au cœur de la vie de foi, les professeurs en formation catéchétique puisent dans divers textes de Vatican II la matière substantielle de leur contenu, une matière soucieuse de maintenir un dialogue entre le dire de la théologie et les transformations du monde. En 1965, les cours du père Tillard, domi-

5 Manuscrit, « Cours du Révérend Père Gignac, O.P. » (1964), 1.

6 Jacques Laforest, *Introduction à la catéchèse*, Sainte-Foy, Presses de l'Université Laval, 1966, p. 32-33.

7 Jean Daniélou, *Conférence prononcée à Lyon le 12 mars 1970* (Dubeau-Legentil, 16), p. 19-20.

nicain d'Ottawa, abordent sous plusieurs angles le thème de l'« Église dans le monde ». D'emblée, il soulève cette question qui montre bien les défis de l'Église face au monde :

> Pourquoi vivre tendu vers un « avenir » et une promesse de bonheur surnaturel, dont on ne sait guère beaucoup de choses précises, alors que le *hic et nunc* de l'histoire et de l'Univers sont en eux-mêmes déjà enivrants, capables de satisfaire une générosité d'homme et porteurs de promesses dont on devine déjà la réalité ? L'homme contemporain ne veut la foi que si elle le pousse à aimer ce monde, à s'enivrer de son progrès.

Et il conclut :

> Que faire en face de cette constatation ? Si l'Église ne se pose pas cette question et n'en cherche pas la réponse avec ardeur, elle est infidèle à la vocation et à la mission reçue de son Seigneur. Elle tente l'Esprit de Dieu ! C'est pourquoi le fameux schéma 13 veut s'en occuper[8].

Ce genre d'interrogation opère un déplacement dans la formation visée. Le professeur ne veut pas tant faire de ses destinataires des théologiens qui connaissent la dogmatique :

> J'espère avoir réussi à vous faire saisir avec acuité à la fois la situation dramatique de l'Évangile dans le monde d'aujourd'hui et sa merveilleuse puissance de salut pour ce monde d'aujourd'hui. [...] Le concile œcuménique ne portera son fruit que si les chrétiens qui l'accueillent se décident une fois pour toutes à ouvrir leur christianisme aux dimensions de l'Évangile, qui sont celles du Dieu créateur... celui qui a « créé les univers » et qui continue de les aimer[9].

Ce projet de formation d'hommes d'Église et de laïcs conscients de leur responsabilité en tant qu'acteurs de la vie ecclésiale et de la vie de foi est également au cœur des enseignements dispensés par André Liégé entre 1965 et 1968. Dans son cours intitulé « Théologie pastorale générale », il consacre une leçon au thème « Les institutions

---

8 Jean-Marie Tillard, *L'Église dans le monde* (Dubeau-Legentil, 1.7.3), p. 2.

9 Jean-Marie Tillard, *L'Église consent-elle au péché du monde* (Dubeau-Legentil, 1.7.5), p. 12.

chrétiennes ont-elles encore leur chance ? » Au départ, il apostrophe ses étudiants en disant, fort de son expérience, que les « Institutions chrétiennes [...] doivent faire partie de l'*aggiornamento* conciliaire : beaucoup le concèdent dans l'Église [...] mais tous ne sont pas d'accord pour apprécier ce que doit être la mise à jour[10] » !

Selon l'éminent professeur, les futurs catéchètes ont besoin de comprendre qu'il y a une difficulté majeure à passer d'un monde de chrétienté traditionnelle, avec sa pastorale de chrétienté, à un renouveau pastoral :

> Nous constatons que le Concile a remis en question les options profondes de cette pastorale de chrétienté, et a choisi des options, non forcément contraires, mais différentes. Cela ne revient pas à dire que la pastorale de chrétienté fut erronée, mais que les signes des temps obligent l'Église à reconsidérer son agir pour le rendre plus véritable et plus actuel[11].

Une des grandes avenues de Vatican II consiste en cette importante ouverture sur le monde, en cette ouverture au monde, c'est-à-dire en une nouvelle façon de se positionner par rapport à ce monde et, dans le même mouvement, en cette nouvelle façon de se vivre et de se positionner à l'intérieur même de la vie de l'Église. On peut certes parler, à ce propos, d'une grande « réception du monde » par Vatican II. Cela a des implications directes sur la manière même de vivre et de se situer à l'intérieur de l'Église.

Aux catéchètes en formation, André Liégé propose une série de cinq grandes conférences, en lien direct avec les « voies de la démocratisation dans l'Église ». Il s'agit ni plus ni moins que d'aborder, à la lumière des textes de Vatican II, « comment se cherchent de nouvelles expressions de l'autorité pastorale dans l'Église, que signifie la participation de tous, comment vivre une obéissance plus libre et quel est le sens de la contestation dans la communauté[12] ». Pour le professeur,

---

[10] André LIÉGÉ, « Les institutions chrétiennes ont-elles encore leur chance? » (Dubeau-Legentil, 1.6.2), p. 1.

[11] André LIÉGÉ, « De la pastorale de chrétienté au renouveau pastoral de Vatican II » (Dubeau-Legentil, 1.6.3), p. 15.

[12] André LIÉGÉ, « Les voies de la démocratisation dans l'Église » (Dubeau-Legentil, 1.5.1), p. 1.

il est manifeste « que le concile dans les décisions, dans les paroles, dans les discours et donc dans les engagements a introduit un temps révolutionnaire dans l'Église par rapport à ce qu'elle était avant[13] ». Toutefois, ces changements sont loin de faire l'unanimité dans l'Église et dans le monde. Il se dit même « quelquefois étonné de voir qu'un certain nombre de chrétiens qui ont lu superficiellement [...] les textes du concile ne s'en rendent pas compte et qu'un certain nombre de colères et d'impatiences aujourd'hui s'expriment en faisant appel à ce que l'Église était dans les premiers siècles[14] ».

Après d'importants développements sur les possibilités et les dangers de cette démocratisation, ce spécialiste de la théologie pastorale veut approfondir avec ses auditeurs trois aspects particuliers qui se dégagent de la constitution dogmatique *Gaudium et spes* : a) la redécouverte du peuple de Dieu, avec en particulier une réflexion sur les responsabilités des membres de l'Église ; b) la responsabilité et la liberté des laïcs ; et enfin c) l'institution de dialogue, de conseil et d'opinion[15].

En lien étroit avec la nouvelle façon d'être présent au monde, un des documents de Vatican II qui contribue également à mettre en perspective la nature même et la responsabilité non seulement des chrétiens, mais de toute personne humaine, est la déclaration sur la liberté. Au cours de l'année 1969-1970, le dominicain Christian Duquoc donne

---

13 André Liégé, *ibid.*, p. 4.

14 *Ibidem.*

15 *Ibid.*, p. 5-8. Le professeur Liégé insinue une certaine mise en garde sur la dynamique même de cette démocratisation : « Mais en quoi va consister ce renouveau, cette redécouverte du concile, un renouveau et une redécouverte qui me paraissent aussi importants que l'insistance mise sur les évêques [...] et il y aurait encore un grand danger à ne retenir que la revalorisation des évêques. C'est vrai que le concile a été généreux pour les évêques comme Vatican I avait été généreux pour le pape.
« Mais cette générosité pour les évêques qui pourrait être mal comprise si on la retenait unilatéralement, car tout ce dont on se plaignait concernant la Curie Romaine, on pourrait aujourd'hui s'en plaindre concernant les évêques qui ont retrouvé un pouvoir et quelquefois un pouvoir beaucoup plus médiocre que celui de la Curie Romaine parce que moins universel ou allant moins loin et il pourrait, en effet, se faire que dans l'Église d'après Vatican II, il y ait une tyrannie épiscopale dans l'Église qui soit bien pire que la tyrannie de la Curie romaine qu'on a remise en question. C'est pourquoi je pense qu'il est très important que les Chrétiens d'aujourd'hui, en même temps que reconnaissant cette générosité tout à fait normale pour les évêques, reconnaissent que le concile a dit autre chose qui doit être pris avec et qui rééquilibre au cas où un déséquilibre serait menaçant ce qui a été dit concernant les évêques. »

un cours intitulé « La liberté religieuse et la mission de l'Église ». C'est l'occasion privilégiée pour approfondir le sens même de la liberté au sein d'un monde de plus en plus pluriel. À partir de là, une vaste réflexion est engagée pour chercher à comprendre comment concilier le respect absolu dû à la liberté de chacun dans sa recherche de la vérité et l'absolue certitude qui se fonde sur la foi en Jésus Christ. Prendre au sérieux cette liberté a des incidences radicales sur tout projet de formation catéchétique.

Dans un autre ordre d'idée, des cours voués de manière plus immédiate à la catéchèse, tels ceux des jésuites belges Pierre Ranwez et Marcel van Casters, puisent également avec abondance dans les textes du concile. En 1965, Pierre Ranwez introduit son cours sur le développement psychoreligieux des jeunes enfants par une section entière intitulée « l'enseignement du magistère ». Son objectif est de faire saisir à ses étudiants l'importance que *Lumen gentium* accorde aux époux unis par le mariage et l'importance de la famille pour une bonne éducation de la foi. Attention, il ne s'agit pas simplement, comme dans des mandements anciens, d'inciter les parents à accomplir leur devoir d'état sous la direction de l'évêque et de leur curé, mais bien de définir le rôle et la responsabilité des parents en tant qu'acteurs constitutifs de l'Église :

> Par la vertu du sacrement de mariage qui leur donne de signifier en y participant le mystère de l'unité et de l'amour fécond entre le Christ et l'Église, les époux chrétiens s'aident mutuellement à se sanctifier par la vie conjugale, par l'accueil et l'éducation des enfants : en leur état de vie et dans leur ordre, ils ont ainsi dans le peuple de Dieu leurs dons propres. De leur union, en effet, procède la famille où naissent des membres nouveaux de la cité des hommes dont la grâce de l'Esprit Saint fera par le baptême des fils de Dieu pour que le peuple de Dieu se perpétue tout le long des siècles. Il faut que, par la parole et par l'exemple, dans cette sorte d'Église qu'est le foyer, les parents soient pour leurs enfants les premiers hérauts de la foi, au service de la vocation propre de chacun et tout spécialement de la vocation sacrée[16].

---

16 Pierre RANWEZ, Manuscrit, *Psychologie religieuse de l'enfance*, p. 10.

Pour sa part, en 1966, Marcel van Caster donne un cours intitulé « L'activité humaine ». La première partie de son enseignement traite de ce qu'il appelle « l'activité axiologique » telle que promue par *Gaudium et spes*. Ce long excursus est plus qu'un préalable à la seconde partie intitulée : « Pédagogie de l'unité dynamique entre les niveaux d'existence », laquelle est développée dans la perspective de la « Démarche catéchétique » (p. 22sq). Le professeur van Caster œuvre à une intégration, une corrélation même de la dogmatique et de la pratique : le cœur de la pédagogie de la foi ne sera jamais dans l'ordre des éphémérides ou de la surface des événements, mais bien au cœur même, dans la profondeur des activités humaines.

De ce tour d'horizon, on peut retenir que Vatican II est bien présent dans la formation dispensée aux étudiants de l'Institut de catéchèse. Cette présence se manifeste de façon à la fois très explicite par d'abondantes citations puisées directement dans les productions émanant du concile, et implicitement par les mouvements mêmes d'Église suscités par le concile et qui circulent entre les professeurs et les nombreux étudiants qui fréquentent ces cours et participent à la vie et à la réflexion qui affleurent durant ces années. Pour mieux saisir le type d'animation, de réception et d'intégration que le concile suscite, il est éclairant de s'arrêter aux productions intellectuelles que représente la rédaction des mémoires de licence.

Vatican II dans les mémoires de catéchèse

Avant de nous arrêter au contenu de ces mémoires, une précision s'impose sur leurs auteurs et également sur le type de mémoire concerné. Les étudiants dont il est question ici, entre 1962 et 1970, ne sont pas d'abord des maîtres en formation — les écoles normales existent toujours à cette époque —, mais une majorité de prêtres, de religieux et de religieuses d'expérience, enseignants ou missionnaires, et quelques laïcs qui se donnent un temps de ressourcement et de « recyclage[17] » en catéchèse. Donc, plusieurs des mémoires écrits à cette époque sont produits par des gens qui avaient soit une formation de licencié en

[17] Il s'agit là d'une expression courante à l'époque, servant à désigner une formation d'appoint que se donnaient des femmes et des hommes au seuil d'une nouvelle orientation professionnelle ou vocationnelle.

théologie, soit une bonne expérience dans le monde de l'enseignement. Pour ce qui est des mémoires eux-mêmes, ceux-ci correspondaient à un travail long d'une valeur de 15 crédits de premier cycle, travail long qui complétait une formation globale de 45 crédits sanctionnée par un diplôme de licence en catéchèse[18]. En moyenne, ces mémoires comptaient une centaine de pages.

À la bibliothèque de l'Université Laval se retrouvent 125 thèses de licence en catéchèse écrites entre 1968 et 1973. De ce nombre, on repère 7 mémoires dont le titre fait une mention directe à Vatican II et 32 dont la bibliographie comporte une ou plusieurs références au concile. Un tableau permet de répartir suivant les années le nombre respectif de mémoires produits et de ceux qui réfèrent au concile.

1968	18	(5 citent)
1969	34	(4 citent)
1970	38	(19 citent)
1971	26	(7 citent)
1972	7	(3 citent)
1973	2	(1 cite)
Total	**125**	**(39 citent)**

Comme on peut s'y attendre, bon nombre de thésards disent reconnaître dans le concile la prise en compte des préoccupations qui les tenaillent. Ainsi, René Bégin affirme : « La constitution *Gaudium et Spes* est précisément dans la ligne du sujet que nous traitons : c'est un effort de l'Église qui, comme le Christ son fondateur, va vers les hommes d'aujourd'hui pour s'incarner et y apporter sa Révélation[19]. » Au-delà de l'analyse et du commentaire du texte, Bégin entre dans un processus d'interprétation qui rejoint son désir et son être le plus profond :

> Tout au long du document conciliaire on sent le souci de l'Église d'être vraiment la Mère des hommes, de se mettre à leur service, sûre de leur apporter quelque chose d'essentiel mais en même

[18] À compter de l'année 1971, la réforme globale des études à l'Université Laval conduira à remplacer cette licence de 45 crédits par un baccalauréat de 90 crédits dispensé sur une période de trois années.

[19] René Bégin, *Christianisme incarné*, 1968.

> temps scrupuleusement respectueuse des libertés. Finie cette période triomphaliste dans l'Église. Elle veut ses interventions beaucoup plus discrètes, elle veut être le levain dans la pâte qui semble perdre son identité mais qui fait lever toute la pâte. Elle veut accompagner le monde dans sa marche, dialoguer avec lui, quelles que soient ses préventions idéologiques à son endroit, se faire le Christ des pèlerins d'Emmaüs qui éclaire l'esprit, réchauffe le cœur et se retire discrètement, plutôt que le Christ de Damas qui éblouit Paul de sa clarté, ce qui, pour nos susceptibilités contemporaines, paraîtrait une grâce contraignante[20].

Pour sa part, Denis Cossette retient, dans son étude intitulée *Le sens de Dieu et le sens du péché*, ce « passage d'une Église royaume de Dieu à une Église en marche. Passage d'une Église du "déjà" à une Église du "pas encore", une Église-étape-vers-le-royaume. De plus, c'est le passage d'une primauté du prêtre à une primauté du laïc et de ses tâches. Signe de ce que le Salut donne à l'homme[21]. » Quant à Maurice Boilard, sa recherche sur l'*Étude catéchétique du rôle du prêtre dans l'Église à la lumière de la révélation et de Vatican II* l'amène également à un regard renouvelé sur le monde et sur l'Église. Dans un texte d'une très grande beauté, il écrit :

> Pour les uns, l'Église va trop vite, pour les autres, elle ne bouge pas assez. Il y a désormais un fait que personne ne peut nier, nous vivons dans un monde nouveau. Nous n'avons pas pour mission de regretter le passé, mais le devoir de rejoindre le présent. Et pour cela, nous devons être prêts à répondre aux exigences du moment, notre mission sacerdotale est toujours la même : « amener les hommes à la rencontre personnelle de Dieu à travers la révélation vivifiante »[22].

Par rapport à toutes ces mutations, J.P. Tessier découvre ce que peut signifier « l'obéissance au service d'un engagement ». Comme il l'écrit dans sa conclusion : « Le Décret sur la liberté religieuse ne propose-t-il

---

20 *Ibid.*

21 Denis Cossette, *Le sens de Dieu et le sens du péché*, 1970.

22 Maurice Boilard, ptre, *Étude catéchétique du rôle du prêtre dans l'Église à la lumière de la révélation et de Vatican II*, 1970.

pas de favoriser davantage les initiatives en éduquant la liberté personnelle par la réflexion et l'action dans l'interdépendance[23] ?... »

Alors que Jean-Noël Gagné, sous le titre *L'Église découvre son visage et se découvre : être du Christ et être du monde*, s'attache à montrer l'évolution de l'Église de Vatican I à Vatican II[24], Fernand Gauthier estime pour sa part que, « avec Vatican II, tout un courant nouveau d'anthropologie a modifié sensiblement cette vision statique et étroite de l'homme. [...] La constitution pastorale *L'Église dans le monde de ce temps* analyse d'une façon toute neuve, je dirais, l'homme qui vit et évolue dans l'univers[25]. » Jacques Garon va, quant à lui, s'efforcer de démontrer comment le concile a su accueillir les perspectives nouvelles reconnues par Vatican II aux sciences naturelles pour une meilleure connaissance de l'homme, connaissance indispensable pour développer un accompagnement pastoral compétent et adapté[26].

En 1969, le *Directoire sur la catéchèse* n'existe pas encore. Néanmoins, Robert Talbot constate que, bien « qu'on ne retrouve dans les textes conciliaires aucun schéma consacré explicitement et systématiquement à la catéchèse, [...] Vatican II parle très souvent soit de la catéchèse, soit de la prédication de l'évangile[27] ». Dans son mémoire intitulé *Ministère et objectifs de la catéchèse selon Vatican II*, il puise au sein de tous les textes de Vatican II les passages se référant au ministère de la catéchèse, afin d'en constituer, en quelque sorte, un schéma concernant la catéchèse elle-même.

Conclusion

Peut-on parler de réception de Vatican II dans la formation catéchétique dispensée à l'Institut de catéchèse de Québec ? Et comment peut-on entendre cette réception ?

---

[23] J.P. TESSIER, *L'obéissance au service d'un engagement*, 1971, p. 168.

[24] Jean-Noël GAGNÉ, *L'Église découvre son visage et se découvre : être du Christ et être du monde*, 1971.

[25] Fernand GAUTHIER, *Un aspect de la théologie de l'homme à Vatican II et son impact dans un renouveau de la catéchèse*, mai 1969, p. 3.

[26] Jacques GARON, *L'enseignement de Vatican II sur les sciences naturelles concernant le fait religieux*, 1970.

[27] Robert TALBOT, *Ministère et objectifs de la catéchèse selon Vatican II*, 1969, p. 1.

Le survol des cours dispensés et des thèses de licence produites démontre bien que pour cette population enseignante et étudiante Vatican II était présent et occupait une place déterminante. Dans la formation catéchétique qui se met en place, on peut reconnaître ce désir, cette soif, cette aspiration à ce que propose et accomplit Vatican II. On est dans une mouvance de Vatican II, ce qui n'est pas à confondre avec une transmission des édits de Vatican II. C'est Vatican II « en mode actif », pourrait-on dire. Vatican II qui mobilise et amorce, comme par onde de choc, un mouvement qui se propage. Autrement dit, il y a une réception de Vatican II qui est vraiment à entendre comme une réception au sens d'un rassemblement festif : on reçoit le monde ! Et le monde, y compris celui qui gravite autour de l'Institut de catéchèse de Québec, se sent effectivement « reçu » par le concile, partie prenante de l'événement. On est reçu et on reçoit Vatican II avant même et au-delà de ce que la théologie peut en dire dans l'instant où se déroule l'événement.

Il y a un souffle conciliaire qui semble avoir une connivence certaine avec le monde de la catéchèse. Un souffle de célébration. Un concile, ça se célèbre. Un concile, ça célèbre ! En concile, on célèbre ! Une célébration conciliaire, c'est comme un sommet : bien sûr, on y parle de diverses choses, mais d'abord et avant tout, on plonge de tout son être, on s'immerge dans un « être avec » qui nous révèle qui on est dans l'acte même qui nous fait advenir comme sujet personnel et collectif. Et cela nous plonge déjà dans des enjeux d'un nouvel ordre catéchétique qui prend ses distances avec le mode de la transmission infléchi par la production et la diffusion des catéchismes imprimés depuis le XVIIe siècle. La formation de cette nouvelle génération de catéchètes ne cherche pas tant à préparer des agents de transmission de vérités dogmatiques approuvées par l'Ordinaire que des acteurs de plus en plus conscients et en quelque sorte partenaires de la mission ecclésiale et sociale qu'implique le projet catéchétique.

Religious Education: From Dogma to Method

Myrtle Power and John van den Hengel,
Saint Paul University

Approaches to religious education had begun to change in the Western Church long before the Second Vatican Council gathered in 1962. The heritage of the famous Roman Catechism of the Council of Trent, with its various national editions and its memorization method of question and answer, endured generally until the 1960s, but voices for transformation had been gathering strength decades earlier.[1]

There were various reasons for the transformation of the catechetical method. One reason stands out as a powerful driving force behind the catechetical movement. By the late nineteenth and early twentieth centuries, the massive reshaping of the religious landscape in Europe brought on by the Enlightenment had begun to pervade popular consciousness.[2] The Enlightenment was no longer the language and worldview only of the elite. Enlightenment consciousness, with its narrowly defined epistemology, its reduction of reality to the measurable and the empirical, and its reshaping of the economic life, had shown its power

[1] The original Roman Catechism that issued from the Council of Trent was not in the form of questions and answers. It encouraged a methodology adapted to the hearers. Only with Robert Bellarmine, at the end of the sixteenth century, did the catechism take this form. Liam Kelly, *Catechesis Revisited: Handing on Faith Today* (London: Darton, Longman and Todd, 2000), 27.

[2] See Charles Taylor, *A Secular Age* (Cambridge: The Belknap Press of Harvard University, 2007).

to wipe away the horizons of religious worldviews. The everyday lives of people had begun to dissolve their previous dependencies on nature and God, leading them to adopt the view that their future depended on technological solutions and human know-how.

As a result, the language of the catechisms, which presumed a self-understanding and worldview of the pre-critical age, began to lose its power of persuasion. The schema of the previous worldview was no longer the common self-reference for an increasing number of people. With this loss of a religious culture and the emptying out of the ostensive reference of religious language and rituals of faith, Catholics found themselves more and more in a religious wasteland. They were being pushed in two different directions. By the end of the nineteenth and the beginning of the twentieth centuries, some religious educators became convinced that the traditional religious language had lost its rootedness in life and common experience. The questions of the catechism were no longer authentic questions; their underlying foundation had been eroded. The search began for a new approach.

To explore the pivotal role that Vatican II played in reshaping the catechetical process, we begin by presenting briefly the catechetical renewal movement prior to Vatican II both in Europe and in Canada. Two women, Françoise Darcy-Berubé and Christiane Brusselmans, are recognized as bringing this renewal movement to Canada. The article then describes the impact of Vatican II on religious education, particularly through the documents that subsequently interpreted the teachings of Vatican II. The article illustrates how the Canadian catechetical process incorporated the orientations of the Vatican documents in the *Born of the Spirit* series, published by the Canadian Conference of Catholic Bishops (CCCB) for use in Canada.[3] In conclusion, the article proposes that the principles of a practical hermeneutics, inspired by the philosophy of Paul Ricœur, underlie the Canadian catechetical process.

3 The *Born of the Spirit* series of catechetical resources is the successor to the *Viens au Père* or *Come to the Father* series initiated by Françoise Darcy-Berubé and the catechetical team assembled in Montréal in 1962. The *Born of the Spirit* series (CCCB) had its origins in English-speaking Canada in 1978 and, in its second edition, is still in use in English-speaking Canada.

The Preconciliar "Catechetical Movement"

The preconciliar catechetical movement recognized the need for the Church to move out of its ahistorical self-understanding with its eternal verities and to link up with the emerging historical worldview. The first stirrings of this movement are found in the nineteenth century.

It began in Central Europe. There, a search was undertaken to find better methodologies to teach the doctrines of the faith.[4] For many, this search for new methods came from a realization that the approach of the national catechisms was no longer up to the task of bringing the new generation into an understanding and living of the faith. The main impetus for this renewal came from Germany, Switzerland, and France.

Otto Willmann (1839–20), a leading German Catholic pedagogue, began to encourage catechists to open up to new educational principles, and promoted a "learning by doing" approach. Others also thought that a change of approach that attended to the new cultural environment would help religious education. The Munich Method, developed toward the end of the nineteenth century, began to look into the psychology of human learning. It proposed the use of the triad: presentation (a Gospel story), explanation (doctrine), and application (to daily life). These early attempts, however, did not change the content. The Roman Catechism remained the catechetical text, but catechists began to make use of better pedagogy to make the doctrinal texts understood.

The push toward new pedagogical approaches came particularly through the impact of new pedagogical and educational theories. In other words, at the same time that the first attempts were being made to soften the unremittingly dogmatic approach of the catechism, significant shifts in the field of pedagogy began to surface as well. These theories, which were more experimental, began to affect the process and orientation of teaching religious education. Most of these new theories were about the process of children's learning. For instance, John Dewey (1859–1952) promoted a theory on the social influences on knowledge, insisting that all knowledge is socially constructed and that only an experimentalist or experiential language can lay claim to

[4] Marie Mongoven, *The Prophetic Spirit of Catechesis* (New York: Paulist Press, 2000), 44.

truth. Dewey insisted on a more active educational method and took a special interest in the aesthetics of teaching and learning.[5] Within his educational theory there is hardly room for a one-size-fits-all textbook. Teaching that used non-contextual and non-experiential language became more and more unacceptable.

A second educational theory in the first part of the twentieth century had equal power to sway methods in education away from content and toward process in education. Jean Piaget (1896–1980) proposed a cognitive theory of moral development from early childhood. Insisting that moral development did not take place all at once, he created a map to show the moral development of persons from childhood to maturity. According to these theorists, all education—including religious education—must attend to the learning and developmental process of children. The conceptual framework of the catechism was found to lack an appropriate pedagogy. In many ways, it was much beyond the capacity of the learner, and certainly of the early learner.[6] Religious education was being pushed to appropriate child-oriented methods.

Overall, the twentieth century can undoubtedly be considered the most active catechetical century since the apostolic age. Decade after decade brought new horizons of interpretation and fresh approaches that shifted the Church from its understanding of religious instruction as rote learning by children to catechesis as critical inquiry into the relationship of life and faith by adults.[7] The insights were radical—not so much in the sense of being "far out," but in the sense of inspiring and summoning catechists to rethink the foundations of catechesis. Gradually, the preconciliar catechetical movement began to return to the Church's rich catechetical roots, shift out of its ahistorical self-understanding, and link up with the emerging worldview.

---

5 Sara Lawrence-Lightfoot and Jessica Hoffman-Davis, *The Art and Science of Portraiture* (San Francisco: Jossey-Bass, 1997), 6.

6 Historically, John Dewey and Jean Piaget have had a great influence in the development of religious education because of new insights into the way children learn. Their writings continue to influence writers. It is not that their views have remained uncontested. See, for instance, Mary Donaldson, *The Language and Thought of a Child* (London: Routledge and Kegan Paul, 1966), and Dan Batson, Patricia Schoenrode, and Larry Ventes, *Religion and the Individual* (New York: Oxford University Press, 1993).

7 Mongoven, *The Prophetic Spirit of Catechesis*, 42–43.

The renewal of catechetics, happily, began in conjunction with the liturgical renewal in the latter part of the nineteenth and the early twentieth centuries. This renewal latched on to the attempts to recover the wealth of the authentic and traditional *lex orandi* of the Church. If the child-oriented pedagogical theories became inserted in the first phase of the preconciliar catechetical movement, the liturgical renewal opened up a second avenue for the preconciliar phase of renewal in the field of religious education. It became known as kerygmatic catechesis. Kerygmatic catechesis was grounded in the search for the foundations of catechesis in the Scriptures and in the Church's early liturgical life.

The chief artisan of this movement was an Austrian Jesuit, Joseph Jungmann (1889–1976).[8] Jungmann was an early supporter of methodological reform by way of a new pedagogy, but he insisted that a change in method was not enough. He was convinced that the Christian message needed to be rejuvenated with the dynamism it held in apostolic times. He "described church life as impoverished, due to a static theology that did not speak to people's lives" and labelled its form of instruction an "arid intellectualism."[9] An avid liturgist, Jungmann took every effort to recover the ancient liturgical traditions. He insisted that liturgy may not be divorced from the people.

Jungmann's basic premise was that the message presented in catechesis ought to include not only creeds and doctrinal formulations but also Scripture and liturgy. He advocated that catechesis return to an exploration of these fundamental sources of Christian faith and determine how they interrelate with one another and with a fourth source, the witness of daily life.[10] Jungmann's thought had an impact in Canada. In his work *The Modern Challenge to Religious Education*, G. Emmett Carter (1912–2003), later archbishop of Toronto, paid tribute to the accomplishments of Jungmann in his costly endeavour to shift the emphasis from method to content in catechetical development.[11]

---

[8] Ibid., 45.

[9] Ibid., 46.

[10] Ibid., 47.

[11] G. Emmett Carter, *The Modern Challenge to Religious Education* (New York: William H. Sadlier, 1961), 89.

A second contributor to kerygmatic catechesis was Joseph Colomb (1902–79). Like Jungmann, Colomb insisted on going back to the sources of Scripture, liturgy, and doctrine, but instead of calling the fourth source "witness," he called it "human experience." He urged catechists to attend to the spiritual dimensions of those being catechetized by drawing out the Christian meaning of their human experiences.[12] He wondered how people could understand a lesson on prayer if they had never prayed. If people had no experience of a parish community, what could a lesson on the parish offer them?[13] Colomb argued that in catechesis, "it is on the child's religious experience that we must build, not on the textbook."[14] He is also known for his insights on developmental learning.

A third great influence in the development of a kerygmatic catechesis was Johannes Hofinger (1905–84). To help spread the idea of Jungmann's kerygmatic catechesis, Hofinger organized a series of International Catechetical Study Weeks held on five continents during the late 1950s and the 1960s. These events finally made the breakthrough from being regional interests to becoming part of the mainstream of the catechetical movement. The study weeks, particularly the one held in Medellín, Colombia, in 1968, began to be heard beyond the narrow circle of their participants. As Marie Mongoven notes in her account of these events, "Some participants in the Study Weeks were later bishops or *periti* (consultants) at the Second Vatican Council. They brought to the Study Weeks theological and pastoral insights of the council, and to the council the catechetical insights of the Study Weeks."[15]

Described as "a landmark in the history of modern catechetics,"[16] the second study week, held in Eichstatt, Germany, in 1960, brought an end, on an international scale, to the narrow vision of catechesis as

12 Mongoven, *The Prophetic Spirit of Catechesis*, 48.

13 Ibid., 49.

14 Joseph Colomb, *Catéchisme progressif*, Guide 1, trans. Georges Delcuve (Lyons/Paris: Emmanuel Vitte, 1950), 5.

15 Mongoven, *The Prophetic Spirit of Catechesis*, 51.

16 Bernard L. Marthaler, "The Modern Catechetical Movement in Roman Catholicism: Issues and Personalities," in *Sourcebook for Modern Catechetics*, Vol. 1, ed. Michael Warren (Winona, MN: St. Mary's Press, 1983), 280.

only instruction in doctrine. The Eichstatt study week concluded that "catechesis embraces a fourfold presentation of the faith: through liturgy, Bible, systematic teaching and the testimony of Christian living."[17] Eichstatt also provided a forum for bringing together the principles of the developmental approach to learning of Colomb and other French thinkers with the kerygmatic approach of the Jungmann school.

The third study week, held in Bangkok in 1962, presented further shifts in catechetical reform. On the one hand, Bangkok moved the emphasis away from the catechesis of children to the catechesis of adults; on the other hand, it changed the focus from concern about the content of catechesis to concern about the subjects of catechesis. This anthropological concern about the life experience and culture of those being catechized continued to occupy a central place in subsequent study weeks, both in Katigondo (1964) and Manila (1967). The study week in Katigondo was the first to be held following the promulgation of the Constitution on the Sacred Liturgy (*Sacrosanctum Concilium*). The week emphasized the importance of adapting liturgical catechesis to the culture of the people. The anthropological or subject-centred focus in catechesis was further advanced in Manila, with the critical impact of the discussions and documents that emerged from the Second Vatican Council, particularly the Pastoral Constitution on the Church in the Modern World (*Gaudium et Spes*) and the Decree on the Church's Missionary Activity (*Ad Gentes*), both of which were promulgated in 1965.[18]

The conclusions of the sixth and final study week, in Medellín (1968), were subsequently incorporated into a Vatican document of the Congregation for the Clergy, addressed to the whole Church. The *General Catechetical Directory* of 1971 summarized what, for the participants, were exciting times of revolutionary social change and Church

---

[17] Mongoven, *The Prophetic Spirit of Catechesis*, 53. Mongoven notes that in accepting the four signs as content and recognizing that catechesis seeks the response of a change of heart, Eichstatt initiated a new search into the nature of conversion and of the catechetical act.

[18] Ibid., 53–55. Mongoven notes that a primary question occupying the minds of participants during the study week in Manila revolved around how one might carry out such an anthropological catechesis in pastoral practice.

reform. Here the preconciliar met up with the postconciliar.[19] The conclusions reflect the excitement of the time and the participants' thrust for a renewed form of catechetical ministry: 1. the beginning point of catechesis ought to be the life experience of the group; 2. catechesis needs to interpret and critique culture, society, and the Church; 3. there must be a diversity of catechetical forms to respond to the plurality of life-situations throughout the world; and 4. the method and content of catechesis must not be separated.[20]

Catechetical Renewal in Canada before Vatican II

The winds of change that were blowing through Europe in the early part of the twentieth century also reached Canada.[21] From an historical perspective, two women pioneers were enormously instrumental in bringing the catechetical shift to Canada and in laying the foundations for catechesis in Canada in the second half of the twentieth century. The first important figure is Françoise Darcy-Berubé. The second is Christiane Brusselmans.

Françoise Darcy-Berubé

Born in Paris in 1922, Françoise Darcy-Berubé was growing up when the first phase of the catechetical renewal was underway. Reflecting on her catechetical journey, Darcy-Berubé recalled the enthusiasm of moving from one catechetical discovery to another as the biblical, liturgical, theological, and catechetical developments of the century were progressing, before and after Vatican II.[22] She cited several prophetic figures who significantly influenced her vision and work: Congar, Chenu, Rahner, Schillebeeckx, Häring, Teilhard de Chardin, Daniélou, de Lubac, Jungmann, and Hofinger. Among educational

---

19 Mongoven, *The Prophetic Spirit of Catechesis*, 58. The participants at Medellín made a concerted appeal to Cardinal Jean Villot, prefect of the Congregation for the Clergy, to include the Medellín conclusions in deliberations of the committee preparing the *General Catechetical Directory* (1971).

20 Ibid., 57.

21 Ibid., 42–43.

22 Francoise Darcy-Berubé, *Religious Education at the Crossroads* (New York: Paulist Press, 1995), 9.

theorists she cited Piaget, Erickson, Kohlberg, Maria Montessori, A. Vergote, Helene Lubienska de Lenval, Sophia Cavaletti, and Otto Willmann.[23]

In the early 1960s, just as a third phase in the catechetical movement was emerging—what Hofinger called the anthropological or experiential phase[24]—Darcy-Berubé was receiving international recognition for her insights in curriculum development, which brought her an invitation in 1962 to join a writing team developing a new catechetical series at the Provincial Catechetical Office in Montréal, Québec. It was here that she would make her mark in Canadian catechesis. In 1961 a thirty-person team of Canadian catechists, theologians, psychologists, sociologists, and teachers, including Darcy-Berubé, began work on the series that was published as *The Canadian Catechism*, later known as the *Come to the Father* series. By 1965 the series was being used by 125,000 students in 6,000 classrooms.[25] It was a radical departure from traditional catechisms for a number of reasons.

First, the catechesis was grounded in "a Trinitarian perspective that invited children into a relationship with God, experienced in the loving outreach of Father, Son, and Spirit."[26] In Berubé's words, "What is important for the children is to put them in contact with the divine persons, not to provide them with a theological definition of the Trinity."[27] Communion and relationship are at the heart of the mystery of the Trinity.

Second, the series saw the task of catechesis as a developmental process of moral and spiritual awakening and not as the intellectual presentation of a body of truths to be learned. "The young child has a capacity for religious experience, for an intuitive global acceptance of God's revelation," Berubé writes. Hence, religious education should not be "indoctrination" but "the slow awakening in the child of an awareness

---

23 Ibid., 7–13.

24 Johannes Hofinger, "Looking Backward and Forward: Journey of Catechesis," in *Living Light* 20, no. 4 (1984): 348–57.

25 Fayette Veverka, "Francoise Darcy-Berube," accessed February 13, 2010, http://www.talbot.edu/ce20/educators/view.cfm?n=francoise_darcy-berube

26 Ibid.

27 Ibid.

of God's loving presence right in the threads of his experience of life."[28] It was a "psychologically oriented" series written for the child's age level, taking into account the child's personality, world, and way of knowing.[29] A third shift of the *Come to the Father* series was the integration of Scripture stories and texts into lessons in a way that taught children how to pray, and led them to contemplation and celebration.

Finally, the program placed a strong emphasis on the role of the family as "the natural environment for Christian education."[30] It offered a special component for parents to involve them more actively in the faith formation of their children. Overall, the *Come to the Father* series introduced theological and pedagogical orientations that are still considered central in the practice of religious education and catechetics today.

Christiane Brusselmans

Born in Leuven, Belgium, in 1930, and raised in the small country town of Korbeek-Lo,[31] Christiane Brusselmans is considered one of the most influential catechetical pioneers of the twentieth century.[32] Her vision on postconciliar catechetical renewal in Canada and, in particular, on catechist formation and religious education curriculum, had an impact in three key areas:

1. Liturgical Initiation

In catechetical workshops and liturgical institutes, Christiane Brusselmans influenced the lives of numerous catechists, catechetical

28 Ibid.

29 Ibid.

30 Ibid.

31 Korbeek-Lo, where the Brusselmans family settled, was situated very close to the Benedictine Abbey of Mont-César, a key centre for European liturgical renewal.

32 Damien Lundy, "A Vision for Catechists in the 1990s," in *The Candles Are Still Burning: Directions in Sacrament and Spirituality*, ed. M. Grey, A. Heaton and D. Sullivan. (Collegeville, MN: The Liturgical Press, 1995), 42–57. In an interview on the topic of the legacy of Christian Brusselmans, Canadian Bishop Remi De Roo expressed these views: "I would see Christiane Brusselmans' legacy as that of a pioneer lay woman who incarnated the spirit of Vatican II as few people have done, who was relentless in the pursuit of her vision. I am certain that many people embraced a career as catechist or religious educator as a result of her undaunted leadership." Interview by author M. Power. Notes. Victoria, BC, March 2005.

leaders, and religious educators in Canada "with a vision of the sacraments which touched the deepest roots of their human experience."[33] Her understanding of the sacraments was "deeply theological in drawing on the sacramental vision of the early church, and deeply ecclesial in locating the sacramental heart in the local church community."[34]

In August 1964, less than a year after the Second Vatican Council's promulgation of the Constitution on the Sacred Liturgy, Brusselmans addressed more than 20,000 lay people, bishops, priests, seminarians, and members of religious communities at the twenty-fifth annual North American Liturgical Week in St. Louis, Missouri. In her address, entitled "The Relationship between Teaching and Celebration,"[35] she insisted on the relationship of catechesis and living faith:

> If however we wish to make true Christians of our children, it does not suffice to teach them their religion. We must make them parishioners, that is, we must prepare them to enter into the liturgy of the Church. We must give them a liturgical initiation.[36]

For Brusselmans, liturgical initiation has to do with awakening a sense of the sacred by: 1. praying in a liturgical way; 2. teaching how to listen and respond to the Word of God; 3. learning how to express oneself in the language of Scripture and the liturgy; 4. learning how to express oneself through the language of gestures; and 5. Eucharistic initiation and the celebration of Sunday.[37] For Brusselmans, it is not "our explanations and lessons" that will make children enter into the mystery of the Eucharist; it is, rather, "*the attitude of the adults*" who participate in the Eucharistic celebration "*with their children*."[38] In shifting the focus from text to action, her catechetical pedagogy bears the mark of a mutual relationship between liturgy, lived faith, and community life.

---

33 Grey, Heaton, and Sullivan, *The Candles Are Still Burning*, vii.

34 Ibid.

35 Christiane Brusselmans, "The Relationship between Teaching and Celebration," in *The Challenge of the Council: Person, Parish, World* (Washington, DC: The Liturgical Conference, 1964).

36 Ibid., 210.

37 Ibid., 212–15.

38 Ibid., 216.

2. *Pilgrim People of God*

Christiane Brusselmans was convinced of the importance of the family and of the vocation of the laity for the mission of the Church. For her, this was a central message of Vatican II. Her view is similar to that of Gabriel Moran, who saw the entire council as an exercise in Christian or religious education—particularly the council documents that changed authority and worship patterns within the Church. Especially important were the Constitution on the Sacred Liturgy and the Pastoral Constitution on the Church in the Modern World.[39] As Mary Grey says of Brusselmans:

> Christiane enabled and empowered ordinary people to discover their roots as truly the "Pilgrim People of God," as truly an expression of local church with full sacramental expression. These roots had little to do with hierarchical power and status: instead she directed us towards a sense of those who were powerless in the Church – to women, to mothers and to children. Hers was a vision and interpretation of the Kingdom of God as the place where the powerless receive dignity and consecration to their true vocation.[40]

The zeal of her thinking began to take root in Leuven and Paris in the early 1960s, enabling her "to make the needs of children in their family situation the touchstone of her theology."[41] In her own words:

> In the fall of 1960, I found myself seeking a center where I could study pastoral catechetics and liturgy. Four years of theological studies at the Catholic University of Louvain (Belgium) and a dissertation on "Sponsorship and Infant Baptism during the First

[39] Gabriel Moran, "Religious Education After Vatican II," in *Open Catholicism: The Tradition at Its Best: Essays in Honour of Gerard Sloyan*, ed. Gerard S. Sloyan, David Efroymson, and John Raines (Collegeville, MN: Liturgical Press, 1997), 152–54. Moran notes that Vatican II as a whole was an exercise in Christian or religious education because it began an educational reshaping of the Catholic Church, and it fundamentally altered the relationship between Roman Catholicism and the rest of the world.

[40] Mary Grey, "Beyond Exclusion: Towards a Feminist Eucharistic Ecclesiology," in *The Candles Are Still Burning*, 169–70.

[41] Grey, Heaton, and Sullivan, *The Candles Are Still Burning*, vii.

Four Centuries of the Church," not to mention non-stop celebration of infant baptism of 58 nephews and nieces, gave me a deep yearning to develop better ways to incorporate children in the sacramental life of the church.[42]

Over the course of her catechetical ministry, Christiane Brusselmans helped redefine the boundaries of sacramental initiation and "showed us how the experience of community—in particular the family or domestic church—is the necessary context for initiation and faith experience."[43]

3. *Implementation of the Rite of Christian Initiation of Adults*

When Brusselmans arrived in Paris in the fall of 1960, the Centre national de pastorale liturgique was a flourishing centre of liturgical renewal. The Diocese of Paris had organized sixty-three catechumenal centres.[44] Here, Brusselmans learned first-hand the principles of the adult catechumenate and how to apply them to the Christian initiation of children. She came to appreciate the pivotal importance "of incorporating liturgical rites as celebrations of growth in the faith journey."[45]

In Paris, Brusselmans studied under some of the key liturgists and theologians in France,[46] and met the White Fathers, who had gained extensive experience in their efforts to evangelize Native peoples in Africa. Upon returning to France following World War II, the White Fathers and the Holy Ghost Fathers shared with the French Church leaders "the four-year formation process that they offered to those asking to become Christians."[47] Although it still lacked a proper liturgical

42 Christiane Brusselmans, "The Christian Initiation of Children," in *Readings in the Christian Initiation of Children*, ed., Victoria M. Tufano (Chicago: Liturgy Training Publications, 1994), 35–43.

43 Richard Moudry, "Regarding Christiane Brusselmans," *Catholic Bulletin* (December 1991): 11.

44 Marian Zimmermann, *Christiane Brusselmans: Bridge Builder and Visionary of the Contemporary Liturgical Movement* (Master's thesis, St. John's University, Collegeville, MN, 1987), 16–17.

45 Ibid., 18.

46 Ibid., 18. Included among her professors were Yves Congar for theology of the laity, Dom Bernard Botte for liturgy, Jean Daniélou for Patristics, and Louis Bouyer for Protestant theology.

47 Ibid., 19.

dimension,[48] the process was, in reality, a first version of a restored catechumenate. In the course of their evangelizing, the missionaries came to understand that "placing the formation process in the context of the total community was essential; either conversion occurred as a communal process, where all were baptized into Jesus Christ or no one was converted."[49] Through these experiences, Christiane Brusselmans came to recognize the importance that a restored catechumenate holds for the renewal of the contemporary Church.

Convinced of the need to restore the Order of Christian Initiation of Adults in the English-speaking world, Brusselmans organized an international symposium in June 1978 at the Cistercian Abbey of Senanque near Avignon, France, to bring together key leaders of the catechumenate to share their experiences of the Order of Christian Initiation of Adults. As an offshoot of the Senanque event, workshops on implementing the catechumenate began to spread.[50]

In July 1979, just a year after this symposium, the headline in western Canada's Catholic newspaper, *The Prairie Messenger*, announced, "Adult Initiation Rite Challenges Church." The story described a five-day Christian initiation institute in the Diocese of Victoria, British Columbia, that Christiane Brusselmans and her catechumenate team conducted—the first institute of its kind in Canada. Quoting Brusselmans, the story said: "There are many catechumens at our doors ... we are blind if we do not see how myopic our churches are."[51] From here on, Christian initiation institutes began to flourish in Canada.

In October 1981 Brusselmans once more spearheaded a gathering of initiation ministers, this time at Estes Park, Colorado. More than two hundred people took part. From this event, The North American Forum on the Catechumenate was born.[52] As Canadian author Muriel Loftus said: "Christiane came to the Rite of Christian Initiation of Adults as a

48 Michel Dujarier, *A History of the Catechumenate: The First Six Centuries* (New York: William H. Sadlier, Inc., 1979), 139.

49 Zimmermann, "Christiane Brusselmans," 19.

50 Ibid., 26.

51 Martin Brodner, "Adult Initiation Rite Challenges Church," *Prairie Messenger* (July 1979): 1.

52 Richard Moudry, "Regarding Christiane Brusselmans," 11.

catechist supported by a rich background in liturgy. With the vision that the best liturgy is always catechetical and the best catechesis is always liturgical, she was able to put flesh on the bare bones."[53]

Religious Education at Vatican II

On first glance, religious education was not at the forefront of the deliberations at Vatican II. Only on two occasions were direct references made to it: once in the Decree on the Pastoral Office of Bishops (*Christus Dominus*), which urges that a new directory of catechetical instruction be created, and once in the council's Declaration on Christian Education (*Gravissimum Educationis*), promulgated on October 28, 1965, which in veiled terms confirmed the thrust set by the catechetical movement prior to the council.

Gravissimum Educationis mentions four key points. Least controversial among these proposals is the insistence that parents be involved in religious education and that training be provided for catechists. Of greater interest is its lobbying for the use of modern pedagogy in presenting the content of catechesis, and for a Christian milieu to be nurtured to pass on the faith. The document recognizes that a cultural change had taken place in the reception of the faith and that this gap needed to be filled. Catechists were asked to be attentive to the changed circumstances. This position, of course, was fully in line with Pope John XXIII's call for an *aggiornamento* of the Church.

Yet these two seemingly offhand references are not the full story of Vatican II's impact on catechesis. By their very nature, the four pivotal documents of the council, the Dogmatic Constitution on Divine Revelation (*Dei Verbum*), the Dogmatic Constitution on the Church (*Lumen Gentium*), the Constitution on the Liturgy (*Sacrosanctum Concilium*), and the Pastoral Constitution on the Church in the Modern World (*Gaudium et Spes*), were a call to reflect anew on the objectives and process, as well as the content, of religious education. Those who had sought to find new ways for religious education before Vatican II saw their work reflected in these documents. These precursors and their disciples were to forge the new face of religious education after the council.

---

53 Interview by author M. Power, Notes, Ottawa, October 2003.

One cannot avoid the impression that lurking behind these documents that steered religious education in new directions there remained the model of the original Roman Catechism. Despite the publication of documents that fully endorsed the principles of the catechetical movement, such as the *General Directory for Catechesis* of 1997, the original catechism remained the unspoken criterion for subsequent development. The hidden presumption was that the validity of the catechism had not changed, and that the accomplishments of Vatican II were ambiguous as a renewal. New methods were needed to make the original content more accessible; as yet, these texts did not contain a clear call to rethink the whole catechetical process.

Post–Vatican II Official Documents on Religious Education

Before we turn to the development of religious education in Canada after the council, it is helpful to refer to several official documents since Vatican II that have impacted religious education. In most of these documents we see reflected a new spirit regarding the content and pedagogy of religious education. However, not all post–Vatican II documents breathe the same spirit. Some leave enough ambiguity to allow for other interpretations.

First, six years after the council, in 1971, the first *General Catechetical Directory* (GCD) appeared. A significant contribution of this directory is that it establishes the documents of the council as the foundation of a renewed catechetical ministry.[54] The directory was an attempt to articulate what had been the focus of discussion of the Catechetical Study Weeks, particularly the study week held in Medellín in 1968. This first GCD set forth the basic principles of pastoral theology and provided a list of criteria of the Christian message. It also urged that psychology, education, and pedagogy be introduced into religious education resources. Also, it proposed a core theme that would allow for a hierarchy of themes. The GCD was the first official document to

[54] Mongoven, *The Prophetic Spirit of Catechesis*, 66. Mongoven notes that fourteen of the sixteen council documents are referred to in the text, and there are approximately 150 such references in the 134 articles of the GCD. Only the Decree on the Appropriate Renewal of Religious Life and the Decree on the Ministry and Life of Priests are not included as references.

insist that catechesis be Christ-centred. Although many considered the first GCD to be too prescriptive, it was a step in the right direction in setting a structure for religious education. This is a principle that, for instance, the structure of the *Catechism of the Catholic Church* (1992) could not incorporate; it reverted to the structure of the Catechism of the Council of Trent.

Second, the apostolic exhortation *Evangelii Nuntiandi* (1975), published ten years after the close of Vatican II, summarized the council's conclusions on evangelization. The document redefined catechesis as a phase in the project of evangelization, which is a valuable distinction in itself. It sees catechesis as part of the process of becoming a Christian and taking on the Gospel. The document also sets catechesis in the historical context of today's secular culture, moving catechesis out of its previous ahistorical hermeneutic.

Third, the synod on Catechesis in Our Time (1977) and its summary document, *Catechesi Tradendae* (1979), confirmed the need for a Christ-centred catechesis. Synod participants hoped that with this core theme it would be possible to arrive at an organic systematic instruction in the faith.

Fourth, the *Catechism of the Catholic Church* (1992) departed from the Tridentine catechetical tradition by being presented in a more expository form rather than the question-and-answer format. Like the Roman Catechism, however, it is structured by four landmarks of the Catholic tradition: the Creed (faith), the Seven Sacraments (worship/liturgy), the Ten Words (moral life), and the Our Father (prayer). Its expository format allows for the introduction of a great diversity of theological positions within the same text, but it does not allow for a clear formulation of the hierarchy of truths. The previously enunciated principle of Christo-centricity at the heart of catechesis did not play a role in shaping the text. In this sense, the text is a step backwards. The great diversity and length of the catechism soon made it desirable to provide a summary known as the *Compendium*. Here it became evident that old habits never die but only mutate. The *Compendium* reverted to the old question-and-answer form in an attempt to provide a grand overview of the catechism. One can only wonder whether, at some point, it will become the Catechism of Vatican II.

Fifth, John Paul II's encyclical *Redemptoris Missio* (1992) spoke once again of the need for the Church to become missionary in a postmodern world. The document insists that outside of the *mission ad gentes*, to those who have never heard of Christ, there is a need to provide a new hearing of the Gospel for those who have forgotten or rejected it. This document's most dynamic and creative suggestion is to address the pluralism of our time, calling for a search today for the unknown God—in line with Paul's remarks at the Greek Areopagus. The God who is still unknown in our time must be sought with new ears and new imagination.

Sixth, in 1997, a new revised edition of the *General Directory for Catechesis* was published. This is, beyond a doubt, the most forward-looking catechetical document to emerge from the postconciliar period. This new edition, which is a grand summary of the catechetical thrust developed during the twentieth century, builds upon the *General Catechetical Directory* of 1971. It gives more emphasis than did the earlier GCD on the need to seek inculturation of the Gospel message,[55] or its indigenization into every context.[56] It amplifies the importance of the Rite of Christian Initiation of Adults and insists that the baptismal catechumenate is the inspiration for catechesis in the Church.[57] Like its predecessor, it will likely set the tone and tenor of catechesis throughout the whole Church for another quarter century.[58] It is also a prophetic document of the mission and method of religious education. This is not the place to summarize the directory. But in its vision of the mission and method of catechesis, it provides the best summary of the vision of religious education of any Church document. Within it is articulated the best of Vatican II's legacy in the field of religious education. The important impact of the GDC in establishing foundational principles for the Canadian catechetical series *Born of the Spirit* is reflected in the next segment of this article, which focuses on the Canadian approach to catechesis.

---

55 Mongoven, *The Prophetic Spirit of Catechesis*, 83.

56 Thomas Groome, "Holistic, Inclusive, Comprehensive Catechesis: The GDC Revisited," *Living Light* 34, no. 4 (1998): 74.

57 Congregation for the Clergy, *General Directory for Catechesis* (Ottawa: Canadian Conference of Catholic Bishops, 1997), no. 90.

58 Groome, "Holistic, Inclusive, Comprehensive Catechesis," 66.

The Canadian Approach to Catechesis

Informed by the *General Directory for Catechesis* (1997) and inspired by the process of initiation into faith, as set forth in the *Rite of Christian Initiation of Adults* (1987), the catechetical texts of the *Born of the Spirit* series are grounded in the following ten guiding principles:

1. The chief *structure* of each catechetical text in the series is the Church's liturgical year. In this way, the catechesis is intimately linked with the liturgical experience of the wider Church community.[59]

2. The catechesis reaffirms that the heart and *context* of the catechetical ministry must be found in the home and the parish community as they celebrate the mystery of Christ in the liturgical year.[60]

3. The *starting point* of the catechesis is always incarnational and begins with the real human experience of those being catechized. The *General Directory for Catechesis* states that experience "assumed by faith, becomes in a certain manner, a locus for the manifestation and realization of salvation...."[61]

4. The *content* of the catechesis is Scripture-based. Celebrations of the Word are central in all catechetical processes, especially during Advent and Lent.[62]

5. The liturgical nature of the catechesis demands integral participation not only in *preparing* and *celebrating* rituals of the Word but also in *remembering* and *savouring* them so that links can be made between our human experience and the story of Jesus.[63] This mystagogical approach stresses the importance of faith in the ritual

---

[59] The *General Directory for Catechesis* (1997), no. 30, identifies the frequent problem of a weak and fragmentary link with liturgy in the practice of catechetics.

[60] See GDC (1997), nos. 253–58, for an emphasis on the Christian community as origin and locus of catechesis, and parents as primary educators in the faith.

[61] See GDC (1997), no. 152, on the topic of human experience in catechesis.

[62] See *The Rite of Christian Initiation of Adults* [RCIA] (Ottawa, ON: CCCB, 1987), no. 82, for the main purpose of celebrations of the Word. See also the *Directory for Masses with Children* (Ottawa: CCCB, 1990), no. 14, which insists on frequent celebrations of the Word, especially in Advent and Lent.

[63] The initial theme of each catechetical text in the *Born of the Spirit* series offers a section on the topic of celebrating the Word.

event and forms those being catechized in a language of faith that they can use to name their experience.

6. The catechesis is trinitarian and Christo-centric in scope and spirit and bears a markedly Paschal character. These fundamental characteristics are in line with the *General Directory for Catechesis* as it outlines the essential criteria for presenting the Gospel message and describes the fundamental tasks of catechesis: "helping to know, to celebrate and to contemplate the mystery of Christ."[64]

7. The catechesis is gradual, taking the form of a spiritual journey that helps participants become more familiar with the Christian way of life.[65] In this approach, the focus is on conversion, in that the catechetical instruction is not an end in itself but is directed to worship, mission, and Christian witness.[66] "Conversion does not come at the end of a journey as in arrival . . . , but within the journey as in *paschal mystery*."[67] The emphasis in this catechesis is on the journey and what happens on the way.

8. The catechesis helps form participants in the primary symbols, rituals, and gestures of the faith: gathering around God's Word, lighting the Paschal candle, signing with the cross, proclaiming the Word, giving praise and thanks together, immersing hands in blessed water, offering each other a sign of peace. These symbols, rites, and gestures build on the day-to-day human experiences of "community activity, exchange of greetings, capacity to listen and to seek and grant pardon, expression of gratitude, experience of symbolic actions," and become a powerful, non-verbal form of catechesis that is experienced rather than explained. This ritual catechesis taps into the memory and the imagination, and offers

64 See GDC (1997), nos. 97–117, for criteria for presenting the Gospel message in catechesis. See GDC (1997), nos. 85–86, for tasks of catechesis.

65 See RCIA, no. 75.2. Paragraph 75 of the RCIA outlines the tenets or chief principles of formation in catechesis.

66 See GDC (1997), no. 109, on the call "to bring the power of the Gospel into the very heart of culture and cultures."

67 Barbara Hixon, *RCIA Ministry: An Adventure into Mayhem and Mystery* (San Jose, CA: Resource Publications, Inc., 1989), 43.

participants "a 'vocabulary,' a language of faith, that opens up and unfolds into a way of life."[68]

9. The holistic sense of Christian faith reclaimed in the Second Vatican Council and echoed throughout the *General Directory for Catechesis* is integral to the catechesis of the *Born of the Spirit* series. The catechesis touches on the growth of participants and makes a difference at cognitive, practical, and aesthetic levels:

   The cognitive indicates the additional knowledge to be gained by the [participant] in the [catechesis].

   The practical looks to the new abilities the [participant] acquires through the activities of the [catechesis]. If the cognitive answers to what the [participant] will know, the practical manifests itself in what they will be able to do with greater facility than before. In the field of religion, the practical indicates all those actions and abilities that come from being a full member of the Church.

   The aesthetic dimension touches the deepest level of growth for the [person]. It goes beyond knowing and beyond abilities to the level of being. The aesthetic touches the change or transformation that the [participant] undergoes in his or her person as faith takes root more and more. The aesthetic operates at the level of feeling and attitudes. It is ultimately caught up with our stance before God. At the level of catechesis, this is most important.[69]

   Underscoring a catechumenal style and approach for catechesis, the GDC insists on integral formation that "comprises but surpasses mere instruction."[70]

10. The chief emphasis of the final principle is the Second Vatican Council's reclaiming of baptism and the sense of the holy,[71] which

---

[68] Catherine Dooley, "Baptismal Catechesis for Children of Catechetical Age," in *Issues in the Christian Initiation of Children*, ed. Kathy Brown and Frank C. Sokol (Chicago: Liturgy Training Publications, 1989), 52.

[69] See "Catechetical Focus," in *Introductory Booklet: You Shall Be My Witnesses* (Ottawa, ON: CCCB, 2000), 23.

[70] See GDC (1997), nos. 29 and 68.

[71] See "The Call of the Whole Church to Holiness," in *Lumen Gentium*, Chapter V. See also "The Laity," in *Lumen Gentium*, Chapter IV. *The Documents of Vatican II*, Walter M. Abbott, SJ (General Editor) (New York: The America Press, 1966).

undergirds the *Born of the Spirit* catechesis and the explosion of catechetical ministries that emerged alongside its development and implementation in homes, parishes, and schools in Canada. The recovered recognition of a common baptism brought into focus the royal heritage of the people of God and "a restored apostolic attitude about the holiness of ordinary Christian life."[72] The recognition of this unearned inheritance of holiness with which we are abundantly gifted continues to inspire a participatory catechesis that is primarily an inclusive communal affair.

The Hermeneutical Framework of the Catechetical Process: A Project of Understanding

In conclusion, the development of a truly Canadian approach to catechesis can be understood only if we see it as a hermeneutical venture. The hermeneutical method can best be described in the language of Paul Ricœur, as a practical hermeneutics.[73] The Canadian resources are not alone in promoting this approach.[74] This form of hermeneutics recognizes that the cognitive dimension of religious education, which so dominated the Church's concerns, is superseded by the celebration of Christian life and the capacity of the catechized to act in a religious way. The cognitive penetration of the mystery of God in Christ is but one aspect of the catechetical process, however important.

Because the Canadian resources have taken the liturgical—exemplified in the RCIA—as their point of departure, that is, have accepted the priority of the *lex orandi* over the *lex credendi*, these resources turned to the practical hermeneutics of Paul Ricœur to give form to their pedagogy and to the structuring of their vision. In order to grasp the implications of such a practical hermeneutics for religious education,

---

72 Hixon, *RCIA Ministry*, 64.

73 See John van den Hengel, "Practical Theology and the Emergence of a New Self," in *La théologie pratique, pratique de théologie*, ed. L. Tardif and K. Demasure (University of Ottawa Press, forthcoming 2011).

74 See the proceedings of the catechetical conference held in Leuven: *Hermeneutics and Religious Education*, ed. H. Lombaerts and D. Pollefeyt (Leuven: University of Leuven Press, 2004).

one needs to explore first the centrality of the concept of understanding in Ricœur's hermeneutics.

For Ricœur, understanding is the goal of hermeneutics; it is not a primarily theoretical exercise but a practical one. In religious education, we intend that someone—a child or an adult—will have not only a notional knowledge of some aspect of Christian faith, but will be at home in it; it will become like second nature in him or her. To understand, for Ricœur, is something like that. It is the capability to insert oneself in a particular world—in this case, the world of faith—and to find oneself at home there. It is the capacity to act within that world as a free person. Riçœur defined understanding as a capacity to "orient ourselves comprehensively"[75] in situations. This means knowing what one can do, or knowing that one is capable of doing something in a particular situation. As such, understanding brings one to a point where one can become creative and insert oneself actively into an historical process. Understanding is, therefore, much more than a cognitive penetration into a status quo. It is a capacity to be in situations where one initiates things. Understanding is a way of being in the world.

Along these lines, religious education aims to give people the capacity to help shape a world in which Christians can live and act as Christians, and be persons who reshape the world in the image of Christ. For this reason, religious education is a projective discipline that opens the world as a possibility. It is not enough to know the doctrines and be able to articulate them. If one is unable to place doctrines in a sphere of life in which they operate concretely and recognize what forces of life they orient, no amount of doctrine will generate life, and certainly not eternal life. As in all education, religious education is an education into the freedom of the children of God so that learners can act creatively in our world with and for others in just institutions.[76]

The questions are these: How can religious education accomplish this goal? What sorts of resources can it call upon to achieve this goal? Religious education in Canada has become increasingly focused in areas where human faith agency is most closely approximated. That is,

---

[75] Paul Ricœur, *Interpretation Theory* (Austin: Texas Christian University, 1976), 20–21.

[76] Paul Ricœur, *Oneself as Another*, trans. Kathleen Blamey (Chicago: University of Chicago Press, 1992), 171.

first of all, in liturgy, where the Christian community enacts itself and calls upon the Holy Spirit to make it into the Body of Christ, into "one body and one spirit" (Eucharistic Prayer III). Without liturgical enactment and celebration, it is difficult to maintain oneself in the encounter with God in Christ, and thus in the transformative work in creation. The liturgical remains, therefore, a central aspect of the process. Yet the question arises of how effective it is when there is a massive lack of youth participation in the liturgical life of the Church.

However, there is a second reason why catechetics makes use of a practical hermeneutical approach. The main focus of practical hermeneutics is human agency. Human agency, because of its myriad possibilities, does not permit itself to be easily reflected on. Linguistic analysis has attempted to do so, but it has only come up with a formal framework or network of human actions. This framework recognizes that human actions are not some kind of essence or substance. They are not a "something" but an energy. Linguistic analysis insists, therefore, that one best approaches human agency by means of a network of questions, such as these: Who is acting? What is being enacted? Why is someone acting? Where? When? Against whom and with whom is one acting? Under what circumstances?

Paul Ricœur expanded on this conceptual framework of human action, pointing out that there is another way of approaching human action that has cognitive, practical, and aesthetic dimensions: the narrative form. For him, what most closely approximates human action as action, what gives insight into action and is able to motivate human action, is narrative. In narratives, Ricœur says, the countless expressions of human desire and the effort to exist are acted out. This finding is best exemplified in the almost unending series of narratives that humanity has produced. But what are the narratives that best articulate the capacity to act for religious education?

The Canadian resources have not taken their lead from the grand narrative that has been used over the centuries as the overriding story of Christianity. This grand narrative was shaped by the triad: creation, fall, and redemption. For many, this triad of creation, fall, and redemption in Christ has operated—and, for some, still operates—as the overriding paradigm for catechesis and proclamation.[77] For a variety of reasons, not the least of which is the loss of many people's ability to live out of such an overriding paradigm, the grand narrative has lost its cogency and its capacity to convince. In past centuries, this simplified story as a sort of summary of the Bible was, for many Christians, how the world and world history made sense. History was a history of salvation. The sense of that story became eroded and collapsed in the eighteenth century. What broke it down, according to German theologian Hans Frei, was the replacement of this story with another story: a story of human progress brought about by human reason and human ingenuity—the story we pointed out in the beginning of the article as the story that emptied out the Christian story.

But what is most significant for religious education is that the story of the Enlightenment collapsed in the twentieth century. We are left today with the detritus of that story's collapse. The salvation promised by reason and technology was shattered by wars, the ecological crisis, the new awareness of the breakdown of the possibility of absolute knowledge in the theory of relativity and quantum physics, the sudden awareness of the all-too-human weakness and corruption of most institutions of Western society, and the stultifying reduction of the human imagination to the measurable and the tangible. But the damage of this overreaching story of human progress has not been removed. It is still not possible to undertake a complete retrieval of the anterior Christian narrative.

But what of Christian narrative *can* be retrieved? Ulrich Simon, in his marvellous small book *Story and Faith*, suggested that there is a crisis of faith because there is a crisis of narrative.[78] The Canadian catechetical resources have taken this crisis of narrative to heart in a number of ways. Faith is not some monolithic block of tenets and doctrines. It is enmeshed in daily living. This means that faith is bound up with the flux of life, with its ups and downs, with its crises and satisfactions. If it is only narrative that can adequately work with this flux and with discordant sequences and changes of fortune of everyday life, and if we

---

[77] See the seminal account of this event in Hans Frei, *The Eclipse of the Biblical Narrative* (New Haven: Yale University Press, 1974).

[78] Ulrich Simon, *Story and Faith* (London: SPCK, 1975), 16.

wish to have those stories interact with the scriptural stories, we may have to ask this question: What narrative in the Scriptures can bring us back to the interaction between God and humanity?

The grand narrative that Judaism and Christianity constructed from the Bible was fashioned by the great number of narratives that are found in the Bible. The Bible is constructed of a series of narratives. It is built on the awareness that narrative is the most appropriate way to tell the story of the covenant of God with people. That is why narrative is the dominant genre of the Bible, in both the Old and the New Testament. Narrative insists that only in the space of a story of a people with God, and the story of the coming of God's kingdom in Jesus, is our faith anchored.

If the compact story of the triad—creation, sin, and redemption—is too overriding a story to enter into with the creative imagination today, one must go back to the larger network of biblical stories, in all their individuality and ambiguity, to hear once again the vagaries of God's Name in the midst of the human story. This is what the Canadian resources have attempted to do. They turned to the broadened scope of the great number of biblical narratives, which in their interaction with each other and with other biblical genres seek to name God. The crisis of today, the resources insist, is the crisis of the naming of God. To retrieve the name of God for our time, the narrative genre is indispensible. It means that for contemporaries, faith is intrinsically historical.

How do the Canadian catechetical resources articulate this idea? We name here only two ways, to give a sense of the direction the resources have taken.

First, as was stated above, the Canadian resources sought to reground catechesis in the liturgical agency of the Church. To do so, they turned to the narratives of the liturgical year. At the liturgical centre lies the story of the resurrection and, in its immediate shadow, the story of the birth and second coming of Christ. The telling of the story of God in the story of Jesus follows, therefore, the constant retelling of the story of Jesus in the liturgy of the Church. The story of Jesus is never told in a straightforward logical sequence. It is told, as the liturgy tells it, from the perspective of the resurrection. All the stories of Jesus—his own stories as well as his deeds—are stories of the Risen One who is brought into our human midst symbolically and liturgically. All the resources of religious education for children up to age twelve follow this pattern.

Second, the Canadian resources construct these liturgical stories into a story about God: Father, Son, and Spirit. These resources take seriously the words of Pope John Paul II in *Redemptoris Missio* (1992), where he talked about the need to find a new Areopagus where we can explore the naming of God in our time. The biblical story must, therefore, as it does in the Bible, intermesh with the story of humans today. Religious education wants to explore in the pluralist world around us the ways in which children, youth, and adults can discover the richness of the mystery of God in our time. In order to do that, religious education must also make use of the treasury of stories of our culture, allowing this culture to interact in a new way with the great treasury of the biblical narratives.

Conclusion

Where is religious education in Canada now? Vatican II—in its rich liturgical legacy, in the renewal of the cycle of readings from the Scriptures, in the reintroduction of the RCIA, in the use of the vernacular, and in its encouragement of a biblical liturgical spirituality—has opened up new avenues of religious education beyond the earlier ahistorical catechism. These avenues have found a resonance in the Canadian resources of the *Born of the Spirit* series.

We are currently in a time of transition. The *Born of the Spirit* resources require a reworking to bring them up to date and to respond to the needs of young people today—not so much in schools as in parishes and in the home. In 2007 the Canadian bishops began the process of developing a syllabus or criteria of religious education in Canada.[79] The criteria was not to be primarily school based but based on age. The criteria promises to continue the method and approach that has been developing in Canada since the 1960s.

[79] The current authors are part of the CCCB writing team that has undertaken to write the criteria for students aged from infancy to eighteen years. Parts of the criteria were presented to the Canadian Conference of Catholic Bishops at their 2009 fall assembly in Cornwall, Ontario.

Vatican II, in its own fashion, gave a direction to the way religious education might take place. The 1997 *General Directory for Catechesis* offered a promising example and vision of this possibility. In the challenges of the present climate, religious educators need courage and faith to pursue this vision and not allow themselves to succumb to the current search for identities based on fear. In the reach for new and wider horizons in religious education and catechesis in Canada in this twenty-first century, it is our hope that the spirit with which Pope John XXIII called for an *aggiornamento* of the Church will prevail as inspiration and strength for the journey.

SECTION II

Religious Life and Laity / Vie religieuse et les laïcs

Imaging *Perfectae Caritatis*: Viewing the Consecrated Life through the Mother House Museums of Canadian Women Religious[1]

Heidi MacDonald,
University of Lethbridge,
and Elizabeth Smyth,
University of Toronto

Introduction

In the 1960s some 60,000 Canadian women belonged to 183 congregations and orders. These congregations were diverse in historical roots and governance. Some were provinces of international communities; others were indigenous Canadian foundations. Regardless of their origins or orientations, Vatican II marked a significant event in

[1] The authors acknowledge the University of Lethbridge (Research Services) and the Social Sciences and Humanities Research Council for their support for the research reported here. The authors thank the congregations and archivists who responded to their survey on mother house museums.

their history. While many of the council's documents both directly and indirectly impacted on their identities and caused some to question the very nature of the vowed life (e.g., the Dogmatic Constitution on the Church [*Lumen Gentium*] in its call to holiness of all the faithful), this essay will focus on the response of some of these religious communities to the Decree on the Adaptation and Renewal of Religious Life (*Perfectae Caritatis*), promulgated by Pope Paul VI on October 28, 1965.

Perfectae Caritatis directed religious communities to look both backwards and forwards, advising that "The adaptation and renewal of the religious life includes both the constant return to the sources of all Christian life and to the original spirit of the institutes and their adaptation to the changed conditions of our time."[2] Communities were encouraged to retrieve their founding identity by studying their community's founder or its original identity. Second, they were to adapt themselves and their work or ministry to the times and to the needs of the times, and to educate and train their members in order that they may carry out the work of the community today most effectively. Third, they were to revise their foundational documents to reflect their renewed identity. Fourth, they were to change their religious habit if it no longer suited their work or ministry. Pope Paul VI reflected:

> The religious habit, an outward mark of consecration to God, should be simple and modest, poor and at the same, becoming. In addition it must meet the requirements of health and be suited to the circumstances of time and place and to the needs of the ministry involved. The habits of both men and women religious which do not conform to these norms must be changed.[3]

This essay focuses on how some congregations of Canadian women have represented their pre- and postconciliar congregational identities through their congregational mother house museums—unique spaces

---

2 Decree on the Adaptation and Renewal of Religious Life, *Perfectae Caritatis*, Proclaimed by His Holiness Pope Paul VI on October 28, 1965, art. **2,** accessed 4 January 2011, http://www.vatican.va/archive/hist_councils/ii_vatican_council/documents/vat-ii_decree_19651028_perfectae-caritatis_en.html.
Leon Joseph Cardinal Suenens, *The Nun in the World: New Dimensions in the Modern Apostolate* (Westminister, ML: The Newman Press, 1963), 130–31.

3 Decree on the Adaptation and Renewal of Religious Life, art. 17.

in which congregations present their historical roots and identities to their members and to members of the public. The essay develops in three broadly constructed sections. It begins by setting a context and methodology for the study. It then explores and analyzes the data collected, focusing on how the museums responded to the directives of Vatican II: to explore the charism of the founders, to modify the habit and regulation of daily life, and to alter the missionary activity of the congregations to address changing needs. The essay concludes with directions for further study.

Context and Method

Mother houses are significant historical spaces that have always played a critical role in the creation of identity and historical memory. For most of its history, a key feature of vowed religious life was living within an intergenerational community where young postulants and middle-aged active professionals shared their space with senior sisters. While community members may have been stationed across the region, country, or continents, they returned to their mother houses annually for retreats, respite, and congregational meetings. Since Vatican II and the move away from institutional living, mother houses remain a place of community gathering and celebration.

Mother houses are also the places where a community's records and stories were housed. The Code of Canon Law directs congregations to preserve their records, and this came to be interpreted as preserving the material cultural elements of their heritage. As a result, many mother houses contain museums, heritage rooms, and historical displays. Museologist and cultural historian Simon Knell and his colleagues note, "Museums are about people, and collections are merely manifestations of human desires."[4] For this reason a great deal can be gleaned from what congregations choose to display in their mother house museums and other heritage spaces.

In the summer of 2008 the authors approached The Catholic Archivists' Group, whose mandate is to maintain and promote the ar-

4 Simon J. Knell, Suzanne MacLeod, and Sheila Watson, "Introduction," in *Museum Revolutions: How Museums Change and are Changed*, ed. Simon J. Knell, Suzanne MacLeod, and Sheila Watson (New York: Routledge, 2007), xix.

chives of Canadian Catholic institutions, dioceses, and congregations, and asked its support in creating and distributing a questionnaire among their members. The archivists' group is comprised of fifty individuals who work either full or part time in English-speaking women's religious congregational archives, usually in the congregation's mother house. This essay draws data from responses received from the following nine congregations:

- Congregation of the Sisters of Saint Martha of Antigonish, Nova Scotia
- Congregation of the Sisters of St. Joseph, Peterborough, Ontario
- Sisters of the Presentation of Newfoundland and Labrador, St. John's, Newfoundland
- School Sisters of Notre Dame, Waterdown, Ontario
- Sisters of Charity of the Immaculate Conception, Saint John, New Brunswick
- Sisters of Providence of St. Vincent de Paul, Kingston, Ontario
- Sisters of St. Joseph, Toronto, Ontario
- Les Sœurs de Sainte-Anne (Sisters of Saint Anne, Lachine, Québec
- Sister Servants of Mary Immaculate, Toronto, Ontario

While the respondents are from five provinces (Newfoundland, Nova Scotia, New Brunswick, Ontario, and Québec), the congregations have served in every Canadian province, as well as in the United States, Africa, and Central and South America. Thus the museums studied include a history of missionary activity in every province and in many nations.

Mother house museums followed the historical trajectory of museum development in Canada, growing from curio cabinets in convent parlors to purposefully built heritage rooms. Significantly, the stimulus of *Perfectae Caritatis* coincided with the professionalization of Canadian museum displays, and some congregations took advantage of these developments to assist them in their presentations. While most museums were opened in the 1980s or 1990s, the broad founding dates for the mother house museums under study are from 1964 to 2008. Thus, the Canadian mother house museum can be viewed as a response to and an extension of the congregation's response to *Perfectae Caritatis*.

Findings and Analysis

It is most striking that the displays presented in the museums under study clearly reflect the directions of Vatican II to study the charism of the founder, to reconsider missionary activity (particularly away from institutions), and to modify the habit. Thus, the museums emphasize three topics: the founding, missionary activity, and the habit. Within these topics, what can be said of museums generally can also be said of the mother house museums under study: "[They] were established to capture and concretize progress – to gather up things as they became known and valued and keep them unchanged."[5] Mother house museum displays present a snapshot of images frozen in time. At the same time they celebrate the vibrancy of, nostalgia, and even yearning for the past, as well as the uncertainty of the future. Controversy is rarely hinted at and never explored. As museologist Chia-Li Chen writes, "the museum is an institution which officially decides what is worthy of preservation and what is not. On the one hand, it constructs what is to be remembered, but on the other hand, it chooses what is to be forgotten."[6] Thus deconstructing the absences in mother house museums is as significant as analyzing what is most prominently displayed.

Purpose and Audience

Each of the museums under study is a designated space; some are purpose built and others are adapted. The museums or heritage rooms under study range in size from 107 square metres (352 ft^2) to 366 square metres (1200 ft^2) with the average being almost 274 square metres (900 ft^2), approximately the size of a small bungalow. The locations of

---

5 Ibid., xix.

6 Chia-Li Chen, "Museums and the Shaping of Cultural Identities: visitors' recollections in local museums in Taiwan," in Knell, MacLeod, and Watson, *Museum Revolutions*, 174. See also Chen's references to Elizabeth Hallam and Jenny Hockey's *Death, Memory and Material Culture* (Oxford: Berg, 2001), and J. Urry's "How Societies Remember the Past," in *Theorizing Museums*, ed. S. Macdonald and G.Fyfe (Oxford: Blackwell Publishers, 1996), 45–65.

the museums or heritage rooms are very significant in signalling their intention. Four of the museums are located near the public entrance of the mother house for the ease of visitors' access, one is located next to the chapel so it is very visible to the sisters on a daily basis, one is close to the congregation's administrative office, and two are in separate buildings.

The survey asked congregations to explain the rationale for their museum's existence—either its written statement of purpose or the commonly understood reason for its presence. Only one had a formal statement. Two noted that the museum's purpose was connected to the larger mission statement of the congregation, which included preserving the heritage of the congregation. Responses emphasized "capturing our history" rather than inferring what purpose providing the history would actually serve. It is possible that the original intentions for founding the museums have been lost and that the museums serve different purposes for different sisters, even within congregations. What is more telling is the acceptance that every congregation should preserve its history, without questioning precisely *why* it should. The mission statement of the Sisters of Providence's museum collection goes further than any other summary we received and explicitly connects the history to members' ongoing faith and work. It is public history as inspiration and nostalgia:

> The museum collection in the Heritage Room and the Printing Room preserve the material culture of the Sisters of Providence of St. Vincent de Paul and the Providence Associates. The museum collection consists of artifacts and other materials (books, photographs) related to the past and the on-going account of the interaction with God of those called to be Sisters of Providence of St. Vincent de Paul and of those called to be Providence Associates. The collection assists the Sisters and Associates in tracing the roots of the Congregation, in following its traditions, and in moving into the future in fidelity to the charism, spirituality and mission.[7]

[7] "Sisters of Providence of St. Vincent de Paul (Kingston, ON) Policy and Procedures Manual," Congregational Museum—Mandate.

The museum of Les Sœurs de Sainte-Anne has a dual objective of preservation and public education:

> … conserver, inventorier, cataloguer, mettre en valeur et assurer la gestion et la documentation des objets qui ont une valeur historique et/ou artistique et qui sont reliés à l'évolution de la Congrégation, dans les secteurs de la vie religieuse et apostolique.
>
> - assurer des activités de promotion et d'animation en regard de la vie et de l'œuvre de la fondatrice.[8]

It is notable that both of these examples emphasize the strengthening of the identity of their respective congregations, which is a major theme in the literature of museums and public history. When combined with the consideration of the intended audience, the emphasis on identity is more significant. Most obviously, the entrances to these two museums indicate the differing intended audiences. The museum of the Sisters of Providence of St. Vincent de Paul (Kingston) is located near the main entrance to the mother house complex, while the museum of Les Sœurs de Sainte-Anne, Lachine, offers a rare example of a museum with its own entrance. These two examples offer an interesting perspective to the visitor—who is the intended audience? In the first example, the designers of the museum intended visitors to have a connection to the congregation to know about the museum, while in the second example, there is more of an intention that the general public will visit.

The survey further explored the question of intended audience by asking the nine congregations to rank the categories into which most visitors fell:

1. Relatives of the community
2. Associates of the community
3. Visiting religious and priests
4. Members of the community
5. Members of the general public
6. Other

---

[8] Centre historique des Sœurs de Sainte-Anne. »Mission du Musée ». See http://www.ssacong.org/musee/mission.htm Accessed January 17, 2011.

The responses varied widely. There was some pooling of answers that indicate a private/public or insider/outsider split, suggesting that some congregations were most interested in promoting their history to the general public (outsiders) while others saw their museum's purpose as providing a service for insiders, the sisters themselves. For the younger sisters it was education and for the older ones it was inspiration/nostalgia. In between were those responses that illustrated the desire to share their history with friends of the sisters and the congregations, including relatives of the sisters, visiting sisters and priests from other congregations, and associates of the congregation, cases in which education and inspiration/nostalgia were dual purposes. The three congregations that clearly identified the general public as their main audience were not necessarily the congregations with the highest number of annual visitors, which suggests they were not actually trying to promote the museum to the public—or if they were, they were unsuccessful. In fact the congregation that reported the highest number of visitors annually, 2000, placed visiting priests and sisters as the most prolific visitors to their museum, even though it was the only museum to report participating in a community heritage open house, during which they received 876 visitors in one week in February 2008. Even with their participation in this community event, the congregation did not indicate that educating the wider public was a priority for its museum. The reported number of annual visitors ranged from 24 to 2000 with a mean of approximately 700.

The authors have concluded, based on our sample of nine museums, that these museums are mostly intended for "insiders," that is, sisters and clergy. This connects to another important phenomenon: These museums are sites of identity formation and identity affirmation for the sisters themselves. It is widely accepted that "consumption of meaning in museums contributes to the construction of personal and shared memories."[9] In the post–Vatican II era of the declining influence and significance of women religious, this construction of meaning takes on a great importance in validating the congregations' histories of service. As Beth Lord, whose work on philosophy and museums is helpful in this

[9] Sheila Watson, "History Museums, Community Identities and a Sense of Place: Rewriting Histories," in Knell, MacDonald, and Watson, *Museum Revolutions*, 160.

context, notes, "The present visitor 'remembers' the object by 'replaying' in the present the truth of the object that was fixed in the past."[10] In other words, the generous and skilled service the sisters performed in the past may be recognized and remembered in a visit to a mother house museum.

Displays

The content of museum displays in the sample of museums studied focuses on three elements: the founding, the community's missionary activity or ministry, and the habit. In each of these elements, the directives of Vatican II can clearly be observed.

The Founding

The content of displays is quite consistent in that the majority of the displays in every museum portrays the founding of the community and its missionary activity. Studying the founding vision of the congregation had not only been a Vatican II directive, but as Rosa Bruno-Jofré has argued, the "founding myth"[11] of a congregation was central to collective and individual memory. Our respondents' museums place a strong emphasis on their founders. Given the Vatican II directive to study the charism of the founder, these displays are three dimensional representations of the findings of that exercise.

The Centre historique des Sœurs de Sainte-Anne in Lachine, Québec, which is also the most professional and the newest of the museums studied,[12] interprets the life of the congregation's foundress, Mother Marie-Anne Blondin, in a 100-square-metre (328-ft^2) corridor. Interestingly, a major emphasis is placed on a conflict between the bishop and the first superior, in which Bishop Bourget demanded Mother Blondin's resignation: "… As for you, my good Mother, you will resign willingly and you will tell your sisters that you are authorized

---

10 Beth Lord, "From the Document to the Monument: Museums and the Philosophy of History," in Knell, MacDonald, and Watson, *Museum Revolutions*, 358.

11 For a further discussion of the concept of a "founding myth," see Rosa Bruno-Jofré, *The Missionary Oblate Sisters: Vision and Mission* (Montréal and Kingston: McGill-Queen's Press, 2005)

12 It was founded in 1942 but opened in a new location in 2008.

never again to accept the superiorship even if they wish you to assume it."[13] Not only is this passage displayed in the museum but a bronze sculpture, entitled "I have surrendered all," was commissioned to represent the incident and is now on permanent display in the corridor devoted to Mother Blondin's memory. The plaque reads:

> The sculpture illustrates the surrender of authority; the giving hand, a symbol of Marie Anne Blondin's renunciation, and another hand, receiving, a symbol of the continuity of the Congregation and the hope that its work will continue to go forward. The glass section that lights up separates the two hands and represents the obstacle that led to the Foundress' renunciation. The transparency of the glass expresses the vision that transcends the trials of life. The illumination of the glass section suggests the elevation of the spirit and the Foundress' ability to rise above the visible in her actions.[14]

This is a powerful example of how Les Sœurs de Sainte-Anne use their museum and collection to reclaim a painful event and acknowledge their respect for Mother Blondin's authority; they concretize that respect by giving a "final word" on the matter within their museum.

The Sister Servants of Mary Immaculate, whose whole museum is based on ninety-one display boards, use five display boards to portray their founding. In addition they commissioned an original painting by Manitoba artist Jeanette Shewchuk of the co-foundress, Josaphata Hordashevska, with the first seven postulants.

The Sisters of Saint Martha of Antigonish have five display cases. One of these contains artifacts that belonged to their bishop, John Cameron, who they noted "founded the congregation along with the first fifteen women." Bishop Cameron's gloves and scull cap are displayed. Another display case contains artifacts from one of the first fifteen sisters, including a cup and saucer, cream pitcher, and writing case. The relatively equal space allotted to male founders (especially bishops of diocesan congregations) and the early sisters clearly reflects

[13] Bishop Bourget to Mother Marie Anne, 1854, Sisters of Saint Anne, Lachine, Historic Centre.

[14] Jules Lasalle, sculptor.

a 1960s, Vatican II era that was less blindly patriarchal and hierarchical than earlier decades.

The Sisters of Providence of Kingston, Ontario, portray their first general superior very prominently rather than doing so for their founder. The Sisters of Providence of Kingston came about as a result of negotiations among Kingston Bishop Edward John Horan and Mother Philomène Bourbonnière, superior of the Sisters of Providence of Montréal and her ecclesiastical superior, Bishop Ignace Bourget. According to the contract drawn up by these individuals, four sisters were to journey to Kingston to establish a foundation and, once it was established, return to Montréal. Catherine McKinley, born in Kingston, Upper Canada, in 1837, was the first postulant to present herself as a candidate for the new congregation. Known by her religious name Mother Mary Edward, she is celebrated in the Heritage Room as the pivotal figure in the history of the community. Her work as a pioneer educator, administrator, mission founder, and practical and metaphorical builder (she oversaw much of the purpose built structures for the enterprises and the growth of the community from four members in 1862 to 404 members a century later) forms the core of the historical display.

It is notable that these museums interpret the congregation's founding through the lens of *Perfectae Caritatis*, which asked them to consider their roots. Both congregations situate their founders in history, exploring how the founders responded to the needs of their times and actualized their mandate of service of God through service of neighbour through a variety of initiatives. Thus, the museums focus less on representing a single moment or series of moments from the congregation's founding, and instead interpret more broadly how the congregations were formed organically over a period of years.

The understanding of the founding is also clearly tied to the congregations' constitutions and rules. The School Sisters of Notre Dame display a copy of their rule in their museums, while the Sister Servants of Mary Immaculate display their mission statement, which is a modern version of other congregations' rules or constitutions.

While the intentions of the displays in portraying foundings is present in each congregation, the chosen media for doing so ranged widely. Artifacts from the founders' lives are the most common items in most of the congregational museums. From the gloves of the bishop-founder to the tea cups used by the first sisters to congregational habits—these were the types of artifacts consistently judged to be worthy of preservation and display in mother house museums. Paintings and photographs are the next most common way to portray history. Only half of the nine congregations used video or reliquaries, and only one third had working websites at the time of the study. While there is much variety among the museums studied regarding the amount of interpretive text accompanying the artifacts, they tend toward minimalism. This suggests that the objects were judged to speak for themselves, and that the intended audience would be familiar with the broad history and purpose of women religious and not require significant assistance to understand the artifacts.

Missionary Activity

Mother house museums focus on how the congregation responded to the dual mandates of service of God through service of neighbour and how their ministry changed over time. The three-pronged approach of engagement in education, social service, and health care is well documented through a number of artifacts including photographs, instructional materials, and task-specific garb, such as white hospital habits. There is little reference, however, to how labour inside of these institutions was stratified between the "professional sisters" and the "house sisters."

In some of their ministerial activities, the religious communities became agents of the state, and this was no more apparent than in the realms of the orphanages and residential schools. These more contested elements, such as the involvement of the communities in residential schools, in orphanages, and in "homes for wayward children and youth," are usually absent from museums, even though we know of their existence through photographic collections.

Further, the move away from the creation and management of large institutions also presents a challenge to those preparing displays. How does one present the history of the community's involvement in institutions that have closed? How does a community portray its recent history of withdrawing from institutions and closing enterprises without creating a sense of useless and unappreciated efforts?

Also apparent in the museums are new opportunities in ministry. Vatican II opened up the study of theology to women, and women religious were among the first to take advantage of this opportunity. Studying theology led women religious to assume new roles in ecclesiastical governance, becoming chancellors of dioceses, canon lawyers, and professors in faculties of theology. Images of these women are included in some of the museums.

For many communities, Vatican II broadened the definition of the mission field, from involvement in missionary activity at home to engagement in activity overseas.[15] While communities such as the Grey Sisters of the Immaculate Conception engaged in mission work in China in the 1930s, it was not until the middle years of Vatican II and the work of Canadian brother bishops, Bishop Alex and Gerald Emmett Cardinal Carter, that Canadian congregations were encouraged to explore the mission fields in Central and South America. In response to *Ad Gentes* and *Lumen Gentium*, and especially to the initiatives arising from the Latin American bishops' meeting in Medellín, Colombia, in 1968, many communities extended their missions into Latin and South America. This new direction presented new opportunities and new challenges: how to reconcile liberation theology with current practices; how to respond to government repression that resulted in psychological and physical torture of community members; where and how to educate novices preparing for work in these fields. These are just some of the topics associated with the impact of Vatican II on congregational missions that need much more analysis not only in mother house museums but also in the broader literature.

The Habit

The habit is the primary artifact of most displays and it is prominently featured. Not surprisingly, the representation of the habit presented us with our most interesting findings. Many communities choose to represent their history through habits, and habits become an

[15] For further analysis, see the essays in the collection Elizabeth Smyth, ed., *Changing Habits: Women's Religious Orders in Canada* (Ottawa: Novalis, 2007).

important element of the material culture of historical memory. Only two congregations did not have actual habits on display at the time of our questionnaire, and one of these had many images of the habit on its poster boards. The single respondent without either a three-dimensional or two-dimensional habit on display was in the process of moving to a new location and did not yet have their new museum set up.

The presentation of the habits is generally devoid of any theological, historical, or anthropological context, in spite of the fact that habits have been the subject of scholarly analysis in a number of academic disciplines. Displays do not situate the habit and the controversies it has engendered. The habit had spiritual, symbolic, and regulatory value. While most recognize the habit as an element of boundary setting that provided tangible evidence that the wearer was both a part of and apart from the secular world in which she served, scholars also note that the habit was not static. Originally designed to be the dress of respectable widows, the construction, display, and significance of the habit came to be highly regularized, and its wearing ritualized. Constitutions and books of customs outlined in miniscule detail how the habit was to be worn.[16]

Most communities trace the changes in religious dress to Vatican II, with none outlining the role played by Pope Pius XII in its modification. Addressing the fact that some aspects of the habit had become highly problematic (the wimple and veil impaired peripheral vision, and made driving cars dangerous) and that rather than serving as a

---

16 *Sisters of St Joseph of Toronto. Constitution of the Sisters of St Joseph in the Archdiocese of Toronto* (Toronto: 1881), 15. The Constitution of the Sisters of St Joseph of Toronto offers this example: The dress of the Sisters shall be simple and modest as becomes virgins who are consecrated to God. Their habit shall be black, made of common material and quite plain; the sleeves shall extend to the end of the hand and be ten inches wide; the skirt shall not quite touch the ground and shall be nearly two yards wide. The shoes shall be black and plain. Their head dress hall consist:

1. of a black veil which shall extend six inches below the waist;
2. of an under veil of the same material;
3. of a cornet which shall be joined under the chin;
4. of a band across the middle of the forehead;
5. of a gimple which shall cover the breast; the last three articles shall be made of white linen.

They shall wear a brassbound crucifix which shall hang before the breast. A black rosary shall be attached by a cord to the left side of their cincture.

feature that would attract young women to religious life, the habit was in fact becoming an impediment, Pope Pius XII addressed the 1951 First International Congress of Teaching Sisters, commenting: "The religious habit: choose it in such a way that it becomes the expression of inward naturalness, of simplicity and spiritual modesty. Thus it will edify everyone, even modern young people."[17]

Leo-Joseph Cardinal Suenens, author of *The Nun in the World*, the 1963 groundbreaking book that became the guide to congregational change, described the habit thus:

> ... some sort of habit which is a distinctive sign is therefore necessary. It has its own nobility, it reminds us of the nun's exclusive dedication to God ... makes it easier to keep conversation on a spiritual plane, renders people more open to discuss personal matters, and is always a joy and a help to those who wear it.
>
> But the habit must be in keeping with the needs of our time. The world today has no patience with mere ornamentation, useless complications, gofferings and other oddities whether starched or floating in the wind, which belong to another age: anything contrived or lacking in simplicity is rejected and anything unpractical or unhygienic, anything that gives the impression that the nun is not only apart from the world but also a complete stranger to its evolution. The habit must be fully adapted to the nun's apostolate: as it is today it often inhibits her social contacts. In de-christianized circles it acts as counter-propaganda, giving the impression that Christianity is out of date, archaic.[18]

If the message of historical change is lost, then the medium used for its presentation becomes even more significant. The historical role of the habit is one of identity and boundary setting. The main medium of display in the museums studied—the department store mannequins or the gendered childhood toy, the doll—presents to the viewer contradictory messages; sisters are either infantilized or sexualized.

---

[17] Pius XII to the First International Congress of Teaching Sisters, 15 September 1951, accessed 4 January 2011, http://www.rc.net/australia/aprel/Counsel.TSisters.htm.

[18] Leon Joseph Suenens, *The Nun in the World: Religious and the Apostolate* (London: Burns and Oates, 1963), 134.

The use of children's dolls to display congregational habits is also a case of the medium interfering with the message. While there are practical reasons for this (it requires less space; presents the opportunity to show modifications of the habit over time, habits for different levels of profession, or habits for special occupations, such as healthcare or warm climates), there is a contradictory message embedded in the use of artifacts of childhood to represent the work of professional women over time. By displaying the habit without interpretation, congregations seem to assume that it is too well known to require comment, an assumption that does not appreciate that "visitors give complex, often contradictory, meanings to museum objects, meanings which are representations of their personal perceptions of identity."[19]

Conclusion

Like the archives of congregations, mother house museums are unique public spaces within private, cloistered landscapes. They are also lenses that enable the visitor and the researcher to gain deeper understanding of how the congregations responded to the directives of Vatican II to explore their founding identity, to adapt to the needs of the time, to revise their foundational documents, and to change their religious habits. Thus, they serve many functions: to preserve congregational heritage, to concretize collective memory, and to educate outsiders.

All congregations that responded to our questionnaire seem to accept the value and duty to preserve and display their history. Their displays run along a wide continuum of what seems to be amateur and professional museum practices. While some invest little money into what are almost curiosity closets and do not have a collection policy, others invest in more expensive and professional displays. Yet correlating low-cost amateur displays with professional displays that have access to more money is naïve and does not address the larger issue: some congregations seem to go beyond displaying their histories to themselves and appreciate the social capital that museums can offer.

---

19 Andrew Newman and Fiona McLean, "The Impact of Museums upon Identity," *International Journal of Heritage Studies* 12, no. 1 (January 2006): 62.

It is notable that, collectively, congregational museums lag far behind congregational archives regarding policy and professionalization.

Like other museums, one finds within the congregational museums the opposition between what is presented and what is absent—what the images are and where there is silence. While it is important to celebrate the achievements of the past, it is also essential to recognize the complexities therein. These tensions are frequently absent. The founding moment is perhaps the most deconstructed of the elements. Influenced by feminist theology, the powerful role played by the founding sisters is frequently celebrated and points to communal identities of women helping women. In the words of the Ursulines of the Chatham Union:

> We are listening women who leave the beaten path to listen to the Earth and its inhabitants, especially the marginalized ones.
>
> We are treasuring women, sprung from a living tradition, who walk in mutuality with others, cherishing life in all its stages.
>
> We are daring women who challenge the status quo, who dream of new possibilities, who explore alternatives.
>
> We are women who follow Angela Merici, herself a woman of adventure, of prophetic vision, of gospel values.[20]

The displays of the religious habits are touchstones, links to the past, and symbols of a lost world. Yet none of these congregational displays highlight the controversies that have surrounded the habit and its recent history. None comment that the decision to move away from the religious habit has become a symbol for the lost "glory" of the Roman Catholic Church. Traditional habits also decorate the covers of books under such provocative titles as *Sisters in Crisis: The Tragic Unraveling of Women's Religious Communities* by Ann Carey[21] and *Double Crossed: Uncovering the Catholic Church's Betrayal of American Nuns*[22] by Kenneth Briggs, books that rally Catholics around a pre–

20 Accessed 17 January 2011. http://www.vocations.ca/Directory/ursulines_chatham.php.

21 A. Carey, *Sisters in Crisis: The Tragic Unraveling of Women's Religious Communities* (Huntington, IN: Our Sunday Visitor Publishing, 1997).

22 Kenneth Brigg, *Double Crossed: Uncovering the Catholic Church's Betrayal of American Nuns* (New York: Doubleday, 2006).

Vatican II world. Not only American lay figures but also New Zealand priests, such as Father G. H. Duggan, praise communities who retained the habit, commenting, "The religious habit is, as it were, the uniform of a regiment of the Church Militant in her never-ending war against the world."[23] Nor do any of the museums engage their audience in habit debate that is very much a part of the institutional landscape. From the pronouncement of Pope John Paul II, to the announcement of an apostolic visitation, to congregations of women religious of the United States, the role of the habit is very much a media darling. Speaking on March 25, 1996, and reporting on the end of the Synod on the Future of the Consecrated Life, John Paul II stated:

> The Church must always seek to make her presence visible in everyday life, especially in contemporary culture, which is often very secularized and yet sensitive to the language of signs. In this regard the Church has a right to expect a significant contribution from consecrated persons, called as they are in every situation to bear clear witness that they belong to Christ. Since the habit is a sign of consecration, poverty and membership in a particular Religious family, I join the Fathers of the Synod in strongly recommending to men and women religious that they wear their proper habit, suitably adapted to the conditions of time and place. Where valid reasons of their apostolate call for it, Religious, in conformity with the norms of their Institute, may also dress in a simple and modest manner, with an appropriate symbol, in such a way that their consecration is recognizable. Institutes which from their origin or by provision of their Constitutions do not have a specific habit should ensure that the dress of their members corresponds in dignity and simplicity to the nature of their vocation.[24]

---

23 Fr. G. H. Duggan, SM, "Religious Habits," *AD2000* 18, no 3 (April 2005): 15, accessed 4 January 2011, http://www.ad2000.com.au/articles/2005/apr2005p15_1909.html.

24 Pope John Paul II, Post-Synodal Apostolic Exhortation, *Vita Consecrata*, of the Holy Father John Paul II to the Bishops and Clergy Religious Orders and Congregations Socieities of Apostolic Life, Secular Institutes, and All the Faithful on the Consecrated Life and Its Mission in the Church and in the World, 25 March 1996, accessed 4 January 2011, http://www.vatican.va/holy_father/john_paul_ii/apost_exhortations/documents/hf_jp-ii_exh_25031996_vita-consecrata_en.html

On December 22, 2008, Mother Mary Care Millea of the Apostles of the Sacred Heart of Jesus was appointed apostolic visitor by Cardinal Franc Rodé, prefect of the Congregation for Institutes of Consecrated Life and Society, and given the task "to inquire and report into the quality of the life of women religious in the United States."[25] Undoubtedly religious garb will be an element of the inquiry and will be reported upon.

Mother house museums are important lenses through which researchers can view both the experience of women religious and how they portray that image to the public. The broader changes in the world and in Catholicism since Vatican II led many women in the Western World to question the value of vowed life. This was evident both within congregations themselves and without the congregation in the pool of Roman Catholic women who might respond to the call to lead a vowed life. Between 1960 and 2000 the number of women religious in Canada decreased by 52 per cent, from 59,712 to 28,639. Since 2004 the Canadian Religious Conference has ceased to keep discrete statistics on women religious. In that year, there were 18,410 women religious in Canada.[26] Moreover, with few new entrants, the average age of women religious in Canada is now over 73. Mother house museums may soon be the only vestiges of the once vibrant convent culture. As such, they will surely gain importance as "flexible mirrors"[27] constructing and reconstructing our pasts. Unfortunately, few congregations have the human or financial resources to construct and maintain museums that do justice to the histories of their congregations. Much work remains to be done on this topic, which is so closely associated with the directives of Vatican II and yet one that also remains very much a part of popular discourse—within the congregations, within the Church, and beyond, among the public at large.

---

25 "Nuns," *New York Times* 2 July 2009, accessed 18 January 2011, http://topics.nytimes.com/topics/reference/timestopics/subjects/n/nuns/index.html.

26 Data are now reported for men and women religious, including sisters, nuns, priests, and brothers. See Canadian Religious Conference, accessed 4 January 2011, http://www.crc-canada.org/bd/fichierNouveaute/482_2.pdf.

27 Susan A. Crane, "Chapter 32: Memory Distortion, and History in the Museum," in *Museum Studies: An Anthology of Contexts*, ed., Bettina Messias Carbonnel (Oxford: Blackwell, 2007), 332.

The Spiritual Journey of Alice Trudeau, MO, in the Postconciliar Context

Rosa Bruno-Jofré,
Queen's University

Alice Trudeau entered the Missionary Oblate Sisters of the Sacred Heart and Mary Immaculate in Saint-Boniface, Manitoba, in 1953 when the congregation's spirituality and culture still had to come to terms with late modernity.[1] The sisters had started to experience an increasing contradiction between their own culture, their own universe, and the world around them, even at the religious level. The journey of Alice Trudeau as a religious was largely defined by her early years as a daughter in a large Franco-Manitoban Catholic family, her personal experience as an orphan, her losses, her experience with Catholic Action, and the drastic late transition to modernity, at the threshold of postmodernity, led by the Church through Vatican II and its aftermath.

This essay focuses on Sister Alice Trudeau, her vision, her prophetic understanding of the role of the congregation, and the limits she encountered. Her journey opens a window to understand the sisters' attempts to reconstruct their identity, liberate themselves, and engage in the social issues of the day. It elucidates the relationship between the process of rebuilding identity as a community and the sisters' own

1 See Rosa Bruno-Jofré, *Missionary Oblate Sisters: Vision and Mission* (Montréal and Kingston: McGill-Queen's University Press, 2005).

discovery of themselves as ethical, autonomous, and reflexive subjects. The latter would lead to new apostolic endeavours. Trudeau's personal letters, her writings on various issues related to the congregation, documents from the congregation, and oral interviews with her and other sisters will be used as sources. Regrettably, Alice Trudeau destroyed her personal journal and most of her correspondence.

The theoretical framework bears an eclectic tone. I embrace the notion developed by gender studies researcher Nickie Charles, among others, that identity formation is linked to culture and that different cultures and subcultures are associated with some form of unique identity.[2] The concept of symbolic universe developed by sociologists of knowledge Peter L. Berger and Thomas Luckman as a level of legitimation that integrates different provinces of meaning and encompasses the institutional order in a symbolic totality serves as a starting heuristic tool to analyze the renewal process.[3] The understanding of the subject is relevant to this essay since the development of an autonomous self, the reconstitution of the self, became a central concern in the life of the congregation after Vatican II and played a central part in the journey of Alice Trudeau.

While this essay centres on Alice Trudeau and the analysis of her leadership, it is also a biography of the community in which Trudeau worked and lived. The latter provides a means to explain the cultural changes that Trudeau envisioned and helps ground the social reality of the community and its interactions with macro-structures such as the Church. The conscious building of the community's identity is placed against a multilevel background.

This essay will be divided into three parts. First, I will explore Trudeau's early life and her initiation into the congregation; unfortunately, I have limited resources for this period of her life. Her life

---

2 Nickie Charles, "Feminist Practices: Identity, Difference, Power," in *Practicing Feminism: Identity, Difference, Power*, ed., Nickie Charles and Felicia Hughes-Freeland (London and New York: Routledge, 1996), 1–37. However, I do not subscribe to an empiricist theory of knowledge that assumes that knowledge is given directly by experience and if you do not have that experience your knowledge is not as valid. Of course, knowledge must account for experience.

3 Peter Berger and Thomas Luckman, *The Social Construction of Reality: A Treatise on the Sociology of Knowledge* (Garden City, NY: Anchor Books, 1966).

history is used here as a retrospective account of her early years and of her spiritual development as a religious as narrated by her orally or in writing. The narration is placed in the historical context of the time in relation to the Catholic Church. The second part of the essay is devoted to Trudeau's leadership as general superior, including her interest in Ignatian spirituality and Christian meditation. The narration and analysis is done in relation to the congregation and the wider Catholic and secular world. Finally, the third part will find its centre in the enriching convergence of previous developments with the theories and practices of the Institut de Formation Humaine Intégrale de Montréal (IFHIM), which gave her the means, in her view, to generate individual and social transformation within a reconstituted vision of the humane. These developments took her to Africa.

I will argue that one may find both continuity and practical eclectic articulations when studying the congregation's search for identity alongside the spiritual journey of Alice Trudeau. The congregation's early quest for freedom was embodied in the sister poet, the deinstitutionalizer Sister Albina Laberge, who put great emphasis on education. Her influence and unofficial memories of her became a point of reference in the congregation's process of renewal and in its involvement with Father André Rochais's program. Rochais, a French educator, had been inspired by the work of psychologist Carl Rogers, in particular *On Becoming a Person*, which provided him the conceptual tools to address human development and a reconstituted relationship with God.[4] Sister Trudeau's spiritual journey—influenced by Laberge's mentorship, her familiarity with Ignatian spirituality, her vision of prophetic leadership, her humanist modern notion of the subject, and her involvement with the reconstruction of persons in Africa through IFHIM—reveals a complex continuity in the search for autonomy, personal growth, and the realization of a social vision. However, the continuity of her journey followed a rather truncated path in her work inside the congregation. One of the theses running through this essay is that the prophetic call articulated by Alice Trudeau was trumped by the community's internal

4 Rosa Bruno-Jofré, "The Process of Renewal of the Missionary Oblate Sisters, 1963–1989," in *Changing Habits: Women's Religious Orders in Canada*, ed. Elizabeth Smyth (Ottawa: Novalis, 2007), 247–73.

renewal process itself and by the structural limits set by the institution to which she was bound. There was little space in which she could lead the community's renewal, in the sense of generating a vital reality that would energize a new direction and a new life. As a result there was a change in the sisters' symbolic universe, but one that led to individual new ministries—as in the cases of Trudeau and Fortier, and Boutin, among others—and not to the reconstitution of the congregational community as a whole.

The Making of a Prophetic Leader

Alice Trudeau was born in a small Manitoba town, Île-de-Chênes, the youngest of fifteen children, in a Franco-Manitoban rural Catholic community. Narratives of her life at home stressed love, joy of living, and a great sense of intuition, but also painful events, such as the death of her mother when she was nine and the death of her father when she was eleven. She was uprooted, separated from her immediate family, and, in her words, she was a "lost child" who left behind security, love, and warmth. After living with an uncle and aunt, she moved in with her sister, Thérèse, when she was fifteen to help her take care of nine orphan children and a chronically ill sister, Rolande. Alice Trudeau found refuge in God to deal with the death and pain around her, and with her own pain. At age seventeen, while involved as a leader in the Catholic Action movement, she fell in love with the young male president, who proposed to her. However, after a prolonged inner struggle, she decided to choose religious life instead and entered the Missionary Oblate Sisters in August 1953. She was eighteen. She said in an intimate conversation, "Il y a une personne dont je suis absolument sûre, c'est mon Dieu" ("There is one person of whom I am absolutely sure, that is my God"). When she joined the sisters, she brought with her an awareness of injustice as a Franco-Manitoban Catholic and her experience as an active member of the Catholic Action.[5]

[5] Alice Trudeau, "Gene`se d'un appel," manuscript, Archives of the Missionary Oblate Sisters, Winnipeg, Manitoba (AMO); Alice Trudeau, "Mon histoire," typed manuscript, 5 August 2001, AMO; Alice Trudeau, *Curriculum vitae* and supporting documents, typed manuscripts, AMO; Alice Trudeau, "Obediences," typed manuscript, AMO; Alice Trudeau, "Dynamic Memory," typed manuscript, AMO; Dora Tetreault, "IFHIM, re: Alice Trudeau," typed manuscript written for IFHIM when Alice Trudeau died, AMO;

Alice caught the attention of Sister Louis-de-France (Albina Laberge), who was in charge of studies and strongly believed from an early age (she entered the congregation in 1910 when she was nineteen) that education was a means to empower the sisters. She was a de-institutionalizer who paid attention to the quality of life and chose to live, for periods of time, on the margins of regular community life. All the while she was perceived as the most powerful member of the community. She had no great attachment to rules, rising late in the morning, studying late at night, and missing morning mass. Her transgressions and her liberal-mindedness became part of the oral memories of the community; she was a window into common sense in a universe made of the rules and complex legitimizations of a regimented environment.[6] Under Albina Laberge's guidance, Alice Trudeau completed high school, a Bachelor of Arts, and obtained teaching certification. Sister Alice described the years between 1959 and 1963 as years of expansion of her inner world, during which she got in touch with inner resources while experiencing moments of painful questioning and a call to a deeper spiritual life.[7]

Sister Trudeau entered the congregation at a time when the sisters, under Albina Laberge's influence, had started to go back to school and obtain degrees and were exposed to contemporary authors in education, psychology, and theology. The Sisters' Formation Movement had reached Canada, as well. Access to the liberal ideas of Karl Rahner and Yves Congar, theologians who resituated the Church in the modern world and revisited ecumenism, accentuated the internal questioning of a "symbolic universe" that could not integrate new meanings and new experiences. This process took place while the superior, Mother Jean-de-la-Croix, led an authoritarian denial of change until the election of a new superior, Jeanne Boucher, in 1963.[8]

"Joseph, 1892–1947," pamphlet describing Alice Trudeau's family life (Joseph was her father) n.d., AMO.

6 Bruno-Jofré, *Missionary Oblate Sisters*, 58–61.

7 Trudeau, "Dynamic Memory." See also Sister Alice Trudeau, interview by Rosa Bruno-Jofré and Sister Dora Tétreault, 21 October 1994, AMO.

8 Bruno-Jofré, "The Process of Renewal," 249.

The phase that opened in 1963 and went to 1973 was later characterized as a therapeutic phase by the congregation. The impact of Vatican II, which started deliberations in 1962, and the developments motivated by the council and the Vatican documents—among them the Pastoral Constitution on the Church in the Modern World (*Gaudium et Spes*) with its emphasis on personal responsibility and freedom, and the Decree on the Adaptation and Renewal of Religious Life (*Perfectae Caritatis*)—set the frame of reference for the renewal process. This phase was characterized by a rapid and uneasy process of changing obsolete customs and traditions that affected daily life and by a reconstruction of the sisters' universe, including their spirituality and their own selves. The general chapter of *aggiornamento* held in 1968 and 1969, and the previous preparations, led the congregation to an internal grassroots approach and to a personal and communal search for identity.[9] The congregation turned, as did many others, to the program offered by Father André Rochais to deal with their own selves and the building of a new relationship with God. Rochais's Personality and Human Relations program included an acknowledgment of and search for the subjective, existential freedom, discovering meanings within oneself, listening to one's self-experience, paying attention to felt experiences (sensations), and a personal relationship with God.[10]

A central issue for the sisters at this time was the loss of the main instrumental mission sustaining the congregation.[11] The two major components of that mission were the sisters' work as a French-English teaching congregation that aimed at building French-Canadian identity

9 Bruno-Jofré, "The Process of Renewal," 249–55.

10 Fondation Personnalité et Relations Humaines, *André Rochais: Founder of PRH*, special edition of the PRH-France 1991 Newsletter (Canada: Winnipeg: D.W. Friesen, 1994). Also Personnalité et Relations Humaines-International, *La personne et sa croissance: Fondements anthropologiques et psychologiques de la formation PRH* (Poitiers, France: Personnalité et Relations Humaines-International, 1997).

11 The concept of instrumental motivation is taken from Margaret Susan Thompson, "Charism or Deep Story? Towards Understanding Better the 19th Century Origins of American Women's Congregations," *Review for Religious* (May–June 1999): 230–50. See also Bruno-Jofré, *The Missionary Oblate Sisters*, Chapter 5.

and their role as an auxiliary to the Oblate fathers in the residential schools. The understanding of Québec as the "basic polity" of French Canada in the 1960s and the movement away from the building of a common identity for all French Canadians created a new political scenario with which the congregation had to contend.[12] Meanwhile, in the late 1960s and early 1970s, the entire ideological configuration sustaining the residential schools collapsed under serious questioning and closures. In other words, one of the most comprehensive levels of legitimation of the existence of the congregation had crumbled.

Between 1964 and 1976, Alice Trudeau served as a teacher in Manitoba, Saskatchewan, and then in Alberta. It was for her a time of inner conflict, questioning, and inward quest. She took the Rochais session in Edmonton in 1970 in her search for meaning in her life. Meanwhile, she built spaces by generating new approaches to teaching and administration, involving parents in the classroom, and even played a role in Assiniboia in the amalgamation of the separate school with the public system in 1970. These experiences, she said, "opened me to the reality of the world, bigger than the Oblates, larger than us."[13] Two elements that link Trudeau to Albina Laberge and the contesting memories present in the congregation were her openness to the world (Laberge used to tell her, "open up, open up"), and her search for freedom and common sense. Trudeau would challenge traditions and customary ways of doing things.[14]

In the fall of 1973, a retreat with Jean Vanier in Gimli, Manitoba, pushed Trudeau even further along her path and had a powerful impact on her spiritual growth and her growth as a woman. Vanier was founder of L'Arche International, a non-profit corporation that provided community living for adults with intellectual disabilities. His message, radical lifestyle, and commitment to building community with the poor and marginalized and to integrate them fully into society had a transformative effect on the sisters who attended. Alice Trudeau

---

12 Marcel Martel, *French Canada: An Account of its Creation and Break-up, 1850–1967*, The Canadian Historical Association, Canada's Ethnic Group Series, no. 24, 3–5.

13 Sister Alice Trudeau, interview by Rosa Bruno-Jofré and Sister Dora Tétreault, 21 October 1994, AMO.

14 Ibid.

recalled "hearing Vanier calling us forth to open up to the world, to the pain of the world, to the people of the world. That was for me a stepping stone."[15] It nourished Trudeau's vision of universal love and transformative social change.

The rapid disintegration of the legitimizing rules and values governing life and the encounter with freedom and theological knowledge led the congregation to a new understanding of the vows, to tensions and fears, as well as to individualism in the congregation.

Sister Lea Boutin was elected general superior in 1973. She opened a phase of spiritual renewal and reintegration. When looking back on this era in retrospect, Boutin said, "We needed freedom and independence. Now more and more we feel the need of others, the need of structures in as much as they help us to live in relationship with others. The Rule is perceived, not so much as an activity to be accomplished but more as a means of entering into relationship, first with God, then with our sisters and the poor to whom we are sent."[16] Sister Boutin was aware that the changes in vision and attitude were not happening in all the sisters at the same time and there was individualism. Many sisters did not feel the need to share their faith, to communicate in depth, and to give themselves periods of silence and reflection.[17] Sister Lea Boutin led the development of a new model of governance, participatory in character, and engaged the community in spiritual renewal and personal development, which included workshops on Personality and Human Relations (Rochais's Group). Sister Boutin and Sister Dora Tétreault tried to rediscover the original inspiration of the congregation (as mandated by *Perfectae Caritatis*). The understanding of the theological concept of reparation was revisited. There was a shift from a language of mortification and grace to a language of social justice that was rooted in congregation founder Archbishop Adélard Langevin's vision of justice for the Catholic people in Manitoba and for Franco-Manitobans.[18] As Dora Tétreault explained to me during an interview

15 Ibid.

16 "Report of the Outgoing General Superior (Sister Lea Boutin) General Chapter of July 1977," manuscript, 16, AMO.

17 Ibid.

18 Sister Dora Tétreault, MO, "Notre oblation et l'esprit de réparation," manuscript

we both conducted with Sister Jeanne Boucher and Sister Lea Boutin, "reparation in the past was part of our identity, but it was reparation to God for offenses committed against Him [*sic*] of course by us, but also by the world, by sinners. So it was a contemplative, cloistered notion of reparation, of adorers who would pray day and night, fast and do all kind of sacrifices to atone."[19] Sister Lea interrupted to say that this notion of reparation came from a theology of atonement and redemption. Sister Dora concluded that the new notion of reparation centred on social justice became restoration, growth, and transformation.[20] The new notion embraced the understanding that people were wounded and that it was necessary to repair (heal) the woundedness in all of us. Instead of an atonement theology from above, the sisters embraced a theology rooted in human experience that moved away from a notion of a God that had to be appeased.[21] The new notion influenced the ministry of the sisters, who had moved from teaching in public, Catholic, and residential schools to a variety of ministries. The sisters' newly embraced theology was further elaborated and reframed, and became particularly meaningful in the context of the work of Alice Trudeau and Cecile Fortier in Africa. Rebuilding harmony between humanity and the individual and within the individual herself was an enduring theme.

In 1976 Sister Alice Trudeau, at the request of Lea Boutin, left school teaching (as many of the sisters in the congregation did at the time) to pursue a one-year Ignatian formation program in spiritual direction at the Jesuit Institute of formation in St. Louis, Missouri. This formation was followed by a thirty-day retreat in Manresa, Spain.[22] Trudeau then started her ministry in spiritual direction and education of the faith. When writing her personal reflections, Trudeau said that she adopted the Rogerian approach (which she learned through Rochais) in her

---

written and presented to the congregation in February 1977, revised and corrected in January 1978, AMO. Also Sister Dora Tétreault, "The Spirit of Oblation and Reparation of the Missionary Oblate Sisters," 1981, AMO. See also Bruno-Jofré, *Missionary Oblate Sisters*, Chapter 6.

19 Bruno-Jofré, "The Process of Renewal," 257.

20 Ibid.

21 Bruno-Jofré, "The Process of Renewal," 257.

22 Written communication from Sister Dora Tétreault, 15 August 2009.

Ignatian formation in spirituality. She writes, "This non-directive and subjective approach characterized by listening, mirroring back, and clarifying was my manner of interacting in a helping relationship."[23] She was talking of her work as an educator and her work in spiritual accompaniment. She believed that a person who becomes conscious of her feelings and emotions could make changes in her behaviour.[24] Through her experience she also noticed that individuals sometimes became narcissistic, downcast, losing sight of their own means and personal resources. Trudeau realized that she was not equipped to help these individuals access their resources or strengths.[25]

The Acts of the General Chapter of 1977 show strong reliance on *Evangelica Testificatio* and encourage an integrative process, a slight movement away from searching the self in order to favour community-rebuilding action.[26] The members of the chapter discussed the mission, although there was no mention of the residential schools or the historical French issue in Manitoba. Instead, they proposed to "conscientize" the sisters on the importance of their role as educators of the faith and the need to revalorize that role.[27] The sisters continued to seek a new alignment of their charism (their *raison d'être*) and the reality surrounding them. Their symbolic universe needed reconstruction to develop a new legitimizing framework. Meanwhile, during the second term of Sister Lea Boutin (1977–81), the sisters continued taking courses on theology, social justice, and pastoral studies and became conversant with Basic Christian Communities that developed in Latin America, the Canadian bishops' letters and documents on social justice, liberation theologians (some sisters went to Spokane's Jesuit Gonzaga University in the late 1970s), and feminist theologians. The commitment to social justice took deeper roots in the congregation.[28]

---

23 Alice Trudeau, "Personal Reflections," (on her personal style of accompaniment), manuscript provided by Dora Tétreault, property of the congregation, AMO.

24 Ibid.

25 Ibid.

26 "Report of the Outgoing General Superior (Sister Lea Boutin)," General Chapter of July 1977, manuscript, 4, AMO.

27 "Report of the Outgoing General Superior (Sister Lea Boutin)," 9.

28 Bruno-Jofré, "The Process of Renewal," 258–59.

Sister Alice served as a member of the General Council from 1977 to 1981. At the same time, she also accepted the direction of a house of twenty-one sisters at Saint-Charles, Manitoba, where she started her ministry in spiritual direction. After considering the needs of lay people, women and men who came regularly for spiritual direction, and after consultation, Trudeau created the St. Charles Retreat Centre. As the driving force behind this means of renewal and spiritual growth for the sisters, she put great emphasis on the Spiritual Exercises of St. Ignatius, which she organized and co-ordinated, working with a team of spiritual directors, among them Fathers Fernand Bédard and Luc Guérin, both Jesuits. However, in 1981, writing the only personal memoir that she did not destroy, entitled "Dynamic Memory," she noted that she had a hard time starting these new ministries and sometimes even felt alienated, rejected, and hurt.[29] The following year, however, she experienced an inner healing, felt whole, in touch with deeper feelings of love, and grew in freedom. In 1981, after Trudeau was elected general superior, Sister Dora Tétreault took over the co-ordination of the Spiritual Exercises in Daily Life program for lay people launched by Trudeau in 1980. The project was transferred to the Renewal Centre at the mother house on 601 Aulneau Street, Saint-Boniface, from where it expanded to other parishes.

Sister Trudeau's quest for experience, meaning, and wisdom led her to embrace Christian meditation, which became her preferred way of praying. In 1977 she was introduced to this form of prayer by Father John Main, an English Benedictine, at the Christian Meditation Centre that had opened in Montréal in 1975. She disseminated Christian meditation among the sisters and beyond by creating meditation groups. She believed with Laurence Freeman, OSB, that meditation provided a path to universal love and peace beyond cultural and religious barriers and a way to heal wounds.[30] Alice Trudeau was always trying to get in touch with her inner self as a woman religious, something that the institutional culture did not favour. Her concern with the place of women in the Church was early and intuitive. She said in an interview,

[29] Trudeau, "Dynamic Memory."

[30] Written communication from Sister Dora Tétreault, 15 August 2009.

"But I always had a feeling for women. Even with Vatican II opening many doors, I recall as a religious beginning to ask myself, is there a place for women in the Church?"[31] During her tenure as general superior she brought the women's religious and spiritual experience to the forefront and confronted bishops and the Oblate fathers when she thought the sisters were not treated fairly.

Reintegration and the Call to Prophetic Leadership: Alice Trudeau, General Superior (1981–1989)

Alice Trudeau was elected general superior in 1981; she was re-elected in 1985 for a second four-year term until July 1989. Sister Lea Boutin had built a reconstituted model of governance that moved away from authoritarianism and, together with Sister Dora Tétreault, had developed new avenues, in tune with the times, to express the congregation's spirituality. However, the congregation was polarized between those who wanted to continue the renewal process, conceived as growth, and those who more and more resisted change.[32] The congregation had difficulties building a legitimating framework as part of their new configuration of values. Their new symbolic universe remained in gestation.

Sister Trudeau had as a starting point the need to reconfigure the ministry in relation to the world and to reposition the leadership at the interface with society and the Church. She had a commitment to social justice and to the oppressed and was open to building a new understanding with Aboriginal peoples.[33] Through a process of consultation and collaboration, and having as framework the 1983 constitution, Sister Alice led the sisters to articulate a mission statement that embodied her vision. The points of reference were "the needs of a suffering world," the call to follow in the footsteps of the compassionate Jesus, and, empowered by faith and audacity, to be in solidarity with the promoters of peace, justice, and unity. Sister Alice defined the mission and vocation of

---

31 Sister Alice Trudeau, interview by Bruno-Jofré and Tétreault.

32 Ibid.

33 Bruno-Jofré, "The Process of Renewal," 261.

the sisters as missionary-educators who enable individuals and groups, especially those who are most deprived, to undertake their personal growth and self-actualization in order to build a more compassionate society and change the world.[34] In her 1985 circular "Onward in Hope," Sister Alice called on the sisters to become challengers in their own communities, to serve in line with the radical character of the Oblate mission statement, and to exercise prophetic leadership as a way of life, contesting the established order and injustice. Her call was neither unique nor new.[35]

Sister Alice's understanding of leadership and spirituality was nourished by women's experiences of spiritual life and an assertive approach in her pursuit of work on equal grounds with men in the Church. At the core was her preoccupation with healing, the development of a sense of freedom, and the restoration of the sisters as persons in all phases of personal growth and communal integration. Having as a goal the generation of situations in which the Christian experience became a lived experience, she envisioned the Missionary Oblate Sisters as "Women of Good News," creators of unity, at the forefront of detecting what is most needed in the world, and thus radiating life.[36] Perhaps one of the most incisive documents she wrote is "Une religieuse interpelle les Oblats," which was a presentation to the congress of the Oblate fathers, in 1983. Teaching in residential schools had become a fundamental component of the sisters' missionary work, though many sisters believed it was not their deepest purpose as a congregation. Sister Alice conveyed to the Oblate fathers the sisters' painful memories, which one can easily trace in the journals of the houses, their feelings of being exploited, considered inferior, and poorly compensated by inadequate arrange-

34 Sister Alice Trudeau, m.o., General Superior, Circular Letter 13, 4 January 1984, theme: Personal Renewal;."Together in Hope: New Evangelical Challenges," Capitular Documents of the 13th General Chapter of the Missionary Oblate Sisters of the Sacred Heart and of Mary Immaculate, held at the motherhouse, St. Boniface, Manitoba, July 4-25, 1985; Sister Alice Trudeau, m.o, Circular Letter 16, "Onward in Hope," 23 July 1985, AMO.

35 See for example Conférence religieuse canadienne, *Rôle prophétique des religieux*, collection Donum Dei, 23 (1977).

36 "Together in Hope: New Evangelical Challenges"; and, Circular Letter 16, "Onward in Hope," 5.

ments that went back to 1909. She made clear that times had changed and that women religious were not any longer at the service of the clergy but of the people of God. She stressed the fact that women religious were moving away from a status of subordination to that of equality, co-responsibility, and complementarity.[37] In practice, early in her tenure, Sister Alice was successful in her struggle with the bishops when she demanded that the sisters in pastoral ministry in parishes have a contract. The Canadian Religious Conference provided support.

In the 1980s and 1990s the sisters became conversant with feminist theologians such as Elisabeth Schüssler Fiorenza, Mary Daly, Rosemary Radford Ruether, and later on Barbara Fiand, among others. In 1991 Sister Lea Boutin authored *Women in the Church: The Pain, the Challenge, the Hope* and made the case for a theology of service for women.[38] With new tools, the sisters continued exploring what the charism (or spirit) of the congregation was and what it would be in light of the new times. The internal documents and manuscripts reveal a critique of the persistent hierarchical, dualistic, and patriarchal character of the Church. The renewal process under Sister Alice also signified empowerment. The Personality and Human Relations workshops were offered again under Trudeau's leadership as a program of adult formation, discernment, and understanding the rhythm personal of growth. The exercises of St. Ignatius and spiritual direction continued.

The same need persisted over time to heal and to reintegrate the community. There was an urgency to rebuild a new symbolic universe that would justify and help integrate in a meaningful way the sisters' daily life, as well as their ministries, within the umbrella of the congregation. The "endurance" of old cultural values and ways of doing things, fear of change, awareness of the limits set by the Church, the discovery of individualism and of a poorly articulated multi-faceted self were all reflected in the continuing polarization of the community. When the time came for the chapter to elect a new superior, in 1989,

---

37 Alice Trudeau, "Une religieuse interpelle les Oblats," typed manuscript, 1983, AMO.

38 Lea Boutin, MO, *Women in the Church: The Pain, the Challenge, the Hope* (Aurora, ON: Emmanuel Convalescent Foundations, 1991). Sister Lea Boutin did both a master's in pastoral studies (University of Ottawa and Saint Paul University) and a doctorate in ministry (University of Toronto and the University of St. Michael's College) in the 1980s.

the Church had moved to dissolve Basic Christian Communities in Latin America, severely questioned liberation theology, and asserted conservative positions regarding the role of women in the Church. Sister Alice's prophetic vision had gone beyond the boundaries set by the Church, boundaries that many sisters felt uncomfortable pushing within a culture that had valued obedience (submission) for such a long time.[39] However, the entire process of renewal and the impact of her vision translated into new apostolates. The Aulneau Renewal Centre, founded in 1979 at the mother house in Saint-Boniface, became a counselling service centre, mainly for low-income people, and an avenue to channel visions both of social justice (in a limited way) and of the renewed meaning of reparation.

Toward the end of her mandate in October 1988, Sister Alice wrote a document to encourage the sisters to move ahead and made the case, once more, for change and prophetic leadership. She hoped that the process of change would continue. At the core of the document was the call to be innovators. She used John Baptist Metz as a reference for the notion of innovation in religious life as a way to become "effective models" for the Church. She also cited the document "Mutual Relations," produced in 1978 by the Sacred Congregation for Religious and Secular Institutes, which insists on the innovative role of religious, and quoted Article 76 of the congregation's own 1983 constitutions that reads "[we] are sent by Christ ... to cooperate with the Spirit who is continually recreating the world."[40]

In order for the congregation to play an innovative role through radical evangelization, Sister Alice wrote, there is the need for prophetic leadership. She understood this leadership as an agent of change in Oblate culture as well as the symbolic incarnation of values in which the Oblates believed. For this kind of evangelization to happen, it was necessary to have the wisdom to make decisions that would be crucial to the values the congregation wanted to instill and the goals it wanted to achieve. Finally, Sister Alice said that the sisters had to have creative energy and will to action to accomplish the objectives of the congrega-

39 Bruno-Jofré, "The Process of Renewal," 264–66.

40 Alice Trudeau, "Prophetic Leadership," manuscript, October 1988, 1–2, AMO.

tion's mission.[41] She borrowed definitions of leadership from cultural anthropology to make the point that a leader must have virtue and vision and recognize the potential in people while creating an environment in which individuals may develop and maximize their contributions.[42] In her attempt to motivate the sisters to embrace a successor who could continue her work, she turned to Walter Brueggemann's *The Prophetic Imagination* to define the task of a prophetic leader as expressing a future full of hope, bringing those hopes to the public, speaking concretely about real newness, and speaking the language of amazement.[43] The main issue that afflicted her leadership remained her preoccupation for the future: the collective inspiration to lead the community to the point of a united vision for change.[44]

The new leadership that succeeded Sister Alice was reflective of the contradictions and changes that emerged during the renewal process. To an important extent, it represented a challenge to prophetic renewal and the work of Lea Boutin and Alice Trudeau. However, the grassroots movement of sisters committed to change in the community and to questioning, and rich in visionary insights, continued its journey.

The Reconstruction of Persons: The Ministry in Africa

After ending her second term as general superior and having tested the limits of her own resources, of the congregation itself, and of the Church as an institution, in 1989, Sister Alice Trudeau and Sister Cecile Fortier undertook a three-year formation at the Institut de Formation Humaine Intégrale de Montréal with the goal of being prepared to accompany persons and groups following the processes of actualization of human vital strengths. Sister Alice had found in the Personality and Human Relations workshops the means to pursue her growth ("there is within me more than me"),[45] to understand and turn childhood wounds

41 Ibid., 2.

42 Ibid., 3–4.

43 Ibid., 8–9.

44 Ibid., 4.

45 PRH-France Newsletter, special edition, André Rochais, Founder of PRH *(Personnalité et Relations Humaines). English translation* (Manitoba: D.W. Friesen, 1994), 56.

into growth, to cultivate openness to relationships ("the personal relation is not opposed to the communal"),[46] to live in harmony with herself, and to exercise complete freedom by being true to her conscience. She fully shared with Rochais the vision of a truly human world and a trust in the value and innate goodness of each person.[47] However, she perceived the limits of Rochais's practice. She needed theoretical and practical tools to generate individual and social transformation. In one of her personal reflections she writes:

> In practice, I noticed that mirroring back, even in the person's own words, in her own concrete experience was perceived as a "platitude." She had difficulty to arrive at making connections and getting involved in an autonomous and responsible way in the process of her personal growth. On the other hand, I felt within myself a dynamic power when I asked more direct questions. For example, in regard to a decision: "What is it that you want?" In the case of a conflict: "You, what can you do?" etc. I realized that questions pertaining to the person's journey could start things moving. Thus, I was inventing my own way of reaching a person in her lived experience. However, I was never sure of my personal tools and moreover I could not verbalize them adequately.[48]

These reflections were obviously written before Sister Alice discovered the human vital strengths approach created by Jeannine Guindon that she adopted so wholeheartedly at the Institut de Formation Humaine Intégrale de Montréal.[49]

The institute, founded in 1976 by Dr. Jeannine Guindon in cooperation with Sister Marie-Marcelle Desmarais, is mandated to lead persons to become conscious of their vital human strengths and to realize how the strengths can be actualized in spite of traumatic experi-

46 Ibid., 57

47 Ibid., 61-62.

48 Trudeau, "Personal Reflections."

49 Jeannine Guindon, PhD, founder of L'Institut de Formation Humaine Intégrale de Montréal (IFHIM), was the founding director of École de Psycho-éducation, Faculté des arts et sciences de l'Université de Montréal and later professor emerita. She was the author of books and articles including *Vers l'autonomie psychique: de la naissance à la mort* (Paris: Editions Fleurus, 1982). Alice Trudeau used this book during her studies at the institute. For general information see http://www.ifhim.ca.

ences. The concept of energy that can be mobile, autonomous, or bound is central to the process the institute teaches. The harnessing of this energy could lead to corporal, psychological, and spiritual autonomy. The development of personal autonomy, so dear to Sister Trudeau, was central to Guindon's theories.[50] Trudeau said that during her formation at the institute she was able to interconnect the human vital strengths approach with the spiritual journey according to the Ignatian Spiritual Exercises, thus opening up a new avenue for the facilitation of the actualization of forces in the spiritual dimension while developing internal freedom and psychological autonomy; she felt that her combined approach dislodged the counter-forces of the subconscious mind.[51]

Sister Alice Trudeau and Sister Cecile Fortier, current superior of the Missionary Oblates, graduated from the institute in 1992. During 1993 and 1994, the sisters exercised the new ministry with lay people, Aboriginal groups, and groups of women at the Renewal Centre at the mother house in Saint-Boniface.[52] In 1995, after the terrible genocide that took place in Rwanda, Sister Alice and Sister Cecile joined an international team of counsellors to minister to the refugee caregivers, including teachers who, in turn, worked with Rwandan refugee children in crisis. The headquarters were in Goma, Democratic Republic of Congo, which is on the border of Rwanda. Oxfam Québec and Terre Sans Frontières sponsored the project, as well. The first assignment

---

50 See Jeannine Guindon, *Vers l'autonomie psychique*. Materials related to the workshops offered by Alice Trudeau, MO, during 1992 and 1993 entitled "Enhancing the Quality of your Leadership through the Actualization of your Vital Human Strengths." See also Marie-Marcelle Desmarais, "L'actualisation des forces vitales humaines: Un Chemin de développement social," *L'Église canadienne* 22, no. 24 (5 October 1989): 747–52.

51 Alice Trudeau, "Résumé de mes engagements antérieurs et de mon cheminement à travers les EVC," n.d., 2, included in binder titled "All what Alice accomplished between 1993 and August 1994 in Winnipeg after her IFHIM training." Also Alice Trudeau, "Exposé Synthèse," presented at the Congrès de spiritualité ignatienne: Pédagogie de croissance humaine et spirituelle: des approches complémentaires, Villa Manrèse, Ste-Foy, Québec, 30–31 octobre 1993, AMO; Jeannine Guindon, interview by Alice Trudeau (Exercices de Saint-Ignace dans la vie courante et Approches des forces vitales humaines), 24 August 1993, St. Boniface, Manitoba, AMO; Marie-Marcelle Desmarais, interview by Alice Trudeau (Exercices de Saint-Ignace dans la vie courante et Approches des forces vitales humaines), 27 August 1993, St. Boniface, Manitoba, AMO.

52 See materials prepared by Alice Trudeau for the workshops included in the binder titled "All what Alice accomplished between 1993 and August 1994 in Winnipeg after her IFHIM training."

of the project, known as Aid to the Reconstruction of Persons, was in Camp Buhimba, working with educators of children who were not accompanied by anyone (orphans). A similar project was launched in May 1996 for the Congolese population of Goma.[53] The project ended abruptly due to the civil war. Between 1997 and 2002 the Aid to the Reconstruction of Persons project was developed in Bujumbura, Burundi, while there were follow-ups in Goma with the Congolese. Between 2002 and 2004 Sister Alice and Sister Cecile jointly ministered to the Congolese people of Goma at their request.[54]

Before leaving Canada to fulfill her mission in Goma, Alice said to me: "And therefore, let's say for myself this new project is like a second wind for me … I don't know how long I will last, that is if my health gives in. I do not know that. It is an unknown. But what I know is maybe that is where I can best bring my contribution."[55] Sister Alice died on October 27, 2004, in Nairobi, where she had been transferred by air ambulance from Goma, ever faithful to her vision.

Conclusion

The journeys of Alice Trudeau and her congregation converged in their desires to reconstitute themselves as individuals and as a community in tune with the signs of the times. The renewal process led to a new model of governance and to a rich engagement with the spirituality of the congregation, to a discovery of the uniqueness of women religious, and a new way to relate to the world. The latter was translated in different ministries inspired by a revisited notion of reparation. However, it did not give life to a new universe of values, legitimizations, and points of reference that would integrate the sisters' new experiences, new and various meanings.

---

53 See Formatrices ARP, "Projet Recherche-Action auprès des éducateurs/trices des ENA du Camp Buhimba," Goma, Zaire, February–April 1996; Alice Trudeau and Cécile Fortier, "*À nos parents, amis, amies bienfaiteurs et bienfaitrices*," booklet, Équipe Ressource MO, 26 March 1997, AMO; Materials provided by Dora Tétreault, MO, *Un petit grain … La congrégation des Missionnaires Oblates du Sacré-Cœur et de Marie Immaculée, cent ans d'histoire: 1904–2004*, booklet, Maison-Chapelle, Saint-Boniface, Manitoba, 2004, AMO

54 The congregation has kept all the letters from Alice Trudeau and Cécile Fortier for this period, as well as related documents. Property of the congregation.

55 Sister Alice Trudeau, interviewed by Bruno-Jofré and Tétreault, 3–5.

The journey of Alice Trudeau as general superior was marked by a prophetic vision that was resisted by many, misunderstood by some, and embraced by others. Internalization of habits, dispositions, and institutional boundaries set the limits to her vision and her projects. The congregation's newly discovered individualism did not converge into a common direction. Alice left the congregation in Canada for Africa to give life to her call to work toward transformative personal and social change with the poor and those who suffered. Her inclusive universal sense of love is partly present in the Alneau Renewal Centre founded by the congregation in 1979 which has provided counselling services to underprivileged families, children, and adults since 1989. This Centre embodies the many components of the congregation's renewal process in its mission to the community. Sister Alice's commitment to the equality of women religious with men in the Church and her women-centred approach to leadership and spirituality has become part of the history of the congregation and beyond.

Vatican II and the Changing Mission of the Catholic Women's League of Canada

Sarah Jardine,
Saint Paul University

English-speaking Canadian lay Roman Catholic women have had a long and vital role in creating community and parish life in the twentieth century.[1] In 1891 Pope Leo XIII's encyclical *Rerum Novarum* was issued in response to societal pressures. As a result, opportunities for lay people, particularly women, to minister in the Church were greatly increased. While the call to personal piety as a way of seeking grace and building the Church was still emphasized, working in the world with and for other people was encouraged. Both Pope Pius X and Pope Pius XI issued calls to the laity to become involved in Catholic Action. Catholics were asked to strengthen their spiritual lives by increasing their devotional piety and becoming officially involved in providing social services to those in need. For effective Catholic Action in the body of the Church, the laity was to carry out their work under the supervision of the local bishops. This qualified the work as being done as part of the apostolate of the Church.[2] A whole new range of

1 In the context of this paper, the term "lay women" refers to women who have not taken vows in a religious order or community.

2 Terence Fay, *A History of Canadian Catholics: Gallicanism, Romanism, and Canadianism*, McGill-Queen's Studies in the History of Religion, Vol. 20 (Montréal: McGill-Queen's University Press, 2002), 260.

activities associated with the Church opened up and, for Catholic lay women, there was an opportunity to move from the private sphere of the home into the public and political domain. Although Roman Catholic women had long been active in parish and community life, with the founding of a national organization, the Catholic Women's League of Canada in 1920, their actions were made more visible. Notes from the first annual convention indicate:

> The Convention which started on Wednesday, June 1st and continued until Sunday, June 5th was the first in the lifetime of Canada that a body of Catholic women convened as a national organization. This does not mean that Canadian women of our glorious Church had before been inactive, either as individuals or as members of the countless parishes that honeycomb the continent, but it does point out that never before had the one million Catholic women of the Dominion been represented as a national unit such as they were on that occasion.[3]

This formation of a national organization of Catholic lay women mainly had its roots in two earlier events. The first was the organizing of local units of the Catholic Women's League (CWL) in major Canadian cities from East to West from 1912 to 1919.[4] The second came when a government employee of the Women's Division of the Canadian Immigration Department, Loretta Kneil, realized that women were not represented at the federal talks for resettling immigrants after World War I. Her connections with the Western CWL encouraged the formation of a national group of Catholic Canadian women involved, among other things, with issues of immigration.[5] The significance of immigra-

---

[3] Valerie Fall, *"Except the Lord Build the House ..." A History of the Catholic Women's League of Canada 1920–1990* (Winnipeg: The Catholic Women's League of Canada, 1990), 23. From Editorial, *The Canadian League* (July 1921).

[4] Fall, *Except the Lord Build,* 7. A note is made that seven out of nine provinces were represented. The delegates listed appear to come from six provinces with Manitoba, British Columbia, and Prince Edward Island missing.

[5] Sheila Ross, "'For God and Canada': The Early Years of the Catholic Women's League in Alberta," CCHA *Historical Studies* 62 (1996): 97. There is a discrepancy about the government position held by the minister who called the meetings about reconstruction and immigration. On page 6 of *Except the Lord Build,* Valerie Fall refers to him as the Hon. C. J. Doherty, Minister of Reconstruction and Immigration. She does not specifically mention his wife but, on page 7, cites Mrs. C. J. Doherty of Ottawa (wife

tion issues for the CWL can be seen in the July 1921 speech to the first National CWL Convention when President Bellelle Guerin stated:

> The Catholic Women's League has already taken some means of meeting Catholic immigrants on the arrival of the ships and we have a dream ...it is that in every city the CWL should have an Immigration Committee, making a chain from the Atlantic to the Pacific, and that these poor forlorn strangers shall be passed on through friendly hands from one Committee to another until they reach their destination and are placed under the care of a Pastor in their own beloved Cross-crowned Catholic Church.[6]

This national organization discussed, debated, voted on, and put forward areas of concern to be addressed. The main areas were: education, social welfare, and national unity[7] and were seen to be carried out through the organizational levels of Church, home, school, and nation.[8] Specific interests of the CWL were: membership, hospitality,

---

of the cabinet minister) as having had "a prominent part in the proceedings ...." Sheila Ross, on page 97 of "For God and Canada," says that the wife of Justice Minister C. J. Doherty was a member of the Ottawa CWL. Ross says that the Justice Minister suggested she contact Bellelle Guerin, president of the Catholic Women's League of Montréal. It seems likely that: i) Mrs. C. J. Doherty suggested the contact with Miss Bellelle Guerin, and ii) that Mr. Doherty was both Justice Minister and Minister of Reconstruction and Immigration. Record of the Hon. C. J. Doherty as Minister of Justice can be found in other sources. There is another discrepancy between Mrs. R. H. Kneil being a former resident of Edmonton [Fall, *Except the Lord Build,* 6] versus her being a former president of the Edmonton unit [Ross, "For God and Canada," 97). A report on Katherine Hughes published for the *Western Catholic Reporter* indicates that Katherine Hughes did found the Catholic Women's League of Edmonton in 1912 and that her sister, Loretta Kneil, served as president of the Edmonton League. Accessed 26 January 2010, http://www.wcr.ab.ca/news/2005/0905/hughes090505.shtml.

6 Fall, *Except the Lord Build*, 14.

7 Ibid., 22. The league chose "For God and Canada" as its motto in 1922. Difficulties encountered by immigrants from the "Ruthenian States," Italian immigrants, and Irish immigrants are the underlying reason for the Catholic Women's League being concerned about "Racial Harmony," and this accounts for the focus on patriotism and citizenship highlighted in their motto. The tension between Catholic Irish immigrants and the ruling Protestant establishment is well documented by Mark McGowan in his article, "Toronto's English-Speaking Catholics, Immigration, and the Making of a Canadian Catholic Identity, 1900–30," in *Creed and Culture*, ed. Brian Murphy and Gerald Stortz (Montréal: McGill-Queen's University Press, 1993), 204–45. He shows how, through education, assistance from the Church community, concerned bishops, such as Bishop Neil McNeil, intermarriage with Protestants, and other factors, Irish Canadians eventually moved beyond their Irish national identity and became accepted as patriotic Canadians.

8 *The Canadian League* 1, no. 1 (April 1921): 3.

education, literature, debates, history, music, art, citizenship, and social service work (including sociology, immigration, hygiene, child welfare, women's welfare, divorce, recreation centres, hostels, hospitals, jails, detention homes, Traveler's Aid, and the Big Sister movement).[9]

Over the decades that followed, the league actively worked to address these interests in a variety of ways. In early 1923 the CWL formally agreed to take on the project of a newly formed religious order, the Sisters of Service, whose founding mission was to work with poor rural immigrant Catholics in the West. To fund the sisters' work, CWL agreed to contribute $3,500 a year to help establish the order.[10] In 1923 the Catholic Women's League of Canada also became federally incorporated as an officially recognized Canadian national organization. A National Girl Guide Convener was appointed.[11] The national scholarship for a Catholic woman doing graduate studies in social work was established in 1927.[12] The droughts and crop failures experienced in the prairies and the hardships of the Depression led to the creation of "The Regina Fund," a national relief fund for people in southwest Saskatchewan. In addition to financial support, clothes, bedding, and books were collected and processed by league members and shipped at no charge by the railways.[13] Over $1.5 million for charity and Catholic education had been raised by the women of the CWL by the end of 1937.[14] In 1938 Business and Professional Women's Subdivisions and some junior subdivisions were organized in major cities. By 1939, 50,000

9 *The Canadian League* 1, no. 1 (April 1921): 4.

10 Fall, *Except the Lord Build*, 25. Note that Jeanne Beck, talking about the formation of the Sisters of Service, found a different amount for the donation. On page 23 she reports that $6,000 per year was given by the Catholic Women's League. Her source is letter Fr. Coughlan, CSsR, to Catherine Donnelly, 21 September 1921. SOSA [Sisters of Service Archive], RG1-01, box 1, file 6. On page 25, Beck comments in footnote 42: "In September 1922 Daly appealed to the Catholic Women's League for individual contributions, 'Remember the small amounts make big sums .... The figures that appear in today's paper of $1,500,000 collected by the Women's Methodist Missionary Soc. tells us eloquently – may I add reproachfully – what continued effort can produce.'" Daly, notes of his address to the CWL Second Annual Convention, 26–30 September 1922. SOSA, RG5-2, box 1, file 7.

11 Fall, *Except the Lord Build*, 26.

12 Ibid., 27.

13 Ibid.

14 Ibid.

members in 554 subdivisions were reporting to the Annual National Convention.[15] The 1940 CWL registration under the War Charities Act meant that charitable actions performed by the league had to be carefully noted, resulting in accurate records showing the large amount and broad scope of the work the women had done.[16]

The great volume of social services work done by the women of the CWL was mostly unpaid and was most often done in addition to their own family responsibilities. The emotional content in the social services work done by the women is significant. The activities were done in response to the needs of someone else. The interests of the league were set out nationally, but support had to come from the bottom up. Individual members participated with their time, talents, and fundraising efforts to further the aims and interests of the group. However, while this was emotional work, the road to and the achievement of these goals of social service were sources of support for both the women and the recipients involved.

The author of a March 1937 article in *The Canadian League* tells how surprised and impressed she was with the friendly and professional reception she received at her first CWL meeting. She expressed her amazement when a woman she knew as "[a] mother of several small children immediately offered to have the dime card[17] filled .... 'Sure, that will be easy,' she said. 'I will return it next meeting.'"[18] Another powerful memory is recorded in the June 1938 *The Canadian League* at a time when the effects of the Great Depression and crop-destroying droughts in western Canada caused tremendous hardship to many western families. The letter reads as follows:

> Dear Miss Dillon:
>
> I have filled in our report, as best I could, as the crop was a total failure in this district again last year. Please find enclosed $1.20 postal note for 12 members, per capita fee for 1938.

---

15 Ibid.

16 Ibid.

17 The dime card was modelled after the 1930s American polio fundraising campaign where people filled a slotted postcard with dimes or bills and mailed it to the White House.

18 *The Canadian League* 16, no. 11 (March 1937): 10.

I hope we have a larger membership soon, but we do well to try to keep alive. We hold regular meetings to keep up our interest, and say daily a prayer for rain, besides one Mass a Month for same. I am sending this prayer, and please say a prayer at the Eucharistic Congress for us all, who cannot go to it.

Sincerely yours [name not included][19]

The financial and emotional support women offered each other provided friendship and hope both ways. The fundraising activities of the Catholic Women's League of Canada were diverse and can be categorized into feeding, gathering, and social/educational activities. They were an important source not only of funding but also of companionship and training.

Over the years, the membership of the CWL grew and waned and although it never reached the one million potential members imagined when the movement was first founded, a significant number of Catholic lay women joined and worked in CWL activities effectively participating in lay action for the Church. They worked to build the Church and community for themselves and their neighbours through actions of social service informed by their faith and supported by their active fundraising that allowed them to fund the projects they saw as important.[20] Organizing themselves under the oversight of local bishops, rather than being directly affiliated with individual parishes, allowed women the opportunity to focus on larger issues that were more effectively addressed with provincial and national planning and implementation.[21] In terms of ministry, the women of the CWL individually and collectively demonstrated the Church's mission toward its members (and others) in the practical work they carried out.

I will now turn to the question of how this history of women in the CWL in the first half of the twentieth century is important today. In a similar spirit to that demonstrated by women in the early years

---

19 *The Canadian League* 18, no. 2 (June 1938): 20.

20 Sarah Jardine, *'The Catholic Women's League of Canada and the Joy of Chicken Salad Sandwiches': English-Speaking Lay Roman Catholic Women of 20th Century Ontario Working in the Communion of Saints.* (Master's thesis, Saint Paul University, Ottawa, 2008), 52.

21 Sheila Ross, "'For God and Canada': The Early Years of the Catholic Women's League in Alberta," in CCHA *Historical Studies* 62 (1996): 92.

of the CWL, Roman Catholic women were optimistic about changes prior to and issuing from the Second Vatican Council held from 1962 to 1965. There were indications in key documents that the institutional Church was aware of the importance of recognizing the full equality and dignity of women in the Church.

The Church response to "the signs of the times," when understood in light of the tremendous societal shifts happening at this time, gave rise to the possibility for a far more equal and extensive role for women in the Catholic Church. Canadian theologian Elisabeth Lacelle sees an emphasis on the "new creation" with the recognition of the co-humanity of woman and man in the text of the Pastoral Constitution on the Church in the Modern World (*Gaudium et Spes*), Article 12. The text reads:

> But God did not create man [humankind] to be alone: from the beginning, 'He created man and women' [Gen. 1, 27]. That society of man and woman is the first expression of the communion of people. For man [humankind], by its basic nature, is social and can neither live nor flourish without others. [22]

Mary Ellen Sheehan explores John XXIII's perception of three signs of the times—workers' rights, women's rights, and global political self-determination—in his encyclical *Pacem in Terris*. Concerning women, he says,

> the part that women are now playing in political life is everywhere evident. This is a development that is perhaps of swifter growth among Christian nations, but it is also happening extensively, if more slowly, among nations that are heirs to different traditions and imbued with a different culture. Women are gaining an increasing awareness of their natural dignity. Far from being content with a purely passive role or allowing themselves to be regarded as a kind of instrument, they are demanding both in domestic and in public life the rights and duties which belong to them as human persons.[23]

---

22 Elisabeth Lacelle, "From Today to Tomorrow: Women in the Canadian Catholic Church," *Grail* (June 1985): 30. Note that the wording of the Vatican text is the original found in Lacelle's article.

23 *Pacem in Terris*, no. 41 in *The Encyclicals and Other Messages of John XXIII*

In regard to issues of progress on justice and equal rights for women, Sheehan refers to Article 29 of the Pastoral Constitution on the Church in the Modern World and reminds the reader that the council clearly stated that discrimination "whether based on sex, race, color, social conditions, language, or religion, must be curbed and eradicated as incompatible with God's design."[24]

After Vatican II, women became involved in ministry serving as lectors, extraordinary ministers of communion, and altar servers. Working as theologians, teachers, pastoral associates, pastoral assistants, pastoral counsellors, and as advisors on a number of significant Church committees became a possibility for many women.[25] Texts on justice and equality found in pre- and postconciliar documents did allow for some movement of women into positions previously closed to them.

In the Canadian context, Jean Forest, long-time CWL member and Canadian Senator from 1996–98, was a contributor to the 1984 Canadian Conference of Catholic Bishops' Ad Hoc Committee on the Role of Women in the Church. In this capacity she brought forward recommendations presented and approved by the ad hoc committee of the Catholic Women's League of Canada on the impact of feminism on Catholic women and families.[26] Some sections contained in the CWL report were: support of feminism, women in the schools, women in the family, and women in the workplace. The report called for an approach of reason and compassion rather than confrontation on issues where people were not in agreement.[27] Commenting on Canadian Catholic

(Washington: The Pope Speaks Press, 1964). Mary Ellen Sheehan, "Women and Ministry in the Roman Catholic Church," in *Heavy Blessings, Light Burdens: Challenges of Church and Culture in the Post Vatican II Era*, ed., Mary Heather MacKinnon, SSND, Moni McIntyre, and Mary Ellen Sheehan, IHM (Quincy, IL: Franciscan Press, 2000), 57.

24 Sheehan, *Heavy Blessings*, 59. Note that Jean Forest, in her article, "Women in the Canadian Context," understands the Pastoral Constitution on the Church in the Modern World to be in keeping with St. Paul's Galatian text—"There are no more distinctions between Jew and Greek, slave and free, male and female but all of you are one in Christ Jesus"—in the sense of a promise to get rid of racist and sexist discrimination. In *Grail* 4 (December 1985): 15.

25 Sheehan, *Heavy Blessings*, 57.

26 Michael W. Higgins and Douglas R. Letson, *Portraits of Canadian Catholicism* (Toronto: Griffin House, 1986), 163.

27 Forest, "Women in the Canadian Context," 16.

women, Jean Forest identified three groups in the Roman Catholic Church. Women in the first group were content and happy with the way they were accepted by the Church. Women in the second group more or less accepted their roles in the Church without a lot of reflection on the status quo or on proposed changes. Women in the third group were hurting and suffering badly and were at risk of being lost to the Church.[28] Of the three groups, Forest said:

> Most of the women we heard from were committed, faithful members of the Church who had experienced both highs and lows in their spiritual lives. When they had been deeply touched by 'the Church,' it had, invariably, been through the healing ministry of one or more of her members – parent, teacher, priest, nun, lay minister, friend. When they had been turned off by 'the Church,' it had, most often, been because the administrative Church – either by structure or design – made it difficult or impossible for her members to minister to each other as their baptismal commitment demanded they should. Many of these women expressed personal pain at the limits placed, by the Church, upon their own opportunities to minister to others, but it went much deeper than that. They were distressed for those who, because of these limitations, might not experience that needed healing ministry. They were grieved by the loss which the whole church will suffer if, to use the words of one woman, these healing gifts "God given, lie dormant, wasted and uncelebrated."[29].

For Catholic lay women to continue to find support and to minister in the Church, Jean Forest reiterated the position in the Catholic Women's League position paper from the CWL Ad Hoc Committee on the Role of Women in the Church delivered to the CCCB committee of the same name. It advocated for people to hold each other in dignity and to offer a healing hand and healing heart to all those they encountered.[30]

28 Ibid., 18.

29 Higgins and Letson, *Portraits of Canadian Catholicism*, 163.

30 Forest, "Women in the Canadian Context," 22.

Although women's ministries in the Church still face challenges today, this brief review of the history of the CWL of Canada shows how women's work of care for their neighbours and one another can create networks of assistance, support, companionship, and hope. In light of this, two questions can be asked regarding the continuing mission of the Catholic Women's League of Canada today: "How can the CWL of today minister to women of all three of the groups described by Jean Forest?" and, "Reaching back to its founding vision, how does the CWL today continue to help the widow, the orphan, and the stranger?"

SECTION III

Ecumenism and Religious Liberty / Œcuménisme et liberté religieuse

La question de la liberté religieuse au Québec à l'heure du concile

Gilles Routhier,
Université Laval

L'origine de cette étude se trouve dans une lettre envoyée par Philippe Delhaye à André Laurentin, à l'été 1965. Delhaye, qui n'avait pas obtenu de poste à Louvain et qui, de ce fait, avait dû s'expatrier à Lille et à Montréal, enseignait alors à temps partiel au nouvel Institut de sciences religieuses à l'Université de Montréal. Ses contacts avec les milieux montréalais lui avaient valu d'être nommé, à la demande du cardinal Léger, *peritus* au concile en 1962.

À l'été 1965, à la suite d'une conférence sur la liberté religieuse qu'il donnait à Montréal, il écrivait à André Laurentin, également proche des milieux montréalais qu'il fréquentait régulièrement, avec lequel il entretenait une correspondance suivie. Ces personnes avaient vite perçu que le cardinal Léger jouait un rôle important au concile et qu'il exerçait une réelle influence sur le cours des affaires conciliaires, autant par ses interventions *in aula* que par ses prises de position à la Commission doctrinale, voire en raison de ses contacts directs avec le pape. Il ne s'agit pas d'un cas unique, l'histoire du concile nous apprenant que l'on se sert ainsi des figures de proue pour faire aboutir les projets d'un petit groupe qui a l'ambition de faire valoir ses idées. Là n'est toutefois pas mon sujet, et je reviens à cette lettre de l'été 1965.

À la suite de sa conférence sur la liberté religieuse, Philippe Delhaye écrivait donc ces quelques mots à André Laurentin : « Ici, plusieurs n'en [liberté religieuse] connaissent même pas le mot… » J'avoue avoir été assez surpris à la lecture de ce jugement et je me suis demandé s'il correspondait un peu à la réalité ou s'il fallait simplement y voir l'expression du sentiment de supériorité d'un Européen à l'égard des habitants du Nouveau Monde, l'expression, en quelque sorte, de l'habitus colonial, les Européens ne pouvant qu'éclairer ces pauvres Nord-Américains à peine sortis des forêts. Cela a suffisamment piqué ma curiosité pour que j'entreprenne de documenter un peu le débat sur la liberté religieuse au Québec au cours de la période conciliaire, sans connaître à l'avance ce que je pourrais trouver sur le sujet.

À mon grand étonnement, la récolte est plutôt abondante, et j'essaierai de fournir ici quelques éléments de ce dossier, en présentant les pièces que j'ai pu mettre à jour, tentant une première reconstruction de ce débat. Je me limiterai à la période conciliaire, soit les années 1959 à 1965, et je puiserai à la fois dans les déclarations des évêques (publiques ou privées) et dans les prises de position de théologiens ou d'intellectuels catholiques.

En fait, la réflexion sur la liberté religieuse au Québec accompagne d'abord la discussion sur la confessionnalité des syndicats, avant d'être de nouveau soulevée lors de la discussion sur la réforme de l'éducation.

Au vu des dossiers des évêques du Québec, le débat sur la liberté religieuse était engagé ici bien avant l'ouverture de Vatican II, en 1962. Ainsi, avant le début des assises conciliaires, les positions me semblent déjà assez arrêtées. Je mènerai mon enquête à partir de deux centres, Montréal et Québec, en raison du fait que s'y concentrent les débats publics. Cela tient naturellement aux foyers intellectuels qu'on trouve dans ces deux villes : centres universitaires, revues, presse, etc., autant d'institutions propices au débat.

1. La prise de position des évêques

Intéressons-nous d'abord aux prises de position des évêques de Montréal et de Québec à propos de la liberté religieuse, le cardinal Léger, seul évêque québécois alors membre du Sacré-Collège, et Mgr Roy, archevêque de Québec et primat du Canada. L'un et l'autre traitent de cette question, mais de manière différente, en raison de leur tempérament, certes, mais également en raison du milieu social qu'ils habitent, Montréal présentant une situation de pluralisme religieux plus accentué que Québec, et des fonctions respectives qu'ils occupent dans la marche du concile et de sa préparation.

Commençons par Montréal et par le membre le plus éminent de l'épiscopat du Québec à l'époque, le cardinal Léger. Ses *vota*[1] comportent, déjà en 1959, un appel à une révision en profondeur des positions classiques (thèse et antithèse) sur la liberté religieuse. Par la suite, dans son allocution lors de la deuxième rencontre nationale des Comités diocésains d'Action catholique, le 21 mai 1961, il déclarait :

> Au plan social, le milieu canadien-français est entré en contact plus que jamais avec le monde pluraliste ou non confessionnel qui l'entoure et il a senti le besoin de s'y adapter. Il serait vain de vouloir vivre chez nous dans un Moyen Âge illusoire où les structures seraient parfois elles-mêmes plus chrétiennes encore que les hommes. Au Canada français d'aujourd'hui, le chrétien doit très souvent témoigner de sa foi dans des cadres qui n'ont aucune référence à la religion[2].

Par la suite, ses prises de position sur la liberté religieuse lors du débat à la septième session de la Commission centrale préparatoire (12-19 juin 1962) sont éloquentes. Je ne reprends ici que quelques éléments de son long *votum* (6 pages) présenté lors de la discussion du chapitre IX du *De Ecclesia*, intitulé *De relationibus inter Ecclesiam et Statum necnon de Tolentia religiosa*, préparé par la Commission théologique et introduit par le cardinal Ottaviani, et du schéma *De libertate religiosa*, préparé par le Secrétariat pour l'unité des chrétiens et introduit par le cardinal Bea[3].

---

1 Voir *Acta et Documenta Concilio Vatican II Apparando*, Series I, Antepraeparatoria, volumen II, *Consilia et Vota Episcoporum ac Praelatorum*, Pars VI, America Septentrionalis et Centralis, Cité du Vatican, 1960, p. 38-58.

2 Service d'information de la CCC, nº 96 (25 mai 1961), p. 6.

3 Nous avons les textes préparatoires de ces *vota* donnés lors de la septième session de

Ce schéma avait été élaboré par une sous-commission du Secrétariat, sous-commission à laquelle participait Gregory Baum.

La position de Léger est très tranchée et elle témoigne de son exaspération de plus en plus manifeste à l'égard des schémas qui sont envoyés à la Commission centrale préparatoire. Léger est alors le troisième à prendre la parole (après les cardinaux Frings et Ruffini), si bien que l'on peut penser que son *votum* soit simplement influencé par l'opinion des autres membres de la Commission. Il s'agit d'un *votum* préparé à Montréal avant que Léger ne se rende à Rome. Au sujet du chapitre sur la tolérance religieuse, il commence en indiquant que « le présent schéma présente une thèse qui valait pour les siècles passés mais qui ne convenait plus dans les conditions politiques et sociologiques actuelles ». Il observe ensuite que « cette thèse [de la tolérance] diffère profondément de celle proposée dans le *De libertate religiosa* du Secrétariat pour l'unité ». Il poursuit en relevant le fait que, selon ce schéma, il y aurait une thèse qui s'appliquerait là où l'État est catholique et une autre qui s'appliquerait là où l'État n'est pas catholique. Cela contredit la doctrine universelle de la liberté religieuse qui s'applique partout, aussi bien dans les États catholiques que dans les États non catholiques. « Ce sont là les raisons pour lesquelles, à mon jugement, le présent schéma *non placet.* »

Il en remet en soulignant que, « en matière de doctrine, le schéma ne convient pas puisqu'il ne comporte aucun argument en matière du progrès de la science et aucune explication de type sociologique ou politique ». De plus, « on parle toujours de la société et de l'État comme s'il s'agissait d'une seule et même réalité », sans compter que l'on personnifie les institutions et les fonctions. Ainsi, « on parle de "pouvoir civil non catholique" ». C'est oublier que « seuls les hommes (les princes, les chefs et les rois), i.e. des personnes humaines seulement peuvent professer une religion et non une fonction que l'on désigne du nom de "*potestas civilis*". Cette manière de parler appartient à un temps dépassé ». « Je ne crois pas nécessaire de faire une distinction entre "Pouvoir civil catholique" et "Pouvoir civil non catholique" parce

---

la Commission centrale préparatoire. Voir Archives conciliaires Paul-Émile Léger, [Naud, A.], *Votum de capite : De libertate religiosa*, AL 2034, (annotations de P. Lafortune), 4 p., et [Lafortune, P., et A. Naud?], *De libertate religiosa*, AL 2035, 5 p.

qu'un pouvoir civil n'est pas religieux, il est civil ; ceux qui exercent le pouvoir peuvent être catholiques, protestants, juifs, mais non le pouvoir lui-même. » De surcroît, « la théorie suivant laquelle le roi ou le chef de l'État récapitule toute la société civile et leur religion déterminerait celle du peuple (*Cujus regio ejus religio*) ne vaut plus. Aussi, l'État n'a aucune compétence dans la détermination de ce qu'est la véritable religion. Si l'on acceptait une telle compétence, alors on devrait admettre leur droit de s'immiscer dans le domaine religieux. » Suit une série de remarques particulières et de questions qui mettent profondément en cause le schéma. Vient ensuite la conclusion :

> D'un point de vue prudentiel, le présent schéma ne convient pas, parce que dans les conditions politiques du monde d'aujourd'hui, ses thèses sont imprudentes et inopportunes. De telles thèses justifient tous les totalitarismes à l'endroit des non-catholiques. Selon la logique de telles thèses, il y a des États protestants, islamiques, bouddhistes, etc., où il est impossible à l'Église catholique de s'implanter. Je me demande comment un non-catholique peut accepter la double théorie suivant laquelle, quand les catholiques sont en majorité, ils reconnaissent une vague tolérance et quand ils sont en minorité, ils réclament la pleine liberté pour tous. Cette théorie apparaît odieuse aux non-catholiques. Je crains qu'avec un tel schéma sur les relations entre l'Église et l'État, l'Église catholique elle-même soit condamnée. En conséquence, mon humble jugement pourrait se formuler comme suit : je pense sincèrement qu'il serait déplorable, pour le développement de l'Église et la paix des nations, si la théorie du présent schéma était proposée au concile et je crois que la discussion devrait porter sur le schéma du Secrétariat du cardinal Bea[4].

Un peu auparavant, dans l'entrevue qu'il accordait à la revue jésuite états-unienne *America*, le 11 mai 1962, il exprimait un jugement tout aussi net sur la question : « Notre respect de la liberté des autres

4 Pour l'ensemble de son intervention, voir *Acta et documenta Concilio œcumenico Vaticano II apparando*, Series II, *Praeparatoria*, Volumen II, Pars IV (Rome : Typis polyglottis, 1965), p. 695-701. La prise de position de Léger allait être appuyée par les cardinaux Liénart (724), McGuigan (724), Montini (729), König (732), Ritter (735), Mgr Graner (742), Suhr (744).

n'est pas une concession inspirée par la prudence, mais un nouveau développement des principes permanents de notre religion. » Même position dans son adresse devant 1 000 ligueurs du Sacré-Cœur de son diocèse réunis sur le Plateau Mont-Royal et qui venaient de se proclamer « des troupes de choc contre l'école neutre, contre l'alcool le dimanche, etc. » « Ce n'est pas avec la faux ou avec des matraques [disait-il] que le Seigneur nous a envoyés dans son champ, mais avec la semence de sa Parole ! », ajoutant « qu'il fallait bien comprendre ce que signifie troupes de choc sur la ligne de feu[5] ».

Toujours à Montréal, au cours de la même période (plus précisément de mai à septembre 1962), la revue *Relations* publie une série d'articles de John Courtney Murray sur « La liberté de religion ». Annoncée au mois d'avril 1962, la revue des Jésuites, dont la proposition d'ouvrir une université à Montréal venait d'essuyer un refus, fait précéder ce dossier d'un éditorial où s'exprime la conviction que le Québec doit envisager une autre solution politique à la question de la liberté de religion au Québec, compte tenu du pluralisme religieux qui le caractérise de plus en plus.

Ainsi, on peut constater qu'avant même l'ouverture du concile, le cardinal Léger non seulement connaissait le mot « liberté religieuse », mais avait des idées claires sur le sujet. Au surplus, ces idées ne lui avaient pas été soufflées par des experts belges ou européens.

Du côté de Québec, on ne semblait pas non plus vivre dans l'ignorance de la réalité de la liberté religieuse. Les dossiers des archives de Mgr Maurice Roy nous donnent à penser que sa préoccupation sur ce sujet remonte au moins à 1960, au moment de la rédaction de ses *vota*[6].

---

5 Compte-rendu de la CCC, juin 1962, repris dans *Perspectives sociales,* vol. 17, n° 3 (mai-juin 1962), p. 43.

6 Quant à eux, les dossiers des archives conciliaires de Maurice Roy nous donnent à penser que sa préoccupation sur ce sujet remonte à 1960. G. Dion envoie à Mgr Roy un volume, avec une lettre datée du 5 octobre 1960. Mgr Roy lui adresse une réponse le 25 du même mois. De plus, au moment d'écrire ses *vota,* en 1960, l'archevêque consulte le théologien Lorenzo Roy sur la question de la liberté religieuse. L'année suivante, au moment de la phase préparatoire du concile, G. Dion adresse de nouveau (2 janvier 1961) à Mgr Roy une lettre à propos de la recherche de la vérité et du respect de la liberté. Enfin, on trouve un texte de R. Laflamme, intitulé *De benignitate dei in Fide.* Ce texte n'est probablement pas étranger au débat sur la liberté religieuse qui agite alors les milieux intellectuels et ecclésiastiques de Québec et dont nous ferons état plus bas.

Par la suite, sans s'engager publiquement, il suit attentivement le débat, demande conseil et recueille les avis, en particulier chez les professeurs de l'Université Laval (G. Dion, L. Roy, R. Laflamme, etc.), dont il est le chancelier. Surtout, il laisse les théologiens et les philosophes de l'Université Laval s'exprimer sur le sujet.

On pourrait étoffer le dossier de l'évolution des évêques du Québec avant l'ouverture du concile en versant beaucoup d'autres pièces au dossier, notamment la *Supplique* qu'adressait le cardinal Léger à Jean XXIII, quelques mois avant l'ouverture du concile[7]. Il serait aussi utile de mentionner que c'est l'épiscopat du Québec qui, le 29 août 1963, proposa à Jean Lesage de faire précéder le bill 60 sur la réforme de l'éducation d'un préambule interprétatif qui définirait les droits de chaque citoyen, quelle que soit sa confession religieuse ; droit notamment des parents « de choisir les institutions qui, selon leur conviction, assurent le mieux le respect des droits de leurs enfants » ; « droit pour les personnes et les groupes de créer des institutions d'enseignement autonomes et, les exigences du bien commun étant sauves, de bénéficier des moyens administratifs et financiers nécessaires à la poursuite de leurs fins[8] ». Cette déclaration des droits en préambule de la loi réformant l'éducation au Québec — qui anticipait la future charte des droits et libertés — n'arrivait pas à l'improviste.

2. Un débat public

Dans l'espace public, la question de la liberté religieuse allait occuper le devant de la scène, surtout à partir de l'année 1962. Elle couve déjà depuis la fin des années 1950, comme nous allons le voir, dans les pages de *Perspectives sociales,* le bulletin bimestriel de pastorale sociale rédigé en collaboration et sous la direction de l'abbé Gérard Dion du Département de relations industrielles de l'Université Laval et qui prend

---

7 Pour le texte lui-même, voir « Lettre inédite du cardinal Paul-Émile Léger au pape Jean XXIII en août 1962 », dans Brigitte Caulier et Gilles Routhier (dir.), *Mémoires de Vatican II,* Montréal, Fides, 1997, p. 93-113. J'en retrace l'origine et en fais l'analyse dans « Les réactions du cardinal Léger à la préparation de Vatican II », *Revue d'histoire de l'Église de France,* vol. LXX, n° 205, p. 281-302.

8 Assemblée des évêques catholiques de la province de Québec, Amendements proposés au bill 60 (29 août 1963).

le relais de *Ad usum sacerdotum* en janvier 1960. Plusieurs articles de ce *Bulletin* sont en effet consacrés au « pluralisme religieux ».

En plus du débat dans la presse, la discussion se poursuit à travers des médias au public plus restreint et plus près de l'archevêché, mais surtout à travers le *Bulletin* dirigé par Gérard Dion à l'Université Laval. Sont alors discutées les notions de liberté de conscience, de liberté religieuse, de tolérance, de pluralisme, de neutralité de l'État en matière de religion, du droit positif des non-chrétiens, etc.

Déjà, au cours de la période préparatoire du concile, Gérard Dion, consulté par son archevêque[9], dresse un inventaire des « problèmes les plus urgents à étudier » : « le problème de la liberté aussi bien au sens psychologique qu'au plan moral (v.g. liberté de conscience, les minorités, le droit à l'information, etc.), les rapports entre l'Église et l'État, la démocratie chrétienne, l'œcuménisme, la théologie de l'histoire[10] ». Dans la version longue et préliminaire de sa réponse, l'énumération de ses préoccupations est encore plus explicite : « liberté de conscience, liberté d'expression, droits des dissidents, rapports de l'Église et de l'État, démocratie et christianisme, œcuménisme, théologie de l'histoire. Et le fameux problème de la limitation des naissances[11] ». Comme intellectuel, dans le contexte de l'époque, il est particulièrement sensible au problème de la liberté et s'en ouvre à son recteur.

La lecture des diverses livraisons de *Perspectives sociales,* tout au long de la phase antépréparatoire (1959) et préparatoire au concile (1960-1962), nous révèle bon nombre de préoccupations en conso-

---

[9] Mgr Vachon, recteur de l'Université Laval, le consultera, par exemple, au moment de la phase préparatoire du concile, « sur les moyens de promouvoir l'influence du catholicisme chez ceux qui cultivent la philosophie et les autres sciences ». La réponse de G. Dion est datée du 2 janvier 1962 (AUL P117/B5.47). On peut supposer que cela est relié à la consultation des prêtres du diocèse de Québec réalisée au cours de la même période, Dion faisant référence au « questionnaire venant de la Commission préparatoire au Concile ». Toutefois, sa réponse ne fait pas partie de l'ensemble conservé aux AAQ. Sur le sujet, voir P. Allaire, « La consultation du clergé de Québec », dans G. Routhier (dir.), *L'Église canadienne et Vatican II*, Montréal, Fides, 1999, p. 99-112. On peut aussi penser qu'il s'agit des rencontres préconciliaires convoquées par Mgr Roy à l'Université Laval. Sur le sujet, voir S. Serré, « Les consultations préconciliaires des laïcs au Québec entre 1959 et 1962 », dans *L'Église canadienne et Vatican II*, p. 113-144.

[10] « Simples suggestions », P117/B5.47.

[11] « Réponse au questionnaire sur les moyens de promouvoir l'influence du catholicisme chez ceux qui cultivent la philosophie et les autres sciences », P 117/B5.47.

nance avec le concile à venir. En effet, déjà en 1959, la revue *Ad usum sacerdotum* consacre un numéro spécial à la question de la tolérance religieuse. Cela n'est d'ailleurs pas sans rapport avec les questions de l'heure, notamment celle de la confessionnalité des syndicats, et en particulier de la CTCC[12]. Dion s'intéresse donc de très près à la question de la liberté religieuse. À titre d'exemple, dans une lettre qui accompagne l'envoi du livre *Roman Catholicism and Religious Liberty* au recteur de l'Université Laval, Mgr Louis-Albert Vachon, le 21 septembre 1960, Dion observe : « Il s'agit là, à mon sens, d'un sujet des plus importants à l'heure actuelle dans l'Église. » Éveilleur d'idées comme on le connaît, il a acheté « quelques exemplaires » de ce volume « pour passer à des amis à qui je crois que cela peut être utile[13] ». Et il conclut, à l'adresse du recteur : « Je pense que, dans ta situation, la lecture de cet ouvrage est pour toi indispensable. Si tu veux le lire, garde-le. Si tu ne le lis pas, renvoie-le-moi afin que je le passe à quelqu'un d'autre[14]. »

Par la suite, à partir de 1961, mais surtout à partir de 1962, certains thèmes affleurent constamment dans sa revue : la confessionnalité des œuvres et des institutions, la laïcité de l'État et la neutralité de l'école, les rapports de l'Église et de l'État, le respect et la « tolérance » à l'égard des non-catholiques, le droit à la liberté de conscience. Ces thèmes reviennent de mille manières. Celui de la confessionnalité, d'abord, à l'occasion du débat sur la confessionnalité des syndicats, du changement de nom de *L'Action catholique* pour *L'Action*, de l'école neutre, etc. C'est sans doute le débat scolaire occasionné par la Commission Parent et les prises de position du Mouvement laïque qui provoque toute cette réflexion. Prenant largement appui sur les déclarations du cardinal Léger souvent appelé à la barre, on tente alors de penser la « société pluraliste »

12 Cet article fera beaucoup de bruit à l'assemblée épiscopale. Mgr Bernier (Gaspé) est prêt à dénoncer G. Dion au Conseil doctrinal de l'Université Laval pour son article sur la confessionnalité des syndicats, alors que Mgr Lemieux (Ottawa) croit que « l'article Dion-O'Neill n'a pas fait tant de mal que ça dans les autres provinces ». Pour sa part, Mgr Roy « désapprouve l'un et l'autre article, mais tous deux ont été censurés : celui des anciens aumôniers et celui des Abbés Dion-O'Neill ». Archives Bernier, Notes manuscrites sur les débats de la réunion de l'Assemblée épiscopale du Québec (14 décembre 1959).

13 On a vu plus haut que G. Dion avait également envoyé un exemplaire de ce volume à son archevêque, Mgr Roy.

14 AUL P117/A5.52.

et « non confessionnelle »[15], les Canadiens français ayant de plus en plus à vivre dans un monde ne comportant aucune référence à la religion. Devant ce fait, l'équipe de *Perspectives sociales* s'oppose à la « politique de l'immobilisme[16] », posant plutôt « l'exigence du dialogue » qu'on oppose à la peur et au refus, et veut établir le « fondement de la tolérance[17] », en se référant au cardinal Lercaro et à l'expérience états-unienne de la séparation entre l'Église et l'État[18].

La discussion sur la liberté religieuse reprendra de plus belle en 1962, alors que se développe le débat scolaire et que l'on assiste à des réclamations de la part du Mouvement laïque en faveur de l'école neutre. Quelques textes importants nourriront alors la controverse. Toutefois, c'est surtout un petit article publié à la fin de l'année 1962 qui alimentera le débat.

La discussion commence dès le début de l'année, au moment où la question de l'Université Sainte-Marie est dans l'air et que la Commission Parent a engagé ses travaux. La livraison de janvier-février 1962 de *Perspectives sociales* ouvre le débat. Cette livraison consacre déjà un important dossier à la question scolaire, dans lequel J.-M. Hamelin signe trois articles[19]. Il commente ainsi trois prises de position, notamment celle contenue dans le mémoire présenté à la Commission Parent par les Chevaliers de Colomb. Hamelin, spécialiste du dossier scolaire au sein de l'équipe de rédaction, prend position en faveur de la liberté de conscience, l'État n'ayant pas la responsabilité de jouer aux arbitres en matière de religion. Il se dit surpris que des catholiques demandent à l'État de « refuser aux agnostiques des écoles neutres ou athées[20] » et gêné de constater, lors de la réunion d'information à Québec du MLF, « un sens sur-aigu du danger grave qui menace la religion chez quelques

15 J.-M. Hamelin, « Le problème de l'éducation », vol. 16, n° 5 (1961), p. 99.

16 « Le problème de l'éducation », p. 98.

17 « Le problème de l'éducation », p. 100-101.

18 « Le problème de l'éducation », p. 98-101.

19 On y trouve trois articles de J.-M. Hamelin : « Un bon Jésuite et l'école neutre », « Les Chevaliers de Colomb et l'école neutre » et « Mouvement laïque de langue française à Québec ».

20 J.-M. Hamelin, « Un bon Jésuite et l'école neutre », *Perspectives sociales*, vol. 17, n° 1 (1962), p. 8.

catholiques sincères mais d'une intransigeance gênante[21] ». Pour lui, il serait « possible de reconnaître un secteur non confessionnel, ouvert au fait religieux (contrairement au secteur neutre), à côté du secteur confessionnel, seul valable pour les catholiques[22] ». Surtout, « le dialogue doit se continuer ».

Aux mois de mars et d'avril, un nouveau dossier sur le même sujet est présenté dans la deuxième livraison de la revue. Dans « Propos sereins sur des problèmes brûlants », J.-M. Hamelin invite à réfléchir au problème de l'éducation dans la « société industrialisée et pluraliste actuelle[23] », aux rapports entre l'Église et l'État et à la question de l'école confessionnelle et de l'école neutre. Au terme de sa réflexion, Hamelin conclut ainsi : « L'Église respecte le droit des nouvelles minorités et les catholiques doivent être prêts à manifester à leur endroit justice et charité par amour de la vérité et des personnes. Il est odieux de parler de faveur ou d'aumône. L'intolérance dogmatique ne doit pas détruire la tolérance civile[24]. »

Le débat ne cessait de s'amplifier en raison notamment du bruit que faisait le Mouvement laïque de langue française naissant. Le 1er avril 1962, la fondation de la section de Québec du Mouvement au Château Frontenac allait mettre le feu aux poudres. Lors de ce lancement, en présence de 300 délégués, intervinrent en effet l'abbé Jean-Marie Hamelin de l'Université Laval, très engagé dans *Perspectives sociales*, et *in absentia,* Charles de Koninck, professeur à la Faculté de théologie et de philosophie de la même université[25]. C'est sans doute l'en-

---

21 J.-M. HAMELIN, « Mouvement laïque de langue française à Québec », *Perspectives sociales*, vol. 17, nº 1 (1962), p. 10.

22 « Un bon Jésuite et l'école neutre », p. 8.

23 J.-M. HAMELIN, « Propos sereins sur des problèmes brûlants », *Perspectives sociales*, vol. 17, nº 2 (1962), p. 23.

24 « Propos sereins sur des problèmes brûlants », p. 31. Il en avait appelé au passage à une intervention du cardinal Léger qui soulignait que la foi catholique ne devait pas empêcher de « traiter justement et dignement ceux qui représentent chez nous la minorité religieuse » (p. 29) et à une autre de P.A. Liégé suivant lequel « Il serait grave que l'opinion catholique, inconsciente du pluralisme dans lequel est aujourd'hui l'Église, se refuse, ou même ne s'intéresse pas, à la reconnaissance des droits scolaires des minorités idéologiques » (p. 32).

25 Prirent aussi la parole MM. Bertrand Rioux et Marc Lacoste de l'Université de Montréal.

trevue de Charles de Koninck, proche de Dion, lue par Marcel Trudel, directeur de l'Institut d'histoire et de géographie de l'Université Laval, qui agitera le plus les esprits. Sa déclaration, publiée d'abord dans *Le Devoir* du 3 avril 1962[26], puis dans *L'Action catholique* le 4 mai suivant, provoqua une vive controverse et a été à la source d'un véritable débat sur le rôle de l'État en matière de religion, débat auquel participeront d'éminents professeurs de l'Université Laval[27]. Charles de Koninck doit même publier un nouveau texte, car il craint, écrit-il au rédacteur de *L'Action catholique*, que sa déclaration « ne laisse croire à certains de vos lecteurs que je me suis éloigné de la doctrine catholique et que je la contredis dans les termes[28] ». Comme si cela ne suffisait pas, il doit en remettre, en consentant de publier, la semaine suivante, dans *La Semaine religieuse de Québec*, l'organe officiel de l'archevêché, un entretien qu'il a eu avec Lorenzo Roy, secrétaire de la Faculté de théologie de l'Université Laval[29].

Le débat sera particulièrement animé dans les pages de *L'Action catholique*, quotidien de l'archevêché de Québec. Comme l'écrivait

---

26 On trouvait, sous le titre « M. de Koninck : l'école laïque doit être, mais la moins répandue possible… », l'entrevue complète accordée par M. de Koninck à Marcel Trudel. Le journaliste Marcel Thivierge rapportait la rencontre de Québec sous le titre « Le Mouvement laïque : les parents agnostiques ont le devoir d'exiger, pour leurs enfants, l'école non confessionnelle », s'appuyant sur les propos tenus lors de ce rassemblement par l'abbé Jean-Marie Hamelin.

27 On retrouve des échos de ce débat jusque dans les archives de Ch. Moeller, pièces 2669 à 2672. En plus du débat dans la presse, voir aussi l'entretien entre C. de Koninck et L. Roy dans *La Semaine religieuse de Québec*, vol. 37 (17 mai 1962), p. 585-596.

28 Cet article, publié d'abord dans *L'Action catholique*, est ensuite repris dans *Le Devoir*. Charles de Koninck publiera un autre texte dans les pages de l'opinion du lecteur dans *Le Devoir*, « La bénignité du chrétien ».

29 « À propos de l'éducation », *La Semaine religieuse de Québec*, vol. 37 (17 mai 1962), p. 585-596. L'entrevue avait été réalisée le 30 avril 1962. Cette longue entrevue constitue ce qu'on appellerait aujourd'hui une opération de *damage control*. Elle permet à Charles de Koninck de s'expliquer sur sa prise de position lors du Congrès du Mouvement laïque de langue française. Il faut observer que, suite à la déclaration de C. de Koninck, la revue diocésaine publie pas moins de trois articles sur l'école neutre et l'éducation. Un premier, le 19 avril, un extrait de l'encyclique *Divini illius magistri* de Pie XI sous le titre « Ce qu'un catholique doit penser de l'école neutre ou laïque » et, dans la même livraison, l'extrait d'un article de Ch. J. Ledit, publié dans *Relations*, « L'expérience des écoles neutres en France ». Ces deux articles sont sans doute une réponse à la publication de l'entrevue de C. de Koninck dans *Le Devoir* et d'un second, le 10 mai, un article signé de Mgr Ernest Lemieux, « Les écoles doivent-elles être confessionnelles? ».

l'éditeur du quotidien, sous le titre « Agnosticisme et neutralité. Droit ou tolérance ? » :

> Depuis la déclaration de M. Charles de Koninck à l'occasion de la formation de la section québécoise du MLF, nous avons reçu plusieurs lettres attaquant la thèse de ce professeur. Déjà nous avons nous-mêmes contesté certaines de ses affirmations et publié d'autres réfutations partielles. Or des correspondants se sont donné la peine de nous adresser à ce sujet des réfutations complètes et systématiques qu'il serait vraiment trop long de publier au texte, et un peu trop abstrait[30].

Dans les mois qui suivirent l'ouverture du concile, le débat ne s'apaisera pas, bien au contraire. Dans le dernier numéro de 1962, le court article (une page) cosigné par Dion et trois autres prêtres du diocèse de Québec, « Assez de tergiversations », allait mettre le feu aux poudres[31]. Relevant que « des citoyens de Québec se sentent parfois gênés dans l'exercice de leur liberté de conscience en raison des insuffisances de la législation civile », le groupe souhaite que la législation élargisse le droit à la liberté de conscience, de sorte qu'il soit accordé aux non-catholiques qui n'ont pas la faculté de contracter un mariage, si ce n'est en présence d'un ministre du culte ou en étant forcés de prêter serment sur la Bible. On plaide pour un ajustement de la législation de manière à ce qu'elle corresponde davantage à une société pluraliste et à une « saine et légitime laïcité de l'État ». Les signataires plaident pour que justice soit rendue à ces individus et avancent que, « en vertu du respect dû à la liberté des consciences dans une société pluraliste, ces personnes ont droit de voir leurs légitimes réclamations respectées ». Autrement, il faut craindre « de provoquer l'exaspération de citoyens dont certaines réclamations s'appuient sur des droits qui sont indiscutables » et que les catholiques passent « pour un groupe d'intransigeants, inconscients devant des problèmes réels qui se posent ou insensibles aux appels de

---

30 *L'Action catholique* (4 mai 1962). Plusieurs interventions contre la position de C. de Koninck sont publiées dans les pages du quotidien. On en retrouve également dans *Le Devoir.*

31 Voir G. Dion, L. O'Neill, J.-M. Hamelin et D. Duval, « Assez de tergiversations », *Perspectives sociales,* vol. 17, n° 6 (novembre-décembre 1962), p. 119-120. On verra ensuite la réaction de Louis-Philippe Roy de l'*Action.*

la justice », installés « dans une tradition routinière qui refuse de reconnaître l'autre, ses droits et ses légitimes exigences ».

Publié ensuite dans *L'Action,* cet article provoquera une véritable polémique. Scandalisé de voir quatre prêtres du diocèse réclamer des droits pour les agnostiques, Louis-Philippe Roy écrira dans les pages du quotidien propriété de l'archidiocèse de Québec un commentaire assez sévère de cet article. Lors d'une rencontre dans les bureaux du quotidien de Québec[32], Dion propose alors une rencontre entre les quatre abbés et le comité de rédaction du quotidien (Paré, Roy, Arteau, Revelin, Plamondon, Paquet, Dorion et Hamel), sous la conduite du Dr Jobin, président de *L'Action.* Il espère pouvoir « expliquer notre position et amener ainsi *L'Action* à écrire un commentaire qui soit formateur pour ses lecteurs ». Le but de cette rencontre serait de favoriser un échange de vues et de « s'accorder entre catholiques sur une attitude à prendre en face du problème discuté ». Même si « le Dr Jobin est enthousiasmé du projet et appelle Lorenzo Paré [qui] accepte d'abord », cette rencontre n'aura jamais lieu, Paré changeant d'idée quelques minutes plus tard, n'acceptant pas « de "parader" devant ses supérieurs et de discuter cette question avec nous devant le comité de rédaction ».

Ici comme ailleurs, ce qui est en jeu, c'est d'arriver à penser la présence de l'Église dans une société pluraliste et de penser l'exercice de la liberté religieuse. Selon les auteurs de l'article, « la première session du concile nous a montré qu'il ne faut pas craindre de reconnaître des retards et qu'il faut avoir le courage de nous adapter aux situations nouvelles[33] ».

Cette question rebondit de nouveau dans la livraison de janvier-février 1963, presque entièrement consacrée à la question de la liberté religieuse. En ouverture du dossier, G. Dion insiste : « C'est là une question[34] que nous estimons très importante », soulignant que, depuis 1959, il est vivement préoccupé par cette question. Le dossier reprend les

---

32 La rencontre Dion-Jobin a lieu le 4 février 1963. Voir memorandum Dion, 1 page (AUL P117/B5.14).

33 « Assez de tergiversations », p. 120.

34 Il s'agit, comme il l'indique, du « problème de la liberté des consciences, de la tolérance religieuse, de la laïcité de l'État [...] considéré par plusieurs comme primordial pour l'expansion de l'Église dans le monde... » G. Dion, « Liminaire », *Perspectives sociales*, vol. 18, nº 1 (1963), p. 1.

propos tenus lors d'une soirée organisée par des étudiants des facultés de droit, de lettres et de philosophie de l'Université Laval, au Palais Montcalm, le 30 avril 1962, à l'occasion de la réunion de fondation de la section québécoise du Mouvement laïque de langue française (MLF)[35]. Ce dossier était constitué des interventions de Charles de Koninck, de Marcel Trudel[36] et de Gérard Pelletier. Comme le dira L. Paré, rédacteur en chef de *L'Action*, celui-là même qui avait refusé la tenue d'une table ronde au journal sur cette question, mais à qui *Perspectives sociales* avaient demandé une réplique, « L'Histoire, la Philosophie, le Droit et l'Actualité avaient été assis côte à côte[37] ». Dénonçant « Le dialogue des laïcistes », il regrette que les quatre panellistes, plutôt que d'entrer en débat, se contentent, dans ce « monologue à plusieurs voix », d'exposer la même pensée, leur présence dans ce débat n'ayant qu'un but : « de perspectives différentes en arriver, par convergence, à l'idée fixe[38] ». Ce dossier, qui faisait écho à un débat animé, était précédé d'un article du cardinal Bea, président du Secrétariat pour l'unité des chrétiens, sur « La liberté des consciences[39] ». On concluait par la reprise du chapitre « Une légitime et saine laïcité de l'État », du livre de Dion et O'Neill, *Le chrétien en démocratie*.

Dans sa contribution, C. de Koninck, qui avait été férocement attaqué l'année précédente, passe en revue la doctrine catholique en matière de rapports entre l'Église et l'État et constate, comme l'avait montré John Courtney Murray, le « progrès dans l'intelligence des principes de l'enseignement chrétien ». Il observe que « la liberté des consciences entraîne éventuellement un pluralisme humainement inéluctable ». De sa réflexion, il tire quelques conclusions, que je livre ici en vrac :

---

35 Voir C. de Koninck, « Le domaine de César », M. Trudel, « À la recherche d'une solution honnête », et G. Pelletier, « Discussion et intervention », *Perspectives sociales*, vol. 18, n° 1 (1963), p. 2-4, 4-8, 8-12.

36 Marcel Trudel avait montré comment, dans notre histoire, on avait déjà été mis en situation de pluralisme religieux et comment s'était définie la séparation de l'Église et de l'État.

37 Voir L. Paré, « Le dialogue des laïcistes », *Perspectives sociales*, vol. 18, n° 1 (1963), p. 15-17.

38 « Le dialogue des laïcistes », p. 15.

39 Il s'agit d'une allocution qu'il avait donnée le 13 janvier 1963. Voir Cardinal Bea, « La liberté des consciences », *Perspectives sociales*, vol. 18, n° 1 (1963), p. 2-4.

> Je ne crois pas que mon Église me permette d'être injuste envers mon prochain, quel qu'il soit.
>
> Comme catholique, je vois dans la laïcité de l'État un pouvoir salutaire qui réprime les injustices de qui que ce soit.
>
> Le respect de cette liberté [des consciences] et par la suite des diversités confessionnelles et non confessionnelles est le signe d'une légitime et saine laïcité qui, pour les chrétiens, est un principe de doctrine[40].

La question de la liberté religieuse (et celles corrélatives de la neutralité de l'école et des relations entre l'Église et l'État) demeure alors la préoccupation centrale de l'équipe de rédaction de *Perspectives sociales.* Le *Bulletin* y consacre de nouveau un long texte en janvier-février 1964, celui de Mgr J. De Smedt, rapporteur du schéma sur la liberté religieuse au concile[41]. « De tous les problèmes discutés au Concile [croit G. Dion], celui qui a trait à la liberté religieuse est sûrement un de ceux qui auront le plus de répercussions sur les rapports entre l'Église et le monde. »

Par la suite, les pages de la revue sont ouvertes à des acteurs de premier plan au concile : le cardinal Bea, Mgr De Smedt (deux articles), Edward Schillebeeckx, etc. Au cours de cette période, il revient également à Mgr Paul-Émile Charbonneau (Hull) de publier dans *Perspectives sociales* un long article sur le schéma XIII, qui traite notamment des relations entre l'Église et l'État et de la place de l'Église dans la société[42].

---

[40] C. de Koninck, « Le domaine de César », p. 6.

[41] Il s'agit de la *relatio antedisceptationem* présentée par De Smedt lors de la 70e congrégation générale, le 19 novembre 1963, avant l'ouverture de la discussion sur cette question. Gérard Dion consacre un autre article à la question, « La liberté religieuse et la couronne britannique », dans *Perspectives sociales* (mars-avril 1964), p. 37-38.

[42] « L'Église à l'heure du schéma XIII », *Perspectives sociales*, vol. 20, nº 3 (mai-juin 1965), p. 54-61.

Si l'on compare de nouveau ce qui se publie dans *Perspectives sociales* et ce qui s'écrit dans les pages de *L'Action catholique* ou dans *La Semaine religieuse de Québec*, le décalage est important[43].

Conclusion

Faut-il tirer une conclusion, au terme de cette enquête ? Celle-ci semble s'imposer d'elle-même. Ce n'est certainement pas Ph. Delhaye qui, à l'été 1965, a ouvert les yeux des Québécois sur la question de la liberté religieuse[44]. Inutile de commenter davantage. Retenons que cette préoccupation ne surgit pas des débats conciliaires, puisque le débat sur cette question s'éteint de lui-même en 1963, avant même de commencer pour vrai dans l'*aula* conciliaire. La discussion est ici liée à la question de la confessionnalité, débat amorcé en 1943 par une publication du P. Lévesque sur la confessionnalité des coopératives et qui traverse toute la décennie 1950, avant que n'aboutisse la déconfessionnalisation de la CTCC. Ce débat reprend de plus belle au cours des années 1960. Il engage alors d'autres questions, celle de la laïcité de l'État et des rapports entre l'Église et l'État, puisque la question resurgit à propos de la question scolaire : d'abord la création de l'Université Sainte-Marie, ensuite à l'occasion de la tenue des audiences de la Commission Parent. Il est alors surtout alimenté par le Mouvement laïque de langue française.

On peut observer que la terminologie n'est pas encore tout à fait au point. On parlera surtout de liberté de conscience. Enfin, les références ne sont pas d'abord européennes : elles sont surtout états-uniennes. En effet, l'auteur le plus souvent cité est John Courtney Murray, et l'exemple auquel on a le plus souvent recours est la situation de la religion aux États-Unis.

---

43 Par exemple, *La Semaine religieuse* publie deux textes en 1963 sur l'école neutre. Le premier reprend un extrait du mémoire déposé par la Fédération des ligues du Sacré-Cœur contestant aux agnostiques le droit à des écoles neutres et une conférence donnée par un juriste (Me Yves Prévost) à l'occasion d'un colloque organisé par la Société St-Jean-Baptiste de Québec. Ces positions ne vont pas dans le sens de celles promues par les intellectuels de l'Université Laval, ni même par les figures de proue de l'épiscopat, le cardinal Léger et Maurice Roy, voire les positions d'autres évêques, tels Mgr Charbonneau ou Coderre.

44 S'il fallait trouver une inspiration belge dans les prises de position des évêques du Québec, on pourrait se référer au texte de Mgr Onclin, transmis par G. Thils au nom de Ch. Moeller au cardinal Léger, le 3 octobre 1962, sur la question scolaire. Toutefois, les positions de Léger sont arrêtées bien avant la réception de ce texte, même s'il a pu lui permettre d'approfondir sa propre position.

On pourrait ajouter que ce débat est surtout intracatholique, plutôt qu'un affrontement entre catholiques et non-chrétiens. Les discussions révèlent qu'un groupe de catholiques « intransigeants » s'opposait aux élites catholiques, membres de l'épiscopat ou universitaires. Ce débat portait en définitive sur la conception de la place du catholicisme dans la définition de la société et, cela est manifeste à Québec, a été favorisé par l'attitude d'écoute de l'archevêque qui faisait confiance aux professeurs de l'Université Laval et qui, régulièrement, faisait appel à leur expertise.

Anglican–Roman Catholic Dialogue in Canada: Receiving *Unitatis Redintegratio*

Catherine E. Clifford,
Saint Paul University

One of the principal motives in calling the Second Vatican Council, as signified in John XXIII's decision to announce it in the Week of Prayer for Christian Unity on January 25, 1959, was the restoration of Christian unity. The council made the Catholic Church's full commitment to ecumenism explicit in its Decree on Ecumenism (*Unitatis Redintegratio*).[1] Among the many practical ways that this engagement in the search for the full visible unity of the divided churches was to be carried out, the decree set out the conditions for the establishment of formal commissions of "dialogue between competent experts from different Churches and Communities." Such meetings were to be conducted "in a religious spirit," and would lead to a deeper mutual understanding of both the "teaching and religious life of both communions." Official dialogue would be essential to establishing the conditions for diverse forms of mutual collaboration and common prayer. Ultimately, the dialogues were to foster an examination of

1 Second Vatican Council, Decree on Ecumenism, *Unitatis Redintegratio* [*UR*], especially art. 1, accessed 4 January 2011, http://www.vatican.va/archive/hist_councils/ii_vatican_council/documents/vat-ii_decree_19641121_unitatis-redintegratio_en.html.

conscience within each dialogue partner and to lead each communion to "undertake with vigor the task of renewal and reform."[2] Ecumenical dialogue, then, was to become both an expression of and a vehicle for the renewal of inter-ecclesial relationships as the churches grow together on the path toward full communion.

In Canada, one of the most significant signs of the reception of this teaching is the establishment of an officially mandated commission for Anglican–Roman Catholic dialogue (ARC Canada). This essay seeks to examine the historical origins of ARC Canada[3] in the events of the Second Vatican Council itself and to explore the process of its foundation in the ten years following the promulgation of the council's Decree on Ecumenism from 1964 to 1974. As will soon become apparent, the first protagonists of this dialogue were active in the council itself and envisioned the establishment and the activity of such a dialogue as both a direct fruit of and an agent for the conciliar renewal. It is hoped that such a historical investigation might enlighten those engaged in the work of Anglican-Catholic dialogue in our own day, as ARC Canada approaches the fortieth anniversary of its founding.

Anglican-Catholic Relations in Canada Prior to Vatican II

In order to appreciate the full effect of the Second Vatican Council in changing the course of Anglican-Catholic relations in Canada, it is worth noting the tenor of that relationship in the preconciliar period. Beginning from 1943, the Church of England in of Canada[4]—as it was then called—embarked upon a series of negotiations in view of estab-

---

2 *UR*, art. 4.

3 This paper is based on research conducted at a number of archives, including the following:
1. The papers of Canon Dr. Eugene R. Fairweather, Trinity College Archives, Toronto. (Fonds Fairweather)
2. The records of the National Office for Ecumenism and Interfaith Relations, including the Anglican–Roman Catholic dialogue of Canada, in the Archives of the Canadian Conference of Catholic Bishops, Ottawa. (CCCB Archives)
3. The archives of the Anglican-Roman Catholic International Commission (ARCIC), of which a copy exists in the archives of Saint Paul University, Ottawa. (ARCIC Archives)
I am most grateful to the archivists in all of these centres for their kind assistance.

4 The name was revised in 1955 to the Anglican Church of Canada.

lishing full communion with The United Church of Canada. Among the committees of General Synod, the Anglican Church of Canada counted the Committee on Ecumenical Relations. But because the Roman Catholic Church continued to stand outside the wider ecumenical movement, a separate committee was established for Anglican–Catholic Relationships. It sought largely to follow developments within the Catholic Church with concern for their impact on the lives of Anglicans in Canada and elsewhere.

A report on reunion conversations submitted to the General Synod of the Anglican Church of Canada in 1957 noted that from the establishment of the Conversations on Reunion in 1943, there had always been a desire to invite other Christian bodies in Canada to the table. However, the prospect of including Catholics in such a conversation continued to be overshadowed by Pius XI's *Mortalium Animos* (1927), and the teachings of Pius XII in *Mystici Corporis Christi* (1943) and *Humani Generis* (1950).[5] The report to General Synod observed,

> It was not possible to ascertain to whom in the Roman Catholic Church the invitation should be sent. At that time there was no Primate in the Roman communion in Canada. The Apostolic delegate in Ottawa was the personal representative of the Pope, but not of Canadian Roman Catholics. Just at that time the Pope issued orders forbidding any in his communion to have official conversations with other bodies. It was thought best not to invite a rebuff by sending an invitation, much as that was desired.[6]

5 Pius XI, papal encyclical *Mortalium Animos* (12 January 1928), written in response to the invitation to send Catholic theologians to the first meeting of Faith and Order in Lausanne, in 1927, repeats an interdiction of Catholic participation in meetings with non-Catholics and reiterates an ecumenism of "return."
See especially art. 10–11, accessed 4 January 2011, http://www.vatican.va/holy_father/pius_xi/encyclicals/documents/hf_p-xi_enc_19280106_mortalium-animos_en.html. Pius XII, papal encylical *Mystici Corporis Christi* (29 June 1943), which identified the "true Church of Jesus Christ" and the "One, Holy, Catholic, Apostolic and Roman Church," art. 13, accessed 4 January 2011, http://www.vatican.va/holy_father/pius_xii/encyclicals/documents/hf_p-xii_enc_29061943_mystici-corporis-christi_en.html; and *Humani generis* (12 August 1950), warns against "imprudent eirenism," see especially art. 11–12, accessed 4 January 2011, http://www.vatican.va/holy_father/pius_xii/encyclicals/documents/hf_p-xii_enc_12081950_humani-generis_en.html.

6 "Review of Conversations on Reunion – General Synod of the Anglican Church of Canada, 1943–1957," in File 987-0012/010 (15), Fonds Fairweather. Little attention seems

The Commission on Church Union, which brought together representatives of the United and Anglican churches, was established at about the same time that the Canadian Catholic Conference of Bishops was forming.[7] Two decades later, the conference and its new Commission on Ecumenism would serve as an interlocutor for the General Commission on Church Union. It would take the event of the Second Vatican Council itself, which committed the Catholic Church to enter fully into the ecumenical movement, to clear a path for the initiation of official Anglican-Catholic relations in Canada. Two personalities would serve to "bridge" the event of the council to the life of the Anglican and Catholic churches in Canada: Reverend Dr. Eugene Rathbone Fairweather and Paulist Father John Keating.

Canon Eugene R. Fairweather

The hand of friendship was first extended from Roman Catholics to Anglicans in a formal way through the invitation to send observers to the Second Vatican Council. In December of 1963—between the second and third conciliar sessions—Eugene Fairweather received a letter of invitation from the office of the Council on Foreign Relations at Lambeth Palace, to represent the Anglican Communion as an official observer at Vatican II.[8] Born in Ottawa, Fairweather obtained a doctorate in theology at Union Theological Seminary in New York in

---

to have been accorded by the report to the first authorization of Catholic participation in ecumenical conversations in the 1949 instruction by the Vatican's Holy Office, *Ecclesia Catholica* (20 December 1949) in *AAS* 2 (1950): 12–17, a belated response to the invitation to send Catholic delegates to the first Assembly of the World Council of Churches held in Amsterdam, in August 1948. It stated, "Mixed gatherings, are not then, forbidden outright, but they are not to be held without the previous sanction of the competent ecclesiastical authority."

[7] The "founding meeting" of the conference was the fourth quinquennial meeting of the Canadian bishops held in Québec City, 12–13 October 1943. Its constitution and name were approved at a gathering on 26–28 September 1945. See Bernard M. Daly, *Remembering for Tomorrow: A History of the Canadian Conference of Catholic Bishops 1943–1993* (Ottawa: CCCB, 1995), 20–21.

[8] Letter from Canon John Satterthwaite, general secretary, Church of England Council on Foreign Relations, to Eugene R. Fairweather, 20 December 1963. An official letter of invitation followed from Michael Cantuar [Ramsey], 19 February 1964. Bishop Jan Willebrands addressed a formal letter of welcome to Fairweather on behalf of the Vatican Secretariat for Promoting Christian Unity, 25 May 1964. File 987-0012/005 (03), Fonds Fairweather.

1949 and returned to Trinity College, Toronto, where he taught dogmatics and ethics. In his council diary, Fairweather reports that future Anglican-Catholic relations were discussed directly by the delegation of Anglican observers in their meeting with Pope Paul VI on November 13, 1965, toward the end of the fourth session. They conferred, he writes, regarding

> a visit from Canterbury to the Pope—the latter asked when the former could come to see him—and it was agreed that something would be worked out after the council. We also discussed the prospects of Roman-Anglican dialogue, and indicated that we wanted such bilateral dialogue, involving the Anglican Communion as a whole. The pope asked just how the Church of England and other Anglican Churches would collaborate in such a project, and was reminded that our delegation of observers at each session had been chosen to represent the communion at large.[9]

Fairweather's diary entries indicate that the subject of future bilateral dialogue was pursued further in a conversation with Canadian Catholics at the council in the days that followed this meeting with Paul VI. He notes that over dinner with Bishop Hayes of Halifax, Bill Norgren, and Father Kingston, CSC, on November 16, 1965, "We talked at length about ecumenical prospects, especially for Roman-Anglican relations. Norgren and I were both persuaded that our people in North America would be enthusiastic about any *rapprochement*."[10] The next day, in a meeting between the Anglican observers and the apostolic delegate to Great Britain to discuss future relations, Archbishop Cardinale observed that "we would naturally find dialogue easier in Canada … because the 'historical background' was different."[11]

These early conversations set the wheels in motion for the visit of Archbishop Michael Ramsey to Pope Paul VI in Rome in March of

9 Eugene R. Fairweather, Council Diary, 13 November 1965, 265. According to this account, those present included: "Uncle Ripon" [John Moorman, Bishop of Ripon], Canon John Satterthwaite, Canon John Findlow, Dr. John W. Lawrence, Canon Eugene Fairweather, and Bishop Jan Willebrands of the Secretariat for Christian Unity. File 987-0012/004 (07), Fonds Fairweather.

10 Fairweather, Council Diary, 16 November 1965, 276.

11 Ibid., 17 November 1965, 279.

1966,[12] and for the subsequent establishment of the Anglican–Roman Catholic Joint Preparatory Commission (ARCJPC), which met three times in 1967[13] to consider the mandate and direction of an official international commission for an Anglican-Catholic bilateral dialogue. Eugene Fairweather was named as a member of that commission, together with a Canadian Catholic, Father John Keating, who had been appointed by the Canadian Catholic Conference as the first director of the new English-language office of the National Secretariat for Ecumenism. At the meetings of the ARCJPC, Fairweather presented two papers: the first entitled "Where Should Dialogue Begin?" and the second, "How the Word of God Creates and Sustains the Church."[14] Fairweather was subsequently named as a member of the first Anglican–Roman Catholic International Commission (ARCIC). Once a national dialogue was established in Canada and he was appointed a member, he would again serve as a "bridge" figure between the international and national dialogues.

John J. Keating, CSP

John J. Keating was born in Stratford, Ontario, and educated in Washington, DC, and Rome. A professor of theology at St. Augustine's Seminary and a staff member of the Paulists' Catholic Information Centre in Toronto, he was present during the fourth session of the Second Vatican Council where he assisted the Canadian bishops in establishing a national commission for ecumenism. Discussions were underway as early as 1964 to establish the National Office for Ecumenism after the style of the ecumenical secretariat for the United States Conference of Catholic Bishops. The annual meeting of the

12 See "The Common Declaration by Pope Paul VI and the Archbishop of Canterbury, Rome, Saint Paul Outside the Walls, March 24, 1966," in *Called to Full Unity: Documents on Anglican–Roman Catholic Relations 1966–1983*, ed. Joseph W. Witmer and J. Robert Wright (Washington, DC: NCCB, 1986), 3–4.

13 9–13 January, Gazzada; 30 August–3 September, Huntercombe Manor; 31 December 1967–3 January 1968, Malta. This last meeting produced the "Malta Report," which provided the orientation for ARCIC's work. In Anglican Roman Catholic International Committee (ARCIC), *The Final Report* (London: SPCK / Catholic Truth Society, 1982), 108–16.

14 The documents cited are listed as ARCJPC nos. 3 and 7 respectively. ARCIC Archives.

Canadian Catholic Conference of Bishops took place in Rome in the fall of 1964, against the background of the conciliar vote in favour of the Decree on Ecumenism (*Unitatis Redintegratio*). At that meeting, Francis V. Allen, auxiliary bishop of Toronto, and Paul Grégoire, then auxiliary bishop of Montréal (who would become archbishop of Montréal in 1968, and was elevated to the rank of cardinal in 1988), were named to a new episcopal committee on ecumenical affairs.[15]

In January 1965 Edward Bader wrote to Bishop Allen to nominate John Keating as national director and to lay out the mandate for such a commission. Its purpose would be to "interpret the Council's Decree On Ecumenism; aid the Diocesan Ecumenical Commissions, especially in their establishment; foster dialogue with other religious groups and organizations; appoint representatives to attend interfaith meetings; and act as liaison for the Canadian Bishops with the Secretariat for Christian Unity in Rome."[16] In April of 1965 it was decided to establish two offices for the new national secretariat, an English-language office located in Toronto and a French-language office, under the direction of Father Irénée Beaubien, located in Montréal.[17] Keating officially assumed his post as director of the Toronto office on January 1, 1966.

From his earliest days in this new post Keating was in direct contact with Anglican representatives and indicated a keen interest in the establishment of a national bilateral dialogue. Though I have been unable to document direct contact with Fairweather during the conciliar sessions and intersessions, it is clear that Keating was in communication with the staff of the Secretariat for Christian Unity. It is not unlikely that he had opportunities to interact with a number of the observers either informally or in the Tuesday afternoon sessions organized for the

15 "Report – National Ecumenical Secretariat, December 21, 1965," CCCB Archives. See also Daly, *Remembering for Tomorrow*, 54, n. 74. At the 1965 meeting of the Canadian Catholic Conference, also held in Rome, the membership of the bishops' Committee on Ecumenical Affairs was expanded to include: Archbishop Martin Michael Johnson (Vancouver), Bishop J. R. Windle (then auxiliary in the Archdiocese of Ottawa), Bishop Antoine Haucault (St. Boniface), and Bishop Adolphe Proulx (Sault Ste. Marie). At this meeting plans were approved for the new national secretariat.

16 Letter from Edward Bader, CSP, to Bishop Francis Allen, 8 January 1965, CCCB Archives.

17 Letter from Irénée Beaubien to John Keating, 1 May 1965, CCCB Archives.

observers by the secretariat. In February of 1966 the Anglican–Catholic Relationships Committee of General Synod passed a resolution requesting that a case of rebaptism of an Anglican preparing to enter into a mixed marriage with a Roman Catholic be brought to the attention of the national secretariat with a request that policies regarding mixed marriage and the recognition of baptism be more clearly communicated to Catholic clergy.[18] In an account of the activities of his office from the first three months of his mandate in 1966, Keating reports that he had been invited to address the Anglican Commission on Roman Catholic Relations on the council's Decree on Ecumenism. He states, "I did not feel that we were prepared to negotiate for regular dialogue sessions at this time, but the way was prepared for this." He indicates further, "I have been in close touch with Canon Puxley, a member of the commission, but also the head of the Ecumenical Institute of the Canadian Council [of Churches]. He will be my point of contact for working out any formal dialogue between ourselves and the Anglicans."[19] In early 1967 Keating mentions that he had raised the matter of formal dialogue at the November 1966 meeting of the same commission of the Anglican Church of Canada and notes that "The matter is now under study."[20] The

18 Letter from Canon H. L. Puxley, Ecumenical Institute of Canada, to Fr. John Keating, 18 February 1966, CCCB Archives. Indeed, the pastoral care of mixed marriages was of such concern that a special joint study commission was established at the international level. The ARCIC Commission on the Theology of Marriage and its Application to Mixed Marriage worked from 1968 to 1975. (See "Commission on the Theology of Marriage and Its Application to Mixed Marriages (Final Report)," in *Called to Full Unity*, 99–131.) As well, the Canadian Council of Churches addressed a letter of concern to the Canadian conference, expressing dissatisfaction with the Decree on Mixed Marriage issued by the Congregation for the Doctrine of Faith on 18 March 1966. Keating was instrumental in the establishment of a study commission on mixed marriages in Canada that would "recommend changes to the Instruction received from Rome in March 1966" (see "Report July–December 1966"). Father Keating was subsequently appointed as a consultant to a commission on mixed marriage by the Secretariat for Promoting Christian Unity in 1968. The work of this commission and these dialogues were to mark the subsequent guidelines on interchurch marriage that appeared in the 1970 Directory on Ecumenism and the 1983 Code of Canon Law.

19 "Report to the Bishops Commission on Ecumenism (English Section), January 1 to March 31, 1966," CCCB Archives.

20 "At the November meeting of the above commission I raised the question of the advisability of commencing theological dialogue in Canada between the Anglican Church and the Roman Catholic." "Report to the Bishops Commission on Ecumenism July-December 1966." In the summer of 1967 Keating records, "In a subsequent meeting

following year Keating reports that, given their joint participation in the ARCJPC, both he and Dr. Fairweather had been invited "on several occasions" to address the members of the Anglican Committee on Roman Catholic Relations. He records that "At the last meeting in February the question of a national dialogue was raised again in view of a projected dialogue with the Lutherans. Nothing was decided, but the Anglicans have determined to give serious study to the possibility."[21]

In this same 1968 report, Keating notes that both he and Irénée Beaubien, director of the francophone office for ecumenism in Montréal, were now attending the meetings of the church union talks between the Anglican and United churches of Canada as official observers. The desire that was present from the outset, to broaden these conversations to include other church bodies in Canada, was expressed anew in a letter of April 1969 from the General Commission on Church Union to the executive of the Canadian Catholic Conference. The commission had passed a motion reaffirming that its church union negotiations were "open to any and all Christian bodies in Canada who are willing to accept the Principles of Union." It now wished to extend to the Catholic Church in Canada a "warm invitation to become full participants in the current negotiations leading to organic union."[22] While the Canadian Conference of Bishops was not able to accept such an invitation, this attempted initiative is indicative of the spirit of the times. A new spirit of goodwill characterized relationships in this period.

The Establishment of Official Dialogue: 1970–1974

After years of study and consideration, the first official invitation to establish a national dialogue came from a resolution of the Anglican

we discussed having such a dialogue in regions rather than nationally. This seems more acceptable, but as yet there is no commitment on either side. I believe they would try to do whatever we want. Our relationship with the Anglicans is excellent." "Activity Report Summer 1966 – Summer 1967 [31 July 1966]," CCCB Archives.

21 "Report to Bishops Commission on Ecumenism, August 1, 1967 to April 21, 1968," CCCB Archives.

22 Letter of Executive Commissioners of the General Commission on Church Union, Canon Ralph Latimer (ACC) and Rev. Robert B. Craig (UCC) to Most Rev. Stephane Valiquette and John Keating, CSP, 3 April 1969, CCCB Archives.

Commission on Roman Catholic Relations in 1970: "That the Bishop of Athabaska [viz., Reginald Pierce] be asked to chair a committee of four to explore with Roman Catholics the possibility of dialogue, and be given the authority to name his three colleagues." On the advice of Keating, Pierce wrote to the members of the Catholic bishops' Commission on Ecumenism on August 21, 1970, to inform them of this resolution and ask for their collaboration.[23] In that same letter he indicated his preferred collaborators: Canon H. L. James Puxley, Eugene Fairweather, and Reginald F. Stackhouse. These four Anglicans were joined by Bishop Joseph Windle, John Keating, Irénée Beaubien, and Gilles Langevin, SJ, to form a "Preparatory Committee for Anglican–Roman Catholic Dialogue," which met at the Ecumenical Institute on Madison Avenue, Toronto, on January 21, 1971. In his opening remarks at that meeting, Canon Puxley indicated the importance of the ongoing conversation between himself and Father John Keating, going back to 1965 in preparing the way for the founding of a formal bilateral dialogue in Canada.[24]

Among the concerns that were raised at this meeting was the desire on both sides to avoid contributing to any perception that the establishment of official Anglican-Catholic dialogue would detract in any way from the energies devoted to church union negotiations between the Anglican and United churches of Canada.[25] To reassure United Church leaders, the committee agreed to invite a United Church observer to any future dialogue meetings. Much of the conversation at this initial meeting focused on the purpose of such a dialogue, including its relationship to ARCIC, and to the churches in Canada. Should it focus on theological issues or on issues of common pastoral concern?

> Should the priority be a practical dialogue looking to the resolution of common problems and the intensification of present

[23] Letter from Bishop Reginald Pierce (Athabaska) to J. R. Windle (Coadjutor, Pembroke), 21 August 1970, CCCB Archives.

[24] "Minutes of the Preparatory Committee for Anglican/Roman Catholic Dialogue," 21 January 1971, F2010 987-0012/003 (12), Fonds Fairweather.

[25] By 1975 the *Plan of Union* was set aside by the Anglican House of Bishops. See General Commission on Church Union, *Plan of Union* (Toronto: Anglican Church Publishing House / United Church Publishing, 1973). The Christian Church (Disciples of Christ) in Canada assumed official observer status in these talks from 1969.

engagements, or should dialogue be largely doctrinal? It was argued persuasively that practical issues arose from doctrinal discussion. No vote was taken, but the apparent consensus was that the dialogue should commence with a doctrinal flavour and that practical questions would be dealt with according to emergence and need.[26]

A brief report was drafted by Keating and Puxley to summarize the recommendations of the meeting and submitted to the Canadian Catholic Conference and the national office of the Anglican Church. That report recommended that five or six members from each Church be designated to serve on an official dialogue that would be staffed by John Keating and Irénée Beaubien on the Catholic side, and Canon Puxley for the Anglicans.[27] The formal establishment of the dialogue was quickly approved by the board of the National Office for Ecumenism in April 1971.

The first official meeting of the new commission for Anglican–Roman Catholic dialogue in Canada was held on November 16, 1971. In addition to the two bishop co-chairs, Pierce and Windle, and staff (Puxley, Keating, Beaubien, and Sister Diane Willey, NDS, who had recently joined the national secretariat in Toronto), six theologians were invited from each side.[28] The following were appointed by the Canadian Catholic Conference: Jean-Marie Tillard, OP, of the Dominican College, Ottawa; Joseph Hardy of London, Ontario; Johannes Pristl of Saint Paul University, Ottawa; Jacques Chenevert, SJ, of Trois-Rivières; and Robert Ouellette of Toronto. The Anglican representatives included: Dr. Eric Jay of McGill University; Jacob Jocz of Wycliffe College, Toronto; Dr. Eugene Fairweather; the Right Rev. Lewis Garnsworthy, then suffragan bishop, and soon after, Bishop of Toronto; Very Rev. Richard Flemming. The United Church named Hugh Rose as its official observer to the dialogue. Initially the dialogue planned to meet at a rhythm of

26 "Draft of a Report of the Exploratory Committee Examining the Question of Anglican/Roman Catholic Dialogue," F2010 987-0012/003 (12), Fonds Fairweather.

27 "Recommendations," F2010 987-0012/003 (12), Fonds Fairweather.

28 Notes and correspondence of National Secretariat for Ecumenism, 1971, CCCB Archives. See also "Minutes of the Second Meeting of the Anglican/Roman Catholic Dialogue," 18 March 1972, F2010 987-0012/003 (12), Fonds Fairweather.

one day three times annually. In this early period a number of notes suggest that the Canadians looked to other regional dialogues for a model. They were aware of the work already accomplished by ARC dialogues in South Africa and the United States. Indeed, in these early years, Canon Puxley and Bishop Pierce both attended meetings of the American ARC (established since 1966) as guests and observers.

Links to ARCIC

The members of ARC Canada found themselves immediately in the thick of the significant work emerging from ARCIC. Indeed, the Windsor Report on Eucharistic Doctrine was circulated soon after the September 1–8, 1971 ARCIC meeting.[29] The Canadian dialogue was at once engaged in the work of promoting the reception of ARCIC's agreed Statement on Eucharistic Doctrine, and enlisted to prepare a background study that would contribute to the subsequent agreed Statement on Ministry and Ordination.[30] The dialogue enjoyed a direct window into the work of the international commission through the presence of Eugene Fairweather and Jean-Marie Tillard, OP, both of whom provided regular reports on ARCIC's progress. In October of 1972 Fairweather presented an extensive proposal for a full schedule of work on the theme of "priesthood," suggesting that members could contribute to the drafting of material being prepared by Tillard and himself in view of a provisional document to be submitted to ARCIC in March 1973.[31] As an indication of the intensity of this period, the dialogue met three times between October 1972 and March 1973. George Tavard, a member of ARC (USA) and also of ARCIC, attended at least one of these working sessions on the subject of ministry. The dialogue

[29] Anglican–Roman Catholic International Commission (ARCIC), "Eucharistic Doctrine (1971)," in *The Final Report*, 12–16.

[30] ARCIC, "Ministry and Ordination (1973)," in *The Final Report*, 30–39.

[31] "Anglican/Roman Catholic Dialogue (Canada): Suggestion for Programme, 1972–73," signed "Eugene Fairweather," 9 October 1972, F2010 987-0012/003 (12), Fonds Fairweather. The broader plan of ARCIC is indicated in a press release following its meeting at Gazzada, 30 August–7 September 1972, and attached to Fairweather's proposal: "At its Gazzada meeting, the Commission began its study of Ministry. … At the end of this work there emerged an outline which, during the coming year, groups meeting in a number of centres in various countries will expand into a draft on the doctrine of ministry." The text of the press release can also be found at ARCIC No. 57, ARCIC Archives.

contributed to a paper entitled "Ministerial Priesthood in Relation to Christ and the Church," which was submitted for the consideration of those drafting ARCIC's agreed Statement on Ministry and Ordination, to be released following its meeting in Canterbury in September of that same year.[32]

The Establishment of the Canadian ARC Bishops' Dialogue

Another significant and pioneering feature of the Canadian dialogue in this early period was the establishment of a permanent dialogue between a representative group of Anglican and Catholic bishops, a rather unique experiment among the regional dialogues. This ARC bishops' dialogue was born out of the theologians' efforts to mobilize the episcopate of each Church to implement the practical suggestions contained in the "Malta Report" published by the ARCJPC in 1968. The "Malta Report" had outlined a vision of unity in stages. Among its recommendations for immediate action was the following: "In every region where each Communion has hierarchy, we propose an annual joint meeting of either the whole or some considerable representation of the two hierarchies."[33] Other recommendations included the conclusion of "agreements for joint use of churches and other ecclesiastical buildings," for the sharing of "facilities for theological education," increasing opportunities for common prayer, the consideration of common lectionaries and common texts for liturgical prayers, and renewed study of the theology and pastoral care of mixed marriage.[34] All of these topics were the object of ARC Canada's discussion.

To bring the bishops together, Beaubien and Keating introduced a formal motion in May of 1973 that the dialogue write to the bishops and encourage them to schedule their future meetings at the same place and time, and allot a space in their schedule "to discuss paragraph 7 of the

---

32 A brief account of these activities is found in "Memorandum From Sr Diane Willey to Bishops of the Office of Ecumenism," 29 March 1973, CCCB Archives. The document in question can be found in ARCIC No. 69, ARCIC Archives.

33 Anglican-Roman Catholic Joint Preparatory Commission, "The Malta Report," in *The Final Report* (London: SPCK / Catholic Truth Society), no. 8, p. 111.

34 Ibid., nos. 9-16, pp. 111-113.

Malta Report and the practical implementation of the latter for the renewal of the Christian faith in our Canadian society."[35] Puxley drafted a letter to the bishops on August 9, 1973, suggesting a joint meeting of the bishops. The proposal was discussed at a meeting of the Administrative Board of the Canadian Catholic Conference on January 23–24, 1974. Though the practicalities were not determined, the board suggested the discussion of "eucharist, ministry, and evangelization"[36] as tentative items for the agenda of such a meeting. The plan was considered by the Anglican House of Bishops at its gathering in May of 1974.

The initiative for the establishment of a bishops' dialogue was somewhat delayed in late 1974 by a transition of personnel in the national offices of both churches. The National Secretariat for Ecumenism of the Catholic Conference was moved to Ottawa in November of 1974. At about the same time, John Keating retired from the directorship, and Sister Diane Willey left the staff. Monsignor Michael O'Connell became the new director of the office for ecumenism, now located in Ottawa. Canon Puxley would resign from the dialogue in November of 1975, but already in 1974 Father James B. Boyles, general secretary of the Anglican Church of Canada, joined the dialogue and began to undertake a number of key organizational tasks.[37] Boyles indicated that,

---

35 "The Anglican/Roman Catholic Dialogue: Minutes of the Sixth Meeting," May 9, 1973. F2012 987-0012/003 (13). Fonds Fairweather. Paragraph 7 of the "Malta Report" relates to the mutual recognition of common faith by the highest levels of authority in each church: "We recommend that the second stage in our growing together begin with an official and explicit affirmation of mutual recognition from the highest authorities of each Communion. It would acknowledge that both Communions are at one in the faith that the Church is founded upon the revelation of God the Father, made known to us in the Person and work of Jesus Christ, who is present through the Holy Spirit in the Scriptures and his Church, and is the only Mediator between God and Man, the ultimate Authority for all our doctrine. Each accepts the basic truths set forth in the ecumenical Creeds and the common tradition of the ancient Church, although neither Communion is tied to a positive acceptance of all the beliefs and devotional practices of the other." For complete text, see *The Final Report*, 110–11.

36 "Agenda: Administrative Board of Canadian Catholic Conference, 23-24 January 1974," File: Anglican-R.C. Dialogue (Canada) 1970-79, CCCB Archives.

37 He writes to O'Connell on 26 November 1974, "With the resignation of Father John Keating, and Bishop Pierce from the Anglican/Roman Catholic dialogue, the group has really been very inactive. We had subsequently appointed Bishop Maguire of Montréal to the dialogue, but just recently he has announced his retirement, and wishes to withdraw from the dialogue also. Our House of Bishops will be meeting during the first week of December, and will make a further appointment to the dialogue. At that

though it was hoped initially that the bishops might meet in the fall of 1974, it was now necessary to consider a date in 1975.

A possible agenda for the ARC bishops' gathering was discussed at length by the members of ARC Canada on March 7, 1975.[38] Recognizing the need for careful preparation of such a meeting, the members established a small subcommittee to prepare an agenda and consider which bishops to invite. Meeting on April 12, the subcommittee clearly outlined the purpose of such a dialogue: "To bring together representatives of the two hierarchies that they may discuss theological and pastoral questions, deepen their understanding of one another, and communicate their experience to their brothers in the episcopacy, and to their churches."[39] In their letter of invitation to the bishops, Boyles and O'Connell indicated that "such meetings were suggested by the Malta Report in January of 1968, and endorsed by Cardinal Bea in his letter to the Archbishop of Canterbury in June 1968."[40]

The first meeting of the bishops' dialogue took place on October 24, 1975, at the King Edward Hotel in Toronto. Eugene Fairweather and Jean-Marie Tillard gave an overview of the important developments in Anglican-Catholic dialogue since the establishment of formal relations in 1966, with particular attention to the work of ARCIC on marriage, Eucharist, ministry, and authority in the Church. The bishops were invited to reflect on all of these issues, as well as on the pastoral challenges in northern regions. Such meetings would become a permanent feature of Anglican–Roman Catholic relations in Canada.

---

point, we may be able to make plans to reactivate the group, setting time and place and agenda for its next meeting. ... One other item of business from the dialogue was the proposal that representatives of the Bishops of both Churches meet together. This was originally scheduled for fall 1974, is now planned for spring 1975. I think we must explore carefully the purpose for such a meeting, and carefully prepare it." Letter from J. Boyles to M. O'Connell, 26 November 1974, in File: "National Secretariat – Correspondence 1970-74," CCCB Archives.

38 "Anglican/Roman Catholic Dialogue: Minutes, March 7, 1975," F2010 Unprocessed, Box 20, Fonds Fairweather.

39 "Report of Ad Hoc Committee for Meeting of Bishops," [22 April 1975], F2010 Unprocessed, Box 20, Fonds Fairweather. The committee members were: W. Zion, J. Boyles, I. Beaubien, and M. O'Connell.

40 "Letter from J. Boyles and M. O'Connell to Archbishop Scott and Archbishop Fortier, May 20, 1975," CCCB Archive.

Conclusion

This brief survey of the history of the establishment of the Anglican–Roman Catholic dialogue in Canada reveals the direct influence of the Second Vatican Council in reshaping the consciousness of the churches. Though several years transpired between the event of the council itself and the establishment of an official commission for theological dialogue and an official dialogue between Anglican and Catholic bishops, the council was clearly the impetus for the development of new networks of communication and a new spirit of collaboration between the churches. A cursory survey of the early years of ARC Canada reveals a concern that remains a perennial preoccupation of ARC Canada: to contribute to the work of theological reflection being done on the international level by ARCIC, and to promote the reception of ARCIC's work within the Canadian context through education, communication, and practical initiatives. ARC Canada also showed an "activist" side, if I may use the term here, in the sense of proposing initiatives, such as the establishment of the bishop's dialogue, and later recommending the organization of colloquia on a regional level across Canada to promote the reception of the growing agreement emerging from across our communions. It is striking to reread the notes and minutes of the early meetings of ARC Canada and to discover in them a constant effort to balance the international and national or regional concerns, the theological and the pastoral, the search for a more satisfactory expression of our common faith with pastoral implementation and the reception of new insights. These remain the enduring concerns of ARC Canada in our day.

Collaborateurs et collaboratrices / Contributors

Michael Attridge is Associate Professor of Theology at the Faculty of Theology, University of St. Michael's College, Toronto. His current research project is to study the contributions of the two Carter brothers—Bishop Alexander and Bishop Emmett—to the Second Vatican Council and the implementation of the council in their respective dioceses in the years immediately following Vatican II. His most recent book is an edited collection of essays entitled *Jews and Catholics Together: Celebrating the Legacy of Nostra Aetate* (Novalis, 2007).

Peter E. Baltutis is a doctoral candidate in the History of Christianity at the Faculty of Theology, University of St. Michael's College, Toronto. Specializing in the history of Catholicism in North America, he is currently completing his dissertation on the Canadian Catholic Organization for Development and Peace from 1967 to 2000. This research is supported by a Social Sciences and Humanities Research Council of Canada (SSHRC) Doctoral Fellowship.

Gregory Baum is Professor Emeritus of the Faculty of Religious Studies, McGill University. His academic training is in Catholic theology and sociology. His areas of research are liberation theology and the interaction of religion and society. For many years he edited *The Ecumenist*. Recent publications are *Nationalism, Religion and Ethics* (McGill-Queen's University Press, 2001), *Amazing Church* (Novalis, 2005), *Signs of the Times* (Novalis, 2006), and *The Theology of Tariq Ramadan: A Catholic Perspective* (Novalis, 2009.)

Raymond Brodeur détient un doctorat conjoint en théologie et en sciences des religions de l'Institut catholique de Paris et de l'Université de Sorbonne-Paris IV (1982). Il est professeur titulaire à la Faculté de théologie et de sciences religieuses de l'Université Laval, responsable du Groupe de recherche sur les catéchismes en Amérique française et l'histoire de l'enseignement religieux, et responsable scientifique du Centre d'études Marie-de-l'Incarnation (CÉMI). Il est auteur d'articles et directeur d'édition d'ouvrages sur la pédagogie catéchétique, l'histoire des catéchismes et Marie de l'Incarnation.

Rosa Bruno-Jofré is Professor and Dean of the Faculty of Education at Queen's University. She holds a Ph.D. from the University of Calgary and specializes in the history of education in Canada and beyond. She is founding co-editor of *Encounters on Education/Encuentros/Rencontres*, published jointly by the Faculty of Education at Queen's and the Department of Theory and History of Education, Universidad Complutense de Madrid. She also serves as senior co-editor of *Historical Studies in Education/Revue d'histoire de l'éducation*. Her most recent book is *The Missionary Oblate Sisters: Vision and Mission* (McGill/Queen's University Press, 2005).

Catherine E. Clifford is Associate Professor and Vice Dean of the Faculty of Theology, Saint Paul University. She holds an S.T.L. from the University of Fribourg, Switzerland, and a Ph.D. in theology from St. Michael's College, Toronto. Her recent publications include *A Century of Prayer for Christian Unity* (Eerdmans, 2009), *For the Communion of the Churches: The Contribution of the Groupe des Dombes* (Eerdmans, 2010), and a translation of the Groupe des Dombes study *"One Teacher": Doctrinal Authority in the Church* (Eerdmans, 2010).

Indre Cuplinskas is Assistant Professor at St. Joseph's College, University of Alberta. She is a historian of Christianity specializing in twentieth-century Catholicism in Canada and Europe with a focus on lay religious movements such as Catholic Action. She has published on the Jeunesse étudiante catholique in Québec and is currently working on a Catholic student organization in early-twentieth-century Lithuania.

Darren J. Dias, OP, is Assistant Professor of Theology at the University of St. Michael's College, Toronto, where he is also Director of the Israel Study Program. His areas of research and teaching include Trinitarian theology, religious diversity, and the thought of Bernard Lonergan. He is currently examining how religious diversity affects an understanding of both doctrine and pastoral praxis. Darren serves on the Provincial Council of the Friars of the Order of Preachers (Dominicans) in Canada.

Michael A. Fahey, SJ, is Research Professor of Systematic Theology in the Department of Theology, Boston College. His areas of specialization are ecclesiology and ecumenism. He is former Dean at the Faculty of Theology, University of St. Michael's College, Toronto, and former president of the Catholic Theological Society of America. He has recently published "The Church," in *Systematic Theology: Roman Catholic Perspectives* (rev. ed. Fortress, 2011) and "The Contribution of the Belgians to Vatican Council II," in *Vatican II and the Contribution of the Belgians* (Peeters, 2008).

Peter Galadza is Kule Family Professor of Liturgy at the Sheptytsky Institute of Eastern Christian Studies, Saint Paul University, Ottawa, and a presbyter of the Ukrainian Greco-Catholic Church. He is the author of *The Theology and Liturgical Work of Andrei Sheptytsky, 1865–1944* (Rome: Orientalia Christiana Analecta, 2004) as well as the editor of two other books. In 2003–2004 he was a fellow at Harvard University's Dumbarton Oaks Byzantine Research Center. In 1999–2000 he served as Dean of the Lviv Theological Academy in Ukraine (presently The Ukrainian Catholic University). He has also served as editor and as editor-in-chief of *Logos: A Journal of Eastern Christian Studies*.

Alan L. Hayes is Bishops Frederick and Heber Wilkinson Professor of the History of Christianity at Wycliffe College at the University of Toronto and Director of the Toronto School of Theology. His areas of specialization include Canadian church history. He is an editor of the journal *Anglican and Episcopal History*; his books include *Anglicans in Canada: Controversy and Identity in Historical Perspective* (University of Illinois, 2004).

Sarah Jardine holds an M.A. in Theology and is currently a Ph.D. candidate in the Faculty of Theology, Saint Paul University. Her thesis will explore the history of the Catholic Women's League of Canada, an important chapter in the lives of lay Catholic women.

Léo Laberge, o.m.i., est professeur émérite de la Faculté de théologie, Université Saint-Paul, où il enseignait en Écriture sainte (1958-1960, 1969-1998) et où il a aussi servi comme Vice-recteur (1988-1994). Il détient la L.Ph. et L.Th. (Angelicum, Rome, 1954 et 1958) et le S.S.D. (Commission Biblique, Rome, 1968). Il a travaillé au secrétariat de la Commission de théologie préparatoire, puis à la commission « *fides et mores* » durant le deuxième concile du Vatican (janvier 1961-décembre 1963). Il était rédacteur en chef de la revue *Église et Théologie / Theoforum* (1969-2008).

The Rev. Dr. Stuart Macdonald is currently Professor of Church and Society at Knox College, Toronto School of Theology, University of Toronto. Dr. Macdonald's published works have looked at witch hunting in Scotland and developments in Christianity, including developments within the Presbyterian Church in Canada, since World War II. Recent publications include *The Witches of Fife: 1560–1710* (East Linton [Scotland]: John Tuckwell Publishers, 2002) and "Divining the Entrails: One Challenge in Studying How the Presbyterian Church in Canada Looked at Itself and Its Future, 1945–2000" (Papers, Canadian Society of Presbyterian History, 2006).

Heidi MacDonald is Associate Professor and past Chair in the Department of History at the University of Lethbridge. Her publications have appeared in *Acadiensis*, *Atlantis*, *Historical Studies* (Canadian Catholic Historical Association), *Histoire Sociale/Social History*, and several collections on women in Canada. She is currently writing a book on youth during the Great Depression.

Peter Meehan is Chair of the School of Liberal Arts at Seneca College at York University in Toronto and Adjunct Professor of Church History at St. Augustine's Seminary in the Toronto School of Theology. He is President General of the Canadian Catholic Historical Association and served for five years as editor of the refereed journal *Historical Studies* (2002–2007). He is presently working on the biography of Philip Pocock, seventh archbishop of Toronto, commissioned by the Archdiocese of Toronto. His article *"Purified Socialism" and the Church in Saskatchewan: Tommy Douglas, Philip Pocock and Hospitalization, 1944–1948"* was published in the Spring 2011 edition of *Historical Studies.*

Pierre Pagé est professeur associé à l'Université du Québec à Montréal. Spécialiste de l'histoire culturelle des médias, il a dirigé la revue *Fréquence/Frequency* et publié plusieurs ouvrages, notamment une *Histoire de la radio au Québec.* Il a été chroniqueur à la revue *L'Église canadienne*, réalisateur et chroniqueur à Radio Ville-Marie, et président de cette station. Il a publié plusieurs articles sur les relations entre l'Église catholique et les médias, le journalisme radio, la littérature radiophonique, ainsi que trois études dans *Encyclopedia of Radio*. Il prépare un livre sur « Claude Ryan, éditorialiste devant le fait religieux ».

Marc Pelchat est professeur titulaire en ecclésiologie et en théologie pratique à la Faculté de théologie et de sciences religieuses de l'Université Laval. Sa thèse doctorale, réalisée à l'Université grégorienne, portait sur l'ecclésiologie dans l'œuvre de Henri de Lubac, autour des concepts centraux de mystère et de communion. Ses principaux travaux ont porté jusqu'ici sur la théologie des ministères, notamment ceux accomplis par des laïques, le système paroissial, l'évangélisation et l'éducation de la foi des adultes.

Margaret Myrtle Power is Assistant Professor in the Faculty of Theology, Saint Paul University, Ottawa, and director of the Summer Institutes in Pastoral Liturgy and Religious Education there. She holds a Ph.D. in Religious Education from Fordham University, New York. Her recent contributions include a chapter in *La théologie pratique, pratique de théologie*, edited by Luc Tardif and Karlijn Demasure (Les Presses de l'Université d'Ottawa, 2011) and articles in *Journal of Religious Education* and *Theoforum.* She was editor of a special issue of *Theororum* 41/1 (2010) on the theme "Religious Education and Vatican II: The Aftermath."

Jacques Racine est professeur émérite de la Faculté de théologie et de sciences religieuses de l'Université Laval. Il a été professeur de théologie pratique, d'éthique sociale et d'éthique organisationnelle. Ses principaux champs de recherche sont le catholicisme québécois et l'éducation. Il a participé à divers organismes de l'État et de l'Église (Comité des ministères et Comité des affaires sociales de l'Assemblée des évêques catholiques du Québec). Il a été Vice-recteur exécutif de l'Université Laval.

Gilles Routhier est professeur titulaire à la Faculté de théologie et de sciences religieuses de l'Université Laval. Spécialiste de Vatican II, il a contribué à l'histoire du concile en cinq volumes, publiée en huit langues, dirigée par le prof. G. Alberigo. Ses recherches se concentrent sur Vatican II, son histoire, son herméneutique et sa réception et sur le devenir du catholicisme, en particulier au Québec et au Canada depuis le concile Vatican II. Il a publié de nombreux ouvrages dans le domaine.

Philippe J. Roy est historien et chargé de cours à la Faculté de théologie et de sciences religieuses de l'Université Laval. Il prépare actuellement une thèse de doctorat sur le *Cœtus Internationalis Patrum* au concile Vatican II en cotutelle entre le Département d'histoire de l'Université de Lyon 3 et la Faculté de théologie et de sciences religieuses de l'Université Laval.

Karim Schelkens holds a Ph.D. (2007) in Theology (contemporary church history) from the Catholic University of Leuven, and has studied at the Université Laval. He has published extensively on the history of the Second Vatican Council, including a monograph on *Catholic Revelation Theology on the Eve of Vatican II* (Brill, 2010) and an edition of the *Council Notes of Edward Schillebeeckx* (Peeters, 2011).

Jaroslav Z. Skira is Associate Professor of Historical Theology and Director of the Eastern Christian Studies Program at Regis College (University of Toronto). He has also taught for the Ukrainian Catholic University, Ukraine. His research interests include Eastern Orthodox ecclesiology and ecumenism. He has co-edited *Windows to the East* (Novalis, 2001) and *In God's Hands: Essays on the Church and Ecumenism in Honour of Michael A. Fahey, S.J.* (Peeters, 2006), and is currently completing a translation of Met. Maxim Hermaniuk's Vatican II council diaries.

Elizabeth Smyth is Professor and Vice Dean (Programs) at the School of Graduate Studies, University of Toronto. Her current SSHRC-funded research includes principal investigator on *Leading Sisters, Changing Times: Women Religious in English Canada in the Post Vatican II World* and collaborating investigator on *Disciplining Academics: The Tenure Process in Social Science* and *The State of the Consecrated Life in Contemporary Canada*. She is the editor of *Changing Habits: Women's Religious Orders in Canada* (Novalis, 2007).

Andrea Spatafora M.S.F. is Associate Professor and Dean of the Faculty of Theology at Saint Paul University. He holds a Licentiate in Sacred Scripture from the Pontifical Biblical Institute (1992) and a doctorate from the Pontifical Gregorian University (1997). His teaching and research are in the areas of Wisdom literature, the Psalms, the Gospel of John, the Apocalypse, and canon studies. His most recent book is *Symbolic Language and the Apocalypse* (Novalis, 2008).

Myroslaw Tataryn is Professor of Religious Studies and Vice-President/Academic Dean at St. Jerome's University, federated to the University of Waterloo, and is a married Ukrainian Catholic priest. He works in the area of Eastern Christian theology as well as the history of Eastern Christians in Canada. His most recent work includes "Between Patriarch and Pope: The Theological Struggle of Sergei Bulgakov" and a chapter on "Canada's Eastern Christians," in *Christianity and Ethnicity in Canada*.

John van den Hengel, scj, is Professor Emeritus of the Faculty of Theology, Saint Paul University. His teaching and publications have specialized in the thought of Paul Ricœur. He has contributed to the development of important resources for religious education and catechesis for use across Canada, most recently acting as Theologian and Editor-in-Chief for *World Religions: A Canadian Catholic Perspective* (Novalis-Nelson, 2011). He presently serves in Rome as a member of the General Council of his religious congregation, the priests of the Sacred Heart.

John H. Young is Assistant Professor at the Queen's School of Religion, Queen's University. His current research interests are the history of The United Church of Canada and the Antigonish Movement. Recent publications include "Evangelism in The United Church of Canada: Charles Templeton to Emerging Spirit" (*Touchstone* 27, no. 1 [January 2009]: 26–35) and "A Golden Age: The United Church of Canada, 1946–1960" in *The United Church of Canada: A History*, edited by Donald Schweitzer (forthcoming in 2011, Wilfrid Laurier University Press).

Index

Les entrées d'index sont présentées par langue, mais certaines références apparaissent dans les deux langues. Dans ces cas, on trouve des entrées d'index en anglais et en français.

Entries are separated by language, but cross-referenced. In cases where the reference to both languages is found on the same page(s), the term appears in two locations, under both English and French entries.

A

B

C

D

E

F

G

H

I

J

K

L

M

N

O

P

Q

R

S

T

U

V

W

Y

Z

RECYCLÉ
Papier fait à partir de matériaux recyclés
FSC® C103567
FSC www.fsc.org

Marquis imprimeur inc.

Québec, Canada
2011

Imprimé sur du papier Silva Enviro 100% postconsommation traité sans chlore, accrédité Éco-Logo et fait à partir de biogaz.

100%
PERMANENT